Celebrating What Is Important to Me

West
Grades 7-12
Fall 2009

Celebrating What Is Important to Me
West
Grades 7-12
Fall 2009

An Anthology Compiled By Creative Communication, Inc.

Published by:

1488 NORTH 200 WEST • LOGAN, UTAH 84341
TEL. 435-713-4411 • WWW.POETICPOWER.COM

Authors are responsible for the originality of the writing submitted.

All rights reserved. No part of this book may be reproduced or transmitted in any form or by any means, electronic or mechanical without written permission of the author and publisher.

Copyright © 2010 by Creative Communication, Inc.
Printed in the United States of America

ISBN: 978-1-60050-306-1

FOREWORD

What is important to me….as events occur in the world, the concept of "what is important to me" changes. When these essays were written, the world was not concerned with an earthquake in Haiti. When this book goes to print, it will be several weeks after the earthquake that took over 100,000 lives. Yet, as I write this forward, days after the earthquake, I return to the question of "what is important to me."

The writers who were chosen to contribute to this edition of the essay book wrote on topics that were important to them. The subjects vary greatly and at the time they were written, they may have been written with conviction or maybe just an assigned classroom topic. If you were to ask these students what is important to them today, at this instant, the topic may be different. However, to many of these writers, the things that are most important, are also the things that are timelessly important: family, friends, beliefs. To the families devastated by the earthquake in Haiti, what may have once been important to their lives, became trivial, when all that was left in the aftermath was what was really important: family, friends and beliefs. And to many of them, even that was gone and what became important was survival.

For myself, I am humbled. As I sit in my home, drive my car, or even open a refrigerator, I come to the realization of the transient nature of the things with which I am surrounded. The realization that many of the things which give comfort are not things that give meaning. As you read each essay, I hope you will reflect into the lives of each of these writers. I hope you will reflect into your life and assess what you feel is most important. As our world changes, I hope what we find important are not the *things* we surround ourselves with, but the *relationships* that bless our lives.

Thomas Worthen, Ph.D.
Editor
Creative Communication

WRITING CONTESTS!

Enter our next POETRY contest!

Enter our next ESSAY contest!

Why should I enter?
Win prizes and get published! Each year thousands of dollars in prizes are awarded throughout North America. The top writers in each division receive a monetary award and a free book that includes their published poem or essay. Entries of merit are also selected to be published in our anthology.

Who may enter?
There are four divisions in the poetry contest. The poetry divisions are grades K-3, 4-6, 7-9, and 10-12. There are three divisions in the essay contest. The essay divisions are grades 3-6, 7-9, and 10-12.

What is needed to enter the contest?
To enter the poetry contest send in one original poem, 21 lines or less. To enter the essay contest send in one original non-fiction essay, 250 words or less, on any topic. Please submit each poem and essay with a title, and the following information clearly printed: the writer's name, current grade, home address (optional), school name, school address, teacher's name and teacher's email address (optional). Contact information will only be used to provide information about the contest. For complete contest information go to www.poeticpower.com.

How do I enter?

Enter a poem online at:
www.poeticpower.com
or
Mail your poem to:
  Poetry Contest
  1488 North 200 West
  Logan, UT 84341

Enter an essay online at:
www.studentessaycontest.com
or
Mail your essay to:
  Essay Contest
  1488 North 200 West
  Logan, UT 84341

When is the deadline?
Poetry contest deadlines are April 13th, August 18th, and December 2nd. Essay contest deadlines are July 15th, October 19th, and February 17th. Students can enter one poem and one essay for each spring, summer, and fall contest deadline.

Are there benefits for my school?
Yes. We award $15,000 each year in grants to help with Language Arts programs. Schools qualify to apply for a grant by having 15 or more accepted entries.

Are there benefits for my teacher?
Yes. Teachers with five or more students published receive a free anthology that includes their students' writing.

For more information please go to our website at **www.poeticpower.com**, email us at editor@poeticpower.com or call 435-713-4411.

TABLE OF CONTENTS

Writing Achievement Honor Schools 1

Language Arts Grant Recipients 5

Grades 10-11-12 High Merit Essays 9

Grades 7-8-9 High Merit Essays 103

Index 243

States included in this edition:

Alaska
California
Hawaii
Montana
Nevada
New Mexico
Oregon
Texas
Utah
Washington
Wyoming

Fall 2009 Writing Achievement Honor Schools

* Teachers who had fifteen or more students accepted to be published

The following schools are recognized as receiving a "Writing Achievement Award." This award is given to schools who have a large number of entries of which over fifty percent are accepted for publication. With hundreds of schools entering our contest, only a small percent of these schools are honored with this award. The purpose of this award is to recognize schools with excellent Language Arts programs. This award qualifies these schools to receive a complimentary copy of this anthology. In addition, these schools are eligible to apply for a Creative Communication Language Arts Grant. Grants of two hundred and fifty dollars each are awarded to further develop writing in our schools.

Coronado High School
   Lubbock, TX
      Sara Stevens*

Corpus Christi School
   San Francisco, CA
      Theodore R. Langlais*

Deweyville Middle School
   Deweyville, TX
      Merrilyn Williams*

Faith Christian Jr/Sr High School
   Yuba City, CA
      Paula Finlay*

Flour Bluff High School
   Corpus Christi, TX
      Myriam Bell*

Granbury High School
   Granbury, TX
      Heather Cook*
      Murphy Cook
      Jana Reid*
      Linda Stewart*

Holliday Middle School
   Holliday, TX
      Donna Lewis*

Isbell Middle School
   Santa Paula, CA
      Mark Lopez*

Kaufer High School
   Riviera, TX
      DeAnna Hamblin*

New Caney High School
   New Caney, TX
      J. Powell
      Michele Powell*

Our Lady of the Rosary School
   Paramount, CA
      Sr. Ellen Mary Conefrey
      Sr. Brigid Mary McGuire

Pine Tree High School
   Longview, TX
      Miriam Lancaster*

Celebrating What Is Important to Me – West Grades 7-12 Fall 2009

Placerita Jr High School
Newhall, CA
Sophia Fernandez*

Post High School
Post, TX
Leslie Tatum*

REACH High School
Fort Worth, TX
Stefanie Macdonald*

Reagan County Middle School
Big Lake, TX
Judy Michalewicz*

Rio Bravo Middle School
El Paso, TX
Gloria Gomez*

Santa Teresa Middle School
Santa Teresa, NM
Rhonda Haberkamp*

Seminole Jr High School
Seminole, TX
Mrs. K. Exline*

South Jordan Middle School
South Jordan, UT
Jill Jenkins*

St Elizabeth Ann Seton School
Keller, TX
Amanda Migura*

St Michael's Episcopal Day School
Carmichael, CA
Joe Monroe*

St Thomas Aquinas School
Rio Rancho, NM
JoAnne Rickard*

Thora B Gardiner Middle School
Oregon City, OR
Leslie Bennet-McCue*
Jeannie Ray

University Preparatory School
Redding, CA
Andy Hedman*

Valley Christian High School
San Jose, CA
Judy Marc*

Valley Christian School
Spokane Valley, WA
Julie Hicks*

Vista Ridge High School
Leander, TX
Penny Billingsley*

Wall High School
Wall, TX
Shelly Nelson*

Zia Middle School
Las Cruces, NM
Chriss Martinez*

Language Arts Grant Recipients 2009-2010

After receiving a "Writing Achievement Award" schools are encouraged to apply for a Creative Communication Language Arts Grant. The following is a list of schools who received a two hundred and fifty dollar grant for the 2009-2010 school year.

Arrowhead Union High School, Hartland, WI
Blessed Sacrament School, Seminole, FL
Booneville Jr High School, Booneville, AR
Buckhannon-Upshur Middle School, Buckhannon, WV
Campbell High School, Ewa Beach, HI
Chickahominy Middle School, Mechanicsville, VA
Clarkston Jr High School, Clarkston, MI
Covenant Life School, Gaithersburg, MD
CW Rice Middle School, Northumberland, PA
Eason Elementary School, Waukee, IA
East Elementary School, Kodiak, AK
Florence M Gaudineer Middle School, Springfield, NJ
Foxborough Regional Charter School, Foxborough, MA
Gideon High School, Gideon, MO
Holy Child Academy, Drexel Hill, PA
Home Choice Academy, Vancouver, WA
Jeff Davis Elementary School, Biloxi, MS
Lower Alloways Creek Elementary School, Salem, NJ
Maple Wood Elementary School, Somersworth, NH
Mary Walter Elementary School, Bealeton, VA
Mater Dei High School, Evansville, IN
Mercy High School, Farmington Hills, MI
Monroeville Elementary School, Monroeville, OH
Nautilus Middle School, Miami Beach, FL
Our Lady Star of the Sea School, Grosse Pointe Woods, MI
Overton High School, Memphis, TN
Pond Road Middle School, Robbinsville, NJ
Providence Hall Charter School, Herriman, UT
Reuben Johnson Elementary School, McKinney, TX
Rivelon Elementary School, Orangeburg, SC
Rose Hill Elementary School, Omaha, NE

Language Arts Grant Winners cont.

Runnels School, Baton Rouge, LA
Santa Fe Springs Christian School, Santa Fe Springs, CA
Serra Catholic High School, Mckeesport, PA
Shadowlawn Elementary School, Green Cove Springs, FL
Spectrum Elementary School, Gilbert, AZ
St Edmund Parish School, Oak Park, IL
St Joseph Institute for the Deaf, Chesterfield, MO
St Joseph Regional Jr High School, Manchester, NH
St Mary of Czestochowa School, Middletown, CT
St Monica Elementary School, Garfield Heights, OH
St Vincent De Paul Elementary School, Cape Girardeau, MO
Stevensville Middle School, Stevensville, MD
Tashua School, Trumbull, CT
The New York Institute for Special Education, Bronx, NY
The Selwyn School, Denton, TX
Tonganoxie Middle School, Tonganoxie, KS
Westside Academy, Prince George, BC
Willa Cather Elementary School, Omaha, NE
Willow Hill Elementary School, Traverse City, MI

Grades 10-11-12 Top Ten Winners

List of Top Ten Winners for 10-12, listed alphabetically

Ela Banerjee*	Grade 11	Roseville High School	Roseville, CA
Rheanna Buursma	Grade 12	Grimsby Secondary School	Grimsby, ON
Ebony Cooper	Grade 11	Lake View High School	Lake View, SC
Nicole DeLiberis	Grade 12	Coventry High School	Coventry, RI
Diana Folla	Grade 12	LaGuardia Arts School	New York, NY
Yeonsoo Kim	Grade 11	Holy Cross High School	Delran, NJ
Michelley Pinson	Grade 12	Chamblee Charter High School	Chamblee, GA
Connor Stonesifer	Grade 10	Berkeley Preparatory School	Tampa, FL
Melanie Tyler	Grade 12	Applewood Heights Secondary School	Mississauga, ON
Emilie Whitman*	Grade 12	Wenatchee High School	Wenatchee, WA

*Students with an asterisk by their name can be found in this anthology.
All Top Ten Essays can be read at www.poeticpower.com

Note: The Top Ten essays were finalized through an online voting system. Creative Communication's judges first picked out the top essays. These essays were then posted online. The final step involved thousands of students and teachers who registered as online judges and voted for the Top Ten essays. We hope you enjoy these selections.

Teenage Pregnancy

Stacy is a normal sixteen year old teenager; she has friends, she has a boyfriend, but there is one thing about her that is not normal; she's pregnant. This year, over twenty-thousand teenage girls will get pregnant by accident and only half of these babies are carried full term and born; the other half are thrown away. Teenage pregnancy is the leading cause of high school dropouts, poverty, and high blood pressure in babies.

Any teen mother you come across will tell you that it is not easy raising a baby at such a young age. Teenage girls are usually thinking about a new car, piles of homework, their boyfriends, and prom; but add a baby in this hectic mess and the thoughts of school get transformed into diapers, rent, arguments with boyfriends, and expensive formula. This leaves no time for school and makes it nearly impossible to get homework done while focusing on a newborn baby. This leads many teen girls to drop out of high school.

A doctor once told me, "Pregnancy is poverty unless you have a good job." Statistics show that a person with a high school diploma makes twenty thousand less than a person makes with a college degree. People with no high school diploma are forced to subside to a life of working an indigent job and going nowhere.

Not much good comes from teen pregnancy. This epidemic is like a spreading disease. America needs to find a cure for it, and quickly.

Courtney Basquez, Grade 12
Post High School, TX

My Mother

In my lifetime I have been through many things that I couldn't have made it through without my mother. Unlike other people in my life, I know she will always love and be there for me no matter what happens. This is why she is the most important person in my life. As a teenage girl, it is hard for me to express to my mother how much she means to me. Every bad thing that happens in my life I take out on her. But even after I yell and scream at her she still loves and accepts me for everything I am. This unconditional love she has for me is one of the biggest things that keeps me going. My mother does more for me than any person should do for someone and she asks for nothing in return. When she walks into a room people cannot help but smile. She is always happy and lives life to the fullest. She is the most unselfish, nicest, accepting, person I know. She treats everybody she meets like they are the most important person in the world. I hope to one day be even half the person she is. I don't think my mother will ever know how much I love and appreciate her. It will be very hard one day to live without her but she could not have done a better job at preparing me for life. She is the best mother anyone could ever ask for. I could never do enough to deserve her. But I could not be happier to have her.

Kaitlin Bush, Grade 11
Pine Tree High School, TX

Letting Go

We're in the middle of a normal everyday sort of conversation and I'm feeling really good because I think you've made progress. You prove me wrong. I can feel you slowly slipping out of reality, your eyes glaze over and you have this stupid dazed look on your face and you start mouthing the words that I can't make out. I try to pull you back to your senses; I say your name over and over again, louder each time to the point where I am practically yelling in your ears. You've left.

You aren't yourself, you're not anyone, and you're everyone. Just a shell full of personalities and conversations with people you don't know. You'll come back; you always do, but who knows how long you'll be out this time. You're usually gone for a couple of minutes, ten at the most, but I know you can be gone for days.

It's gotten to the point to where I can't handle you in my life anymore. I can't trust a word you say to me. It's all just meaningless dribble. I want to believe in you so badly, but I know better. You've put me through enough already. I am distancing myself from you. From now on, you and I will no longer speak.

I realized that every time you leave, you never come back the same; you have been gone for quite some time. When you left me the first time, you left for good.

Amber Bazan, Grade 11
Cypress Creek High School, TX

War in Iraq

A big controversy in America right now is, if we should stay or leave Iraq. Many people say we have done all we can do, and it's time to bring all of our troops home. I disagree, I think the U.S. being in Iraq and Afghanistan has done and keeps doing a lot of good.

If you look at Iraq before the American invasion and then look at it today, it's like trying to compare night to day. Before we went there, they had a dictator who told them what to do and when to do it, if they did not do it, they were killed. Now the dictator is gone, and they get to elect who leads them. They have also gained much more, now they have more roads, hospitals, schools, and they have their own military.

Many people look past the good we have done, and only focus on the bad. They say this war is only about oil, and we staged everything that has happened, just so we can invade the Middle East and have cheaper oil. I think that is true to some extent. I don't think there was a government conspiracy so we could invade Iraq and have cheaper oil. But I do think that since Iraq and neighboring countries are so rich with oil that helped with convincing people to go in. Now the U.S. can say to the Iraqi government, "Since we helped you, you can help us."

Thomas Vasko Jr., Grade 12
Coronado High School, TX

The Mind and Fear

The sound of my own heart pounding like a jackhammer in my chest sent my mind into panic. Cold shivers ran through me like a thousand needles clawing their way through me. Heavy sounds of growling came from deep down below the darkened attic causing more poison to run through my beating veins.

For many years, fear has tortured the human mind and body. Most of the time fear can lead to death, other times psychologically damaging anyone it meets. It can affect the important emotions that are most frequently used, such as joy, anger, and sorry eventually leading to paranoia. This in turn causes anxiety attacks putting pressure on the human body that causes much more damage. So is it danger that sends fear to us? Alternatively, is it merely our minds playing tricks on us? Think on this can fear actually tell our future? Can it control us, our future? You decide and remember don't let fear find you.

Alexandra Castilleja, Grade 12
Coronado High School, TX

Family First

Some say that blood is thicker than water. I'm one of those people. I believe family comes before anything else. I know it doesn't seem like it but I don't have much family here. Half my family is in Ohio and the other half is in Puerto Rico. Distance doesn't matter. I stay in touch with them through the phone and computer, and when thoughts get too overbearing to talk about I write them in letters.

Who doesn't text these days? As you may know, texting is my favorite hobby. That's how I keep in touch with my distant relatives most of the time. Just as much as I text them, I talk to them on the phone. It's interesting to know what's going on in other places.

Texting is fun, but what happens when they tell you they just had a baby girl and you want to see her but no picture messaging? That's why I'm so glad they invented computers. MySpace isn't just for friends; I've found a lot of family and they found me too. I love to look at the pictures and see how they've changed. Sometimes I like to switch it up and talk to them on web cam.

I just have so much on my mind that it's just overwhelming to talk about. It's like I'm having word vomit. I sit in my room and write a letter to make myself feel better. When I'm done I know that I'm going to feel better and somebody who loves me is reading it. That's the way I relieve stress and talk to my family.

In conclusion, there are a trillion ways to talk to your distant family without having to travel. I believe that family comes before friends. But, in general, distance doesn't matter.

Pamela Carter, Grade 11
Omega High School, CA

The Truth

The words flooded out of my mouth in rapids of misery. My face was hot and clammy as I confessed to my mother the horrid events of the day, trying to get through them as quickly as possible so I could be reassured and hugged by her, for that's what I truly wanted.

My day had consisted of getting told off by a nasty girl and having my best friend stab me in the back by not coming to my defense. The nasty girl and I had been arguing about weather Santa was real or not, an annual tradition. When I turned to Emily for help she confessed no longer being a believer. That's what had hurt the most. Santa had been sacred to me and Emily. Saying you no longer believed in him was practically saying you didn't believe in God either.

I looked to my mother expecting reassurance, love, and comfort, but what I got instead was the truth.

Franchesca Samaniego, Grade 12
Granbury High School, TX

What Matters to Me

There are many things that are important to me; one of them is my learning. If you don't learn anything like reading, writing, or math you will never be able to get a decent job, if a job at all. Besides, no money or job, you will always be unnecessarily dependent on other people. Life will be a never ending circle of disappointments that will make you miserable which can include begging on the streets, drinking, and doing drugs. Also you will not be able to drive and your circle of friends will be very limited. Learning certain things which you now think might be pointless could help you be more successful as your knowledge and understanding grows.

Lynda Sorensen, Grade 11
Valley Christian School, WA

Go Hard or Go Home

"Go hard every play. You don't want to leave anything behind and regret it years down the road that you didn't give it all when you could have," said Ashley DeBuhr, pitcher, University of Nebraska. Softball is a big part of my life. I have to work hard to keep my spot on the team. Giving it my all gets me awards, college scholarships, and a win. Little kids look up to me when I give it my all, and it makes me play harder. Also, playing hard and giving your all earns respect from people that come and watch you play. "Love it, experience it, and when you step on the field just do what you do," said Kirk Walker, coach, Oregon State University. Not only in softball do you have to give it your all, but you have to give it your all in life. During school, you have to give it your all so that you can pass the class and get awards for your hard work and scholarships to colleges. In business work, you have to give it your all so that you can get a superior pay check and will be able to pay for your bills. Working hard and giving it your all will get you great things in life, whether it is a spot on the softball team, an education, or a pay check.

Alisha Brooke Morris, Grade 12
Post High School, TX

Respect

As the years scamper by, respect fades or is even scarcely visible as a result of human blindness regarding the significance of this quality. Unlike other words, respect has a whole complex meaning that will keep vanishing, becoming less and less evident in this society while its brightness is obscured in every family, home and school, by coarse and unfriendly actions. Such actions contribute to the world's unstoppable wave of rebellious and disrespectful behavior.

Respect is not simply a word, it is an attitude of consideration towards others rights. In the human relations, respect cannot be demanded but earned. It is merited although some falsely think they can claim such civil and courteous manners. By offering this characteristic to others, you will get the satisfaction of receiving it back in times in which it was unnecessary to demand. Would it be possible to earn anything, appearing to be prideful, arrogant or abusive? Yes, maybe some things such as objects or money, but one thing that those incorrect deeds could never allow a person to gain is sincere admiration or genuine respect. In some cases, favors are done due to fear but not to respect and with this in mind, to a father give honor, to a child, give guidance, living an exemplary life, and to all men, show respect. Someone once said, "Respect to the rights of others is peace." This quality is one that will undoubtedly lead to a tranquil and prosperous life.

Cindy Mondejar, Grade 11
New Caney High School, TX

Impact on My Life

One person who has made a big impact on my life is my brother Richard Bruner. On July 6th of 2005, my mom Diana Bruner, passed away from a heart attack in her sleep. I was the one who found my mom around noon. When I found out what had happened the paramedics arrived at the house. Richard was the first family member who showed up to see if I was ok after I called.

At the time, my sister, Mary Hayes, was at her friend's house. I was put in the back of a cop car until the sheriff talked to me. Every now and then Richard would ask if he could give me a bottle of water so I wouldn't be thirsty. He didn't talk to me until a few hours later. When the sheriff finally talked to me and asked me questions about my side of the story of what had happened, he put me back in the cop car until me and Mary were taken to a shelter.

When Mary and I were taken to the shelter, we didn't get there until one in the morning. Richard was making many phone calls to see if he could get guardianship over her and me so we can live with him and his girlfriend. After we were in the shelter for three days, he was able to pick us up and take us home.

William Hayes, Grade 12
Coronado High School, TX

Poverty's Reality

Poverty effects millions of people in the world, and can be caused by individual and geographical factors. Due to individual factors there isn't access to employment for non-educated people, fathers get discharged from their jobs and have to face their children with hunger in their eyes when they come home. Geographic factors affect poverty because living in rural areas makes it difficult for nations to provide basic necessities such as purified water, food, education, and primary health care. Medical centers are uncommon in rural areas, and usually there's none that can provide the essential antibiotics for citizens in that area due to the lack of funding. Diseases infest these little towns and kill thousands of people and children who don't even reach the age of two. These individual deaths are unnoticed, completely isolated from the scrutiny of urban cities and the conscience of the world. Millions of people in Africa, India, and other countries are on the streets unable to walk from the fatigue of starvation, denial of medical attention, and are unable to sustain themselves. Poverty never takes a holiday, and is a crime against humanity. People who are fortunate need to eradicate this specific crime from human sight. Who wants to see the fear in a poor woman's eyes clenching her child close not knowing if there's going to be a tomorrow? Fortunate countries need to unite and help repay loans, guarantee free resources, and denounce poverty.

Evelyn Santillan, Grade 11
New Caney High School, TX

How a Life Can Change

This past summer, between my eleventh and twelfth grade year, I had the most amazing and educational time of my life. I was able to attend a program with a youth group from Redondo Beach, California entitled, Sierra Service Project (SSP). We took a road trip down to Tsaile, Arizona, where SSP had assigned our youth group, and we prepared ourselves to help rebuild the Navajo Nation.

During the week, I got to meet many wonderful people from other churches that have been through a lot in their life, but still had the heart to lend a helping hand to those less fortunate. I also had the opportunity of meeting under-privileged Indians that are looking for kind-hearted people to give them a break. SSP taught me that there are other people in the world that need help, and it was a wonderful feeling knowing that I was the one that was able to help these people. However, the Navajos are not that fortunate. These people have gone through so much horror in their life, and it continues to this day. By learning information about these Indians throughout the week, I continued to feel more and more sorry for them.

That week changed me forever, because I got to witness another way of life. With living in the suburbs my whole life, I did grow to have a some what sheltered life, but SSP helped to expand my original ways of thinking. I will never forget this experience.

BreeAna Fileccia, Grade 12
Vista Murrieta High School, CA

High Merit Essays – Grades 10, 11 and 12

Help a Horse

Sometimes the most important things go unnoticed. Sometimes things that hurt quietly are the ones that suffer the most. People don't notice this because ignorance is an easy solution to an "unfixable" issue. Sadly unwanted horses are continuing to be a growing problem. About 150,000 horses are sent to slaughter houses every year in the United States because it is their only option. It's just not humane for something so beautiful and powerful to be destroyed! Horses are amazing creatures! For hundreds of years they have been there for us. In time of war, transportation, recreation, competition, and pleasure, horses have and still are helping us. People take and take from them and they loyally give to us. Horses and people also build more than a work relationship, but it grows deeper than that, in a more personal way. Isn't it only fair that we care for our responsibly, since horses rely on it for their lives? About 81% of horse owners give up their horses because they can no longer afford their high expenses. Many people don't understand that death is not their only option. Horse rescue programs nationwide (although filling up) are always willing to accept a horse in need. Although people would rather overlook this increasing issue, the more people that can help the better off all horses will be. Because after all "These birds and animals and fish cannot speak, but they can suffer." — George Q. Cannon

Alyssa Peyatt, Grade 12
Mililani High School, HI

The Gift of Life

Since 1954, organ donation has been possible; however, there are many people that are sentenced to die unnecessarily because there are no organs available to them. Your own organs could save many peoples' lives. If you choose to donate your organs after your death, your family can still receive and bury your body; just your organs will be missing and still working at keeping another person alive.

Instead of rotting in my coffin, I have decided to donate my own organs once I am gone. I plan to put that I am an organ donor on my driver's license in case I am in an accident. I have made this decision because of several personal reasons. I wish to be a better person and help all those in need. By stepping back and looking at the bigger picture, I have concluded that donating my organs could better the entire world. My kidney could go to a future legislature, or my heart to an Olympic competitor. I chose to save lives with my death. Instead of just leaving one less person in the world, I might be ensuring that several others remain.

People die every day because there are no donorees to save them. Organ donation can be accomplished by simply specifying your willingness on your driver's license. In this way, you can ensure that someone is surviving through your own demise. If you are in a fatal accident, your ending may be the beginning for someone else.

Carson Alsop, Grade 10
Kaufer High School, TX

Sister in Christ

Over many years I have learned the powerful influence of friendship. We will always have those friends who we can have fun with, but then we have that truly special person whom will never be forgotten. For a friendship so rare, I thank God for bringing Lisalette Garza into my life.

It all began three years ago, at a Christian based camp where kids got to enjoy the goodness of the Lord. Not only did God bless me with an amazing group of girls, but provided me with an incredible counselor as well. Above all, Lisalette exhibits something truly special which makes me incredibly thankful that our friendship did not end at camp.

How ironic that I have only known her for a few months, yet it genuinely feels like we have been best friends for years. I am fortunate enough to have her as a mentor to assist me through the hard times. For instance, being a junior this year, I have faced numerous temptations and have gone through countless struggles. She understands what I have gone through and I am relieved that I am able to converse with her honestly and not fear being judged. She points me in the right direction and aids me through my difficulties.

Lisalette's unconditional love for the Lord sets her apart from the rest. In short, she has always been there for me, and I feel so blessed to have her in my life as a sister in Christ.

Hailey Robinson, Grade 11
Flour Bluff High School, TX

From a Shattered Cocoon, Emerged a Butterfly

Among my friends, I am the social, outgoing one. I can transition between different cliques with ease. My ability to connect with people comes naturally, now at least. In my younger years, I was "the" awkward child, afraid of the world and all that was in it. I did as I was told with complaints being rare. I recall the beginning of every school year. I always felt the butterflies. For the beginning weeks I would cry, begging my mother for a way out, an escape from the shame and insecurity I often felt.

My insecurities were due to family issues. My family was far from a family. We were divided by our own personal agendas, bewildered by the thought of an actual family. The physical and mental abuse I took broke me, but with age, I shed the wounded interior, and gained confidence when I realized I deserved better. I was simply fed up.

Present day, my parents are separated. I can barely talk to my father without feeling the pain that he caused me and at times I cry at the thought of a lost childhood. Although the experiences in childhood I had were ones I would not relive, they made me stronger. I shed my insecurities the day I stood up to my father's abuse. From a shattered cocoon, I emerged something greater than I had ever expected.

Brianna Fernandez, Grade 10
American Renaissance Academy, HI

High School

High school! When you think of high school the first thing that pops into your mind is the teenagers roaming the hallways, hanging with buddies, and enjoying life without any worries. Much more goes on in school than you may think. Bullying, narcotics, and sexual activity are all common in my high school. In my opinion dealing with the issues behind the scenes of high school life can be very stressful and life threatening for some students.

Drugs are in the schools. Teachers incorrectly think that posting a sign at the doorway proclaiming the school to be drug free makes it drug free. It is my belief that random drug testing among selected students is not the answer. The students using and dealing drugs are the students exempt from the testing. In addition to drug abuse some kids are constantly being bullied. This cruelty causes a great deal of pain to the victim. Who wants to come to school to endure daily abuse from fellow classmates? These students are defenseless against their tormentors. Another problem that I feel needs to be addressed is the sexual activity among the students. It is not uncommon to see a pregnant teenager ambling through the corridors. These students cannot take care of themselves much less a baby.

High school should be a great experience but in my opinion this isn't always the case. Don't just look at the lines, look between the lines to see what is really going down in the halls.

Britt Reynolds, Grade 10
Kaufer High School, TX

Ice

Heart pounding, adrenaline pulsing, and butterflies inside of me. A crowd of people watching, a panel of judges waiting, the door opens, and I step inside. My name is announced, the music begins, and I start to skate. This is what I feel before every competition. I am a competitive figure skater.

Every time I step onto the ice, all of my troubles disappear. Once I am on the ice, I only hear my music and think of what is in my routine. The ice numbs me from all of my problems, like it numbs a body's injury. But skating is not only an escape; it is also a form of expression. Like dancers, skaters need to listen to their music and convey the emotion or story to the audience. In addition to artistic expression, a skater must also keep focused in order to execute the jumps and spins in a program. Skating is a test of mental strength. It tests how well your mind can balance technique and structure with artistic freedom and creativity. Then, the skater is placed in a high-pressure scenario and must perform, while contemplating all of these points.

I believe skating is a balance between athletic, artistic, and mental strength. I try to fuse the three together in an effortless manner. Though a million thoughts and doubts may pass through my mind, everything is hushed when my music begins and I make my first move.

Katrina Phan, Grade 11
Valley Christian High School, CA

The Underbed Underworld

Laying here in my Barbie bed, I look to my left and see my Barbie night light with her yellow hair shining next to the window looking out into the dark, windy night. I turn right and see the door cracked, where the light is flooding in, yet it's still very dark in my room. My mom is a couple feet down the hall, but it feels like she's twenty miles away. All of a sudden, I freeze in terror. The noise, SCRAAAATCH SCRAAATCH, makes it impossible to move; it sounded like Freddy Kruger dragging his long knife fingers down a pole. Then, the horrible thought. The hand that comes out from under the bed. What if it pulls me into its underworld? He would put me into hot buckets of lava with sharks and then salts and seasons me up for dinner! I looked up and saw another monster on the wall; it was a shadow of branches reaching into the window for me. I ducked under my electric blanket, put all my body parts under and tucked in tight. But it was my feet I worried about most. The whole night, I stayed awake in fear of being taken to the hot, smoky, flaming red kingdom. My only safety was my hot pink electric blanket. I was secure in a cocoon, fortress. That shield of armor would electrocute his large, green, slimy, smelly hand the moment that he touched it…

Shalyn Nettles, Grade 12
REACH High School, TX

Different and Same

What makes people so different from each other? We all have skin, hair, bones, faces, beating hearts, and a mind that constantly keeps us going so what's so different? We all have different personalities, beliefs, features, and how we think that makes us different but is it enough to keep us apart? We walk day by day judging others as if we are perfect with no faults. News flash here, no one is perfect. I know that it is human nature to judge others and weed out the weak links, but is that right? The things people get into fights over are land, money, power, religion, and the opposite sex. Things won't ever be peaceful as long as everyone wants and desires what others have.

Are you wondering why I am writing about this, well first of all it's not nonsense. Second, I am typing to let you all see that there really isn't much difference between people. Instead of looking down on someone maybe we should try thinking of them as equals. If we think in that state of mind then you will find that you have many friends that love and respect you. Those you normally wouldn't think of hanging with could be the one person who gets you out of a trouble or even stands up for you when you need it the most. So just think about getting to know someone before you make a judgment on them it could make the greatest difference in your life.

Erika D'Andrea, Grade 12
Granbury High School, TX

High Merit Essays – Grades 10, 11 and 12

What Lies Beneath the Surface

"Is there something you want to talk about?" I asked him.

"Well Melissa, I feel you should know about my dad," so many things went through my head as soon as Taylor said this, but I shoved it aside with all my might and let him tell his story.

For the next hour, he told me how six months prior to that time, the wheelchair bound, loving father he thought he knew turned into a crazy, psycho guy. He told me how his dad set his room on fire and tried to kill his entire family. How they lived in a safe house, how his dad stalked them and how his parents are now getting a divorce. When he finished all I could think was wow.

"Wow, I'm so sorry." That's all I said, all I could do was look him in the eyes and try to comprehend what he had just said. A few months before I met this kid he had been through a living hell. If he didn't tell me I wouldn't have known. It just seems so unrealistic it's almost like what you would see in a movie or a book. Except it's not, it's reality for this boy. He has inspired me in every way to have the same attitude as him and be as nice as him. If Taylor can go through what he did and not let it affect his life in a negative way then I sure can be just as nice as he is.

Melissa Rendeiro, Grade 12
Granbury High School, TX

One, Two, Three. One…

We take our positions. In front of her dry house full of loneliness. Six cousins, five boys and one girl, one princess, we line up together. Every Monday we fill the street and begin our practice. One, two, three, one, two, three, one. As our voices echo down the road they create one single reply. It is our unity as we drift in the waltz that calms such thirst for joy. What seemed to be a lawn, turns into a garden, what used to be dry becomes fully hydrated, what seemed to be lonely becomes a family. It only has one tree in the front lawn, and it has grown uneven, it has grown isolated from the rest of the trees located behind.

It is my cousin's house. He lives with his wife and child. Aligned at an angle just like that one tree, he has lived a life disconnected from the rest of the family trees. He has created his own world.

However, one road, one home, one new world, coming together echo a single voice. So we drift with beautiful music waltzing up and down. Six people creating one dance. Unity is perfection and practice makes perfect. That is why we are there. A quinceañera will be crowned, a lady will be born, and every family member will be there to support the beginning of a new tree. They will form a foundation in order for the lady to grow strong in a beautiful garden on the other side of the home.

Octavio Medina, Grade 11
San Clemente High School, CA

Love

The heavenly light that I dream about melts me with its gaze. It seems to wrap me in its wings; it makes me feel loved again. Life seems to have a purpose when there's love. Love never fails; love is a foundation that can never be shaken. Love is deep and when stirred, it fills the room with fragrant smells. Love pushes darkness away, and consumes the hearts of those with the purity of a child. The world aches, it has lost true love and has replaced it with lust. Have our hearts grown cold in this "Perfect" world? Where is the love that makes you warm, and truly happy? Love is a pure beacon of hope, hope that doesn't question honesty. I know that this love is still among us, that only one Savior can fulfill.

Aaron Mitchell, Grade 12
University Preparatory School, CA

The Transition

When I was eleven years old, my parents informed my sister and I that we would be moving. I went through numerous hardships that came with adjusting to life in a new country. The school system was a lot different, and the way people handled things was completely new to me. It was hard to adjust. After six years in the United States, I have noticed that the move has truly affected my life. It is the longest I have ever lived in any country. I realized that the way I look at things is different than the way my friends look at things. I have experienced many cultures and ways of life. It has broadened the way I view situations and international events. I feel as if my mind is opened to diverse circumstances, because I have been part of those situations. Moving was a huge obstacle, but I am a different person because of it. I wouldn't give the experience up for the world because it has added richness and diversity in my life.

Jessica Van Gelder, Grade 12
Valley Christian School, WA

Expected News

It was like a nightmare I never woke up from; I wished and prayed I would get up. But no, I couldn't. It was real. The mistake was made; it was incurable. My life of being a dancer in high school was over. My dream of becoming a successful woman was over. I had to think, not only for myself, but for anther person, too!!! I know she would depend on me, so I could not get rid of her!!! She was a piece of my life I could not let go.

Six months later, I was in the delivery room. It was three days after my birthday. I was fifteen with a baby in my arms and the man I loved in the other. He was there support me!! That's when my nightmare became a new dream…I was going to be a mother I would always be there for her, when she is sick, when she does something wrong. Yisell is six months old now, crawling around the house with her daddy crawling next to her. Our lives are perfect. Everything turned out for the best. We are a happy family and we love one another.

Daisy Mendez, Grade 10
REACH High School, TX

Wake Up Call

After sixteen years of life and the gathering of knowledge, I have found the ultimate question to life. I have found the most insignificant yet most thought-provoking and insightful question that everyone takes for granted. I know the number one question that people all around the world ask themselves every day of their lives, but know the answer less than a portion of the time: "What happens next?"

Relating back to my sixteen years of age, my future thrives on this single question on account of the millions of possibilities that await me after my high school graduation. Do I go to college? For how long will I attend college? Which college do I go to? What will I major in? What do I do after college? I resent these choices due to the fact that there are simply too many to fathom, yet I graciously accept all the answers for I trust that my decisions will define where my character rightfully resides.

My future is a scary, wild, massive, magical thing that taunts me with its esoteric mysteriousness reflecting upon my every action and thought. In other words, my future makes me want to scream. I know for a fact that I will attend college; however I have not the slightest clue as to which university I will attend. (With today's economy, I am lucky to even think about college.) My interests change like the wind, so I have no aim at a major. So what happens next?

Michael Todd, Grade 11
Pine Tree High School, TX

An Early Start

My sophomore year was full of surprises. I had a new school, old friends and new coaches. One thing that I didn't expect was to have the news that I could do something extraordinary. From there on out, life for me would change drastically.

I was in fifth period, Spanish with Mrs. Daniels. We were writing a story over our favorite food. I never really liked Spanish, so I always hoped to be called out for some reason. Well I guess it was just my day because finally an office aid walked in. She handed a slip of paper to Mrs. Daniels, who then said my name and handed me the slip of paper. I didn't waste any time getting out of there.

When I arrived at the counselors' office, I was greeted by Mrs. Langley. "Good afternoon," she said. I returned the gesture with a smile, "How you doing?" We walked into her office and she pulled up my transcript, she then said, "You have enough credits to graduate early if you're willing to put forth the effort."

So this year I will graduate with the senior class of 2010. It was hard work and a lot of things to take care of in a short amount of time. Somehow I made it through. I am having some trouble but it will be better towards the end of the year.

Sebastian Chain, Grade 12
Granbury High School, TX

My Own Escape

When I was a child, I always said, at least once a day. "I want to be an adult."

I feel as if I grew up at a very quick rate, which I realize now that I didn't. None of this mattered though — I was having fun and learning.

Those moments came three times a year. During summer, there was one thing I always looked forward to. Tornado Terry's!

What on the face of Earth is that? Every little kid's, or at least was at the time, dream — a store that was full of ARCADE GAMES! When I was here, in this (what seemed 'massive' at the time) building, I was free. We emerged into the icy cold building, escaping the fiery Texas heat, and instantly we all sprinted to the games that we all wanted to beat.

What made it so great? Honestly, I have yet to figure that out. Something about this place just made me a happy kid. I was with friends, and I was doing what I loved to do most: kick butt at video games. For the hours that we were here, we played the games so much, yet they never got boring. We were laughing and enjoying life with our friends.

I miss being a child, but at the same time, I'm glad I've learned my lessons in life. I enjoy finally having the responsibility that I've had a desire for my entire life. I've enjoyed it, and I plan on enjoying it for a long time.

David Duckworth, Grade 12
Granbury High School, TX

The Family Factor

Success in life is sought by many, yet achieved by few. One of the most important aspects of my life which has assisted me in gaining success has been that of family unity. The bond that I have with my family began when I was a child and has developed in strength throughout the course of my life. Upon entering my home, the love that exists for me is immediately made known. Individual members of my family inquire about my day expressing a genuine interest in the minor details of my life. When I have overcome a difficult feat, my rejoicing is shared and is greatly enhanced by each individual family member. At times when I face disappointment and discouragement my family expresses concern and a willingness to assist me in any way possible. Such unity and support creates a unique bond which cannot be found elsewhere.

The standards observed within my family unit have become an important part of my life. In practicing the high standards which have been set, I have developed a positive reputation and defined who I am as a person. High standards and the qualities possessed by an individual have an impact on society and others associated with that individual. As a result of the values I have been taught by my family from my youth, I will be able to make a positive contribution to society. My family defines who I am, and is therefore the most important aspect of my life.

Michael Cope, Grade 12
Spanish Fork High School, UT

High Merit Essays – Grades 10, 11 and 12

My Hero

Once lost in society of utter darkness and the conformity of worldly ways, I started losing hope in finding a leader worth following. Suddenly, a picture of a being that showed all the traits of a loyal, respectable, courageous, self-sacrificing servant of others was placed in my heart. I meditated on this individual who was different from the rest.

Some had heard of whom I was searching and said with great enthusiasm that this person was the answer to all my problems and tribulations. When told of my dilemma, some simply spat at me and said no such perfection can be found. A quest for this undiversified legend was set upon my mind.

Venturing high and low, never did my heart seem to confront the flourishing grace that made the lives of so many filled with delight. I pondered over people such as preachers, teachers, leaders of positive influence, and businessmen of great stature that I had crossed paths with, but none compared to the face of elegant righteousness that rattled my brains and shook my soul.

At the brink of ending my conquest, I took interest in a bright light that shone through the darkness that surrounded and choked me. It was a florescent figure that showered day through my night. The splendor that sweetened my sourness was called Jesus; the strong, gentle pair of arms picked me up from where I had fallen. He was the one I was looking for! He was the loyal friend anyone could entrust with a secret, the only pure form of innocence! He was a man given respect beyond measure when He presented more courage than the mightiest soldier to become the sacrificial lamb that served in the place of every single person that has lived, is living, and will live.

Kent Kirby, Grade 12
North Lamar High School, TX

The Divorce

My parents got divorced in the summer when I was going to 9th grade. They were talking about it and arguing a lot before this. I hated it and I never stayed home with my parents. My evil grandma got into it and started hitting my dad. I couldn't take it anymore; she made me so mad that I started crying. Then, I left to stay with my nice grandma, the one I stay with on the weekends. That's how the whole me-living-with-my-grandma-thing started. I've always wanted to live with her. My dad, my brother, and I all lived at my grandma's house. My dad took us back and forth from Blue Mound to Haltom City, just to go to school. That didn't last long. My mom bribed me into living with her and her boyfriend at that time in Colorado. I liked it at first. Then things got messed up. I wasn't going to school, so I pretty much dropped out for a year. It was ok, but now that I look back, it isn't. I moved back down to Texas and moved in with my boyfriend. He got me into REACH. Now I will hopefully get things back together and graduate in 2011 like I should have and not 2012. All I have to do is keep up the good work.

Shanna Weisbeck, Grade 10
REACH High School, TX

Above the Influence

Children can only be described as naive. They are dependent on the world and people around them without question. Every place, person and small detail has an impact on the child's development for better or worse.

My father attempted to kill my mother and was stopped by myself and siblings when I was ten years old. The thought that my father would harm my mother was unbelievable. It made me question my entire life that I believed to be happy. I was soon pushed into a world of screaming, fighting and pain. Being a child there was nothing I could do to escape the hell formally known as my childhood. There was not a night that I couldn't hear my mother cry in her room.

Being the oldest child I did my best to grow up quickly, but I grew distant from my friends and old life. I had new responsibilities to attend to. I did not have time to be a child, nor will I ever get that time back.

The conditions of my "childhood" shaped me to become a responsible and independent young adult. These trials did not come without a cost. I became unable to trust the world around me and I soon found that no matter how much I detested my father, he had played a key role in shaping my development and for that I was thankful.

Children can only be described as naive, but they are no more so than the people, that surround them.

Mollie Wheeler, Grade 12
Granbury High School, TX

Friends

Friends are the most important thing in my life, not because I have to go to school with them, but because they make school, and the rest of my life in general, so much fun! Being able to talk to somebody, going to fun activities, and knowing they are always there are the main reasons I love my friends. Life in general is a stressful process, but when you have people to share it with, the task becomes easier. There are so many aspects of life, and being able to slow down once in a while and just talk with a friend makes me feel so much better. My friends and I have planned and attended so many fun activities. My personal favorite was bridge jumping, but we have also gone to the corn maze, been sledding, and we also play sports together. When life gets tough, it is always inspiring to know that you have someone behind you. Sometimes it's that one compliment or encouraging word that changes your day from lame to delightful. The only people that can do that are my friends. My friends are always there, either to encourage me or just talk to me, and it's the fun activities we do together that make our lives exciting. I hope that during the course of my whole life, I will have friends as close as I do now. Even better, I hope that the friends I have now are friends for life!

Meaghan Miller, Grade 12
Valley Christian School, WA

A True Hero

Often times, a hero is seen as a daring prince, courageous super hero, or one who becomes famous. While these exemplify qualities of a hero, a person does not need to slay a dragon or fight off evildoers to be called one. Irene Sendler, for example, did not possess any supernatural powers; however, her acts of courage definitely made her a hero. Irene lived during the time of the Holocaust as a health worker. When the Germans invaded her country, she began to work in the canteens. Here, she became the savior of the Jewish children. Motivated by her care for the young, Irene smuggled the children out of the camps to religious centers. The children then grew to become men and women. Even when the Nazis found out and tortured her for her "crimes," she remained faithful to her mission by refusing to reveal the hiding places of the young Jews. By the end of the war, an estimated 2,500 Jews were saved by Irene. Despite her noble deeds, many Americans today do not know she exists. This does not however, make her any less heroic. People do not need to earn a title to be a hero. In fact, some of the most renowned heroes do not even consider themselves to be one. Rather, like Irene, they continue to serve others despite the lack of recognition. Irene Sendler and many other heroes have impacted the world by simply opening their eyes to the suffering and acting upon it.

Jordan Yoshihara, Grade 10
Whittier Christian High School, CA

The Blessing of Music

Music is the essence of life. It has the power to uplift, tear down, energize, introduce new ideas, depress, revamp thoughts, direct actions, invigorate one with passion, release emotion, move someone to tears, relieve stress, encourage, lead someone in worship, and inspire. In my life, music is evident throughout. Its presence is always there, in the car, at home, and even at school. Life is viewed differently through the veil of music, giving it color, beauty, and purpose. During some stress-filled days and nights of tiresome heartache, an experience can be aided and soothed through the wondrous help of music. Hearing a beautiful piece of music moves me to tears, as something deeper than this Earth speaks to me. With encouraging lyrics, music can strengthen me throughout the day and show me my worth in life. Uplifting me when I am depressed and filling my soul with passion, music changes my outlook on life. Powerful choruses and verses with great chord progressions prove music's power to transform a life. God can speak to a person through music, showing us there is more to life than what is visible. If anger fills one's character, music can alleviate the strong emotion. Music outlines every aspect of life; movies, parties, dances, concerts, schools, churches, weddings, funerals, and processionals would not be the same without music. The blessing of music on Earth gives a beauty to life that only something greater than this world can give.

Paul Hoffman, Grade 10
Whittier Christian High School, CA

Life Lessons

As Dan Gable once said, "Once you have wrestled everything else in life is easy." Having wrestled throughout my life I know this statement as a true fact. During wrestling practice you are using everything in your body; from your head to your feet, even your mind. Wrestling isn't an easy sport, on average a wrestler at Spanish Fork High loses 5-7 pounds a practice. Wrestling doesn't just teach you how to be physically tough, but it teaches you how to be mentally tough and how to handle problems in life.

Coach Webb who coaches locally in Spanish Fork teaches his students how to become great, hard nosed wrestlers. Along with that he tells them that once they learn how to do certain things in a match the rest is mental. Once you learn how to overcome problems in a wrestling match you start to win on the mat. After that, you win in life.

If you are mentally tough and determined not to give up on your goals, you succeed at some point in time. I play football along with wrestling and I always hear my teammates complaining about how hard it is to remember the plays or how hard conditioning is. Because of wrestling I know that if I tell myself "this is easy" it becomes easy and I don't struggle with it. This also helps me in my life never to give in to a challenge, to do my best and to never sell myself short. Win Forever!

Michael Stone, Grade 12
Spanish Fork High School, UT

What Can You See in Yellowstone?

During June, I went to Yellowstone National Park for the first time in my life. We left home at noon, and drove to Yellowstone. We got to our campground at about six o'clock. We got out of our car, and felt the cool mountain air. As we set up camp, it started raining, and as we set up, we got very wet. As we toured the park over the next week, we saw many beautiful hot pots, geysers, and many animals. As we walked on the boardwalks around the hot pots, we smelled the sulfur in the water and the steam. At Mammoth Hot Springs, we touched some runoff from the hot springs. The water had run down a bright orange mountain side, so it had lost some of its heat, but it was still much warmer than body temperature. After that, we went to see Old Faithful erupt. We saw it start to erupt, and we could feel water droplets, blown in our direction. As it continued to erupt, we could hear the water spewing up and splashing down onto the ground. As we were driving back to our campground, we saw a black bear eating. We could hear it moving through the tall grass. As we saw more hot pots, some smelled so strong that I could almost taste the sulfur in the air! My trip to Yellowstone was great, and I saw many things that I had never imagined before.

Ty Haws, Grade 12
Woods Cross High School, UT

High Merit Essays – Grades 10, 11 and 12

Abortion: Is It Really Necessary?

Today we are subjected with debates about how certain procedures could be used to enhance and save people's lives; however these procedures have recently been classified as "inhumane," "unethical," and as "blasphemous." What is the reason for these medical procedures to be labeled as a taboo? Is it because of religion or moral standards? Well to me these procedures are undoubtedly inhumane, and I do hope one day these procedures can be stopped.

Let's take a look at abortion. Abortion is a procedure used for pregnant women who "abort" their child while it's still in the process of becoming an infant. Abortion is done with the consent of the woman, knowing that in the process it would "eliminate" the child permanently. Now this is where it's controversial. The "eliminating" of the child has caused many debates, especially by those who rely on religious or moral beliefs to guide their decision making. Personally, I believe that abortion is considered immoral because killing is wrong, even if the victim has yet to be born.

Although many people have different opinions about abortion, as well as the procedure, I feel that people must realize what moral boundaries they are breaking when they take a life of a human being — no matter how young the victim.

Lucas Ruiz, Grade 10
Kaufer High School, TX

The Camera

I hastily paced back and forth in the eerie hallway that smelled of musty back drops and hairspray. As I waited, all I remember thinking was how much easier this would be if my aunt Tammy could have made it. Aunt Tammy had always supported me and when needed she gave me a shoulder to cry on. She helped me whenever I needed it. She would always help anyone, despite the selfish and self-centered thoughts of others.

Just then the short, but very pretty photographer stepped through the door with a gust of wind that swam around me and wrapped me up like a cocoon. I was sick with anxiety with each step that she took. I had never liked the camera, or being in front of people, and I was on my own this time. My Aunt Tammy had always told me that I could do anything I set my mind to, but as I waited to take my senior pictures I was beginning to doubt this. The photographer finished setting up and we got started. As the bright lights went on my fears melted away. I just knew that my aunt would be so proud of me. If it wasn't for her advice and words of wisdom I would have never gone through with what was probably one of the best experiences in my life. Through all of this I realized sometimes you have to overcome your fears with or without the ones you love by your side.

Jessica Copeland, Grade 12
Granbury High School, TX

Black and White

The memories in black and white always seem a little more elusive, as if the lack of color constitutes a lack of memory. The tired roar of a dead philosopher's voice always seems more distant when there's only a first name and you can't relate with the era. There's more to what I hear than the white noise that seems to come and go, spattering conversation with little pieces of nonsense, that somewhere, in some other conversation or galaxy, might have meaning. The grainy reception in a TV is no different from the grainy reception I perceive from reality, and the smoke signals in Darfur are no different than the ones I see in my own backyard.

The parts of the whole never come together unless they were once apart, and this means as little to me as anything else. I'm starting to think what one person says is as true as anything else. Truth is a lie and lies are lies and truths inside of lies are masked as truth and who really understands what the truth is anymore? Is truth more important than faith and plain human imagination? I'm sure if I didn't know the grass was green because of chlorophyll that I would wonder what made it that way; the wonder though, the questioning, is what makes this life so much more interesting. The truth is, even if life is just some steps in a process, who's to say those steps aren't on beds of hot coals?

Payton Ritchey, Grade 10
Memorial High School Senior Campus, TX

A Little Wit, Please

Trying to ease my boredom after the first five hours of my train journey through the barren landscapes of Nevada, I had just sat down in a new location to read. I sighed and delved into the story, only to be interrupted eleven pages later by a total stranger around my age. We began to converse, but at the back of my mind I was wondering when I could return to my book. Twelve hours later, I was reluctant to abandon the train and my new acquaintance's conversation. I never did go back to reading.

Thinking back, I wondered what in the world could have entertained me in conversation for twelve hours! For me, that was quite a feat; usually I can barely keep up a conversation for one or two hours, let alone twelve, and I tend not to talk much with strangers. However, when I thought about the content of our conversation, I discovered it was his wit which had kept me intrigued. We had been constantly laughing, but cleverness had never ceased to be present in our joking.

As a girl who tends to over-think and overanalyze everything, intelligence is incredibly important to me. The frivolousness of "girly-girls" and crude guys really gets on my nerves. On the other hand, when I find someone who can joke cleverly without resorting to crudeness, it really sparks my interest. Really all I ask for an interesting conversation is "A little wit, please."

Katherine McLain, Grade 12
Faith Christian Jr/Sr High School, CA

Lamb of God

"You are my strength when I am weak. You are the treasure that I seek. You are my all in all. When I fall down you pick me up. When I am dry you fill my cup…" God stands as the most important person in my life and without Him my life would not be the same. God places many people in my life to help me learn and make my faith grow even stronger. He also allows me to experience Him in ways that encourage me to trust Him and put my life in His hands. One reason I consider God the most important person in my life is because He always cares for me and watches over me through the good times and the bad. I love that no matter what I do, He will forgive me. Growing up in a Christian family, I believe, has helped me immensely in my walk with God. Having a wonderful, loving, encouraging, and most important, spiritual family, created the foundation for my eternally growing relationship with Him. I have endured many hard times with friends, but we usually seek God for His guidance and we receive it. I have made a promise to myself that my kids will grow up in a great Christian home like me. God plays a very big part in my life and He will continue to do so forever. "…You are my all in all."

Kinsey Jeffers, Grade 11
Pine Tree High School, TX

Something of Importance

Everything is important to me in one way or another. I have my family, my sister and my mom whom I love very much and would do anything for, and I have my friends, whom I would do mostly anything for. I have my materialistic items that have become a little more important to me than I'd care to admit, and I have my own ideals and things that are important to me in various ways. However, I have a particularly odd affinity for plotlines. I'm not all that picky, really — any type of plot has the potential to be good and intriguing. Plots bring things, people, whole worlds, and strange events to life. The ability, the *power* to bring something that isn't even a whole idea, just a small whisper of a thought, to life is an amazing skill in my opinion. It's important to me, because while I'm not very good at it right now, I hope one day to become as skillful at it as some of the writers and authors of my time. I have every intention to do so. I want the ability to weave lives in to an unbreakable web made of nothing but the words and thoughts that are my own, and yet seemingly belonging to someone else, or several others. In a really odd sense, it's like controlling the world. There's really no rhyme or reason for it…but everyone's dreams have to start somewhere.

Miranda Samford, Grade 11
Pine Tree High School, TX

The Perseverance That Began a Reformation

"I cannot and will not recant anything, for to against conscience is neither right nor safe. Here I stand, I can do no other, so help me God. Amen." Martin Luther. In early sixteenth century churches, people were led to believe that they could buy their eternal salvation. In 1517 a Protestant reformer, Martin Luther, combated these beliefs and teachings in *The Ninty-Five Theses* and nailed his theses to the front door of the Castle Church in Whittenberg. In his theses, Luther negated the beliefs imposed upon the people of Europe by the pope and by Charles V. Since Luther refused to go against his beliefs that salvation is through grace which is given as a gift from God, he became an enemy to the high officials in both religion and the government. The ideas in Luther's theses spread quickly across the European countryside, because Luther's negation to the church meant that all mankind had opportunity to receive their salvation through grace instead of paying for the absolvence of their sins. This idea gave birth to Protestant Reformation and the forming of the Lutheran church. Protestant reformers, like Martin Luther, were persecuted by high authorities and by many of the Roman Catholic denomination. Luther bared his cross as a martyr. "Even if I knew that tomorrow the world would go to pieces, I would still plant my apple tree." Luther knew that in the worst case scenario, he would be put to death, and that eternal salvation was his reward.

John Bocko, Grade 12
Post High School, TX

It Was Sunday

It was Sunday, March 2, 2008.

I had been in a great mood all day. I was extremely hyper and bouncing off the walls. That was soon about to change.

My best friend had called, and she gravely informed me that a girl in my Algebra class, Alyssa, had just been in a horrific car accident. She was on her way home from church choir with her two sisters when her oldest sister took a turn too fast, causing them to slide into oncoming traffic. Alyssa died on impact.

Alyssa was the most devout Christian I had ever encountered throughout my life, and she didn't deserve to die.

Two or so weeks before Alyssa's accident, one of my very close friends and I had gotten into a dispute about typical high school stuff that is never important. We hadn't even spoken to each other and I was beginning to think that we never would make amends. As I walked towards my Algebra class my friend approached me. We started talking. At the end of the conversation she simply stated, "You know, this really makes you think how stupid some things are. How we let something so small get in the way of our friendship."

And just like that, the argument was over.

Not many people ever think to live each day like it was their last. Everything you know and love can be gone in a matter of seconds. I now know that and implement it in my everyday life, thanks to Alyssa.

Carpe Diem.

Ruth Morris, Grade 12
Granbury High School, TX

Beyond the Music

For some people, a stage complete with a microphone and a spotlight represents nervousness, or fear. But to me, it symbolizes something that is very important in my life, which is singing praises to God, my Creator. The very first time I sang in my church's adult praise band, I experienced a shocking peace inside my heart that whisked away my anxiety. It dawned on me that I finally found a way to share my talents in a way that glorified the Lord. Christian music contains hundreds of different spiritual messages, praises and emotions. I truly love to use that music to express my heart. Sometimes, if I feel discouraged or lost, that spiritual emotion will bubble up my throat and morph into a song. I used to fear what others thought about my voice, my looks, or my way of worship. To reveal my voice was to reveal something very personal. But because I sing to my Father, I gladly open up my heart to Him. Now, I do not worry about what others think of me when I lift my voice and worship my king. When I sing to Jesus, it feels like a father wrapping his arms around his daughter, smiling and saying, "I am proud of you, my child." Each time the final notes of the ending praise song resonate in the sanctuary, I look into the faces of the audience to see if they feel the joy that is beyond the music.

Victoria Coleman, Grade 11
Pine Tree High School, TX

Striving for Purpose

We, as a community, continue to live our "insignificant" lives on a teardrop sized stretch of time, as if everything revolves around us. Media, social construction, and interaction with others does not detract from this fact whatsoever; it only adds to the belief that we are important. Are we important? More than 6 billion people are living today, with innumerable amounts that have previously existed. Can we truly believe that we have a purpose? That one person, out of tens of billions, has a certain importance that is specific to him alone? As a teenager, living in this age, I cannot comprehend how all of mankind assumes importance out of the seemingly unimportant. Can we truly say that we have any meaning at all?

This train of thought leads to an individual's doubt of whether or not living has any meaning. I believe it is the essential foundation of human achievement, an effort for humankind to strive for a purpose. Without this underlying question in every human's mind, people wouldn't accomplish anything. What would be the point? It would all be irrelevant. We feel happy after doing something worthwhile because it gives us a sense of fulfilling our purpose, to however small a degree. We see this in the Declaration of Independence, with our right to the *pursuit of happiness*. In ancient Greek, the definition of happiness was to "fulfill one's purpose." So we can conclude that striving for importance is itself, important, because it is the cause for our continued happiness and progression as a species.

Ethan Lie, Grade 11
Valley Christian High School, CA

Something Important to Me

A child cries as he watches his father walk through the front door for the last time, his two year old lungs can't take much more, and eventually he cries himself to sleep. A six year old girl watches over him, holding her own painful cries deep inside. In that moment, eleven years ago, my brother became the most important thing to me, our father left and our broken mother cried in the bathroom. With no father to protect his son, I stepped in; a six year old took on her father's responsibilities. My brother and I grew closer over that time, we cried together, stuck together through thick and thin, together we brought our mother back from the abyss. Then again, our father had to ruin it all.

Years later his words dripped from his deceiving mouth just as venom dripped from a serpent. Our father was back; his selfish mind thinking only of himself. In a tragic accident I was separated from my brother, a knee injury kept me from him. In that time we grew apart. He fell under the man's unfaithful promises and again our father had torn the family. It took time and the fight was hard, but my brother returned, and in time he will realize he is still the most important thing to me. But, for now, I quietly watch over him waiting for the next time he will need me.

Jessica Mohler, Grade 12
Northridge High School, UT

Strength and Weakness

According to Myers-Briggs, my type is the Idealist. Three traits of an Idealist would be humane, imaginative, and sympathetic. My subtype is Teacher. Three traits of my subtype would be benevolent, romantic, and supportive.

I believe being humane is a strength for me. I am characterized by kindness and compassion. I also believe being supportive is a strength. My aunt just recently lost her job. She has two small children, and she is barely making it. Because I care, I have offered to help. I now give her half my check and help care for my cousins as she goes out to find a job. If she needs me, I am there. I will always help her with whatever it is I can.

At times, being sympathetic is a weakness for me. I have been stepped over for being too sympathetic. I was giving someone money to buy food, since I was told they were going through hard times. I later found out it was all a lie, it was all being used to buy alcohol. I can make this trait into strength. I just need to draw that line and know when I really should show sympathy and when I shouldn't.

Overall, my traits suit me well. I wouldn't change them. My subtype was teacher. I can turn out to be a teacher. Being kind, compassionate, and supportive are amazing traits for a teacher to have. Students need help and understanding, which I can surely give.

Michelle Morazán, Grade 12
Coronado High School, TX

Friend Forever

In our small Texas town, the soil is usually hard and dry. But not today. Today, our shovels easily pull the earth from its long staked home. It gives way without struggle, as if wanting to help us as we toil. The terra is moist from the rain that has fallen with our tears for most of the week. We work in silence, my friends and I. We reflect on the past year, and just what it means for us to be working here.

We stood in a large group facing the tree. On the cue of my history teacher, I stepped forward and recited the poem I had written for the occasion:

The **A** is for attentiveness
For she had nerve to care
The **M** is for the memory
She left for us to share
The **B** is for the bravery
That was inside of her
The **E** is for everything
Of which she had made sure
The **R** is for remembrance of her caring love
And we'll remember AMBER
As she smiles up above

And then everyone — myself, and my macho football playing friends included — burst into tears, realizing for a final time, that our friend had left us. She wasn't coming back this time.

Collyn Glaspie, Grade 10
Wall High School, TX

Soccer

As I run toward the goal, and I hear friends cheering and crowds chanting, I can feel my energy rising and spirits lifting. The ball moves from foot to foot, as if floating gracefully on a cloud. I know exactly how to control its movement and flow through the grass. The rush I get from playing soccer is so indescribable that it can change my mood in an instant. Watching my team play is like watching a dance performance in a ballroom. The way players assemble themselves with such natural ability makes you wonder how God is able to bless so many people with extraordinary gifts. I can see our team attacking as we pass one defender, and another, until we score and win the game! No story or tale ever told lives up to the experience of scoring your very first goal as a child. Soccer gives you the opportunity of reliving those childhood memories or creating new ones with the loved ones around you. This sport is played all around the world. It is no wonder why people love it so much!

Soccer is a sport that includes everyone, whether tall or short; looks or brains don't matter. All that matters is having a willing spirit, a fun filled attitude, and being ready to play! Soccer is able to bring joy to an individual practicing or a whole team. Whether you are just learning or have been playing your whole life, playing soccer gives a person the thrill of experiencing the beauty of one elegant sport.

Alejandra Alvarado, Grade 11
Valley Christian High School, CA

Bigger Is Better

As a child, bragging about how many family members you had meant complete domination. Every kid on the playground could not top my number, the big eight. I told them all I actually had nine though, because my mother had a miscarriage with a baby girl. The years went on and still arriving at top, I stayed awesome. With four boys and two girls, we had a lot of fun and were never alone. Bigger really is always better. Even though having lots of friends makes you the cool kid at school, at the end of the day, the love that comes from family conquers any amount of friends you could ever have. Some days I would wish I was an only child, because they received more presents from their parents, they never wore hand-me-downs, and they never had to share. Looking back on those thoughts, the realization that I would actually rather spend the rest of my life never getting any presents, always wearing hand-me-downs, and sharing everything I had, than never having my brothers and sisters. The most important thing is family. Without that center focus, many people would become lost and hopeless. Always having the support system and love from them, remains a blessing to the world. Knowing that no matter how bad I mess up, Mama will wipe away the tears, Daddy will help fix the mistake, and my siblings will make me smile, makes my life worth living.

Sophia Rossow, Grade 11
Pine Tree High School, TX

The Beast

I came home from school one day and my dad told me to go out the back door and that he had a surprise for me. I leapt out of the house, looking. "Nothing?" In anger I screamed out, "Dad!!" with my pupils lashing out of my head. "THUD!!!" I fell to the ground with a snarling beast lying on top of me. At first I figured I should play dead, but he kept licking my face, so I screamed with terror and disgust.

My dad yelled, "Elvis" and the beast jumped off me, ready to eat me. I stumbled to my feet.

"His name is Elvis and he is our dog and I blah, blah, blah, blah, blah." All I could hear was "our dog" in my ear. I am going to die. This is not a dog, it's a killing machine. I ran for the door to try to get away.

"BAM!" Stupid glass screen, why do I keep running into you? My dad went inside laughing at my pain. I tried getting away from the beast.

I fell to the ground with a thud. This dog my dad called Elvis stopped and looked at me like I was strange! This dog is kind of cute. He fell to the ground expecting a belly rub. So I scratched his belly and calmed down. So I played with him a little bit then went inside to rest.

"BAM!" Stupid glass screen.

Ryan Belote, Grade 10
Wall High School, TX

Sisterly Love

I awoke to the sound of tears and immediately expected to hear troubling news. I slowly rose out of bed, quietly opened up my creaky door, and tiptoed down the dark hallway, where I halted right outside my sister's door. As I softly pressed my ear against the wooden door, I could hear her soft cries. I wrapped my trembling hand around the doorknob and cautiously opened the door.

As I crept in, I saw my sister sitting in the soft glow of the lamp light with a tear-streaked face. When she saw me, she began to cry again and explained that she and her boyfriend had broken up. As she cried, I comforted her the best way I knew how. She did not want to listen to me at first, but she eventually did.

I informed her that the ending of this relationship could be good, and she needed to see the positives. Then, I repeatedly convinced her that better relationships would come in her future, which consisted of love and respect. Finally, the correctness of my position occurred to her, and her sorrows disappeared. She thanked me, and then embraced me in a way that only sisters can do.

I gave good advice to my best friend that day and helped a wounded goose fly again. From then on, I have been pleased to help with all of her problems, to ensure she gets out of every troubling situation and is prepared to fly to a new destination.

Caitlyn Espitia, Grade 11
Flour Bluff High School, TX

The Runner

It all started at the track. The gun sounded and everybody took off. I thought I would just walk in there like nobody's business and win the race, but I quickly found out that running is more difficult than it looks, a lot more difficult. So difficult that I got dead last, they actually got tired of waiting for me and started the next race. Although this was humiliating, for some reason it motivated me at the same time. I got a thrill from running around this circle, feeling the breeze across my face, hearing the crowd scream with excitement. From this I decided how I was going to spend my summer, improving myself as a runner. I remember the first day of training. I wish it was my last. There was no way that I would be able to do this every day for the entire summer, but miraculously I managed to drag myself onto the hard paved road every day. The days seemed to stretch longer in time, and the road seemed to grow further every day, but I was determined to get faster. People never seemed to understand why I ran without a coach, but they never realized that I didn't need a coach, desire was my coach and it fueled me to run down that road faster and faster every day.

Andrew Cantu, Grade 11
New Caney High School, TX

Love of My Life

Aside from God, family, and friends, there is one thing that has kept me going through all the stress and hardships of life. Although it seems ridiculous to think such a thing could bring so much happiness, soccer is my pride and joy. After ten years of playing, I can't imagine my life without the beautiful game that has helped me emotionally and physically. Soccer has shaped who I am today.

The people I have met throughout my career have been some of my best friends on and off the field. I have grown close to them after years of working together as teammates. Staying united as a team has helped our relationships grow as friends because it forces us to support and build each other up. It is the most amazing feeling to do something you love with great people surrounding me.

Soccer has disciplined me and shown me how hard work pays off. Soccer is a physically demanding sport that has taught me to not give up even when I am faced with a challenge. I have been faced with mean coaches, who have made me want to quit, but my passion for the sport overpowers people who try to take away my love for the game.

I can't imagine my life without soccer since it has taken up so much of my time and energy throughout the years. No matter how frustrating and tiring it has become over the years, soccer is my joyous escape from reality.

Lindsay Cole, Grade 11
Valley Christian High School, CA

Warning, New Sickness

It's flu season once again, and I'm reminding you to wash your hands and cover your mouth with your inner elbow. Hey, I'm just trying to prevent the H1N1 (Swine Flu) and the common cold. I don't want anyone to catch the contagious germs. However there is a new virus brandishing its sword in the air. In the past, it rarely affected the human species. But for some reason, the virus is coming back in full force. What should we call it? Aha, the Outburst Flu.

In September, celebrities and political leaders alike have failed to suppress the urge to keep their inner thoughts to themselves. Symptoms include: screaming "You lie!" while President Obama is speaking like Rep. Joe Wilson; being a Serena Williams and threatening a tennis official that you would shove a ball down their throat; or pulling a Kanye and stealing the microphone and voice your opinion during someone else's acceptance speech. There is no cure or medicine so far, but I advise patients to seek anger-management, take yoga, or simply hold your tongue. If at any time you feel like the Outburst Flu is starting to take over again, please write in a journal or express your feelings to some who cares about your problems. Side effects may include sheer foolishness, embarrassment, getting booed, and being ostracized. Please call your local friend or clinic and help yourself today.

Ebony McCaskill, Grade 10
View Park Preparatory Accelerated Charter High School, CA

Music!

The sweet melody gently lulls me to sleep; the loud crash of cymbals and the scream of the guitar awaken my deepest emotions. Music controls my emotions, thoughts, and actions. I noticed when I am downtrodden or angry listening to hard rock that has intense screaming in it intensifies those feelings. When I feel emotional pain, I can turn on my music as loud as I can and blast away my pain. This music also affects the way I drive in the sense that I drive a lot faster when I hear it because my driving has a direct connection with my emotions. Classical music does the exact opposite slowing down my emotions and balancing them with its sweet harmonies. Music plays such a big role in my life, whether I'm performing it or just listening to it. Unfortunately, today's society has forgotten music and its emotional values it contains. A lot of the music in today's society is just words empty and flavorless. Music should stir your very soul when listening to it. Therefore, I ask you to listen to music in a different way to separate the real soul moving music and the plain dry crap society offers today!

Colton Astwood, Grade 12
Coronado High School, TX

Fearful Warrior

I have never given a second thought to my name before. Sure, I have googled Kellie a few times, but I have never thought about the results. Coming from the ancient Gaelic name Ceallach, Kellie means warrior, yet I prefer peace. I also prefer to think of warrior as simply aggressive and driven, which does describe me.

As a child, I received the nickname Beans, but that related to my lanky appearance, not my name. My mother named me after Kelly Bundy, on the television show *Married…with Children*. Michelle, my middle name, comes from my father's name, Michael. My name, a whispering river, flows when spoken, and looks lovely when written. Though the meaning of my name does not quite fit my personality, I would never change my name.

The myths behind my name capture my interest. Two legends relating to my name deal with a saint and a goddess. Though St. Ceallach actually uses the old form of Kellie, I relate less to it. Meanwhile, in prehistoric Ireland, priestesses called Kelles devoted themselves to the Goddess Kele. Mysterious, religious, and powerful, Kele bore an eerie resemblance to the Hindu goddess, Kali. While I do not inspire fear, or have four arms, I find it incredibly intriguing that my personal identity, Kellie, relates to such a strong, sinister woman. I will not lash out like a snarling tiger, or an angry goddess, but I will fight for what I believe in, just like my name suggests.

Kellie Cyrus, Grade 11
Flour Bluff High School, TX

Music

Do you ever get that feeling of purpose or know you were meant to do whatever it is you are doing? Well, I feel exactly that way when I play the guitar. As I pluck each string, the next one just comes naturally to me with each sounding note, echoing in my ears and bringing peace to me after any kind of day I just had. Energy flows from the guitar, through my fingers to my chest after each song that I play, along with the feeling of great achievement.

Even when I mess up, I get the feeling of motivation that makes me want to be better at what I'm doing, and as I end my session, everything I just played rings in my ears in perfect harmony through the next day, and the next day, and the next day.

Brian Patterson, Grade 11
Valley Christian High School, CA

Trust

If there is anything I've learned from life so far, it's to trust few people, if anyone at all.

You never really know who could be a Judas, just waiting to betray you for his own 30 pieces of silver.

As time goes by you learn to keep you internal guard up, letting few into your personal side. Don't get me wrong though, you shouldn't take it too far to the point where you shut everyone else around you out, but just learn to be cautious.

The friends you want to have fun with are not always the friends that would stick around when you really need their help. Unfortunately, I learned this information a little too late and had to learn the hard way.

So trust few, and keep the people that you can trust close, because I've learned those people are the hardest to find.

Eric Grace, Grade 12
Vista Ridge High School, TX

Relative

It was one late afternoon and my sister Erin and I went down to the lake with my mom. Erin wanted to swing down by the water. I agreed and we walked down together. I went first, as we took turns pushing each other on the swing. We got bored pretty fast so we decided to just pass the swing back and fourth. Erin was standing on one side and I was on the other. When I passed Erin the swing, I accidentally threw it really hard. It hit Erin in the head and knocked her onto the ground. She started crying and screaming so I went to go get my mom as fast as I could. My mom reached down to pick her up and there was blood covering the ground. I was really shocked and scared. My mom took her upstairs and put her in the tub to wash off the blood. I had cut a huge slice in her head. My mom parted her hair away for the cut so she could clean it. It was a lot bigger than I thought. Thankfully, Erin didn't have to go to the hospital. I learned a good lesson from that. Never play around with a swing.

Shannon McBride, Grade 11
Vista Ridge High School, TX

High Merit Essays – Grades 10, 11 and 12

From Chicago to Fort Worth

I had just graduated from middle school. My friends and I were getting ready to go celebrate when my mom gave me the horrible news, I couldn't believe what I was hearing. After spending five amazing years in Chicago I was told I had to move back to Fort Worth. I was angry, but since it was my last night in Illinois with my friends I wasn't going to let it get to me. I tried to have the best time I could, knowing that after that night I was going to have to start a new life. The celebrations were coming to an end and it was time to say our goodbyes. I tried to keep a positive mood but I knew I was going to miss my friends and family. I headed back home feeling lonely. As my brother and I packed up more and more memories kept going through my mind. My bags were packed and my brother and I were sitting on our porch remembering old times. We were going to miss the windy city. Feeling like lost puppies because there was nothing we could do we drifted off to sleep. The next morning our aunt dropped us off at the train station. We said our goodbyes and before I knew it we were heading to Fort Worth Texas. As I stared out the train window I knew there was nothing I could do but hope for the best, and that's exactly what I did…

Jose Rodriguez, Grade 12
REACH High School, TX

Stories in Music

I sat in the choir room, empty of sound after the singing youths had gone. Mr. Doss entered, his hands cradling pages of music.

His eyes showed the exhaustion in his 25 years of work. Despite this, his greetings would always add a smile to anyone around him.

"Let's get started," he said. The silence that had once shrouded the room had now become engulfed with a river of sounds and words. "There's a feeling that you give," he said. "Have you ever considered going into a career in music?"

The question had been asked before, though not in such a direct way. However, there existed another desire that dwelled within my mind, something I found more appealing.

"I want to write," I responded. "Send people to another world, to new dimensions."

"But there's so much more that you can accomplish," Doss responded. "Why don't you try music?"

"I'll always try to be in choir, but it isn't me." Despite my words, Doss wasn't disappointed, just happy to know that I loved what I did.

"What if you wrote lyrics?" Pondering, I wasn't sure of what to say. "Songs tell stories as well." To create those worlds through song was something I barely thought about. The smile that he always gave me, as well as all the other students, still shined.

"Thanks, maybe I will." We continued working on my solo for the rest of the time. My mind would soon open to whole new worlds, and whole new possibilities.

Chad Eaton, Grade 12
Granbury High School, TX

Life's Paths

"Two roads diverged in a wood, and I — I took the one less traveled by, and that has made all the difference." The poem by Robert Frost teaches valuable lessons about the choices and consequences that each of us deal with daily. The whirlwind of decisions we are faced with can leave us feeling overwhelmed and perplexed. All too often we feel the crushing pressure of following the crowd and all too often we would have been better off if we had not.

The fear can be petrifying and each movement heavy as we head down the path that has not yet been blazed. The thought that the path has yet to be touched even by a slightest foot print is breathtaking. The shelter that is provided by following the crowd is overcome by the desire to find myself. Each step in the sand is new and unmarked leading me to be all that I can be. Untouched, unmoved and blessed by being just me.

Andrea Anderson, Grade 12
South Sevier High School, UT

Dancing Sunshine

I lay on my bare stomach in the warm sand, kicking my feet into the air as I drew light circles with the edge of my pinky. Every so often I could feel the cool ocean tickle my skin as it escaped it's barrier.

"Heather, look what daddy helped me find!"

Glancing up, I found my younger brother Mark standing before me, face lit up with excitement.

"What is it baby?" I asked, lifting myself up on my elbows. Already, I was nearly his height.

I smiled to myself as he opened his chubby fists, which had previously been clenched behind his back.

"Look!" Mark exclaimed, tilting his small palms toward me. Inside lay several shards of sea glass, various shapes and sizes, made smooth by the continuous weathering of the ocean's current.

"Daddy says they're glass, but I don't believe him," Mark stated matter-of-factly, shaking his head. "Glass gives you cuts, but these, these are soooooper smooooth."

I laughed as he stroked the sea glass's surfaces, the sunlight playing off the vivid colors.

"They're very pretty."

"Sister, will you come look for more with daddy and me?"

"Of course!" I stood up as he reached over to place his tiny hand in mine, the left still clutching the sea glass.

"Yaaaaaayyyyy!" Mark sang as he ran down the beach, tugging me along.

Running down the shoreline, I watched as, one by one, the sea glass pieces fell to the sand, leaving a trail of rainbow colors behind us.

Heather Bush, Grade 11
Vista Ridge High School, TX

The Power of Beauty

Nothing is more powerful than beauty in a wicked world. Can you find that beauty? It is all around. Most of the time, it is right in front of our eyes, and we just never take the moment to notice it. Being a teenager, for the most part, high school is basically what my world consists of because it is where my time is most often spent. Constantly being surrounded by other students, most of which apathy has taken over and respect has ceased, makes for not the most peaceful and diplomatic time. I walk down the halls every day and cannot help but notice what hatred people have for their world. It is a sad sight to see, but then again, this is what makes beauty so powerful. On the other hand, I see students who choose to be different. I see students who are helping one another. I see students who cannot help but be kind to their peers, who find joy in building up other students, and love to befriend. Mohandas Gandhi once said, "Be the change you wish to see in the world." If one chooses to conform instead of reform, then beauty easily becomes shadowed. On the other hand, choosing to take hold of what is right in front of us, and embrace the beauty that lies within and all around us, change can occur and beauty can be found. After all, beauty is in the eye of the beholder.

Lindsey Morrow, Grade 12
Post High School, TX

Fighting the Consequences

You can always choose your choices, but you can never choose or even anticipate your consequences. I learned this valuable lesson the hard way. Last year I was involved in a fight. It was a locker room fight, and the coaches had made it seem like there would be absolutely no repercussions for my actions. They made me feel safe and said nothing would happen if I stood up for the honor of my team. Everyone felt that the situation should be resolved in the football program with a lot of running, but the law had different plans. To the amazement of everyone involved, the other guy's parents called the cops and filed charges against me. Over the years, there have been countless locker room fights, and all of them resulted in running until you threw up and then resuming your normal activities. The parents blew it way out of proportion, and because of that, I've been put in jail and face ridiculous monetary fines. This event was a huge lesson for me that will affect my decisions for the rest of my life. I will always consider any possible consequences when making any kind of major decision.

Talyne Bitner, Grade 12
Granbury High School, TX

My Vision of Success

As I sit in my advanced placement courses, I notice that I always happen to be one of the few African-American students in the class. This is a stark contrast to my regular courses, where I am one of many African American students. Initially, this realization saddened and upset me. For several weeks, I could only contemplate this unfortunate imbalance. An uneasiness haunted my thoughts and actions, as I reflected upon my new insight. It took a long while for me to overcome my dismay. Once I did, I began to notice the positives in the situation. It gave me opportunity to learn from those unlike myself, and for those unlike myself to learn from me. I realized that my school, being so diverse, naturally fosters multicultural acceptance and understating. The environment fosters learning, and positively impacts the intellectual advancement of every student. People are often surprised when an African-American succeeds in school. To many, the occurrence is unheard of or unexpected. My desire to eradicate this sentiment has influenced me to pursue goals, like becoming an orthopedic surgeon, so advantageous that they can only be accomplished by one who is adamantly determined to succeed. I work tirelessly in my studies to ensure that my vision comes to fruition. I will not rest until I have proved to at least one doubtful, ignorant, or close-minded person that when a member of a discounted minority works determinedly towards his or her goals, they have no option but to find success.

Jennifer Oradiegwu, Grade 12
DeBakey High School for Health Professions, TX

Exercise: the Word from Hell or Heaven's Gift?

If you were to say the word "exercise" to a group of regular people and ask for their first response, most likely you'd get something along the lines of groans and moans. Exercise is something that most people see as a chore, but it doesn't have to be.

Exercising is incredibly good for your mind, body, and soul. Exercising helps to increase your metabolism and allows you to burn off more calories than if you were to stay sedentary. Regular exercise will also allow your body to fall asleep faster and deeper because you have worked harder throughout your day. As well as increased metabolism and deeper sleep you will also have higher energy and mood levels.

Besides the amazing benefits on your mind and body you can also have fun while you work out. You don't have to do the classic 100 pushups. Nowadays there are a lot of workouts that aren't so intense and are easy to start.

One example is yoga. Yoga is a very low impact exercise that involved using your own body and weight to work on muscle tone, flexibility, and balance while strengthening your core muscles. If you're a busy person and can't fit in a routine work out, replacing a desk chair with a balance ball will work your core muscles and improve balance.

All in all, exercise is something that can very easily fit into your daily life and the sooner you start the sooner you will reap the amazing benefits.

Alisa Green, Grade 12
Nestucca High School, OR

Through the Lenses

Art is my escape. With art there are no boundaries, no rules, nothing, I am free to run wild and express myself in any way I feel is fitting. I am the one in charge. There are so many different kinds of art that I love, but my favorite art is photography. I love photography because I am able to capture a specific moment that will create a memory. The moment I take hold of the camera and look through the lens I see nothing but my subject. A picture can make someone feel so many emotions: it can make a change, or make someone's day, or bring back memories. With my camera I can capture someone's most inner thoughts, beautiful breathtaking scenery, or a once-in-a-lifetime event. Taking pictures has opened my eyes and shown me how unique and diverse our world is. By looking at pictures I have learned that no one is the same; everyone has their own style, personality, and uniqueness. I also appreciate the beauty in nature: the delicate colors in flowers, the intricate design on a leaf, or the way the sun shines through the tree leaves. Our world is so beautiful, but very rarely do we take the time to notice. Photography allows us to take time and see the amazing world around us.

Analisa Miyashiro, Grade 11
Valley Christian High School, CA

Love

Love: a strong, positive emotion of regard and affection. One hears the word love used a lot because it has a large diversity of uses and meanings. But it is truly one of the most powerful and wonderful impressions that a human can feel, experience, or give off. Many deem love as a power greater than themselves. Some also think of it as a manner to live by.

The secular approach to love seems to be focused on the emotional and physical side. Destiny is believed to bring two people together in the union of 'true love.' But look where that has brought America now. The divorce rate is unbelievable! And the youth of today is handling the whole concept of love in the wrong way. This should afflict those of us who understand the situation.

There is one thing that comforts me at all times though, the most pure, precious, true, beautiful, and perfect thing: God's love. For He is love! That is the reason for everything and anything! Trying to live by this love revealed to us through Him is my life's mission. Everything else in life will come better to all those who realize what true love is and who it comes from.

This true and faithful love is the most amazing thing one can have in their heart. And it is something worth celebrating every day! I desire to get to know this kind of love increasingly throughout my life.

Alina Stefoglo, Grade 11
Valley Christian School, WA

The History in Me

History is meaningful to me because I learn from past mistakes, and that can help me make wiser choices for the future. I've learned not to discriminate, and that all races are equal. Learning about other cultures helps me know who I am more fully. Also, it gives me the knowledge of others' backgrounds so I can be respectful for what They've been through, or who they are. One way I can be respectful is by not judging. First impressions are usually wrong.

Everyone wonders what the future holds, right? For me, the future is completely predictable. All we have to do is look back on the past so that we don't repeat mistakes in the future. I know that I want to always be caught up on current events. Current events keep me involved with the world around me. Staying involved means giving me an opinion about certain subjects, therefore, I can be more aware of politics.

Most consider history boring. I think of history as pure knowledge. Without histories of other people, we'd cease to have a government, the bill of rights, the scriptures or any other important document. The people before us have molded us into who we are today. Nothing would happen without a past. Let's all hope for the future, and remember that history teaches us what not to repeat again. Nobody wants to go through a depression again. Stay updated on history, and the future will be grand.

Jenessa Jorgensen, Grade 12
Spanish Fork High School, UT

The Rhythm of the Heart

What makes up rhythm? Something you can sing, move, and listen to. The beat comes alive in every rhythm. Dance uses many styles of beats. Moving fast, slow, soft, and hard all make me strive to become a better dancer. When I get angry or sad, I take my emotions and put them into my dancing. This way dance lets me release all my rage and anger throughout my movements. When I dance, I put in as much emotion as I can so I can free my mind from all its misery. If I feel like the world is turning against me and nothing is going right, I listen to fast upbeat songs that let me throw all my anger out onto the dance floor. Taking in the loss of a loved one sets my mood to a soft mellow movement. Everything I go through in life I easily express through my dancing.

I also show my own kind of style when I move. The individuality of each step shows part of my personality. Putting the two together creates an explosion through my body. When I get caught in the moment, it feels like nothing else exists. If I did not have dance as a way to express my feelings, life would be uncomfortable and strange. The rush of every movement symbolizes a conflict going on in my life. A beat makes up the rhythm in dancing, and that beat is in my heart.

Brittany Liu, Grade 11
Pine Tree High School, TX

Grandma's House

Some of my dearest memories come from visits with the family. When I was young, my great grandparents lived in a rural town in Oregon about 850 miles away. I can remember Dad driving for fourteen wearisome hours until we arrived late at night, when my loving grandparents welcomed us with many hugs and kisses. Quickly unloading the car, we made our beds in the basement. The basement was always my favorite part of Grandma's house.

After a good night's sleep, the delicious aroma of a hearty breakfast awoke me. The mouth watering bacon and eggs and scrumptious canned fruits from the cellar adorned the table. My Grandma was a phenomenal cook and always made the best food. After breakfast, we would wander near the railroad tracks and try to have the oncoming trains smash our pennies. It was exciting to hear the deafening whistle and thunderous engine of the trains roar passed us as we desperately tried to find our smashed pennies.

However, the best part about going to Grandma's house was the family reunions. My great grandparents lived long enough to celebrate their seventieth wedding anniversary, and when that day came, it was the biggest event that small town had seen in years! Grandma loved to be around people, and she always kept in touch with all of the extended family and friends via letters. It was fun meeting cousins that I never knew existed! I still cherish these wonderful memories of my Grandma's house to this day.

Kevin Dorn, Grade 11
Valley Christian High School, CA

My Condolences

My mother neglected to bake me a birthday cake this year. After explaining that she was too tired, she took my silent response as typical teenage sulking and commenced her teasing.

"Aww, do you feel neglected? Are you upset?" she prodded.

"No, I'm okay," I said, hoping to stop her before she really got going. "Don't worry about me, I'm self-actualized."

"What's that supposed to mean?" she asked. Score one for AP Psychology.

Smug about gaining conversational superiority, I explained, "It means that I've reached my full potential."

My mother was silent for a moment. I almost took it as a sign of victory. It looked like I had finally won a battle of wits. But the silence was shattered, along with any hope of success, by the sound of her hysterical laughter.

Clutching onto our kitchen's door frame for support, literally gasping for breath, my mother offered me her condolences.

Kimberly Ong, Grade 12
Alhambra High School, CA

Bad Day

I pulled up to my friend's house not knowing the day would end in disaster due to my young teenage stupidity.

I got this idea that it would be fun to drive around even though I had little driving experience and no license. So I turned to my friend and asked her very politely if I could take her car around the block. She then got her keys. Turning the key it made all sorts of noises that couldn't be explained. Then finally it turned over and started up. Right before I put it into reverse one of my friends got in and said "I'm not letting you drive alone." Throwing the car into reverse I stomped on the accelerator throwing dust and rocks everywhere. Putting it now into drive she said three words to me "don't hurt it." Letting those words pass through my head numerous times, I decided that there was no way I could hurt her car. Turning right out of her driveway I started to drift, the tires were squealing and my friend was holding on to everything possible. The back end started to slide out from behind me and I tried to get the car back under control but it was too late. Heading toward what seemed was a never ending ditch. On the other side of the ditch was a steel fence. Slamming into the steel fence I knew that my next month was going to be spent in my house grounded.

Dylan Archer, Grade 12
Granbury High School, TX

The Cycle of Music

Music is the lifeblood of creativity. Music is that which makes us able to express our deepest emotions. Without music, we as humans would be severely lacking in the single most important portion of our lives, expression. What started as simple euphonies has branched out to complex rhythms filled with lyrics that inspire, entertain, and ease pain. Though the changing pop culture has changed music, much of the deep creative styling's that make it so enchanting have remained.

Music spans generations and from the Broadway musicals of yesteryear to the indie bands of today, it still has the same profound effect. Music is universal and all reaching. In every culture today, music is a common sight to see. It expresses not only personal beliefs, but can also entertain the listener with stories of the past. Even though music relates to every person differently, it holds the same ability to carve one's being. Music is not something that is meant to influence one individual, but something that defies race, age, and gender and brings people together for a common goal of creativity and expression. This universality enables anyone to create music, furthering its common goal to inspire and bring expression to newer generations. Music is not a fad or temporary notion, but a cycle of expression that will continue until humans no longer have the ability to express themselves. This cycle is the foundation of music, and it enables music to reach out to all.

Zachary Warman, Grade 11
New Caney High School, TX

High Merit Essays – Grades 10, 11 and 12

The Winding Paths of Halloween

One school day, I was anxiously awaiting for the last bell to ring, to enjoy my night of haunting. It was Halloween. My eyes were intensely locked onto the clock. The clock's hands seemed to be moving as if they were being held back by iron chains. I counted down, five, four, three, two, one — "Ring!" Yes, the onset of my ghoulish night had finally arrived.

My mom drove up with precise timing. I pounced into the back seat, eagerly awaiting my arrival home. I jumped into my costume, with the accuracy of an arrow hitting its target. My make-up was finished. I was ready. I was now the frightening phantom of King Tut! I was to be honored and feared by all who encountered my power. I was off to reign the night of Halloween!

I made my way down the winding paths. I imagined them as the great limestones of the Great Pyramids of Egypt. As I made my presence known along the paths, people bowed in my honor, saying, "All hail, the Great Tutankhamen." I proceeded to collect all of the delicious treasures I had set out to obtain.

As my haunting reign of power ceased, I laid back remembering the spectacular night I had encountered. Thoughts of sweet chocolatey, and creamy treasures swam beneath my glistening crown of jewels. My night of haunting had come to an end. It was all I had imagined. Next year, I shall again, walk down the winding paths of Halloween!

Kyle Logan, Grade 10
Sierra Charter School, CA

The Philosopher

Our lives aren't the future, or the past; those are moments in life that have already happened or will happen. Life is now, the present, the moment you see in front of you. My life is grand; I'm only sixteen and I have learned so much, but I still have some chapters to read before the end of my story. I have both my parents that love me, and siblings I would die for. My room is my place of serenity, my food is my source of energy and life, my friends are my teachers and students, sharing ideas and absorbing information from each other. I thank God, life, or whatever granted me the time to enjoy the breaths I take, to wake up every day and to have a feeling of misery or joy.

We see all negatives in life, like chaos and hatred, but without these things, these gears and sparks in life, we would never really know what peace was, what happiness is, and even how to love and cherish things. I am happy to live, I've probably said it many times but that's just the way I feel. I love to see birds soaring in the sky, like angels of earth. I love to be annoyed by the cries of children, like alarms to your ears. I love to see the same old faces every day and know that we are alive and breathing. My conclusion, life's short so live it while it's here.

Humberto Badillo, Grade 11
REACH High School, TX

The Most Important Thing in My Life

The most important thing in my life is living a successful future. I am 17 years young. I am a senior at Omega High School. After graduation, I would like to major in criminology or become a criminal lawyer. I will attend a community college for required classes. Then, after I accomplish my required classes, I will attend a university for my degree; I really want to attend Sonoma State University.

After graduating from college hopefully I would be 25. I will join a police department as a criminologist or open my own law firm as a lawyer. After a year in that business I will then earn some money to buy my first car which will be a Cadillac SRX 2010. After buying my first real car out of the lot, I will then buy a house in the Bay area: a two story family home with 5 bedrooms and 2 1/2 baths.

After I make it to where I need to be I will start saving for my kids. I want my kids to have successful futures and without money that wouldn't happen. I want my kids to have great education and material things. I will shower myself with beautiful designer handbags, clothing, and beautiful jewelry. I want a pearl white Pomeranian as my house dog. On Friday nights I will enjoy it with my girls, go out for drinks and party! After all that's said and done I will be married to my wonderful baby's daddy!

Cindy Saelee, Grade 12
Omega High School, CA

Destination Graduation

There is a saying that my little sister Kay would tell me sometimes, "When life gives you lemons, squirt it in someone's eye!" Now, it's probably the unethical thing to do, but it sure does make you laugh hard. What she was referring to was that even though life can be rough and throw some curve balls on your way, just smile and know that this too shall pass.

Being a senior has its ups and downs, but it's supposed to be this way. There is no perfect senior year. I believe the perfect senior year is learning from the mistakes you make; that way when the day comes for you to go to college, you'll be prepared to go through situations and fix them as well. The one thing you have to learn is once you've fallen down, that's the easy step. The hard step is getting up from where you fell and continuing to move on.

One thing that I can compare my senior year to is a GPS system. You program your destination in to the GPS and just drive forward. The unique thing about GPS is that if you make a wrong turn or miss a sign, it will redirect you to your destination. Although we miss signs and make wrong turns during our senior year, it will always redirect us and get us back on track to our destination, graduation day.

Kathryn Villalon, Grade 12
Post High School, TX

Writing Abilities

There are many ways to express myself. Mine are both in writing and action. Writing is the easier way to tell someone how I feel. I was the shy type, and never expected to become a writer. There were things I needed to learn though. With the thing I enjoy most, I needed schooling, and practice a lot on writing. So far I have been writing for one year. Never to stop my biggest dream, which is to become a professional writer. Yes, I have some things to work on, but if I work on them with gratitude then I am sure to make it.

My writing skills are no competition to the professionals, for I have not gotten to the professional stage yet. That may take me a couple years, but I never know what will pop out at me from behind the bushes. When I write, I can express how I'm feeling. Sometimes, I write about my class, but in fun ways. The last essay I did about my class was, some of my class mates were clouds, and some birds, and some airplanes. It all depended on how I felt. I always like to make things fun for everyone. Now if there is one person left out of the fun, I try to include them.

Writing is always a good way to show people where you have been in life. Whether it be a real place, or in your own little world. What I have learned about writing, is that if it is pushed onto a child too much, when they are younger, then they are worse at it. That goes for any subject for that matter.

Anyone can write, just like on *Ratatouille*, 'anyone can cook', cause anyone can, they just get to believe in themselves.

Shae Jensen, Grade 10
Heritage Foundation School, UT

Going International

International studies are a great interest of mine. I have always longed to go to a foreign country to visit and tour; however, just recently I have learned that you can do these things while receiving a much needed education.

There are many programs that offer studying abroad as a part of their curriculum or an extracurricular activity. One that I know of personally that provides many extra bonuses in accompany with being sent overseas, is Rotary International. This program allows students to spend a year in a foreign country, attending school as usual and not only academically learning, but also experiencing life to the fullest. While there, the youth live with 2-3 different host families to experience every aspect of life in a foreign country. From speaking with current members of the Rotary International program this summer, I learned that they not only send you to the country of your choosing, the main host member from Rotary also makes weekly to monthly visits to the host kids to check on them. In some of these visits they take trips to national Rotary meetings in order to speak, Rotary conferences, and even ski trips and cross-country tours by train. The feelings and experiences related to me by these students only further piqued my interest in attending such a program.

I am a very adventurous person and believe that my life would be greatly impacted by getting such an opportunity as this. Perhaps, I can.

Bethany Berry, Grade 12
Post High School, TX

Key

The smallest things sometimes lead to the biggest possibilities. A single piece of metal with a couple of teeth in it can lead to amazing power. A key can open whatever it's made for, but the key I'm talking about opens up the world of horsepower and torque. This key opens up the world to the thing I care most about in my life. This key goes into the ignition of my Mitsubishi Lancer Evolution 8 and when turned reveals what a car should be like. Every time I get in my car I expect a whole new experience and thrill. With each drive that my car and I go on we try new things and always push the laws of nature, but not the laws of the cops. I always enjoy pushing my car to see what its limits are and thankfully it can easily handle it, which is why I put time, effort, and money into my Evo. Working on my car makes me feel on top of the world, knowing that the smallest adjustment to anything can either improve and make my experience more enjoyable or kill me in an instant. I believe, though, that there is a pact between my precious car and me. The pact is that it will keep me safe and in one piece as long as I keep it maintained and in perfect condition. Oh, there also might be a little love involved, but I think that's a one way thing.

Andrei Savastru, Grade 11
Valley Christian High School, CA

The Human Mind

The hmuan mind is vrey complex. Studeis show that the hmuan mind can read things even thuogh the words are misslped as lnog as the frist and the last lteters are in their corerct place. Poeple can figrue out excatly waht is bieng said becuase thier brian aldreay has the wrod, spleled coerrctly, progarmmed in thier memroy. The biran deosn't look at evrey lteter by istelf but it raeds the wrod as a wlhoe. We raed missllped wrods sometmies wtihout raelizing the wrod is missllepped. Becuase poeple can esaily oevr look missllepped wrods, we all mkae misatkes, and this makes the eidting porccess mroe diffcult. So I raelly look up to eidtors who go thruogh this porccess wtihout rpiping out thier hiar. Sometmies we can also leave out leters, and the mnd can stll read wat is bing said. Leaving out leters is jst like misspelling words; because the mnd reads paterns, and not the word itslf. Also people can read sentences that leave out words such as, of, the, is, and it. This because mind skips these words anyway when reading. Mind doesn't need read all words understand. This how speed readers are good reading fast; they train themselves skip unimportant words.

Kristen Jones, Grade 12
Coronado High School, TX

Leaders of the Pact

In our generation, we have many kids that do not take a stand and go with what they feel is right because they want to fit in and do what their friends are doing. If their friends are doing drugs and going to parties and not coming home at night, if one is not a leader, they are most likely going to participate and do the same thing. Our generation needs to take a stand and start following their beliefs, rather than doing what is cool. Half the kids that go out and partly know that it is not right, but because of their lack of leadership and peer pressure, they feel that they have to do this to fit in. If kids, teenagers, and young adults would learn how to make their own choices in life, we would not have so many kids getting in trouble, or dying of drug overdose or even alcohol poisoning. Parents need to start teaching and showing their kids leadership, so there will be changes made in our generation. We all need to take a stand and do what we feel is right, because we have younger kids watching what we do every day. As our 6th president, John Quincy Adams once said, "If your actions inspire others to dream more, learn more, do more and become more, you are a leader." Wouldn't you rather someone follow your actions, rather than following the actions of someone else?

Branda Stevens, Grade 12
Post High School, TX

School Experience

My hopes and dreams were crushed as I walked into our high school the first day of our senior year. I sat in sadness in my first period choir class starring at my schedule in total disbelief. I almost cried as the teacher went over the rules of the class and told us everything that was suppose to happen. I even went and talked to my counselor during the summer about it and we fixed it. Apparently not.

They put in a hard core math class and stuck me in another computer class seventh period. I'm not that skilled in math so I was not ready to tackle on this new math class and I had already taken a computer class so I didn't need that; however the new school administration decided that I didn't need to get out of school early.

However, I was excited at the fact that they decided to make two lunches instead of three. That way there was a greater chance I would be able to have lunch with my friends. Yet, they put me in the lunch that had no one I knew in it. What a great start to the "best year of high school."

Not only that but they messed up just about every other seniors schedule in the entire high school. The waiting line just to see the counselor was, at the least, 2 weeks. Senior year. The best year of high school. Ya right. Got to love the new school administration.

Nathaniel Delaney, Grade 12
Granbury High School, TX

What Does Love Mean to You?

What does love mean to you? I was asked that question on a church retreat. Instead of writing, I drew it out. When I was asked to present my answer, I passed my paper around and started talking about the pictures. There must have been something I said or how I said it. Everyone was gaping at me and they said that it was deep. I'll try and repeat my words.

To me, love is many things. It's the light in the darkness. It's the warmth of a nice campfire. Love is a warm, soft, fluffy pillow. And, it's the ferocity of a protective mother.

I meant a lot when I said those words, and I don't remember them all. It was that one question "What does love mean to you," that changed my views on what love is. Now I see love in all shapes and sizes, colors and textures. I think about what love is when I don't expect it.

I have also seen how love is viewed by other people. Some think that love is sex. It has become a large part, and for some a huge problem of society. If you love someone, you HAVE to have sex with them on the spot. That's how they see love, but don't question them. They may one day find someone or something that changes their view of love.

Olivia Zizzi, Grade 11
American Renaissance Academy, HI

The Purpose of Writing

My bed is more than just that, it is a home.

My bed is the dull sensibility of sleep, enveloping, like sinking in to a bath half a degree too hot.

It's all the promises I'll deal with tomorrow, and all the ones I'll never keep. It is an eternity made tangible on long eight-year-old nights, wondering what happens when you die, deciding (hoping) that it's something like sleep.

It's waking up tomorrow, half asleep, wholeheartedly half-humming a nursery rhyme when it's half-past half the day, slept away.

More importantly, my bed is soft.

Not my bed, but somewhere else's, is where I began, and my bed, not someone else's, is where I'll end.

On uninspired nights, I sit, stare out the window at a cold, cold cul-de-sac, a street lamp's unblinking eye, wondering why I'm not asleep yet.

It is sleep: an empty canvas, a blank page, dreams, the still-life impressionist portrait of summer painted upon it.

My bed is good night moon, full moons, half moons, moons than grin like Cheshire cats, moons never observed because I was already asleep.

It is the dividing line between the duality of dark and light — nightmares, daydreams, starlight from across the street, lamplight from across the stars — most importantly, night lights from down the stairs, the one light that let me sleep.

It is a smuggled popsicle that ends up a stain on sheets.

It is always where I'd rather be right now: My Bed.

18 September, 2009   3:48 am

Benjamin Manry, Grade 11
Vista Ridge High School, TX

A Kiss, a Reminiscence, and an Uncertainty

Seamlessly, effortlessly, summer has glided into autumn. I feel the cold nip in the air as I tug the sleeves of my sweatshirt over my chapped knuckles. Flaxen leaves fall like fluttering confetti around my head as I pass beneath a birch; the sun that filters through the boughs seems somehow weaker, less assured than the exuberant rays of August. Beneath my sneakers the leaves crunch like saltine crackers. What internal clock told the seasons to swap the sticky, hot "popsicle" days for these passing moments of gold and gray?

My thoughts waver and then solidify: what is there to discern about this transitory season known as fall? What if my life is spent only in the lazy haze of summer, and suddenly winter rushes upon me like an icy northeaster?

My high school career is drawing to a close. I feel that my seventeenth year is one of transition, much like autumn — fleeting, anticipatory of the future, and almost lonely. I am no longer the happy-go-lucky teenager that I was in past summers. Now I know I must gather in the harvest of my education, and prepare for the winter. I must look back on my life thus far and give thanks for family, for friends, for the laughter and tears that wind their way through the memories. I don't want winter to catch me unawares. I want every season of my life, no matter how warm or frigid or ephemeral, to be filled with purpose.

Emilie Whitman, Grade 12
Wenatchee High School, WA

Keep Your Friends Close, and Your Family Closer

The room was cold and lifeless. White walls closed in on grim faces. The buzz of the television screamed, but no one was listening. Red and tearful were the faces in the waiting room of Kingwood Medical Center. All gathered in one small corner, my family waited, feet tapping impatiently, for an update on my mom.

Days passed by, and we moved from that small, dark corner to the side of my mom's hospital bed. Once a dull white hospital room was now littered with colorful cards, flowers, and hope. She was never alone there. No matter how small the room was, it was always full of people who loved her.

Recovering from a stroke is hard, not only for the victim, but for the loved ones as well. That is why it is so important to stay close to one another. Support and love are the best gifts one person can give to another. I never realized that until they were given to me. Even though friends can leave you, family can never truly turn their backs. That is why family is the single most important thing any person can have, and I thank God every day that I have a family like I do. My mom may have never made it through without them.

Sarah Lester, Grade 11
New Caney High School, TX

The Inexorable Nightmare

September 13, 2008 is the date I will remember the most. That's the day Hurricane Ike devastated my home town, Bridge City. The small town was no match for the hurricane's storm.

I thought it wouldn't be as bad as Hurricane Rita, or any other hurricane my family has been through since we lived in Bridge City, because the weather reporter stated that the hurricane would be a tropical storm. Two days before the hurricane hit my family evacuated to the Dallas/Fort Worth area. There was one particular day that I remember while at the evacuation destination. My dad went on kogt.com and saw pictures of our high school, Jack in the Box, and McDonalds. It had 3 feet of water in it. When it was time to return to our homes my family was anxious to get there.

Upon arrival my father did something that surprised me, but confused me. My father drove around Bridge City looking at other people's homes and how local stores were doing. By the time my family and I arrived home I found the answer as to why he did that. He wanted me and my sister to know what we might face in our own home. When we walked inside our home, our carpet was drenched, we had only 7 inches of water, and almost everything was destroyed. The nightmare was that I had to rebuild something so precious in my life when the hurricane was completely irrelevant to my life. There was one particular quote I heard my mom say during the hurricane disaster, "If you find yourself in complete darkness remember one thing, there will always be light." That's always true, in this hurricane Galveston got wiped out but they're currently reconstructing and my prayers will always be with them.

David Ferris, Grade 11
Bridge City High School, TX

My Importances

Trust, friends, a sense of knowing and belonging! The most amazing feelings in the world!

If I can't trust you then we have problems. Trust is very important to me and with trust comes happiness and better relationships. After our "trust bond" is broken, you most likely won't get it back.

My friends know me better than anyone. They know if I can't trust you, I won't have anything to do with you. They know when I'm happy and when I'm sad. They have my back and I have theirs! The inside stories that we share bring us even closer! I don't know where I would be in life without them.

Getting attention from that "special someone" gives me an energetic rush of sensation! It's like I belong here with everyone and that I'm special in my own way, not that I was just another unexpected mistake. Also, getting affection from "him" tells me I'm loved, I mean something to someone. With trust, love and friends, I am happily alive!

Savannah Haggard, Grade 11
New Caney High School, TX

What It Means to Me

If we, as mankind, received a grade in life, we would have a failing grade in respect. Respect has diminished through the ages. Where did it go? Somewhere between my grandparents' generation and my own, the teaching of respect took a back seat to sign language and Spanish.

How can we begin to think that the world will take us seriously as an individual when we don't have respect? Respect is like gift giving. It's better to give than receive. Respecting others helps us to understand how to respect ourselves. If you give someone respect, you are empowering them and thus empowering yourself.

Respect should be an active part in everyone's daily life, it's not hard. Really, all you have to do is add the Mrs., Mr., or Ms. to your teacher's name, open doors for others, wish your grocery bagger a nice day before you leave, and as always, there's the tried and true "Please" and "Thank you." If that's too much to integrate into your life, then try this: tone. The basic rule of respect comes from my grandma, "It doesn't matter what you say, but how you say it."

Respect is not dead, yet. It pops up from time to time in places and people I would never expect it to flow from. Every time I see it, even if it's not directed at me, it's inspiring and reminds me that to keep it alive, it needs to be shared.

Have a nice day.

Jenna Matsumura, Grade 11
Northridge High School, UT

Equality

An important issue to me is being treated equally. Some say they treat everyone equal, but they're lying.

For example, parents always say they treat their kids equal. However, they tend to show more attention to the younger kids. Many parents have "favorites," as in a father treating a son more special than he would if he also had a daughter. If parents have more than one child, they will more than likely be treated differently.

Another issue with equality is setting rules. Rules are set for everyone to follow, once broken they get in trouble. However, that is not always true! One can get away with doing something wrong while another gets punished for the same thing. This mostly is to be done in school. A teacher can choose if they want to punish a student for doing wrong. If a student was late they could get a tardy, but the teacher does not mind the tardy because she likes the student. While another student walks in late and she writes him up for being late. It is all based on favorites, and whether they want to treat the students equally or not.

Being treated equally most likely won't happen. I personally think everyone has a favorite and is going to treat them better than another. Although that is how our society is. We have to get used to being treated differently. Some won't like it but have to deal with the way life really is.

Matthew Zepeda, Grade 12
Coronado High School, TX

Student Gang Involvement

The concept of student gang involvement depends critically on the treatment that an individual receives at home. It has been revealed by recent studies, taken by distinctive students at Garfield High School in Los Angeles, CA, that three out of four students attending high school, between the ages of fourteen and seventeen, tend to have a higher level of involvement in such gangs as a result of family violence.

An anonymous speaker, who we will call John, once shared that getting involved with gangs was the only way out of such a stressful life that he had going on at home. He assured that having the attention and respect from people on the streets most merely substitutes the attention and respect that you should be receiving from your folks at home. Another anonymous speaker agreed that having people look up to you on the streets is an accomplishment. He stated that getting good grades is nothing but marks on a paper that will fade away with time. This speaker, however, disagrees strongly with the previously presented argument. He believes that nobody has the ability to substitute attention from one's family and states that having been neglected by family members contributes to student involvement in gangs. Therefore proving the point of the studies and providing physical proof about what is being written.

Jonathan Corralejo, Grade 12
John J Cairns Continuation High School, CA

Changes Perfectly Planned

When you have gone to nine schools in twelve years, along with four different houses in two states, one might wonder how this person made it and did they. Although the odds may have been stacked against me, I made it, am happy, and even glad for the changes I experienced. Although it wasn't always easy, I did survive and will again. With new schools came new friends to make and with new homes came different rooms to move into, but I always tried to stay positive. Adaptability and a positive attitude was key. I needed to adapt to new places, new friends, and new ways of life. As I step into yet another new circumstance as I move into the family role of the oldest child at home, I think it's good to reflect on handling change.

Being able to adapt, for me, meant doing what I might not normally do. I always took time to watch others. I wanted to observe to see how I might fit in. Adapting for me also meant being sure of who I was and what I believed, all the while staying positive. As a result, I do know who I am and what I believe. My family kept me positive, building within me a courage to take on new situations. With a positive attitude and a certainty of who I am, I can embrace change and praise God that He orchestrated it wonderfully.

Jack Basalone, Grade 10
Whittier Christian High School, CA

Never Mind Me

Just a passerby, you may say, but that is just what you could say to describe anybody you see pass on the street that can be visible in a window. Dusty as it may be, this picture can be seen through the interior of a coffee shop nearby. Seemingly like the perfect place to read the paper, discuss to self the exact root problem in society today, and then walk out the golden/bronze door of the shop to continue life again.

As I walked down the intersection of 40th and 5th Street, I became aware that this was the start of a different day. Not an ordinary day, if, for this split moment we both decided to agree there was such a thing as this "ordinary" madness. I could not describe, really, what I felt, but what I know for sure was that there was a sudden gush of air that had left me out of breath for a moment that assured me that this day was to be taken to be extraordinary, once it had unfolded.

I had gotten across the street, when I had an uncontrollable urge of wanting a cup of espresso. I looked around and I saw the coffee shop of "Walsh and Creetan's Coffee Brew." At that moment, I comprehended that the day's moments of my life were steadily unfolding before my eyes as I had described earlier. I had set my life in motion.

Briana Gomez, Grade 12
Eastwood High School, TX

More Than Cookies

"Would you like to buy some Girl Scout cookies?" When people think of girl scouting, little girls in vibrant green vests singing cookie songs outside of stores come to mind. Despite the occasional reality of this stereotype, girl scouting represents more than little girls with charming smiles that sell Thin Mints. Girls of all ages, from kindergarten to the twelfth grade, are making significant changes in their communities through Girl Scout programs. Service projects range from Daisy Girl Scouts planting flowers on elementary school campuses to Senior Girl Scouts earning their Gold Awards through sixty-five hour community service and leadership projects as extravagant as gathering books and other materials for disadvantaged children in Africa.

As a junior in high school, I am currently entering my tenth year of girl scouting. My troop consists of eleven committed juniors and completes many projects that positively impact the community. But more importantly, though we have benefited greatly from these service experiences, girl scouting allows us to maintain close relationships with each other as we grow older and change schools and social groups. One of our troop members recently lost her mom, who battled for two years with lung cancer. Because of girl scouting, she has a troop of ten girls she has known for many years supporting her. For these reasons, still in the eleventh grade, I am proud to be a cookie-selling, service-project-completing, and friend-supporting Girl Scout of Northern California.

Lauren Speers, Grade 11
Valley Christian High School, CA

Life and Death

Life. The beginning of all things. Death. The end of all things. Why do we take for granted that which is a gift unto us? The past is history, the future is a mystery, but today is a gift. Life is a gift. Each day we live, we live for a reason, for tomorrow we know not whether we wake the next day to see the sun shining in through the curtains in our rooms. Each day, we fight to stay alive, and those who do not, those who think that each day they should be dead, are missing the whole point of why they exist. For every day we live, we affect the lives of those around us. The world would be gray and empty if we all acted gray and empty. We live today so that we can bring light into the lives of those who love us, even if we don't see it. We must live each day as if this were our last day, and we would die tomorrow. Don't waste it. Live every moment like it's your last. Breathe it in. Taste it. Feel it. Love it. For if we do not do this, then it would be better if we were not born. Take up this sword. Take up this shield. Fight the battle of life, for death has already been defeated. So, we must be the best, do the best, feel the best. We have life. Take it.

Branson Tanner, Grade 12
Vista Ridge High School, TX

What We All Need

The church body was nicely dressed for the weekly invitational. People wearing nicely pressed clothes with checkered ties, slacks and button down shirts entered the holy sanctuary. Also a large dignified pastor stood speaking fire and brimstone. In this perfect situation, perfect for capturing lost souls, I knowingly sinned. I slept for the entire service.

My father's unshakable hand of order would not be moved. Still my parched lips desired new fun things. On February 4, 2002 I wanted to go to Roger's sleepover. I would die if I didn't. I finally got to go, and I did stay up late until 9:45 before we went to bed. The next day was quick to come. I attended church where the pastor's lullabies of timeless tales of murders and Satan worshipers rocked me to sleep. The whole service I slept, as the pastor captured other sinners' hearts and changed the heathens.

I told my dad I was sorry in the parking lot. He listened but still walked swiftly to the car. Then bracing myself for the shock, I heard the most powerful, awful thing I have ever heard from my father. He said with sweet tenderness and sincerity as if he was apologizing to me, "Son, I want you to know that I love you and will always love you no matter what." "What?" I thought. How could he take away discipline to say kind words of encouragement. However I now realize that he does love me.

Nicholas Henney, Grade 12
Granbury High School, TX

My Color

Art is most important to me. It is my religion. I am saved by the feeling of completing a painting that conveys everything I am. Art sings to me like music. It provides the rhythm I choose to live by. The diverse colors I use reflect my multilayered personality. On the outside I am the brightest shade of lighthearted gold; likewise, the lighter turquoises and salmon pinks leap off of my canvas and greet your eye first. At this stage, I am Louis Armstrong's trumpet telling you how wonderful the world is. However, if you gaze deeper past my pleasing colors then you will find a sharp contrast of mood. Beyond the foreground is where darker hues begin to transform the meaning and purpose of what is in front of you. Ominous blues and purples reveal what is hidden. Only the canvas knows my history full of secrets. The painting makes itself my closest companion. Through the wet paint, I share the weight of my problems and discover a taste of freedom. I embrace my future and share my past all in one single present moment when the brush strokes against the canvas. My color is most important to me because it sets me free.

Dylan Bailey, Grade 11
Pine Tree High School, TX

What Expression Means to Me

Expression stands as one of the most important factors in determining both individualism and our society as a while, especially expression through the arts. My individuality frequently reflects through music, for the plethora of inner thoughts and desires I possess can then permissibly roam free. Music and I hold a closer relationship than words can ever illustrate, and over a course of sixteen years, our connection continues every today. However, a time arose when I abandoned music and all hold on reality in a desperate attempt to control and cope with my emotions, and thus music and I separated. I no longer knew myself, for life signified a dark, frightening, and unpredictable existence. A year later, though, music and I suddenly reconciled, and simultaneously the Earth stood motionless and time ceased to progress; immediately I realized that music, my art, represented oxygen. Never do I feel more vibrant than when surrounded by notes, chords, melodies, and harmonies as they flow from an instrument or from one's lips to my ears. Ultimately, expression serves as a powerful vehicle for communication and a method to express visions that lie beyond the capacity of words, as well as a means for cultural enlightenment. Knowledge of the arts provides an essential foundation for humans to possess in order to maintain personality in an increasingly complicated world. Overall, art represents a universal language that, when utilized by the human being, holds significant potential to make a difference.

Veronica Vasquez, Grade 11
Pine Tree High School, TX

Push It to the Limit

"It was character that got us out of bed, commitment that moved us into action, and discipline that enabled us to follow through," was one of the many amazing quotes by Zig Ziglar. In life, everyone has a goal they plan to achieve. Whether it is working hard in sports, receiving an A in Physics, or finding a job, one must be committed to accomplish that goal. In order to be successful, one must be fully committed to his or her destination. Laziness is not acceptable in the word commitment. Commitment consists of hard work, discipline, dedication, and determination. Although this might sound like a large quantity of work, it all pays off in the end when one receives a scholarship to a university or a raise at a large company. Whoever said life was to be handed to us on a golden platter? Did Barack Obama become the president by chance? No. He was committed to showing the world his opinions, and open to helping the world become a better place. With commitment, anyone can achieve anything. I use this broad statement to emphasize that the sky is the limit when one is committed.

Alex Miller, Grade 12
Post High School, TX

Influence of Literature

Throughout time, literature has been a tremendous part of society. It's helped change social views, transfer moral messages, teach ethics, and more. Literature has changed people's views and thoughts, making people think with a broader view. It's had a huge impact on society, one that's so huge it's unbelievable. Literature's influence is truly great.

One of the most important influences, is literature affecting social views. Examples such as Upton Sinclair's novel *The Jungle*. This novel depicted the vile U.S. meat packaging conditions in the meatpacking industry. This caused a public uproar, which led to important acts that changed the laws of meat packaging. A piece of literature had the ability to do this.

Sometimes, moral messages can be forgotten. Literature has been used to transfer these messages. Messages such as the famous, "don't judge a book by its cover," was explored in the novel *The Outsiders* by S.E. Hinton. It brilliantly delivers this message by showing the story through the eyes of a boy that seemed like a hood at first glance. He's really the opposite of a hood though.

Ethics was taught in the novel *To Kill a Mockingbird* by Harper Lee. The lawyer's personal ethics prevailed, making him defend an innocent African-American man in a racist time period. This teaches us to trust our own ethics no matter the obstacle.

Through ethics, moral messages, and changing social views, literature has been dynamic. It's proven to be astounding throughout history, providing so much in appealing stories.

Maddison Rodriguez, Grade 11
Lodi High School, CA

A Testament of Forgiveness

As a part of our society I find myself often assailed by the nature of others, and as a willing participant I find myself being trampled eagerly by those who know no better. I have since come to favor a very simple action of forgiveness. I am often quite angry at others, thus I assure you that I lack no human qualities of expressing and venting these emotions. However, in contrast to some, I forgive, I move on.

Forgiveness is a hard emotion, it can be viewed as though looking upon a flower: the petals represent a built up anger around a very small center, and these centers represent the ultimate anger, the part we hardly wish to even acknowledge. This is the main cause of our resentment. In time of course, but in order to forgive, one must peel away the petals, plucking them from their once thriving, but now vulnerable and revealed core. And this core must be destroyed, not forgotten really, for human tendencies often repeat. This core of irritation and pain must be completely eliminated; otherwise it is likely that it will produce seeds of other problems.

We, in this society amongst one another, can learn the power of forgiveness through each other within trial and error. But in all honesty, who can enter into the future if completely trapped within the past and unable to forgive? Forgiveness is divine, give and accept it.

Ashley Vance, Grade 10
Regents School of Austin, TX

Texas Tech Football

Texas Tech football is on the rise of becoming not only a powerhouse in the Big Twelve but also in the whole nation. The whole idea that Texas Tech is not as powerful as Texas or Oklahoma may have been true in the past. Now Texas Tech has beaten one of the two teams 5 of the last 6 years. Texas Tech has continued to pepper the top national rankings year after year. The year that they come and consistently win, and stay in the top five will be the year that finally puts Tech above all. Texas Tech is a very underrated powerhouse that not only can get the big win when they need it, but can pull recruits in away from the major universities such as OU, Texas and Florida now. The recruits are what set the foundation of a university football team. In the past Tech could not pull in the best recruits but now the recruits are loving Tech. The new recruits could be what Tech needs to stay in the top five consistently for the upcoming years. Last year Tech tied Texas and Oklahoma for the Big Twelve Championship and has maybe started the next level of success in the program. Texas Tech has and will continue to grow, at the rate they are growing, it won't be long before they pass the other big universities.

Keith Scioli, Grade 12
Coronado High School, TX

Creative Connections

One day I was over at my friends' house, playing soccer and eating peaches; they tasted like delicious honeysuckles. We played soccer until late, but then my friend accidentally kicked the soccer ball and hit her mom in the head. She got into trouble, so I had to go home.

When I arrived home I heard my dad call me to come downstairs, so I went downstairs and found him. I looked at him and he seemed to be grieving, so I asked him what was wrong. He told me to sit down because he needed to tell me something. So I went and sat down next to him, the basement smelled of mildew because the basement had flooded two days before. My dad started to cry and then he told me the worst news I have ever heard my dog, Rambo, died.

I started to cry and yell, "No, it's not true." I swung and hit him in his jaw. He didn't get mad, he just hugged me and said, "I'm sorry son, he was chasing after the neighbors' duck then ran out into the road and got hit by a truck." When I finally stopped crying, my dad and I went out to our field to bury him. My dad wouldn't let me see Rambo; he didn't want me to be scarred. When we finished we went inside and drank hot cocoa, it burnt my tongue; it felt like my tongue was being stabbed with needles.

Dylan Grimaud, Grade 12
Woods Cross High School, UT

Loss

Loss. It's usually unexpected, sometimes tragic, and almost always painful. There are different kinds of losses. The most common type is forgetting where you put the remote, or misplacing your phone. It's typically not very painful, unless what's lost has some kind of sentimental value, or is accidentally sat on.

Then there's the feeling of being lost. I don't mean the confusion of what road you think you should be on, but of what you want to do, and who you are. Some people know what they want to do in life, but others have no idea. A lot of people who ask themselves who they are, often find the answer to be simple, and unsatisfying.

The most painful loss is that of someone who is close to you. Everybody deals with a personal loss differently. One person may cry for a week after a death, while someone else cries for a day. The reaction from someone leaving doesn't vary that far from a death. There is still the feeling of anger, sadness, and regret, but there are usually stronger feelings of responsibility.

Loss is part of life, and some people realize that, but those who don't, tend to take it harder than those who do. A common reaction is to not think about it, or forget. I find that makes dealing with it even harder. There will always be grieving, but acceptance is the best, easiest way to handle the loss of someone.

Brandon Bush, Grade 12
Northridge High School, UT

Religious Freedom

We live in the greatest country in the world. We have the ability to become whatever we want to be. The United States of America is the land of opportunity. Many other countries have rules and restrictions that hold people back from their true potential. Here in the United States, we enjoy many freedoms. We have the ability to express freedom of religion.

The first amendment in the constitution gives the people of the United States many freedoms. "Congress shall make no law respect an establishment of religion, or prohibiting the free exercise thereof." The one that is most meaningful to me is freedom of religion. I am so grateful to be able to worship how, when, and where I want to. Our forefathers came to the American continent for this very reason. They wanted to be able to enjoy religious freedom. There are countries that still do not have this freedom.

In the early 1800's, a religious revival was taking place in America. People were coming from all over the world to exercise this freedom. Many new churches were established during this time. Americans were learning to accept different views on religion. This is when the Constitution was put to the test.

I am thankful to the forefathers of this country, for making freedom of religion possible for every citizen. We must remember the sacrifices that were made on our behalf and make sure that the future generations will be able to enjoy these same freedoms.

Gavin Hales, Grade 12
Spanish Fork High School, UT

Serving It Up

"A perfect combination of violent action taking place in an atmosphere of total tranquility" (http://www.quotegarden.com/tennis.html). Those are the words of Billie Jean King, one of the greatest female tennis players to ever walk the earth. And King is right, tennis may look very graceful and tranquil to the untrained eye, but to a tennis player like myself, it is a game of struggle, fight and battle. The battles in tennis are not only with your opponent on the other side of the net, but with yourself. You have to fight back the emotion of losing that one crucial point, fight back the tears after losing a fifth and deciding set, fight back after missing an easy shot that would have won you a game. Also the game wears you down over time, as you are running around for three straight hours, lunging, jumping and sprinting to every ball that bounces on your side, all to get that one point closer to an elusive win. No matter how hard you try, there is still your opponent on the other side, trying to force you into making mistakes. He will try with all his might to get you to hit that easy winner outside of the court and want you to shout at yourself and throw your racquet. All of these elements that make this game so fierce and hard just add to the beauty of this wonderful sport of tennis.

Philip Ambler, Grade 11
Valley Christian High School, CA

The Unheard Sufferers

The sparking blue surface takes my breath away and the gentle waves sweep my spirit to the shore. Then my eyes glance downward toward the soft grains of silk and I have to do a double take. For laying right before my feet is torn up trash and bottles that have algae growing inside them. A small floating fish looks at me with his unclosing eye as if to inspire me to save his friends. A sense of guilt overtakes me and I trot around picking up all of people's waste that has caused the death of innocent animals such as Mr. Fish. After a while I believe that at least a portion of the lake is pure and peaceful for God's creatures to relax in. However to my horrible surprise only hours later there is more junk taking up Earth's precious water. I jump into action but the miserable conclusion comes upon me that while I can continue helping Mother Nature every day it will only do so much good, I need to start something big. Something bigger than big. Something huge! I need to get more people involved to be the voice of the helpless muted creatures. Then I pray that in the future animals will have a clean and safe environment to swim around in.

Cassaundra Braaten, Grade 10
Bullard High School, TX

Family

The basic family, children with their mother and father living together, happily married, is a dying breed. It's so common to hear a child say, "I'm going to over to my dad's this weekend." Some people are so afraid of getting a divorce, they say, "If you really love each other, it doesn't matter," and are "together" without getting married. They are wrong. There is no commitment to that and it only can end in tears.

At the same time marriage isn't just a game and it isn't doomed to failure. Marriage is what two people do when they want to be with each other for the rest of their lives, and it's one of the most important decisions of our lives. Too often now, this decision is taken lightly because divorce makes it so easy to get out of it. Marriage itself is hard, but it can be wonderful if two people marry for the right reasons. If a marriage is based on the superficial, it will shatter the second hardships arise and divorce is eminent.

Divorce between two people is hard enough when they haven't had any children yet, but it's far more complex when children are in the equation. If there's any way to save a marriage and spare them the emotional pain, it should be done. Children deserve to have both parents together and married while growing up and unless death occurs or there are problems that can't be fixed, you should give that to your child.

Michal Smith, Grade 12
Northridge High School, UT

Warm Metal

"Does everyone have their black socks?" Maxwell yelled to the band.

"Yeah," everyone replied.

"Get on the bus!"

We piled on the bus, and got the party started by singing, dancing, and downing Pixi-Stix. Once we arrived, I could see that people were tense. I was hoping one of my cymbal straps didn't break. I went to where percussion was standing, got my cymbals out of the bag, and put them on. Next thing you hear is the line playing Eights. The crashes sounded crisp and clean; the cleanest we've done. You could see the concentration perspiring on everyone's faces. Another quick tightening of the straps and we went through the show.

The whole band got in line at the gates. Everyone was dead silent. Nothing else mattered. Cheers. We were marching out.

"Granbury High School, is your band ready?" the unknown voice asked.

The drum majors salute.

"Granbury High School may now take the field in competition."

It was over in seconds. We threw down our cymbals and the crowd roared. You could barely hear the four faint little taps signaling us to go.

Awards came surprisingly fast. They started by announcing the "Best Sections." Our line was queasy with anticipation.

"Best Snare Line-Aledo." Cheers. We started getting chills.

"Best Bass Line-Aledo." More cheers. We got a sick feeling in us.

"Best Cymbal Line-Granbury." We all hugged each other in the stands, jumping up and down. The USSBA's a regional competition, which means we're the best in North Texas.

Stephanie Looney, Grade 12
Granbury High School, TX

Blast from the Past

"Study for SATs! Study for AP exams! Write an essay!" The things I have to endure during high school; things like parents screaming at me because I failed a test, or the stress that comes from studying for a test. All night, I lose sleep and become exhausted. I grow tired of freaking out about which college I want to go to. I wish I could go back to a time where homework took ten minutes. Or to a time when all I had to do was keep out of trouble and be a good child. Looking back, I realize that I had a great childhood, with parents that love me. I didn't have to focus on college or SATs and I could just sleep and eat. I miss that childhood. I want to go back and enjoy it again. Life was great as a kid. When I did not have to worry about losing sleep or taking the SATs, or getting accepted into college, or what I was going to be in the future. Being a kid was great, and if I could be a kid again for at least one day, I would be happy.

Dustin Truong, Grade 11
Valley Christian High School, CA

Land of the Free, Home of the Brave

The United States is, without question, one of the most blessed nations on the face of the Earth. Having only been in existence for the past 233 years, what this nation has accomplished is unmatched by any other in history. It is important, however, to remember our humble beginnings. It started when a group of puritan's came over from an oppressed England, looking for a land to worship there God freely. They knew that the new world would not be hospitable; nevertheless, they were willing to venture into it, with their faith put in God. Little did they know that the country they were establishing would come to be the most powerful nation on Earth. Since the time of the Puritans, our nation has experienced a variety of situations. It has gone through numerous wars and depression. The difference with the U.S.A. is that it has always put its faith in God. This faith is visible to our day. It's in our pledge, our anthem, it's written on our currency, and so much more. God has honored this faith, and blessed our nation. No matter what the circumstance, we have always come out victorious. Lately, a trend moving away from God has been popularized, but this country will always have its roots in Christianity. History never changes, people who fear God are many, and while this is true, our nation will forever stand strong.

Franklin Espinoza, Grade 10
Whittier Christian High School, CA

My Grandparents

Being raised by my grandparents is the best thing that has ever happened to me. I can only dream of what it would be like if I was raised by my mom. I can see drugs, alcohol, possibly even prostitution, if I'd been raised by her. Life with my mom would only be a nightmare to me now.

Not long after I was born, I was taken away from my mother and was put in my grandparent's house. They weren't surprised; they knew it would happen. I am the fourth oldest of eleven children. My grandparents have raised each and everyone one of us.

Growing up, not really knowing my parents has been hard! I hear people always talking about how cool their parents are, or how they wish they could get away from them. What they don't realize, is that their parents play a key role in their life. I love my grandparents: I consider them my mom and dad. I even call them "Mom and Dad." They have always been there for me. And through good and bad, they support my every decision. I look up to them, they are my heroes. I could only wish for everyone to have parents that love them, support them, acknowledge their good deeds, and punish their bad. Over all, my grandparents are AMAZING, and I wouldn't be the person I am today without them.

Brieanna Boisa, Grade 12
Nestucca High School, OR

Drew Swank

This year, Junior Drew Swank died from a serious injury due to a football tackle. His death made me totally reevaluate my life and priorities. I was not a close friend of Drew's, but by observing the effect that this had on those close to him, I've gained a new perspective on my relationships with family, friends, and acquaintances. No one knows how long we have here on Earth, so we need to take time to build relationships with people while we still have them.

After Drew died, his classmates were in deep sorrow. Because I did not know Drew as well, I became more of a comforter and encourager for those who were hurting. I realized that I need to be doing this on a regular basis. God created us to need each other so I need to be willing to be there for those who are struggling as a listener, comforter, or whatever they need at the time.

Drew is not remembered for how he looked, how much money he had, or how popular he was. He is remembered for how he treated others and the impact he made on their lives. In the end, our relationships with God and with people are the most important things for which to live.

Katie Worley, Grade 12
Valley Christian School, WA

Ryan Blake Johnson

It was 5 am he just got done dropping his girlfriend off at home from coming from his senior prom. He was a mile away from home in Golden, Colorado. He fell asleep at the wheel and didn't have his seat belt on. He drove off the side of a cliff; it didn't have any guard railings or road bumps to wake him up. As he went off, he flew out the front window and crushed his chest. It killed him instantly. A woman saw him drive off and called 911. About an hour later, they came to my aunt's house and told us what happened. They pronounced him dead at 5:52 am. Seventeen years young, a month away from being eighteen, our beloved son, brother, grandson, cousin, Ryan Blake Johnson, was gone from this world to live in our hearts forever.

April 24, 2004. The day he drove off a cliff to his death. He didn't mean to, it wasn't his fault. He was just coming home from his prom. He was still a child, just seventeen, never getting the chance to become a man. He had everything: a loving family, a girlfriend how cared for him dearly, a house to live in, friends to support him. He was such a trustworthy person. His happiness and ease rained on us all, a warm safe trickling of love. So, why did it have to happen to you? Why that way? I don't understand. Did you do something wrong, or was it just your time?

Summer Morse, Grade 12
REACH High School, TX

The Reality Deception

The worst thing about reality is you can never truly escape it. Reality will always be there, pulling you back to it, like gravity to Earth. But unlike gravity, reality can sometimes be deceived. Unfortunately, those ignorant of the secret try to take other routes that are never successful. The true key to deceiving reality has three elements: faith, hope, and a limitless imagination.

Faith is believing in something, usually without a sensible reason. Reality calls for us to put our trust in things we can see and touch. Believing in something beyond our perception is risky; it involves reaching out not with our nerves, but with our feelings. Still, there is more to faith than believing and feeling. Faith must have hope. You may believe in a perception, but you need to want it to happen. If you can hope with all your heart that something unrealistic will come true, then you are one step closer to fooling real life. Faith and hope elevate you above the present; however, they do not take it away. To deal with the present, you must constantly practice optimism and imagination. You must be able to find the good in anyone and the benefit of everything. If your imagination is strong enough to see past every wrong, and if you have faith and hope in a better tomorrow, you can cheat reality of your soul.

The worst thing about reality is you can never truly escape it…or can you?

Shannon Murphy, Grade 11
Insight School of Washington, WA

Pa Bill

I remember when the phone call finally came. I remember the silence it delivered and the pain that twisted inside of me. Knowing it would come had only caused anxious dread and in no way could have prepared me for the inevitable news. He was gone. My grandfather, my hero, my teacher, my role model, all crashed down in one moment.

The lessons my grandfather, William Patrick McGuire, Jr., whom I fondly called Pa Bill, taught me in the last sixteen of his ninety busy years hold enormous value in my life and will forever impact my identity. As a Southern gentleman, Pa Bill taught me to act politely and mind my "P's and Q's." He inspired me to work my hardest at everything I undertake through his encouraging words that always showed his pride in me and silent example of hard work which spoke volumes. Witnessing his cheerful spirit and seeing him whistle or sing the upbeat song in his heart taught me the value of a positive attitude. He lived out his walk with the Lord, letting me see the courageousness and surrender of a true Christ-follower. He lived as an example even in his last weeks, bravely facing death and gracefully awaiting the day he would meet his Master.

Pa Bill taught me many of life's important lessons and modeled a Christlike existence. As I strive, in my own life, to follow my Savior, Jesus Christ, I will always remember Pa Bill's example.

Molly McGuire, Grade 11
Pine Tree High School, TX

Rain

A single, followed by a million droplets falls from the sky. In mere seconds the world is transformed into a whole different realm. Though seemingly impossible, in this realm, time slows and timelessness presides, as if the world itself wants to preserve this moment of wonder. Each volley of activity becomes a slice of eternity; each contact with the skin, a new burst of energy; each droplet, a splash of golden ichor that revives the five senses of life.

When the great sky sheds its tears, it feels as if one is experiencing the world at the advent of its awakening. Under the icy veil, one can see the world through a mosaic of glass, hear the rain as falling stars, taste the water of purity, breathe in the crisp, clean scent of both earth and sky, and feels the cool sensation of a brisk shower.

The rain, like a million freezing crystals shattering through the soul all at once, washes away all identities, worries, and physical tethers to the world. It leaves nothing but the raw sense of freedom and the feeling of tranquility.

When it rains the world holds its breath from the rhythmic cycle of time. When it rains, one looks up and sends one's soul to the limitless reaches of the sky. When it rains, a million droplets are charged with a million purposes to bring laughter to the sky.

Kevin Hsu, Grade 11
Vintage High School, CA

The Longevity of Society

Our society today. Has mankind simply gone blind? Or have we just ceased to care? Selfishness, deceit, cruelty, wrongdoing. Corruption is spreading, and people fail to open their eyes to such matters. The unjust conquer the world. It is unfair.

I am terrified. Terrified of what tomorrow holds. Terrified of what mankind will do next. Is it a sickness, is it contagious, is there a cure? Savageness is spreading, corrupting, like an evil plague. Humans are without a doubt an extraordinary lot. The way we live and interact is something we fail to see the wonder in every day. So, are we not supposed to be progressing? Every day, uniting as we grow smarter and stronger? Why is it that we are steadily becoming worse? Every day, people are shoving aside the things that are in desperate need of our attention for their selfish desires. Every day, people form grudges on others for things that affect them in no way, and do no harm to society. Every day, people deceive, mistreat, ignore, and harm each other for completely ridiculous reasons. The handful of people in the world who bear hearts and mindsets of righteousness are forced to yield to such wrongdoing.

While society continues to live on, it can still fall to the great force of wrong, which is in fact, the weakest force of all. As long as there are few in the world with morality, civilization will thrive. The strongest man in the world can never amount to a just and noble heart.

Tyler Maricle, Grade 11
New Caney High School, TX

The Media

Why is it that the media that tells us what is good and bad? Why can't the media be humble? Have their thoughts be presented without the emphasis. Imagine how much easier life would be. No more coming to school worrying what you look like or how you're dressed. Today's media is showing racism, not necessarily in skin color but in character life rankings. Newer generations should put down the controller and turn off the television because nowadays television producers and directors are pushing the envelope in their movies and shows. 20 years ago media mostly consisted of television. With new technology booming, imagine in another 20 years how much media will affect the lives of our new generation of kids. If older kids like me are supposed to be the role models to younger kids, then "Why are my role models affecting every aspect of my life and of my peers?" Will there ever be a generation in which media won't affect their taste but only will their feelings and thoughts affect how each teen will live their life? The lives of teens and kids should not be offset by money but by the joy and beauty of life. When will the media teach that family, friends, and education are the most important things in life excluding survival?

Michael Bangal, Grade 10
Kapolei High School, HI

Swim with a Purpose

My heart was already in race mode. It beat fast and hard, as I watched the race before me. It's always like this, the anxiety, the adrenaline rush, the breathlessness. Everything else pales in importance compared to the next twenty three seconds. That's how long it took me to complete this race. A sprint; a race in which the swimmer uses explosive power throughout his entire body without breathing the whole time, down twenty-five yards then back. I picked my head up to watch the last heat in front of me. There's nothing too special about it. It's just another pool. Only it's the pool that would decide who would go or not go to State. "Swim with a Purpose." This was our team motto for this year. Swim with a purpose, swim with a goal, echoed in my mind. Crouched down in the start position, I tensed ready for the buzzer. Then the tight feeling in my chest that signals to me that I can't keep anymore of my pent up energy inside any longer, hit me. The buzzer went off and I dove. It felt good, the water streaming all around me. I began my sprint. It felt good, the best it's ever felt, I swam with a purpose. I finished second in that race; didn't advance to state or break a school record. It came close though and that's good enough for me. Now I know what swimming with a purpose feels like.

Bradley Kade, Grade 12
Granbury High School, TX

National Health Care

Have you ever been denied medical attention because you didn't have insurance or couldn't afford the medical bills? This is a common problem among Americans. There are around 46 million uninsured Americans today and if something doesn't change, that number may increase. Insurance prices have increased so much that people just can't afford it especially in today's economy. There needs to be a change and fast. The problem can be solved with free healthcare. While some people and politicians may say it's only going to hurt us because people are going to take advantage of it, think about the good it could do. Think about all the good people it could help. The people that work as hard as they can for their families but they still just can't afford insurance or the medical bills. Consider the less fortunate families with a child that may need serious medical attention because of a life threatening disease. Should he die just because his family doesn't have the money to provide the treatment he needs? Not here in America he shouldn't. It seems that sometimes we help other countries with their sick, more than we do our own. We shouldn't let our own country suffer just because insurance companies and doctors want more money. We need to change our health care system as soon as possible. This problem has gone on long enough and things need to change.

Jonathan Cavazos, Grade 12
Coronado High School, TX

The Ultimate Goal

Everyone has dreams of what they want to do in life. My dream has always been to become a doctor. There are many who want to be doctors for the money. My motivation is that smile and "thank you" that doctors receive from little children after an appointment. My motivation is the feeling that I will get when I am driving home in the evening knowing that because of me, someone is feeling better and more assured. Many complain of the difficulties of medical school, but to me, all the blood, sweat, and tears I give up are worth it.

As Thomas Fuller once said, "One that would have the fruit must climb the tree."

I know that in order to achieve my lofty goal, I will have to sacrifice much. I know that to become a doctor requires a student to study for eight years in college and medical school, and at least another three years in residency. Many people cringe at the thought of spending that much time in school. But to me, that long and arduous journey will lead to a rewarding future.

Accomplishing your dreams is not easy no matter what they are. A basketball star works hard in the gym to be successful and, likewise, a doctor has to study hard to become who he is. My dream is to become a doctor, and hopefully, with perseverance and hard work, I will fulfill it.

Bilal Jilani, Grade 11
New Caney High School, TX

The Man in the Plaid Shirt

I was riding in the car; my dad was taking me to my second day of fourth grade. This year, I hated school — I was too shy to even make eye contact with my peers.

As we drove past the cemetery, I watched the empty streets of early morning. Bushes and trees raced by, the old used car dealership, up and over the train tracks, then, a ratty old shirt.

I watched this ratty old shirt approach, and realized its folds draped over a skinny old man. He walked face towards the ground, with shuttering steps. He wore a plaid shirt. It used to be red, its sleeves were rolled up. The buttons in the middle were almost up to his neck.

I saw my homeless man every school day for the next five years.

In the fifth grade, I realized that my shyness in school was hindering my performance. I decided that I would start to make eye contact with people. First, I tried to make eye contact with the man in the plaid shirt. However, he never once looked up from his sandals. I began to wave at him whenever we passed, hoping to catch his attention.

I'd like to think that the man noticed me, benefited from the little girl that waved at him every morning for five years. But that could have been a reflection of my own progress. Slowly, as slowly as the man's stuttering steps became steady, I began to gain confidence.

Hannah Southall, Grade 12
Granbury High School, TX

To Love and Be Loved

As a junior in high school, I'm getting hit from every direction: varsity volleyball, AP exams, school dances, homework, SATs, friends, church, the list goes on. And on top of all that, I realize that now is the time that I should start figuring out who I am in relation to who I want to be. That is a lot for a 16 year old to be carrying around. It's overwhelming! It is so easy to get lost in all these priorities and forget what is really important. But just when I think I've taken all I can take from my coach or my history homework, my mom always knows how to set me straight. She said it best one day when we were just talking in the car, "It's all about relationships: to love and be loved. The rest will take care of itself." I'll admit, it'd be cool to be known as the girl with the best arm swing, highest GPA, and the girl who's got it all figured out. But I realize that is not, and never will be, the definition of me. I feel like I am known as the girl who is fun to be around, who tries to improve herself daily, and the girl who can never take herself too seriously. And in the end, I'd rather spend time with her than with the girl who's got it all figured out.

Lauren Sutton, Grade 11
Valley Christian High School, CA

Sex Education

An issue of importance that is made into a discussion when brought up, to me is sex education. Sometimes there is no right answer. I personally believe that it is both the parent's and the school's job to inform the children. Although some schools have a sex education class available, it is the parent's duty. Some parents do not care when the word "sex" comes into the picture; while other parents do. The ones that sit down with their kids and have the "sex talk" are more responsible. I believe all parents should at least attempt to talk to their children. Some parents are oblivious. Usually the stuff you educate them about, they've known for a while. Although parents should make an attempt, it is sometimes less awkward to talk about sex an abstinence with your peers, rather than a parent. My opinion would have to be that the school boards should force a "sex-ed" class throughout the years of your school education. For these kids that have non-caring parents, they should have the opportunity to be educated as well. Along with offering the class teenagers respond better to photos. Photos should include babies, diseases, and consequences of their actions. Either way, I believe that all kids should be sex educated. In one way or another, this is a very important subject in today's society. Think back to your childhood, were you sex educated?

Ashley Sorensen, Grade 12
Coronado High School, TX

My Emergency

There's nothing better than spending Sunday afternoon with my grandma. On this day, however, such was not the case. I walked in to see grandma in her usual chair. Moments later I heard a strange noise from the living room. Confused, I turned to investigate and found my grandma in her chair, trembling. She was unresponsive.

It is a powerful feeling, being powerless. My grandmother was shaking and cold, and the only thing left was to call 911. Dialing tested my wits, and I made the most important call of my life. I had to do everything I could to take care of this woman.

A voice came through the phone, and everything spilled out. It assured me everything would be okay. The ambulance then arrived and I immediately went to grandma's side and said all I could. "I love you, Grandmother…I love you." "I love you too, Ryan," was her slow, simple reply. She was then lifted into the back of the ambulance, and I mustered a low, "I'll see you soon," before my emotions overtook me. Powerless still, but no longer without power.

I saw her later that day. "I'm sorry I put you through all that," she said. "It's okay, Grandma, I'm just glad you are okay now." My grandmother had a stroke that day; luckily, I was able to provide the attention she needed during her emergency. The day then ended peacefully, and all was well.

Ryan Reyes, Grade 12
New Waverly High School, TX

The Moment Before

There are many things that happen before a game. For instance, there is all the pressure built up between the teams. You brutally train for hours on end for the opponent. You are taught to make everything as perfect as humanly possible. You are yelled at for making mistakes, punished if you cannot correct them fast enough. After all of that, you run until you get sick. The whole week you get bruised, beaten up and exhausted. You have to push yourself past the breaking point, and keep going. The enemy then comes to your own town. They are going to try to humiliate you in front of your family and friends. You warm up on the opposite side of the field, sneaking a peak at them. You have to go through a couple of plays to make any last minute changes. The team gets in the tunnel, all you can think about is destroying the other team. When you run out of the tunnel in front of your home crowd, you get this indescribable feeling of pride; it becomes clear to you that you will not let them defeat you. The sweat runs slowly down your face; you can feel your heart beating faster and your blood coursing through your veins. Both teams line up as the band plays the national anthem. The only sound you hear is your heart beating in harmony with your slow breathing. You run onto the field and the rest is history.

Cody Dean, Grade 12
Post High School, TX

My Family

God has blessed me with an amazing family. There are six people in my family including me. I have two parents, a brother, a sister, and a sister-in-law. I love my family very much, and they are extremely important to me.

My family gets along very well. We do not fight, but mostly share laughs. I am so blessed to be in my family. God created us to fit together wonderfully. We all love each other so much, and we would do anything for each other. My father will surprise my family in the morning sometimes with Starbucks coffee and Mike's Donuts (two of our favorite things). My mother cooks us fabulous meals and desserts every day. My brother introduces us to new things all the time. He taught us to like coffee and made us realize tattoos were ok. His wife is so sweet, and helps out around the house whenever the two of them come to visit. Everyone gets along with her. My sister makes us all laugh. I am there to keep everybody happy. My family goes out to eat, we watch movies, and celebrate holidays together.

It is always so much fun to get together with my family because we always have a great time. Everybody has a place in my family, to make us get along. After God, my family is the most important thing in my life.

Callie Johnson, Grade 11
Valley Christian School, WA

In an Instant

I debated the question every young person contemplates during car rides: the seat belt. Such a hassle, but I finally strapped myself in.

Rain pouring, thunder vibrating, we rolled up to the four-way intersection. Infectious laughter traveled through the suburban. Then in an instant, the car became silent. We rolled to a stop in the middle of the intersection as a piercing scream shot through the car like lightning. Heads spun to see a dump truck bearing down on us. My head whirled around to see our driver, and he slowly looked over and realized our fate. Seconds passed and all our lives flash before our eyes, while nothing but prayer and tension could be felt in our midst.

The impact of the truck forced the car across the road, spinning as if it was a rickety old fair ride. One full circle around and we swayed sideways as the impact of a second car smashed into us. Silence. Eyes wandered throughout the car, with everyone speechless. Glass. Everywhere. I heard the ringing noises coming closer, while at the same time those few moments felt like a lifetime.

That was the day I walked away with a new realization. A realization that life is what you make it and you must take full advantage of each day. Flowers will keep growing, and fish will keep swimming, but it's up to you to live and learn to appreciate what moments you do have, because in an instant it can all disappear.

Nina Cates, Grade 12
Granbury High School, TX

What My Education Means to Me

To some people their high school education is making as close as they can to a failing grade, but still passing for the six weeks. Many do not care how their grades are going to affect them when they get into college or more importantly out into the real world. For me that is very different.

I have had dreams ever since I was a little girl to grow up and be one of the most successful women on the planet. Without a great education, that dream I still have, would be nothing.

At this very moment in time, I am doing all I can to apply myself and do the very best I can to get the education I need to get into a great college and make my dream come true.

My education means the world to me and I will not let anybody take it away. I was blessed with a smart brain and it is a very good gift. I promised myself that I would not let it go to waste and I plan to keep that promise.

My mother and older sister made a mistake by not finishing college and they are both really paying for their mistake now. I do not plan on making that same mistake.

Kierra Hart, Grade 10
Alto High School, TX

Intensity

Although winning is not everything in life, the exhilaration that flows through my body after winning a game is priceless. At school people may view me as a smart, introverted girl, but in a game my personality comes alive. No matter the time, place, or opponent, whenever I step on to the volleyball court I become an entirely different person. Similar to the fictitious werewolf who is transformed by the setting of the sun each night, I transform into a hard core ambitious warrior.

Because I live and breathe volleyball, I anticipate each game; without it I feel incomplete. Every time I walk into the gym before a game, I prepare for a battle against my opponents. As the national anthem plays and my heartbeat accelerates, the passion deep within me is jump-started and my personality roars with intensity. The competition begins at the blow of the whistle. When my adrenaline is pumping through my veins, my fervor suddenly takes control of my actions.

I feel a spirit lifting me higher with every pass, jump, and block as the game gets more intense. The cheering in the crowd and the constant faith of my teammates keep me pushing on towards the prize. After winning the game point, I join in my teams' screaming of absolute fulfillment and accomplishment. There is no greater feeling than when I leave the gym walking on "cloud nine" with a smile on my face without a care in my mind.

Megan McKinley, Grade 11
Valley Christian High School, CA

Influential Person

The day started surprisingly hot, humid, and cloudy. I could feel the warm stone bridge getting splashed from the rushing surf below. I was eager to get to the other side of the beach.

Then unexpectedly, I lost my footing and tumbled into the murky water below. Instinctively, I grabbed onto the side of the rock bridge. My head was submerged, and my feet couldn't reach the bottom. I could feel my grip quickly losing hold of the rock. I just knew at any moment now, I would lose my holding and be washed downstream. I thought my life would end there and then.

Then I used all of my strength to pull me up just far enough so my head could pop above the surface. As soon as I was up, I let out a cry for help. It was loud enough where someone passing by noticed me.

Suddenly, I felt a hand grasp my wrist, and hoisted me free from the water's grip. When I was lifted onto the bridge, the man who pulled me out asked me if I was okay, but I was too dazed by what had just happened to answer him. As the daze passed, I thanked him and he went back on his way.

Shortly after, I realized that if he hadn't pulled me out, I might not be here today. That man influenced me to always exercise caution and to help people in need of it.

Ryan Hilton, Grade 12
Granbury High School, TX

Unexpected News

It was October 1, 2008. I was sound asleep in my bed when heard my phone ringing. The sound was like an alarm going off underneath my pillow. I squinted to see who was calling. I saw it was a friend of mine, Ernesto. I answered and heard my best friend, Carla's, voice on the phone. Her voice had a tone that I had never heard before. She was crying so hard I could not understand her. My friend Ernesto got on the phone and told me what Carla could not say. I got off the phone cried my eyes out. One of our friends had been in a car accident the night before and had died. I just saw him the night before last and never thought that it would be the last time I would ever see him.

His funeral was four days later. It was the saddest funeral I had ever attended. It's been a year this month, and it still feels like it was just yesterday that I was laughing and joking around with my friend, David Solis. May he rest in peace.

Losing a person close is like a rose thorn poking your finger as you reach to smell its pretty aroma. The pain stings you all of a sudden and takes a minute to fade away. Life goes on, though, and you learn to cherish what you have and celebrate the life they did have.

Marcy Madrigal, Grade 11
REACH High School, TX

A Rich Curry

"I don't care how poor a man is; if he has family, he's rich." — Dan Wilcox and Thad Mumford

Love, happiness, and a high standard of values are important to me. However, my family serves as the most essential of these. They are the ones who taught me the values to live by, and they nurtured my childhood with love and happiness.

I come from a rich, Indian background which greatly influenced me as a person. Even though I was born in New Jersey, I spent the first five years of my life in India. Because the Indian culture emphasizes the unity of family, our house was packed with cousins, aunts, uncles, grandparents, nieces, and nephews at any given time. Of course, there were many conflicts, usually over trivial matters, but for the most part, we felt truly blessed to be a part of the family. When I was growing up, I noticed a common thread that laced our family together. We all had almost the same values, such as treating a guest as a family member and caring for the well-being of others, no matter the cost.

My family truly cares about my well-being, which ultimately underscores its importance to me. They shaped who I am today by teaching me the correct values. My family has always protected and nurtured me, and for that, I love them.

Pooja Reddy, Grade 11
Pine Tree High School, TX

Changing

I believe all people change for the better or worse.

When I was younger I saw my friends all fawn over boys when they came around, changing everything about themselves just to impress them. Seeing them change started to change me too. One day my best friend, whom I thought would never change her especially weird self, "fell in love." They "dated" for a month. They never talked more then two times but she was hopelessly in love with him. When he broke up with her she changed everything about herself to get him back.

That was when I realized people change themselves for all the wrong reasons, I believe in myself and if people don't like me for who I am, they were never worth my time anyway. I finally gained the courage to be my own person and not follow the crowd, especially when I saw most of the people with a ton of friends were all talking bad about each other. I guess I never saw the point in having a lot of friends I don't actually like.

I've made plenty of mistakes in the past that I could say I regret, but I really don't because they've made me the person I am today. Although I'll never be the most popular girl in the school, I don't care because those things don't matter to me. I'm glad I realized that if I'm going to change, it should be for me, and not for anyone else.

Jenifer Schwartz, Grade 12
University Preparatory School, CA

Escape Route

Self-expression, whether it's in sports, music, or art, everyone has a creative outlet that they can plug into and escape. There's always something we rely on to take us away so we can forget all the pressure and stress that is going on. A photographer takes pictures that capture precious moments in time. A soccer player might practice shooting until she gets that perfect goal. A dancer might move to the rhythm until she finds her beat. The guitarist strums then gets the right chord. A skater flips until he nails that ollie kick flip. A BMX rider spins in anticipation of landing his first triple tail whip. A mathematician solves that one equation to crack the code. Even a daydreamer is dreaming of his perfect scene. Through the stress of everyday life there's always an outlet we can depend on to take us away, to put us into a trance and let us forget the pressure put on us, as if nothing in that moment matters, a pause in time. When you escape, whether it's in your sketchbook or your iPod, you come alive, free of all restraints and free to express yourself in whatever way you want, something they don't always teach at school. Self-expression helps us change the way we see things, through another perspective. Without expression of our own unique interests everything would be bland, the same. Expression isn't just for you to get away, but it models everything we know and how we are today.

Taylor Rush, Grade 11
Valley Christian High School, CA

Beating the Odds

My official bipolar disorder diagnosis came at the tender age of eight, and I have endured many struggles throughout my life. A move from Colorado to Texas triggered many severe problems.

As I helped my mother prepare for our move, thoughts darted through my mind. Will I make new friends? Will everybody hate me? Eventually moving day arrived. I began to settle into my new home, making more quality friends than ever before. However, nothing could foreshadow the problems ahead.

As time passed, my symptoms became increasingly worse. Attempts to halt my illness with therapy and medication failed. To this day, it pains me to think about what I went through, including time in a residential treatment center. Insurance problems forced my premature release. Thrilled to be out, my problems were not over. To everyone's relief, I finally started to improve. After much hard work, the bulk of my problems were over at last.

Over the years, I have made great strides to overcome many challenges. I still have to pay attention to symptoms, but ever since that dreadful year, I have never experienced such an enormous amount of hardship. As a senior in high school, I look back on my struggles with great reluctance, but also with pride. I have learned that the sky is the limit for me. When I have hard times, I look back knowing full well that I can beat anything and that these hard times have made me a stronger person.

Casey Fogel, Grade 12
Vista Ridge High School, TX

Under the Bed

I have just moved into a new house. I'm not used to the place and already weary. Ever since I was little, I have had the fear that there would be some monster hiding under my bed, waiting to grab my leg as soon as the lights went off. I do my routine: turning off the lights, running across the room, jumping on the bed…a quick sigh of relief, and then adjusting to fall asleep. A few minutes pass by and I am quickly awoken from my halfway sleep by my bed slightly moving. I am holding my breath. Nothing happens, so I go back to sleep. Within a few minutes, there is a push. My bed comes off the ground. I am so quiet. I can hear my heart pounding. I know either something is under my bed. I know I have to get out of my room. I decide to make a run for it. I jump off my bed, but as soon as my foot hits the floor, something grabs me by the ankle. I scream horrifically, clawing for one of my stuffed holiday bunnies. I start swinging away at the evil bat creature that has my foot. My sister hears my crying and runs in my room, turning on the light to expose the mutant. She laughs hysterically, along with my brother who was halfway out from under my bed.

Samantha Smith, Grade 11
REACH High School, TX

Life of Axel Rose

Axel Rose, the lead singer of Guns and Roses, formed the band in 1985 and has become one of the many rock legends releasing over 100 million albums worldwide. The peers in the music industry often spoke highly of the band: Ozzy Osbourne called Guns and Roses "the next Rolling Stones." Axel Rose hasn't been freed of criticism. Like Axel's alcohol and drug abuse, his fondness of Charles Manson T-shirts, and was used by the media as a poor and negative influence on the younger fans of Guns and Roses. Axel Rose has become a source of both controversy and criticism since the owner founding members left the group in 2002, but Axel Rose brought the band back with a comeback with new performers in the band (Stitson, keyboardist Dizzy Reed, multi-instrumental Chris Pitman, and guitarist Robin Finck). And with a lot more live concerts singing both old and new songs which put them back onto the charts and amazing the rock media with many new albums like Chinese Democracy, and getting nominated for many awards which finally made Axel a rock legend.

Kobie Gray, Grade 12
Coronado High School, TX

Depression and What It Can Lead To

Rollo May once said, "Depression is the inability to construct a future." By saying that he meant that when you aren't clearly focused and not able to do, get up and be happy about life, or you aren't able to create a good future for yourself.

Depression and teenagers do not mix well. According to teendepression.org, about 20% of all teens suffer from some sort of depression. Many factors are the cause of this. Teenagers need to enjoy their life and have fun with it, though the efforts of pleasing parents and almost everyone around can get to a person. Also school and friends play a huge role in this too as a great cause of stress.

When you think of depression you don't think that it can lead to a worse cause. In fact according to teendepression.org, 1 out of 5 kids have thought about suicide. When the illness becomes too great to handle, they seem to find that the best way to deal with the problem is suicide.

I have a friend who needed help after battling with depression. She felt the only way to overcome everything was to kill herself. When I found out about that, I talked to her and helped her out with some of her problems that she was dealing with. I stepped in because I was slowly losing my friend and I didn't want to lose her forever. Knowing about depression and what you can do can really help and possibly save someone's life.

Mary Jo Figueroa, Grade 10
Kaufer High School, TX

Blissfully Unaware?

I think the very condition of being human, in and of itself, presents some inherent difficulties. Human versus animal brings up a core struggle; ignorance and bliss versus knowledge and power. Obviously, each seems infinitely superior from within. If one is oblivious and happy, unaware of any malignancy in their surroundings, their personal orb, and is truly, exquisitely content with their state of being, why would they want to change it? If they are so truly fulfilled by what they have, why is the knowledge of anything more even necessary? Furthermore, what good does power do them any ways, if they are inhabiting their own personal Eden?

Conversely, those possessing knowledge and power — the informed autonomous — cannot possibly settle. They may, at times, be the malcontents, and skeptics, the critics and pragmatists, but, they get things done. They are so acutely attuned to the nuances of the world that in ignorance, they would not find bliss, but torture; they would be in agony at their own oblivion.

These two factions can never be at peace. They are polar opposites in the truest sense, diametrically opposed. Rendered wholly incapable of seeing the value of the opponent's argument by virtue of the lens through which they see the world. Those partaking in ignorant bliss cannot see any alternative to their unencumbered insouciance; after all, life is bliss. The empowered and knowledgeable look at their adversaries with condescension, satisfaction, even supercilious pity at their unenviable state. Mutually exclusive, neither can know the other without first losing itself.

Marie Sbrocca, Grade 12
University Preparatory School, CA

Learning

There are very few of us that don't like listening to music. We listen to songs over and over again and never get bored, as if an addiction controlled us. I had seen people using magical instruments to create amazing sounds. I didn't understand how that was possible, but the mystery intrigued me. When I found out about a class in middle school that taught children how to make music, it immediately caught my attention. So I signed up for band to check it out. When class began I was given a mouthpiece and asked to try and make a sound, but I had no idea what to do. It took me a while, but I eventually got the hang of it. I still sounded weird, but I decided to stick with it. Most of the other kids had been in band for a while, and they sounded amazing when I heard them play. I dreamed of one day becoming as great as they were. And as time went by the dream started becoming a reality. It wasn't long before I was the best in the class, and the more time that passed the easier it got. It felt great to make good sounds so effortlessly. The music gets harder as time passes, but I keep working hard to be the best I can.

Armando Cepeda, Grade 11
New Caney High School, TX

My Leap

Today is the day I will finally exert myself and build enough courage to ask out the girl whom I have had a crush on. The lunch bell rang and I was slowly gliding over to her locker when a solid wall of nervousness came out of nowhere. What am I going to say to convince the girl that I would be a good boyfriend to her? What marvelous traits do I have that would prove to her that I am the right guy for her? As I am approaching her locker my mind went on frenzy. "Ask her! Ask her!" my mind is shouting but the words cannot breach my mouth. As she finished she headed over to the table. Shamefaced, I followed her and even the taste of my sandwich didn't repel the defeat. "At least I have tonight at the football game," I told myself.

That night after she played in the school band we were alone. My mind went on lock down once again. My first couple words were a stutter and she laughed at me turning my face tomato red. "Would you care to take a chance and be my girlfriend?" I managed to muster. It came out the only way it could. She smiled at me and said yes, filling my heart with joy. As it turned out my leap of faith proved to give me courage and a person to take the leap with.

Jimmy Maldonado, Grade 12
Granbury High School, TX

Transforming the American Life

It has been 400 years since the first American colony was settled. Today, if asked, the majority of the American people would say that America has come a long way since it was founded. Examining this closely brings an entirely different perspective into mind, however. This is not to say that we haven't accomplished many things since the very beginning, but I simply state that we have lost our focus and our direction. We have strayed from our Founding Fathers' goals and ambitions for this country and we have come to a point where no one is sure what to do.

Today, morality is a thing of the past. A person's sexuality is flaunted in the media and in the streets, gang violence and poverty levels have risen significantly, and you can't watch the news without hearing about a recent scandal. Our country is burdened with debt, building and investing in new structures that tear down the land and waste away our country's beautiful natural resources. Progress came to a peak long ago, and what we have left to do now is change our ways. It's the desire of every parent that their children live in a peaceful world, and it's doubtful at this point in time that generations to come will look back on what we've done and be proud. Repairing our country now will spare our children and our children's children the blood, sweat, and tears that no doubt will accompany their predicament.

Eva Wickliffe, Grade 11
Warrenton High School, OR

High Merit Essays – Grades 10, 11 and 12

The Behemoth!

Why did fishing on this blustery, frigid, foggy, abysmal day seem like a good one? It was day break, my brother and I headed out to our secret fishing spot in hopes to hook the big one. We set up our rigs tossed them into the water and began to sit, waiting for that big bite that would bend our pole over backwards.

We had been fishing for about an hour now when we started to get some action on one of our little poles that was rigged for small lingcod. We caught about 5 baby lingcod and were hoping that the mother of all fish would be close behind. After a good 15 to 20 minutes of catching these small fish we got a bite on the big pole, it was her. My brother grabbed the pole and began the gruesome fight to reel in the big one. The fish was fighting hard, not wanting to be bagged up and put on the barbecue for our dinner that night. The fish was starting to get closer and closer on shore, we could see the behemoth's shadow in the water being force towards us, I grabbed the gaff and prepared myself. The fish got in range and BAM I stuck the fish right under the gills, we had caught the big one. The fish was weighed at 33 lbs. We headed home, cooked it up and had ourselves the best fish feast we had ever had.

Jarod Vance, Grade 12
University Preparatory School, CA

Be the Change You Wish to See in the World

"Never look down on anyone unless you're helping him up," were the great words of Jesse Jackson. We should thrive to live by this statement because it is often easy to get wrapped up in the ways of the world when talking about putting people down. To be quite honest, it usually makes us feel better about ourselves when we put others beneath us. As humans, we feel a sense of superiority when we denounce people, but we must keep in mind the feelings of the person we are putting down. We have all been made fun of or teased, probably for unnecessary reasons, so the next time that we feel the urge to tease someone, we should remember how we felt in a similar situation. Respect is a very important lesson to learn in life. Not only should we respect our elders such as teachers, parents, and managers, but we should respect anyone we come in contact with on a daily basis. I've learned that if you show others respect, you will receive the same amount in return. The statement also urges the readers to help others. Everyone could help someone and, on the same note, everyone could use help. Whether you can tutor a little brother or sister or help an elderly woman with her groceries, as humans, we need to start working together to better the lives of others because if you help people, you will get help when you need it the most.

Toni Wait, Grade 12
Post High School, TX

What's More Important Than the Present?

When asked about writing this essay I had to think for at least a day to find out what was important to me. I'm normally a lazy man, I don't like to do anything but eat and sleep. However, when I seriously pondered my life to figure out what is important to me, I came up with two relatively simple ideas. My ideas were food and sleep, and that's when it hit me. I don't have anything that is really important to me. So I thought harder, and after thinking, I finally realized that it isn't a "thing" that is important to me, it's a concept. My important concept isn't religion, family, education, or any of that. It is simply time. I realized then and there that I don't have a job, girlfriend, or much to really live for. I don't do anything besides march on Friday nights. All I have going for me is that I have all the time in the world to do whatever I want to. If you knew me you'd know that the title, the saying "What better time than the present?" doesn't really fit me. I almost always procrastinate to the last possible second. However, during my thoughts, I realized how little time I actually did have, and how soon I need to utilize it. So, what's important to me? Why, the very realization that I can be something great, if I can make better use of the present.

Chuk Maples, Grade 11
Pine Tree High School, TX

Of Twisted Stories

Ever since we were little we've listened to them. In fact, many of us could repeat them with the effortless ease associated with memorizing a story often repeated. Fairy tales. They're everywhere, seemingly from the beginning of time itself. Don't deny it — we know these whimsical stories better than the back of our very hands. A 'once upon a time' is necessary; a 'happily ever after' is only natural. But why? When did the terrifying stories meant to invoke fear and instill practical lessons transfigure into the light, cheery, pixie-dusted fictions they are now? What in the world caused the rapid 360?

It's supremely ironic...think about it. As our society swiftly grows more violent and unmerciful, we feed ridiculously blithe fabrications to the naïve; when years ago terrible deeds were at a considerable low and every child was scared out of his or her wits with impossibly terrifying snippets of extreme peril. Our modern time holds a type of morbid theme never tested to any such limits before, yet we are impelled to tell only stories of unrivaled moral to youth. Perhaps we need those euphoric tales to whisk us away to a fantastic world full of magic and selfless love, where the "good guy" *always* wins and your happily ever after is only guaranteed. Perhaps the child in us all would rather our realities be manipulated into something more innocent; to be twisted into something far more merry and carefree.

...If only it were that easy.

Priscilla Ortiz, Grade 10
Coronado High School, TX

The Perfect Gift

Snow insulates the earth beneath with a glistening coat of diamonds painted across a bleak whiteness overnight. Christmas sparkles golds, silvers, reds, blues, whites, and greens. Smells of hot chocolate and peppermint in the house mingle with the scent of fir boughs. Christmas music plays softly in the background while husband and wife dance in the candlelight before the children awake. A warm fire crackles and pops in vibrant oranges and yellows as it chases the chill from inside the house back to the snowy wonderland outside. The children return home from a lovely trip to Slumberland as couples whisper sweet nothings in each other's ears on a cozy couch.

Christmas is waiting…waiting for the children to awaken and squeal and laugh in delight; staring with mouths agape, awed at the brilliance and enormity of the tree, or the gifts that sit atop one another, protected beneath a covering of needles. The Nativity story is told. Memories of Christmases past flood peoples minds and they can't remember a better Christmas than this one. December 25th can do that to a person, make them forget everything while they laugh and smile with everybody else. Christmas brings an infectious peace and joy to people around the globe, even if it's just for one day. Christmas is a marker in history that vividly shows God's amazing love because He sent His son, Jesus, to Earth over 2,000 years ago. Jesus is the ultimate image of love. The First Gift. The Perfect Gift.

Ember Trembley, Grade 10
Cam Jr/Sr High School, WA

A Time I Was Scared

My baby's due date was on the 28th of May, 2009. I was nervous and scared because my mom-in-law was telling me it wasn't contractions, but I could tell they were contractions because it was in that time frame of what my doctor had been telling me. They took me to the hospital. I was so nervous, because throughout my whole pregnancy, I had been hearing how bad it hurts and that it's the worst feeling ever. My doctor came in and said I was dilated to a two and that I was having contractions, so he said that he was just going to go ahead and induce my labor. A couple hours passed, and they broke my water. I started getting more contractions, but not enough, so they upped my contractions three or four times until I was dilated at a 5.5. They told me that the baby's head was stuck and getting swollen from where it was trying to come out. They needed to do a c-section to get the baby out. They gave me a lot of medicine so I didn't feel a thing during the c-section, which was nice. I was asleep during the whole thing when I suddenly heard my baby crying. It was the best feeling in the world when I got to finally hold her.

Vanessa Cortez, Grade 10
REACH High School, TX

The Importance of Warm Laundry

What if warm laundry disappeared? To think of a world with no warm laundry makes me wonder, how could we forget the impact warm laundry has, not just on human vitality but for the essence of life?

Cold. That word makes you cringe. There is an explicit happiness you get when opening a dryer and getting that blast of warm air on your face. Most of the enjoyment of doing laundry comes from having warm fabric touching you. In all the laundry commercials you always have someone touching, feeling the laundry. The way they treat fresh laundry, you would think it was a precious heirloom to humanity.

Warmth, not just in commercials, is also depicted in words like home, family, and love. What is the cozy feeling you get when you arrive at home? Home is where the heart is. It is a warm feeling that you get in your heart. When one talks about love, it is a burning they feel. It is because of warmth that we can all grow in our relationships. Warmth can be taken farther.

The ultimate source of warmth is the sun. The warmth and light the sun gives off is what keeps the Earth operating. With no sunlight, life would cease to exist as we know it.

Warmth is essential to life. Having warm laundry gives us an insight as to the importance of warmth that is needed in our lives.

Eliza Wilson, Grade 12
Lone Peak High School, UT

Believing Is Achieving

Believing in yourself is one of the most important qualities you need. When you believe in yourself you set yourself up to do the best of your abilities. When you believe in yourself you set your mind into a focus which will lead to determination and hard work. You can only achieve what you put your mind and body into and if you believe you can do something then do it to the fullest. No matter how you show it, you must believe in yourself in order to achieve. If you don't believe in yourself then you are automatically a failure. When you don't believe in yourself you are quitting, telling yourself you can't do anything. In reality millions of people set themselves up for failure by not believing in themselves. This lack of confidence brings them down. Likewise, there are also millions of people in the world who don't want to see you succeed. Those people are always trying to bring you down and say you can't do it. Dream killers are what they are called, people who don't believe in themselves so they try to put you down to their level. If you really think about it, you are already achieving more then them because believing in yourself is the first step to doing something. With this in mind, you can achieve anything you want to do or become. Whether it is completing calculus class to becoming an astronaut you can achieve it as long as you believe.

Shawn Meas, Grade 12
Vista Murrieta High School, CA

Value of High Grades

Something that has always been important to me is success, in particular success in school or good grades. Good grades in my mind show hard work, responsibility, and a desire for self improvement. There are many benefits to having good grades including better opportunities in college and the military, and many schools have a mandatory grade level to be maintained before the student can be allowed to play sports. Also having good grades is a major part of presenting yourself as a good student which is useful when applying for a job, to a college, or for a scholarship.

In order to get good grades a student must generally pay attention in class, be responsible to turn his work in on time, work to learn and understand the material, and have a general desire to make himself better than he currently is and set himself above the standard. It is also important for the student to be challenged in attaining his grades because if the material is at a lower level than the student is capable of success should be considered standard not exceptional.

Having good grades is important because they are a common reference for determining one's aptitude and general level of achievement. Which are both things you want to be viewed as high by anyone determining whether or not you are a good choice for a job or student they want at their college.

Sam Gilmore, Grade 12
Valley Christian School, WA

Losing Someone Precious

"It was Alyssa..." my eyes glazed over and the impact shook me. My knees hit the floor as my heart rate increased. Tears flowed out of my blank eyes but I realized the overwhelming pain wouldn't go away with tears. All I could do was climb slowly to my feet and move my legs, weighed down with this horrific news, one by one back to my welcoming bed so I could crash on top of it, grab tight to my teddy bear, and curl up in a ball to somehow hold myself together through the night.

The pain of losing a best friend is unlike any other. A broken arm could heal but a broken heart continues to break with every mention of her name or a song that blares cruelly out of the speakers. The numbness of the first week passed and left in its wake a stabbing, crushing pain that I had never felt before.

Alyssa Dix was not only a best friend to me but a friend to everyone. She loved without question and hurt when others hurt. I want to be like her but I could never replicate the outpouring of love she showed to everyone. That is why at her funeral people from all groups came to mourn the loss of a girl who linked us all together.

It was a car accident that took her too soon from this Earth but before she left she taught me something. To try harder, love better, and to hold on because God has a plan.

Riley Goodman, Grade 12
Granbury High School, TX

A Life Begun in Thirty-Seven Measures

My life, in the musical sense, started with a simple waltz. Just the piano playing solo; the song barely over a minute long, with only a mere thirty-seven measures behind its structure. Little did I know, hearing those simple chords changed the entire meaning of my life, and gave me the thing most important to me in the entire world: music.

My music, whether it be my piano playing, singing, or compositions, allows me to truly express myself on a level of emotion that words cannot even begin to describe. When I concentrate on nothing but the music within me, I always slip temporarily from the world around me into a place where there is only me, my instrument, and the sweet, sweet sounds that the two forces combine into one. Music has been the one thing that has helped my sanity throughout the tough times that being a teenager in this world bring; I am so very fortunate and grateful that I have such an escape that cannot be taken away from me. I know that the bond between my music and myself is truly a gift from God, and I thank Him every day for letting His love flow through my music.

Music, without a doubt, is the greatest thing that has ever happened to me, and it will for now and forever, remain the most important thing in my life. And to think, it all started with a short, little waltz...

Austin Ferguson, Grade 11
Pine Tree High School, TX

Wakeboarding

Wakeboarding is one thing in my life where there is no stress involved. Going to school and cramming in homework late at night, while studying for tests and having intense baseball practices with coaches yelling is never too exciting. I look forward to summer where my friends, family and I can go out on the lake and have no cares in the world.

More people are starting to wakeboard, and I think that is great. There's nothing better than waking up early on a summer morning and looking outside seeing not a cloud in the sky. Hooking the boat up to the truck and packing food and driving to the delta is the way I love to spend my summer days. Launching the boat and pulling away from the dock with the music blaring is so much fun. I get excited once we're outside the 5 mile per hour zone because now I know it is time to get my board on. I pick the song I want to ride to, drop into the water and say, "Hit it!" I glide over the water like it is glass with the wall of water shooting out from under by board as I cut in hard toward the wake. I feel like I'm flying when I soar over the wake and land on the other side. I cut out into the flats and look at the horizon and think, "There is nowhere else I'd rather be."

Jason McCracken, Grade 11
Valley Christian High School, CA

Not My Usual Morning

For once, I knew this would be a good morning. I knew it the minute I awoke without rolling out of bed slamming the snooze button with my half sleeping hand. For the first time all school year, I was up half an hour before my alarm clock awoke me from my slumber. I turned off the alarm, as not to wake the parents, and hopped in the shower. After doing my daily routine in about 30 minutes, instead of 10. I then wandered downstairs, opened the cupboard and drawer to retrieve a bowl and spoon respectively. I'm used to running out the door catching a nearby banana in flight, so this was new. The box of unopened Raisin Bran sat on the counter. Dad bought it for me, but I hadn't eaten any, never having the time. I tried to open the bag without alarming the house with the crunch of the plastic. I then poured a nice big bowl and proceeded to pour myself some milk too. I continued to eat my delicious breakfast item. I then went out to my old fashioned truck, still with plenty of time before school, and slid right on into the driver's seat. I flipped the car into gear and waited for my station to tune in, as usual. For once, there was a talk show going on, not my standard tunes. I checked my phone to see if I had the wrong car time. It said today was Saturday! Oh great!

Tennyson Jones, Grade 12
University Preparatory School, CA

Out of the Dark

All I saw was blackness; I could hear the faint voice of Kolton as it got louder. I started to realize what was happening. I slowly opened my eyes to see that I had come out of the blackness.

Will and I were in the car when Kolton decided to pass the car in front of us. It all happened so fast. The car had turned into our truck right as we went to pass it. The truck was thrown to the side of the road, and all I could hear was tire squealing, screams and a huge BAMMM!

I remember seeing our cars collide and thinking, "Am I going to die?" I saw all black and heard Kolton yell, "Maddie, are you OK?" I opened my eyes and immediately saw my jeans drenched in blood. As I stood there waiting for help I glanced over my shoulder and saw the damage we had done in a split second. You could see our cars twisted together in a strange knot. It was really scary to see the vehicles and how bad of shape they were in, and to think everyone came out of the crash alive.

I will never forget "the wreck." This accident made me realize that life can end so fast with no warning. So I intend to live my life to the fullest in case something like this happens but I don't come out of the blackness.

Maddie Davidson, Grade 10
Wall High School, TX

I Love You

That morning, December 5th, I awoke earlier than usual so that I would look perfect for that evening. Every time I saw him my heart would race, and the frantic high school hallways would melt away to a world where it was just me and him. I spent my classes trying to build up enough courage to ensure myself I would not back out.

Soon after dinner we were off to the park, we donned our jackets and walked to his car. We arrived to the park shortly after nightfall. We spent the next perfect hour enjoying each other's conversation while we walked hand-in-hand in the freezing cold.

"Ready to go?" he asked.

"Almost." I replied as I started walking towards the garland and light covered bridge. When we reached the small set of stairs I stopped him, he looked at me quizzically.

"What?" he asked.

I began to tell him all the things that I liked about him, stumbling all over my words. I stepped closer to him and raised myself onto my tippy-toes. I leaned a little closer to him and whispered in his ear "I love you." He looked at me with extreme joy and total disbelief, his eyes brimming with tears as he flashed the largest smile.

"Really?" he asked. I smiled and nodded my head yes. He leaned forward and his lips gently brushed against my ear as he whispered "I love you, too."

Brieghanna Chase, Grade 12
Granbury High School, TX

Behind the Dance

The audience, in awe at her beautiful extensions, sweet smile, and the graceful movements of her hands and feet. Their eyes follow her every movement, from her toes lightly moving across the stage to the expression on her face. Each of her movements tell a story without verbal communication. Dance is not only a movement, it is an expression. It is more than what the audience can see with their eyes. It is about the story behind the dance that matters.

Many children are not able to dance because they are either disabled, or simply cannot afford the bills that come with dance. Some dancers fail to realize the talents that they have, and put it aside like it is nothing. Other dancers use dance as a way to communicate their feelings. For some, dance is the only good thing that they have done in their lives. A dancer may not have to have the best technique, but if they put their heart and soul into it, the audience will feel their pain or happiness. Professionals train for years before they can finally achieve the level they are at.

That is what's so beautiful about dance. It is the hard-work and dedication put into it, to make something so difficult look effortless. I, myself, still have a long way to go, but dance is something so important to me, that it is a lifestyle. Without dance, I do not know who I would be today.

Alyssandra Baniqued, Grade 11
American Renaissance Academy, HI

My Passion

Wrestling is my passion. I want to be a wrestling coach and show people some of their abilities they didn't know they had. I want to help people make something of their lives. I want to see others go on to better things in life. Wrestling is a sport that takes a lot of dedication and the will to want to win. You have to be willing to work hard and give it your all.

Wrestling was the first sport I was committed in. It taught me the meaning of CDR; Character, Discipline, and Respect. It showed me a different meaning of life, it helped me realize all of my abilities I didn't know I had. My first coach was H.E. Burchard. He was a tough coach, but he showed me everything in life has a different meaning and a different point of view. Because of wrestling, I have a chance to do something with my life.

I wrestled two college girls from Lockhaven, Pennsylvania and because my coach was there, I was able to win both of my matches. The coach is looking to give my sister and me a wrestling scholarship to Lockhaven. I want to follow coach B's footsteps. He helped me find out what I want to do with my life and that is to wrestle. Because I was in wrestling, I was in more.

Wrestling made me want to do more in life and be involved in more.

Jessica Hise, Grade 12
Coronado High School, TX

Passion

Ted Ray once said, "Golf is like a love affair. If you don't take it seriously it's no fun, if you do take it seriously it will break your heart." This man perfectly described, in one sentence, the whole of my feelings for a sport that has consumed my passion. I have played for two years and lettered my freshman year as our number one player, taking second in district. But to me, winning is a menial part of my love for the game. Merely setting foot on a golf course gives me butterflies, and those butterflies flutter away with all the frustration and the evil that may have filled my head. Golf is my escape. I find myself thinking about it constantly. When I'm not playing, I'm thinking about playing. Whether I have a good day or a bad day, I always leave wanting to play more. If golf is taken away from me by anything, like an injury, or the weather, it's all I can do to keep from going absolutely crazy. My life would change drastically if I could never play golf again; starting with depression. I'm suffering from torn cartilage right now, so I'm getting a small taste of it presently. Golf has taught me a lot about myself and about life. Through the sport I have met a lot of incredible people including my golf coach. All that aside, I've discovered one major thing, my heart is shaped like a golf ball.

Maddison Malone, Grade 10
Bullard High School, TX

Masks

When you look in the mirror, what do you see? Do you look at yourself in the eyes and smile, being proud of yourself? Or do you find yourself hiding from your reflection? Many of us look in the mirror and do not know what to think. We look right past our faces and try to look into our souls and hearts. And when we find who we really are, we are disgusted and turn away. We do not know ourselves. The fear of not knowing ourselves sends us into a frenzy. We try to look beautiful in the mirrors. We try to deceive ourselves. But, we only put on a mask, a mask that can be easily taken off. Yet it suffocates us; Makes us blind, causing us to stumble and run into the dangerous and obvious. We are so concerned with our image and our pride, that we keep the mask on. We pull the mask on and make it tighter and tighter, pressing it into our faces. Eventually that mask we put on becomes us. Like a clown who puts on makeup and goes into character, so are we who hide our faces.

Joseph Domingo, Grade 11
The Bear Creek School, WA

Commitment

I've thought and thought about this word. What's its significance? I've come to realize that of all of our morals, commitment is the one that is iffy, but can make a world of difference. To commit to someone or something is to make a promise, if you ask my opinion. A promise of never letting go, holding on to that one thing that could make you, or break you. A promise that no matter what the outcome is, you've done your part, and you've achieved what you set out to accomplish. You have your self-esteem and your pride swell to know that whatever you've committed to has become a part of your life or life accomplishments. It can be hard, but with commitment, pushing through and accomplishing the final destination is just a step away.

Chauncey Willis, Grade 12
REACH High School, TX

Story of My Life

I felt the fresh rush of mystic water, for I was a new soul on this earth ugly on the outside, but more beautiful than an angel on the inside. I was welcomed to a small apartment on the out skirts of Venezia, Italy, close to the ocean. I was a small child, and I do not really remember much of my past, but I do recall tales that my mother used to tell me when I was a young child. She would tell me tales of when we lived in Italy; the beauty of the buildings and how romantic it was for her and my father, how they would take long walks on the docks while sipping on champagne. I see pictures of where I was born and it was magnificently beautiful. I wish one day I could go back with my mother and see all the beauty with my own eyes.

Jessica Saenz, Grade 12
REACH High School, TX

Idol

My mom just recently became a single mother of four. She does a great job at caring for my siblings and I. She is incredibly organized, has certain schedules for us, and works hard. Life is not simple, but no matter how difficult it gets or what problems are thrown her way, she never gives up. She is there for us, at all times.

It has hardly ever been easy for her. I have not always been a decent child. She had to deal with all my problems, and I never really showed her that I loved her. But she made sure that I knew she loved me and cared about me.

My mother is an extremely strong woman. She relies on no one but herself. Her independence stands out and makes her who she is. In my eyes she seems fearless. She would do anything for her children.

I want to be just like my mom. If it was not for her I am sure I would not have a good life. She has taught me everything she knows, she is extremely smart. She makes life look effortless. She is an amazing mother and best friend. I would not be here without my mom, my idol.

Ariana Bogdon, Grade 11
New Caney High School, TX

Embrace

The key to any achievement in life: hard work. One could be given all the innate qualities ever desired and still be unsuccessful, because he did not take advantage of his God-given talents. In order for one to succeed, he must set forth an effort to achieve his goals despite any unwanted situations that may confront him.

Leaders such as Gandhi, Martin Luther King Jr., and Michael Jordan fought through adversity and as a result are looked to as revered statures. Though the British ruled about two-thirds of the world at the time, that wasn't enough to stop Gandhi from protecting his country through nonviolent action; MLK did not step down when his house was nefariously bombed, and Michael Jordan never quit, despite being cut from his high school varsity basketball team. It is these kinds of leaders that keep our world from falling apart; they not only are fully determined themselves, but also seem to give off a ubiquitous aura that fills those around them with marvelous work ethic. Through these increased motivation levels, people begin to understand that they have all the potential in the world, and that they just have to set their minds to their goals.

Those who sit around and play video games all day instead of getting outside and chasing their dreams are wasting away their copious potential. While on the other hand, those who embrace their inherited qualities end up achieving far more than they could ever imagine.

Neil Verma, Grade 12
University Preparatory School, CA

America's Wonder Woman

Beauty may be in the eye of the beholder, however, often times, people seem to forget that beauty is based on so much more than ones physical appearance. Beauty can be found everywhere you look in the world both in nature, and in manmade things. And it is safe to say that none, after actually seeing her with their own two eyes, can consciously deny her splendor.

She was by far the most beautiful woman I had ever seen. Her dark brown eyes glimmered in the sunlight; her flawless copper skin sparkled like a brand new penny. She carried herself in such a way that even the most prestigious of individuals humbled themselves in her presence and the seven-spiked crown upon her head proclaimed her unspoken royalty.

The overall atmosphere at her location was one of respect, thankfulness, and gratitude. People of all different cultures and native tongues flocked from the four corners of the earth to admire not only her beauty, but also the bigger picture of what she stands for.

Lady Liberty or as we know her, the Statue of Liberty, stands tall and unwavering on the shores of Ellis Island and continues to breathe hope and optimism into the air. She watches over America from her post at the most famous New York City as America's Wonder Woman. When admiring her grandness, one cannot help but to feel instantly empowered in knowing that deep inside her, the stories of so many others dwell.

Kryshawna Charleston, Grade 12
James Bowie High School, TX

Stop Being Lazy!

As time goes by I notice that more and more people are getting lazy. I don't understand how someone can sit there and stare at a television set or just lie on their bed and not do anything for hours upon hours. I know that with society the way it is, it's very easy to give in to the technology. What people need to realize is that in order to keep their bodies, and minds, from turning to slush is good old fashioned fresh air and plenty of exercise.

Now that TV can be accessed anywhere there are kids, granted their outdoors, that are sitting on a curb watching TV on their phones, or texting, playing games, going on the internet, the possibilities are endless. That's why I think that this has gone way too far and parents, school officials, or any adult needs to take away these devices every now and then and force children to notice what's around them. They need to be encouraged to use their imagination and they need to be able to entertain themselves. These are valuable skills for life that are just being completely wasted. Action needs to be taken and I don't know if it ever will be but hey, why not hope for the best.

April Davis, Grade 12
University Preparatory School, CA

City Limits

On the brink of adolescence, I challenged a standard of society. I liked someone of a different race. It was a silly puppy love, yet my parents still challenged it. Unsuitable, they said. I was just too young to handle the social responsibility. That was that.

Even at that age, I didn't like being told what to do.

"I thought we handled this."

My father fumed. His brow furrowed and I could see his thoughts ramming into each other as they attempted to collect themselves. He spoke slowly; about disappointment, about what people were saying about him, about the shame I was bringing upon our family. My eyes burned and my chest ached. Realization struck: my father was ashamed of me.

His words lost meaning. My hurt turned to rage. The injustice of it all had sunk in, weighing me down. Emotions choked me as I bit back everything I wanted to say. Dad, why does this matter? Why aren't you who I thought you were. How could you be so unfair? I had never questioned his judgment. This time I knew he was wrong. The color of someone's skin should not dictate anything. This was not equality. How could he be willing to sacrifice my happiness because of petty gossip? Realizing for the first time my own father was severely flawed, my heart broke.

Mallory Eastland, Grade 12
New Waverly High School, TX

Family

When posed with the question of what is most important to me in my life, my brain was overwhelmed. Many things are essential in my life. While pondering ideas in my room, I spotted my favorite family photo framed on my desk. It hit me that the most important thing to me was right here under my nose, my family.

My family began in 1986 when Marion Burns and Larry Murray were married. It received its first add-on in 1989 when Brenna Murray was born. Claire Murray was the next to join in 1991. I took my role in the Murray family in 1993. The year 1996 brought the family its first boy, Nolan Murray. The family was big, loud, chaotic, and in need of a bigger house. The emigration from Tacoma to Fircrest took place in 1999. The year 2000 brought us a family miracle. Marion Murray was hit by a car while pregnant with the next and last incomer, Shane Murray. The incident had made the family closer, calmer, and more loving. Days later we were the loud, big, notorious Murray family again.

Being part of a family of seven has taught me many things; hand-me-downs take up most of your closet, quarrels with siblings and/or parents is part of a daily routine, road trips are the worst vacations, a toilet is always plugged, food must be bought every three days, and most importantly that I would not change it for the world.

Kara Murray, Grade 10
Bellarmine Preparatory School, WA

Why Do Young Writers Matter?

Today there are young writers all over the world who are able to express their thoughts in essays and poems and short stories. These pieces are expressive and imaginative, yet their ideas are solid and true. Young writers have a voice by the use of written words — just like adult writers — that should be recognized and never ignored.

Children and adolescents are full of great imagination. When these minds write, there are many possibilities to what and how these people can express each other. Every individual has his or her own idea made up by the use of imagination, so each piece should be recognized for its uniqueness and originality. These pieces are also different from adults' works, so the ideas of young writers and adult writers are no more or less great.

The thought put into a young writer's work is not fast and simple. There is no easy way out when trying to express one's idea precisely, and to attempt is a brave step. The perseverance put into writing should be known and praised no matter the age, thus work should not be judged and discriminated just because the writer is young.

There is always a purpose when writing; it is the same for adolescents and adults alike. Young writer's work should be known and recognized despite age. A young writer puts equivalent time, effort, and thought into each piece and with the imagination young ones hold, great work can be from anyone.

Kelli Yamane, Grade 12
Mililani High School, HI

Hopeless

Every night as I lay in bed thinking, can life get any better? With everything that has happened, I constantly have to ask myself this question. Every once in a while after a long day has passed, I lay down thinking to myself, life is great, and pray that it stays this way. But of course, it doesn't; the next day everything goes horribly wrong and after everything possible goes wrong, the impossible happens, never imagining that the day would come that I would never see his face again, but it did. On March 10, 2006, the worst day of my life occurred; it was the day my daddy passed away. I never imagined life would turn out this horrible, but it did. Ever since that day I ask God, knowing it will never happen, to bring him back. If he would just answer this one prayer I would never ask for anything again, because my daddy is the only person I can add to my life that would make everything perfect. Every day I think, "Can life get any worse?" but then I tell myself, of course it can, but if I lost the two other most important people in my life I would not be able to live on with my already hopeless life.

Carolyn Castro, Grade 12
Post High School, TX

Dying Angel

On April 1st, my cousin gave birth to a beautiful baby boy. This bundle of joy was born with half of his heart missing. Everyone soaked in every minute that we could with him, because we never knew when it would be his last. If I was the parent of this broken child, I don't know if I would have made it out in one piece.

The waiting room filled every day with anxious faces just waiting to see the little boy cooped up in his hospital room. Dim lighting and machines covered every empty space. In the center of the room laid a helpless little baby in a clear plastic box. Tubes came out of every part of him. His skin was no longer pink and healthy, but pale and sickly. It became hard for me to look at him without feeling sad. Then it got worse. I looked down at this helpless baby in front of me and saw him get upset. But instead of the room being filled with cries the room filled with utter silence. Tears rolled down his face but no sound came out. This was the first time that I had been able to take my eyes off of the little angel in front of me and look at his mom. I was holding back the tears and she stood strong. If I was the parent in this situation, I know I would not have been this strong.

Jessica McKamy, Grade 12
Granbury High School, TX

You Have Earned It

"Just stick with it and I'm sure you will play, God knows you have earned it." The words stuck in my head all day, especially the "you have earned it" part. I really have earned it. Last year I moved up onto the JVA team and was safety. During off season I worked out the hardest I ever have to keep my spot as a starting safety on Varsity the next year. And I did, but all good things must come to an end, and it did, in the way of a separated shoulder during soccer season. The coaches who always wanted you to be with your team didn't like it when I would go to the trainers during football and then go play soccer for the school team afterward. So I got moved to the bottom of the chart. I ran against our starting defense as a tight end during spring training, and I did such a good job that I was second string tight end. So, I started coming back. When the season came around, I was back at the bottom of the chart again. After I had a really good day of defense against our starting offense, I became a defensive lineman as a pass rusher. I did such a good job that first game that I became a starting defensive end. I guess this shows you that perseverance is the key to success.

Callum Wright, Grade 12
Granbury High School, TX

Thrill Ride

Driving down the road coming home from school, in the passenger's seat of my sister's car I glanced into the rear-view mirror to see a trail of cars behind us, Johnna and me leading the pack.

Everyone parked when we arrived and walked inside, immediately spying in the back yard the All-Terrain-Vehicle that my neighbors let me use to travel to their house to feed their dogs when they vacationed. Twinkles shone in their eyes, grins stretched across their faces like rubber bands. I knew what they were thinking and decided to let each person drive just once a simple path, down the street, turn onto the dirt road of our field and into the back yard.

Boredom enveloped me once everyone took their turn, I decided to dismount, but still let them ride. Hour after hour the ATV stormed across the road, leaving behind a cloud of smoke and the overwhelming smell of burning fuel. I grew worried as time passed. I thought to call my parents but decided that they wouldn't listen.

Finally, their thrill ride ended. It came time for CCD. I wanted to feed the dogs before leaving. I climbed onto the leather seat and turned the key in the ignition, nothing. I called the mechanic next door to ask him for help, but he could barely start it. The ATV wouldn't be fully repaired without a professional repair costing $1,600.

From this experience I've learned to always stand up for myself despite the circumstance.

Kim Schwartz, Grade 10
Wall High School, TX

Remembering Alyssa

My phone vibrated in my lap. I looked at the lit up screen to find my friend Amy calling. Expecting to hear a juicy gossiping story, the subject was somewhat less exciting.

"Hey Chels, it's Amy," her voice was tender with care although I sensed a feeling of worry and sadness through her mellow tone. She stuttered the first few words, continuing with the horrifying story. Alyssa Dix had passed away.

My heart sank immediately. I felt as if someone had just punched me so hard in the stomach that the breath was knocked out of me. My face started to turn pale. Tears were built up in my eyes continuously falling one by one down my cheeks.

A ceremony for Alyssa was held that weekend at Acton Baptist Church. Alyssa was the perfect example of an amazing Christian along with a loyal friend. You could feel her presence, even though she wasn't visually there. The feeling of grief and pain was filtered heavily in the air. Her high school friends all sat in one section and started to gather in prayer, holding each other's hands for comfort. Then the moment came. It was like a huge lapse of grace swept over us all. Words can't describe the emotions let out. Finally, the flood escaped from my eyes, streaming like a waterfall.

From that day on, I have learned to be thankful for my friends and family members; we only have one life, and I plan to cherish every moment.

Chelsea White, Grade 12
Granbury High School, TX

High Merit Essays – Grades 10, 11 and 12

The Importance of My Family

Out of all of the important things in my life, family would have to be number one on my list. Not only is my loving family important to me but also to the handfuls of people that walk among us. Why does family outweigh other important aspects of my life, because those are the people you can always count on and they got your back no matter what. That is the case for me, since I was born I had problems breathing while I slept, and was diagnosed with sleep apnea at the age of five. All that led to long surgeries that required lengthy recovery time and guess who was by my side with get well balloons and all sorts of toys I couldn't resist, my family. Although not all of my family would always make it to one of these events regardless I still felt a sense of warmth and love swirling the room. Ten years later I am happy to announce I am sleep apnea free, and thank all of my family for being there when it counted most. What is important to me? Family, because they always support you and aren't shy to give you that extra push once in a while when you need it.

Brando Vargas, Grade 11
Pine Tree High School, TX

Apathy

Wracked with fear that I would be disowned, my ninth-grade day was quite ruined. I didn't know then that paper would break me.

Surprisingly, I was not disowned for, "Geometry: B." However, I blame this occurrence for planting a dangerous seed into my developing mind; apathy.

I sat back and rode on the laurels of my inherited intelligence. While my peers suffered from heads bowed with stress, I relaxed. I now accepted C's with an emphatic, "eh."

My love, English, never reached my back burner. However I overlooked that school is a package deal. Surely nothing could touch my 100 English average. But I grew farther behind in all classes.

"English: 86." Instead of parental punishments, I was now afraid I wouldn't escape my own disappointment. When I had endured temporary failure, this B evoked inward reflection. The constant catch up game I played had me worn and haggard, my boyfriend became truant, my parents constantly felt angry or skeptical of me. And so, I changed. I took my experiences I had had and fused them with who I had been. I studied, I did my work, and yet I allowed myself to have fun; took disappointment in failures, but moved on. Extremes, on either side of the spectrum, do no good.

"AP World History Exam: 3." A smile. "AP English III Exam: 5." A toothy grin. I held in my hands my crowning glory, absorbing its cool redemption. I would be better. College, future, life; I've decided to come.

Lauren Cutler, Grade 12
Granbury High School, TX

The Pink Haired Girl

She was short, and her pink hair stood out among all the normal haired people. Her family was new to our church, and I couldn't wait to meet her. Her children, Savannah, who she adopted, and Malachi, her handsome little boy, were a joy to watch and spend time with. Although she had wonderful children, she also had an amazing relationship with God. Parish could go on and on about how He has blessed her and her family, so I knew I wanted what she had.

Since I have put my life in Jesus, He has led me to serve in the Children's Ministry. I have decided to go to Life Christian Bible Institute to earn my degree in theology and Children's Ministry, so I can teach children at a young age that Jesus is here, and He loves them very much.

My life has changed so much because of Jesus, and I want other kids to have what I have now. With Jesus all things are possible, and now that I know that, I pray to Him and all my problems are solved, and I thank Him for the blessings He has given me.

In a way Parish has become my hero. I don't think she even realizes what an inspiration she is. Thanks to Parish, I now walk the path Jesus has laid for me, and I thank both of them for my friends, my family, and my boyfriend.

Jessie Cole, Grade 12
Granbury High School, TX

Unoriginally Original

When asked the question, "What is important to you?" I'm afraid I must choose the topic that hundreds, if not thousands of students will select for their essays. But because the subject rings so true for me, I have no choice but to be unoriginal. Freedom and liberty demonstrate two great things that reflect great importance for me. But my reasons differ from other students. My great-great-great-grandfather fought during the Civil War for freedom, against his own brothers. My late grandfather, Andrew Jackson Burns, served as an army cook during World War II. Though never considered a "hero," he stood in the background, making food for the men who fought and died. His wife, my grandmother Dolly Dimples Burns, worked in a fighter plane factory. They both used their gifts and abilities to further advance the nation they loved. My grandfather on the other side of my family served in the navy for a considerable number of years. He flew helicopters off the huge navy vessels. Many of the stories have stayed with me to this day. Once, he had to fly a rescue mission for a friend who had crashed in the ocean. I remember as Papa Joe told that story, he got a little quieter and remembered that fateful day his friend died. Freedom is earned by sacrifice, and today we must remember those who have paid the ultimate price. As for me, it's personal and I feel proud to live as a descendant of these heroes.

Kristin Burns, Grade 11
Pine Tree High School, TX

One Summer Day

I stood there on the California soil, while the scent of fresh oranges filled the air. I could feel the warm sun beating down on my shirtless back. This was how a normal day always started in my life. But little did I know this would be the last California day I would ever have.

My brother and I decided to go in for lunch; when I opened the thick wooden door we could hear screaming, "get away from me!" I sprinted into the kitchen to see what was wrong. When I entered the room I couldn't believe my eyes. I could see the fury in my dad's eyes, and he was standing over my mom with his fist clenched tight.

My mother had already called the police. They came in and arrested my dad around five minutes later. My mother told us that we needed to pack all of our stuff up and get ready to leave for Texas. Sure enough, the next day I was in Texas. I had no friends and I had no idea what to do. No more dirt bikes. No more beaches. No more cool summer days.

I knew that my mom always worked hard so she could give me and my brothers the best life we could possibly have. She sacrificed everything for us. I learned from this life changing experience that I had the best mom in the world.

Justin Essman, Grade 12
Granbury High School, TX

I Wonder Why?

I wonder why things happen the way they do. Why people get hurt, why people love, why people cry? Why does the world go round? Why does a dog bark and a cat meow? Why do some people love with everything they have while others only give half their heart? Why do families break and why do mothers go away? Why do people expect so much from everyone else but don't put out as much effort themselves? Why are so many people so arrogant and cruel? Why are people only worried about themselves? I wonder why rain smells so good and why the snow makes everything beautiful. Why are emotions so strong? Why is a moment with the one you love worth a lifetime of happiness? Why can one person affect you so much? Why do people break hearts? I wonder why waking up on a rainy day makes you feel so relaxed or why laying in bed on a cloudy day is the most comforting. I wonder why I hurt so much. Why do the actions of others affect me so much, but they don't even realize what they did? Why do the people around me always give up on me? Why do they always move on with life and leave me in the dark fending for myself? Why do the most important people to me always just leave? Why can't happiness last forever? Why do you have to live a full life to completely understand?

Trinda Garza, Grade 12
Coronado High School, TX

The Music Box

Many would see an ordinary music box as an inanimate object. Not I. I consider my music box as one of a kind, alive, and with a story eager to tell. When it plays its melody, the whole room lights up and everyone listens attentively to its curious music. I received the rusty and worn-out music box from my mother, which she inherited from my grandmother.

My grandmother obtained the music box as a birthday present from her parents. As the youngest child of seven brothers and sisters, my grandma rarely acquired new things. She considered the music box a treasure and always kept it hidden under her bed. Since seven other children lived in the same house, their mother rarely had individual time with each child. So my grandmother listened to the music box's melody to comfort her. She kept the music box for 40 years before she bequeathed it to my mother. After my grandmother deceased, my mother stored the music box in a secure place.

I feel honored to have received the music box my grandmother considered so precious. It has sentimental value, because it reminds me of the love and happiness she brought to everyone. It motivates me to do what I love, play music.

Brenda Arras, Grade 11
Pine Tree High School, TX

Robotics

While other children played football and soccer, at the age of seven, I was picking up my soldering gun and creating my first circuit. I have always dreamed about building and designing machines. This passion for creating led me to the robotics club at my high school.

Robotics has become a huge part of my life and what is important to me. In competitive robotics, students have six weeks to create a fully functional robot that will compete with other robots from across the country. Competitive robotics immerses students in real world engineering scenarios. It is the challenge of creating something while being under funded and with a limited time frame that keeps me interested.

Aside from the challenge, the learning experience makes robotics important to me. Everything about robotics can be used in the future in industry. Robotics is a great way for students to learn basic programming, electronic, and mechanical skills. But robotics is so much more than learning how to build a robot. This year, as head builder, I am learning how to build a team. One of the responsibilities I have is to make sure the robot is completed on time. Because of this responsibility, I have to get students to work together and be committed to robotics. The basic skills and values learned in robotics will follow students for the rest of their lives and prove vital in the workplace. Because of the challenge and the skills learned, robotics is important to me.

Chad Nijim, Grade 11
Valley Christian High School, CA

Kicking

"Here's the snap, it's a good hold, and the kick goes right through the middle of the uprights." It sounds easy, right? Well contrary to popular belief, being a successful kicker is a challenging job.

Some people might say that all you have to do is kick a ball down the field or through the uprights, but there is more to it than just kicking a ball. There is also a technical side to being a kicker. There are many different styles of kicking. The two main styles are strait or soccer style. Strait on is easier to learn and master, but it limits how far and how high you can kick. Soccer style is more complicated and technical, but once you get it figured out, the possibilities of how far you can kick are limitless. Being successful means that you have to develop you're kicking style until it becomes as natural as brushing your teeth. Getting your style to where it is natural requires hours upon hours of practice and going to a few camps. Sure, all the work sounds daunting, but it is a unique talent for people to learn and master.

Being a kicker can be a pain sometimes, but it has its good points. Maybe one day you might wind up like Matt Williams, kicking a field goal at half time and getting an invitation to play for Texas Tech. Kicking can be a challenge, but at the same time, it is rewarding.

Reed Williams, Grade 12
Post High School, TX

Water Polo Warrior

I am a warrior and the pool is my kingdom. I find my peace and tranquility during five o'clock practices in the morning, running miles in the dark, and lying on the football field doing workouts while gazing at the numerous sparkling stars in the sky. I am in my element when I pick up the yellow gripped ball and shoot. I can feel the adrenaline rush through my body when the whistle blows and I swim with the ball. I can think big and set my goals without limits. The pool is my canvas and my final masterpiece is left to my own creativity in the water.

In the pool I can do anything. I put on my cap and I feel different; I am no longer just a name, I am a warrior ready to fight, pass, shoot, and score. I no longer worry about trivial things, but focus on my game and make my every movement with intention. I am in control, and can make my own choices and decisions in the water. Here, my teammates are family. No matter what the result, we always laugh it off and have fun. Even through the worst of games and toxic pools that burn my eyes, my teammates are always there. So, you may ask, who am I? I am a water polo player. Water polo is my life and although it may seem like an unimportant sport to some, it means the world to me.

Myvy Ngo, Grade 11
Valley Christian High School, CA

Home Is Where Importance Lies

I have lived in Spokane, Washington for sixteen years, three months and eleven days. How incredibly boring. But that doesn't matter, as long as I know my friends, family, and everything I enjoy will be here. I know that no matter where life takes me, no matter how far away my feet may wander, Spokane will always be my home, and to me, home is as important as air.

Now, Spokane may seem fun, but after being here so long, it can get some what overrated. The crucial point to understand is that it doesn't matter where I go, because home will always be with me. Many people don't know what to call home; their houses have been destroyed, maybe they have run from danger. I find myself one of the lucky people to recognize that I am blessed, and even though boredom still tends to find its way through the cracks, I know my situation and where I dig my roots. Though Spokane is drab, I still love where I live.

My life continues on, the clouds outside roiling with heavy rains, and I can't seem to see myself any other place. The people I love are here. The scenes I have seen a thousand times become a comfort when I have been away. I know that Spokane will always remain an important part of me. "Home is a place you grow up wanting to leave, and grow old wanting to get back to." — John Ed Pearce.

Ashley Hansen, Grade 10
Valley Christian School, WA

Sorry

I felt sorry for myself in a dimly lit space I call my room. As I glanced around, heart thumping slowly against my weary soul; I wanted to weep. I was alone in a nest that lay battered at my feet. The art I created from my being held no comfort, just lines on paper. Everything collapsed as I fell against a wall with endless engraved pictures. I sat motionlessly with eyes fixed on a clouded ceiling and thought.

I unwillingly reflected on my common flaws and cried. Weeping on a stained carpet that gave me no comfort I hated that I could never do what I wanted in life. I hated that my vivid dreams never looked as good as anyone else's. My sniffles echoed loudly, while my flawed tears fell down my hot face. My blurry glance landed on an opened door.

The room changed its dreary appearance because my hero was there to save me. My sister briskly opened her arms and talked. Her persistent face turned glossy with tears, while I took her hands and prayed. She unsealed my red eyes to the instilled love and qualities God had given me. My mournful tears no longer cried in bitterness and pity. I cried because I felt lifted and healed, no longer broken and weary. I clutched my sister's hands and prayed for strength. I prayed for the part of my life that was missing, and then I prayed for the settled girl in the dimly lit space of room.

Julia Allen, Grade 11
Flour Bluff High School, TX

Beauty

If I were able to relive one event of my life, it would be a summer afternoon I spent with a friend I really loved, sitting on the roof, watching the sun go down. It might seem odd to choose this simple evening out of all my life, but it made me truly happy and that's something worth reliving. I don't remember the exact day or month but I remember that it was beautiful to me, something I can't say for many things I've experienced, and that I'll never forget.

Out of every bad experience, dark memory, and gloomy emotion that are all so easy to recall, that even sticks out like a bright light. To me that moment was perfect; I was having problems at home with my parents, with myself, but for those couple of hours everything ceased to exist. It was a dream made of multi-colored clouds, a warm sunset, and colors fluttering in the pool underneath us. Easy talk and even easier laughter, the best friend I could've wished for and a case of cold Mountain Dew. Like all good things I knew that it would have to come to an end, but that was a superfluous detail that wasn't going to wreck the evening that defined the reason why life is worth living. To me, it was an afternoon from God Himself and I treated it like nothing less, soaking up every second of it. It's awfully easy to remember the bad times in life. For some reason that I'll never know, they seem to fade from our memories so much slower than the events that bring us joy. I believe that it's important to hang on to precious memories to keep us from sinking to low. That's why I would relive that evening.

Kevin Brandon O'Baker, Grade 12
Redwood High School, CA

My Trip

On the plane ride there, I started noticing the difference. New things I'd never seen huge houses that looked like mansions; it was a beautiful sight. Getting off the plane, driving to the hotel, palm trees everywhere, buildings on the sides of the road, cars suffocating the streets with traffic, and diverse people everywhere. At the hotel, the men were polite and proper; they got our luggage off the taxi and transferred it all the way to our room. The time was two hours ahead. When we were ready to eat lunch, every restaurant was serving breakfast. Driving through the streets, we saw thing that we saw in movies. I felt rich and famous. The beach was blue, clear, and beautiful. The weather was perfect; the sky was blue, the sun was out, and there was a nice breeze of air. The mountains were green and enormous. It all seemed like it was a dream, but when I opened my eyes, I realized I was in California. I felt like the luckiest person, being able to see new things. My cousin and I got to walk the streets of Hollywood; the shopping part was very fun. We saw the Kodak Theatre, the wax museum, and the Hollywood sign on the mountain. Everything there was all amazing.

Maritza Uribe, Grade 10
REACH High School, TX

The Gift of Passion

Music is my passion. Music opens doors for me that I used to find locked. Beyond those doors is a world that I love. I find myself in a world that lets me express myself in a unique way. Music can be played at any time of day, no matter what your emotion. While sometimes it is hard to sing through your tears, your voice is still heard. Sometimes the guitar is out of tune, but your song is still valid. With one song, someone can fall in love, find peace within themselves, and even save a life. Music is a gift that is meant to be shared with the world.

That is my goal, to impact the world in some way with my music. I plan on using my gift and make sure it keeps on giving. This gift, as any gift, should not be locked away in a tall tower or even set aside in a box for later. When someone has a passion for something, it is important to go for whatever that may be. One needs to find that key to the locked door in their life. Then, the first steps need to be taken into that world. While this may take a lot of work, it is important to know that with patience, perseverance, and passion, that world you were once afraid of, can become something you will fall in love with.

Emily Faulkner, Grade 11
Valley Christian High School, CA

Beauty

Beauty is far and wide, in a bottomless sapphire ocean of in a vivid cotton sky. It shines radiantly on the surface of our earth. From the crystalline eyes of an innocent child to the wise wrinkles upon a father's face. It sometimes lies profound in a heart, with a calloused facade, but a tender truth. Beauty surrounds us and is not always perceptible. It is not always physical. It's a distraught ravenous dreamer hoping for better on a frosty night. A mindset of a conqueror, when failure mischievously awaits. It is a lonesome silence in an abandoned room waiting to be filled with a melodic harmony. Its ambiance evokes inspiration and enlightens minds. It evokes life-changing ideas that were never thought before. True beauty is natural and never superficial. True beauty loiters on immense contagious smiles and reflects on a lively mesmerizing sunrise. Beauty lingers in darkness, as distant dazzling lights that allow you to dream dreams that are as far-fetched as the stars themselves. It flows smoothly in the silk black waves of a young mother's hair and runs swiftly in an emerald lagoon where a father bonds with his thirteen-year old son. Beauty is present at all times, in the smell of zesty barbecue sizzling on a smoking grill. It hangs in the echo of exploding fireworks on a summer in July. It passes on to the warm colors and crunchy crispy leaves of a gusty fall. Beauty is everything.

Darlene Araiza, Grade 12
Post High School, TX

The Plight of Asphalt Angels

A push and a shove; the eternal clock is ticking. The city streets are overrun with a myriad of people scurrying off to meet their ultimate destinations, disregarding the copious amounts of jostling they commit; another's displacement means nothing in comparison with their own goals and agendas, reflecting an inherent comprehension of the constitution-granted right to a pursuit of happiness.

Each fails to note the tragic beauty visible in the tumbling cumulus clouds above and none pause to smell the sweet scent emanating from scattered roadside rosebushes. In light of their own trials and tribulations, people fail to distinguish true value from that which is worthless, the everyday smells and sights from that which will forever remain breathtakingly beautiful, and the boundary line between the proverbial right and wrong.

Welcome to the scene of society's degeneration. The digression within our society is sickening. People have fallen to Orwellian standards, emotions and thought at the bottom of their priority list. The enjoyment of simplistic beauty has fallen due to the dizzying pace which we incessantly keep up. In our vertigo, we fail to search for the meaning which resides in every action perpetrated and the beauty in our surroundings and human emotion.

We don't possess the capacity to feel the regret needed to initiate us to take a step back and correct the blindness which has possessed us. We're falling to the effects of desensitization. We are like asphalt, stone-cold angels, existing yet lacking the eyes to perceive that which has befallen us.

Keisha Bedwell, Grade 12
Granbury High School, TX

A Photographer's Journey

Before high school, the biggest thrill of my life was performing. Where I come from, most kids get their "kicks" from playing some ball-oriented sport. I, on the other hand, spent my extracurricular time in uniquely, different venues, namely actual stages all over the SF region. I sang with the San Francisco Symphony and enjoyed numerous standing ovations in community, regional and professional theatre, even performing with the national tour of Evita. I always knew my journey was somewhat different than other kids. What I didn't expect was that a new passion would soon take center stage.

Photography. It was as simple as that. Extensive travel locally and internationally found me with my camera in tow. I explored nooks and secret places of seemingly regular life with my camera strapped securely around my neck. I was keenly aware that I didn't want to wake up at age 50 with these experiences a far too distant memory. Grateful to this new hobby and talent, I began to memorialize new adventures.

And what adventures photography brought to me! Photography gave me the determination needed to hold numerous jobs to finance equipment and travel expenses. It broadened my social network and eventually brought the position of photo editor for my school newspaper. Perhaps, most importantly, photography took me down new avenues to express myself. My love for documentation has taken me beyond my familiar world and into the physical and emotional places that I needed for personal development. Photography completely and utterly captivates me.

Jake Sigl, Grade 12
California High School, CA

That One Person That Understands You

Do you have that one friend that just gets everything about you? One who is always there for you and helps you whenever you need her? I know I do, in fact I call this person my best friend. She is that one person that understands me and knows everything about me. When we are together there is never a dull moment and we always have such a good time. I know I could go to her whenever I need her and we could talk about anything that is on our hearts. She knows when I am upset or sad without me even telling her, and does everything she can to cheer me up.

My best friend is the person I talk to every day and who I always text when something good happens in my life. She guides me to do the right things, but also tells me when I mess up. We might not agree on everything in life, but through the hard and good times we are always there for each other, no matter what. That is why she is my best friend.

Lauren Coco, Grade 11
Valley Christian High School, CA

Writing

One of the most daunting tasks I've ever faced is writing. Thousands upon thousands of images fill my mind, but I often can't find the words to express them. Between my mind and the paper something is often lost in translation. Sometimes inspiration hits me like a bolt of lightning and the dam between my hand and mind disappear and I can set some of those scenes to paper, but like the glowing after image of the sun it does not last because the scene is often based on another scene that I have not yet found words for or I can't find the words for what happens next; and so another fragment of a story is added to one of my many discarded notebooks. When faced with writing assignments in school I receive them with mixed results. Sometimes the prompts spark the fires in the forge of my mind and other times they leave me with nothing to write about, much less a desire to try. Ironically perhaps I aspire to be a writer. All my life I have tried to find the words and translate completely the great story that has been locked away in my head all my life.

Sean Bertrand, Grade 11
Vista Ridge High School, TX

The Importance of Family

Family is not a given, it's a blessing. To have people that will stand behind you no matter what is something that many people take for granted until it is too late. Family is an important part of society that advances in technology, busier schedules, and cultural changes have hindered.

Technology has advanced society beyond what people twenty years ago could have even imagined. However, all the big screen televisions, fancy cell phones, and other advances have created a rift in many households. People do not connect with their families like they used to. I have many friends who would rather sit by themselves and watch television instead of have a family dinner. This is detrimental because families lose the closeness and friendship that they can have through having a discussion at the dinner table.

Cultural changes also play a huge factor in a families unity. Americans do not treasure family as they once did. People put other things first, such as their jobs, sports, or hobbies. That is why sixty percent of couples in America get a divorce.

The speed of our everyday lives also contributes to loss of family unity. With people so busy, whether it be with a job, school, or sport, families have no time to sit down to a meal together. It is especially difficult for mothers to find time in their busy day to make a home cooked meal to be enjoyed together, while being the family chauffeur.

All of these distractions take away from family unity. Family is something that should be cherished, not taken for granted.

Nathan Van Ryn, Grade 10
Oakdale High School, CA

This Is Me

The referee shoots his gun, and splash! The crowd goes wild, I feel the adrenaline flow through me, and I gasp for air. This continuous routine for eight laps, and finally at the touch of the pad, I get 3rd place. Where would I be without this sport? I have swum since I was seven for the pleasure of it, and to this day every time my body lunges into the pool I cannot help but to feel energetic and happy. I never swam with the intention to compete, I swam to feel serene, to pretend that I was a mermaid, to free myself from the real world for as long as I could. When I am in the water, it is as if I am in my own little world, and no one can bring me down. It is a place of my own, a dwelling for my thoughts to linger as long as I desire. It has taught me to be patient and to process all thoughts and actions in life, to become a critical thinker. As I have grown up I have come to love this hobby more, it's no longer a hobby it is a sport. Most importantly it is a way of life; my passion.

Stephanie Lopez, Grade 11
La Serna High School, CA

My Bike Bash

When my eyes finally fluttered open a shock of pain fell over me. My whole left side ached and when I lifted my hand to touch my face, my trembling fingers glided over a warm disgustingly thick liquid running down my face.

"Hey let's try and race down that hill again!", I remember my sister Bethany huff as she sprinted up to me. That would be the third attempt to race our bikes down the steepest hill in our neighborhood, even though our mother told us not to.

"Okay so when I say go, we'll see who makes it first!"

Bethany was hysterical and I was confused. "Why was I laying on the road?" I kept thinking. Since I could barely walk Bethany had to half carry me home. Later I found out that I blacked out on my bike and slid about six feet on the road.

I had a concussion so I never got any sleep, I could barely walk, and my face looked like Two Face from *Batman: The Dark Knight*. Now ten years later all I have to show for the crash is a tiny scar on my forehead. I'm so lucky that nothing more severe came out of it.

Every time I look back on the accident I scold myself for not having enough common sense to stop while I was still ahead. Ever since then, I think everything over many times before I do anything irrational.

Maryssa Mathis, Grade 12
Granbury High School, TX

Life in the Suburbs

Deriving from the Los Angeles region, life has been nothing short of a world defining experience. Life was full of struggles and sacrifices that enriched my perspective on several issues regarding poverty and immigration. The ghetto-rodent infested dwellings were what I called home for the first few years of my adolescence. My family had immigrated to America not knowing how they would sustain a family of ten. Our journey through America first came to the all too flashy city of Los Angeles; which portrays the image of success, fame, and capital. However, a quick trip towards the surrounding suburbs, one is quickly overcome by a wave of poverty, violence, and death.

Life emulates an individual's perspective the issue itself. In order to become successful, one must never be condescending or pessimistic upon life. My father is my inspiration because not only did he provide the essentials of life for ten bodies; he accomplished this while living as an impoverished immigrant working back breaking labor occupations. His persistence through difficult times made me feel as if I could accomplish anything I desired. As I began pondering about my past, I saw a grim oppressive past with no hope. It was then when I realized that what I aspired in life was to liberate myself from the stereotypes unfairly bestowed upon me and succeed in life.

Oscar Montano, Grade 12
Fontana High School, CA

Reaping Individuality

"As you sow, so shall you reap." I had heard this proverb numerous times while growing up. As a naïve child, these were just words rambled together to make a sentence that was beyond my comprehension. I didn't care much to learn what it meant, but as the years passed by and it was more frequently used by my parents, my curiosity steadily rose.

It was at the age of ten when I decided to do some research, and it was only then that I had a better understanding of the Biblical quote. I made a literal connection to a farmer harvesting his crops; if he plants bad seeds, he will reap bad crops, but if he plants good seeds, he will have a good harvest. There had to be more to the quote than just that. After pondering it for a while, I came to a realization that it could be figuratively applied to any circumstance in life. This proverb was the foundation to my ethical and religious upbringing, the base of my morals and values, all without me knowing it.

I truly feel that it is the extent to which we choose to follow this wise saying that makes each of us individual. Everything in life revolves around how much effort you put forth to achieve the desired goal. Everybody has the ability to choose between good and bad seeds, but it is your actions that will determine the outcome; what you reap is what you sow.

Miriam Martinez, Grade 11
New Caney High School, TX

The Question of Importance

What is important to me? Perhaps one of the broadest questions of all time, yet also a question that requires a great deal of introspection before coming up with a very specific answer. The most important thing to a person speaks volumes about how they view life and their place in it. So when I asked myself what is important to me I thought about how I try to live my life, and after doing so I determined that decisiveness is most important to me.

My decisiveness demonstrated itself in the writing of this essay because when I came to the conclusion of writing about decisiveness I stuck to it and did not sway. Decisiveness disguises laziness, another one of my favorite things, at least the way I utilize it. Some would interpret this as a negative, however; I prefer to view it as a part of my character, which determines my personality today. Decisiveness can also have positive effects in some situations, such as when a person must make a very important decision quickly. Nothing annoys me more than someone who whines and questions everything; I just want to yell, "Get Over It!" I try not to dwell on the past too much because what's done is done and I do not want to waste time worrying about the past when I could make better decisions for the future.

So what is important to me? My inflated sense of decisiveness and everyone else's lack thereof.

Adam Allen, Grade 11
Pine Tree High School, TX

Beauty

Beauty is a look. Beauty is an emotion. Beauty is a feeling. Beauty is a way of life. Beauty is a way to look. What is beauty?

Some would say that "beauty is anything that provokes a strong, emotional feeling." This is not true. The Holocaust provokes many strong feelings, but it was most definitely not beautiful. Others would say, "beauty is anything that provokes a strong, POSITIVE, emotional feeling." This is also not true. In the movie, *The Notebook*, at the end, one of the main characters dies. If one is truly sucked in to the movie, it is a very sad ending, but it is beautiful nonetheless.

Beauty is hard to explain. It is many things. There isn't one way to describe it. Beauty is a professional runway model, but also the new girl, tripping and stumbling while she practices. Beauty is the feeling one gets from watching a loved one go off to war; it is also the feeling from watching them get off of the plane coming home. Beauty is a funeral for a friend, but also knowing his legacy will be carried on. Beauty is one lone rose, standing tall in a raging storm. Beauty is the withered bodies and souls of those who can't take much more punishment from the world.

Beauty is in the eyes of the beholder, but it takes the heart to see what beauty really is.

Brandon McDaniel, Grade 11
Northridge High School, UT

Mi Familia

My name is Tracy Wade; full name is actually Tracy Vann Wade Jr. I have a very entertaining and awesome family, and I love them so much. My mom, Belinda is a very loving and caring woman. She's supportive and is involved in everything that her kids do. She usually hangs around me and my siblings. Next is my dad, I call him Pal. His name is Tracy too. My dad is a pretty strict guy but he can be so fun to be around. His job is pretty time consuming, he's a police officer. My dad is crazy, like he should be in an asylum crazy. But no matter how many times he gets on to me I still love my Pal. Next is my little brother, Xavier. Basically he's going to be the guy nobody messes with when he gets older. Don't let his appearance intimidate you, he's a lovable guy. I try to be a role model to both my siblings, especially him. Next is my little sister Brittany, she resembles me, A LOT. Brittany is growing up and it's kind of hard for me to face that. I guess I have to let her go and let her do her own thing for now. But we share a lot of interests in music and some TV shows. I love my family, and would do anything for them. No matter how many times we get mad at each other we always remember "love always conquers hate."

Tracy Wade, Grade 11
New Caney High School, TX

Behind the Wheel

It is impossible for me to find a better seat than the one behind the wheel.

When that ignition is turned on I become one with the car, hugging every curve and rolling along every inch of asphalt. Each single part of that engine becomes another vital organ in our joint bodies. Every turn of the piston is an entirely unique experience unmatched by anything else in this world. Shift into first and watch as the world passes by in the rearview in a flash. Put the windows down and feel the wind rush through your hair like a tornado. Turn the wheel and feel how the great machine responds to your every whim in an instant. Push the gas again and feel all of those horses pull you forward on your journey. When it's finally time to rest, park your car in the garage and put your baby to bed for the night. Through all of the twists and turns your car will always be your noble steed and will carry you until the end. No matter what car and no matter what road, there is nothing quite like the true driving experience you can only get in one place, the driver's seat.

Richard Gonzales, Grade 11
Valley Christian High School, CA

Celluloid Impact

Movies, we have all seen them, ones we love and those we hate. Every day millions of people all around the world watch movies. Whether it be at home with family or in the theater with strangers, movies have always impacted people in one way or another. Through movies we learn how to live, love, and laugh. We look to the screen and are transported into another world. Filmmaker Roman Polanski once said "Cinema should make you forget you are sitting in a theater."

I myself want to be a part of this. I want to be a filmmaker. I want to make an impact on people, the same impact I felt when I first started recognizing film as an art form. Even though so many films are made just to make money, there are artists involved who work behind the lens: it may be in the special effects department, or the sound department. Film is a team effort; it's not just the director that makes a film great. It's everyone working together, all striving to make a perfect film that will stay with people after the credits roll. I want to be a part of that, even after I'm dead and gone, I want my ideas to impact people.

Caydon LiRocchi, Grade 11
Valley Christian High School, CA

Breaking Down Walls

In American schools today, there are numerous issues of importance that are plainly overlooked. Many students believe that since these matters do not have a direct impact on them, they are not imperative to mend. The most important of these is the lack of leadership in high schools. Most schools around the nation are plagued by walls put up between the various cliques within them. A lone historical example flawlessly exemplifies what schools here in the United States need.

Erin Gruwell, a first-year teacher at Wilson High school in Los Angeles, was utterly stunned whenever she witnessed the color of her students' skin ignite a vicious racial war inside the school. While teaching one afternoon, Gruwell intercepted a racist caricature of one of her students. This instance sparked teachings on the Holocaust in her classes. Just like Anne Frank, Miss Gruwell's students kept a journal, telling of their hard lives in East L.A. Through Erin Gruwell's teaching, journal writing, and multiple field trips, racial walls were broken down and Wilson High School was once again united.

Many so-called "leaders" in my high school see this ultimate goal as irrelevant. According to these "leaders," the leadership that they offer in their small, departmentalized arenas is sufficient for the whole school. Many of these students take the, "I'm not the only one accountable, so it's not my responsibility," stance regarding the issue. If each of these students fused for a common purpose of uniting the school, they would truly be unstoppable.

Michael Porter, Grade 12
Post High School, TX

Trampoline Troubles

Lying on the trampoline that warm April day, Jalyn and I stared at the puffy clouds. Standing to jump, Jalyn pulled me up with her. As she started to do a back flip, her feet landed on the hard springs, she lost her balance, and fell on her lower back.

Her mom convinced us that Jalyn needed to go to the hospital. After hours of waiting in the cramped, miserable emergency room, the doctors called her in. My mom picked me up, but I waited impatiently by the phone for the next few hours and I jumped when it rang. A million questions raced through my mind.

"She will have a brace because of the fractured bones in her lower back. The doctor said that if she had fallen any further up on her back, she would have been paralyzed for life…" her mom told me. A few days later, I finally got to see Jalyn. Walking into her room, I nearly cried. Miserably immobile, she laid there on the bed, looking pitiful.

Confined to her house for the next six weeks, Jalyn loved that I visited often. The time for her final checkup eventually rolled around, and the doctor said that her back was completely healed.

Just like a goose does not leave another member of the flock, I did not leave my friend when she needed me the most. That whole experience has strengthened our friendship, and it showed me that true friends never leave each other behind.

Gracie Gibbon, Grade 11
Flour Bluff High School, TX

Another World

The wood is cold and smooth beneath my touch as my fingers grasp the neck of the guitar. The touch is familiar and the feeling electrifying as I draw the instrument near and it comes to rest on my restless leg. Leaving its cushioned cradle of quietness and emptiness behind, another world is opened. A world in which there are no bounds, no limits, and no walls. Just me and the guitar. It is a place where my imagination and creativity can roam freely without fear of being rejected, a place where I can express myself through the music flowing through me. It is not only a place where only I can venture, but my brother, my sisters, and my friends as well. It is at that moment, when we come together in this endless world of possibilities that we find that there are truly no bounds to what we can accomplish.

My musical capabilities have given me an outlet from the troubles and stresses of this world. My dedication and hard labor have allowed me talents that no amount of homework can teach. These talents allow me to think with an open and creative mind that have no bounds but the physical ones encompassing it. They have also allowed me to use my imagination to play and construct pleasing pieces of music. More importantly, these talents have showed me that my dreams and my aspirations no matter how difficult, can be achieved through hard work and perseverance.

Jonathan Huff, Grade 12
Angelo Rodriguez High School, CA

Faith

My faith and my relationship with God have always had a big impact on my life. Even as a young girl, I attended church. I think that one's relationships with God should be a top priority because He created life. Attending church dominates a major part of my life. I enjoy learning about the Bible and how much God loves each person. It amazes me that every individual person has a special place in God's heart. At times, I do not feel as close to God as I usually do, which makes me have an empty feeling. I try not to get really busy so that does not happen. I think He deserves our whole attention because He gave His son to die for us. In my opinion, Bible study helps one's relationship with God strengthen. Learning about how great He is makes me want to praise Him more. Prayer helps with my faith. Talking to God is essential to having a relationships with Him. Some people feel that they do not have to pray because God already knows everything. To me, if I tell God all my problems and talk to Him, He seems more real. I think that helps me believe even more. I continue to grow in my Christian life and I have many more amazing experiences to come. I cannot wait to see what God has in store for me.

Paige Lackey, Grade 11
Pine Tree High School, TX

More Than Just an Extra-Curricular

As I finish up my senior year in marching band, I've come to realize my passion for Drumline. I first joined because I thought it was something cool. It turned out to be pure fun. Another upside was the time away from the real world of stress and drama. But as I trek through my final year as Drumline captain, I start tearing because I know that I'll have to leave it all behind in just a couple of months.

During the tough times, when we're being wrongly accused by our director for tempo issues, the Drumline sticks up for me and backs up whatever decision I make to go solve this issue. I frequently receive the comment, "If he's giving you pushups, I'm doing them with you." Unfortunately, this silent fight got to the point where I broke down and almost quit. But in the back of my head, I know I would be letting those kids down and abandoning something I absolutely love. During these times, I remind myself that these kids are the reason I decided to come back for my senior year. And I don't regret it one bit. They really stepped up and formed one drumline; "one," which has become the theme for this year's line. When one of us hurts, all of us hurt. And I am willing to give my all for the line this year because I know, even if we don't take first place, this will be my most memorable season.

Jordan Tansiongco, Grade 12
Mililani High School, HI

Pushed to Perfection

All our lives, we are told to look our best, which in itself is not terrible, but often our best becomes trying to reach perfection. Billboards, magazines, commercials, movies, etc. tell us that beauty is an outward appearance that can only be achieved if you buy this "magic lotion" or if you purchase this line of makeup. Whatever happened to knowing that you are beautiful, because you are you?

Throughout one year in a child's life, they see roughly 40,000 commercials, most of which are pertaining to how to enhance your appearance. From the start of our lives, we are told that we are never good enough. Celebrities and models, who are featured in most magazines and commercials, portray beauty as being skinny, wearing makeup and having nice clothes, but what about having character or morals, what about personality? Do these things make us beautiful or is piling on the foundation the only way you can truly look your best. Looking your best is not just about the outside, to look your best you must feel your best and to feel your best you must be you.

Outward beauty will die, you will get wrinkles, sun spots and gray hair, but your soul will last forever. Perfection is impossible, we will never reach it. So, instead of spending all your time, energy and money on materials that are supposed to help you get closer to perfection, just enjoy who you are and be yourself.

Taylor Murray, Grade 11
Whittier Christian High School, CA

The Importance of Dancing in My Life

For fifteen of my seventeen years of life, there remains one thing that always keeps me happy, motivates me to excel, and calms me when I get upset. Each time I walk into my dance studio, I feel a strong sense of excitement and splendor. Dancing is my outlet for emotions and the one thing in my life that actually means something important for me.

No time can I remember that I did not have dance in my life. As most little girls announce when they turn two years old, I told everyone I would be a ballet dancer when I would grow up. My mother, with her reasonability and sensibility, signed me up for a summer dance class, believing I would hate it and never give dancing another thought. When that summer ended, she inquired of me how I enjoyed dancing. I proceeded to tell her that I absolutely loved it. My mother looked shocked and amazed. After the stun had worn off, she agreed to let me register for tap and ballet dance classes.

Fifteen years later, that love remains just as strong as my two year old self exclaimed. Throughout the years, I expanded my dancing range to include jazz, lyrical, ballroom, and hip hop. Each one gives me such pleasure and accomplishment that I could not picture my life without any one of them. Dancing truly is a very important piece of my life.

Catrine Johansen, Grade 11
Pine Tree High School, TX

My Family

There are many important things to me, but nothing's more important than family. What would you do without family? Without anyone to share past memories and experiences with? Family makes us feel loved. Family brings the worst and best in each of us. I think family should be important to all of us.

Our day-by-day interaction with our family makes us aware of their attitudes, personalities and who they really are. They are important to me because families help each other, as for mine also. They help me in any problems; I know I can go to anyone in my family to talk about a problem or a difficulty I'm facing. My parents are the most important part of my family, they are the ones who love me selflessly and sacrifices so much to raise me all these sixteen years. My brothers are the only ones I really can tell anything to, I know I have their trust. I tell them any problems and they help me with them, they know the teenage stage I'm passing through and want me not make the same mistakes that they did when they were teenagers.

Our family holds the key to understanding and appreciating ourselves. Family is important because we are important and we need support through thick and thin. Nobody else cares more about us than our family members. That's the most important thing in my life that is important to me. Together we make memories and pass experiences that are either good or bad, that we can always look back to, and maybe learn from them or just laugh at them.

Josh Diaz, Grade 11
Pine Tree High School, TX

The Door Unlocked

It is hard to wait around for something that may never happen, but it is even harder when you know it is everything you desire. When you lock your heart, hide away the key, and tell yourself that you are not going to let anything or anyone in, there still remains the key hole to where things come through. I believe I will not carry out my life alone, but let God take everything in control. Yet it never fails for things to fall through.

Through pain and hard times, I gained more than a boy could give. I have gained respect for myself and have learned to guard my heart 'til the time is right. Rely on the one and only Creator and realize my desires and wants will be filled if I stand still in patience. I broke my promise to God, giving away the key to my heart, but learning from my mistakes made me grow stronger as a person. Now I firmly place my feet on solid ground, I move towards no one without thought. I am who I am. I am who I will be. I am who I will always be because of what I have learned through a broken heart. "God determines who walks into your life, it's up to you to decide who you let walk away, who you let stay, and who you refuse to let go" (Dade).

Kelsi Cathey, Grade 12
Granbury High School, TX

The Choice

You're at a bar with your friends having a good time and having a few beers. It's time to go home and you are having trouble standing and unlocking your car. What do you do? Well here are some things to think about while you're making that life or death decision. Every 22 minutes in the United States a person dies or is seriously injured by an alcohol related car accident. Every 22 minutes…a person dies that is someone's mom or dad or child just because a selfish person made a selfish choice to drink and drive. Let's say there is a family of five, on a Friday night Mom decides to run to the store for a thing of milk and takes the baby with her. Well right when Mom turns out on the main road she and her baby have a 20 percent chance that they will never make it home or be seriously injured because of a drunk driver. I could go on and on with the scary statistics and scare you with all the hefty fines and jail time for drunk driving, but I won't because when it's just you outside an empty bar struggling to get your keys in the ignition, only you can make that right choice that will save another's life and also your own. So, what will you choose?

Stephen Harris, Grade 12
Coronado High School, TX

Family Matters

Bishop Desmond Tutu once said that, "You don't choose your family. They are God's gift to you, as you are to them." This true statement helped me to realize the importance of my family. Every day I gaze into their eyes and behold something special, something beautiful, something made specifically for me.

Having a family that cares enables you to release stress. Sometimes I break down in a puddle of tears when my life turns sour. My mother appears and knows exactly what to do. My mother comes off as "bittersweet," but I would never replace her. Everything I can and cannot think of she blesses me with. My father is not the greatest when it comes to the gooey stuff, but I give him his props for handling my smart attitude. A true family takes you as you come. If you once heard the myth of the "overprotective brother," it is an understatement compared to my brother. I cannot even go to the movies without hearing, "Momma look at those tight pants. Who do you want to impress Shanise?" My boyfriend better beware. The cat and dog relationship with my brother makes my day (whether he thinks so or not). I love my family, and I would never wish for another.

People do not truly understand the importance of family. If people realized that not everyone has a good family they would appreciate theirs more. Happiness with one's gifts will make you truly appreciate those gifts.

Shanise Walker, Grade 11
Pine Tree High School, TX

A Place for Us

In *The Goose Girl* by Shannon Hale, there is a line that reads, "And she felt sure as bones and deep as blood that she had found her place." Every time I read this simple sentence, a chill runs down my spine, for within me (and I am sure within each of us) there is a primal longing to have a place in which we belong, fully and without compromise or doubt. Sometimes the longing is so great I feel as if my very soul is reaching out, pulling my heart strings as it struggles to break free and *find* it, this elusive location with a special spot made exactly for me. I imagine that finding it will be like slipping my hand into a warm glove, filling out the fingers, feeling soft wool fit itself around my hand as if it was always meant to be there…a puzzle piece to my heart a tonic for my brain, a bulwark for my soul.

I have seen people who fill a special place in the world, and light seems to shine from their faces like a soft and temporal sun. Every move is made with confidence, for they know that whatever happens to them in this life they will never be alone, and once found a place is never truly lost. You may wander far in your travels, but always there is a shining thread, like Ariadne's magic ball of yarn which led Theseus safely home.

Hannah Nielsen, Grade 11
Northridge High School, UT

Intergalactic Space Ninja Warrior

Intergalactic space ninja warrior, that's what I was. I choose the almighty lightning sword as my weapon, and a huge star destroyer as my ship. Ok really, I was just a little kid with a stick, a swing set, and a huge imagination.

So, my story begins on what seemed a normal day, but turned bad when Slade, the most evil, hated man in the galaxy, decided to attack. Since I was the best, I had to be the one to face him.

When he arrived I suited up, a bandana and a stick, and I flew (swung) to face him. And then, the epic battle began.

I wielded my sword and took the first swing. He dodged and struck back. I blocked him then released my lightning which he stopped easily with one hand. The battle raged on for hours, more like five minutes, and I was exhausted. In my exhaustion he knocked me down and readied his sword to finish me. "Is this it?" I asked myself, "Had I really lost?" But right before he finished me I used all my strength to lunge at him and we rolled across the yard, I mean the battlefield. "He had to be defeated," but as I said those words he stood up, raised his sword, and swung to kill me. And as that blade fell on my neck I heard, "Kevin Michael, stop rolling around in the yard. You just look silly. Now get cleaned for dinner."

Kevin Michael Keating, Grade 12
Granbury High School, TX

Angel

I remember waiting outside the delivery room holding my grandmother's hand, tears rolling down my white puffy face. I heard an infant's cry and I melted to the floor. He is here, and I could not wait to hold him in my arms. Atreyu Isac Gamboa weighed seven pounds five ounces, was welcomed into this world at 5:35 p.m. on June 28, 2007, and looked like a monkey alien. My monkey alien. I ran inside the room to make sure my mother was okay. I looked at my father and saw his back was to me and his hands were on his face. I've never seen him cry except for today. That must mean something.

The name Atreyu was decided after watching our family's favorite movie. In the movie the young warrior is selected and sent to do brave and heroic duties. My family and I have a feeling that Atreyu is going to do something extraordinary in life. We feel it and we know it.

I kiss him on the cheek and forehead every possible moment I am with him and we can make each other laugh hours on end, but I receive the utmost happiness when he runs into my arms and lies his head on my shoulder and we simultaneously close our eyes. I live for him and love him with all that I am. He was put on this Earth to remind us what love is. He is my warrior. He is my Angel.

Jessica Livesey, Grade 11
Pine Tree High School, TX

Influential State of Mind

"Close your eyes, fade it out, God will help and come about!" Rocking back and forth I repetitively shouted amongst myself. The floor began to rumble, and there was so much rage in their voices. Suddenly, it became quiet, and this silence had answered my prayers. That would be the end of it! The hurt, pain, and suffering. My parents were getting a divorce! Hope, inspiration, and self esteem issues were the problems I began to face. Only one person could eliminate my worries in this situation; my sister Samantha.

The day my mother moved out of the house became the day my mind became crazy. I turned to Sam for guidance. She was open, honest, and comforting. "Hold your head up high, pumpkin," Sam said to me. "Don't let the troubled times bring you down, yet they are there to make you stronger." Crying all day and every night worrying about my father and mother; who knew how things were going to end up.

Learning from Samantha's knowledge and my experience going through this tragedy, it became easier to see a light at the end of the tunnel. I couldn't do it without the people in my life that support me, like Samantha did. Cherish the ones surrounding you and pay attention to them as they will do for you. Most importantly, never give up on anything because there is always hope in something or someone!

Emily Antley, Grade 12
Granbury High School, TX

My Aunt Johnnie

"Mom, do I really have to go with you? I don't know these people," I asked with an attitude as I climbed into the car. My aunt Johnnie called us and asked us if her and her daughter could move in with us. I had to sit in a car to go pick up someone I didn't know. I was wishing that we would hurry up and get back home. When we pulled up to the house where she was staying, she was holding her daughter tightly in her arms. When I walked into the house, I saw how bad everything was. I had noticed that they had no electricity or running water. It smelled horrible. The house had trash all over it. I was feeling queasy so I walked outside. My aunt Johnnie called me over to help her move boxes. When I got to her, she had an exhausted look on her face. I knew she was determined to make her and her daughter's life better. I went to put the boxes in the back of the car. When I was done, I noticed that her daughter was sitting on the porch. I asked her if she was happy that she was moving in with us. She said yes and went back inside. When I got back inside the house, my aunt Tammy was apologizing to my aunt Johnnie. I knew she was doing the best for her daughter. I knew that everything would be better for them.

Jennifer Sims, Grade 12
Granbury High School, TX

2 Shots?

The water was smooth as glass in the pond not far away from our tent. The moon gently shone, reflecting off the water to bring light to the whole camp. All the hunters gathered around the fire telling stories.

It had seemed an eternity I had been waiting for my hunt. Ever since I was born there was one weekend in November that my father held a youth hunt. I was shaking with excitement for the hunt to come. My mother held my rifle as I scrambled to get in the bed of the pickup.

We finally arrived, got out of the bed of the truck and wandered to our stand through the thick mesquite. We came to our stand, which wasn't much more than a box on stilts. We just entered the stand when the sun began to rise. The deer began to make their way to the feeder. One deer grabbed my attention. I loaded my gun and held my crosshairs steady.

The moment arrived I slowly squeezed the trigger then POW. The deer was down, my mom congratulated me and we made our way down. My mom grabbed the rifle from my hands and loaded another round. We were about four feet from the deer when a shot rang out from beside me. It was my mom and she had almost taken off my foot. We looked at each other nervously then began to laugh. I will always remember my near foot losing experience.

Austin Morrow, Grade 10
Wall High School, TX

My Companion

Spring was in bloom as much as spring could be in bloom when we got our sweet little puppy. He was so happy that his tongue often hung out of the side of his mouth and had so much joy that he would breathe so hard his cheeks stretched back revealing a large grin.

In time he grew to be a bigger, stronger, faster puppy, but he still had a lovable clumsiness. Every day of school, he would wag his big, fluffy, yellow tail at my arrival home from school showing nothing but unconditional love.

Over the next few years, time kept on moving, and he grew weaker and fatter than ever before, but he was always just as lovable. Lumps began to appear on his body, and we later found out he had a tumor wrapped around his large intestine.

There was an uncommonly cool breeze the day my dad and I took a walk with him to the lake. That day, my whole family sat with him in the claustrophobically small white-walled room. I shared a stare with the brown eyes of my friend who had always been there for me. I left the room when I saw the man in white enter; I never wanted to see my cheerful, fat puppy covered in hair be anything besides that, so I decided I never would. I now often come home to an empty house missing my sweet puppy's unconditional love; inside, I know he is in a happier place.

Jason Pavik, Grade 12
Granbury High School, TX

Unconditional Love

The importance of things for many people changes over a course of time. I believe there exists many things that define and describe why we value the things we value. Therefore, the atmosphere at home and around my family represents and conveys the kind of person I display and will display toward the outside world.

If my life with my family happens to display tension and depression, then my representation of which I desire to convey disintegrates. A family contributes marvelous and affectionate experiences, but love stands forth as the most considerable affection that a family shares with one. Eva Burrows once said, "In family life, love is the oil that eases friction, the cement that binds closer together, and the music that brings harmony." The unconditional love that a family shares with one another is priceless. One can have the best clothing, hair, and dwell in abundance of money, but without the love and affection that my family bestows upon me, life would have no meaning. The importance of having a family that cares for me conveys my value of life.

Now that I think about how important and valuable my family is, I thank God each and every day for the family I have. I would not change a thing about them. Life consists of many opportunities and chances; family remains one within one's life.

Raquel Fuertes, Grade 11
Pine Tree High School, TX

My Big Decision

Life has not been easy for me. Until now my views on life have been very vague, to the point of me trying to take my own life. By vague, I mean that I didn't have any better goals set for myself, other than the typical goals that my mom had for me. She expected me to end up like her, pregnant at the age of seventeen and no important career or life ahead of her. Not only was she a failure by choice, due to laziness, she was very abusive toward me. She did not love me just because "I was my father's kid," were the words that she used every time I asked her why she was mean to me and not my sister. This continual reminder that she "tattooed" to my forehead was a painful wound that I could not understand. This is what drove me to my deep depression and to the biggest decision that I have ever made which turned out to be almost deadly. The question that always was on my mind was "Why does she not love me and what did I do to deserve a life like mine?" Of course, this question still remains unanswered to this day. Having to live with the painful remembrance of my mother shunning me was very hard to overcome, but I learned to live with it. I have decided that I will not let this monster defeat me and stop me from living a fulfilling life.

Jennifer Gomez, Grade 12
Granbury High School, TX

Reading

Reading can be a wonderful get away for all who enter into the pages of a book. All it takes is a little time, a book, and some privacy, but a little imagination does not hurt at all. Opening a book is like opening a portal to distant lands, seas, and planets. Through the world of books you can be put in the middle of an epic adventure you can never take or the middle of a romantic get away. Whatever sparks your interest.

After all, without books where would we be? If it was not for the written word there would not be movies or television which some might argue is a bad thing, but it has sparked the creativity of today's youth and has captured most everyone's attention. I believe that even though movies and television are great they in no way compare to reading a book, even if I have seen the movie based on the book a thousand times.

Americans have become too fast paced to sit down and talk with their family let alone read a book but they do not know what they are missing. I believe that books can present a much more favorable world than the one we live in. Through books daily troubles can disappear along with the worries of tomorrow. So pick up a book and lose yourself today.

Steven Parks Jr., Grade 12
Nestucca High School, OR

Freedom

America is the home of the free and the land of the brave. Well at least it used to be. You doubt me? Just look at the path our country has traveled down the last couple of months. It sure looks like the government is regulating more and more. More than it was designed to, which leads us to the question, what is the purpose of government?

Now just take a look at what the government is in charge of and what it is still after. It has a foothold in several large companies. It controls the nation's currency. It has also forced CEOs to step down. Deservedly or not, this is wrong. The government also wants to control healthcare; bad idea. This is something the government is not good at. It is horribly inefficient which would mean that everyone would end up worse. It just wants the power to control our lives.

When our government was created, there were checks and balances put in place. Ever since these checks and balances were set in place, politicians have tried to circumvent these measures. The most ingenious get through. Things like Medicare/Medicaid, income tax, and this new health plan. There was a time without an income tax. Try and imagine that today.

As the old saying goes "power corrupts." Our politicians received power when we elected them. Now since being elected they look for more power. We must seek a different path.

Kevin Gilmartin, Grade 12
Valley Christian School, WA

The Education of a Master

Benjamin Franklin was a jack of all trades. He was a writer, publisher, scientist, inventor, diplomat, and politician. But where did he learn, at some illustrious college? No! He taught himself by reading good books and watching others! The most formal schooling he attained was at a grammar school for two years when he was young. Ben read all the famous writers of the day: Bunyan, Defoe, Locke, Steele and many others. He taught himself how to write by reading one of the editions of the Spectators and taking certain important words out of the sentences, then without looking at the book, he would reconstruct the sentences in his own words. He would then compare his sentence with the Spectator's. Gradually he learned how to write efficiently and eloquently. Ben also taught himself geometry, French, Italian, Spanish, Latin and law. Franklin, who was a printer all of his life, printed many important papers, including Poor Richard's Almanac, which he authored and published. Ben had a system of checking his virtues each day. The virtues that he drew up were temperance, silence, order, resolution, frugality, industry, sincerity, justice, moderation, cleanliness, chastity, and humility. Because Ben continually worked on his virtues and education all his life, he became well respected for his talents and a master at everything he did.

Jessica Vassar, Grade 10
Victory in Jesus Academy, AK

Another Day, Another Lesson

Again I scratched at my itchy legs covered in black hose while the preacher continued his rant on faith and love. It was another day at church with me squirming in my seat while my grandfather sat next to me nodding along to the sermon and flipping through his Bible. I could hear the other children outside running and playing on the playground and again I imagined getting out of that stiff wooden pew and running around with the other kids. They didn't have to stay inside and listen to a preacher talk on and on about nothing important to me while my legs got stiff and my belly growled for the want of food. Again I asked myself what I was doing there. I could have been sleeping in or watching cartoons while eating a Pop-tart. Though many times I considered ditching it never actually occurred. With a lot of time and patience I grew out of those fidgety elementary years and became a teenager who looked forward to dressing up on Sundays and going out to eat afterwards. Is there a moral to the story? No, but there is something between the lines. Ditching the stiff dress and never ending sermon might have changed who I am, and maybe it wouldn't have. But right now I'm glad that sitting there next to my grandpa has made me the woman I am now.

Marnie Cannon, Grade 12
Star Charter School, TX

Driving

Hands on the wheel. Foot on the pedal. Finally Freedom. Being able to go where I want, when I want. Driving is indispensable to me. I can no longer imagine what I would do if I had no car and no driver's license.

I love driving for fun and going places with friends. I can drive out to the rolling Buttes or go to the movies with friends. I feel like there are no limits. Driving relaxes me. It can be my alone time and I just think. I blast the music and sing along not caring who sees, there is no embarrassment. I roll down the window at night, in summer, or during spring when the weather is great. It is so much fun to feel the wind blowing into the car and to put my hand out the window. There is no stressing and no worrying when I drive.

The changing scenery, from city to country, along with the mood of the music affecting me. I listen to fun music and am upbeat or slower music and am mellow and thoughtful.

When I drive it's just me and the car. I am in control. Just my hands on the wheel and my foot on the pedal.

Marla Strong, Grade 12
Faith Christian Jr/Sr High School, CA

A War Waged too Long

It is in the best interest of the state of Texas, the United States, and its governing body to move toward federal decriminalization of marijuana. The war on drugs has been by far the lengthiest and costliest war the United States has ever embarked upon, one for which the nation has paid too steep a price. It continues to exhaust valuable time, money, lives, and resources that can be used elsewhere in more laudable and worthwhile projects.

Opponents of the legalization of marijuana argue that it will lead to its increased abuse. The only relevant and prevailing argument here is: under what justifications confirm that legalizing marijuana will inevitably lead to a substantial increase in marijuana use? When abortions were legalized, did every pregnant woman in America race to get an abortion? Legalizing marijuana does not necessarily mean that every American would be well on their way to a path of abuse and addiction.

It's human nature to yearn for what we cannot have. Legalizing marijuana could very well dismiss the increased crime and violence, corruption, the undeserved profits of smugglers, and the entity of the drug trafficking business itself.

It's time we recognize a lost cause when we see one. In taking all of the above into consideration and in representing the adamant opinion of the public majority, I plead that you help support and further drug law reform in Congress. Forty years waged in this unwinnable, wasteful war is forty years too long.

Leslie Nguyen-Okwu, Grade 11
Pflugerville High School, TX

Attached

Interpretation…the same story always turns out different. This proves especially true when the story comes from people with completely different views on life and on each other. I have often thought this could be the cause of confusion, the confusion of my curious name. My dad claims he heard my name and immediately realized its beauty and elegance. Kris, his ex-wife, however says he simply came home from a night out and demanded his daughter be named Angelica. Despite the uncertainty, I received my label and am now attached for the rest of my life.

An angel sent from the heavens or a messenger from God provides the meaning of my spice of a name. However, I do not hear that angelic title too often, because I have so many other names. I blame this as another source of the indecision of my name.

My name possesses no history, nor does it serve a particular purpose. I cannot connect it to anything important, a family member, or a past. But if you had asked me if I would like to change my name, I would shake my head no and laugh. For my name fits like a well-seamed dress, perfect and exact. A name usually exists as just that, a name, a label, or an undeserving title. However, my name acts as a mirror, reflecting the angel within myself. Whether through a bar or through deep thought, "Angelica" found me and remains attached to my heart.

Angelica Montano, Grade 11
Flour Bluff High School, TX

My Life

What is life? Is it something that I can control? Is it something that I will always have? I have never thought about it deeply until now. On September 27th, 2009, a known schoolmate passed away. I have known him through all of high school and was privileged to take three years of math with him. He was sitting right across the desk from me the day of his injury. The next school day, I find out that he is gone. God's Word says, "Why, you do not even know what will happen tomorrow. What is your life? You are a mist that appears for a little while and then vanishes" (*New International Version*, James 4:14). What have I done with my life?

Andrew Swank was a junior at Valley Christian School. During a football game on Friday, Sep. 25th, Drew received a severe head injury that killed him two days later. He strongly believed in the Lord, and now, he is in a better place. His faith was deeply enrooted in the Word and what it says. Drew always showed a Christlike lifestyle, being called "the peacemaker" of the family. He did what he loved to do, and accomplished it well. Drew gave the gift of life through donating organs after being pronounced brain dead.

So what is my life? My life is not my own, I belong to the One that created me, who controls my every breath, my every step, my every heart beat. Yes, I belong to Jesus.

Nadia Fedchun, Grade 10
Valley Christian School, WA

Under the Waves

As I go down, deeper and deeper into the depths of the ocean, I see a trail of bubbles floating to the top. Ten, twenty, thirty feet, I descend to the ocean floor, enjoying my favorite activity. Scuba diving is an important part of my life. The freedom I experience when among the aquatic life is awe-inspiring. The surrounding marine environment gives me a sense of closeness to God and nature. My hobby of scuba diving allows me to learn and be aware of everything that I otherwise would not be able to see, such as the life and vegetation in the ocean. This sport enables me to become skilled at new ways of communicating other than verbal language. I use hand signals and different sounds to get my point across to fellow divers. Through the extensive training to become a certified scuba diver, I realize the importance of being well disciplined and applying the knowledge that I have gained. The tranquility of the ocean water provides me with a sensation of relaxation. Scuba diving is not only adventurous, but it will also help me attain my goal in life which is to be a marine biologist. As I ascend, closer and closer to the surface, I see the ocean floor slowly vanishing, but the images are still vivid in my mind.

Daniel Pense, Grade 11
Valley Christian High School, CA

The Meaning of Family

What is family? Family is a net that is always there to catch you when you fall. They're a pick me up when you're down. Family is a canopy to shelter you from harm. They're support when you're weak and feeble. Family is a hot cup of cocoa on a cold, stormy night. This is what family should be.

Helping each other through hard times is important in a family. When my parents come home from a hard work day, I cheer them up the best way I can. As soon as I come home from a tough day at school, I know my parents will be there to make me laugh. Without family, I would go to bed thinking about my bad day, with a sliver of hope that tomorrow will be better.

Another meaning of family is support. My family will support me and the decisions that I make. Family is also there to help me make big life decisions such as where to go to college and what I should do for a living. These decisions are scary, but not with a good support system.

The final meaning of family is love. My family wants me to do excellent in the things I do and I know they are there every step of the way. Even if I don't do well, my family still loves me. And I love them.

Alexandria Sholtis, Grade 10
Kaufer High School, TX

Beauty Is in the World

When I look up into the sky, I become a watcher of beautiful clouds that pirouette in a sea of blue. A breeze whips up my hair and brings the scent of spring. Sometimes, when I step into the night, I am greeted by stars that twinkle from dark lands above. The air is frigid but refreshing — a shiver runs down my spine as I gently relax my muscles. Other times, on a rare wet day, thunderous mountains weep of the sun's departure. Puddles splash their soft fingers at my feet, soaking my socks until I agree to play. When the sun finally peers out from behind its stormy parents, I happily relinquish my hold on time and place, relaxing in eternity.

The vastness of the world ignites my wonder at the beauty of it all, the uniqueness of each day. However, the same cannot be said for the rest of society. Under pressure from the world, the people around me drown in stress, despair, and breakdowns. If they could once smile on a bad day, then the day would get that much better. If they could breakaway from the currents of civilization and enjoy what we already have, the world would be that much more dazzling. Finally, if we could reach out to the people in need, the connections between us all would get that much stronger. Beauty is in the world — if only we could open a gateway of radiance that everyone could enter with ease.

Samantha Zhang, Grade 10
Troy High School, CA

Being Yourself

"Be yourself" is a moral taught to children in this culture from a very young age. However, once younger kids become older kids, most of them spend much of their time worrying about whether or not they are liked by their companions. This is ironic, considering that they were raised to "be themselves," and not worry what other children think.

The problem is not that they have blatantly decided to ignore the idea of being themselves. The problem is that they begin to question who they actually are. When children goes from Elementary School to Junior High, this is usually about the same time that said children become self-aware enough to stop being totally self-absorbed, as so many young children are. However, once they have decided to stop being this selfish brat that they once were, they don't know what to become. It is impossible to be yourself if you don't know who you are.

This is when peer pressure becomes so important in a child or preteen's life. Not knowing who they are, they figure that if they can become someone that everyone else likes, at least they will have pleased someone. However, becoming someone that you truly want to be is far more important than pleasing other people, or than fitting into a mold that they want to put you in. Children need to remember this as they grow into the person they will become.

Chandra Bergmann, Grade 11
Valley Christian High School, CA

Stringed Music Maker

The wood sits on the wall with a brilliance like that of a diamond ring. The light from my window caresses the fierce fireburst paint and bounces off of the glistening metal magnets beneath the tightly woven brass wire. I carefully reach my hand to grasp the long fretted rosewood neck, accented with creamy mother-of-pearl inlays. As my skin makes contact with the smooth paint, I carefully bring the instrument to my side, like a mother with her newborn baby. My finger runs across the surface, just to check for impurities. The jet black cord, inserted into the metal hole cut out of the maple body, slithers like a snake into the bulky amplifier that occupies the dark corner. The knob that reads "Volume" spins clockwise and a faint buzz echoes around the room and fills my ears. This white noise had made its presence before, which brings a sense of security and comfort to me. I observe the small creamy white sliver of plastic, wedged between my index finger and thumb, worn down from a sharp point to a dull flat curve from years of slamming it against the silver strings. I lift up my hand while positioning my fingers against the slightly dusty fret board. My right hand thrashes down, hitting the strings with a thunderous force. The harmonious chord rings like the heavens, leaving my mind in a state of euphoria. My guitar.

Zach Ramsey, Grade 11
Pine Tree High School, TX

Letter from 2022

If you could write a letter to yourself at 15 what would you tell yourself? Would you try to alter things from your past? Well here is the letter I would write.

Dear Destiny,

I'm you from the future. It's inconceivable right? Wrong. Everything is imaginable if you just believe. Here I'll prove it's me. You keep a picture of you and your best friend in your pillowcase. I know he may say he loves you, but you're 15. Your first true love has yet to come. High school can be so rough, but you'll learn to make it through it. Don't let it get you dispirited. You may feel like your grandma is being too narrow-minded, but she's really not, she is just preparing you for college and life. You'll learn you and Beth turned out to be each other's best friend. You need to keep your grades up because if you don't then you can't get into any distinguished colleges. You make acquaintances so easy. They may cause you heartache, but you will make new friends to replace the dreadful acquaintances. Don't change or regret one thing you've done or have yet to come across in your magnificent life. Keep it up.

Love me…

Destiny Cannon, Grade 12
Coronado High School, TX

What a Best Friend Is

I met Justin the second semester of my high school freshmen year. I went after school to Pre AP Geometry tutorials to check if my grade was up to my normal high A standards. After checking it, I saw him in the classroom working on the homework that was due the next day. He seemed to be struggling as I watched him erase his answers for number one over and over again. I sat next to him and from the corner of his eye I saw him watching me. I offered my help and from that day on we stuck to each other's backs as if we were forced to. As any other teenage relationship we went through the everlasting drama the last half of our freshmen year. But through it all, we gave each other a shoulder to cry on and a hand to pull ourselves back up. He made me appreciate him for who he is. Through the tears and fights I would still count on him to pick me back up when I fall and defend me at my weakest moments. Over the two years of our friendship we built the perfect bond of trust, honesty, and love for each other.

That's what's important to me: a true best friend.

Nancy Gutierrez, Grade 11
New Caney High School, TX

We Are Who We Are

Yes, we are all different. Yes, we have different mindsets, values, customs and live different lives, but we are all united under the same principle: equality. Each and every one of us, no matter what origin, nationality or background we come from, are connected through the difficulties and struggles we face. The core of our unification is our heart containing our feelings and most precious being. It does not matter what we wear, what we have, or even how rich or poor we are. All that matters is that we choose to be the best of ourselves, those which we were created to be. We must not give into the temptations and wrong doings of this world. We must not follow these corrupted and deceitful minds that we see every day. We must not tear the world apart anymore than it is already broken. We must dare to be different. Our life's mission is not to see how much money we can make, in order to acquire all the "cool" priceless items we can buy. Our mission is to share the gifts that God has given us. We are to share our talents, wisdom, knowledge, wealth, and hope with the world. Most of all, we are to love, respect and accept each other as we are, not as who the world wants us to be. If we put into effect these principles, our world will become an indestructible beautifully united ideal place to live.

Carmen Farhat, Grade 11
Valley Christian High School, CA

Health Epidemic

How does it feel to know that each and every second someone, somewhere in America is dying from deadly worldwide epidemics that are being spread? On Earth, sickness revolves around everything, attacking without a warning. If America had free health insurance, we would not hear of these horrifying realities. If America came together and looked deeper at the realities happening around us, free health insurance could save us all.

Nearly 65 million Americans are uninsured and are suffering each day because of the incapability of paying for health insurance. If America changed its ways and decided to pass having free health insurance for everyone, a tidal wave of people could be saved. Due to the lack of free health insurance in America, many jobs have gone out of business for the simple fact that people do not want to work if health insurance is not one of the benefits within the job. Health insurance affects everyone more than we may think. Millions of people are dying out on the streets because of money problems and because they are not in access for the right immediate medical attention needed. America lacking free health insurance is a huge problem with a simple solution.

Children are slipping out of our hands every day in a blink of an eye because of no free health insurance in America. If our world changed, even just a little, more lives could possibly be saved. After all, shouldn't we be saving more instead of losing more?

Kelly Chapa, Grade 12
Post High School, TX

My Guardian Angel

My grandmother was the epitome of selflessness. She was my family's guardian angel. She was in her eighties and she still worked. She still provided for herself. She was a very independent woman. She was very frugal and always had money to give to her kids and her grandkids. She never really said much, but when she spoke, everyone listened. She was short, about my height, with curly white hair and she always smelled like smoke, but I looked up to her. She had a very cute, soft, lovely laugh.

There was one time at my niece's birthday party that I always remember. Jaymi, a cousin's girlfriend, came to the party with my cousin and her son. She was wearing a very short, revealing skirt. Gran happened to look at Jaymi when she was bending over to get something. Gran turns back to the rest of us, and with wide eyes, she simply states, "I can see up her skirt!" Everyone burst into laughter.

Gran was very frank and had a very cute sense of humor. She never waited for her kids to ask for help financially. She always seemed to know the exact time we needed help and she was always there for us.

She died recently and at her funeral, I don't think there was a dry eye in the room. She was such an influential woman. She touched everyone she met. I love you, Gran, I miss you, and I can't wait to see you in Heaven…

Carissa Dickey, Grade 11
Vista Ridge High School, TX

Invincible?

Tearing your ACL is never a minor aspect you should overlook; it is a very serious injury that takes six months recovery or even a year before you can participate in any sporting events. My experience tearing my ACL was shocking; however, it made me realize that I am not invincible.

Before my injury, I thought I was indestructible; I spent years involved in sports with minor or no injuries. I had few worries about what might happen to me during my sporting events. When my injury happened it was an accident that many people thought was minor, mostly because I got up and walked off of the basketball court, and I also played our last game. However, my injury never got worse, but it never got any better. Needless to say, what I thought was minor turned out to be major. It shocked everyone including me, mostly because I never thought an injury I got would be as serious as tearing my ACL. After my injury and all the rehab I had to endure, I started to realize that I was vulnerable to any injury that may come my way.

I have become cautious in my sporting events that I partake in after tearing my ACL. It has made me consider what could happen to me without thinking about it. Although my injury was serious, it made me look around at everyone else and I realized how lucky I was. Luke the saying goes, "Everything happens for a reason."

Trent Babb, Grade 12
Post High School, TX

Carly

When the blue PT Cruiser drove away for the first time, all I could think was "Now what?" I always knew my sister would have to leave me for the wondrous adventures college has to offer. However, I never thought that I would be as emotional as I was that day.

Carly has supported me my entire life. She is my best friend and the only person to whom I tell everything. We never fight, we share clothes, and we even entertain each other throughout boring family dinners. I will never find anyone as important to me as she is.

Learning to live life without her nearby has been a struggle, and I still find myself running to tell her about my ninety-seven on a math test or my bruise the size of a baseball. Carly and I miss each other, but we find ways to work around the distance.

So when she left, I cried oceans and lakes because I realized everything worthwhile in my life happened because of my sister. Without her I would not be half the person I have become. We may never be able to see each other every day like we used to, but we will always be there for each other when a support system is needed.

Caitlyn Hayworth, Grade 11
Pine Tree High School, TX

May 27th

One of the best days of my life was the day my little girl Nadia was born. It was 2 a.m. on May 27th when my girlfriend woke me up yelling, "Ow-ow-ow, GET UP!" I was so tired, like a bear woken from hibernating. What got me on the move was her saying, "Call your mom, I'm having contractions!" I jumped up out of bed and ran to my parent's room to wake them. We rushed to Baylor All Saints Hospital emergency room. We hadn't come to a complete stop in the parking lot before I jumped out the moving car to find a wheelchair. After walking through the long, pale hallways, we came to room D42. They hooked on the I.V. and the contraction monitor. After seventeen long hours in labor, Vanessa was unable to dilate past four, so the doctor broke her water to induce. When they brought her back to her room, I saw the most beautiful little girl I had ever seen laying on her chest. From that day till today, I have been and always will be the luckiest father alive. Having this whole experience with Vanessa and my baby, Nadia, made me very happy. I am proud of myself, because I stuck with Vanessa through the whole pregnancy. Thanks to God, we are still together today, and I hope someday we can get married.

Jose Escamilla, Grade 11
REACH High School, TX

The Best Experience Ever

With mumbling around I couldn't help someone understand right from wrong. It's hard to teach someone something when you are a fifth grader. I had an awesome experience with my kinderbubbies, Kelly and Jane.

Kelly and Jane were wonderful little girls. They were smart, fun, and outgoing. They didn't know each other well enough, so they didn't get along. At first, I wouldn't see them talk to each other. We would read together, but that was all they interacted.

I remember the intense aroma in the room, smelled like vanilla. Kelly came up to me and said, "I don't like Jane." I asked, "Why?" She answered, "She's a little brat." I said, "You have to know her before you say anything." At that moment, I wished she had said I'll try. I worried they wouldn't be able to get along. Then I told myself, "They can really get to know each other."

Kelly came up to me and hugged me so tight. She said, "Thank you Martha, you taught me not to talk about others before I get to know them." When she said that, I felt like crying. That was the best thing I had ever heard in my life. I hugged her and felt her comfort. I felt special since then.

It was a lifetime experience. A child teaching another child is a wonderful experience. Teaching right from wrong to a child is extremely important. If you teach them something little or big you will experience a bond.

Martha Martinez, Grade 12
Granbury High School, TX

Who Wants to Be a Robot?

When I was a child, I never sat still. I was constantly playing games; not the games you needed a game board for, either. When I was a child, imagination was my most used resource. I was constantly going to far off lands and battling pirates or saving royalty. My imagination and creativity flourished.

Today's youth, however, seems to have a lack of interest in using their imaginations, and why should they? With all the TV and video games giving them the stories, they don't need their imagination to think of stories on their own. Today's children are losing their imagination and it may not seem like that big of a deal, but it truly is.

By not using their imaginations the youth of today are losing their creativity and individuality. Who wants to be an individual when we could all be like Hannah Montana and SpongeBob SquarePants? Even reading books would be better, if a book is read right, by a person with a real imagination, it can take you to a whole new world. If it isn't, then a book is just words on a page. No wonder the percentage of children who enjoy reading has dropped so dramatically; without their imaginations, they are only seeing words on a page, not a story. The loss of imaginations in our youth is turning them into robots. What will the future be like if we are all just robots.

Andrea C. Kenagy, Grade 11
Nestucca High School, OR

Playoffs

Goaaaaaal! We had scored with barely any time left in the game. That imperative goal put us into a shootout giving us a second chance to win. Each team had to choose five shooters to go one-on-one with the opposing team's goalkeeper. I was selected to take a shootout, I knew what I had to do. As I waited for my turn we missed our two previous shots and the pressure was all on my shoulders. I had to convert this one-on-one to keep our hopes alive. The pressure was overwhelming. I stepped up to the ball feeling extremely nauseous. The crowd began chanting my name.

"You got this Tyler," I could hear my teammates yelling at me. The referee blew his high pitched whistle and I started to run with the ball at my feet. I watched the other team's goalkeeper start moving out at me. I had to make a decision quick. As he neared me, I dropped my right shoulder and faked a shot pushing the bright white ball to the left of my torso. The keeper bit on my fake and flew by me. The only thing left that could stop me was the time limit. I had to score. The referee counted down "Three, two, one" and right as he blurted out "one" I nailed the ball with my shiny white cleats towards the goal sending the ball into the back of the net. I had never felt better in my life.

Tyler Brabec, Grade 12
Granbury High School, TX

The Joys of Snow

I was flying down the mountain with the wind whistling in my ears and tiny ice shards pelting me in the face. The cold air penetrated my skin straight to the bone regardless of the many layers of clothing I wore. The torrent of snow swirling in the air made is impossible to see more than fifteen feet away. I was new to skiing and was not very skilled at turning yet. I knew that my mom was considerably far behind me so I began to turn to slow myself down. However, once I began to turn right I didn't know how to turn back to the left. I ended up straightening out just before I hit the tree's but by then I had reached a blue black mountain. On that section of the mountain lay something that I had never skied before; Moguls. I flew through the air over the large bumps hitting the ground hard and not knowing how to stop. My mom screamed for me to get out of there, so I turned to the left hoping to break free. Just as I reached the last mogul of the mountain I flew too far and flipped through the air not knowing which way was up or down. I landed onto the hard packed snow on my shoulder and cracked my collar bone. I was not able to play baseball at all that season. From then on I was more careful when I went on ski trips.

Clayton Young, Grade 11
Vista Ridge High School, TX

Gift of Freedom

"We hold these truths to be self-evident, that all men are created equal, that they are endowed by their Creator with certain unalienable rights, that among these are life, liberty, and the pursuit of happiness..." Every citizen in the United States is granted the right to have liberty which cannot be taken away.

What is liberty? Liberty is different for every individual. Personally, I believe liberty is the freedom I am granted to do what I want as long as I abide by the limits that are set by the government. Liberty as defined on Merriam-Webster Online Dictionary is "the positive enjoyment of various social, political, or economic rights and privileges." Having liberty is a privilege, because in some countries, people do not have freedoms that Americans are granted. As an example, if I were in a different country such as China, I would not be able to practice religion at my own will because religious freedom is not allowed in China and citizens must follow the specified religious rules. However, because I am an American, I am allowed to decide to which religion I will be faithful. This is a liberty that I appreciate greatly.

Liberty is the difference between deciding what I want in my life and having someone else tell me what must be in my life. Every day in the United States of America, people take this liberty for granted and disobey the laws.

Latasha Soto, Grade 12
Post High School, TX

Kindness

The way people interact with one another is a basic part of life, but attitude plays a distinct role in the way we treat each other. When you go to a job interview or want to make a good impression, it is human nature to display kindness. For some, showing such generosity is a sacrifice and for others it is a gift, but for Irena Sendler it was a sacrifice she was willing to make. During WWII, Irena smuggled 2500 children out of the danger of Nazi's until she was caught and severely beaten for her heroic actions. Once someone like Irena Sendler takes the time to exhibit good deeds, it becomes contagious and easier to bestow upon others. Like Mother Teresa once said, "Kind words can be short and easy to speak, but their echoes are truly endless." Though kindness is not always easy to possess in times of struggle or in difficult situations, it builds up strength in others as well as ourselves. For me I would like to show kindness by mentoring younger girls who might be able to learn from my experiences. I hope to by a shining light to girls when they are entering their teen years and don't know how to sort through their feelings. When I have a bad day it always makes me feel better to see a smiling face and hear a few kind words.

Lauren Gale, Grade 10
Brookside Christian School, CA

Joy

It was joy.

That was what enveloped the fingertips of the conductor, propelling them to curve this way and that, as if tracing the air, as if they glided through water. Even from my living room, watching the symphony play on my television set, I could see the perfect bliss shining brightly from the conductor's features, his hands moving as if to sculpt the notes.

I had seen this joy before. It was in the sole of a ballerina's outstretched foot, as she spun faster and faster, gaining speed until she was just a blur of sparkling color. It was in the first brushstroke of an artist's canvas, the paint already smeared like a streak of light across his hand. It was in the last drops of ink in a writer's notebook, her hand struggling to keep steady, to flood those final syllables with her entire thought and being.

I've always wanted to feel that joy, to love something with that much conviction and power. But I know now that joy doesn't have to come with genius or talent. It happens in each day and in every moment. Joy spills out when the rain hits the roof, when the sunshine strikes the window. Joy blooms when we sprint ahead of the clouds before dawn, when we pull the stars over our heads for night. Joy comes in the fact that I speak, that I see, that I breathe.

As Betty Smith said, "We should all fall in love with life."

Ela Banerjee, Grade 11
Roseville High School, CA

Dependence on Technology

Every day, someone says, "I could live without television, phones, or mp3 players," but the reality is that humanity has become entirely dependent upon the usage of technology. Around the globe, millions of individuals rely upon several devices just to get through the day. Technology has become so prominent in our lives that hundreds of people were stranded in the streets when the New York power grid went down, because none of them knew in what direction they lived or because they had always relied upon the subway to take them to their destination. Even medical teams have become too reliant upon our technological advances. Beepers, equipment, and medicinal distribution has all been a wonderful convenience to the medical staffs of hospitals across the world because of the advances in technology, but we can take these for granted. Because of the high reliance on our technology, hospitals have to have backup generators in case of an electrical failure. What would occur if all the electrical sources that humanity has failed? Would we be able to continue with our normal lives, or would we struggle? With the increasingly high addiction to technology, I begin to doubt that we could perform our routine activities, would could spell disaster if for some reason we no longer had the use of electrical power. So with all the wonderful and magnificent pieces of technology, we need to be wary of taking them for granted just because we use them for everyday usage.

Colt Deen, Grade 12
Post High School, TX

Shame versus Guilt

Shame is something that is brought upon a person by those that surround him, whether it is a stranger or not. A person can be said to wear shame like an overcoat, since it is brought upon by others. A person feels no shame for an action that they committed until someone acts superior to the offender because of poor judgment, poor judgment in a taboo subject of society. Shame is not an enjoyable feeling whatsoever, but, one can put a stop to their shame by simply relocating and starting over; living a new life on a clean slate. However, guilt is much more different.

Guilt, on the other hand, is brought about internally. Guilt arises in a person, even without the knowledge of any other person; stranger or not. It is something that is an internal struggle, something that may emotionally consume a person if it goes uncared for. Although both guilt and shame can weigh down one's heart, guilt does not leave until one comes to peace with what they have done and learns to accept it, because what they have done is what makes them the character with the personality they withhold today.

David M. Meza, Grade 11
La Serna High School, CA

High Merit Essays – Grades 10, 11 and 12

Life Time Rhyme

My life so far has had its up and its downs, you could say something like the Rocky Mounds. I was born in Fort Worth, or best known as funky town. The year was 91, when I was finally brought around. It was the creation of a new kind and you could see it in my eyes.

As a child I didn't have much growing up, all I had was my mom, but for me that was just enough. Roaming the streets was like an adventure for me, discovering new things that you would rarely see. To an outsider we were seen as different, living on my block they should have been more specific. As the years passed my independence grew with, something like a loner or smoke in the wind. Middle school was cool, laughing acting a fool. It wasn't till the 9th grade when I got off on the wrong page. Soon after my bad ways, my cousins told me to quit, saying it was just a phase and he would learn from it. The negative aspects, I was never involved. Positives what drove me and my talent to draw?

It was until I switched schools when I really got on track, I left Castleberry High and haven't looked back.

Informing the people on my life time, telling my story in the art of a rhyme.

Joshua Ramirez, Grade 12
REACH High School, TX

Until the End

Oh the agony and sadness I would feel for months. These thoughts filled my head August 30th two thousand eight. Juan Carlos Rodriguez, my brother, would be leaving to Marine boot camp that day.

As kids we had the same friends, had our own two people member club called VCR, and he would defend me from everyone. As we grew up things changed a little, I knew he still loved me, but we didn't hang out as much mainly because he was busy with his girl and weekend job.

When it was time for him to leave, He went in my room and he hugged me tight. The only thing he could say to me was "I love you, take care, and I will make you the proudest little sister." Those words meant the world to me. The only thing I could reply was "I love you and will miss you, take care" and even those words came out as a mere whisper.

October 31st two thousand eight, my brother graduated, and was officially a United States Marine. He never gave up. He held his head high, and kept giving it his all. That day I felt prouder than ever before! He had accomplished his dream. He taught me the biggest lesson of my life. The saying you can do anything you put your mind to is true. Carlos accomplished something no one thought he would. He changed and became a better person and made me the proudest little sister.

Sagrario Rodriguez, Grade 12
Granbury High School, TX

The Movie Star Name

My parents gifted me with a sophisticated, formal name: Kimberlyn. A combination of two pretty names, it seems almost made up. Naming me like a movie star child, my name follows the movie star trend. I say this because celebrities constantly name their children names like Apple or Reign Beau.

My name had belonged to a soap opera star named Kimberlin Brown. My name originates from Old English and means "from the royal fortress meadow." It means I have a vibrant, witty personality and it apparently ensures popularity, but the meaning has nothing to do with why my parents chose it. While my mother waited long hours in labor, my parents watched *Family Feud*, with Kimberlin Brown on the show. When my mother heard the name, she told my dad how much she liked it, and he responded, said that they could name the next girl that after my sister had already been born and named. When my mom got surprised by a twin, me, she knew the name she wanted, so they christened me Kimberlyn Michelle. My parents awarded me with the wonderful name Kimberlyn for the beauty in the name, and Michelle because my mother thought the two names sounded good together.

Years ago I could not stand my name. I thought it too long and too common.

The older I become, I look back and see how silly I acted. I define myself with the meaning of this name, and I never want to trade it.

Kimberlyn Kasperitis, Grade 11
Flour Bluff High School, TX

My New Job

Being there for my family has always been important to me, but especially over the past few months. My mom and my step dad were divorced in February of this year, and ever since then I have had to step up and take the role as the man of the house. This job is never ending. I have to do the physical tasks around the house such as mowing the lawn and repairing non-working objects, besides the normal everyday jobs I have had to step up and become the protector of the house.

This lately has been a full time job. Over the past month or so there have been a lot of events that have taken place at my home. I have had to be brave for my family and go outside when there is a loud noise or when we hear the gate being opened or when my dogs are growling and barking at something or someone. Though I have been fortunate as of yet and have never found myself in any immediate danger. I am scared that there may come a time where I might be in danger. This fear will not stop me. I love my family too much to take the chance and have something happen to them.

Mark Thorpe, Grade 11
Faith Christian Jr/Sr High School, CA

Crushed Dreams

I found out I had torn my ACL and needed to have surgery. This was a terribly painful moment for me. I have never been in a tougher situation than those few minutes when I was told I would require surgery on my ACL.

One word that strikes fear into the heart of all athletes is the word "surgery." The realization that I needed surgery on my ACL presented a whole different level of a heart-wrenching injury. The moment when Dr. Jesse Ward told me my ACL had been unattached was a painful moment.

The feeling of failure and disappointment was far greater than any physical pain I encountered from the surgery. My dad slid down into his chair in shock and utter horror after Dr. Ward announced the news. I experienced the stark realization that I had just lost something I loved doing, and I would never experience it again. Football is more than just a sport or a game played for fun; it is a way of life.

I still haven't quite fully analyzed exactly what took place in the room that day. That moment when Dr. Ward proclaimed I would need surgery to fix my ACL was such a painful moment. Already recovery is taking place in leaps and bounds and before I know it, I will be achieving all my hopes and dreams.

Matthew Gray, Grade 12
New Waverly High School, TX

To Text or Not to Text

Most teenagers over the age of 16, around the U.S., have a car. There are so many responsibilities that go along with driving. It seems as technology progresses, focus, and lack of attention seem to become more of a problem.

The cell phone companies are coming out with more and more phones; it seems like every day they release a new one. They all have awesome, different features, but the one thing they have in common is the text messaging feature. Pretty much everyone knows how to send a text on their phone. The average number of texts sent in a month by one person is 188 (Wikipedia.com/text_messaging). Unfortunately, this has become a problem while driving, especially with teenagers. For some reason, it seems so very important that when you get a text no matter where you are, you feel the need to respond right away and send it, even if you are driving. In 2007, from the ages of 16-17 years old, there have been nearly 1,000 crashes related to texting and driving, many died from the accidents, not because of them texting someone else was (http://www.edgarsnyder.com/car-accident/cell/statistics.html). So, is this going to be you? Are you going to be the one to injure maybe even kill someone, simply because you HAD to send that text message? Think twice it could save a life, YOUR life.

Mariah Montoya, Grade 12
Coronado High School, TX

Hunter

Growing up with an Autistic sister is not a burden, but a blessing. Hunter is 9 years old, has blonde hair, blue eyes and contains the most innocent laugh a child can embrace. When she was brought into this world, her eyes said it all. She was different, in an odd but peaceful way. We all knew instantly there was something about this little girl that was unexplainable. Weeks after we brought her home we noticed a pattern in her vocals and eye contact that we knew right away was not normal. After months of testing, the doctors finally had an explanation, she had Autism. To a lot of families, this is devastating news, and it was at first. Years would show that this was a very unique child that brought laughter, happiness, joy and loving heartache into our lives. Today she is the blessing of my life and words cannot explain the impact she has had on me and my family. This blonde haired, blue eyed little girl is the most impeccable child with the most outstanding sense of humor a person can have. I thank God every day for her and the change she has brought.

Kayla Bullard, Grade 12
REACH High School, TX

Words Count

Two-hundred fifty is a big number when you talk about years, people, or languages. It is not a big number when you are talking about words. To write an essay or story that is no longer than two-hundred fifty words is like trying to talk without moving your mouth; it is writing a nation's constitution on Twitter; it is frankly impossible.

There is nothing closer to artistic slavery than a low word count. Sure, a great paper can be written with great brevity, but the sheer idea of restricting words scares most writers away. For any essay or short-story contest there should either be no limit, or a suggested target far in the back of the contest website, otherwise writers far and wide will freeze at the glowering number scowling at them on the requirements page.

Is a word count an attempt to force writers to use excessively long words to cut down on chat-speakers? Nay, it is the opposite — it is embracing the world of bare bones concision and a deficit of detail. Writing today has become a great machine of archetypes — if your story isn't short or easily recognized as a certain category of story like boy meets girl, vampire sex novel, or geeky dystopia of nerd-dom, then it is shunned.

And so I demand: rid the world of draconian word counts, swim against the mainstream like a great salmon in shining armor, and let raw creativity flood back into the great ocean of literary lackluster, RAGE AGAINST THE*

*(Essay cut off from word count)

Dylan Mahood, Grade 11
Washington High School, CA

Aroma of Rice

Winter in San Francisco is freezing; it froze my entire face to a pale color. Right after I get off the B.A.R.T. the wind blew strongly against me as I carried my backpack from school in Union City. I always noticed the many people who passed by me in their cars followed by other cars. I was followed only by my shadow. My backpack carried every subject I had in my school, and I carried all my parents' hopes and dreams. My shadow carried nothing. Sometimes I feel as if my shadow was mocking me in its own way, it carried nothing, but it gets to have every adventure I've ever had.

On my walk I look at local coffee shops, grocery stores, and bakeries. The sweet smell of bread always brought me back when I was a kid eating sweet bread, delectable. Unfortunately I didn't have enough cash to buy me a slice of bread or a small warm drink on our trail. A Muni roars and passes me in it's own trail. My imagination becomes wild and my shadow tells me that I walk extremely slowly, which annoys me. I take a few turns and get to a church. A choir sings harmonious psalms as I walk, but a dog starts barking and creates discordance. I come up to my house, open the doors and smell the sweet aroma of rice that is cooked by my dad. I feel ecstasy for my shadow doesn't get to taste love.

Leonard Chan, Grade 11
Purple Lotus International Institute, CA

The Power of Music

When people play music, it often becomes a window to their soul and mind. For me, that very idea lives in the music that I play. When I was nine years old, I had a desire to pick up an instrument and chose the cello because of Yo-Yo Ma, one of the greatest cellists today, due to his graceful tone and effortless ability. I remember picking up a cello for the first time and it had a sound that told me that this was my instrument. From that time, music and my cello have been a constant part of my life. I studied music, practiced it, and was eventually able to gain an understanding of it. As the pieces became more physically and emotionally difficult, I began to infuse the emotional energy from my mind into the music. Because of this, the cello has become a lot like a mentor to me. It has helped me to learn about controlling my emotions and releasing them into the music. The music lets me feel like I am floating above my emotional worries and fears. It has also taught me discipline by always pushing me to do better and causing me to strive to become the best I can because I want to be good at what I do. I look forward to the day when I will see the pinnacle of myself playing the cello with that graceful tone and the effortless ability I admired in Yo-Yo Ma.

Jonathan Ho, Grade 11
Valley Christian High School, CA

A Wonderful Accomplishment

Slam. Thud. "Oww!" I was at UT in Austin for my solo in band. It was a dreadfully hot day, and my legs were tired from walking and exploring all that morning.

I was in the ninth grade, and at state! To get here was a tremendous amount of effort. I chose a piece of music that was three pages long. At first I didn't bother to learn the music. I had expected my teacher to tell me how to play it. Soon I began practicing for hours in my room. This would help me learn the music. Help me better myself. Then, the day came for state.

Upon entering the room, I was trembling. I had just jumped a mile in the air from the slamming of the door, dropped my stand, and tripped over the chair. "Have a seat please," she was a pretty lady with long straight brunette hair. Sitting down, I took a few deep breaths. At first the music was shaky, but, as the song went on, it became smoother, graceful and confident, a light melodic sound. When the song ended, it surprised me. I got up, said "Thank you," and waited for my results. Three agonizing hours later, shock, pride, joy, success, and excitement coursed through my veins. I, a ninth grader, had made a one at state.

This accomplishment made me realize that I have to work at my goals in order to accomplish them. No one else can do it for me.

Amanda Heard, Grade 12
Granbury High School, TX

Winning Fair and Square

The smell of barbecue begged my tastebud's attention. Carefully powdered funnel cakes demanded to be eaten. Frenetic screams from Zipper riders pierced my ears. The local fair filled me with anticipation.

For eight months, I had prepared my plant project for the county fair's horticulture judging. I knew my antique chair planter was well done. After initial judging, I was incredibly upset because the winner had cheated. I was devastated at first, then angry. During final judging, I began chatting with Chase, a 4H kid in junior high; he was exhibiting his first fair project. Sadly, I learned his dad died in a car accident two years earlier. I was horrified. How could he focus on the fair? Suddenly I felt guilty for my selfish desire.

Later that evening, the young lady who 'won' first in the horticulture division withdrew. I could now sell my fanciful horticulture project (for a decent amount of college cash) or I could sell my apple pie for less money. I decided on my pie, so when my friend Chase sold his leafy green project (his only fair entry), I knew I had made the right decision. Seeing Chase's smile during the sale was perhaps my greatest joy; I earned less for my college fund, but my personal reward was much greater. Winning in 4H is tough; winning in life is tougher. That day, both of us won.

Clint Brown, Grade 12
New Waverly High School, TX

Why Am I Doing This?

"Why am I doing this?" is a question that comes to mind at around 3:30 after school every day. At this time I am usually in the middle of a cross-country practice that consists of anywhere from four to eight miles of running. As I feel my heart beat and lungs pump while everything else is numb, I ask this same question. It is a habit that I have probably developed trying to distract my brain from its desire to quit. Cross-country is a sport that is 50% physical conditioning and 50% mental conditioning.

So when I want to quit and start to wonder what I am doing this for I tell myself, "Why shouldn't I be able to do this when many people before me have gone through much worse." The Jews felt it as they were fleeing across the Jordan River from the pharaoh and a couple thousand years later again, through miles of snow, while pursued by Nazi soldiers. Jesus Himself was beaten and then forced to carry a cross a great distance also. As I draw all these connections I am able to distract myself for a good amount of time and finally finish the race. Cross-country running forces me to occupy my brain with many different thoughts as I conquer the desire to quit, and I believe I am a better person for it.

Ross Martinez, Grade 11
Valley Christian High School, CA

Music to "My" Ears

There is something I could not imagine life without, without it my life would have little, if any happiness. It is Music. There was actually a time when I only heard music and thought nothing more of it. But, one day I heard something that stopped me instantly. When I first heard it I did not make a sound until it was over when it did I thought "I will do that one day I have to." My breath was taken, and my hair stood on end. I realized I had ignored this beautiful, miraculous thing for reasons I cannot comprehend now. As the sound poured from the speakers it filled my mind, and has remained there since. With music I make anything the way I want it. There is just so much I can do with music. I can take any precious memory and make a song that will be with me for life. Even better I could write a song that everyone would cherish. To be able to have a positive effect on anyone with music is a great feeling. One lifetime would not be near the amount of time I wish to spend with music. Even if I do get to spend my life with music I will never want to sing my "last song."

Kolby Stafford, Grade 11
New Caney High School, TX

Negative Nancy

"Ha, well that doesn't surprise me," were the last words that were spoken. I looked at my mother who was standing by my side in disbelief of what had happened only moments before.

Golf has always been a part of my life. I play it, watch it, and sometimes teach it, but whenever I heard those last words uttered out of her mouth; I raised my white flag in surrender. No longer could I put up with the constant "Negative Nancy" that was a part of my everyday life. No longer could I take the love and fun out of golf only to be replaced by tactics and seriousness to fill the gaps.

As I was contemplating on whether or not I should play for my current team, or go play for another school, my decision hit me like a ton of bricks. I don't have to put up with the everyday "Negative Nancy" because golf is about playing the course, intimidating your opponents, and coming together at the end of the round under one common goal, a team.

The team I am on today is the team I was meant to play for. The obstacles that were overcome were merely stepping stones on the path to my final realization. Any other team doesn't have what it takes to play hard and succeed when all odds are against you, but whenever you have a team like my own, nothing is impossible with us, because the word impossible spells "I'm Possible."

Ryann Warner, Grade 12
Granbury High School, TX

Time Management

Many students are compelled to fill their agendas with many different extracurricular activities in order to become "well rounded" so applications for college look better. Though a well rounded person is more desirable, that person must be able to handle all their activities well in correspondence with everything life has to throw at them. Time management is key to any high school student looking to get involved at their high school.

Students become so involved that many activities interfere with each other. Taking challenging courses in high school is also recommended which leads to more homework and study time. The best time management tool for anyone is a planner. It is important to plan out the entire day and include homework, meetings, rehearsals, practices, or anything that can be forgotten. Frequently checking the planner allows the student to remember events before committing to anything that could become overwhelming. When becoming involved it is important to ensure time to rest and allow time for something that suddenly comes up or for any forgotten or last minute items that need to be taken care of. When a day comes that is not as busy as others, taking the time to reorganize and assess the upcoming days can be extremely beneficiary and prevent over stressing. When going throughout the day, it is helpful to keep a strong mental stamina and remember that anything can be overcome by trying hard and not giving up.

Michael Cole, Grade 11
La Serna High School, CA

Six Important Letters

Family can be just a six letter word or a huge component of our everyday lives. Parents, grandparents, brothers, sisters, aunts and uncles, etc. make my family. Family, the base of ancestry and it makes you who you are. The importance of family in life is having the love, care, and help whenever you need it.

My family is what truly and rightfully makes me who I am. Mostly, the ones always there for me are usually my family members in all my times. Family members can appear nice or mean, but you just have to live with them because they still remain your family. People can come out as polite or ill-mannered, but family remains inexpressible and very unique. Some of the people that I share my feelings with are my family. They can make fun of you, joke around, make you laugh, but when it really matters they are always there for you. Being there for someone whey they're sick, happy, sad, or anything else is the largest thing that I have encompassed.

People that are not appreciative for having a family should not have one because they have not experienced what it feel like to not have one. Good and bad times come and go, but once a family member is lost then it's very hard to get them back or sometimes even impossible. That's the motivation why I wake up every morning and express gratitude to God for giving me a family.

Saad Shams, Grade 11
Pine Tree High School, TX

A Life Changing Event

My name is Kalee Larcade, I am seventeen years old and I have a daughter that is two and a half years old. Her name is Alycia and she means the world to me. She is the best thing that ever happened to me.

I was heading down the wrong path but she took me out of it. I was hanging out with the wrong people, doing stuff that I most definitely should not have been doing, and was overall not a very good kid. But she took me completely out of that state and made me a good person. Because of the added responsibility that I had brought unto myself, I could not hang out with the people that I did or do the things that I was doing, so she saved my life.

Her father, who is eighteen, was also going down the same path that I was headed on during this time. That was how we met and became a couple. He was hanging out with the wrong crowd and made himself become enjoined in something that was not only illegal but completely stupid. Having a daughter is what truly changed him around.

She has brought so much joy into our lives that it is truly unexplainable. We cannot even imagine what it would be like without our little girl to hold in our arms when times are rough. She is beyond doubt a God's blessing gift to the world. She could never be replaced.

Kalee Larcade, Grade 12
University Preparatory School, CA

Another Day a New Dismay

I miss the days of high school when what to wear was the biggest problem. The times where what people thought of you was the issue. Not anymore; almost all the problems that used to seem important really don't seem that problematic anymore. Looking back now, those were all problems that could be fixed or gotten over with a little time. Now, today's issue is the rest of life! There is no getting around it and there is certainly no seeing how it's going to turn out. Everybody is just along for the ride. Right now I'm on the ever so fun college loop of this roller coaster. And I must say it has knocked me off my feet a few times. Luckily, no matter how many times it hits me, I'm always able to get back up and continue on. That's how all of life is I've come to find. How would anyone ever make it if we stayed down when we had a moment of "Oh my gosh I can't do it." Well, it turns out you can do it. That first step is the hardest, but once it has been taken the rest doesn't seem all that bad. I have come to find that life really does come at you fast and that Nationwide really isn't kidding. Car insurance doesn't fix everything but determination sure does. With that you can get through almost anything.

Sapphire McFarland, Grade 12
University Preparatory School, CA

Winter's Ritual

Winter, everyone in our family loves it when it's here and misses it when it's gone. It's in our blood, I suppose, our last name honoring the season the way it does. With winter comes cold. You quiver, snow falls, and it's lovely.

If and only if, the temperature is below fifty degrees does the wonderful thought of a fire enter our minds. Momma plays soft music in the kitchen while she sings along and bakes cookies that we eat until our hearts are content. Daddy puts on his coat and steps slowly into the dark night so that he can gather enough firewood to last us the night. I stay in where the cold is not apparent and make a cup of hot, hot chocolate for each member of the family. Everyone meanders into the room to gather a warm cookie and a cup, filled to the top with liquid love. Enveloped in our own soft blankets, we sit together for hours listening to the wood burn and the fire pop and we watch the flames wisp and fly.

Our cat falls asleep while he lies on his back with his head hanging over the side of the couch. He stretches his body so that he covers two of the three couch cushions, the glow of the fire showing in cloud-like forms in his long, soft fur. The fire quickly disappears, but only temporarily. The next time the thermometer drops, we'll be here again, enjoying the winters' ritual.

Victoria Winters, Grade 12
Granbury High School, TX

Swallowed Up by Sorrow

I heard the sound of crying and the faint ranting of the priest but I could care less. I felt a small hand grip my shoulder firmly. When I looked up, I saw a somber look upon my grandmother's face. Though she tried her best smile, it came out like a grimace.

I couldn't believe how childish I was acting. If my grandmother wasn't going to cry then neither was I. I never understood why she didn't cry until I heard her life story.

Her life was sad to say the least. She got married at a very young age to a cheater that left her with 4 kids. She had to stop pursuing her dream of becoming a RN to take two degrading jobs that barely kept food on the table. It wasn't until a couple years after her kids moved out that she was able to downsize to one job.

Things eventually turned around. My grandmother found her true love named Bill. Soon after they got married, she found a job in a hospital. Though she wasn't a RN, she was still happy to be working somewhere close.

Things turn worse again. Bill had developed cancer. Although he fought for a very long time, the cancer eventually won out. She never left his side until the day he died.

She wasn't being strong for anyone. She just wasn't letting sorrow rule her. She was celebrating Bill's life, not crying over his death. She wasn't letting sorrow stop her life.

Lauren Godinez, Grade 12
Granbury High School, TX

Classic Football

Lacing up your cleats and putting on your first pads are the classic memories of every football player. Your first big hit and your first touchdown are not far behind. These memories are with all football players forever. Football as it is today has not changed very much since the past. The players and coaches may be different but the heart and soul of the game remains pure and true. As a football player in high school I witness accounts of teamwork, unity, and brotherhood on a daily basis. No matter where we are whether it is in the locker room, at school during class, or even on the field during a big game, we are a family. We are there for each other when times get rough, and we stick it out together like any family would. When we are on the field we work together with all of the tools that have been given to us. We play our absolute hardest till the whistle is blown, every single play. When we play we leave it all on the field and play our hearts out. After a crushing defeat or a blow out win, we grow closer as a team. We see each other every day and we all know there is work to be done on the field. We lace up and prepare for battle and are willing to fight on every play. We are the Warriors of Valley Christian and we are classic football.

Matthew Mortensen, Grade 11
Valley Christian High School, CA

Stories of the World That Look Like Our Own

Most girls will never forget the first boy they had a crush on. One day I may forget that, but I will never forget the first time I fell in love. I was exactly three years and eight months old when I saw my first movie. It was *101 Dalmatians* and my eyes were glued to the screen the whole time. Of course, my crazy obsession with movies only started at that young age; it spun out of control when I was about 12. For me a film is more than a film. When I watch a movie, nothing else matters; time seems to stop and for two hours I'm in a world that only looks like my world. For most people a movie is a way to spend a rainy day. For me, movies are a stimulant for my imagination. When I see a movie I cannot help but analyze it. Movies are meant to show us how or how not to live, so I can't help but learn and relate to movies. What I love about movies is that they're a way of telling stories. Stories are a universal phenomenon that everyone understands. People love hearing and telling stories. Movies are unique in storytelling because you see the movement of the story. Storytelling is a force that most people underestimate. Stories and the movies that tell them have taken me to worlds that probably don't exist, yet I have been able to recreate them in my own backyard.

Rachel Hiatt, Grade 11
Valley Christian High School, CA

Interest Turned Passion

I stood up and walked to the middle of the auditorium with the rest of my classmates. Music and instrument in hand, I tried to calm down as I found my seat in the front row in the first chair. I never thought I would be in this position. I never thought that I would even *think* of being in this position. I never thought.

My heart raced as we started to play. I was nervous, so I ran out of breath quickly. I had never played in front of an audience before, and it felt like all eyes were on me. But, beside the frantic nerves I felt a sense of comfort.

I started playing the flute eight years ago. At first it was just an interest, like dance or soccer, but then it turned into something I couldn't live without. Not only was I good, but I knew I wanted to strive to become better. And once I reached that point there was no keeping me away from playing.

I used to practice for hours on end (as soon as I reached junior high and high school, I practiced less), and I would take my practice time very seriously. Anyone who disturbed me would be punished. On countless occasions, my mom had to force me to put my instrument down, come to dinner, and go to bed. She realized that I was inseparable from my talent; this was my passion. I had found where I needed to be.

Nicole Stanger, Grade 12
Northridge High School, UT

Sights and Sounds

Lady Liberty in her green billowy cloak and her matching green crown equipped with a tall row of spikes. She has a sudden case of "disco fever" with the sun's light shining like a disco ball. In the middle of the summer, in the middle of the afternoon, a lady liberty is dancing away as if there is no tomorrow. The sun beats down on every single inch of space in sight; no niche or corner could hide. The usually off-white building shone so bright it was as if an angel herself was in the building. The enormous pod tree across the street that covered the shopping center had refused to provide shade anymore. Instead it acted like a clear tent that was there for no other purpose than just decoration itself.

"What is she doing out there? Is she a street performer?"

I took a second or two to think about it, and then when I read the sign she was holding. It then dawned on me that she was a sign holder for the Liberty Tax Service.

Why would a street performer choose Aiea to showcase their talent? I debated.

Now it all made sense! I suddenly understood as the sun beat down on my face that although she was putting herself up for embarrassment, it was her job after all.

Lauryn Mow, Grade 12
Mililani High School, HI

Broken Heart

"Let my heart be broken with the things that break God's heart," this quote by Bob Pierce represents the children abandoned by society, the hungry going unfed, and the needy not getting their essentials taken care of. Every day these essential needs become dreams to some but not reality to others around the world in some places more than others.

Haiti, a third world country was not just some ordinary vacation; it was a youth group mission trip. The scenery was filled with every different type of trash you could think of covering the deceased grass as if shading it from the sun. Children were lined up at the gate looking at you as if they themselves are prisoners to their nation. The poorer children and adults walking barefoot in the hot dirt carrying fruit baskets, bricks, and other materials on their head either for selling or taking home to the family. This consumed my heart with sorrow for this nation's people.

Children gathered around us as if we were their entertainment. I bent down, a child came up to me and I taught the children patty cake, an original American children game. A trend began and the Haitian children started to bet the American youth. This made my little heart smile to make a Haitian kid's day by getting down and being personal no matter the language barrier. This journey would have once been a place of sorrow for me, but now it's a place where happiness has broken through my heart.

Courtney Reagan, Grade 12
Granbury High School, TX

Self and Swim

Everyone goes through some sort of issue or concern about their health or weight at some point in their life and mine happened to be during my elementary and middle school years. I was always slightly overweight and teased while growing up, which has definitely affected me as a person because I have been really self-conscious about my body. When I was a sophomore in high school, I decided that it was time to get involved in some kind of sport again to stay active and keep fit because eating right would only take me so far. I chose to join my school's swim team, which I was really hesitant about because I had no idea what to expect, but I did it.

Being on the swim team has got me in the best shape that I have ever been in, but it is not easy. Swimming taught me to think positive about what I can do. My coaches made me realize that I am actually stronger and much better than I think I am, which has made a huge impact on my self-confidence and thoughts on many things. I have improved and changed a lot mentally as well as physically since I started swimming, which has been the biggest thing holding me back in life. Experiencing such a great change and having it noticed by the people I know is one of the best feelings I have felt yet.

Raina Okazaki, Grade 11
American Renaissance Academy, HI

More Than Just Four Boys in a Van

The band Fall Out Boy has changed my life. I know it probably sounds cliché to say that about a band, but I really believe this to be true. I found out about this band when I was in the fourth grade by my cousin, who doesn't think much of them now. Before I heard their music, I had never really "heard" music. When I listened to their CD, I heard the voice, the lyrics that were speaking to me in a way I've never heard before. Soon after that, it became my mission to find out everything I could about the band. I felt like I knew them. The way they care so much about their fans just astounds me. More than once, they have set up online scavenger hunts leading up to new songs, or announcements about new albums. I call these hunts, "shenanigans" and they give me a headache most of the time, but I have discovered that most other fans of bands don't get the luxury of having so much interaction with the band members. With lyrics about finding love, losing love, or having it slip through your fingers, their songs helped me through a divorce, moving away, and bad days. All of the lyrics written by their bassist, I felt a deeper connection with his words than I have ever felt before. They are a huge part of me, changing my perspective on life, music, and writing. Without them, I wouldn't be myself.

Marguerite Castaneda, Grade 11
La Serna High School, CA

Taiko Life

I am a taiko performer. Taiko is Japanese drumming in which I have been involved for six years. Taiko has taught me many life skills that have and will help me to succeed in my personal life as well as in the world at large.

Through taiko I have learned self-awareness. I have gained a mental state in which I am happy with myself and not afraid to show who I am. When I was in middle school I was shy and afraid to be myself around others. Through learning how to perform and how to play solos, I learned that it's okay to be who I really am, even if others frown upon me when I do. I now strive to portray my true character and the person I was created to be.

Taiko has also raised my cultural awareness. I have learned about the importance of my heritage. Because of taiko, I have gone to many Japanese festivals and become a part of the tradition of Japanese culture. I have learned respect for my culture.

Taiko also helps create group cooperation. Every day we focus on "ishyoni" or being together. In order to play well, we have to work together. Without unity, the group will fall apart. Through installing this virtue in my everyday life, I know how to cooperate and work together in group situations.

Taiko has taught and instilled these virtues into my life and has created a better person in me.

Chelsea Chida, Grade 11
Valley Christian High School, CA

Not So Material Girl

A lot of people would say that their cell phone, or their house, or their car stakes the claim as the "most important" thing to them. For some reason, though, I cannot understand calling a material possession the "most important" thing to me. Some *things* I would not even call important to the slightest degree. Personally, I think it takes a deeper emotional, maybe even spiritual need for something before it can be declared *truly* important. Therefore, I have chosen drive and determination as an important thing to me.

A person with great determination and a strong drive that makes them want to succeed can push themselves beyond the limits that have been set for them mentally, and force them into a whole different realm of creativity and inspiration. This force could almost be considered supernatural, as it allows people to do things not only far beyond their expectations, but things surpassing the expectations of others.

Nothing even begins to compare to me when I truly want something. It completely consumes me. I think about it while I fall asleep. I make up game plans on how to get it while I dream. I wake up, still dreaming about it. I go all day with thoughts of it constantly burning in the back of my mind, bubbling to the surface whenever they can. Because of this passion and drive, most of the time, I achieve what I want to. Therefore, this quality means a lot to me.

Briatni West, Grade 11
Pine Tree High School, TX

Mi Papi

"You don't get it, and you will never understand!" is a statement used on a daily bases in a relationship between a teen and parent.

The thought of my dad not understanding me sends chills through my body. Who would I turn to when something goes wrong? Who would advise me or who could I trust enough with my problems? Many of my friends could answer these questions without a sweat: friends, other family members, or siblings, but no one in this world could give me support and love like my daddy does.

I believe that when he listens to me, he genuinely cares and wants to help make my life just a bit easier with his advice. A huge part of why I trust him is because of his strong relationship with God. I always hear from peers and family friends that I am so lucky to have someone put me in the center of his world. Sometimes I hardly recognize that this is true; but if I were to examine his life, his love for me is clearly shown. This is not to say that we have a perfect relationship as father and daughter, but there has never been a doubt in mind that everything happens for a reason, and that his intentions are always good.

Martha De La Vega, Grade 11
Faith Christian Jr/Sr High School, CA

Musical Theater

"Life is not a dress rehearsal." I like to live by this saying. I love musical theater. I live, breathe, eat and sleep it. Musical theater has so many aspects: vocal, dance, and acting. It's such a wonderful way to express oneself. I've been doing musical theater almost all my life. It's become a part of who I am. I enjoy every part of a show, from the first audition to the last bow. Even the downfalls shape me as a performer.

Theater can transform you. You can become a new person, live outside yourself. Add costumes, makeup, lights and a stage and voila! You no longer are the same person. Theater allows you to make many new friends, and it can make you a more confident person. Theater can teach you many valuable lessons. It teaches you patience. Rome wasn't built in a day and neither is a show. You have to have patience as piece-by-piece, song-by-song and step-by-step a show emerges. Theater also teaches you to never give up. Maybe you can't nail that pirouette or hit that high C the first time, but when you persevere and keep trying, you will one day! I think performing is one of the best things out there. If you don't believe me, maybe you should try theater yourself! Life is not a dress rehearsal; every day is opening night.

Sara Segal, Grade 11
Valley Christian High School, CA

My First Kiss

As we walked outside I remember thinking: "Wow she is absolutely the most beautiful girl in the entire world!" Her hair a natural golden blonde brighter than the sun. Her eyes green, greener than a flower petal. Her smile, a smile that would make my day better when I saw it. And of course her body. It was shaped perfectly and when I looked at it I got lost in imagination. She defined perfection!

At last, the moment had come. I stretched my shaking arms out and put them around her and pulled her body close to mine. I stared into her gorgeous eyes and smiled. As I leaned in for the kiss my world abruptly stopped spinning. For those few split seconds, it was just I and the girl of my dreams locked in a romantic moment that neither of us will ever forget. I remember clearly the warmth of her smooth lips brushing against mine. I can still feel her arms around my waist and her hands rubbing my back. I was lost in the moment, thinking only about our kiss. As the final seconds of it came to an unwanted end, I kissed her softly one last time and said to her in a sweet voice, "I will never forget this as long as I live."

Dustin Mosley, Grade 12
New Waverly High School, TX

Mother

Many people have come and gone in my life. I've had numerous friends, best friends, boyfriends, teachers, counselors, and very many people who I care for, and love dearly. But, there is one person who I have taken for granted too many times, and that person is my mother. The past couple of years, my mom and I have drifted far from the close relationship we used to have. Although, within the past couple of months, I feel like I have become a lot closer to her. About four weeks ago, her fiancé, and my soon to be step-dad had a heart attack and passed away. Seeing my mom in so much pain really changed the way I saw things. Being a single mom of two kids is never easy, and my whole life, my mom has worked so hard so me and my sister can have what we want and need. It was my turn to be there for her when she needed someone. I am a believer of things happening for a reason, and I think that God wanted me to respect my mother more, and it took the death of someone for me to see how important my mother is in my life. When it comes down to it, my family, Mother especially, is really the only one who has always been there for me since day one, and words truly can't describe how important she is to me, and how much I love her.

Rikki Jackson, Grade 11
Pine Tree High School, TX

Si-Da-Ne-Lv-Hi

This word describes the structure in my life. This word describes the people that are important to me in my Cherokee heritage. This word holds within it ancient wisdom of the ages. This word in Cherokee means family.

When I was young I didn't have a real driving force in life I didn't have anybody to guide me at least that's what I had thought. My family seemed distant from me and I felt as though I was a black sheep. My family was distant from each other and also from me. Then a great tragedy occurred in the family which no one had expected. My grandmother died. It seemed as though a great depression had swept throughout the family and my despair grew deeper. Then something changed on the day of the funeral there was a sense of somber kindness within our family everyone was getting along with one another. The family was happy with each other. My family started talking to me about everything I was going through with the family and they agreed that everyone was being very childish. We forgave one another for the first time.

Although the family suffered a great loss of my grandmother, it was a bittersweet day, because it brought the family back together. Now I have a structure of life and what needs to be done and I am a lot happier and thankful for that.

I love my family.

Brandon Moore, Grade 11
New Caney High School, TX

Clarity

As a young girl, all of my friends had their share of "boyfriends," but I was never one to have a boy hanging on my arm. I blamed it on my weight and my physical appearance, which led to self-consciousness. To this day, I have never had a boyfriend, and that used to really upset me. However, I began to realize that I should consider myself extremely lucky that I have never taken part in any type of relationship, because I still remain so young and so vulnerable to making mistakes. I feel that it renders tremendous importance to keep myself as pure as possible for my future husband, because, hopefully, he feels the same way for me. What many people do not take into consideration these days is that all of those emotions and actions that they willingly hand out like candy will eventually lose their value. Consequently, when those things should matter, they have become less genuine. How is saying "I love you" to your husband any more meaningful than when you said it to that cute boy in ninth grade, whose name you have already forgotten? I thank God that He chose to bless me with the realization of how my actions today could possibly effect my marriage later, rather than having to find out the hard way and wish that I had done something differently in my youth. Believing that my husband will appreciate all of my hard work definitely makes it worth the wait.

Theresa Pisano, Grade 11
Pine Tree High School, TX

Rambling Roadtrip

My mom tells us stories about when we were still really little, when it would take her a half an hour to get all five of us loaded in the car for a "road trip" to the doctor or dentist. She said that she would be exhausted before the trip even started.

But, as we grew, road trips became a little less laborious and a little more fun. We began to travel more often and go farther distances. Now we travel a lot, mostly by car. We have an eleven passenger van that we can cram full of our suitcases and bags, and off we go. Despite the large size of the van, there is never enough room for us to be comfortable, but somehow, that is what makes it all the more fun. We make do with a little bit of ingenuity and a lot of humor. As the scenery changes and the sun makes its way towards the west, we find little games to play or stories to tell. Jokes that would not normally be funny become hilarious, and we find pleasure in talking about the scenery that we see outside the window.

Traveling is my favorite way to spend time with my family. Something about being smashed together for hours on end makes us closer, no pun intended, than we otherwise would be.

Faith Philipp, Grade 12
Faith Christian Jr/Sr High School, CA

Determination

Don't you need determination to perhaps win a game, or put on a show? Of course, my mom told me to reach "for the gold," but my nerves always get the best of me and butterflies always develop in my belly. I have been in dance all my life, but even though I'm used to going on stage in front of a big audience, I still get the chills and my nerves pop in. My teachers give me strength and determination all the time to do my best and put my goals I want to achieve first hand, do you do the same?

Two years ago I knew this girl who went to dance with me but now lives in England. She was a great dancer who wanted to achieve dance as a career and move to big dance companies, but she had one problem, fear. Every time she saw a huge crowd her nerves would tingle up and she would freeze. One recital she was actually so nervous when performing one of her solos that she ran off stage. Even though she was amazing, she didn't realize it, and she couldn't go for all she had because of lack of determination. It didn't matter what anyone told her; she didn't believe in herself enough to go out there and strive to be the best.

Determination is a part of life and if you don't believe in yourself how do you expect to achieve your goals and dreams?

Krystine Mohr, Grade 10
Kaufer High School, TX

Determination

As the great runner Steve Prefontaine once said "To give anything less than your best is to sacrifice the gift." Many people might think that giving your best only applies to running and other sports, but it also includes academics as well. When someone asks me about my best quality, I quickly respond with the answer "my determination" and smile afterwards. I belong to the math/science team at my high school, and I can say that I compete as viciously as others who compete in sports and other activities because I believe math is very entertaining.

As a current state champion in number sense, one of the subjects in math/science, I can honestly say that ninety-nine percent of the battle depends on your will power and the other one percent depends on your natural skill. Although my natural gift to perform math outweighs most, my desire to succeed exceeds even that of my gift. Without the determination to excel in either a sport or in any sort of academics, you will not prosper as well as those who do have the heart to try harder. Whether someone has more innate talent than you or not, nothing can overcome the will to improve. If I did not have the determination I acquire now, I would not be so proud of myself and all of my accomplishments.

Shereef Elhalwagi, Grade 11
Pine Tree High School, TX

The Move

The most dreaded day of my entire young life suddenly arrived. I knew we would be moving away from the only home I had ever known. However, it snuck up on me like a storm forms, quick and ruthless.

As my family entered our time worn light brown Ford van I realized this was the last time I would ever see the familiar red and tan brick of my house. The sparkling canal and our dark red ski boat would evolve from an important aspect of my life to nothing but a memory. Although all of these things were important to me, bigger worries jumped around inside of my head. The reality of moving to a completely different state started filling my brain. Every aspect of our new home in Green Bay, Wisconsin would be alien to me; nonetheless, we would be alien to the people in Green Bay. My best friends from the time I was three years old would live over a thousand miles south back in my hometown Granbury, Texas moving on with their lives while I'll be in a foreign place wishing I was there with them. I realized this move was going to cause more problems than I ever dreamed it could.

Our van was about to turn the corner, blocking the view of my house and everything I had ever known. My life was about to change like day turns to night. I thought to myself, this is the start of long suffering.

Paul Helm, Grade 12
Granbury High School, TX

Childhood Memory

As we got in the car to make our long ride to Schlitterbahn, my heart began frantically pounding. On the ride there I was excited to be finally beginning our journey.

We finally arrived and I couldn't contain my excitement. It seemed like I waited in line for years before I rode my first ride, but eventually we made it. I jumped on the slide and was ready to go. What an amazing feeling, finally going down the endless wet slide.

The slide that I rode down led into one big slide where I would meet with my parents and sister. As I looked ahead of the slide, I noticed this one led into two different slides. I wasn't going to hold mommy's hand. I would stay with my parents and everything would be fine. But no, I went down the other slide and immediately started crying. I felt my heart dropping by the second. I would never be with my family again; I began to cry more and more. I let my lifeless body float in the lazy river and waited. I felt body after body touching me, looking up each and every time hoping it was mom or dad.

After a couple of hours I completely lost all hope. But suddenly I heard "TAYLOR!" I couldn't believe my eyes, and I would never leave my mom or dad's side again. I learned that no matter how old you get, you're never too cool to hold mommy's hand.

Taylor Dollins, Grade 12
Granbury High School, TX

Donating Your Time Pays

"The best thing a person can donate is their time" and "though life can be transient, one's contributions will live on." Volunteering not only gives you a chance to reach out but opens new doors to experience and learning as well. What matters most is that you went out of your way to show that you cared.

For years my family and I occasionally spend time at a nursing home; entertaining and conversing with the seniors. Although I've heard their stories countless times, patience is what it is about and I've come to realize that aging, loneliness, and illness are inevitable. Now, my family and I also spend three to five hours every Saturday at Life Care Center with the residents.

A few of the many other experiences I've had are tutoring others and helping at the Food Bank. We all have our weaknesses and without the help of others, I too wouldn't have made it this far. Billions of people are plagued with poverty and with it comes death that could have been prevented. But we can help make poverty history. As I packed boxes of food at the Food Bank, it occurred to me just how fortunate I am to not have to worry about my meal.

Although I have helped in only these small ways, the experiences have benefited me greatly: rewarding me with a smile and a happiness that money can't buy. After all, the best verb next to "to love" is "to help."

Jessica Chen, Grade 12
Galena High School, NV

War on Terrorism

One of the worst issues to me at this moment in my life is the war on terrorism. This affect me personally in two different ways, and affects the community that surrounds the whole United States of America and me.

The reason why this war on terrorism is affecting me is that I don't know what this war is really for, so I feel that there is no reason to be at war. Ever since this war has started I have tried to find out what it was about, and each time I received something different shall it be we are at war over oil, stop terrorism, rebuilt Iraq, or to save Iraqis' lives.

I feel as there is no real reason for the United States to be at war and they have two of my family members that are over there fighting for the United States risking their lives. I look up to both of my family members and of positive role models. I looked up to them my whole life, and they inspire me to do better for myself.

This doesn't just hurt me but it hurts the United States. It hurts the people who have family who are fighting and have already given their lives for the U.S. in this war.

I feel that the war needs to stop it's hurting America and me. It's good to see troops are evacuating. I just want my family home and the families of the U.S. to be at peace.

Jalen Vazquez, Grade 12
Coronado High School, TX

Having Good Friendships

Friendship, friendship is more than just saying "hello" in the hallways and having someone to keep you company. Friendship is that person who is loyal to you during the hardest times in life: someone you can trust at all times and can rely on for everything. A true friend lifts you up and never tears you down. A good friend who truly loves you will never want to intentionally hurt you in any way. If one of your friends does something purposely to hurt you, you may want to consider asking yourself why you are friends with them. You need to make sure your friends have a good influence in your life and encourage you to make good decisions, as well.

Forgiveness is key to a good relationship. A friend might betray you, but forgiveness is still necessary. You may need to be on your guard with them, but you know in your heart you have forgiven them for what they have done. No one is perfect, everyone has flaws, and we all have issues. We need to be willing to forgive others just like we want them to forgive us. If we expect to be given grace for wrongs we have committed, we should understand that grace will only be given to us if we are willing to give it.

Camille Holm, Grade 11
Valley Christian High School, CA

Drinking in College

It seems like people these days just want to go to college to drink and party. They don't care about their education or their future. Our generation needs to wake up and realize that they won't be able to live their life happy without college. What is drinking going to do for you? You go out, get drunk, and can't remember anything from that night, not to mention you wake up with a headache. College should be fun and a new learning experience; somebody should control drinking in college better. More than 3,000 teens die every year from drinking and driving. Some kids just do it because they think it's cool, or they want the popular kids' attention. I understand drinking to relax, but there is a limit and you should know where to stop. It is ridiculous that people say it's addictive because if you never started drinking in the first place then you wouldn't have a problem. You can go to pep rallies, football games, softball games, soccer games, and wrestling matches and still have fun without drinking. However, some colleges have their pros and cons and you just have to find the right college. College is and should be a place where you decide what you want to do for the rest of your life, not a club or drinking place.

Mary Hise, Grade 12
Coronado High School, TX

To Dream of the Sea

For me, to dream of the sea is breathtaking. You have the sight stretching beyond the horizon for eternity, with the smell that is fresh but salty; the sound of the tide coming in, crashing into the shores is so amazing to see. The touch of the sea is cold but warm caressing your skin with a gentle breeze.

The time of being a part of a sea will always be a part of me. The sea was everything I dreamed of since I was younger. The sight of seeing a jellyfish as small as a penny and as big as a meter stick just a few feet next to me was amazing. The feelings of being able to see dolphins soaring over the waves, being free, were indescribable.

Even though the sea holds dangerous things below as well as above, it brings in a magical sensation when you look upon it, anywhere in the world. The sea represents freedom as well as history and myths. Poseidon and Titanic, the god of the sea and the unsinkable ship, which both have history, as well as a myth to them.

So, the dream of the sea is just a part of me, just like something you believe in is a part of you.

Ashley Jones, Grade 10
Coronado High School, TX

My Guidance Through My Years of High School

It has only been two years since my freshman and sophomore years, they seem like forever ago. I struggled my freshman year with Geometry, and my sophomore year with World History.

For Geometry, I had Mrs. Keyes, who still teaches this course today. Notes did not help me whatsoever. When I looked to my notes for help on homework, I got confused. I went to tutorials every morning for help. Emily Paulison helped me get through this difficulty. As I obtained more help from Emily, my grades improved. I finally obtained the grades I wanted, but it came at a price. I had to actually admit to myself that I needed help, and then go ask for it. I got through this struggle, and moved on to another.

I struggled in World History last year. I received the grades that I wanted to make, but I had a hard time grasping the information. The college level work had levels of difficulty that confused me. World History had strenuous material throughout the course. I also had to endure the dull book issued to us. Emily explained what was going on in that period of time, and I listened intently.

Emily prevails in academics, is selfless, and she remains tolerant of me. She will regularly go out of her way and help me with any tough problems that may come across in my homework. She helped me almost all year long, for the past two years. I extend my gratefulness to Emily.

Kaitlyn Kasperitis, Grade 11
Flour Bluff High School, TX

The Baby Is Finally Here

I was sixteen years old, and nine months pregnant. Everyone wanted the baby to be born all ready. I couldn't go anywhere, nor do anything. I didn't feel like myself anymore. Throughout my whole pregnancy I didn't know whether I was having a girl or boy. My boyfriend, Ivan, and his family were dying to know what gender I was expecting.

It was five thirty in the morning. I woke up and went to the bathroom. I pulled my pants down and felt a lot of water. I went to my mom's room and let her know that my water had just broken. She slowly woke up, and told me not to worry.

My mom said "wake up Ivan, and let's go to the hospital." We got there at six in the morning. I was put in a room; where I was going to be delivering my baby. My pain was getting worse. I had high blood pressure; I couldn't relax.

Twenty one hours had passed by. I couldn't bear the pain; I decided to get the epidermal. It's a shot that pregnant women get when they're in labor. The shot numbs from your waist down. I couldn't feel anything for the next two hours.

My baby was born at four thirty-four on December 27, 2008. She was the most beautiful baby I've ever seen. I was surprised and really happy that I had a girl. I named my baby Kamila Dolores Garcia. I took her home one day later. I was happy to have her there. I wouldn't trade her for the world.

Sabrina Lizama, Grade 12
Omega High School, CA

A Blessing!

You never really know what you have until it's gone. My foster brother Anthony was a huge uplifting part of my life. We have had him since birth of June 1st, 2009 because his mother did drugs while she was pregnant and had to give him up. This child has been a blessing and such a joy in my life.

Today Anthony is a year old and is now living with his mother part time and the other time with my family. I am very grateful that Anthony's mother was able to get her life in order and that Anthony has his mother back, but every day, I pray that she doesn't fall off track because all of her hard work will have gone to waste. I look to Anthony's mother as an example of how I don't want my life to be. I love and adore her, but I feel like the mistakes she made and the people she hung out with were because of the idiotic things that are happening to her now.

Even though she has overcome hard obstacles, her son, my brother deserves to have the best life that he can receive. I always tell my mother how grateful I am to have a mother like her, who loves and supports me and is always there for me. I pray that Anthony's mother will be the mother that her son needs. They will always be in our hearts and in our prayers.

Victoria Cairns, Grade 11
Valley Christian High School, CA

Death, the Renewing of the Soul

Death is a dreadful experience for anyone. Yet it brings reason and insight to a person's soul. My first encounter with death was my seventh grade year. My grandpa was in his late eighties and his physical condition was gradually deteriorating. My grandpa had been in the hospital before, and I thought he would gradually stroll out of there as on previous occasions. But this time I was wrong. One late afternoon my mom called the house. I picked up the phone; in an anxious tone of voice she said, "Yutaka, tell Dad, he and you need to rush to the hospital right now." At first I did not understand what was happening. I had never heard my mom sound so tense and worried before. So my father and I dropped everything and rushed to the Santa Teresa Hospital. My dad drove like a maniac down the highway. He parked the car with haste and promptly made out way to the floor where my grandpa lay. All my cousins surrounded the bed; he was living off the machines, and could not support himself any longer. We all said our goodbyes. His heart rate gradually fell. I didn't have a grandpa anymore. At first my feelings were of loathing and sorrow. But I soon was able to appreciate the small moments in life, the moments that people take for granted. From then on I was by no means the same.

Yutaka Rodriguez, Grade 11
Valley Christian High School, CA

Autobody

Autobody is a wonderful program taught at my high school, Spanish Fork High School. We learn to repair and/or replace body panels on vehicles. We also learn to prepare vehicles for paint, and how to paint the vehicle.

First year students are taught the basics such as small dent repair, priming, sanding, and some welding. Second year students are taught more advanced subjects such as tinting, blending, painting, custom painting, etc. The teacher is awesome and very skilled at autobody and collision repair. When it is time to be out in the shop, he is right out there with us either helping someone, or working on a project of his own. He is constantly helping me or giving me advice on what approach I should take to complete my task.

Second year students will spend most of their time in the shop working usually on their own project vehicles that they bring in. First year students spend a lot of time in the classroom and watching demos, but only until they have the hang of what to do. They then fix a small dent, and pass it off. After that they work on a class project, which is usually an 80's Chevrolet pickup.

Overall autobody is an amazing class and gives me a chance to show my abilities. It has taught me patience and hard work. I would recommend autobody to anyone who is looking for a fun relaxed class and has an interest in cars.

Philip Thomas, Grade 12
Spanish Fork High School, UT

Shelby Lyn Allen

When my best friend Brianna told me that Shelby had died, it didn't hit me for the longest time. I mean, how could somebody that I know, used to go to school with and played on numerous volleyball teams with just overnight be gone? It didn't make sense. I tried to let it sink in, but it wouldn't. After calling my friends to hear their take on the events that happened on the night of December 20, 2009, it started to hit me. No more volleyball team, no more hanging out with friends, no more longboarding, no more school, no more being a teenager, no more living for Shelby Allen. Her very short life had ended because of her choice to drink irresponsibly. To this day, I wish I could have been there when her friends who were partying with her made the decision that she would be fine propped up against the toilet, so I could have intervened. I also thought that God should have not let her life be over like that, not that way, not that early.

But then I think how different so many lives that she had touched would be, how we would of not learned what it is like to loose someone you know, especially to a factor like alcohol that is so easily preventable. I know that for me, my life will be forever changed and I will always have the memory of Shelby living inside of me.

Sofia Prokop, Grade 12
University Preparatory School, CA

Conquering Calvington

Longboarding is my favorite pastime. I build as well ride as longboards. My friends and family have always known me for my ability to create anything I put my mind to. I rushed out the door to a local metal shop. A man appeared out of his office. We cut out the longboard. It was finished; all that was left was to ride it. I called all of my friends with longboards together to go test out my newly invented and freshly finished longboard.

The largest hill in Pecan is on Calvington Court. As I sat at the top of the hill, I stared at the steep drop off that quickly fell downward as if the drop was the side of the earth dropping off into an abyss. I rose to my feet and stepped onto my board. All I could think of was how flimsy it seemed, though just hours before, I had praised how wonderful it was. I pushed off, overcoming my fear, and dropped down the hill. It seemed as if I were flying down the hill. My muscles were tensed. The hard left turn was now here; I leaned hard back into the turn, soaring around the corner. The pressure and stress instantly dropped as the hill sloped gently back up slowing my board. I came to a stop. I stepped off my board, legs shaking, and sank to the ground in relief. I had conquered the hill with my new board.

Riley Toon, Grade 12
Granbury High School, TX

Rookie

I was at the Granbury High School baseball fields. The bleachers were full, and the crowd was cheering. I could hear my dad shout to me, "Come on, son," as I stepped into the batter's box.

The coach was anxious to see what I could do as I started my varsity debut. The voices of the cheering could be heard from a mile away. All of them cheering for me to come through in this clutch situation. If you knew how this moment felt you would understand my actions at that very moment.

As I stepped into the batters box, I could feel the goose bumps start to form on my skin. I was ready for anything.

Here came the pitch. The umpire signaled as he yelled out "strike one!" The next pitch barely caught the corner of the strike zone. "Strike two!" yelled the ump. I stepped out of the box and took a deep breath as I said to myself "this is it." I entered the box again to get my last chance to come through. I could see fire come from him as he approached the pitchers mound. He looked at the catcher for his signs. I have never been this scared in my life. He threw his best pitch, a nasty slider. As Coach Hart told me before the at-bat "just keep your weight and hands back" I did. I waited on the slider and "POW!!" I hit the game winning home run. I was relieved to have finally proven myself.

Bryan Hickey, Grade 12
Granbury High School, TX

They Pay for Our Freedom

Our freedom does not come from being born in the U.S.A., moving here, or even living here. Our freedom comes with a price tag, but not for any specific amount. This cost can never be replaced. Freedom comes from those hearts that are brave, willing, and determined. Freedom physically stands upon the battlefield, freedom waves in the wind — honored as we, the people; possibly its family, salutes it, and freedom sheds wet tears and blistering red blood. Freedom never gives up. Its battles are fought until conquered and even further. It began his journey on July 4th, 1776 and continues *every* day to fight for its country by air, by land, by sea. Freedom fights here, freedom fights there. It's protected, loved, respected, admired, and thanked — just not enough. The United States realizes on *holidays* how important freedom is, but during morning announcements, in newspapers, TV news reports, and even history classes do we then *remember* how grateful American citizens should be for freedom? Those that wake *every* day for freedom are those fighting and dying…so pay your remembrance *every* day for those that bought Freedom.

Morgan Briesmaster, Grade 10
Northridge High School, UT

Selfless

"Therefore I tell you, do not worry about your life, what you will eat or drink; or about your body, what you will wear. Is life not more important than food and the body more important than clothes?" Matthew 6:25-27. For 30 hours, I lived out this verse.

It was Disciple Now weekend, and I was excited as always. I arrived at the church, and everyone was waiting on the bus. This weekend we would be fasting for 30 hours while helping those less fortunate.

We arrived at the apartments. Starting off in our "echo" groups, went around to the apartments, and knocked on the doors. After helping with what needed to be done, we prayed with the residents, and then we moved to the next apartment. We did this for about an hour, and then moved to the apartment playgrounds. All the children who lived there gathered to the yard, and we played many games. Hunger was not on my mind. My focus was fully on Christ and helping these families.

When it was time to hand out lunches to the kids, hunger hit my stomach full blast. I asked God to keep my focus on the good we were doing. The time for us to leave had arrived, and the families were greatly appreciative of everything we had done.

Though this experience was difficult, it showed me to not take everything I have for granted, and to be thankful each day for what is given to me.

Stormi Bailey, Grade 12
Granbury High School, TX

Family

Family is a bond from God that can never be broken; my family has an amazing bond. I was born into a Christian home with loving parents that care for me so much and support me in everything I do. Some children are not lucky enough to have parents that love them, but I do. The first thing I am thankful for is my parents taught me about Jesus Christ. If I did not have the parents I do, I might not have ever learned about a man that is so important to me. Secondly, they taught me about love, and how important it is in every relationship. They don't only teach me about it, they show me love through their actions. They show it through supporting me in my decisions, coming to watch me in all of my activities, and disciplining me when I do something wrong. Some parents think not disciplining their kids is love but I believe discipline is love because they care enough to show you that you are doing wrong. My family also makes an effort to spend time together. It is not an easy thing to get everyone together, but somehow we manage to do so. My family is also very close, we are even close to aunts, uncles, and cousins. I believe the reason we are so close is because our family cares and loves each other. I thank God every day for sending me such an amazing family.

Emily Gothard, Grade 11
New Caney High School, TX

A Life Well Heard

Music, it's everywhere. From the streets of Chicago and New York, to inside your own head. It comes in many different genres, from heavy metal to classical piano. Everyone has a different idea of what music should be. Music has been important to me my whole life, without it I would not be who I am today. I listen to a very diverse group of music. Depending on how I feel at that time, I can listen to the eardrum bursting of Deycfer Down and then jump to the workings of one of my good friends, who writes piano music. Many great musicians have said things like, "Music is what feelings sound like." —Author Unknown, or my favorite, "When words leave off, music begins." —Heinrich Heine. Music is, to me, not something that is just heard, not just words on a page or notes from an instrument, it is something that comes from deep inside you, from your soul. Music is the one thing that people can fall back on when all hope is lost. It is created when we are at a highest of highs, or our lowest of lows in life. That is why music is so important to me, it has stayed by my side through everything, thick or thin. I will always have something to fall back on, — my music.

Rachel Meadows, Grade 11
Pine Tree High School, TX

El Barco

The unneeded half of the board falls from the saw horse after cut by expertise, in the background the clink of nails coming to reside in their final resting places. The cause of these sounds: spending time with my dad.

My dad has played an enormous influential role in my life. He has helped me to become more creative, improvise, how to build things, and the mechanics of how things work. I can think of one time where he incorporated all of these "lessons" and afterwards I admired him even more due to the successfulness of the project. The project itself was a canoe building kit. Supposedly it would be possible to finish this kit in a weekend. However my dad likes to go above and beyond. This extra effort is one of the lessons that have influenced me; meaning that now I see how important taking pride in everything I do, and doing it to the best of my abilities is. For example, after all the woodworking was finished, and a fully formed canoe residing in our garage, my dad decided that the canoe should have end plates, rails, three keels, fiberglass, paint, and name our masterpiece.

At the start of the project I didn't think completion a possibility. However, I am glad we chose to embark upon this journey. Without having done so, I would have not grown closer to my father, or have received all the important influential bits and advice from him that I now carry with me.

Jim Norton, Grade 12
Granbury High School, TX

My Love for Tennis

Playing sports has always interested me. I have played team soccer, basketball, and volleyball. In addition, I have participated in dance, swim, and track. However, tennis ranks as my favorite activity. I have played on Pine Tree High School's varsity tennis team for three years.

My first exposure to tennis occurred at four years of age. I chased balls for my mother when she attended tennis drills. I cherished my first tennis experience as ball girl. My love for tennis developed before I gripped my first racket at nine, and I do not expect to ever put it down.

My other sports experiences have helped my tennis game. For example, the foot work in soccer facilitated my movement on the tennis court. Basketball helped me develop a strategy for competing, knowing when and where to put the ball. Track increased my endurance. I wanted to play tennis because I liked hitting the ball. I have always enjoyed playing, and find winning a match very satisfying. Losing can challenge a player, but always encourages me to try harder.

Tennis players work hard. I have been on the court when the temperature hit a 100 degrees, and I thought the match would never end. I have also attended drills when it seemed I could not hit a ball over the net. In the end, everything always seemed better when I would win that one point that seemed impossible. Sports do not define me; they make me complete.

Anna Chamness, Grade 11
Pine Tree High School, TX

Respected Freedom

Living in a country with as much freedom as we are allowed is not always a positive thing. Although we are very blessed to have a country with such independence, some people take advantage of our liberty.

As our country grows and develops, one may notice the immature people that take our freedom for granted. For example, there are many opinions about President Obama, but no matter what one may think, he is still our president, who we must respect. Therefore, the governor that yelled out, "You're a liar," during his speech should have been removed from his office. As one has the right of freedom of speech by the first amendment, President Obama is still worthy of respect. Furthermore, our country is also one of the few that is self-governed and many want to be a part of our establishment. As our country accepts immigrants from other countries at our own will, there should be a law that pushes for respect to our pledges. I live in a town where we have many different races, as well as immigrants. We have students that sit in their desk during our pledges as respect to their country. If our country is so much better than the one that he or she came from, I don't understand why one refuses to at least stand up and respect our independence.

Although we are known for the land of opportunity, we should be respected for it as well.

Cheyenne Miller, Grade 12
Post High School, TX

Twins

I remember the first time I ever looked at my little brother and sister. So cute, lying in the hospital nursery, all red and their skin all shriveled, looking kind of like little raisins, or old people. I always thought newborn babies looked funny. However, I knew that these two would grow out of their gross-looking newborn stage and be very important to me. I was right.

My little brother and sister are now four year olds, my little twins. They are such a handful it's ridiculous. You can never have a moment of peace and quiet around my house, and they drive everyone crazy. However, they make up for it in everything else they do. It is so worth all the chaos and noise in the house of having them at those moments when they come up to you after a long day, wrap their arms around you in a hug and say "I missed you big sister." Or when you're out in the backyard and one of them picks a flower and says "Look, this pretty flower is for you, Jackie!" I miss them and even talk about them when I am gone away from home for a long time, however much I do enjoy the peace and quiet. They are my little twinners, I've looked out for them ever since they were little babies, they mean everything to me, and no amount of quiet would make me want to trade them.

Jacqlynn Peavler, Grade 12
Northridge High School, UT

Smile

Christopher Carter teaches me to enjoy life. A simple ten-year old kid, who enjoys swimming, playing kickball, and shooting hoops, has no idea of the amount of impact he has had on my life. I have spent much of the past five summers as a day-camp counselor for ages 5-12 at my local recreation center. I spend time with about one hundred children each day, but Christopher Carter stands out. He stands out because he is always smiling, always laughing, always having a great time. Christopher Carter is a child with a severe case of Down syndrome, a genetic condition in which a person has 47 chromosomes instead of the usual 46. When I first met Chris, I was intimidated and did not know how to interact with him; I questioned even approaching him, worried how he would react to me. One day, all the campers were playing in the gym, and I noticed Christopher shooting alone on a basketball goal. He turned and saw me and motioned for me to come his way. I walked next to him, and he took a shot. He makes the shot and began smiling and putting his hand up for a high five. I high-fived him, and immediately, all those unnecessary worries and doubts I brought up in my mind went away. Christopher Carter taught me to enjoy life; he is always smiling, always laughing, always having a great time.

Jordan Bookstaff, Grade 12
Bellaire High School, TX

Aaliah

My mom once told me "give more than you take." That's when I was around 8 years old. I didn't understand what she meant then but now I do, sort of. Life is based on helping others less fortunate, children, and anyone who needs it.

There is this girl named Aaliah she is in 4th grade and she was left to be cared for by her grandparents. Her mother couldn't care for her because her new husband refused to have Aaliah in the house. So the mother made the choice to send her to live with her grandparents. Aaliah thought it was a temporary thing that would last a week max but she then discovered that it was permanent.

Just recently her grandmother was taken to the hospital with something very serious so her grandfather decided to take Aaliah to live with us because he couldn't care for her. His job interfered with taking her to school so she came with us. One night I woke to her crying and we talked for a while and she kept on saying that none of her family wanted her. The only thing I could think of saying is that she will always be part of our family and is always welcome.

I think that family is not based on your blood line but by who will always stick by you and always help you out of the bad times that are in your life.

Tammy Rodriguez, Grade 10
Kaufer High School, TX

Priorities

Slow down! Take a look at your life! What are your priorities?! Your grades? Your college? Your career? Your future? Is that all you think about? Do you look so far ahead that you miss what is standing right in front of you?! Like your friends, family, and God? Would you sacrifice your adolescence for an extra GPA point; a lifelong friend to an overcrowded schedule? For too long I have seen best friends grow apart because one of them has too much work and can't make time; or they have too many extracurricular activities to spend a weekend building their friendship that will outlive any career.

I say to you, my peers, stop worrying! Put your life in God's hands, for through the darkest nights he will provide. He can take care of your needs, but only you can restore your relationships. Do not misinterpret. Grades are important, but they're nothing compared to your relationships with your friends and your Savior! I say to you once again, put your priorities where they will not change. Take time to invest in your entire life rather than just the future.

Eric Bergen, Grade 11
Valley Christian High School, CA

Lessons from a Chocolate Chip Cookie

It is easy to go through your entire life and never be truly happy. English poet Philip Larkin testifies that "most people are unhappy, don't you think?" I however, disagree with Mr. Larkin, the source of my disagreement being a delicious chocolate chip cookie. How can something so simple solve so complex an enigma, one may ask; the answer lies in the question — a chocolate chip cookie is simply delightful.

My enlightenment occurred within the first bite I took of the ambrosial little cake. The appealing aroma, agreeable chocolate chips, and appetizing cookie all came together to perform a veritable symphony in my mouth. I found that I could not help but smile as I consumed the cookie, and in that moment, I discovered true happiness.

This simple dessert solves the riddle of happiness in life. From this cookie, I learned that happiness is not complicated; from this cookie, I learned that happiness derives from finding joy in the numerous little moments throughout life that make you smile. One simply must find a chocolate chip cookie moment every day, and savor each delectable bite. This lesson is best summed up by American novelist Edith Wharton, "If only we'd stop trying to be happy, we'd have a pretty good time." Indeed, this is a lesson everyone should take to heart; instead of being devoured by greed, and the thirst for material wealth in life, we should all slow down, take a deep breath, and enjoy life's simple pleasures.

Brandon Kopper, Grade 12
Coronado High School, TX

My Many Names

Of all the English speaking countries I have been to, no one has been able to pronounce my name correctly. The name has Greek origin, and apparently, my name means "Greek goddess" and "the mother of the sun, moon and the dawn," even though these meanings do not sound quite like me. In Norway, my home country, I have found a lot of other people with the same name, so even though I like the name itself, I have mixed feelings about it. I prefer the name Anna, actually, a name that needs no spelling or pronunciation explanation.

I share names with the one I look up to the most: my grandmother. During World War II, she spent her spare time being a secret spy, which makes her pretty cool in my eyes. I can picture her sneaking behind old, dusty houses without making a sound, but I have to try hard to picture her without white, curly hair.

My name sounds like lemons, strange and sharp, but sometimes sweet. It all depends on who pronounces it, though; some people make the name Thea sound ice cold like a needle poking through old fabric. The first time people try to say it, they put the tip of their tongue on their teeth, and make it sound like spitting. I usually correct them, but after a while I give up, and let them think my name is Theya. It does not really bother me that I have a dozen names; I feel like I have multiple personalities.

Thea Kolmannskog, Grade 12
Flour Bluff High School, TX

That Old Yellow Dog

She was my best friend through thick and thin. I never had something more valuable to me than my yellow dog, Casey. She had thick yellow hair, and a lavish collar that hung just right around her neck. She meant the world to me. I could tell that she knew my feelings. When I was disappointed or stressed, she would cuddle up close to me and help me feel alive and make me feel as if I had a purpose. She also knew when I was happy because she would be willing to play around and she would brighten my day. We had an inseparable bond. Everywhere I went, she followed. I felt as if she needed to be treated just the same as I was. If I could sleep in a nice comfy bed and eat delicious food, then Casey should be allowed to also. Every fiber in my bone wanted to have the best for her. I could not seem to understand why she slept in a cage at night or had hard and mushy food. Many of times my mother explained to me that Casey was a dog, but knew she was just as equal as me. From the day I received her when she was just a pup, to the day she died as an old dog, I loved her the same. My love for her grew over time. Since her death, I still think of her, knowing she will always be in my heart.

Lauren Harris, Grade 11
Pine Tree High School, TX

Photography

Photography can capture a moment in time, freeze an image and create a memory to look back on. My grandpa's mastery of the craft sparked my desire to pursue the dream I have now, of becoming a professional photographer myself. Photography is unlike any other form of art. In photography you do not see paint or pencil marks. Photographs are unique in the way that they reflect the true image of the object, not the artist's personal perspective. With photography I can view the world through something as simple as a lens. I can see things from a different perspective through a camera such as nature, people, places, anything.

Photography gives me the unique ability to capture any moment in time as long I have a camera in my hand. This is where I can find pure, unadulterated happiness. With a simple click of a button I can capture the essence of life itself. Photography opens up my eyes and enables me to view the world a whole new way. There's more than meets the eye when it comes to photographs. No photograph goes without a story; even the simplest picture can become the proverbial "picture worth a thousand words." There is nothing more satisfying than taking a gorgeous photo, knowing that I have captured the beauty of that one moment for all to see and for me to share. Photography is an art, an expression, a story, my passion.

Kyle Paskett, Grade 11
Valley Christian High School, CA

Childhood Stories

I think that everyone has had a childhood of their own. Maybe it was one they would want to forget. Maybe it was one they would want to remember for the rest of their lives. I, for one, would never trade it for the world. I loved my childhood. It was filled with play and laughter and imagination.

There were many times in my youth when I would think nothing of the world outside of my playhouse. It was my own world. It was the place where I could come and be whatever my heart desired. It was the place where my imagination poured out like an ever flowing stream. I pretended I was a doctor and fix the boo-boos my toys had. I pretended I was the waiter at the most magnificent restaurant at the top of the city. I pretended I was everything.

My childhood was the building blocks of the mindset that I have today. It was the time when I experimented with what I wanted my future to become. When all my inhibitions never existed and I could just do as I please in my little sanctuary of a playhouse. Those were the days when I decided on all the things I would do when I grew up. Those were the priceless days that I would never trade it for the world.

Aileen-Ann Patoc, Grade 12
Mililani High School, HI

My Family

The most important thing to me is my family. Yes, we don't always see eye to eye, but we will always love each other. My mom, dad and big brother each play a specific role in my life. My mom is my biggest supporter, while my dad is my encourager. My brother is like my safety net. When I am in trouble or need help with something, he is always there to lend his hand.

When the world around me is crashing down because of stress or a situation at school, my family is there to listen and help me. I could not imagine a more perfect family for myself. I have the perfect combination of love, humor, and rules. My family can get very silly most of the time, but when I do something I know I am not supposed to, my parents can "bring down the hammer." Although I wish my parents were a little less strict sometimes, I know that they do it for my own good and to make sure that I grow up to be an amazing woman. And for that, I am very thankful to have the family that I have.

Kara Kirmse, Grade 11
Valley Christian High School, CA

Questions for the President

Thanks to the economic recession and the ineffectiveness of the stimulus package, some folks have begun to question the Obama administration. Questions have arose about former Green Jobs Czar van Jones, a self-avowed communist, who recently stepped down after video surfaced in which he said that white farmers intentionally poison minority food and that all white farmers should give their farmland to Native Americans in the name of "social justice." Questions have been asked about Mark Lloyd, the Diversity Czar and head of the Federal Communications Commission (FCC), who praised the government takeover of the media by Hugo Chavez in communist Venezuela as a part of the "incredible revolution" that is taking place there. The last, and perhaps most disturbing controversy surrounding the president is the footage of ACORN (Association of Community Organizations for Reform Now) employees giving a couple posing as a pimp and a prostitute. This comes not two years since the president said in December 2007 that, if and when he becomes president, he will consult them before he makes decisions regarding labor.

In response, the president asked van Jones to step down, but has not issued a statement regarding his presence in the White House in the first place. He has said nothing about Lloyd's comments, or the fact that Lloyd thinks that free speech has been over-exercised in America. Finally, when ABC's George Stephanopoulos asked him about ACORN, he shrugged off the question, saying that it is not the most important issue in America.

Brian Owens, Grade 12
University Preparatory School, CA

Reforming Tendencies, Opening Minds

Humans are social by nature. When forces go against the flow of nature, calamity becomes inevitable. Therefore, when humans are forced out of their society, their only option is to resort to depression or resentment.

I believe that people are not meant to be alone. If we are to survive in this pitiless world we must do so though support and collaborative effort. In order to achieve this objective, we must first reform ourselves and become open minded to others.

People by nature, are stubborn. We unknowingly hold high expectations for what qualifies a person to even become our acquaintance. If someone is too fat, too ugly or too stupid by our standards, natural tendency will force us the other way. The problem however, is that we will never know the joys of the potential relationship so readily rejected. Some may say that what we don't know won't hurt us, but have you ever thought about the things you don't do and how it may hurt others?

In the end we are all the same, philosophers searching for meaning, foragers struggling to survive, and adventurers seeking happiness. If we cannot change our standards and soften our hearts and minds, then we do not deserve the company of others and ultimately, the privilege of life.

Dharyl Bongbonga, Grade 12
Mililani High School, HI

Hunting

Hunting has been used for survival since man first was created, but not it is simply a sport for everyone to enjoy. I have experienced many types of hunting, such as quail, dove, pig, and deer, all of which are exhilarating.

My father and grandfather have both always been avid hunters and it seemed the love was equally instilled in me. I began hunting when I was close to six, starting out with only a 4-10 shotgun as my weapon for bird hunting. Those early years were difficult and frustrating, but in the end I learned to shoot accurately. Once I aged a bit, my father felt I was ready to kill a few hogs, so my next weapon became a 30-06 rifle. This is a fairly large rifle and for a ten year old it could have been difficult to handle (luckily I was no ordinary sized 10 year old), and from there the fun began. There is no emotion that could replace the invigorating feeling as you look at an animal through the cross hairs of your scope. Your heart beats faster and faster, your hands begin to sweat, and finally you hold your breath and pull the trigger.

Every hunting experience is special in its own way, no matter what your prey is. I have always enjoyed hunting and always will, even into my latter years. Hunting for sport did not begin in America, but it is definitely one I enjoy thoroughly.

Clint Windham, Grade 12
Post High School, TX

The Struggle with Algebra

Going to school is sometimes complicated for me because some classes are hard and I'm not that smart. For example, I hate math. That's my least favorite class. I've always struggled with math. My 6th grade teacher, Mrs. Gallman, was so old she gave birth to the first dinosaur. Nobody listened to her because she was elderly and stupid. So now, numbers make me mad and I feel like hitting stuff. There's so many numbers, so many steps, too many rules. Then, I say to myself, "I'm not going to make it in this cold world, I'm not going to graduate." I'll never have a job and I'll never have money. The algebra class takes forever, because I hate it so much. Every class feels like a millennium. I look at the numbers in the clock and they mix with the numbers in the books and they make me want to escape the class and drive to Austin and throw all those stupid numbers right in their faces. I hate the politicians that said we have to take algebra in high school. It's easy to make up all these laws for them, because they don't have to do the work themselves. I think the politicians should get in my shoes, then they will figure out the struggle that I am fighting every day.

Rey Limon, Grade 12
REACH High School, TX

Let Your Heart Decide

The judge's gavel hit hard and loud as he called the court to order. At six years old the courtroom was big and menacing. Yet I, in my pretty blue Sunday dress, was the focal point of every person in the room. Sobs still racked my body from the first time the judge had asked the horrible question. After a short pause, he asked again, "Leslie honey, would you rather stay with your mommy or your daddy?"

"I'm just tired of it Walter!" I heard my mom yell just before she slammed the front door. She could never leave the house without World War III erupting in our kitchen first. As she drove me to school, an angry tension clouded the truck cab. The tension was so unbearable. I finally had to ask, "What's wrong Mommy?"

"Leslie I'm leaving your daddy," she said. My world crumpled around me.

I looked around the courtroom and into the faces of the people I loved. On one side was my mother, who meant everything to me. On the other side was my dad, who was my partner in crime. Their divorce had been torturous. Their hate for each other had only hurt me. However, I couldn't live without my mother. "Daddy," I whispered, "would you hate me forever if I chose Mommy?"

Before my eyes flooded with tears, I saw him smile.

From that decision I realized that it's best to just sit back and let your heart decide. It's rarely ever wrong.

Leslie Wimberley, Grade 12
Granbury High School, TX

Growin' Up Country

The engine roared, the seats shook, and my heart pounded faster. Though the noise was deafening and the air dusty, I knew today would be the greatest day ever!

For me at age five, "fun" was getting to spend the day riding in a good ol' fashioned John Deere tractor with my grandpa or dad. It didn't matter whether we were plowing, spraying, picking or stripping, we always had the best of times. My grandpa was a faith-focused, soft spoken man who barely raised his voice. My dad's personality was different, however, much more like that of a rodeo clown who enjoyed making me laugh.

Every now and then I would be presented with the chance to drive, which meant I put my tiny hands on the wheel and let my dad or grandpa control the pedals. Though only five, I felt powerful when I was in charge of steering the tractor, like Columbus sailing out to conquer the New World. I was queen of the field while driving the tractor.

Lately I've realized that I can never relive those moments spent with my grandpa and dad. Someday, they might not be here to listen to my constant talking, though I can make the most out of each moment I have left with them. I can drive the tractor by myself and though it's still enjoyable it's not the same as it was claiming my throne by my dad's and grandpa's side.

Meridith Wilde, Grade 10
Wall High School, TX

An Important Issue to Me

An important issue to me is dyslexia. Dyslexia is a learning disability that anyone can have. I have struggled all my life with dyslexia. Dyslexia has affected my grades, my self-esteem, and my known relationship with my mom. I feel like dyslexia has ruled my life. As far as I have known, dyslexia has affected my grades. When I began to read, I started to notice I was a slower reader than the other kids in my class. I saw words backwards and could not comprehend them well. Dyslexia has also affected my writing and spelling. My grades were very low for many years. Dyslexia has made me feel stupid, dumb, and weird. Dyslexia has ruined my self-esteem. One of my most embarrassing moments was when I was trying to read aloud, I could not sound the words out, and some of my classmates started to make fun of me. It's hard to read, write, and spell still. I have taken classes to help me with dyslexia. Dyslexia affected my relationship with my mom. It would have taken hours on hours to just one of my homework papers done, because we fought so much over me not being able to see the letters and read them right. It was hard for her to be patient and adjust to me having dyslexia. I learn things different than someone without dyslexia. I know there are other kids that are struggling with dyslexia and do not even know they have dyslexia.

Lauren Lear, Grade 12
Coronado High School, TX

The Melody

With the common thought of sports or athletics as the nature of "cool" in high school, music is obscured behind the lead roles of the play known as *High School*.

Being a shy person has left me with few chances to express my inner self. Music, however, provides me with diverse ways to shine. To a specialized ear, the slight conversions of your sound, style, and articulation can alert them to the player's personality.

Music, when played, is not derived from the instrument. It ventures from deep within the composer. The conversion of sounds, styles, and articulations originate from the composer's soul. In essence, the music that flows freely from my instrument portrays what is within my soul.

With the ability to finally reveal what I've hidden for so many years has begun to liberate the repression I have felt upon myself outside of music. With the eloquence of music, I am able to radiate through the lead role of my shyness and render the young explosiveness of my once hidden identity.

Music has allowed my character to flow unrestricted by my coyness. If it were not for the expressive ability of music, my identity would never be seen or noticed, left behind to take back stage.

Joey Jennings, Grade 11
Pine Tree High School, TX

Blue Eyes Crying

Ever since I was born, I'd always thought myself to be Nana's favorite. A visit to her Rogersville, Tennessee home always held the promise of presents and then me laying in bed and Nana serenading me with Willie Nelson's "Blue Eyes Crying in the Rain." That song resembled her Bible; she had every single lyric etched into her heart. She'd sing it to me every night and would promise that as long as she could sing it, I could know that she loved me.

I was twelve when Nana got Alzheimer's. A few years went by, and she forgot everything, even me. She'd look at me and all I would see was a shell of a person, dead behind the eyes. My seventeenth birthday rolled around and my visiting aunt decided it would be a lovely idea to have the Nana shell over for my dinner. After a meal of silence and somberness my parents took her to their room for a screaming match, and I was left with Nana. Lost in thought, I went to rinse my plate in the sink but then I heard a familiar tune from the dining room. I walked back in to see the source of the noise. It was Nana singing "Blue Eyes!" After the final notes rang out she looked at me and in a cracking voice said: "Your Nana loves you, kid," before her mind left her once more. It was okay, though, because I knew her promise still stood strong.

Holley McLane, Grade 12
Granbury High School, TX

Power of a Smile

"Today, give a stranger one of your smiles. It might be the only sunshine he sees all day." — Quoted in *P.S. I Love You*.

Some ask how a smile affects one person. I will tell you a secret. A smile can change a life. It can inspire others. We smile and the world smiles back. All it took was a smile to give me hope, joy, and inspiration. It was an ordinary smile that changed my life in an extraordinary way.

The sun shone through the tree branches. Threads of light glistened through the leaves. Every recess, I ran to this tree and watched other kids play. I never joined the fun. No one asked me to play. While they played, I sat alone and listened to the other kids laugh. Today, something was different.

There was a circle of kids on the playground. I looked at them, and a girl in the circle saw and ran to me. I shrunk down and became nervous. I looked up into the brown eyes of a curly haired girl. She was smiling at me. I gazed at her before she whispered,

"Why don't you play with us?"

I was stunned. She wanted to play. I looked at her and smiled. I stood up and together we skipped towards the circle.

A feeling filled me to the brim, a feeling of pure joy. All because of my best friend with the bright smile. It's that smile that influences me to this day.

Kindra Stapleton, Grade 12
Granbury High School, TX

A Pathetic Situation

As a whole, America is divided amongst itself by many of the trivial things the country should have already forgotten — things like race, sex, religion, political party, and many of the other quirks that come with being a free country. America is divided by things the country should recognize as a part of itself and embrace, divided by things it cannot avoid; even by the country's quality of living.

On one hand, America is a country of wealth, home to some of the richest people in the world who live lives of luxury, without a second thought directed towards the sick and dying living in the streets. Even though America is called a wealthy country, it still has a lower class, the members of which can't manage to pay rent, much less save their dying children. America may not be a third world country, but the division is obvious and between the country's richest rich person and the poorest poor person is staggering. This division in the country is far more important for the immediate future than the division of politics or religions factions. Even so, politicians would rather debate on whether to blow up third world countries than try to help the people living in their own country who live as though they were in a third world country.

It's a pathetic situation, with the people it affects unable to change the situation, and the people who could ignoring it at every turn.

Nikki Savage, Grade 11
Coronado High School, TX

My Greatest Opportunity

The greatest opportunity for me would be getting to go to a university or trade school. I have a high interest in being a successful person in a university. I have many skills in math and would plan on learning even more new things. I think if I got to college I would be able to widen my skills. I also want to be an excellent role model for my younger siblings.

The reason why I want to be a successful person is so I can take care of myself when I grow up. Other reasons on why I want to be a successful person are because I want to be known for what I do. I don't want to be known for a person who can't make it to college. I also want to be known for the things I can accomplish. I also need to do well in life.

I also have many skills in math. The reason why I have so many skills in math is because I had practiced my math skills when I didn't understand what to do. I even took an extra math class just to improve my math skills. I never gave up on my math even when things got tough. I became very successful in math.

To conclude what I have said I am very interested in going to a university. I hope I have a lot of opportunities to attend the college of my choice and will graduate with high honors.

Brenton Haynes, Grade 12
Riverside County High School, CA

Getting Out of the Danger Zone

It was all before I moved away from California to Utah. As most people during the time of filling boxes with stuff to be packed to move away, my brother and I got hungry. It was about 6 p.m. so we started to walk to the corner to go to the burger place called Tom's. As we were halfway there, a drive-by shooting began. We hit the ground and stayed on the ground until they stopped and drove away. As we saw them drive away we saw my father come out and run towards us. The look on his face described how terrified he was.

This was all I had known my whole life, so this was just another day in South Central Los Angeles. My father grabbed us and we walked back home. When we entered my home I looked at the window and I could see the bullet holes. Right then and there I asked myself, will we all move away to a better place that we believed to be better?

Certainly it was a better place. Now I don't have to worry if I will live to see tomorrow. We finished packing quickly. We loaded everything in the truck and we all said our final goodbyes to childhood friends and family as we began to drive away I looked and said goodbye to everything I knew, and said hello to a new life without fear.

Sly Morales, Grade 12
Woods Cross High School, UT

My Best Friend

Every morning I wake up expecting something new, with the exception of the way I am treated by one person. When asked who my best friend was, at first I thought I could easily answer, but when I really started thinking about it there was only one person who has shared every moment of happiness, sadness, frustration, and excitement in my life. I am sure he gets tired of me feeling like "my life is over" and my complaints about everything, but still he listens and cares.

I remember one day in particular, everything was going wrong and all I wanted to do was see him. As I sat there with the tears rolling down my cheeks, I realized that this was one person I could not make it through the day without. Another day I was sitting there listening to him talk to someone, and I began to grasp what it is that makes him so amazing. He is genuinely the sweetest, most real, and most caring person I have ever met, and I am extremely lucky to be able to call him my best friend.

Sarah Hall, Grade 11
Faith Christian Jr/Sr High School, CA

Employment

I believe economic recession is an important issue that a large amount of people struggle with financially. The recession causes struggle and stress toward students and/or the unemployed because it is harder to find decent paying jobs to support oneself and a family. For example, businesses have to pay their employees a certain amount of money for every hour worked whether it's part time or full time, but with the recession, continuously hiring new workers is not very easy for employers to do.

When minimum wage was raised twenty-five cents an hour, businesses gave their employees less hours because they couldn't afford to give them any more than they had. In addition, it's getting more challenging for students to move out of their parents' house when they are of age.

Apartments, duplexes, condominiums, and rent houses are increasing their prices every year. I would assume that most students work part time and then have class part time, earning approximately five hundred to seven hundred dollars a month. Prices of necessities such as gas, clothing and food as well as luxury items involving entertainment and accessories have all increased in value since last year. Totaling all of that up and adding the price of rent and bills each month costs about eight hundred to one thousand dollars a month.

Since it's difficult finding jobs, living on your own after finishing high school is a tough task. Therefore, saving a large amount of money before graduating is extremely important.

Kelsey Barley, Grade 12
Coronado High School, TX

Silent Heroes

Countless lives have been saved by silent heroes. These heroes are organ donors. Although they are commonly overlooked, organ donors play a major role in the lives of many. Without their kindness, many of our loved ones would be lost.

In the saving of a life, there are of course the doctors and nurses. However, the actual organ donor is never given credit. They have literally given up a part of themselves to save a person's life, yet they are commonly forgotten.

Those who donate organs sacrifice quite a bit. Once they have given an organ they only have one to help their body function, sometimes resulting in inability to participate in certain activities the donor previously enjoyed. Such examples include an athlete who gives a lung or a kidney. They would save a life but their own lives would be greatly altered.

In my opinion, being an organ donor is a great deed. To give of yourself to help another is one of the most wonderful things a person can do. The fact that people are willing to donate organs truly shows the brighter side of humanity, and I hope to one day be on that side and donate my own organs when I am deceased.

While doctors and nurses are true heroes, we must also remember those behind the scenes. Organ donors give so much yet ask so little. We can't all save a life, but we all must be grateful to those who can.

Kaitlyn Polly, Grade 10
Kaufer High School, TX

It's All About the Drive

"Dedication is not what others expect of you, it is what you can give to others." This anonymous quote is one that, as a I studied it, I really felt it applied to my life and the way I have tried living. Sports have been an influential aspect in my life. Dedication runs hand-in-hand with sports, yet many take it for granted. I have believed that dedication is what has gotten me to where I am today and will help me excel in the future. "Practice makes perfect" and "repetition, repetition, repetition" have been instilled within me since the day I started athletics and will stay within me till the day I can no longer move. Having a drive to achieve the best in life is something that should help people have a desire to be dedicated. Not only does dedication relate to sports, but it relates to nearly every aspect in life. Being dedicated with your schoolwork and studying every day may help you in your future. Life may throw unexpected obstacles in your way, but with dedication, keeping a level head and overcoming these obstacles can play a vital role. Living your life in a positive way is crucial to becoming an influential character in the world and practicing dedication may help you achieve this task.

Aaron James, Grade 12
Post High School, TX

Influential Person

In life, there is always one person you inspire by your actions and sayings. People that inspire you to act different. For me, there are both kinds of people, and one of them is my best friend Jairo who has been with me every time I need him.

It all started when people from our church got invited to a church retreat, only seven of us decided to go and Jairo went with us. Jairo and I didn't talk as much, we went to school together but we didn't really talk. I remember when we were going to Austin where the retreat was taking place him and I were having a conversation about how we didn't talk even though he was dating my sister, but at the end we just ended up laughing about it.

When the retreat started everyone was silent and nervous. I remember that we picked teams in order for us to get social with everyone and also to get confidence. Well me and Jairo talked about all of the problems we had and gave each other advice on them. This retreat was supposed to help us get closer to God and to me it did, but it also helped me to get closer to people. Jairo has been with me in the toughest moments of my life and he has always helped me through them, so that's why he is someone that has pushed me to be a better person.

Abelardo Hernandez, Grade 12
Granbury High School, TX

A Second Chance

When I was three years old, my parents divorced. At six, my mom married Bob. The first day I met him, climbing into his white Chevrolet truck, I noticed a mini saddle hanging from his dashboard mirror. Bob saw me and took it off the mirror to put in my small hands for the keeping. I immediately loved him.

At the time, my real dad seemed to live in a different place every few years, and have a different girlfriend every few months. His TV shows, workout routine, and girlfriends seemed more important to him. After a while, his house stopped feeling like home.

Since I was six years old, Bob and I have butted heads about everything. Besides that, we are very close. He has shown me what it means to work hard, and how to enjoy life.

Growing up, I caught my dad in countless lies. All he turned out to be was a hypocrite. I was told I would see the truth as I grew up, and when I opened my eyes, I hated it.

I had my mom, and Bob, and they were enough. I was the most important thing to them. Over my life, I was so focused on my father that I never saw what was right in front of my eyes. I have a step-dad who has never left me. I got the chance to have a dad I can call my own.

Cierra McFadden, Grade 12
Granbury High School, TX

Family

Do you have much to deal with at home? I have plenty going on, especially because of my family. I live in a house with 2 younger sisters, and 2 parents. Both of my sisters are stuck-up, but I'm glad to have them. As you can imagine, it's pretty hectic living with four other relatives. With all of the events going on during the week it can be frustrating.

Event wise, I have church Sunday, Tuesday, and Wednesday. Sometimes I have church on Thursdays and it clashes with my sister's football games. She must be at the school to play in the band at the football game.

Sadly, my dad is always at work. He never has time to come home and talk to us. He rarely gets home before 7 o'clock every night. Usually when he is home he's on the phone for something at work. He never gets a break and I miss not being able to actually sit down and talk to him.

In contrast, my mom is always home. She doesn't have a job and is usually doing laundry or running errands of some sort. I'm not sure if she gets bored, but I definitely would. Since she's doesn't work there are so many times that I wish it were my dad that were home instead of her.

In the end, my family isn't very normal. There are many things I wish I could change and fix, but I know I am fortunate to have them.

Chris Keiper, Grade 10
Kaufer High School, TX

My Heritage: An Invaluable Gift

"Ee me rim!" The teacher's shrill voice cut through to my hiding place under the slide. "I'm going to count to three and if you're not out by then…I will call you mother!" My mischievous grin quickly turned into a look of terror. Though my Korean school teacher did not scare me, the wrath of my mother did. Sheepishly, I crawled out and reluctantly went back to Korean school, a place that would teach what living in the United States would cause us to forget: the language and culture of our ethnicity. I was born in the United States, but because I was raised by my grandmother, who's English speaking capacity was limited to "yes" and "no," I did not learn to speak English until I attended preschool. And while being dropped off at a strange address with no way to express myself was a little more than traumatizing, I am glad. To learn English was inevitable, but retaining the ability to speak in my native tongue was an invaluable gift.

With this gift, I can travel between two distinct worlds, learning my life lessons from two cultures. I'm eternally grateful to my grandmother, who taught me the language, my mother, whose iron will drives me even to this day, and, of course, to Korean school. I was forced against my will every week and am now grateful for every hour; for without it, I would not be who I am today.

Angela Lee, Grade 12
Faith Christian Jr/Sr High School, CA

Raging Waters

The powerful current was pulling us faster and faster. We couldn't slow down when BAM. We hit the edge of the bank. That's when they came out by the hundreds.

It started out as a normal cool summer morning when my dad and I got the kayak ready. We met Trent, my dad's friend, on the edge of the river. Soon we were paddling down the river with the flow of the current. I remember just sitting there and thinking about how my dad didn't care about me. Why would he make me do something I didn't want to or didn't need to do?

We came up to a swift flowing current when all of a sudden the powerful current pushed us right into a low hanging branch. As soon as Trent hit the low hanging branch we noticed the huge hornets' nest. A sense of panic spread throughout my trembling body. Then they came out. Hundreds of angry hornets came right for my dad and I. "Watch out!" my dad yelled as he threw himself over my body until the hornets passed. "Are you all right?" my dad asked. "Yes, I think so." I said.

After the ordeal was over, I was relieved to find that my dad had hundreds of hornet stings but every one of them were in his life jacket. That day I realized how much my dad cared about me. He would risk his own well being for my safety.

Caleb Montez, Grade 10
Wall High School, TX

The Story of a Farmer Named Finn

As I stepped down the three steel steps of the big orange tractor and leaped into the field, I was filled with a sense of great satisfaction. I bent down and let the moist, brown dirt run through my fingers and crumble to the ground. Walking back to my truck, I noticed a familiar vehicle driving down the turn row kicking up a cloud of dust as it made its way. I briefly reflected upon my childhood, riding in a fleet of Allis Chalmers tractors with my dad. At the end of the day as we walked back to the truck, I would try to match his stride. Reality came back as he pulled up.

"There's 700 acres I want you to farm, are you up to it?"

"Yeah," I replied with a grin, "I'm up to it."

There's no other experience like putting something in the ground and watching it grow. It's putting everything in God's hands, and praying for Him to give you cooperative weather that year. It is the little miracles that happen every day, as a tiny green stem cracks through the ground searching for warmth from the sun's rays. In my fields, I will grow the crops that go on to feed families, and be used to make new innovative fuels and materials. A wise man once told me, if you do what you love you'll never work a day in your life. Farming is what I love.

Jeff Finn, Grade 12
Granbury High School, TX

A Place I Call Home

Beautiful views, warming sunsets, and fresh smell of nature; this is what life is like when you live on a farm. I have lived on a farm my entire 17 years that I have been on this planet. The farm life to me means the world. Living on a farm has not only created wonderful memories for me, but set up a place I can call home.

Having lived on a farm to this day has made my life great. There are many great aspects when living on a farm. The farm life has taught me to be a respectful man and has also showed me the beauty of Mother Nature. I know that I would be a different person today if I had not been raised on a farm. If I had not been raised on a farm, I figured I would be a stuck-up city boy who does not know how to work and get his hands dirty. The place I call home is our farm just outside of Post. To me, the farm has been a great home because I passed through many experiences on it and had the opportunity to create a great work ethic for myself. The farm is my life.

Living on a farm has made me the happiest person on the earth. The farm has taught me many marvels that I will never forget as long as I live. Our farm may not be very nice, but it is where I call home.

Robert Contreras, Grade 12
Post High School, TX

Learning to Ride

I remember the exhilaration of the speed; the feeling of falling forward, with the wind rushing by as it would a skydiver. I remember worrying that when I applied the brakes on the bike, what if I pressed the wrong brake handle and flew face-first into the pavement, my momentum carrying me down the road? What would it feel like to have the flesh peeled from my face?

I went through three attempts of learning how to ride a bike over the course of two years. I don't respond well to negative reinforcement; when somebody tries to get me to learn a lesson through negativity, I block them out. Thus said, the first two attempts of learning to ride a bike didn't turn out well. My father was the first to try to teach me, using shame to get me to ride a bike by telling me about some drunk old men who were laughing at me; as if I cared about what a drunk guy who's wasting his life on alcohol has to say. My brother was next, and he used anger. However, the man who taught me how to ride was my uncle, and he taught me through love.

It's great to say that my face is intact. Not a single accident occurred through those three sessions. My uncle had shown me the type of man I'd want to be when I grew up; the type of father I would want to be: a patient, kind, and loving father.

Matthias Abraham, Grade 12
Granbury High School, TX

Wushu

Wushu. Just the mention of such an art form makes my heart beat faster, as the adrenaline fills my body and all of a sudden I am excited for the world. I am excited to be alive. Wushu, literally translated as "military art" is my life. I would not be able to live without it.

The first time I went to a Wushu competition in seventh grade, I won several awards. It took a lot of training and practice, but I won something. I had purpose. For the first time ever, I had a huge, overwhelming sense of purpose. I wanted to spend the rest of my life acquiring new abilities, entering more competitions, and perfecting the skills I already had and held so true to. I realized for the very first time that I was somebody. I realized that if I set my mind to something and gave it my time and effort, I could achieve things.

I have a passion for Wushu, the art that makes me feel whole, and I will continue to train and practice to do this art form justice. Wushu is my life.

Jake Trinh, Grade 11
Valley Christian High School, CA

Psychological Warfare

Brainwashing is defined as any method of controlled systematic indoctrination, especially one based on repetition or confusion: i.e., brainwashing by TV commercials. Also, to advertise means, to announce or praise a product in some public medium of communication in order to persuade people to buy or use it. It is strange how these two definitions are similar, however, it is clear to see. Advertisement is a form of subconscious attack trying to subject its viewers to its will. Advertisement aimed toward children is even worse. Who already growing up, are extremely impressionable, ignorant, demanding, and naive. This is the exact idea that almost all major corporations have thought about.

Not only are children perfect targets to be led astray, but they control a large percentage of their parents' money whether they know it or not. Corporations advertise to children who can't walk, who can't talk, and can't even read. The American Psychological Association (APA) has come together to try and reason and find a solution to this growing issue of advertising. Since we cannot completely ban advertising toward all children, the APA has researched and studied to find what age a policy should be set at. Their research shows that children under the age of eight are unable to critically comprehend televised advertising messages and are prone to accept advertiser messages as truthful, accurate, and unbiased. It is not right to advertise toward children who can't comprehend the persuasive intents of advertising and are therefore mislead.

Kimberly Micheletti, Grade 12
University Preparatory School, CA

God, Family, School, Friends and Sports Are Important

The most important is my relationship with God. He is my foundation. Even when I struggle in my spiritual walk, God is always here with me. He will never leave me.

Family is important. They support me in whatever decision I make. They are with me through hard times and triumphs. They will always love me and I will always love them.

School is also important. My parents encourage me to go to school because they want me to succeed in life. Although school has always been a challenge, every failure I encounter is a step up because I am determined to get where I want to be in my academics. I love to work hard at my goals. This is my senior year and my next goal is going to college.

Friends are an important part of my life. They are here when I need them. They are here for the hard times and good. When I feel my parents don't understand, my friends support me.

And finally, sports are important to me. I love being a part of something I can work hard at and glorify God at the same time. I play volleyball and run track and played basketball my freshman year. Sports help me academically because I have to maintain a certain G.P.A in order to continue in athletics.

I always choose to live, work and play for God's glory using the gifts He has given me.

Jordan Stewart, Grade 12
Valley Christian School, WA

The Power of Faith

Faith represents the most meaningful part of my life. Faith involves more than waking up early on Sunday morning to attend church or showing up for activities. A relationship with Jesus constitutes the central focus of faith. To me, faith centers on a personal relationship with Jesus. This relationship requires trust, believing in that which you cannot see.

Some people may say that prayer travels no higher than the ceiling but I have discovered that prayer draws me closer to God. Through prayer God offers answers to life's most difficult questions and strength to face any challenge. In prayer I feel as though I'm leaning on God's strong shoulders. God demonstrated His love for humanity by sacrificing His own Son on the cross as a payment for our sins.

Through faith I received this gift of forgiveness and the promise of eternal life in heaven. Twice in the last two years, I traveled to Africa in order to share my faith with the people of Malawi. This required faith to step out of my comfort zone to enter into a land where I could not speak the language. Through my journey of life, I constantly find myself leaning upon God for support.

Joshua Schulik, Grade 11
Pine Tree High School, TX

All We Had to Do

The shadows emerged from their hiding places, sprinting toward the door. Gasping in fright, I threw my hands over my head and ran for my life. I quickly hid behind the nearest trash can and saw the lion catch its prey. My sister the slowest of the herd was captured. Feeling guilty, I side stepped the trash can and grudgingly turned myself in. The lion, who was a janitor and surprisingly fast for his age, cocked his head to the side as if not expecting another person. He gladly jerked my arm and dragged me and my sister to the office.

We were brutally pushed and pulled to her office; never had I been so frightened. I can't believe that we were caught. We fell into the chairs she provided on shaking legs. We spilt our hearts out; leaving no one and no detail out. Laughing she told us that all we had to do was ask permission. Little did we know that the alpha of the group blatantly forgot to tell us. Guess who got into trouble? My sister and I were the victims.

Cheryl McBride, Grade 12
Granbury High School, TX

Fashion Is Important!

Do you ever wake up 10 minutes before you have to leave for school? Or do you ever figure out your outfit as you are rushing out of the door? To none of those questions I would answer yes, because dressing nice for school is one of the most important things to me. Fashion has always been an interest of mine and if dressing up for school means waking up a couple of hours early, I will. I feel it shows my teachers how interested I am in learning and to my pears that I care about my self image. It makes me feel like I am important in life and that I am set for success. Unfortunately, because I look nice for school, some of my peers, think I'm stuck up, but that is not the case at all. I don't like to flaunt or try to be more seen by what I wear, but would like to earn respect and let everyone know how serious I am. This may seem silly and unimportant to others, but to people like me, fashion and style means everything.

Tayler James, Grade 11
Valley Christian High School, CA

Grades 7-8-9
Top Ten Winners

List of Top Ten Winners for 7-9, listed alphabetically

Conner E. Bennett	Grade 8	Manus Academy	Charlotte, NC
Noah Farrell	Grade 8	Northlawn Jr High School	Streator, IL
Madeline de Figueiredo*	Grade 7	Lindero Canyon Middle School	Agoura Hills, CA
Emma Halley	Grade 7	Glenwood Middle School	Glenwood, MD
Carly Hampton	Grade 8	St Gerard Majella School	Kirkwood, MO
Elizabeth Jaeger	Grade 9	Cambridge Christian School	Cambridge, MN
Madeline Muskrat*	Grade 8	St Elizabeth Ann Seton School	Keller, TX
Ace Robinson	Grade 8	The American Academy	Philadelphia, PA
Claire Taigman	Grade 9	Andover High School	Bloomfield Hills, MI
Patricia Xie	Grade 7	Dr. George M. Weir Elementary School	Vancouver, BC

*Students with an asterisk by their name can be found in this anthology.
All Top Ten Essays can be read at www.poeticpower.com

Note: The Top Ten essays were finalized through an online voting system. Creative Communication's judges first picked out the top essays. These essays were then posted online. The final step involved thousands of students and teachers who registered as online judges and voted for the Top Ten essays. We hope you enjoy these selections.

Cold Sweat and No Mercy

It was early Saturday morning. I was up at the crack of dawn; the sky was still dark outside. I got up, ready for my first day of boot camp. I was very nervous; my stomach was growling. I was dragging from being so tired. I did not know that would be the worst day of my life.

That day, I went through hell! They kept everyone at a state of confusion. It was calm for a few seconds when we got there. They introduced the Sirs, and then the unexpected happened, the calmness went away. They started yelling at us, "stand up; sit down!" I think they said it so fast, nobody could think. I was so scared to even move. When we were in attention, I was barely moving my pinky. One of the Sirs came up to me and said, "if you move your pinky one more time, I will break it!" I wanted to cry so badly, but crying to them is a sign of weakness, so I held it in.

I was the only girl who didn't cry. I made it through that day. I am going this next Saturday. I will make it to be one of the best cadets. I can do it.

Amri Lopez, Grade 8
Rio Bravo Middle School, TX

Tony Romo

Tony Romo is one of the best quarterbacks for the Dallas Cowboys. He was born in San Diego, California on April 21, 1980. He was also voted football player of the year of 2002. He is 29 years old. His parents are still alive. His father is fighting in the United States Navy. His mother is a Polish-German descent.

When his father joined the Navy his mother moved their home town, Burlington, Wisconsin. Meanwhile, Tony Romo was playing for the Burlington Demons all star football team.

Tony Romo went to play national football league. He went to Eastern Illinois University in Charleston, Illinois. Then, before that, he played basketball for Burlington High School.

I chose Tony Romo because he inspired me to play football.

Donovan Evans, Grade 7
Deweyville Middle School, TX

Emmitt Smith

Emmitt James Smith, the best player of all time, set many records. He was born in Pensacola, Florida May 15, 1969. I don't know what school he went to, but I do know that he went to school in Florida. His height is 5 foot, 9 inches and weighs 216 pounds. So you could say he is not very big.

Emmitt Smith's career started when the Dallas Cowboys drafted him to their team in 1990. Smith played for the Cowboys for 12 years, but then in 2003 the Arizona Cardinals drafted him to their team. He played with them for 1 year. In his whole career he had 18,365 career rushing yards and 164 career rushing touchdowns.

After his career was over he went on Dancing with the Stars with Cheryl Burke and won 2006 champion. That is why Emmitt Smith is my favorite football player.

Bailey Freeland, Grade 7
Deweyville Middle School, TX

Taking Luke on a Run

We crossed the street and quickly went up the curb on to the side walk. My sister and I were taking my dog Luke on a walk, but instead of "walking," I stand on a ripstik, and Luke pulls me as fast as he can while following my sister. It's more of a run. Luke then sprinted around a corner and my foot slipped off of the ripstik and I plunged into the ground crushing my side and scraping my elbow. I screamed in pain, then looked up to see an entire family staring at me. After getting up, they came to me asking if I was okay. I said yes and after a minute of small talking began my return home in pain.

Two houses away from mine my neighbor was being followed by two friendly dogs. When Luke saw them, he charged them and my ripstik wheel went into a hole and I crashed again. In pain I dragged Luke back to my house to bandage my elbow. For the next couple days my side was killing me and I walked, and even crawled with a limp. Sitting down was even painful. It took me about a week to get back to going on runs again. But I was happy.

God has given me a drive to do dangerous and stupid things. And doing stupid things is, well, stupid! And stupid things have their consequences. But you simply have to get up and keep on going.

Alexander Samay, Grade 9
Faith Christian Jr/Sr High School, CA

Alaska

Alaska, my favorite state, better known as the "Last Frontier." I only lived there for fourteen months, but those months were the best months of my life. I feel during that time I was the luckiest boy in the world. Some people say that Alaska is a dump, a wasteland, a place of igloos and snow. I say it's a land where there is beauty.

I love to fish; Alaska has some of the best, sought after fishing in the world. I have seen someone catch a King Salmon as big as my little sister, Annie. I have caught fish on both the Kenai and Russian rivers, and even shared a fishing hole with a grizzly sow and her cub.

Alaska is known for its harsh, cold winter, and wild animals. Extreme weather calls for unique adaptations. It wasn't unusual to see a moose in your front yard or walking down the city street. You know you're in Alaska, when the hair in your nose freezes just by taking a breath. Being the lucky boy I am, I loved the snow and cold temperatures. I could build snow forts for hours. My favorite activity was sledding. It wasn't hard to find sledding hills. My family and I spent many days and nights sledding together. Then when we were tired, we headed for home to sip hot chocolate by the fire. So if you get a chance, head to Alaska and I promise you will feel lucky!

George Wolter, Grade 7
St Thomas Aquinas School, NM

Now or Never

Have you ever felt like you were a star? When everyone was focused on you? Because on October 10, 2009 that's exactly how I felt. I drove five hours to Medford, Oregon. I knew that we didn't come here to lose the biggest game of the year. My team and I have been working three days every week, training for this game, and once I stepped onto the field, I knew that it was now or never.

At the end of the first half right before the whistle blew, Ashley got a penalty kick right outside the eighteen yard box. I could see her legs shaking and her heart pounding, she was nervous. When the referee blew the whistle, Ashley took five steps and smacked the ball. It came right at me, I dove and headed it right into the goal as it passed the keeper's hands. Goal!

With five minutes to spare, the other teamed scored. I knew that this was our last chance to score, with twenty seconds remaining on the clock. As Becca headed up the left side the clock kept ticking. Becca crossed me the ball, I jumped in the air, kicked the ball right pass the keeper and the defensive line! As the referee ended the game with the whistle I thought to myself, that right this moment I knew, I was a star, and everyone is truly focused on me.

Cassie Downing, Grade 8
Thora B Gardiner Middle School, OR

Who's Writing What?

My friend and I are writing a book together. At first, it's a lot of fun. We get to express our crazy and zany imagination through paper and pen. When you get farther into the book though, things get a lot harder. We have to deal with writer's block, character personalities, who should write what, and so much more! Talking to each other every day helps, but not that much.

Writer's block is the largest hurdle to overcome. One time, my friend had writer's block for two weeks! It's not as bad as when I had it for a whole summer though. Another thing is printing out and transferring the manuscript back and forth at school. It takes up a lot of paper to print it out and also takes a lot of time. We are on chapter seven so that means we're doing pretty well. Deciding who should write what is another big thing. We've decided to each write three chapters then let the other person write three chapters. Still, what to write about is the real question. Who should do the climax, the rising action, or the falling action.

Writing a book is extremely hard, but also extremely fun. Persevering through it is the best part. We keep each other excited and help them write more. This also helps us with our friendship. The book will hopefully be a bestseller or turn into a movie! We are working together to make something we couldn't possibly do on our own.

Alison Clifford, Grade 8
Monte Vista Christian School, CA

Your Broken Heart

If you are a girl, there is a moment in your life that you get your heart broken in a million pieces. When that day comes, you want to run to your mom and tell her to hold you so tight and never let go and ask her why did I have to go to the big world why couldn't I always be by your side to protect me? But you know at that moment, if it was up to her, she would protect you like a lion protects her cubs. She doesn't want you to go through all that pain, either. You say to yourself, "You're never going to fall in love," and you close your heart to everybody who wants to love you. You don't even give them an opportunity. You don't ever want to cry your eyes out or feel hurt shove a knife in your heart. Your heart is hiding behind a haunted house door and if you try to open that door to a person and they let you down, you become a heartless zombie. So you say to yourself, "I'm not going to fall in love, never again!" and you just lay your head softly on your pillow and cry yourself to sleep.

Jennifer Dimas, Grade 9
REACH High School, TX

The Perfect Gift

Have you gotten that one gift that you'll always treasure your whole life, the one thing you won't trade for all the riches in the world? A gift that brings a happiness that can conquer all the bad in the world? I am very fortunate for I already received such a gift. What is this gift I speak so highly of as if it is priceless? It is love, and it *is* priceless. This love is from my family. The amount of love I get form my family is just tremendous, along with the amount I give them. Yes, it is true that there are times when we have arguments and say hurtful things to one another, but it is also true that no matter how mad we are, we know we don't mean those things, and that we love each other.

Love is such a powerful thing, and it is my special weapon for getting through bad times. This isn't something that every person has, and that makes me realize how fortunate I am. My family's love is my treasure and I would never give it up. It is truly the perfect gift.

Leslie Muñoz, Grade 8
Rio Bravo Middle School, TX

Love

I wish that there was more love in this world. I would really want to buy it, but since I can't, I would have to show it. I can show love by going to church, and by treating others the way I want to be treated.

Love is happiness. It is wonderful to enjoy love with your family. Love is a gift from God to show that He really loves us. Love is sometimes serious, sometimes fun, or just being happy.

Love comes out of one's heart. Sometimes it may be difficult to understand its meaning. Love may sometimes show by how one acts. But the truth will always be in one's heart.

Elsa Orozco, Grade 7
Our Lady of the Rosary School, CA

Video Games

I may not be the most decent human being in the real world, but when I get home and enter the virtual world, I rock! Video games are my passion! I love them! I try to make some time for them every day by getting my homework done really fast. Some days, like Tuesdays, however, my schedule is so full that I don't have time. Oh, well! You can't have everything you want, right? The video game that I'm stuck playing right now is *Paper Mario: The Thousand Year Door*. It's awesome! It's about Mario being paper-thin and turning into a paper airplane, a boat, and other paper forms that help him navigate obstacles. My second favorite game is called Super Smash Bros. Brawl. It's about 39 different Nintendo characters fighting each other. Both of those games are really fun, and not inappropriate one bit! I like them because they are like TV, except you control the main characters instead of watching them! I usually play up to two hours max every time I play. I'm not addicted. I just like playing them. Video games are exciting and help me when I'm under stress.

Nicholas Keough, Grade 8
Faith Christian Jr/Sr High School, CA

Cruelty to Critters

In this country, there is a heartless type of research. It is also known as animal testing. This so-called testing is one of the world's most revolting activities, and it should be brought to a halt immediately.

Animal testing is where companies that manufacture products that we use every day experiment their designs on groups of engineered animals. They either apply or inject the designs into them. This process can harm the critters physically or even worse mentally.

Due to excessive tests the species Rhesus Macaques [a type of monkey] are becoming endangered. IN 2005, scientists tested HIV vaccines on them. This causes many to die within the first week of testing. There is a possibility that this monkey species will be low if these types of testing continue. Once this one species is gone, it can never be replaced.

Another negative is that a company that is caught testing animals will have an impact on the business's reputation. Some corporations not only use the animals for cosmetics, they also use them for medicinal purposes. This can lead to issues with pharmaceutical companies. With bad reputations of cruelty comes great accountability with the law and the public.

In the end, animals should be treated with the same respect that humans have for one another. As innocent as applying your makeup is, remember that a rabbit was the "middleman." Animal testing is inhumane. Remember this next time you open your shampoo bottle.

Carlie Berry, Grade 8
Holliday Middle School, TX

Kitten

There are a lot of differences between kindergarten and eighth grade. Some of the main differences are that in kindergarten you take naps and you are starting to learn addition, and in eighth grade you take algebra and you don't take naps, of course. Others include having eight periods and seven teachers. In kindergarten all you have is one teacher. Eighth grade can put a lot of stress on you and kindergarten is mostly just a play time where you learn things. In eighth grade you get infractions and detentions, but in kindergarten all you get are timeouts and lectures. And in kindergarten you get free snacks during the day. In kindergarten you probably thought girls were gross and had cooties and things of that nature. But now that I'm older I realize that girls are part of society. Also in kindergarten you learn the ABC's, how to write better, and how to read. So like I said, there are a lot of differences between eighth grade and kindergarten…and if you're wondering why the title is kitten it's because kindergartners wouldn't know how to title stuff correctly, and they would probably title it something they like.

Justin Peterson, Grade 8
Monte Vista Christian School, CA

Justice in the Political World

In the political world, justice has been spat in the face. No one cares anymore what Congress does. Justice in the political world has shrunk to a few powerless men.

Justice is important to me because people die every day trying to cross over to this country, even though it's deteriorating. It's not literally deteriorating, but its liberty and justice is. This is not what the founding fathers wanted. On a quarter, it says liberty, but as it gets older it fades away. A quarter describes America in this way. It is important to me that we bring back justice in America before there is no chance to even think about it, and because justice is the only thing keeping this country together even if it's only a thread.

I have a feeling that justice in the political world is not only important to me, but to all those living as refugees around the world. It is important we keep ours during these hard times.

Joseph Manganiello, Grade 7
Lindale Jr High School, TX

Numb

It's a cold morning in El Paso, TX, March 2, 2002. You could feel the grass dancing with the wind, and the ground shook my world. As I hold some flowers, I wait for my good bye to my aunt. As tears fall to the ground, I feel numb inside. My sisters and family kiss her good bye, and as I stand in front of her coffin, looking at her eyes, I said, good bye and touch her hand. I closed my eyes, to keep the tears from streaming down my face. As I left I will always know how she died, and how she feels, numb. When I sat down, I ask my dad how she died (to make sure). He said, "The way she felt now is how she was in the blizzard in New York."

Ezequiel Zaragoza, Grade 8
Rio Bravo Middle School, TX

Basketball

The sound of sneakers screeching the floor makes basketball breathtaking and bouncing the ball, to pass the ball, or go for the shot. It is a great sport for almost anybody, I want to be a basketball player, the fame, fortune, the cars. But it is not about all of that it takes good leadership, good sportsmanship, and a lot of practice and having fun. My coach told me, you win nothing and you lose nothing just have fun. But basketball is a great, challenging sport, but try your best at everything even the sports you think it is stupid just practice all the way and you can accomplish anything. Just believe in yourself and never give up.

Noah Carrillo, Grade 8
Rio Bravo Middle School, TX

Family

There are many important things in life to me but the most important thing to me is my family. When I'm with my family I feel comfortable because I know that everyone there loves me and they know that I love them. On our free time we do all kinds of things like go snowboarding, tubing, wakeboarding, boogie boarding and we go to six flags. Sometimes we all don't get along but we always find a way to work it out.

My family is always there for me when I need them they never let me down. When I get home I can always count on my mom or dad to help me with my homework, or if I have a big volleyball game coming up they will take their time to practice with me. My family loves me enough to send me to a Christian school, because they could just send me back to a public school but they want the best there is for me. I know that even when I get older and move out I can always count on them if I need anything.

Shon Ritchie, Grade 8
Faith Christian Jr/Sr High School, CA

Friendship

Friendship is the best part of living your life. Without friends everyone would dislike each other and the world would be a mess. Together, as one, our ancestors built this world long ago because they cared for one another. As the present human beings, we need to keep that chain linked because we have such power as one.

As children get older, they need friends to keep them strong. To not only fight battles, but also know that they have somebody on their side that is rooting them on in any condition. You may have great classmates, but they will only be with you for a short amount of time. If you make friends then they will be with you as long as you treat each other with tender, loving care. The best type is the long lasting partnership. A long lasting friendship means that they will stick with you until the end. They will be by your side and guide you through the ups and downs. You can share feelings and secrets and not have to worry about getting stressed. This is the friendship you will want to earn and keep forever.

Samantha Omiya, Grade 7
South Lake Middle School, CA

The Biggest Change of My Life

Have you ever thought life is giving up on your family? When bad things happen they can go away or stay with you forever. I've experienced some good and bad memories, but the bad memories seem to be the most important.

It was my thirteenth birthday in 2008. We went to Odessa and went to Town and Country to wait for my dad because he was working in Odessa. When my dad finally arrived, I saw that he looked extremely mad, so I asked him, "what was wrong?" He told me not to worry, so I turned and looked at my mom and she was a little upset. I didn't ask her what was wrong because I knew what she was going to say.

After we finished shopping, we went to go eat and my mom said she was sick, so she stayed in the truck. Then my dad got mad and we went and ate. She did the same thing when we went to the movies. On the ride back home my parents gave us the bad news and told us that they were getting a divorce. At that moment it captured our attention and put my brothers and me in tears.

My parents getting a divorce impacted me by making me take responsibility for myself and my brothers. We learned that the four of us have to stick together if we're going to make it through life.

Micheal Ortiz, Grade 8
Reagan County Middle School, TX

When My Cousin Died

It was Thursday, June 30, 2005. My mom was exhausted, and doing laundry while my brothers and I were in our room playing with our toys. My mom gets a phone call. "Ring, Ring, Ring" we stopped playing to hear what she was talking about, but later wished we hadn't.

As we heard her talking we went to the laundry room where my mom was. When she saw us she began to panic and got her purse. She told my brother that she would probably be gone for a while, but to watch us and finish the laundry.

About an hour later, my uncle came and took us to my grandma's house. When we got to her house, we began asking her "Grandma, where's Mom?" and "Grandma what happened?" She told us "She'll be here in a little bit."

Finally, my mom showed up. I could tell she had been crying just by how red her face was, but I didn't want to say anything. Later she told us the news that my cousin, Lucio Navarro Jr., was in Ropesville, TX, and was killed in an eighteen wheeler accident.

It was a very sad week. On July 6, 2005 my cousin was buried in Seminole, TX. That was an even sadder day, because we would never see him again, and for my dad because him and Lucio were like brothers. It was a day that I will never forget.

Matthew Flores, Grade 7
Seminole Jr High School, TX

Animal Abuse Is Wrong

I believe animal abuse is wrong, because people shouldn't hurt animals for no good reason. At times I think people abuse animals to let out their own personal pains, but that is still not an excuse. These horrible people have no reason to abuse animals and yet they still do. I can clearly state my opinion on this issue because I have tried to see every view point, including the view of someone who would abuse animals. Let me just say I can't find one logical reason as to why they would do such a thing. If these people hated their animals so much, why don't they just give it away? They can take it to an animal shelter or do something besides hurting the innocent animal. If we can help find the animals a new home, then we should. It would benefit both the owner and the animal. I have much more on the topic but it would go on forever, so I will end with saying ANIMAL ABUSE IS WRONG!!!!!!

Ashley Bosquez, Grade 7
Goodson Middle School, TX

The Life of a Columbian Squire

The life of a Columbian Squire is fun and very active. A squire is any Catholic young man from the age of 10-18. I became a Squire two years ago and I love it because I get to hang out with my friends on Sunday, I also do work that helps my faith and community. I myself am a Texas State Council and I am the new deputy chief at my local council. I have gone to two state conventions, one in January and the other in August. They were so much fun because I met new kids and I was appointed my position on state council. I have many duties since I am the new deputy chief and on the state council, but somehow I still come through even though I'm in the 7th grade. I hope that once I get older I will be the Chief Squire at my circle and one day be the Grand Knight at whichever Knights of Columbus circle I will be at when I'm older.

Onassis Puente, Grade 7
St Elizabeth Ann Seton School, TX

Song and Dance

A song and dance is a traditional social gathering. The purpose for a song and dance is to have a good time. You can dress traditional or just dress regular. They have contests to win money. Only first, second, and third are the ones that win money. I won second place in the youth category, and I received fifty-five dollars for dancing. My niece won forty dollars for best dress. You have to dance up to four hours. Song and dances happen throughout the year. This year, I am going to dance at the state fair in Albuquerque, New Mexico. My niece Sie and my nephew Gilbert are going to be there too. I hope I get first place! My mom and dad will be proud that I danced for tradition. This month my sister will have a benefit song and dance. The first prize will be a sack of flour. A benefit song and dance will have no cash prizes. I am going to dance for my sister.

Juan Pedro Apachito III, Grade 7
Pine Hill Schools, NM

A Special Tradition

All families have traditions, and my family has a tradition that is very special to me. I do not know when the tradition started, but I do know that it originally started in Germany. My great-grandparents came to the United States just before World War II started. It was passed down to my grandpa and he carried it on with his family. My mom grew up doing this tradition, and she still participates in it to this day.

This tradition happens every year on Christmas Eve at my grandma's house after church. My mom's side of the family all participate. Our tradition is that each family sings a Christmas carol before they can put their presents under the Christmas tree. After they sing their Christmas carol, they bring their presents out. While they do this, everyone sings "Jingle Bells." Everyone sings until all the presents are under the tree. My grandpa especially loved this tradition, and I always loved listening to him and my grandma sing "I Saw Mommy Kissing Santa Claus." Sadly, my grandpa passed away three years ago. But we still go to his grave every year and sing "Jingle Bells" to him. This tradition is very important to my family and has a special place in my heart. I will carry on this tradition for the rest of my life because I know that my grandpa would be very disappointed if our tradition ended. After all, it does not feel like Christmas without singing "Jingle Bells."

Ashley Lentzner, Grade 8
St Elizabeth Ann Seton School, TX

Combating Animal Cruelty

Every year, thousands of animals are being neglected, abandoned and abused. Animal cruelty occurs too often in the United States and in other countries as well. When these abusers get caught, they usually get a fine and can spend some time in prison depending on the severity of the act. Acts that involve animal cruelty are dog fighting, abandonment and abusing animals to the point of horrific torture. Animal policeman enforce the animal cruelty laws and veterinarians help the animals heal.

Things we can do to combat animal cruelty are to report known acts to the authorities, and get your pet spayed or neutered. In doing this, controlling the pet population will reduce the number of abandoned pets and strays on the streets. Educating others on the proper care of animals will also combat animal cruelty. For myself, I need to study hard and get accepting grades so I can become a vet someday. As a vet, I will assist the community. I also want to assist local animal shelters by performing spays and neuters.

Becoming a vet is important to me because I can play a big role to combat animal cruelty, but we can all do our part so animals can have a good quality of life while enriching and enhancing our lives.

Bianca Olivas, Grade 8
Zia Middle School, NM

Love?

Everyone at my school seems like they want to be in love! But the problem is, I have no idea what it is! My best friend explained it to me, but I still have no clue! In my point of view, well I get this from movies and books, is that, you get these crazy feelings around them, and they're on your mind 24/7. When you wake up, the first thing you want to see is them. When you go to sleep, you're hoping they're okay and they're thinking of you too. But I'm not sure because well, I've never been in love. Love is blind, I hear. I'm not really sure what it means, but I have a feeling it's like you see the person for who they are inside. I hear love is beautiful, kind, awesome, great, and wonderful!! Sometimes I feel like I want to fall for a guy but I know it's way too soon, and I'm so not ready to be in love. I can't wait to be like my parents happily married and still going strong! I never really thought of how all this would go down but I know if it does it will go down with LOVE!! I still don't think I know what love is, but I know I will feel it when the time comes...Love?

Jasmin Samaniego, Grade 8
Rio Bravo Middle School, TX

Our Choices Affect Our Standards

How many times have we been pressured to do something we knew was against our values? The world will try to get you to do things that you know are morally wrong because misery likes company. When we do something wrong, we usually feel guilty for the things we have done. We have all experienced shame, embarrassment, guilt, or remorse resulting from our wrong choices.

Our parents, teachers, and leaders have taught us right and wrong from the time we were born. It is the decisions that we make that affect what our standards are. If we make the right choices, we are setting high expectations for ourselves. For example, if others see your example of kindness, honesty, or general service, they will respect you for your beliefs and are more likely to stand up for you. They trust you to keep doing what you know is right. If you make a wrong decision, then you will lose that trust.

One of the highest contributing factors to our beliefs is religion. Religion helps people to keep order in their lives, and keep them free of sin. Many different religions hold different principles, but everyone should respect other people's different beliefs. Religion also helps us to answer puzzling questions in our life.

Keeping values and standards are a part of law and order in our society. If people don't receive revelation, create guidelines, and follow religious principles, we wouldn't be able to distinguish between right and wrong. Without these principles and knowledge, we wouldn't be able to make decisions or choose to do certain things.

Seth Herbert, Grade 9
Syracuse Jr High School, UT

An Unbreakable Plate in an Unique Ship

When I think of my inner being, I see myself as an unique ship. I may not have the same qualities as others, but each day I discover that others do not have the same qualities as me. I see myself in the center of the big sea. It is as if I am floating all by myself with all the talents and the good things I possess. I also think of myself as an unbreakable plate. I never give up, even if others tell me that it is about time for me to. I never let myself shatter on the floor till I have given it my all. I am not afraid to make mistakes. I may not always get a perfect score on a math test or get in the volleyball or basketball team, but that doesn't stop me from trying. I know I have a nature and intellect of my own which brings out creative or even unique ideas. I am just a person who is unique and likes to be another ship, different from all other ships that were made. I am also a person who does not want to give up just because of my weaknesses in certain areas. Overall, I could say that I am just an unbreakable plate in an unique ship.

Divya Thomas, Grade 9
North Garland High School, TX

Dreams

People always talk about dreams, but how many people actually act on their dreams? Martin Luther King Jr. said I have a dream. Leonardo Da Vinci dreamed of flight. A president once said that we would fly to the moon and back. All of those happened just like they dreamed. There is a poster in my class that says "dreams without actions stay dreams."

If you fail, keep on going. It's very very important that you stick to what you want. "Fight for what you believe in." If you keep on trying then you are bound to get it one of these times. Maybe you will need help, but one way or another your dream will come true.

The world would be so much better if people just believed that they can make a difference. I'm going to keep on dreaming, so should you.

Jake Hogan, Grade 8
Canyon View Jr High School, UT

The Life I Live

I hear your judgmental words; I can't dodge your glares; but what you do can't hurt me; what you say won't affect me. I've built up my walls; put a blockade on myself, so no words can ever break through. I've created my world from these restrictions; somewhere I can escape the lies of my reality; somewhere I can lead a different, imperfect life. The flowers will never die there, and the leaves will never fall. Snow will be more like marshmallows, rather than the sloppy cold blanket. I'll never grow old; my skin will always have a youthful glow and I shall live forever.

Go ahead and say what you think, I'll never change under your negativity, because you can't tell me to quit. Writing is more than just what I do, it's who I am.

Andie Palagi, Grade 8
East Middle School, MT

My Future Profession

For my future job, I want to be a professional chef. The reason why I want that specific profession is because I love watching the Food Network. *Secrets of a Restaurant Chef*, *Good Eats*, *Iron Chef America*, and *Chopped* are my favorite shows. I just like watching how the chefs move around the kitchen in *Iron Chef* and *Chopped*. It's almost like a dance, sometimes fast and hurried, sometimes just gliding around gracefully. With *Good Eats* and *Secrets of a Restaurant Chef*, though, I like how the hosts show what goes on in the cooking process, and how they describe the smell and taste of their dishes.

When I was young, my mom shared her chocolate-chip cookie recipe with me. I thought those cookies were just divine! I loved those cookies, almost as much as my mom, but that wasn't really what got me to do more. I think the real time that I was really propelled to doing bigger things was when my friend's mom was watching TV. My mom had to be somewhere that day, and I went over to my friend's house. Her mom turned on the Food Network and I saw Emeril Lagasse cooking up a storm on *Emeril Live*. I really wanted to stay parked in front of the television and just see what exactly Emeril's techniques were, but that would have been rude. So I went home later that evening and turned on the Food Network. Needless to say, I was hooked!

Meridith Peel, Grade 7
St Elizabeth Ann Seton School, TX

My Family

Webster's Dictionary defines family as, "A group of people in the service on an individual." But, is that what family really means? To me, family means people that are there for you no matter what. They love you for who you are, even if you are not perfect. They provide for you and support you in all you do. Because of this, I would say that family is the most important thing in my life.

My family loves me twenty-four hours a day, seven days a week — even if we do not always get along. My family's love comes with no strings attached, and is one of the constants in my ever-changing world. Next, they provide for me by giving me shelter. Without a stable shelter, and home life, I would not be able to survive. Because of the love in my family, we make our house a home — a home that I would call a stable home. Finally, they give me support to reach for the stars. My family never puts me down; they encourage me to be whoever I want to be and live my life to the fullest.

Not many people are blessed enough to have the kind of family I have. I am loved unconditionally, provided for, and am supported in all I do. The presence of my family will never fade. For these reasons my family is the most important thing in my life and that will never change.

Jennafer Harris, Grade 8
Zia Middle School, NM

General Zaroff: Civilized

General Zaroff is a civilized person. He is an extremely cultured human being. He reads fine literature. His grand château is full of luxurious things. The wine he drinks is only the finest. He is quite knowledgeable and can most likely tell you anything about any subject.

General Zaroff is a cultured man. He can speak many different languages. Many of his possessions come from different places. He has traveled all over the world. He can probably tell you more about a country's cultural background than anyone else. Some may argue that General Zaroff is uncivilized because he hunts fellow human beings

General Zaroff is not afraid of spending big money for his possessions. The wines he drinks are imported from the finest vineyards. He lives in a grand château on his own secluded island. He eats only the finest meals. He dresses himself in the most extravagant clothes with the most intricate designs. General Zaroff has many of the trappings of fine living.

General Zaroff has been well educated. The books he has read are some of the most complex books of all time. He reads all the classics, as well as the more obscure books. Zaroff is smart enough that he can learn several languages and keep them straight. His plans to ambush his prey and get away with it are ingenious.

For all these reasons, General Zaroff is an extremely civilized person. His not being refined is like Hitler not being evil. General Zaroff is just a misjudged person because of what he finds joy in. But he knows that what other people think does not matter. Even if it did, what they think is completely false. Maybe people should be more like General Zaroff. He is, after all, an exceptionally civilized human being.

Taylor Hammer, Grade 9
South Jordan Middle School, UT

Rockey

He was the cutest one foot long and half a foot tall dog in my mom's hands with his brown eyes, black fur, and what my mom calls 'boxing gloves' are all four of his white paws. He showed up outside of our house and ran up to my sister. My mom took him around to everyone's houses wanting to know where he lived. No one knew where he lived so we took him into our house. The next day our neighbor came over and told us that he was thrown out of a passing cars window. We waited a few weeks to see if anyone would claim him but no one did. The next day we took him to the vet and they said that he had heartworms. He was sick for days because of the medicine he was on so, we were all worried about him. Now he is a happy, healthy dog and he can do everything that any other dog can do. We finally decided to call him Rockey because he had a rocky start to life. Rockey has a huge 'Great Dane' dog bed all for himself and two kennels while the other two dogs only have small beds and one kennel each. Rockey grew up to be a great dog that we call 'ours.'

Kelsey Martin, Grade 7
Goodson Middle School, TX

Basketball

I started playing basketball when I was in 5th grade. I never joined a team because I wanted to get better. In 6th grade I tried out for the school team but later I quit because I didn't understand the plays and I didn't know what some words meant.

In the 7th grade I was the manager for the basketball team for about 3 weeks. Then the coach saw me playing and asked me if I want to be on the team and I said yes. The first practice day I learned the plays and my position. But on the first game I played I completely froze and forgot everything they taught me. So the coach only played me in games for a little while. I was officially known as a "bench warmer."

In the summer I would go to Shawver Park with guys twice my age and play against them. I learned a lot of new things and started to get better. I played there every day from 6 to 8 pm.

Now that I got better, I will not be known as a bench warmer any more.

Billy De La Cruz, Grade 8
Rio Bravo Middle School, TX

Applause Theater

Every Wednesday, I go to Applause Theater for musical acting. I love to sing and act, so I'm hoping to become an actress when I get older. Musical theater is really exciting; we get to act out musicals like *Grease*. They teach us how to prepare an audition so that we may get the part we desire. Also, the teacher there helps us warm up our vocal cords and practice projecting our voices. It is very hard not to like theater after the first week because the people there comfort you when you get stage fright, they help you over come your fears. Like maybe when you're acting you think you look dumb or maybe you think you don't sing well, they will help you overcome your fears. I love theater and every week I can't wait until Wednesday!

Alexis Trosclair, Grade 7
Goodson Middle School, TX

Michael Jordan

46-year-old Michael Jordan, born on February 17, 1963, is a legendary basketball player. Michael went to college at North Carolina in eighty-four. Michael was one of a few people elected to be in the basketball hall of fame on April 6, 2009, and on September 11, 2009 he became inducted. His first basketball game began on December 21, 1981 at North Carolina at Chapel Hill with the Tar Heels.

Michael Jordan led them to National Championship in 1982. Jordan became one of the most effectively marketed athletes of his generation, and he joined the NBA Chicago Bulls in 1984. He quickly emerged as a league star, and entertained crowds with his prolific scoring. His leaping ability was illustrated by performing slam dunks from the free throw line at a slam dunk contest. His nickname is "Air Jordan" and "His Ariness."

Kelsey Henry, Grade 7
Deweyville Middle School, TX

Hello Seattle!

As I feel the car come to a slow and complete stop, I open my heavy eyelids as the dim light from the remaining sun pours into our suitcase filled car. I hear the door of my grandma's house slam, and muffled hellos coming from outside. In the distance the Space Needle towers over ant-like people, and the city lights start turning on one by one. I smile to myself and silently say, "Hello Seattle!"

My sweet, little grandmother is always so excited when we come to visit. While walking across the old, creaky porch, memories fill my head like a swarm of bees! Once inside the amazing smells of freshly cooked pork, rice, and my grandma's famous Korean pancakes feel like home. Sitting at the large, glass-topped table, that in its younger days sat many friends and family, we eat, talk, and have a great time!

Lifetime friends are the greatest! No matter how long it's been, it always feels as if they live right next door. As we make our way to West Seattle the excitement of seeing our old friends runs through me, ready to BURST! When we finally arrive at their small, white house I am embraced with what feels like thousands of hugs. Then, sitting in their cozy living room, we make memories and laugh the night away!

As we pull away in the dimming sunlight, leaving our family and friends behind, I silently say, "Goodbye Seattle, 'til next time!"

Mckenzie Morstad, Grade 8
Thora B Gardiner Middle School, OR

Harry Board

One night, a Friday night, in the evening I was outside with my brother, Kevin, my scooter and his skateboard.

I was on my scooter when Kevin decided to wave his skateboard behind my head. I didn't know he was doing it. Unknowingly, I stepped on my scooter brake and spun around.

I saw it and winced knowing it was going to hit me. Then "Bam!" lights out because it hit me hard. I got up and tried to go wash the blood off of my face with the water hose, and my brother kept telling me to not tell mom. He kept on until in ferocity I told him, I was just going to wash the blood off my face with the hose.

My brother Kevin saw how bad it was, so he sheepishly went to tell my parents. Good thing my dad was there because my mom was scared to death. Then my dad said we needed to go to the hospital which scared me even more.

Once we got there my parents, brother, and I went to the emergency room. My mom did all the paper work, and then they let me in with my dad. The doctor said it was a good hit and prepared everything to get me stitched up. When the doctor had finished, he told me I had nineteen stitches!

Then we went home, ate dinner, and went to bed.

Macaulay Noel, Grade 7
Santa Teresa Middle School, NM

Randomicity!

Hi my name is Audrey Alexander, and this is a story about my random life. Ever since I was a little girl, I would always ask to play with the most random things such as a napkin. I would make the napkin a home for my favorite stuffed animal. Now that I am older, I am still just as random as ever! With my allowance or birthday money I will buy a useless piece of junk. I even might just buy it because I think it's cool. I am a major packrat and I don't like getting rid of my things. My mom constantly has to tell me it is just a piece of trash, and she will throw it away. Sometimes I will go and get it from the trash and go put it back in my room, but then I realize that it is trash. Many people describe me as the most random and spontaneous person that they have met because of my constant sayings or what I pull out of my pocket. I always get remarks on my randomness. Whether it is good or bad I don't really care about what people have to say about me. I like the way I am random or not random. That is a small intro into my random life!

Audrey Alexander, Grade 8
St Elizabeth Ann Seton School, TX

Endangered Species

Today there are so many endangered species. Some of the many are polar bears, pandas, beluga whales, and many more. There are many reasons for these animals becoming endangered. There are two main reasons for this. One is global warming, and the second is human actions. Every day 94% of people identify littering as a major environmental problem and yet people still litter.

The main reason why people litter is just out of carelessness. By us littering we are hurting the animals that surround us. For example, when most people go to the beach they leave their trash on the sand thinking others will come and pick it up. But the water comes up, takes it near animals, and just by littering once a day we hurt the animals surrounding us. The solution is simple. We just have to not litter and do some volunteer work and clean up. By doing this we can help the animals survive for future generations.

Jamie Glaser, Grade 7
Placerita Jr High School, CA

Thursday Night Lights

On a Thursday we were playing at Ysleta High School it was Ysleta us Rio Bravo us. When the game started we were doing great two interceptions on one of those interceptions we made a touchdown. They were huge but we know size doesn't matter if you're big, short, skinny, fat, or anorexic as long as you want it more than the other team. The half was over we were up 6 to 0. The coaches gave us a pep talk during half time. After half time, we scored two more but they scored 6 points a touchdown but we had them the rest of the game and after we felt knowing we won. After the game we threw the ball up the ball and when it hit the floor we fell knowing we had a great day and a great game.

David Navarrette, Grade 8
Rio Bravo Middle School, TX

Irony of Invisibility

Out the window, watching the trees roll past, I wished it would all rewind. I was thinking, "Isn't it a little too much to expect someone to survive a whole year at a new school?" Not to mention this was first grade! This wasn't like kindergarten; there were no early releases. Now I was in real school. Mom had tried to make me excited, but it hadn't worked. When we got out of the car, I was in tears. I clung to Mom's leg while we walked. To my horror, my teacher came to take me; I hoped fervently that she wouldn't see me crying. Mom left. Traumatized that everyone would see me in tears, I walked inside. The children sat in a circle in the front of the room. I couldn't bring myself together, so I sat down and wished I could melt into the floor and become invisible. It didn't happen.

The day got better, although I felt out of place because these kids were all friends. During recess, they were playing. I wished I knew them so they would play with me. I had started to become invisible when I didn't want to be. The moment I wanted attention, I was neglected, but before, when attention was the last thing I was looking for, it was all I got. I felt sick. So I just sat and watched the other kids and thought about the irony of invisibility.

Wyatt Stevens, Grade 8
Headwaters Academy, MT

My Horse and I

I am a thirteen year old girl. For as long as I can remember, I have always loved animals, but horses are my favorite.

I didn't know if I would ever get a horse. My mom said to pray about it, so I did. Then one day a friend of mine said her parents had a horse for sale for 1,000 dollars.

I didn't know what my parents would say about me finding a horse, but I had to tell them. So when I got home from school, I told my mom about the horse. She said that I would have to ask my dad. So when he came home, I told him they wanted 1,000 dollars for it, but it also included the saddle and one bag of feed.

The next day we went to look at the horse. To my surprise, my parents bought her! I couldn't believe I had my own horse!

Since she was not completely trained, my dad and I started training her. Before I knew it I was riding her all by myself. I named her Shelby. Now I spend as much time with her as I can. I'm also training her for barrel racing. This last summer, I got to go to the rodeo and barrel race with her.

We didn't win but that did not keep me from trying again. So now I train with her as much as possible, and she's getting better. That's something that's very important to me.

Susie Enns, Grade 7
Seminole Jr High School, TX

Why I Love Marin Headland

Marin Headlands Institute in Sausalito, California, was a remarkable experience I had last year in seventh grade with my class. We had the chance to not only bond together, but learn about our environment and how to protect it. The animals and our surroundings helped me to understand about a different side of our world and a different side of me.

The counselors and the nature I met made me become aware of the fact that there are more things that exist than I thought. I learned facts about animals, plants, and how food sources are taken away from them. It is important to respect the good aspects and change the bad ones such as dishonor to our surroundings.

Having another class from a different school accompany us on this week helped me realize how nice it is to meet and share new challenges with new people. Bonding with my class and the other school, working together as one helped me to realize that we have something in common, and if we listen to others, we may find out something new. The challenges that we had to finish led me to see others perspectives instead of just my ideas.

When our trip came to an end, the things I experienced affected my personal life such as relating to others within my class. Science made me think about other ways I could experiment new changes resembling our ecosystem. Overall this experience changed some ways I view my life and the world.

Jullisa Romani, Grade 8
St Michael's Episcopal Day School, CA

Buckeye

It all started out one day when I had a soccer game. It was really early in the morning, so we went to get donuts afterward. Across the street of the donut shop was a Dollar General. In the parking lot, there was a gentleman selling chocolate lab puppies. I begged my dad to go look at them. He said that was fine, but with one condition. We can't get any. We ended up leaving, but a few hours later, we came back and bought one. We ended up buying the laziest, sleepiest puppy of the bunch.

In her first few months, she pulled a couple of the puppy tricks on us. When she was in our backyard, she chewed up everything in sight. At night, she used to bark because she was hungry or lonely. Buckeye soon grew out of her puppy stage to my mother's relief.

Later, there was this guy that came to our house to fix our door. He soon noticed Buckeye in her crate. He liked her so much that he offered to pain our whole house for free in exchange for our dog. To his dismay, we said no. After that experience, I figured out that I would never trade Buckeye for anything.

Grace Goulet, Grade 7
St Elizabeth Ann Seton School, TX

Empathy

I know I'm young, but feelings are real. When you have so much hatred, and resent towards the people in your life what other choice is left than to push them all away and to go back to where you left in the first place. I live each day going by the regret and loss of my past, of taking everything that ever made me genuinely happy for granted. Every night there's that same star I wish upon hoping one day it will take me back to the state of being where I want to be at, and the passionate love my amazing and beautiful mother once felt. When you have something taken away from you, you realize the price it really is worth. Sometimes, I'm happy I'm so torn apart from the truth I've been facing I have my whole life ahead of me, and this is just the beginning, but there's something in me that keeps addressing that this nightmare I'm going through, will all lead up to something. Day by day, I wonder what would be different if people really understood how I felt, what I feel, what I would do to hit rewind way back to where it all started. Maybe things would be different, maybe I would be different. But, that'd be a fairy tale. Besides, isn't that what everyone else wishes for to? Keep your head up high honey, everything happens for a reason.

Sharon Covary, Grade 9
Desert Oasis High School, NV

There Is a Mysterious Creature in Me

There is a mystery creature in me, waiting for me to figure out what it is…trying to grasp the world with its monkey paws… examining existence with its eagle eyes…using the mentality of a fox to think its way through life… giving me hints about itself, but at the same time, it seems as if it is not ready to let me know yet.

Is there a monkey in me? Playfully swinging from tree to tree beneath the hot rain forest sun…screaming and shrieking its high pitched yell when frustrated, yet still cheerful? Is this monkey really what is inside of me, begging to get out, or is it a fox?

Is there a fox in me? Quick thinking and sly… always finding a way to sneak up on you…lurking in the deep blue darkness, lightened up by only the vivid glow of the night moon…ready to lunge and catch its prey… its intelligent mind and strong senses always prepared for whatever comes next. Is it actually a fox that is buried deep in the layers of my heart or is it an eagle?

Is there an eagle in me? Soaring through the clear blue sky, looking down at the altering landscape… always on the lookout for danger… gathering twigs and grass to build its vast next in the midst of the strongest and sturdiest tree… doing whatever possible to protect its eggs that are soon to blossom into chicks. Is this high-flying bird the creature that defines me?

Or am I a mix of all three? A clever fox, a carefree monkey, and an alert eagle, these animals are what make me, me… the foundation of my soul. All mixed together to form a single mystery creature.

Sofia Paganin, Grade 7
Lindero Canyon Middle School, CA

Roller Coaster Rides

Do you like roller coasters? Well I like roller coasters. I have been on a lot of roller coasters and have been to so many amusement parks. I have been on roller coasters that are fast, slow, tall, and short. Some with loops, spins, and all of that crazy stuff.

My favorite roller coaster is the Top Thrill Dragster in Sandusky, Ohio. That was the best vacation I have been on. It was so fun there because of all of the rides and because of the location. From the top of the Top Thrill Dragster you can see a pretty good view of Canada.

The ride I do not like so much is the Texas Giant in Arlington, Texas. The ride is wooden and more shaky than most rides. It jerks you around like crazy.

The ride with the most loops is the Incredible Hulk in Orlando, Florida. This ride has 8 loops and rides very smoothly.

The ride with the most spins is the Tony Hawks Big Spin in Arlington, Texas. It takes you on about 20 spins per minute. It spins fast; it drops, and has quick turns.

I like roller coasters because of the thrill and the speed of the roller coaster. I think others should like roller coasters too because they are just very fun and people of any age can ride them.

Giraud Mouton, Grade 8
St Elizabeth Ann Seton School, TX

A Joke

Have you ever played a joke that had gone too far? Well, my former best friend did, she played a joke on my close friend Monica. I think Lisa was jealous of Monica because she and I talked a lot to each other and thought she was going to be my new best friend, but that's wasn't going to happen because Lisa and I had been best friends since Kindergarten. Lisa always diatribed Monica.

So on Halloween Lisa told me her plan and persisted for me to help but I denied her proposition. I tried to convince her not to do it and she had promised she wouldn't do it either but I guess her promise meant nothing.

During the Halloween parade, Lisa surreptitiously went to the bathroom and changed into the costume of a scary clown. Suddenly I noticed Monica had gone in the bathroom. Lisa waited for Monica to come and when she got there Lisa shut the door on Monica and then turned off the lights and when they turned on again, the clown was standing in front of Monica. She got scared because there used to be a myth that supposedly a clown killed a girl in the bathroom. So when I got there Lisa was laughing in Monica's face.

After that me and Lisa stopped talking and she knew why. If you don't trust people you care about then eventually you're going to lose them one way or another.

Jessica Devora, Grade 8
Charles Maclay Middle School, CA

Love, Peace, and Friendship

What I want are three things: love, peace and friendship. I want love because I'd be empty without it. When I'm sad I want somebody to hug me and tell it's all right, not a pair of shoes or jeans.

I want friendship because I'd be lonely. I'd watch the other girls play volleyball and basketball while I'm on the bench trying not to get hit by the football. Money can't buy true friends.

I want peace because too many bad things happen to good people. I'm tired of hearing the police siren pass my house. Money can't buy the things I truly want.

Lauren Torrez, Grade 7
Our Lady of the Rosary School, CA

World Peace

What I want most that money can't buy is world peace. World peace is what I really want in life. On the news I hear that there's murder, gun shootings, and fighting. My mom always tells me, "Treat people the way you want to be treated." She only tells me that when I get in a fight with my brother or with one of my cousins.

There are other people who have wanted world peace as well. Martin Luther King, Jr. wanted a special kind of peace. He wanted black people and white people to finally get along. There was Mahatma Gandhi, he didn't want violence in the world. The Nobel Peace Prize was name after Mahatma Gandhi. The most spiritual person was Pope John Paul II. People John Paul II traveled all around the world to try to get different countries to be peaceful.

I want world peace for the Earth, because I want it to be a better place. We can all make a difference. We should all want world peace, to stop fighting, racism, and war. Let's hope and pray that people who want to destroy life, that their hearts will be changed to hearts of love and peace.

Nathalia Padilla, Grade 7
Our Lady of the Rosary School, CA

2009 H1N1 "Swine" Flu

The 2009 H1N1 is a new virus causing many people of all ages to become ill. The virus, commonly called the swine flu, is passed on from person to person, similar to the normal influenza. On the other hand, this sickness is very contagious and severe within five to seven days after the person is diagnosed. H1N1 is often referred to as swine flu, because of the virus' similar genes with the flu passed around in pigs, or swine. Symptoms of H1N1 include fever, cough, sore throat, runny or stuffy nose, body aches, headache, chills and fatigue. In April, when the influenza had just begun to circulate, there was no antidote. However now, vaccines are constantly being produced. Deaths and flu hospitalizations are increasing, and flu activity is now occurring in thirty-seven states in the U.S. The Centers for Disease Control and Prevention continue to monitor the Swine Flu activity, hoping this disease does not travel any further.

Julie Torgerson, Grade 7
Placerita Jr High School, CA

Signs

The trees flew by in a blur as my mom and I drove home from my brother's soccer game. In an attempt to strike up a conversation, my mom said, "It was a good game, huh?"

"Yeah," I replied, "I've never seen them work so hard to score a goal. They played well."

Wasn't exactly a conversation starter and it ended with me turning to glance out my window and stare at the endless hills of dirt. Now, just to clarify, my mom and I weren't in any sort of argument or angry at each other here, just a little disappointed with the turnout of my brother's soccer game.

When I glanced out the window, I saw a "Historical Marker" sign and the only words on the sign that I could read stated, in big bold letters, "Spanish Entrada Site."

"Someday I am going to travel all around New Mexico and read those signs," I stated, "I've always been interested in what they say."

"There must be some interesting stuff on those signs," she responded, "I've often wondered about what they say, myself."

In my mind, I pictured the horses that rode into this land, the banners of the Conquistadors flaying in the wind and the crosses held high portraying their ever loyal lives to Christ.

I was in awe of my Spanish ancestors and the bravery they portrayed when traveling into this new land of unknown dangers, a land of unknown gifts and curses, and a Land of Enchantment.

Ryan Hayden, Grade 8
St Thomas Aquinas School, NM

The Downside of Expression

Although we say we value freedom of expression, most of us are not really very tolerant of people who express unpopular ideas or act in uncomforting ways. Three main ways we do this is through the way we dress, our religions and music.

People judge others by what they wear just because it's different from what they wear themselves. You can choose from many different clothing styles. Heaven forbid someone stand out in a crowd because of their ensemble. We should be able to dress freely.

Others look down on those who express their religion. There are all kinds of religion choices, and there's a certain one for every person. It may not be the same as everyone else's, but it's their own business. So why should people make rude comments about them? Let them go about their lives in peace.

Some people think others are weird because of the music they listen to. What's the big deal? We all have different tastes. People think others are scary or weird because they listen to bands that are different from what they're used to.

Although not everyone does this, many people judge a person by their looks, choice of religion, and musical preferences. It would be so much nicer if we could agree to disagree.

Alissa Stevens, Grade 8
Holliday Middle School, TX

Freedom Helps

The best three things in the United States are liberty, military, and freedom to speak. These are things we have in the U.S.A.

Liberty lets people make good choices. To pick your life and how you want to live it. No one else can tell you what to do and what education to have. There are enough things to do and you can pick and to achieve what you think or want.

The military also helps us and not to do things other countries do. There are no wars, because we have people to go and fight for what we believe in. They help us be free and not be in danger of what is going on in other places.

The good thing about freedom of speech is that you can protest against things you don't like. Also if we say something that someone else doesn't like, we don't have to worry about getting hurt or injured by anyone. We also have the freedom to vote. Now women can vote for president and not just men.

These three things are the best things I like about freedom. They can help us live our lives and not like other people in different countries.

Andrea Ortega, Grade 7
Santa Teresa Middle School, NM

My Favorite Holidays

I am writing an essay about my favorite holidays. My first one is of course Christmas. The reason I like this holiday is because it represents the birth of Baby Jesus. Some people are so lucky to be are born on Christmas. I also like it because everybody is grateful for what they have. All of the things we have now represent how much your family loves you. I thank the Lord for bringing me great parents. They also thank him for bringing me into their lives. Even though we get on each others' nerves, I love them with all my heart. I also love this holiday because of the wonderful gifts that I receive.

My second favorite holiday is Thanksgiving. This is the holiday that shows how much you appreciate everyone and everything. I bless all of my family's hearts. They have very generous hearts. Our families are able to keep us safe and make miracles. This holiday also represents the day the Pilgrims met the Indians.

Halloween is also a great holiday. Some people say that this holiday celebrates the devil. I kind of believe them but it also gives children a chance to dress up and masquerade. My favorite part about this holiday is getting candy. The thing that stinks about it is that it gets really cold every year. Most people think that they are too old to trick or treat. I say that no matter how old you are, you can't stop having fun.

Those are three of my favorite holidays of the year. Each serves a different purpose and each is unique it its own way. I just love them all.

Christian Shaw, Grade 7
Goodson Middle School, TX

Living My Dream Life

I was starting a theatre class at Lifesong Studio and I felt a lot of excitement because I love performing. Since I went to a theatre class there, they informed me about musicals they were having this year. The first musical was *Annie Jr*. They had auditions for *Annie Jr*. on August 22 and then the show nights started in October. So I went home and I asked my mom if I could audition and she said that would be wonderful.

After a week or two, I auditioned for four hours. That night I got a callback. You should have seen me, I was so excited. So the next day I went to callbacks for another four hours. That night my mom got an e-mail and I was on the cast list as an orphan called Kate. I was so thrilled, I was screaming around the house. I had to begin going to rehearsals all the way through September. It was a lot of work and I had so much fun during rehearsals. I was living my dream life.

Olivia Hervey, Grade 7
St Elizabeth Ann Seton School, TX

My Birthday

Wake up! Wake up! Yelled my anxious sister, "It's your birthday." I got up lazily to look at the clock that displayed the time which read eight o'clock in the morning. Still wondering why I had been woke up so early; making my way to the kitchen my family started singing the happy birthday song. When the song finished my parents handed me an envelope, I emptied its contents and found out they were tickets to the band named Kings of Leon. They were going to play at California. As soon as I found out my bags were packed faster than you could say California. When we arrived in the airport we rushed to the hotel and took off for the stadium the lines were so long we had to wait two blocks down. The concert was cool and loud that even after we were left the concert my ears still felt weird. The next day I thanked my parents so much for the best birthday ever.

Joshuah Ochoa, Grade 8
Rio Bravo Middle School, TX

Happiness!

Do you like being happy and have happiness in your life?!
Happiness is a good feeling knowing that there's times when you can be happy or sad. Even if we all love being happy anytime like they say live, love, laugh!

I am mostly happy all the time. I love laughing and making my friends laugh so we can all have a good time!

There are times when you could be happy for other reasons like when something good happens to you or someone makes you smile! and makes your day.

It's always best to be happy and never be down because you can feel upset or sad and everyone knows you should always smile and fill your family with happiness! and joy.

Make your day and do something good so something good can happen to you so you can be happy.

Brisa Quezada, Grade 8
Rio Bravo Middle School, TX

Christmas Time!!!

My family is always excited for Christmas time because it is the holiday we decorate and celebrate the most. On Christmas Eve, it is a tradition to open ONE present from the family near bedtime. We also put out cookies and milk for Santa and leave 9 carrots for the reindeer. We wake up early in the morning and yell "Merry Christmas!" We then run down stairs excited for the day. We open only the Santa presents. My parents get this on camera because they love watching our expressions and keeping them for memories. We then wish our Grandpa in California a Happy Birthday. After we open all the Santa presents, we get ready to go to our Grandma's house. We usually get to her house around 11. Our family brings in different foods so our Grandma doesn't have to cook. We all hang out and play until everyone has arrived and when everyone comes, we gather and say grace. The kids get served and sit in the living room and watch movies. The adults serve themselves and sit at the dining table. Then we let our stomachs rest. When we've waited long enough, we bring out the dessert. All the kids run over each other excited about the treats. Then we decorate our Grandma's tree. We get home around 10 pm and open the rest of the presents. After that, we will go to sleep and wake up for another exciting day (my Mom's birthday). That's what we do during Christmas time.

Alexa Burciaga, Grade 7
St Elizabeth Ann Seton School, TX

Top Priority: God

The most important part in life to me is keeping God as my top priority. God is the most important person to me because He created everything: our families, friends, pets and animals, houses, cars, etc. Even though He himself did not create our houses and cars, He gave others the unique ability to be able to do it.

God is so important to me because He will never let me down and will always be there in my most troubled times. I can trust in Him that my hard times will turn out to be just fine. For example, my puppy, Callie, died a few weeks ago. My family was very sad, but God helped us move through it, and we are now thinking about getting another puppy.

Sometimes, I feel like I don't need anybody to help me, and that I can do it all by myself; but really, I need God. "Achievements are impossible with man, but all things are possible with God." This saying grabs my attention because I need to remember to include God in everything I do. For everything is possible with Him. It can be so simple and easy to get distracted and forget that I need God, but I need to remember that I need Him and He will help me because He loves me and wants the absolute best for me. God is the only way I want to make it through life.

Megan Evans, Grade 8
Faith Christian Jr/Sr High School, CA

Planet Earth

Planet Earth: a tiny speck in the universe. This tiny speck is our home, and our home is endangered. Many plant and animal species may be extinct in our lifetime. Polar bears are now highly endangered because of global warming. No one knows for certain which plants are being destroyed as the rain forests in the Amazon are cut down.

Humanity has lived on Earth for thousands of years. We have used the planet's resources until now without fear of running out. Humans have cut down forests and hunted some animals to extinction. It is now up to us to save planet Earth.

We can all do little things that can make a big difference. Water and energy conservation are great ways to help the earth. Taking shorter showers can save hundreds of gallons of water a year. Unplugging phone chargers and other electronics can save energy. Using CFL (compact fluorescent) light bulbs also saves energy. Dawn dishwashing detergent donates one dollar per bottle to the World Wildlife Fund. Carpooling can help reduce gas emissions.

Recycling also reduces pollution. Plastic bottles, glassware and aluminum can be recycled. Instead of buying plastic water bottles, buying one reusable water bottle cuts down on plastic waste. Planting trees is another good way to help the environment. Forests are being torn down, and in the process, many animal homes.

Our world is disappearing, and soon, there will be nothing left. Planet Earth is in danger. We can save the planet, one step at a time.

Veronica Huber, Grade 8
Zia Middle School, NM

Bowling

One thing that is important to me is bowling. My great grandma put me in a league when I was eight years old, and I didn't really know very much about bowling. I didn't really want to be in the league because I thought it was boring and I thought it wasn't competitive enough. I wasn't very good at first; my first game was ten.

Then, I started getting help from my coaches, practicing more, and going to tournaments. Tournaments are really fun because I like going to new places, and I get to spend time with my family and friends. I get to earn scholarships at the same time I am having fun bowling. When I went to my first tournament, the California State Tournament, I was nine years old. I had a lot of fun, and my team got second place so we got scholarships. When I went to the tournament, I saw how much competition there really was in bowling. That made me want to keep bowling. I am glad I didn't quit bowling, because it is what is most important to me and I love going to tournaments and bowling in league every week.

Stephani Cooksey, Grade 8
Faith Christian Jr/Sr High School, CA

Baseball Fan Forever

I will always be a baseball fan. I have played baseball since I was 3 years old, it is my favorite sport, and I still play it. I like it because you have to have hand-eye coordination and fast reflexes. I play select baseball for a team called the Heat, and I will play with the team until I get to high school. My team is very good. We always win at least 25 games a year, but it depends on how many games we play. My goal in baseball is to bat a .475 average all year.

I have always wanted to be a professional baseball player and I hope I can get to be one. I like baseball because it is fun and exciting, it is very exciting when your team wins a tournament. I think my team has won about ten first place trophies and twenty second place ones. I would love to become a professional baseball player and I think it would be cool to make it my job.

Kevin Lentzner, Grade 7
St Elizabeth Ann Seton School, TX

A Day in the Life of a Disney Fan

I have always loved Disney ever since I was little. My favorite Disney movie has always been *Beauty and the Beast*. When I first visited Disneyland at three years old, I gazed at the wonderful majesty of its castle. I saw the beautiful fireworks, and the magic of it all made me wonder how it was made to be like that. Now we flash forward nine years. I have been a Disney fan for almost my whole life. I have always wanted to go to Tokyo Disneyland but looking at it is nice enough. My love of Disney has made me some enemies, but that is ok with me. Now that Disney is going to go back to the traditional cell animation that was done when Walt Disney was alive, I am loving it even more. When I grow older, I would like to work for Disney very much. That is a peek in the life of a Disney fan.

Alex Gayon, Grade 7
St Elizabeth Ann Seton School, TX

Break Dancing

I was in third grade. My heart was pumping. The music was booming so loud that the room was vibrating. All the kids were chanting my name like a bunch of monkeys in the jungle. This is how it happened.

I woke up Friday morning, and I was getting ready for school. I had known there was a dance, but little did I know what was going to happen. I went to class and the work was very difficult. My teacher scowled like a hawk at me all day. I had gotten a "C" on my test that day.

"THIRD GRADE PLEASE REPORT TO THE DANCE THIRD GRADE THANK YOU." I trudged to the dance thinking of what a day I had! As I was listening to the music I saw a circle of people. I found out that it was a dance off. I maneuvered to the front of the crowd and suddenly this kid I didn't even know challenged me! I danced I had won my first dance off.

I was in third grade my heart was pumping. The music was booming. The kids were chanting my name!

Willie Torres, Grade 7
Santa Teresa Middle School, NM

Ballet

My heart is racing, lights are flashing, and the crowd is chanting my name, "Madison, Madison." The bell rings, not to signify my turn to dance for the title of Miss Dance of America, but to end third period. I rush out the door into the busy hallways thinking to myself, "if only…"

What is a dancer? She is someone who wishes to live, breathe, eat and dance. From pointe shoes to canvas slippers, there is nothing to hate about the sport of ballet. While some may say ballet is not a sport, I disagree. From bruises to broken bones, this is my life and there is certainly nothing wimpy about it. As my teacher once jokingly said, "If ballet were easy, they would call it football."

Although I said we are not fragile little girls, dancers love to "bling" it up every chance we get. From makeup to Swarovski crystals, performances transform you into a different person. When you think of ballet, most people automatically think of classical composers, but ballet has grown a lot more modern. We still dance to composers like Enya, but we also have very fast dances composed to high jumps and difficult spins en pointe.

You have now stepped into the shoes of a dancer. Ballet isn't just tutus and weird shoes. It is training that requires determination, strength, and confidence. Dancers are warriors in the form of beauty and grace.

Madison Cogburn, Grade 7
St Thomas Aquinas School, NM

What I Want Most

I want peace. Peace in school. Peace in homes. Peace in the world.

I want peace in school. By this I mean I don't want to see little or older children fighting. They might fight for a ball, jump rope, or any other equipment or supplies. I wish I could just see everyone happy and sharing with one another.

I want peace in homes. I don't want to go to a house and see a brother and sister fighting. Maybe they are fighting because they didn't agree, or one of them just doesn't want to give the other what he/she is asking for. I would love to see families happy and united. I would love to experience peace in all homes.

Peace in the world. I think this is necessary in life. There shouldn't be war! Why so much killing and loss of innocent lives? Why so many families separated? Instead of war why is there not a constitutional meeting where they would arrange peace between nations. I think peace is a necessity for the world.

Peace in school, homes, and in the world is necessary. Peace is a comforting, relieving, and great feeling to have. The more peace, the more happiness. Peace is what I want most in the world.

Alondra Rodriguez, Grade 8
Our Lady of the Rosary School, CA

My Friends

I have many amazing friends, but I am going to tell you about five of my best friends, Katie, Maryssa, Clare, Lauren, and Amelia. These aren't my only friends by the ones I am closest to.

One of my friends is Katie Ouellette; she has long blonde hair and hazel eyes. When you first meet Katie she seems shy, but when you get to know her she is very outgoing. She is very intelligent and is always eager to help me with homework.

Another friend of mine is Maryssa Buffano; she has long, dark brown hair and brown eyes. She is tall and she is a great dancer. Maryssa is also very fun and outgoing.

My next friend is Lauren Ondarza; she has long, really dark brown hair and brown eyes. She is very fun, yet organized. Lauren is fun to talk to when you just want to be girly and talk about fashion.

Clare Bowman is an amazing friend; she has long blonde hair and green eyes. Although she seems quiet, she is very talkative. Clare is an incredibly nice friend.

Last, but not least is my spectacular friend Amelia Arth. She has long, dark brown hair and brown eyes. She is very extroverted and fun to be around.

My friends are amazing. If I want to have some fun I can always count on them. Although we all have different personalities, we make a great combination.

Alyssa Aduddell, Grade 7
St Elizabeth Ann Seton School, TX

The Importance of Music!

I think that music is very important in life. Music is an outlet for everyone and a way of expressing oneself. I believe that music greatly affects the world and if we didn't have it, the world would be very plain.

To start, it is scientifically proven that playing an instrument actually helps students do better in math, reading, and health because you have to read the notes and count the beat. According to Rosalia Staricoff, who conducted a study, there is scientific evidence that music aids physical changes which can help heal the body. She said, "The physiological benefits have been measured. Music reduces blood pressure, the heart rate, and hormones related to stress." Doctors in the UK and Germany have discovered that listening to just 50 minutes of uplifting dance music increases your levels of antibodies.

Second, music can help one's mood. For example, when I'm angry I listen to "Interloper" by Slipknot because it's fast-paced and has plenty of screaming. Whenever I'm happy I listen to "Yes I Can" by Kerli because it's upbeat and happy. I usually choose music in the tone of my mood.

Last, I believe music is important because it's a universal language. No matter, what part of the world you're in; all music is created through 8 notes. As long as any melody and rhythm makes me feel myself, it's the best doctor I can find, and the best medicine I can recommend.

Jari Rubio, Grade 8
Zia Middle School, NM

My Guide

People should choose what they want to do and what they hope to accomplish but be guided by someone in doing so. Some have parents, family, or close friends to be there for them. There was a time when I felt I had not one of these. No one would help me with my personal problems or anything at all. It may seem selfish but I even thought of hurting myself considering what I should be thankful for. Then I met someone who changed that and helped me realize I had everyone at my side. This person was always there for me. Showing me the right direction, this person was my guide through the dark and showed me the light. All my problems were resolved by this one person, made me want to help others in my same situation. They had made me a better person. I came to the resolution that everyone will find that one person to help them through it all. I had found mine.

Jasmine May Barcelon, Grade 8
San Carlos School, CA

Undie Lockout

Have you ever been dragged from your room and then tossed like a rag doll onto a three story high balcony. I have it's not fun at all. I do not recommend it.

It was about mid day I was changing into my pjs. All of the sudden my big brother Brock walks in. I was in my underwear so I yelled, "Get out!" He didn't like that too much so Brock dragged me to the balcony and threw me over. We lived on the third floor so I couldn't climb down to the ground. I was locked out in my undies in winter. I was nine years old, how could I get out of this? I was a fudgesicle in a freezer it was so cold. I banged on the door, boom, bang, pow!

"Let me in," I yelled, "it's freezing cold!" So my cretin brother threw out a hooded sweatshirt. I pulled it on quicker than a cheetah. In the end I was outside probably twenty minutes. Just goes to show lock your door when you change.

Heath Burns, Grade 7
Santa Teresa Middle School, NM

Dad

Why did you have to go? Why you? I miss you Dad. Ever since they told me you were gone I felt like the world was over me and I couldn't help it. You are my life, Daddy. I hate that I don't even remember you. I have only seen you in pictures. You left me without even getting to say good bye to me. When my mom told me you had passed away it was the worst day of my life. But I got to understand that this kind of stuff happens for a reason. Now I have my step dad and my crazy little brother. I'm not happy that you left, but I'm not sad either that I have a great step dad and great little brother. I will never forget you I will always have you in my heart no matter what, and I know that from where you are you're taking care of me and loving me. We will soon be together Dad again. I miss you a lot, and I love you with all my heart Dad.

Karina Torres, Grade 8
Rio Bravo Middle School, TX

My Obsession

I never thought I'd play a sport until a few years ago. My friends always played sports and had busy weeknights and games every weekend. I hate to say it, but I thought they were crazy. They were always talking about practices and games. At times, I felt left out or bored, but I didn't see myself doing anything.

At a family gathering, my cousin Ali had a volleyball net up. She had decided to try volleyball. Ali let some of our cousins bump the ball around and I got a feeling for the sport. After that, I decided to play volleyball for my school's team.

Three years later I got to play. At my school, you have to be in fifth grade to play most sports. I was able to play that year for a great coach, Coach B. She is an amazing woman who made sure we had a team. We trained hard, played hard and worked together even harder. In sixth and seventh grades, my dad has coached our team, since Coach B coaches another school team. We went to the championship last year and hold a great record this year.

Volleyball is more than just a sport; it's a way of life. It's also more than bump, set, spike. The sport is my life, and I hasten to add, my obsession.

Ann Marcelli, Grade 7
St Thomas Aquinas School, NM

Ping Pong

Pap! Pap! Pap! Back and forth went the ball, and "whoosh," I missed. "Well, that was a good game," I said to my dad. He replied, "15 to 21, your skills improve." I have almost forgotten how long it had been since I started to play ping pong. I played with my dad very often years ago before my mom and I came to America. One thing is sure: I really love ping pong.

The school I used to study in Taiwan had a ping pong club that provided ping pong tables, rackets and balls. Every club member enjoyed playing ping pong after school. I participated in the pin pong club in fourth grade. The reasons why ping pong was one of my favorite sports were: first, there was no need to move leg muscles too often, and second, it was a great exercise to practice reflex action. During that time, the more I practiced, the better I was at it. One time two of my friends wanted to play against me and I agreed. It didn't take long to beat them because they were too exhausted to fight for the ball game. Consequently, I won the game.

In conclusion, ping pong is a sport that I like the most. Particularly, I missed the old time when I played ping pong with my dad and friends, which gave me many unforgettable memories. I think I will keep playing ping pong. Without it, I don't feel like myself.

Jia-luen Yang, Grade 8
Zia Middle School, NM

When I Got Lost

Have you ever been lost in a store, or somewhere where you don't know your way around? I have. It was really scary.

I got lost in the mall when I was about five years old. My parents were in a store. I went to the restroom. When I got back I thought they had left me. I started running to look for them. I got tired and stopped. I started crying. After a while a security guy saw me by myself he got close to me. I thought he was going to take me away so I ran away from him. He caught me. We started looking for my parents. When I found them my mom was crying. I ran to them. I didn't want to get lost anymore. She told me to tell her where I was going before I left. This was the scariest time in my life, so far.

Arturo Valadez, Grade 8
Rio Bravo Middle School, TX

Turkey Day Traditions

My favorite holiday is Thanksgiving. It's my favorite because I like the food and I enjoy being with my family. Along with the food and family, I love the cool air fall brings. Sometimes families from other states come see us. Since our family is a football crazed family, we'll also watch the Thanksgiving football game. Usually after eating, my cousins and I will go play on the swing set. Another part of the reason Thanksgiving is my favorite holiday is because the Christmas feeling starts to affect me. Christmas is another favorite holiday! This Thanksgiving should be extra special because my sister from college is coming to visit us. Another part I love is helping my dad prepare and cook the turkey along with some side dishes. While cooking the food my family and I like to watch the Macy's Day Parade on TV. Mostly I like the idea of Thanksgiving because we give thanks for what we have and who we get to share it with.

Maddie Flores, Grade 7
St Elizabeth Ann Seton School, TX

That Day

Some days are bad, and some days are good. Sometimes you get both days like me. I should have known something was wrong. I should have noticed it at the beginning.

It was a Monday morning. It was October 1 which meant gifts. I woke up and my dad made me do all this work. I was thinking why is my dad like this today of all days?

Why is my dad making me do all this hard work? Why today? Something was wrong. Finally he said, "Hard work pays off."

He made me work for my birthday gift. It was a Polaris 110cc dirt bike with a lot of kicks. I said for me!!! Yes, "Hard work does pay off."

The bike was fast as a cheetah when I tried it however the bike was a nightmare; it had a lot of kick. When I drove it I crashed it, BOOM!! BANG!! right into a tree. I fell to the ground and woke up in a bed. I was dizzy and appalled I decided I would never ride that bike, however when I grow up, I probably will.

Miguel Luna, Grade 7
Santa Teresa Middle School, NM

Learning Responsibility

Responsibility is important while you're a child. When you're a child you don't have a lot of responsibility. The basic chores you have to do when you're a child are things like washing dishes, cleaning your room, or feeding and watering the animals if you have any.

Those are just the easy chores for kids who are ten years old or younger. When you're a teenager, you have to be more independent because you start driving. Your mom may ask you to go grocery shopping for her, or she may ask you to go pick up your brother or sister from somewhere.

When you are an adult, you have much bigger responsibilities. You have to buy a house, pay bills, keep a job, and maybe raise a family. It takes responsibility to keep your job and drive a car!

In everyday life nearly everyone has a responsibility, no matter what age. Babies have a responsibility, too; they have to scream and cry in order for you to notice that they need their diaper changed or if they want to be fed. Being responsible is what gets you through life.

In conclusion, do you think you need to be responsible to get through life? Your answer should be, "Yes," because if it was, "No," then your life is or could be out of order! So you should always be responsible, there's no telling what life will throw at you!!

Ariel Valentine, Grade 8
Holliday Middle School, TX

Music Is My Life!

I always have a song in my head no matter where I am, what I'm feeling, or what I do. It can be classical, alternative, show tunes, anything. I don't like to brag but I'm really good at music. I can play drums, piano, I'm learning guitar, and I'm a really good singer. I even write my own music!

Most of the time when I have an idea for a song I get so frustrated that I can't write it down. So I memorize the lyrics until I get home. Then I start writing. I usually write about personal situations.

The one band that has inspired me the most is Paramore. Their music is so good and deep. Their lyrics are personal and that's the main reason why I like them. Their main song that gets my attention most is "Misguided Ghost." These are my favorite lyrics to that song, "A broken heart and twisted minds so I can find someone to rely on and run to them, full speed ahead oh you are not useless, we are just misguided ghosts." I think I like those words so much because, I sometimes do feel useless and abandoned, and confused about everything.

Music is a powerful thing that can inspire a lot of people to do great things, and I want to be one of those people. Music is my life, and I couldn't live without it!

John Paul Sales, Grade 7
Seminole Jr High School, TX

Friends!!

Friends are always people you can rely on. I'm sure you have experienced having a friendship also. If I didn't have my friends, I don't think I would be here right now.

My best friend's name is Ashley Trevino. She lives in Grape Creek so I don't get to see her often. Although we live so far apart, the distance will never break us. We have the most amazing times together! I know for sure I can count on her. I am always there for her when she is down. When her boyfriend, Jacory, is acting up, I tell her everything's going to be okay. No matter the damage, we're always there for each other.

The things we like to do are usually go to the movies or the mall. The movie crew is usually Carley, Ashley, Jacory, Alex, Sierra, and Sherman. The mall crew is just Ashley and me. When I'm around Ashley, I always have a smile on my face. Our song is called "Break Up to Make Up." We dance in the car to that all the time! I'm just an all around happy person around her. I have no earthly idea what I would do without my Ashley baby! I will never forget our amazing, best friend, crazy, fun memories!

True friends are there for you no matter how much you mess up. They love you and guide you through it all.

Carley Jackson, Grade 8
Reagan County Middle School, TX

Life at St. Michaels During the Shakespeare Festival

At my school, St. Michaels, we have plays that we do each year during our Shakespeare Festival. In the 7th and 8th grade we do a Shakespearean play. In 7th grade my class did *Much Ado About Nothing*. Not everybody received the part that they wanted but we were still happy with what we had. Besides, every role in a play is very important because without all of the roles the play couldn't have gone on without them.

The first thing we do after we receive our parts is we practice our lines and get a sense about what the play is really about. In the play *Much Ado About Nothing*, the story was mainly about two couples: one that were madly in love with each other and the other that at first weren't too fond of each other. Next we focused mainly on rehearsing the play. After that hard work we do the minor things like props and costumes. Then we practice the play a few more times so we know how to use our props. After a couple dress rehearsals we are ready to put on our show.

When we perform these plays in April we are glad that we put all of our energy and time into them because the result is excellent and everyone likes it. The plays are a lot of fun even though they involve hard work. I am glad we do them every year because they bring out the best in everyone.

Savannah Symister, Grade 8
St Michael's Episcopal Day School, CA

Siblings

Do you have an older sibling? If so, you probably get tormented a lot by them. I know exactly how you feel.

I have three older brothers. I was the only girl in my family for a really long time. Being the youngest is hard enough, but I was the little sister. I didn't have to worry so much about my eldest brothers, because they moved out of the house before they became a problem for me. I was stuck with Ben for quite some time.

When I was little, Ben thought it was hilarious that I was afraid of the dark. I would usually get a glass of water before bed. Ben would hide around a corner right when I was about to turn, he would jump out and say, "BOO!" I, being completely terrified of the dark, would scream like the little girl that I was. You would think that after all the times he did this, I would have been used it it. But I never got used to it. He got me every time.

This is only one of the many things that happened to me as the youngest sibling. So, if you are an older sibling, please, have pity on us younger ones.

Rebecka Nisbet, Grade 8
St Thomas Aquinas School, NM

Living Determination

Is determination a noun, verb or adjective? What is it? The dictionary definition from Merriam-Webster is "the act of coming to a decision," "the decision or conclusion reached," "fixing of the character," and "firm purpose." Looking at the definitions, you can tell determination is around you every day in life. It can be pushed by coaches, parents, teachers, etc, or even your own peers. From my experience, I've felt so frustrated and overwhelmed when it comes to the sports I play interfering with my grades. Last year, I never worried about sports interfering with my excellent average of a ninety or above. Now, I'm just fighting to pass my classes as well as excel in sports.

With the difficulty level above my head, being determined to pass with good grades is all I'm focused on. I know that I'm not the only one in this situation, but sometimes I feel like I am. Hopefully, by the end of the six weeks I'll feel relaxed about myself and start off fresh for the next six weeks. I've realized that determination's building me in every way that Webster describes "determination."

Heidi Muery, Grade 9
Kaufer High School, TX

My Future

As I grow every day I have several goals to achieve.

I need my education which is to finish middle school, high school and to move on to college. While going to school I would like to join a soccer team to become a great player of soccer. I hope to do well enough to be a professional player. After this achievement I hope to have enough money to open my own private gym to train to be a boxer. I would want to be a famous lightweight boxer to be an influence to others.

Cesar Camarillo, Grade 8
Rio Bravo Middle School, TX

Children and Divorce

Whether it's because of a fight, adultery, or lack of original love, divorce has a very emotional effect on children. Especially at a young age, divorce leaves children not only angry, but also confused about marriage.

The "Hollywood Family" consists of perfectly in love parents and children who miraculously always get along. I have spent most of my life around children who have suffered divorce. Even though I am lucky enough to have parents who are happily married, I have an idea of what it must be like to be a product of divorce. Children may feel guilty on holidays, birthdays, or just days when they're with one parent. Some may also feel like they have to take sides when they're with one parent.

Shouldn't marriage last forever? I know that divorce leaves children confused about marriage. Children may think that marriage doesn't have to, or isn't supposed to last forever. Once in the third grade I had a friend whose parents were getting divorced. I asked her why and she simply responded that, "They were just married too long." I was very shocked when I heard her say that, but I never understood the impact until now.

The reason for the divorce doesn't change the impact that it has on children. Divorce not only defeats the purpose of marriage to the adults getting the divorce, but also the children facing it. It makes them value marriage less and makes it less likely that they will commit to a lifelong relationship.

Marcela Sosa, Grade 8
St Michael's Episcopal Day School, CA

Ginger and Chubby

Normally I would write about my family or friends, but that would be kind of boring. So, I'll talk about the next best thing. Ginger and Chubby!

No, Ginger and Chubby aren't my sisters. They're Chihuahuas. I've had them for four years now, and they're lots of trouble.

Let's talk about Ginger. Ginger is short and fat, with short light brown hair. She also has a chip on one of her little ears. She's a very nice dog and her favorite toy is a little green rabbit.

Let's talk about Chubby now. She has long legs with short dark brown hair. Unlike Ginger, Chubby has really big ears. Oh, and her favorite food is beans, not dog food. Ginger has a cheerful personality while Chubby has a very boring personality.

Ginger and Chubby are different, but at the same time they have one thing in common, they drive me CRAZY! My mom is thinking about getting another Chihuahua. Oh, great!

Andrew Jurado, Grade 8
Rio Bravo Middle School, TX

H.U.G. Patrol

When I grow up, I'm going to start the H.U.G. Patrol. They will be a group of people who go around doing spontaneously random things for the simple purpose of making someone's day. The motto of the H.U.G. Patrol would be "Hired Under God." There would be agents all around the country doing things to make people smile.

A group in New York would do something such as put on a dance party in Grand Central Station. They'd bring a boom box and one hundred people and dance around. They would go at it for about an hour, encouraging others to participate. Their goal: Do something that no one who witnessed it would ever forget. I think that would definitely get someone's attention.

Agents in Texas would do something like shop around Southlake Town Center dressed up in costumes. They might see a movie or shop around in random stores. They might even go out to eat at a restaurant or get some ice cream. Whatever they do would definitely get noticed and put a smile on someone's face.

I think the H.U.G. Patrol would make a difference in people's lives. If at least two people go from having a bad day to a good day, or from grumpy to happy, then the world would be a much better place. When more people are smiling, less people are frowning. People are more likely to look on the bright side of things if they are in a good mood.

Kelley Schorn, Grade 8
St Elizabeth Ann Seton School, TX

Don't Stop Believing

Failure is an everyday part of life. People fail every day, at school and at work. Without failure, there is no success. Failure doesn't mean you are a failure, it just means you haven't succeeded yet. In order to succeed, we must first believe that we can. Failure is part of the learning process. You fail in order to know what not to do. Albert Einstein failed many times before he found the speed of light. You can't find the key to success until you walk through the door of failure. You will always fail many times before you can succeed.

Believing in yourself is sometimes knowing you will learn from your mistakes. Believing in yourself is very important in life because, if you believe, you can achieve, and you will succeed. When you believe in yourself, you can achieve almost anything. You need to believe in yourself before anyone else can believe in you. Trying to please everyone can lead to failure.

Our failures are like the sticks and stones we trip over on the road to success. Success doesn't come easy, it takes hard work and determination. Believing in yourself is the determination to reach your goals. What starts off as an idea in your mind can become your plans for the future, and only you can that happen. Start each day with a positive attitude, set your goals and follow your dreams, reach for the stars. Don't stop believing in yourself, even if you do fail.

Natali Ochoa, Grade 8
Isbell Middle School, CA

The Scarlet Ibis

Who *is* responsible for Doodle's death? Is it his brother that was disappointed in him from the beginning? The Scarlet Ibis bird that happened to die in their tree earlier that day? Or was it strictly "they were in the wrong place at the wrong time?"

Doodle's brother, the narrator, couldn't have killed Doodle. The narrator may have thought or done things that would give off the feeling that he didn't like Doodle. He may have been ashamed, but he definitely didn't have the heart to kill Doodle himself. Some people may think that Doodle's brother wanted Doodle to die that day in the field. Doodle's brother couldn't control what that lightning did.

The Scarlet Ibis had nothing to do with Doodle's death. How could a bird that is dead kill a young boy? The way Doodle looked when he died, just like the Scarlet Ibis, was just a simile. Even when Doodle helped the bird out by burying it.

Lastly "they were in the wrong place at the wrong time" seems to be the only logical explanation for Doodle's sudden and unexpected death. Doodle was a young boy who was passionate about life, and overcame all hardships that were thrown at him. He looked up to his brother, and trusted him, they had such a great bond, there is no way he could have killed him.

Then who really did kill Doodle? His very own brother couldn't have done it. They loved each other, and the narrator wouldn't do that. A bird could not have had anything to do with Doodle's death. Yes, they looked alike when they died, on the same day, but a bird does not have that power. Being in the wrong place at the wrong time is the only logical explanation for Doodle's death.

Jordyn VanRij, Grade 9
South Jordan Middle School, UT

In a Lifetime…

In a lifetime you will find and go through friends in an instant, but finding that one great friend is worth it in the end. Friends are like stars, always there for you but disappear when you don't pay attention.

When you're down, they know what to do, say and how to act around you. They know your darkest secrets, but won't tell a soul. They will always have a shoulder for you to cry on, and my best friends are who I'm talking about.

They aren't the type of people who are stuck up around others, or will tune you out if they are talking to more popular people than you. Friends like that will go through sticks and stones to help you get through what you're going through. They will knock someone out if they mess with you, or even tell a lie for you, but great friends with great advice don't come along that often so hang on to what's in front of you and don't let go.

So my advice to you is, hold on to that one true friend because a great friend is hard to find, but finding that one true friend is worth a lifetime!

Brianna Smith, Grade 8
Thora B Gardiner Middle School, OR

Seussical

I listened to all the people in the "house." I stopped and took a deep breath. "You're fine. There's nothing to be worried about," I told myself. JoJo started his opening lines. The music started. "Here we go," I thought. At first I was nervous, but then I relaxed; there was nothing to be nervous about. "Just do the steps that you know," I told myself. I saw all of the familiar faces in the audience. I was doing what I loved.

Performing in *Seussical the Musical* was one of the best things that I have ever chosen to do. In order to participate in this play I had to audition, rehearse, and perform.

Auditioning was an exciting but nerve-wracking experience. *Seussical the Musical* required vocal auditions and dance auditions. The final cast list was posted two days later. Approximately ninety-five people were cast in the play.

Rehearsals were held after school every day in the auditorium for two to three hours. Rehearsals were never boring and many times they were physically taxing.

The best part of the whole experience was the performances. They were an amazing experience. It was a feeling that you can't get from doing anything else.

I learned so much during the course of this experience. I learned to do my best, that hard work pays off in the end, and that there is always more to learn in life.

Sarah Herring, Grade 8
Canyon View Jr High School, UT

Friend

I was at my locker and I heard a loud bang! A little stunned, I turned around quickly and saw that Christian hit his head on the corner of his locker. I started laughing, but I also felt bad because it looked like it really hurt.

It was the first day of school, and I walked into my English class looking for my seat; I noticed that Christian was in my class, second row, second seat. Still looking for my seat, I found out that I sat right beside him. He looked scared, so I started talking to him, and that's when I knew that this was going to be an amazing friendship.

Christian is probably the closest thing I have to a best friend. We've been friends for two years now, and we talk to each other about almost everything. We have a really strong bond. He makes me laugh every day, and his personality is the best. His smile lights up my world, and the happiness he exudes makes my whole day. We've actually have had an on and off relationship, but that hasn't stopped us from being extremely close.

Christian might not be what I expected in the beginning, but I'm glad that we're friends and I hope we can stay that way throughout our high school years and beyond.

Amber Martin, Grade 8
Piner Middle School, TX

Montana Bike Tour

Finally, after six months of training, and three days of riding in a packed van for ten hours, we're finally there! The only other sound besides my deep breathing and the bike tires on the road was the Swish, Swish, Swish, of cars rushing pass, less than four feet away. I look up and I see eight other kids and one adult leading our 'bike train.' It is the first day of the Montana-Lewis and Clark, bike tour. We are reaching the halfway point to our rest stop and my mind starts to wonder, it wonders to the rolling green hills all around us, to the sun dancing across the road; to the grass stalks I am whizzing past; to the cows lining the wire fences on our right, and the fields going on and on to our left. As I take this all in I thank myself for choosing to go on this bike ride, I thank myself for pushing myself to the limits and farther; because if I did not I would never had had that opportunity to learn, to grow, and to change.

Scheridan Vorwaller, Grade 8
Palm Desert Charter Middle School, CA

Baseball

Baseball is America's pastime, it is the greatest sport ever invented. It has been around 200 plus years. It certainly is an awesome sport. There has been great athletes in baseball such as Babe Ruth, Mickey Mantel, Joe-D, Roger Marris, Fernando Valenzuela and many more. For me baseball is the greatest game every played. I play every game like it was my last, I play every ball like it was my last, I lose like it was my last loss. Baseball is everything you ever wanted. Getting the winning hit is the best feeling in the world, getting an awesome double play is the best feeling in the world, just playing the game of baseball is the best feeling in the world. So for everyone out there that doesn't believe me BASEBALL IS LIFE!!!

Chris Gonzalez, Grade 8
Rio Bravo Middle School, TX

The Ocean

The ocean covers more than three quarters of Earth and is needed to sustain life. However, only a small portion of it has been explored and very few, compared to the millions, of ocean life have been discovered. The ocean goes to great depths and is quite vast, so it is actually quite amazing that such a giant amount of space has rarely been observed. Ocean life can also be important to people by becoming a new favorite food, being a new medical miracle that is essential to good health, and even teaching us something that could possibly change everything we have thought was true. Therefore, it is very crucial we explore it.

The ocean can also be a great tourist attraction. The cool breezes and warm sand have visitors swarming to wherever the water is. This magical place can also be the beginning to a child's imagination. At the ocean you can do everything from building sand castles to collecting beautiful shells. This proves that the ocean can be a fun tourist attraction.

Cole Christensen, Grade 7
Placerita Jr High School, CA

School

The people that know me are probably going to ask themselves, "Why in the world is he writing about school?" I never would've thought I would be writing this, but school has had the strongest impact in my life.

School has taught me how to learn from my mistakes. For instance, you know when you have homework, but you have, say, history first thing in the morning. After history you go to your locker, throw your book in there, and come the end of the day, I mean even after football practice, you get to the truck, throw your stuff in the back seat, hop in, and BAM you don't have your history book. Well if you're like me then you'll wait until you get home and DON'T tell your parents until they ask you. My mom's the type that if I forget something, she is going to make a big deal about it and call everyone she knows who has a key to the school and makes sure that I have what I need. That's definitely not a bad thing, but it taught me not to forget my books.

School has taught me little things like learning from my mistakes. In life if you learn to learn from your mistakes it makes everything a little easier. Remember this, school lasts eight hours a day, but wisdom will last you forever.

Trenton Gardner, Grade 8
Reagan County Middle School, TX

Our World Today

The depletion to our ozone layer is one of the most important events that is going on in our world today. Things like cars, factories, and simple things, such as smoke from cigarettes are destroying it. What does this do to our world?

Well, at this very moment global warming is occurring. That is when the sun's rays come through our atmosphere and heat the entire surface. The gases from our earth trap the heat. If it gets worse and worse our ice caps could melt and flood many vast lands in our world.

Because of the depletion to our ozone layer, more rays can come through more clearly. This is very harmful to our skin. Things like skin cancer can take place and even lead to death. With the ozone depletion, the sun's rays are becoming more and more harmful.

Global warming could eventually lead a large number of species to extinction. Some scientists predict that one third of all the species in our world today will become extinct by 2050. I know people say "save the polar bears," and people may not take that thought and turn it into action. Help these poor animals.

These are just a few examples why the depletion of our ozone layer is very important in our world today. We need to do something about it. If we all work together, maybe we can help make a change before it's too late.

Tatum Jones, Grade 8
Holliday Middle School, TX

Cell Phones Are Handy Dandy

Texting, calling, internet, and ring tones! What is it? It's a cell phone! A cell phone is HUGELY important to me! For one thing, what would the world do if there were no such things as cell phones?!?! No texting?!?! NO WAY!No calling my friends? GET OUTTA HERE! Using my cell phone happens to be half of my lifeline.

Say, for instance, I fell off the slide at the park and broke my leg, I wouldn't be able to get up and walk to the hospital. With a cell phone, I can just call my mom or even text her without having to get up and walk or yell for someone to help me. I would have my handy dandy cell phone with me, and in minutes, my mom would have picked up her cell phone to come get me!

What could have happened if I didn't have a cell phone? I could have been at the park for hours, maybe even days, until my mom realized I was gone. But with my handy dandy cell phone, I was able to call her and have her rush over to the park and get me. That's just one example of why cell phones are important in our lives. Because without cell phones, people would be lost and possibly hurt without anyone to help them.

Rebecca Barclay, Grade 7
Piner Middle School, TX

Losing My Grandma

My grandma has diabetes, and she had no legs because of that. She was awesome and loved everyone. When she would see us, her smile would be bigger than it already was.

My mom came to school and picked me up and I noticed that she was worried. I asked her what happened, and she told me, "Your grandma is sick." We got our clothes ready and left for Piedras Negras, which was where they had hospitalized my grandma. Before we crossed the border, we stopped at H-E-B to get some supplies, and I got my grandma some flowers. When we arrived to the hospital, where my grandma was at. We said hi to our family because they were outside sitting. My aunt came outside crying, and she told us that my grandma had passed away. I started to cry, and I couldn't stop. I was mad because I didn't even see her or anything. My parents went inside to see the body; I wanted to go but the people who worked there didn't let me. I stayed outside with my brother and sister and family.

My family is not that close anymore, and we mostly don't visit them. We don't really talk to them either like we used to when my grandma was alive. I don't like to see my family because I think they are rude people. I mostly don't like talking about my grandma. Till this day I still miss my awesome grandma. Losing someone you love doesn't mean your life stops yet.

Cynthia Saucedo, Grade 8
Reagan County Middle School, TX

Barry Sanders

Barry Sanders, born on July 16, 1968 in Wichita, Kansas, was one of the world's greatest running backs of all time. He played for OSU (Oklahoma State University) and the Detroit Lions from 1989 to 1998. In his NFL career, which lasted ten years, he rushed for 15,296 yards.

When he was a junior in college in 1988, at OSU, he won the Heisman trophy. He was inducted into the Hall of Fame in 2004. If you don't know already, the Hall of Fame is for the best of the best.

My favorite is Barry Sanders. I picked him because he is one of the best running backs of all time and he is not a big show off. He still calls his home Detroit.

Zackry LaFleur, Grade 7
Deweyville Middle School, TX

Unhealthy Food Choices

There are many ways to avoid unhealthy eating. One thing to avoid is eating sweets, such as candy bars, bubble gum, skittles, chips, and even soda. All of these things are very unhealthy because they have sugar. For example, did you know that if you put a penny or a nail in soda, like root beer, then leave it for about one or two days, it will dissolve!

Your stomach cannot process all of the sweets you eat and the overeating you do. If you keep doing these things, you might get cancer. It is not fun having cancer. I had it once, and it was because of too many white blood cells. It took two years of treatments to make sure that it was gone, but I am better now.

I suggest that everybody should increase the amount of vegetables and fruit that they eat! Your body needs the vitamins and minerals. Eat healthy and try not to get cancer.

Isaac Bennett, Grade 7
St Sebastian School, CA

Feeling of Skateboarding

Feel the wind pushing against your face and brushing through your hair as you're going down a ramp or quarter pipe. That little nervous feeling you get when you're about to try something new, and then you succeed at it. That little tickle you get on your spine when you know people are watching you. That's part of skating.

Kick flips, heel flips, shuvits, and 180s are all some basic tricks, but if you want to look good you got to do more advanced tricks, like varial kick flips, inward heel flips, big spins, pressure flips and many other tricks. It gets so exciting as you're learning more and more stuff, that you'll never want to stop skating once you start.

You'll want to get better and better so that you can get sponsored, then turn into a professional skater. Getting sponsored might be the best part of skating because you can get a free complete deck every month. You also have to get in every skate competition there is in the city. It's all so exciting, and the adrenaline rush you get when you're about to start a skate competition.

Nicolas Villagrana, Grade 8
Rio Bravo Middle School, TX

What a Piece of Paper Can't Buy

The times long ago were not focused around a green piece of paper that we now call money. This piece of paper got a dollar amount, and then finally you have to have it. True, money buys you things. Things that you want, and sometimes things that you need. To me, money is just that; a thing. A thing to which many of us treat like a God. A piece of paper that we carry around and every now and then do something worthwhile with it.

On the other hand, what about the things that we cannot buy with the almighty dollar? In my belief, money cannot purchase happiness, love, and faith in God. These necessities are important to have to live on the right path. If one is to be a person closer to God and have internal grace, money cannot be the focus in life.

Happiness, love and faith in God can be measured as a state of grace. They come in many forms for everyone. Giving to the poor, feeding the hungry, and clothing the naked are forms of brining happiness, love, and faith in God. These feelings cannot be bought. In our society, magazines, television, and radio broadcasts describe happiness and love as something that can be attained by economic status. In reality, love and happiness are something that we give and receive without any conditions. Our faith in God allows us to attain happiness and love without the exchange of money.

Anthony Munoz, Grade 8
Our Lady of the Rosary School, CA

Venerable Viruses

What is a virus? Specifically, a computer virus is a program created to harm or extort the users of a computer. Today however, most virus outbreaks are worms. Worms are in some ways the worst viruses out there.

A worm has two parts: a client file and a server file. A worm will tunnel into its target, and then installs the client file, and then contacts the server file for instructions. Most times, a worm spreads via open connections onto the internet, and then onto the server of a website infecting all computers that connect to the website that are unprotected (ex. No firewall, antivirus programs, etc.) which makes a worm very dangerous. The most dangerous worm in history was the Morris internet worm, which did exactly what it says on the can, it took down the internet in 1996, classifying it as a very high risk virus.

However, the first viruses were very different. ANSI bombs actually reconfigured the root commands of the computer, making them much more dangerous, and much tougher to make. A hacker would usually create a batch file to reformat the hard drive, and make all the keys say, "YES." Malicious eh?

Cole Phelps, Grade 8
Isbell Middle School, CA

The JFK Assassination

It was November 22, 1963. President John F. Kennedy was visiting Dallas; he was riding in a car with his wife and Governor Connolly. Suddenly, 3 shots were fired and President Kennedy slumped down. He was rushed to Parkland Memorial Hospital. The alleged killer was Lee Harvey Oswald. The shots were fired from the Texas School Book Depository. Oswald was arrested in a movie theater after killing Dallas Police Officer J.D. Tippit and for the assassination of John F. Kennedy. Questions were asked; why did he shoot John F. Kennedy? What were his motives? We will never know why Oswald did it because 2 days later he was shot while being transported to a prison by Jack Ruby. There are several reasons we know that Oswald was the killer. The technology that we had helped us, forensics showed his fingerprints on the rifle and the spent bullet cases. Ballistics also helped in proving that he was the killer. Lee Harvey Oswald was the alleged and only killer that shot President John F. Kennedy.

Christopher Lang, Grade 8
St Elizabeth Ann Seton School, TX

Nature Deficit Disorder

Kids nowadays are spending more time indoors on the computer or watching TV and they aren't getting time to enjoy the outdoors. This is really affecting the kids of this generation. The author Richard Louv coined this situation as a "nature deficit disorder." In his book *The Last Child in the Woods* he talks about the way kids' lives have been changing in the last few years. For example a middle school kid can likely tell you about the Amazon rain forest but not about the last time he or she explored the woods in solitude or lay in a field listening to the wind and watching the clouds move. Another reason kids aren't playing outside as much is because parents aren't giving kids enough freedom, they want to know exactly where their kids are all the time. This is really changing kids' lives and I think kids should take time to go outside and play tag, go for a bike ride, catch frogs, or climb a tree.

Tanner Husman, Grade 7
Placerita Jr High School, CA

My Favorite Superstar

Tom Brady was born on August 3, 1977 in San Mateo California. We have one thing in common. We like football. Did I mention he now holds the record for the first quarterback to win 3 Super Bowl rings before he was 28?

Tom Brady was a multi-star when he was in high school. He played catcher for baseball, but now he only plays for the New England Patriots which is my favorite team in all time. Tom Brady got drafted 199th in the year 2000 and has played for them till this day. He is a very successful superstar in quarterback history even though he started out as a backup quarterback and now is doing very good. That is why I chose Tom Brady over all the others as MY FAVORITE SUPERSTAR.

Robert Brinson, Grade 7
Deweyville Middle School, TX

My Future

When I become older there are a lot of things I would like to be. For example, I would like to be a pro NFL or MLB player, but I would have to be really good at those things (by the way I'm pretty good at them). Also I would like to be pro skateboarder, but if I do I would still need to go to college so I can have a backup plan in case I get a lifelong injury. When I go to college I want to study in computer engineer or go into business. Computer engineer because I can make video games and business because if I make it into a skateboarding theme I would get some money out of it. So that's what I want to do in the future, my future.

Ruben Corral, Grade 8
Rio Bravo Middle School, TX

Misty May-Treanor

Champion Misty May-Treanor (or Turtle) is an extremely good beach volleyball player. She has gone to the Olympics three times. Misty was the first ever to win a gold medal for volleyball. In all, she has won five gold medals and one bronze.

Misty first started playing volleyball when she was eight years old, and she danced and participated in soccer and tennis. She started playing volleyball because her dad Robert "Butch" May played. She also played volleyball in college.

Born on July 30, 1977 in Los Angeles, California, she is thirty-two years old. Her hometown is Costa Mesa, California. She married Matt Treanor; they now live in Coral Springs, Florida.

Her current teammate is Kerri Walsh. Troy Tanner is their current coach for volleyball.

Misty tore four major ligaments in her knee (ACL) and was out for five years, almost causing her to quit volleyball.

Jenna Davis, Grade 7
Deweyville Middle School, TX

Dreams, Wishes, Imagination

Everyone dreams. Everyone wishes. Everyone imagines. Without these things we would be nowhere.

Martin Luther King's famous quote "I have a dream" rings in my mind when I think of dreams. Reminding me, and us that we all have a dream, but that he was just open about his. Dreams change lives, as Martin Luther King's did.

Wishing and dreaming come hand-in-hand. No more can you dream without a wish than wish without a dream. The definition of wish is: an object of desire. Half of all the famous people are famous because of their wishes. Because of Thomas Edison's constant desire to learn and to know, our lives were affected.

While imagining, you become free. You let your mind wander and explore with nothing in its way! Adults as well as children can imagine. Adults of what they may. Children of what they wish!

When you dream, dream big! When you wish, go for it! When you imagine, be free!

Gloria James, Grade 8
Canyon View Jr High School, UT

My Parents

Most people love their parents, and most don't. When you love your parents, they feel really good about it because they know they're loved. If you don't love them then they will feel really awful, because you are their child and they should be loved by you. Even when you do something wrong and they are mad about it, it doesn't mean they don't love you. It's just that they're trying to protect you from getting hurt or from something that might happen to you. They care for you and don't want to lose you, if they were to lose you, they would be worried, and so emotional about it. You would also be sad because your parents are the ones who are there for you when you need them the most. When you are happy about something you did for your parents, they are happy too no matter what you did, because something was done for them by their own child that they love. Even if you did it wrong, they'll be happy that you tried. They'll also take really good care of you by feeding you, have a roof to put over your head, trying to get you things you really want. When they can't get you what you want, they still try their hardest to get it for you. Parents also help out other family members in need. They help them by giving them money if needed. When they need comfort, they're there for them.

Jerry Ann Cornejo, Grade 8
Zia Middle School, NM

Tennis

Tennis is a sport played between two players, or two teams of two players each. Each player uses a racquet with strings on it, to hit a rubber ball covered with felt over a net into the opponent's court. If you hit the net, you lose the point. You have to try to get it over the net, and into the green rectangle.

Tennis is a sport that was made from combined elements of two different sports. Between 1859 and 1863, Harry Gem and Augurio Perera developed a game that combined "rackets" and "pelota." This was called "lawn tennis." The first tennis club was founded in Leamington Spa. The first tournament was held in the grounds of Shrubland Hall.

One of the greatest tennis players is Roger Federer. He has won 15 Grand Slam singles titles, which is more than anyone has ever won. He is currently ranked number 1 in the world.

There are 8 basic shots in tennis. The serve, forehand, backhand, volley, half-volley, overhead smash, drop shot, and lob. These shots are hit in certain situations to gain an advantage over the other player.

Tennis goes way back to the 19th century, and is still played today. Not many rules have changed, but we have new racquets and equipment. Tennis is a fun sport enjoyed by everyone.

Winston Limbengco, Grade 8
St Michael's Episcopal Day School, CA

Lovin' Baseball

Kerdink! The baseball was thrown. I swung as hard as I could. The umpire screamed, "Home run!" I hit the ball over the fence. When I got to home plate my team was there to give me a congrats.

Baseball rocks my world! The first time I remember playing, is when I was only five or six. I played on the T-ball league. I started one year early. I played pitcher, short stop, and outfield. I hit seven home runs, and two grand slams.

Now I am playing for the league Babe Ruth and play first base, third base, and pitcher. I only hit one home run.

Baseball is really important to me. It keeps me outside. It also keeps me healthy.

Seth Koedyker, Grade 7
Seminole Jr High School, TX

Babe Ruth

George Herman Ruth began his life on February 6, 1895 in Baltimore, Maryland. When George was in high school he played on his high school baseball team. When he was nineteen he was accepted into a major league.

George played for many teams. George started out playing for the Boston Orioles as a left-handed pitcher. Later on he was promoted to the Boston Red Sox. After a while he was sold to the New York Yankees. He was made full-time outfielder. The Yankees were the first people to call him "Babe." In 1927 he slammed 60 home runs. Babe holds most of baseball's important slugging records, including most years leading a league in home runs and most total bases in a season both in 1920.

Babe Ruth is one of the most well-known baseball players. Babe retired from the Boston Braves in June 1935 with 714 career home runs. Babe died at 53 years old in 1948 in New York.

Katelynn Gibson, Grade 7
Deweyville Middle School, TX

My Soul…

Memorizing each word as I fall asleep every night, listening to my music, listening to part of my world. Music is maybe the only thing that inspires me to draw and write. I listen intently to each word of all the songs I listen to as my eyes close and lips curve into a smile.

I don't have a "thing" for music, I'm passionate about music. Each note being hit on symphonies, each song being sung by famous artists, or just by people trying to be big. Listening, hearing my songs as images fly through my mind, I have a pencil in my hand, eraser in the other. Smiling as I'm drawing my heart out on the paper before me.

Music is my solace for when I'm feeling sad, mad, or anything in between. Some people say music isn't that important, I say it is the most important thing in the place we call a world. Then a person asked me, "If music was a person, and it asked you to jump off a cliff…what would you do?" And I told him, "I'd ask 'Which cliff?'"

Emilee Cunningham, Grade 8
Thora B Gardiner Middle School, OR

Why Not a Dog?

According to the Humane Society of the United States, from 2007-2008 there were approximately 74.8 million owned dogs in America. About 63% of the owners owned one dog, so why shouldn't you be next?

Every household should own a dog. Why? Simply because it is, first and foremost, man's best friend, second, they can actually help you become a better person, and third, because they do not have some of the annoying characteristics that humans have.

Firstly, a dog is man's best friend. Dogs, Golden Retrievers especially, are extremely loyal and when trained properly will listen to whatever you say. They are fun to love and great for just quiet companionship. Dogs follow you around and would join you in a heartbeat if it meant going outside. They also make great guard dogs and have been known to save lives. Hence, dogs are fun, lovable, and loyal, a man's best friend.

Second, dogs are great teachers. A dog can help you to become more responsible. How? By just remembering to brush his hair, walk him, feed him and show unending love. They teach us how to be more responsible and keep us in check by making sure we have a routine involving him.

Thirdly, dogs don't have some of the irritating personalities humans have. They are easily satisfied with just a meal and frequent cuddles and don't spend your money. Dogs are forever faithful and can never let you down. And no matter what, they always stick by you.

Beverley Loo, Grade 7
Lindero Canyon Middle School, CA

Family

There are many important things and people in my life, but I believe the most important is family. My family is always there for me and I care about them so much. We put family first. When I get home from school, someone is always there to greet me and help with my homework. My parents care about me so much that they put me in a Christian school so I can grow to be strong with the Lord.

Even though my family and I don't always get along, we always have each other's backs. I love them so much, even though it doesn't always look like it. My sister and I fight, but it makes us closer by learning how to deal with the problems. She is my best friend and will always be there not like friends, who can turn away and leave. I wish to be like my mom, caring and thoughtful. I wish to be like my dad, fun and giving. My parents help me through rough times and when I'm sad, they make me smile. They teach me when I do something wrong and help me to make it right. Even when I'm older, I know I will always be able to count and lean on family.

Jennifer Spencer, Grade 8
Faith Christian Jr/Sr High School, CA

Favorite Music

There are many types of music. However, I like one particular kind. I like pop/rock type of music. One band that really describes what kind of music I like is Metro Station.

Metro Station is made up of four boys. Their names are Mason Musso, Trace Cyrus, Blake Healy, and Anthony Improgo. Mason is the lead singer and rhythm guitarist, Trace is the other singer and lead guitarist, Blake is the keyboardist, and Anthony is the drummer and percussionist.

I first found about this band last June when my cousins told me about it. So, I decided to go on the computer and have a look for myself. I immediately fell in love with the songs and put them on my Myspace profile playlist.

The reason I like that kind of music is because it has a very unique rhythm. I especially like the keyboard's sound because it sounds retro. For example, on their song, "Kelsey," the keyboard sounds amazing! I also love the vocals. Mason and Trace have great voices separately, and even greater when put together in a song. Their voices just go perfect with the rhythms of the songs.

All bands and artists have their own unique rhythm, but overall, I personally think that if you are looking for a band with a really different sound, I suggest you listen to Metro Station. You may or may not like it but if you don't, it's okay because everyone has different music tastes.

Shayla Garcia, Grade 7
Isbell Middle School, CA

Presidential Stress

Tomorrow I give my presidential speech. I am nervous. So many things are running through my head. Will I win? Will I lose? Will I make a good president? Am I qualified? As the clock counts down the minutes to tomorrow, these questions never leave my head like a haunting or a bad dream. These questions give me doubt; they put me in a place no one should be.

My opponents are strong and wise. They would make great leaders, as would I. There has been so much tension between us this past week. We say we will always be friends, but in the end will we? I mean, two of us are going to look onto the other with jealousy and watch them enjoy what we worked hard for the past two weeks.

Posters! Bookmarks! Speech Drafts! Oh my! Saying speeches on stage in front of the whole middle school with a microphone in your face waiting for you to do something is the most nerve-wracking thing ever. What if I say my speech too fast? What if I stutter? What if…what if…what if. Maybe I am just being hormonal; a regular teenage girl dealing with stress in a dramatic way. Whatever the case is, tomorrow is coming and there is no way to avoid it.

Gracie Gullen, Grade 8
Monte Vista Christian School, CA

Ben Roethlisberger

Ben Roethlisberger is the quarterback for the Pittsburgh Steelers. A 27-year-old rookie with a wife and two kids, and yet somehow he still has time to play. "Big Ben" has won rookie of the year in 2004. He got drafted from Miami University in the year 2000. Big Ben is an idol to me no matter what.

Born in 1982, he is the youngest and most valued quarterback the Steelers have ever had. He loves to play the game so he tried out. His life has always been a game of ball so he says. He is one of the many people I look up to.

This rookie hasn't always played football; he has also played baseball and soccer in his college years. He gets the name from his size, intimidation, and because wherever he goes he brings his entire offensive line with him.

Tanner Doucet, Grade 7
Deweyville Middle School, TX

Vianca

On August 5, was a very special day for me. That was the day I asked out the girl of my dreams and her name is Vianca. I remember the first day I started to talk to her and ever since then I started talking to her I was like wow I really like her. So then I started talking to her more and each day I started liking her more and more and every time I saw her I started getting butterflies. So then one day I decided to tell Vianca that I liked her and when I told her she told me that she liked me too. So then I got all happy and then on August 5 I asked her if she would be my girlfriend and when she said yes it was the best feeling in the world and that was the best day of my life and now we have been together for 3 months and my feelings for her are still getting stronger.

Frankie Lujan, Grade 8
Rio Bravo Middle School, TX

Have Faith

Your faith should be the center of everything. Whether it is intentional or not, you will at one point have faith in someone or something. To have faith is to believe or trust in something without physical evidence of its existence. We should have faith in respectable and helpful things and not evil and merciless things. When we see all of the sinister things in the world, we should have aspiration that it will change. However, nothing will ever happen until we have faith in the world changing. We need to show clemency to those who have done wrong in their lives. Then we can focus on ameliorating the world. We need to take action on what we have faith in. If we have faith in God we should try our best to build a relationship with Him. We can take action by helping others, or simply picking up trash in public places such as parks. We should all show alacrity when it comes to changing the world. Our world would be refulgent if everyone had faith in making it better and we would be able to take delectation in it. Astonishing things can happen if we just have faith.

Torrey Meyer, Grade 8
St Elizabeth Ann Seton School, TX

Ever Glow

The soft tap of the black and white keys — the whisper of wind — the silent tinkling of wind chimes — a bow drawn across a string: All have something special behind them. It takes me back to a simpler time, a different world than the world I live in today.

Throughout the years, music has been something incredibly special to me. In the beginning, I didn't really care much for it, but in my years of playing, a slow fiery passion began to emerge; the warmth of the ever glow was finally beginning to peak for me.

The music I play releases something inside of me. It's one of those small things that keep me holding on throughout the day. Sometimes the epidemics that are going on can make the day seem like nothing can possibly make it better. Being able to pick up my violin, or cradle my cello, or sitting in front of my small piano, and press the keys, or bow a string. My mind begins to relax, and it's just one of those little things in life that make me happy. Music is a dream for me, not a fantasy. In the words of Dave Elkins: "Seeing this fire burn out of control, I finally feel the warmth of the ever glow. Take a dream, light it up and watch it grow, (it is) a combustible explosion."

Emily Waters, Grade 8
Faith Christian Jr/Sr High School, CA

First 49ers Game I Went To!

The first football game I ever went to was when I was six years old. The 49ers were playing the St. Louis Rams. My mom and her friends took me. We waited for ten minutes for a bus to arrive at the restaurant. When we were about to order food, the bus finally arrived. When we got on the bus, I ate chips that my mom's friend brought. When I finished eating the chips, I took a nap because my mom said she would wake me up when we got to the football stadium.

When we got there, all I saw were Rams fans walking into the football stadium. When we got in line to enter the football stadium, it didn't take long to get in. When we got to our seats, we put our stuff down and got food.

Finally, the football game started after the national anthem. Then the 49ers entered through a big replica of their helmet. The Rams won the coin toss. So the 49ers had to kick it off to the Rams. The Rams returned the ball to the 30 yard line.

I stopped watching the game for a while. Then when I started watching again, it was fourth quarter. Two minutes into the fourth quarter, we had to leave. We started listening to the radio. Then we heard that the 49ers won. It was the best game I ever went to because it was my first game. I had lots of fun with my mom.

Kyle Veloro, Grade 7
Corpus Christi School, CA

Freedom in the Oddest Place

I close my eyes, my cares seem to blow away with the breeze, and everything in the world whirls from my view. My hair is blowing back, absent from my face. A small squeak is ringing in my ear, my mind is off dreaming as calm and care free as a young child. My eyes open, and I let out a silent scream when I realize I'm ten feet in the air.

The swing, for me is a stress releaser. Life goes back to its simpler form making me feel as if I am a five year old again! Some may say that simple moments are boring, and are not special, but I would strongly disagree.

In the midst of hectic, crazy lives it is nice to have somewhere I can escape from the loud world. For me that nice, quiet place is in the backyard on the swing, in the coolness and tranquility of the night. Here all my cares slip away. Here is where I am truly free.

Caitlyn Mattice, Grade 9
Faith Christian Jr/Sr High School, CA

Life

Jorge Jasiel Torrez, born September 21, 2009. What can I say about this wonderful baby boy? Well right now he is the youngest of all of my cousins. He looks a lot like his dad but he acts like his mommy. We call him Jasiel and my grandma calls him Jorge. His godmothers are my aunt Tamara (Tammy) and I.

The first time I saw him was from a picture and I cried. The second time I saw him my heart sank because I was sick so I could not carry him. My aunt Tammy took me to her room and she covered my mouth and nose with a muscle shirt. When I carried my godchild he smiled and my aunt Judy (his mom) said that was the first time she has seen him smile. I think that was the best moment in my life so I decided that should be his nickname, Life.

Skyblue Guzman, Grade 8
Rio Bravo Middle School, TX

The Human Mind

The human mind is the most powerful and limitless resource. Many heroes throughout history have become that, simply because of their ability to control their mental power.

The only way anything ever happens in this world is if someone, somewhere makes it happen. To do that they need their mind to tell them to.

If you think something will happen, or hurt, even taste good or bad, it almost always will. Many times someone will get hurt and have no idea until they see it, and their mind tells them it hurts. Every time something really big happens that changes the world, or at least some part of it, there's someone with a good head on their shoulders leading the change.

Everything from the wheel to giant super computers that can combine atoms are here because someone had an idea and pursued it. Nothing happens without the amazing system that is the human mind to spear it into action.

Samuel James, Grade 8
Canyon View Jr High School, UT

High Merit Essays – Grades 7, 8 and 9

My Sister's Quincenera

A quincenera is one of the best parties you can ever have. You get to wear a fluffy, gorgeous dress and you dance with all your guests. I am telling you this because I still remember my sister's quincenera. My sister's dress was white and red; it looked beautiful.

My sister's quincenera was on April 1, 2005. Beatrice and my mom had planned it for two or three months. When Beatrice went to pick her dress, she chose a fluffy one as white as a cloud. My dress was long and as red as an apple with white diamonds on it. It was beautiful!!

Then it was time for the party. Beatrice, my mom, Nancy, Jessica, and I were very excited. YUPPI!! When we got to the party, we all danced. The quincenera was fantastic. I will never forget that day!!

Vanessa Ibarra, Grade 7
Santa Teresa Middle School, NM

Bethany Hamilton

Bethany Hamilton is 19 years old now, but she was attacked at the age of 13 years old and her left arm was torn off almost to the armpit. She was born February 8th, 1990. She was at the Hawaii beach. I am going to explain it so listen up. She was relaxing with her left arm dangling in the water then suddenly she felt something pulling on her left arm. She jerked it and pulled up out of the water. She swam to the bank calmly as could be and fainted. Then the ERs rushed her to the hospital and wrapped her arm up. Then months later she taught herself how to surf with one arm. Once she was really good at it she entered a surfing contest and won best comeback athlete of the year.

So how did she get back on the surf board? She overcame her fears of sharks and all I got to say is that she is one tough little chick.

Lauren McCollough, Grade 7
Deweyville Middle School, TX

My Uncle Eddie

When I was younger I was very close to my uncle, who passed away in the month of November, 2006. My most memorable childhood moments involved him. He meant a lot to me, his name was Eddie. My sister and I used to call him Uncle Eddie though. My uncle used to visit my family and me almost every single day. I would see him in the mornings and after school. I remember that the way I would know he was there was because I would hear him clearing his throat. He would be outside sitting in a chair reading the newspaper. He was an outside person who enjoyed nature. Then when I would come home from school he would be watering the grass. I used to playfully tease about the way he stood while he was watering outside. By imitating the way he was standing and the both of us would laugh. Also on the weekends sometimes he would take my sister and I to the Bronco. My mom would give us money and he would take us.

Gabriel Reyna, Grade 8
Rio Bravo Middle School, TX

The Power of Books

Why are books like a magnet to most people? People stare at pages seemingly oblivious to the world around them. I believe they read books because they get a chance to imagine, to become part of the story, and to learn life lessons.

Unlike in movies and television shows, readers picture the setting and characters, like they are writing the story. They modify the descriptions to their liking and soon grow attached to the places and characters in the book.

Mysteries allow readers to pause and guess what will happen next. While logically sifting through the clues, they wonder "Who committed the crime?" and attempt at the answer before it is revealed to them.

In novels, people gain life experiences and do not have to face the negative consequences that the character goes through. They may learn something like intelligence does not guarantee happiness or success, and that supports their beliefs and gives them confidence.

When I'm in the bookstore, it seems like it is full of portals to worlds instead of books. Every time I read one, I escape to a place where I do not need to worry about real life. Whenever I finish one, I am left wanting more, and start searching for a sequel. I am glad that I have a quiet time with my book. For me and most people, books take me to places I have never been and let me be someone I may never be, even just for a moment.

Danny Shihabi, Grade 8
St Michael's Episcopal Day School, CA

My Heart in Two Lands

In my family I have many different heritages. My dad comes from Wisconsin and my mom comes from Ecuador, which is in South America. Which do I prefer? Well both. I am very proud that I am capable to tell others about my culture. To me having these traditions in my family, makes me unique in my own way. It allows me to feel very proud of my family and our heritage. When I talk about doing things here, in the United States of America, that nobody does in Ecuador I feel privileged to live here. I love to show off my culture around to anyone who will listen. To tell people I can speak English *and* Spanish is very intriguing to others. To see two individuals who are different in many ways, join together shows how many similarities they have.

I have learned many things from living in America and visiting Ecuador. Being able to enjoy both countries is a gift for me. Not very many people have that chance that I have and I am very grateful for that. Once again, I am thankful and proud for having this opportunity. I love my family for who they are and I am glad I have the opportunity to show off my heritage.

Abby Starck, Grade 8
St Elizabeth Ann Seton School, TX

Terrell Owens

Terrell Eldorado Owens plays the position of a starting wide receiver for the Buffalo Bills. He was born on December 7, 1973 in Alexander City, Alabama. Unlike most pro-football players, Terrell did not start playing football because his abusive grandmother (whom he lived with) forbade him to.

He has been cut from teams many times, often the reason being he created firestorms with his fellow teammates. His pro career began in 1997 with the San Francisco 49ers. In 2003 after a bad season he left the 49ers. In 2004 T.O. began a new season with a new team: the Philadelphia Eagles. After three seasons Owens began to voice his displeasure and eventually was cut. The main reason being after suffering a defeat from Dallas, T.O. was seen wearing a Dallas jersey on the plane ride home. In 2006 he signed with the Dallas Cowboys. His work with the cowboys ended this year. The reason he was cut still remains unknown. He currently plays for the Buffalo Bills.

Though T.O. may be a very talented wide receiver he is also known for his notorious touchdown celebrations. His most memorable celebrations include a game where he was playing for the 49ers and caught a touchdown pass. Owens ran to the Famous Dallas Star and began to dance on it. Dallas's safety George Teague then hit him in the face. Other celebrations include the time when he caught a T.D. pass when he played for the Eagles and ran through the end zone and ripped down a hand-made sign that read "T.O. has B.O."

Owens may be passed around from team to team but he's in my opinion one of the most talented wide receivers of our generation.

Talon Shoemake, Grade 7
Deweyville Middle School, TX

Dance

Dance is my sport that I love. I have been doing dance ever since I was three years old. My mom put me in ballet class and I fell in love with it. Dance is one of the best exercises to get into shape. Now, I take ballet and jazz and I love it.

I love learning new steps and new combinations. Sometimes at first, I fail, but I know that when I keep practicing it I will finally get it right. The success keeps me motivated for every other challenge I face in dance and in other life situations. It shows that if I work at something and put my mind to it I know that I will achieve my goal. Maybe when I get a little bit older I intend to do competitions. It will be a big step for me to take because I can show people what I got and show them that I have put my hardest effort into dancing all throughout my life.

I would like to keep doing dance for a long time. When I get older, I would like to teach little kids how to dance because then I could say that I taught them how. It will be a great accomplishment for me to complete. I love to dance and I will continue to do it.

Celine Garcia, Grade 8
Monte Vista Christian School, CA

My Love for Piano

There is no better feeling than walking up on a stage and hearing the clapping of the audience. Just to think that they are clapping for me is the best feeling in the world.

Throughout the years, I have never caught on to anything faster than the piano. I have never had a greater love for any instrument, hobby, or sport. I believe it has a lot to do with my piano teacher, Dianna Ortiz. She has been my teacher since the summer of third grade. She made me excited and eager to learn new songs to play. She encourages me to play and practice. It has now been three years and I still have the same love for the piano as I did in the third grade. Mrs. Dianna Ortiz has never been mad at me for anything, from not practicing, to missing the notes. Her encouragement has caused me to love the piano more. As a result of practicing, I have made it to her top three most advanced students. I now perform in special recitals and soon in a restaurant.

My love for the piano is because of my teacher. I thank Dianna Ortiz for making music a part of my life and giving me a love for the piano.

Tera Lucero, Grade 7
St Thomas Aquinas School, NM

Emmitt Smith

My favorite sports star, 40-year-old Emmitt Smith is a former NFL superstar, who played for the Dallas Cowboys and the Arizona Cardinals. Born on May 15, 1969 in Pensacola, Florida, he weighs 216 pounds and stands 5 feet 9 inches. Emmitt attended Escambia High School and has the second most yardage in the history of high school football. He broke the 2,000 yard barrier twice in one season and ended his high school with 8,804 yards and 106 touchdowns.

After high school he moved on to play for the Florida Gators where he broke the 1,000 yard barrier in his seventh game. He carried the ball 39 times for 224 yards and two touchdowns. Smith finished off his college career with 3,928 yards.

When he moved on to the NFL, he first played for the Dallas Cowboys and then the Arizona Cardinals. He holds the NFL record in career rushing yards with 18,355 yards. He went to the Super Bowl and won 3 times and he ran a combined total of 21,864 yards. He left the Cardinals and signed a one day no-pay contract with the Dallas Cowboys and retired as a Cowboy.

After retirement he judged for a Miss Universe Pageant and won Dancing with the Stars with his partner Cheryl Burke.

I chose Emmitt Smith as my favorite sports star because he had great football talent and still does. I also chose him because even after retirement he kept going.

Gabrielle Henley, Grade 7
Deweyville Middle School, TX

Travel

Traveling is one of the most common things that people enjoy doing. It gives people a chance to experience other cultures and try new things. It gives people the opportunity to visit historical sites and landmarks. They get to view a whole different way of life, new foods, and a new group of people. You see how the people live their daily life. When you visit a new place you see new views and scenery and sometimes they can be prettier than the ones back home. You also may experience a new language when you're in a different country.

When you travel you get to visit historical sites, which include landmarks and museums. When you visit, you learn more firsthand than from a book. They have tours and the tour guides give you loads of information. Visiting a historical spot can make you feel like you were there and help you find out interesting details about the history of the location.

When on vacation you can enjoy lots of things. Getting a chance to live the life of another culture can be a lot of fun. Visiting new sites and seeing new things are chances of a lifetime. Doing all of these things during your experiences of traveling is fantastic!

Shayne Wilson, Grade 8
St Michael's Episcopal Day School, CA

The Worst Christmas Ever!

There I was having all-star basketball practice. My mom's friend Shelly Duncan, had come to pick me up so I knew something bad had happened.

When I walked in the front door there were people there. So something had happened. Then I looked at my dad, and I could tell he had been crying.

Finally after my brother got home, my dad brought us into my brother's room. He said "Papaw died this morning." At first I didn't believe him, then my mom told me it was true. My dad also said that he found Papaw dead out at our farms. I burst into tears. I ran into my room and didn't come out for a long time.

After that night, we had a memorial service. I saw him in his coffin. I felt him, he was cold and very still. My cousin and I had to keep going to the bathroom to wipe our tears away.

The last day I saw him was on a Saturday. That day was the day of his funeral. When we were at church, people were saying stuff about how much of a great man he was. As I was listening, I felt a hot and heavy breath on my neck. I turned around, but nobody was there so, I smiled and cried happy tears. When we got to the cemetery, I saw him go underground. As I saw him go I realized God was ready for him to go home.

Madison Logan, Grade 7
Seminole Jr High School, TX

Kristine Yamaguchi

Kristine Tsua "Kristi" Yamaguchi is a professional ice skater. Born on July 12, 1971 in Hayward, California, Kristi always wanted to skate. When Kristi first started ice skating, she started as a junior pair skater with Rudy Gallendo in the U.S. World Junior Pair Championship in 1986. Two years later, she joined the singles competition. In the 1992 Winter Olympics, she competed as a single competitor.

Kristi Yamaguchi has been skating for more than a decade. That is more than ten years. In 1992 Kristi won the World Championship. She is the greatest female skater this generation has ever seen, and she has won lots of awards and lots of competitions. In 1998 Kristi was in the U.S. Figure Skater Hall of Fame. Kristi Retired at the age of 38. She had two kids. Kristine Tsua "Kristi" Yamaguchi is the best ice skater in the world, and she truly inspired every person who wanted to do what she did.

Kaitlyn Ashworth, Grade 7
Deweyville Middle School, TX

Who Do You Think Killed JFK?

John Fitzgerald Kennedy was assassinated on November 22, 1963. I believe that Lee Harvey Oswald was the only shooter in Dealey Plaza at the time of the shooting. I do believe the shooting may have been part of a conspiracy, though. It may have been a conspiracy because of the picture of Oswald with the rifle used to shoot JFK. Who would have taken a picture of a man with a rifle in a crowded plaza?

Oswald did kill JFK, conspiracy or not. All of the evidence is against him. His rifle was found, the bullets were found, and his sniper nest was found. The only thing that says he may not have done it was how he couldn't live long enough for a fair trial, thanks to Jack Ruby. The shooter was Lee Harvey Oswald, no doubt about it. Whether or not he was in a conspiracy, nobody knows for sure.

Connor Johnson, Grade 8
St Elizabeth Ann Seton School, TX

Regrets

We all have things we're not proud of, whether you said something to your parents or lied to your friends. There are tons of people that struggle with it and there are tons of people that can get over it, but there is not one person on this Earth who hasn't experienced it. When you feel shameful, wrong, or sorry for something you did, you probably regret it. To me regret means to feel bad for a wrongdoing. What does it mean to you?

I've found there are two types of regret, regret for doing something wrong and regret for being in the wrong place at the wrong time. You shouldn't be ashamed of yourself for having regrets, it just makes you human. We all have them and there will be many more in the future, I guarantee it. Sometimes one door opens to another door closed. Just keep walking until you find one that lets you through, and maybe you won't regret it.

Rachel M. Stotler, Grade 7
Placerita Jr High School, CA

My Dream

I started competitive swimming when I was nine. My interest in swimming began when I was eight. It was on a bright sunny day in the summer of 2004. My mom and I were watching the Summer Olympics. Swimming was going on, so we decided to watch it. I was captivated. I saw all the athletes in swimming: Michael Phelps, Natalie Coughlin, Ian Thorpe, and many more athletes. The competition was amazing.

My first year of competitive swimming, I was a lot slower than I am now. I only got a chance for a blue ribbon in relays. I still do, but I am getting faster in the individuals and the relays. When I first started, I could not dive at all! It took me a long time to improve my dive, but now I have become much better. I just learned the butterfly stroke, the hardest stroke ever, this summer. Now I can compete in the individual medley! It is a race in which you swim all four strokes.

When I grow up, I want to go to the Olympics and get the most medals that a woman has won in a single Olympics. Until then, I will keep practicing, and working toward my dream.

Hannah Krebel, Grade 7
St Elizabeth Ann Seton School, TX

Most Embarrassing Day of My Life

Embarrassment is always around everyone and everywhere. When you get embarrassed you might think your life is over, but it's not. For example, last year when I joined the Turkey Trot, I was embarrassed. At the beginning of the race, I was one of the last ones. However, at the end I was like the 7th or 8th with more people behind me. I eventually survived the school year. I thought everybody was going to laugh at me, but they didn't and I thought my life was over too. If you ever get embarrassed, don't give up and face your fears.

Getting embarrassed isn't surprising or new to the world. People deal with it every day. For example, I've seen many people trip, fall, snort soda through their nose, and much other embarrassing stuff. For example, some people even move from school to prevent people from making fun of them and I don't understand why. Another example is that if you ever tear or rip your pants you could always go to your friends, teachers, counselors, or any other staff, but there is nothing to be embarrassed of, it was just an accident. One more example of embarrassment is when you argue with someone about something in front of the whole class and you end up losing and rumors start. I conclusion, if you ever get embarrassed don't just hide, ask a teacher, friend, or someone to help you out.

Yesenia Garcia, Grade 8
Isbell Middle School, CA

A Great Man

His name is Rosalio, but they call him Lee. He's about 75 years old he still walks, drives, and works. Well one day he had a sort of swollen throat, and my family was worried about him. This man is one of those types of men that don't like going to the doctor to find out something's wrong with them since they're older. Well he has diabetes and can rarely eat anything, as you know, so when my family decided to take him to the doctors. We heard the terrible news of him having cancer in his throat! We were all devastated, because everyone who had cancer on his side died from it. He went through all the chemo treatments he lost his hair, weight, and his vocals so you could barely hear him because of the tumor. When he was done with the treatments I prayed that he would get better every night, and before you know it the cancer was successfully cleared! I'm so grateful for that day. He was the only from his side of the family to survive cancer; now slowly day-by-day he is slowly regaining his voice back. He always helps us in our time of need and he is very brave and he's a strong man and I love him. I'm proud to call this wonderful man my grandpa.

Yesenia Gomez, Grade 8
Rio Bravo Middle School, TX

Twinkle Toes!

The first time I walked into the dance studio with my silk ballerina shoes tied to my ankles, I trembled with nervousness. The teacher fixed my crooked tutu and took me by the hand and played a few classical tunes. I stumbled a little. She called me "triple toes" because I would trip constantly and every time she would giggle because I would pout that all the other girls were better than me, but weeks and weeks passed and the name changed to "twinkle toes." My dancing improved drastically! And at my first solo competition I won 2nd! I had a smile from ear to ear. Now every time I hear music it takes me into a zone that's hard to explain. It's peaceful, I forget any problems I have. It's like my own little world, my own escape…

Mikaela Chaides-Reyes, Grade 8
Rio Bravo Middle School, TX

Peace and Love

Peace is freedom from war, harmony, serenity or quiet. Peace can be in so many things. It can be in people, animals, the ocean, the sky, and the Earth. Peace can help us all live in happiness. It can help us understand how to love, to care, and help others.

Love is a strong affection for someone or something. When we love we can't hate, we can't hurt, and we have no guilt. We can love in so many different ways, for so many different things. We can love a parent, we have love for a sport, we can love a pet, and we have love for a spouse. And yet so many more unmentionable loves. But the most important love is for our planet, and it does so much, to love it is the least we can do.

Asalia Arauz, Grade 7
Our Lady of the Rosary School, CA

High Merit Essays – Grades 7, 8 and 9

If I Could Have One Last Wish

If only I could have one last wish, I would want my Uncle Alfonso. I was seven when he died. Ever since he died, I've felt alone, cold, like no one is with me. My uncle was like my father.

My Uncle Alfonso was loving, caring, funny, helpful, and a great friend. He would come to visit every year, and when he did he would take my nephew and me to Shakey's. He had plans to come back and take my nephew to Disneyland. But then he got sick, and sadly, he died. When he was in the hospital his last wish was that we'd take my nephew to Disneyland.

My uncle was my role model. To me he was an angel sent from God. I loved him and I know he and I will meet again. My uncle is still watching over me. I miss my uncle, and my family does too.

Ericka Morales, Grade 8
Our Lady of the Rosary School, CA

Brothers in Arms

Imagine getting one hour of sleep, hearing subtle gun fire around you all day, carrying fifty pounds of armor everywhere you go. Imagine going into a fire fight or losing the life of a friend. This is what our military deals with every single day, all for you and me. This is why the military is very important to our country and to me.

The military fights for our freedom. They place their lives on the line and fight because they love their country and wish to protect it. They deserve a great amount of respect from us because they have the courage most of us don't. They have the courage to go to our enemies and to keep us out of harm's way. We may have many branches of the military, but they all work together to accomplish the same job. The army works hard to keep the enemy where they are and stop them at close quarter combat, the air force bringing in strong attacks to the aid the army, and the navy keeping enemy cargo or attacking ships from coming to our land. Semper Fidelis, or always faithful, is the motto of our best, the marines. All working together to make sure that our country is safe. God bless America.

Chance Ludwick, Grade 8
Faith Christian Jr/Sr High School, CA

Fear

Fear strikes everyone, it burns, stings, and could be a real big thing to get over. It could even mess your life up forever. Hi I'm Anthony Gonzalez and every weekend I fight fear.

Every weekend or so, I go to a track designed for dirt bikes. It's big, it's huge, it's intimidating. It has jumps up to one hundred and twenty feet long and you can reach as high as thirty feet high. It strikes fear into everyone that enters it. This is where I was introduced to fear. It was until I heard a saying that said, "You have to learn to take risk," that I actually started to jump some of the jumps there. Since then fear has been fearing me.

Anthony Gonzalez, Grade 8
Rio Bravo Middle School, TX

Dare to Dream

The adventure began in the 7th grade. The year was awesome! I had many friends and was making good grades. I was also the treasurer of the Student Council. Every Friday, I would have a Student Council meeting, and the President, Stefan Puente, would lead the meetings. At the end of the year, there were sign-ups to run for Student Council President. I was inspired by Stefan to go for it and felt that I could win. I had learned a lot and had gained plenty of experience. So, I made and placed posters around the school, as I had decided to run for President. All was going well until I found out that I had to write a speech and present it to the entire school! The speeches were to be broadcast on the televisions in each classroom. The day came for me to read, and I was dreadfully nervous! I read my speech and found out that it was easier than I thought. I had a lot of fun that day, except that I would not find out who had won until following week. Finally, the results were in. That wonderful morning, the Secretary of the Student Council, Elizabeth Seyer, announced the positions. I had won! I was the new President of the Student Council. I could now start planning for an even better 8th grade year!

A.J. Zaugg, Grade 8
St Elizabeth Ann Seton School, TX

My Brother

"It snowed last year too. I made a snowman and my brother knocked it down and I knocked my brother down, and then we had tea" — Dylan Thomas. This describes the relationship between me and my older brother Matthew. We would always fight, get revenge and make up. Matt is an amazing sibling, and I don't know what I'd do without him.

Matt is 21 years old. He is going to be a father in January. He is my half brother, so we've no resemblance. Over 6 feet tall, he towers over me. His eyes are brown, his hair blonde, and his nose is big. He loves to spend his time playing video games, golfing, and eating.

Ever since we were kids, Matt and I have always fought. He would always pick fights with me and I would pick fights with him. We spent half our time fighting, and the other half playing. We would catch lizards, and we had a whole lizard farm right in our backyard! We would eat prickly pears, and play jokes on our parents. Once, when we were washing dishes, we splashed each other and were soaking wet! We had some great times, and I was really sad when he moved out.

Matt and I have always been very close, even though we may not have shown it. Matt, you are a wonderful brother to have and I know I can always count on you. Thank you for being there and supporting everything I do!!! I love you!

Erin Avilucea, Grade 8
Zia Middle School, NM

Last Day of Sixth Grade

It was a cloudy morning and a start of a new day but it felt like the ending because it was the last day of 6th grade. I trudged to the wet mail box and waited for the start of a sad beginning.

As I arrived to school, it felt like a big blanket tried to cover the school with warmness, but you could still feel the big chunk of ice on your back. I hugged all my friends in the halls. You could see smiles full of happiness and laughter. We talked much about middle school and how we were going to miss 6th grade. Middle school feels like a new story with new characters, setting, and themes.

The classmates and teachers lingered around the school, taking pictures and signing yearbooks. You could hear the noises surrounding the room. The slapping and flips of cards, the twists and turns of the games, and the yelling and talking of the students. When we were clearing up the classroom, they called us to get our sack lunches. We got our backpacks and took off to the cafeteria watching the rain pouring down like a foggy rainfall. As everyone got their lunch, the 6th graders were called up to line up outside the cafeteria doors.

Our sweaty hands held the lunch bags and our backpacks were heavy rocks leaning on our backs. As we busted through the doors, we saw confetti flying everywhere. It was like walking through a parade and heading home into our school buses. Everyone from the building was hugging each and every single 6th grader. This was the moment I'll never forget. As I walked outside hugging my friends, I will always remember the people I love because they will never leave my heart.

Dashia Gallegos, Grade 7
Santa Teresa Middle School, NM

My Dad's Football Career!!

My dad, Samuel Garza Jr., was born July 10, 1965. His parents were Dahlia and Samuel Garza. He grew up in Harlingen, Texas and Corpus Christi, Texas. He attended the University of Texas at El Paso (UTEP). He played football there as the quarterback and moved on with his career when he got a job offer as the quarterback in the Canadian Professional Football League (CFL) in Canada. He played for the Ottawa Rough Riders and the Winnipeg Blue Bombers. He also got drafted into the NFL on the Seattle Chiefs but later was cut and played with St. Louis. He still continued on with a career in football, but had to retire in playing so he began to coach. He starting his coaching with going back to UTEP and got a coaching job as the offensive coach. After that he got another offer in Canada for a coach he has played for in the past, the Rough Riders. He moved back and forth with different coaching jobs, but when he got a job offer for the Dallas Cowboys in 2006, he had to take the offer. By this time he already had 3 kids and was living in Canada. He moved to Dallas and now is a scout for the Dallas Cowboys football team.

Hailey Garza, Grade 7
St Elizabeth Ann Seton School, TX

Pumpkins

When we think of pumpkins we think of fall. Well there is much more to think about. With pumpkins we can make: pumpkin pie, pumpkin purée, pumpkin bath stuff, and pumpkin candy. Jack-o'-lanterns, pumpkin pudding, pumpkin ice cream, pumpkin seeds, pumpkin spices, and much more are also things that pumpkins can make. Pumpkins not only symbolize October and November but they are also one of the symbols of Halloween. Pumpkins are native to America, grown by the first people, the Indians. Pumpkins are grown by seeds, but they no longer grow wild here in America. Pumpkins are related to the squash and sometimes come with warts. Pumpkins also vary in color. They come in white, green, and different shades of orange. There are many types of pumpkins, like the Cinderella pumpkins, Jack-Be-Littles, and Big Maxes. Jack-o'-lanterns are pumpkins with a carved face and candle on the inside. Usually pumpkins are put outside of someone's house or yard on Halloween. There are many uses for pumpkins, especially for recipes and decorations. Pumpkins are a green-stemmed, multicolored, circular reminder of autumn.

Ashley M. Silva, Grade 7
Walter F Dexter Middle School, CA

Every Day

Every day I come to school I feel more distant. I don't know why, but, I think to myself what's happening to me? Am I even alive…? Is this a dream…? Am I invisible…? I feel that I'm tied between two worlds. Every time I talk to somebody, it seems that they just walk through me like I'm a ghost. I'm worried that the great friends that I have will not be there. They will just be a far off memory. Every day I become more upset. I guess I'm the one that is pushing everyone away. Every day, I wish I could start off with a clean slate. Correct the things that I have done wrong and make new friends or go back to the older friends that are a far off memory. Every day, I live knowing that I hurt someone emotionally, but for reason, I'm beginning not to care. I don't know why, but, I guess the reason is that every time I try to apologize, it just makes it worse. Every day that someone talks to me, they make it seem like everything is okay, but it's not. I'm confused and upset. I don't know why, but, every time I look into someone's eyes it gives me a smile, but, at the same time I see a reflection of me. The mistakes that I'm not proud of. I don't know why I can see this, but I'm done with people, because I will just get hurt and be ashamed of myself. The problem is friends give joy and strength, but they can also bring you down. Every day I ponder this, every day I lay on my bed and ask myself why am I here? Why can nobody see me? Is this a dream?

Daniel D'Amico, Grade 8
Centers of Learning, CA

My Friends

My friends are the best of friends anyone can ever ask for. My friend Michelle always makes me laugh every time I'm feeling sad. Then there is Melissa. She is the little cute blondy of our group and we love that about her. Also there is my friend Fabiola. She is the most trustworthy person of our little group. She has lots of problems here in school, but I have actually been able to help her.

Also my other good friend is Audry, she has everything pre-AP and I am so proud of her. She always helps me with my homework. There is also my friend Liliana. She unfortunately broke her leg so all my friends take turns helping her.

Then I saved the best for last, my friend Jovannah is the most cool friend I have ever had. All my friends that I have they are good because we tell each other all our secrets and we never tell anyone. But the sad thing is that I lost a very good friend because of rumors. But I ended up moving on with my other friends.

Abraham Juarez, Grade 8
Rio Bravo Middle School, TX

The Five Stages of Grief

We have all felt grief. Those rolling waves of hopelessness that pound on us like nothing we have felt before. The feeling that will never subside, leaving a deep, burning nostalgia in which we will never feel again. As we struggle to cope with the pain, we come across these obstacles; The Five Stages of Grief.

The first is denial. During this stage, you try to convince yourself this simply *isn't* happening to you. You burn, on the inside. The thought of losing someone, or something, eats you alive. The hope that whatever you desire will come knocking at your door. This feeling will always be there.

The second is rage. While fuming, you ask yourself, "Why is this happening to ME?!" You don't even think about the fact that you, the victim, or the world couldn't have stopped it.

The third is bargaining. "If I am a better person, will you make this go away?" This question, commonly asked, is like a penny thrown into a fountain, but the knowledge your wish has no chance.

The fourth is depression. Like after a blow to the stomach, you feel numb, even though anger and sadness and hatred are welled up inside you, pouring down your face. This feeling lingers for a long time.

The fifth, the hardest, is acceptance. This is where you finally accept the reality of the loss. You finally realize that you must carry on. Some never want to move on. These are just parts of life.

Samantha Nua, Grade 7
Placerita Jr High School, CA

A Special Someone

Do you believe in love at first sight? Well at first I really didn't, but now I think I'm finally beginning to. We used to talk so much last year, he always made me laugh, and would always put a smile on my face when I was feeling down. Now it's the beginning of a new school year in 8th grade, and yet still that warm, comforting feeling comes to me every time I talk or even see him. I finally made up my mind and decided it was time to let him know what my feelings were for him…so I wrote him a note, and gave it to him with no hesitation. The next day turned out to be the best day of my life, because it turned out to be that he liked me too. And from that day on we've been getting closer and closer, which makes me happy knowing I have that special someone in my life.

Anica Villanueva, Grade 8
Rio Bravo Middle School, TX

Integrity

Your integrity is one of the greatest qualities that you have. It must be at its best, even when no one is watching. In the United States during the 1950's and early 1960's racism and segregation were a big part of everyday life. The ethnicity that you were given by God was not enough if you were of color. The government created a separate but equal law, yet this racism in the United States continued.

If you were white and you helped a person of color, your reputation by white people would be shot down to the lowest of the low. Your integrity caused problems. You might have thought about going back to your old selfish racist ways but your incredible integrity told you to stop.

We strive as Americans to do the right thing and it is hard, but whoever said life itself would be easy? Whoever said, when the going gets tough, it's hopeless, give up? We picture ourselves in the near future being great, but if we don't have our integrity, will we be? Next time when someone drops their books in the hallway, don't be embarrassed to pick them up. Remember to always wear your integrity with pride.

Patrick Dodge Clay, Grade 7
Dr Hector P Garcia Middle School, TX

Glacier Upon Earth

Recycling a Pepsi can is supposedly going to save the world from the myth of global warming. The Earth itself has already been polluted since the beginning of time and will continue until the end of time.

I agree with the fact that glaciers are melting into the ocean, but isn't the Earth already seventy something percent water? How much water could a glacier honestly add to the ocean?

Floods happen every year and to places all over the world. The accumulation of all of the water can't possibly overrun and conquer the world. Soon everybody will think that one day we will all drown of a great flood. That happened once and we were promised that it wouldn't happen again.

Stephen Beltran, Grade 8
Piner Middle School, TX

The Ultimate Death

Have you ever stopped to think about how drugs and alcohol slow down, and damage your body? Well, recently I have, and WOW! It does an awesome job of wrecking your body and your mind.

About a month ago, my mom's cousin died at age 53 because all her life she drank alcohol and did drugs such as marijuana and cocaine. Starting during her teenage years and up until only four weeks ago she used those awful things. Drugs and alcohol changed who she was as a person. She was the youngest of three sisters, but with all those harmful drugs, she looked and acted the oldest. She literally went crazy. Her mind and body were no longer working.

If you look at old pictures, she was so beautiful! But if you just would've seen how different she looked after all the destruction due to drugs. She lost almost all her hair, she was missing several teeth, she needed someone to walk her anywhere she went, she was only skin and bone, and she looked about 80 years old. She looked so bad my cousins and I were afraid to go anywhere near her. She was really a very scary looking person.

All of this can happen even with just a few weeks of doing drugs. Once you get hooked, it's forever. Now that I realize how horrible it is to do drugs, I know I'm not ever going to place one finger on any type of drug or alcohol.

Victoria Chacon, Grade 8
Rio Bravo Middle School, TX

My Escape

Life is full of mixed emotions, and sometimes a person can feel as if they are trapped in this world. Well, that's the way I feel, but I know I can escape. Music is my escape, and it's something I feel is very important to me.

To me music is like a portal to a place where I don't have to worry about any problems. I listen to music every day, and I listen to music based on my emotions. Certain emotions I feel lead me to listen to songs that have a meaning to me. A lot of times when I feel down I listen to sad and slow songs such as "Vermilion Part Two" and "Zzyzx Road." The lyrics in those songs are just so deep and emotional. When times are hard and I feel as if I am going to explode, I listen to some heavy metal. I listen to bands such as Slipknot, Bullet for My Valentine, and System of a Down. The music helps me take out my anger. When everything is going great and there is a bright smile in my face, I listen to songs such as "Fully Alive" and "That Green Gentleman."

Life without music is like living life in an empty box. Where there is nothing to make me happy. Music is the one thing I have that helps me forget about all my problems and sets me free.

Rosa Ulibarri, Grade 8
Zia Middle School, NM

Quotes

A quote is something that someone has said. Most famous quotes are something someone else says, that another person admires. People look up to them and try to use them in their own lives. It's like listening to your grandpa tell you one of his "back in the day" stories. Well at least that's what it is to me, because quotes pass down wisdom, from Abraham Lincoln to Martin Luther King Jr., to your own English teacher.

Crystal Parga, Grade 8
Rio Bravo Middle School, TX

Fishing Memory

It was a normal fishing day with my dad. Bright cloudless skies, no one in sight, and I thought I wasn't going to catch anything. Though I was wrong about not catching anything.

My fishing pole was having a spasm like a chipmunk that got shot. The pole was about to jump out of my hands. My grip was getting weakened. Trying to crank the reel handle the hardest I could, but the fish fought hard.

The fish was flopping out of the water everywhere. I could barely see my bait and the hook in the fish's jaw. He was trying the best he could to get loose. Suddenly my dad told me not to give up and I almost had it in the boat.

Then I started to believe what my dad told me. I tried to be even more formidable, with a better grip on the pole and cranking it faster. It got closer and closer, I couldn't believe it, I might catch my first fish in my whole life!

Finally, "I got the fish out of the water," I yelled excitedly. I was springing up and down; also I was so happy that I didn't give up. Even happier that my dad told me not to give up. If you don't give up you'll succeed, if you do you won't go far.

Adam Petruska, Grade 7
Goodson Middle School, TX

Best Friend

I have heard "A friend sees your defects but doesn't say anything. A best friend doesn't see any." My best friends like this are very important to me. They are the ones that pick me up when I fall and are there for me whenever I need them. To me, best friends are a necessity in life. They are the family that I chose; they help me get through life no matter what life has in store for me. They help me through everything, even when I act like a total brat. They love me no matter what I do or say, and will go to the ends of the earth for me, as I would do for them. They are loyal in every way possible. When hard times hit, they are ready to catch me when I will stumble and encourage me through it all.

Last year, my best friends, Bethany, Lydia, Arielle, and I became one, stayed one, and stand as one. They are always there when I fall and pick me up. They are the family when I feel like I need one. They are the heroes of my life, most of the time anyways. They love me and care for me and never leave my side when I need them the most. They are truly best friends and I would never take them for granted.

Frances Childers, Grade 8
Faith Christian Jr/Sr High School, CA

Broken Hand

One beautiful afternoon turned into a horrible afternoon in a flash. I know this by experience. You know how you're not supposed to run backwards in softball? I guess coach "Mando" didn't know this because he had us running backwards all over the place.

It was a Wednesday and I had to go to practice, softball practice. I knew I was going to get yelled at because he had a men's softball team before us. We had to run backwards to get into good condition. While running I felt a rock, so I turned back to see. That's when I fell. My hand twisted all the way back, and I began to cry. He told me angrily "You have to do it 5 more times or until you get it right!"

I ran home and he called me a quitter. I showed my portly hand to my mother. With trepidation I expected the worst…a broken hand! My mother's tone sounded very bad, as she spoke. I was as scarred as a baby seeing a clown. "Your hand looks so lifeless, broken I would say!" The next day we rushed to the hospital to get x-rays. The doctor told me "You will have to get a cast, what color?" I chose pink, then purple, then glow in the dark green. I wasn't going to play softball again.

I was a little chicken with a broken, fractured wing. Three months later I had no more casts and the doctor said I could go back and play softball. I said no way!

Trigal Valencia, Grade 7
Santa Teresa Middle School, NM

Rhinoplasty

What is the one thing that most of the Hollywood stars get… Rhinoplasty! Rhinoplasty is a nose job. It basically means you have a Rhino nose and you get plastic surgery to fix it. This surgery is the sixth most common plastic surgery in the United States.

What stars have had this job done? The answer will come to you: Angelina Jolie, Ashlee Simpson, Michael Jackson, and more. A gorgeous woman like Angelina did this surgery to improve her incredibly good looks. Ashlee Simpson debated whether to get a nose job or not. Finally, her decision was revealed after the job was done. Ashlee Simpson was voted to have had "The Best Nose Job" out of all the performers, which in turn made people more aware of her and her performances. Now what we have all been waiting for: the legendary Michael Jackson. Mr. Jackson had about eight nose jobs. His last couple nose jobs were just to fix his prosthetic nose. My theory to why this man over did the art of Rhinoplasty is because he was addicted to beauty. Michael Jackson was voted to have "The Worst Nose Job." Nose jobs can go well or badly and Michael Jackson proves just that.

If you want a nose job you may want to know who to get it from. My top two choices are Dr. Raymen Simoni and Dr. 90210 himself, Dr. Robert Rey! Both surgeons are in Beverly Hills. They are the crème-de-la crème of biological sculptures.

Natasha Nerenberg, Grade 7
Walter F Dexter Middle School, CA

A Popular Sport Since It Began

Basketball, a long-living sport since it began. It all started with a physical education teacher. With a whole history behind it, basketball has been a long living sport since December 1891.

Dr. James Naismith was a physical education teacher. His superior, Dr. Luther H. Gulick, requested that Dr. James create an indoor sport; at the time, it was winter and Dr. Luther wanted an indoor sport for students. Dr. James knew what kid of game he wanted it to be, one of skill not strength alone. December 1891, Dr. James created his game. The game was called basketball. The goals were two peach baskets attached to the wall and the first ball used was a soccer ball. Basketball was a mixture of hockey, American football, and soccer. There were thirteen rules. Nine players were on the court at a time. Basketball spread quickly around the world and soon everyone was playing.

In the year 1893, iron hoops and hammock styles nets were used. Only ten years later, an open ended net was introduced. In the year 1897, the standard number of players was five. As the game became more popular, so did specific teams. The original Celtics were one of the first greatest professional teams. 1927, was when the Harlem Globetrotters were founded. They were specialists in court stunts and expert ball handling. In 1959, in Springfield, Massachusetts, was when the James Naismith Basketball Hall of Fame was founded. Today, we gladly still hold on to this exhilarating sport.

Amber Herrera, Grade 8
St Thomas Aquinas School, NM

A Day to Remember

It was May 14, 2006. It was just like any other day. I went to a restaurant with my family. It was my uncle's birthday. After we went home, except I went to my cousin's house. I started to play *Rock Band* with them. I left their house at 7:30 p.m. I got back to my house and went to bed. I heard knocking on the front door. I walked to the living room and my mom was talking to a police officer. The first thing I heard was that my uncle passed away. He had a motorcycle accident. I felt bad that I went to my cousin's house, because today was his birthday and also it was Mother's Day. My whole family burst into tears especially my grandmother.

The day of the funeral, I remembered how he would give me rides on this motorcycle. He worked at a plant nursery, which he owned. He would always be there when I needed him. He taught me how to ride a bike, and in the summer I would help him at the nursery. To this day I miss him and wish I could have enjoyed his presence more.

Adrian Lopez, Grade 8
Charles Maclay Middle School, CA

The Best Smell in the World

"Crish, crash, crish, crash." This sound of the crashing waves against the rugged rocks of the beach creates a perfect soundtrack that harmonizes with the fresh, salty aroma of the ocean. This scent is a refreshing burst of a crisp and raw fragrance that is unlike anything else. This briny, unprocessed perfume of the sea is something that almost stings your nostrils, yet it is not harsh, scathing, or caustic. The ocean is an all-around mystical, magical place, but when you get a whiff of this piquant bouquet of salt and the sweetness of nature, it is absolutely sublime. Once you immerse yourself in the water, you have a saline and sprightly smell that is not evanescent, but will stay with you for hours. This brackish, but insanely beautiful scent is the best smell in the world.

Olivia Furano, Grade 8
St Rita Elementary School, CA

The Unimportance of Material Things

Let's face it, we all want material things: a new car, the latest technologies, and even the most stylish clothes. But there are things, not material, that money can't buy. What I want most that money can't buy is friendship.

Friendship is something special. You can't buy friendship even if you had all the money in the world. If you want a good friend you need to be a good friend.

Another thing I want is peace. I think peace in the world is something we should all want. The world would be a much better place to live in if there was peace among people, states, and countries. So you see, the things I want that money can't buy are more important than what it can buy.

Jaimie Ramos, Grade 7
Our Lady of the Rosary School, CA

My Future Job

To me, having a job that I will enjoy is very important. I want a job that I look forward to going to every day, and not one that I will dread. That is why I want my job to be something I love, and that I'm good at. I want to become a musician. In addition to being a musician, I would also like to be an actress.

When I grow up, I want to be on stage playing my guitar, and not stuck in a cubicle. I want to go on stage and have fun. I do not want to be bored. To me, being confined to a small area would not make me happy. Being a musician takes hard work and a lot of practice. It is most definitely worth all of the hard work and practice. I love the feeling that I get when the crowd cheers. It makes me feel very special.

I would also like to be on the big screen. I want to be in many movies, and maybe even write a few. I think that it would be like living a different life with every movie role that I played. To be on stage, or in the movies, what a great adventure!

Marley Reed, Grade 7
TX

Why a Chef!

My goal after high school is to attend culinary arts school and study to become a chef. In culinary arts school I will learn basic food preparation, knife handling, meeting deadlines, basic baking, cake decoration, large party catering, food sanitation, and restaurant operations.

I know what you're thinking, "why do you want to cook?" Well, because it's fun! Pizza is fun to cook because you can pick all the toppings you like and it's pretty easy to make too! But I don't want to be just any cook; I want to be a chef.

It all started in the third grade. My mom always asked me to help her in the kitchen and I would watch her bake and make all these creations. I thought I wanted to try and do that too, because it looked like she was having fun. Ever since then, I love to cook, and that's what I hope to do when I get older.

Sure it won't be easy, and it will be expensive, but it's what I love to do and if I try hard enough I know I can do it. I will take cooking lessons and I will learn new things from my mom. A show that inspires me is *Hell's Kitchen* because Ramzie may seem out of line, but that is just a learning experience. Someday I hope to be on that show like all the other great chefs.

Alexa Allison, Grade 7
Long Valley Charter School, CA

Taking on Responsibility

Children learn responsibility and the value of work by being required to do household chores. When you have chores, you know more about keeping up with things.

You learn responsibility just by working for allowance. When you're an adult, you have to work hard to get paid. It is much easier if you had chores when you were younger so you would understand the system. For the people who never had chores, it is probably difficult. If you have a job on computers, you can't just sit around and expect to get paid; you have to work for it.

With chores you learn how to do things you need to know as an adult. You will need to know how to wash dishes, do the laundry, and the house can't clean itself. IT is better to learn when you're younger so you can clean it right, instead of things being in the closet or under the bed.

Finally you learn how to get things done on time. With chores you have to have them done by the end of the day or you might not get your allowance. As an adult, you may get projects that will have to be done in a couple of days or you might not get paid.

Learning responsibilities will help you as you get older. You can go without chores, but it will teach you things you need to know.

Katelyn Adams, Grade 8
Holliday Middle School, TX

High Merit Essays – Grades 7, 8 and 9

My Trip to Roller-Coaster Paradise

This summer I was at home reading a moon book. My mom came into my room and said "Michael has offered to take you to Lagoon with him. Do you want to come?" I thought for about 2 seconds and exclaimed "Yes!!" When we arrived at the gate I stared around in bug-eyed wonderment at the majestic roller-coasters rising like skyscrapers from the earth. Their tracks looked like train-tracks pulled from the ground, twisted and lifted by a mighty giant. I asked Michael if we could go on the old wooden roller coaster and he said "Sure." We got on the creaky old contraption and the cart started up the rise with a clack-clack-clack. We rounded the top hill, highest on the ride, and shot down like a space capsule returning to Earth. Just as I thought we'd fly off the track, we came back to the starting dock with my hair looking crazy, my eyes bulging and my mouth gaping open. Of course we went again. This time a kid in front of us snuck an ice cream cone on the ride. Half way through the ride, he pulled it out and the ice cream flew back, nearly hitting us and splattered over the sunglasses on a man behind us. We laughed so hard. After five fantabulous hours later, soaking from the water park, it was time to leave the land of speeding fun. My thoughts? We have to go again!

Maxwell Flann, Grade 7
Thomas Edison Charter School - North, UT

My Grandpa, My Hero!

My grandpa is my hero because he has been through so much in his life. My grandpa is a double survivor. First, he survived the Korean War. Second, my grandpa has lived from two strokes in his lifetime and he is planning to live for a while longer.

My grandpa has had 2 strokes in the 1990's. My grandpa had a stroke in 1997. For this stroke it took him about one year to recover, talk, walk, or even go anywhere. His second stroke was in 1999. This stroke took my grandpa a few months to recover, talk, walk, or go anywhere. These two strokes really affected my family because my grandpa is very forgetful, he gets tired easily, and he can't drive so he has to rely on others. The strokes affected him by having no sense of taste, he has a shunt in his head so he must be careful, and he also has to use a cane.

My grandpa was in the Korean War in the 1950's. My grandpa tells me lots of stories about the time when he was in Korea. One story that he told me was about the time when he saw Koreans eating dogs and cats.

He has a big place in my heart because he is very special, tells about family history, and always makes me laugh and smile even if I am having a bad day. So, as you can see my grandpa is my hero for a lot of reasons.

Kandice Garnica, Grade 7
St Sebastian School, CA

The Mood Ring

My most favorite treasure is a mood ring. It's old, and doesn't change colors anymore. To me, though, it's worth more than all the money in the world!

I acquired it from my mother, who received it from hers, and I love it very much! One day, though, I lost it, and couldn't find it! I looked everywhere (I was four, so everywhere meant EVERYWHERE!), but I couldn't find it.

Later that day, I was in the backyard, playing with a friend in the sandbox. We were having lots of fun, when he said, "What's dat in your ear?" I checked, and lo and behold, there it was! It was in my ear!

My friend and I still get a laugh out of it now. That's why the old mood ring is my most prized treasure. I am thirteen now, and still have the ring, and love it more each and every day. If I were to EVER lose it, and never find it, I don't know what I'd do. That's my most prized possession and memory, and it always will be remembered. I encourage you to have a treasure you love.

Lily Pearce, Grade 8
Thora B Gardiner Middle School, OR

Notoriety in Prestige

Oxford University, undoubtedly one of the world's most prestigious institutions, recently stated that they will no longer admit anymore so-called 'deprived students,' students from poorer backgrounds. Oxford University has been focusing on preserving its tradition, yet such an obsolete and biased effort has never been disclosed so apparently. It seems that their fruitless effort to maintain the custom is hampering them from seeking the students with the potential to perform successfully in today's demanding world.

One's social position does not directly represent one's intellectual ability. It is an irrefutable fact that Oxford University, while acknowledging this, has finagled its way out of the government's policy aimed at increasing the number of working-class students going to university. Ministers have been endeavoring for a decade to advocate the middle-class students, while Oxford launched massive fundraising drives to secure their financial independence from government.

Oxford University's grand scheme of having blatant inclination toward independent school pupils has been castigated numerous times due to its paradoxical violation against social justice.

Now it seems that 'multitudinous number of candidates' cannot be an excuse anymore for being excessively fastidious. With their jaundiced view, would they be truly able to admit students who deserve such an honor? Or are they simply searching for individuals whose social positions and backgrounds can represent Oxford University's 'master plan'?

Time has changed and time has come for such a biased attitude to vanish. Positive discrimination is still discrimination. Perhaps Oxford University is a little outdated in that aspect…

Brian Reigh, Grade 9
St Stephens Episcopal School, TX

My Life Hobbies

Today I am going to write about my favorite hobbies. I have many hobbies. My first favorite hobbies are playing sports. I really like to play football and volleyball. When I'm bored I play football with my older brothers. Football is a very exciting and fun sport. I usually play volleyball wit my friends or my cousins. Volleyball and football are two of my top hobbies. I enjoy many other sports, but those are my top two.

One of my other hobbies is drawing. Drawing expresses my feelings and emotions. In other words, it expresses my mood towards life and my family. I draw when I have free time or just when I usually have a bad mood. For me drawing is a way of life. It can also be a style. Art is another one of my top hobbies. Art is my first top hobby.

Last but not least, my favorite hobby is listening to music. Music is my life. Without music, life would have no entertainment or fun. Music is everywhere, in your head, on TV, and well everywhere. I listen to music while I am doing my homework or just simply relaxing at home. I usually take my CD player or my MP3 player with me. People will always find different music. For example: rock, heavy metal, hip hop, Chicano rap, and many more. Every person listens to different music because we have different backgrounds. That is what makes each person special in their own way.

Laura Neria, Grade 8
Isbell Middle School, CA

Cartooning

Cartooning is my life; it's what keeps me going, what makes me happy, and is my biggest talent. Here is how I was inspired to draw and why it is so important to me.

What inspired me to get into cartooning are my idols. One of my idols is Matt Groening because of his unique style. He inspired me to have my own style. Also, I grew up watching his show, *The Simpsons*. Another person who had a big impact on my life was Julie Hanson. She taught me that "if you mess up keep it that way because you might have created something even cooler."

Drawing is important to me because it was something that I was "drawn" to and something I seemed to be naturally good at. Once I became inspired I started to develop my own style. As my drawings evolve I seem to draw more variety. Some of which is drawing animals that I've never drawn before.

My dream is to go to college and major in graphic animation. After college I want to work for South Park Studios. Now you know why cartooning is so important to me. It is something I was born to do and something that I hope to make a living at in the future.

Logan Adam, Grade 8
Thora B Gardiner Middle School, OR

A Fallen Hero

Have you ever had a hero within your family? My family once did, now he is only in our memories and in our hearts, for he has died like many other soldiers in war. He was Major Ivan Rodriguez. I will try and tell you about our fallen hero.

On the morning of September 20, 2008 mom received a call telling her that my cousin Ivan had just been killed in action. My aunt was working so she was unaware of what was going on. My parents got her out of work to let her know about the bad news. It was really hard on her and her other two kids. Everybody gathered at my aunt's house to give her support. Nobody could believe what was going on in our family. It was as if time had stopped and everybody had no lies, and all we had was pain and sadness.

The following days we spent in agony mourning his tragic death for he'd died in a suicide bomb attack. Everybody sees these things happening on TV, and never stop to think, "Could this happen to me?" Could somebody in your family die like this? Well that question was certainly answered the day my cousin was the one on the news.

The funeral took place in Colorado Springs a week after his death. All my family went, aunts, uncles, cousins, everybody took a road trip together. We went to say our final goodbyes to our family hero.

In conclusion, yes we did have a death and yes it was a tragic one. Yet our family is still holding on to Ivan's memories. He will always be with us. To you it's only another soldier killed in action. To us, our family, he will always be our hero, our fallen hero.

Christian Juarez, Grade 8
Rio Bravo Middle School, TX

My Best Friend Kirsten

Everyone knows the feeling of the first day at a new place like school, a sports team, or work. My first day of second grade at St. Malachy School was that exact feeling. That day I met my best friend, Kirsten. Every little kid's first day of school is always scary and confusing. Well, that was the exact feeling I felt when a girl with blonde curls and glasses turned around to me and said, "Hi, my name is Kirsten, do you need a red pen?" I was so nervous as she started talking to me that I almost broke down crying. I was looking at the projector with the thoughts in my head saying, "What am I supposed to do? I don't have a red pen, and I want to go home!" Kirsten talked to me for the rest of the day, sat by me at lunch, helped me in class, and made sure I had everything I needed. I didn't know it then, but Kirsten and I would be friends all through my school years at St. Malachy. I left St. Malachy at the end of my 5th grade year to move to Texas. We were both upset when I found out I was leaving, but we visit each other a lot and still keep our great friendship alive. I never thought this girl who came to my rescue on my first day of school would become my best friend!

Paige Johnson, Grade 8
St Elizabeth Ann Seton School, TX

High Merit Essays – Grades 7, 8 and 9

My Dog Peppy

The day that I turned two I got the best birthday gift in the world. I had got my first dog to share with my cousin Chris. When we saw the dog we were happy so we started to say all kinds of words. One of the words that came out of our mouths was Pepe. Right then and there our parents said his name was Peppy. Both me and my cousin were happy that we had a brand new dog of our own. We had lots of fun with Peppy and he was the perfect dog. Sometimes we would call him Pepper or even Pizza and he would still come to us. We had Peppy for a long time, for about ten years. Well Chris had got other dogs so they were all kept behind a fence. One day Peppy got one of the other bigger, meaner dogs mad by eating its food and that's when the sad trouble began. The other dog bit Peppy on the neck. He had broke Peppy's neck and killed him. We were all sad so we decided to bury him in Chris's back yard to remember him. He was our first dog and always will be. I loved him so much. It was a sad loss. I will never forget him. Peppy.

Jennifer Gonzalez, Grade 8
Rio Bravo Middle School, TX

My Brother, a Pool…Oh No

It was a bright summer afternoon in June around 2:00 p.m. The birds were singing and flowers danced in the breeze. I didn't think this beautiful day could be so ominous.

It all started when my mom, my brother Danny, and I were going to go swimming at our parents' friend's house. I was seven, almost eight, and Danny was twelve.

When we arrived my brother and I raced for the bathroom. Danny ran as fast as a hungry lion at lunchtime. After he changed, I went in.

Danny asked my mom, "Can I go swimming now?"

My mom answered, "Wait for Joey."

When I finished changing Danny had left for the pool already. I was thirsty so I asked my mom for a glass of water, meanwhile my brother was putting on goggles that had the color blue when you look through them. What my brother didn't know was Michelle, mom's friend and owner of the pool, had a blue pool cover over it. When my brother jumped in, SPLASH, he was trapped beneath the pool cover. I didn't know where my brother was, so I went outside and saw that the pool cover was moving! I suddenly realized my brother was under there! I rushed into the house and yelled, "MOM! DANNY IS DROWNING!" We all rushed outside and my mom pulled off the pool cover. Danny started coughing.

Danny said, "Thank you Mom!"

My mom said, "Thank your sister. If she hadn't have gone outside and come back in screaming, you might not have made it." My brother and I shared a big bear hug and then went swimming. My mom and Michelle decided to stay near the pool, just in case.

This shows that even if you think you aren't going to drown, you might.

Joanna Miranda, Grade 7
Santa Teresa Middle School, NM

Why I Like Skateboarding

My favorite sport is skateboarding. Skateboarding is my favorite sport because most of my free time I go outside and skateboard until I get tired. My friends and I like skateboarding because we have nothing to do in our spare time. The first skateboard I ever got was in Christmas by my uncle. From that point on I started skateboarding but after a while I started playing soccer and riding my bike with my brother. My second skateboard I got was by my brother.

My favorite skateboarder is Rodney Mullen. He's my favorite skateboarder because he's a person that goes for the excitement when he's skateboarding. Mullen's full name is John Rodney Mullen and he was born on August 17, 1996 in Gainesville, Florida. He's also my favorite skateboarder because he's one of many people that can do some of the best and hardest tricks ever made. I want to be like him so I could do all the tricks he does.

All in all I like skateboarding because you could meet new people at the skate park. When you have free time it's the best thing to do in my opinion. I have many tricks I like. One of my favorite tricks is the primo because your feet have to be in the right spot when you start it then you lean your feet forward after that you get on the wheels and just lean back this time and land on the board. That's why I like skateboarding as my favorite sport.

Octavio Diaz, Grade 8
Isbell Middle School, CA

Freedom

Freedom…Freedom, some people in the world will never know the meaning. That is why it is so important to me. The freedom of America is the envy of the world. Yet it is taken for granted by so many people like our amount of clean water. Oh yes, our freedom is much taken for granted. So much, in fact, we don't even know how spoiled rotten in freedom we are. To me, freedom is the smell of hot dogs on the Fourth of July as fireworks boom overhead. Reading the Bible and praying, resting assured we will not be murdered for our beliefs. Choosing who our leader will be. Not having to be taken away from our family and having someone choose who we work for or what kind of jobs we have. But it does not mean that I can go one hundred miles per hour down a country road in a car. It does mean I answer to no one except my elders. Freedom, I could go on forever, but I'll sum it up for you. It is an unwritten law that every man should follow not to enslave other men but to be like brothers throughout the world. Only when past grudges are forgotten and every man lays down his weapons of hate will our whole population of the world be free. That's what freedom means to me.

Tanner Lowry, Grade 7
Lindale Jr High School, TX

Photography

Photography…it's a wonderful thing. Without it, life would be dull. Nobody really understands why taking pictures is important. It's to cherish or remember the memories you've had. Photography isn't only about your memories. It can also be of other things too, like nature, people, places, animals, different countries, even things from outer space! I, personally, LOVE to take pictures. When I get older, I want to be a photographer. I take pictures of me and friends, family, pets, and plants. I hate deleting pictures off my camera, because I have wonderful memories from the pictures. If we didn't have cameras, what would happen to yearbooks, calendars, picture books, CD albums, shirts, and way more? Think of how boring and blah life would be without those things. I bet you can pick at least one of those things you love. Now, do you see why photography is important?

Emily Valentine, Grade 7
Lindale Jr High School, TX

Love

Love is this sensation that revolves around our nation. When you love someone they are in every one of your thoughts. There is not one minute or second you don't think about them. That special someone is everything you hoped for, and everything you need. Once they come into your lives there is no ifs or buts.

It's like without them there is no air to breathe. Everything you do is as if it were for them. You would do anything to make them happy or at least smile. It doesn't matter in the end if you give your life. As long as they live a good, long happy life!!

Cindy Rivera, Grade 8
Rio Bravo Middle School, TX

The Journey

The journey I have or am currently on is the journey to school. I grew up in a poor family where I had two sisters and money was scarce. My mom, and other adults would always tell me, "education is the key to success." I thought yeah, I know. No matter how many times I tried to show them this they kept telling me over and over again. Then I thought about it for a while. What would happen if the successful people didn't have the education they needed to get where they are now? So I brushed off an assignment once or twice so I failed a test or two. Does that mean I won't be able to get where I want to be in life? The answer is yes. I know that the effort I put into my work is going to affect me somehow.

So to me my journey is important. I know what it's going to do for me as I grow up. I know that my level of intelligence is going to determine my place in society. Sure the journey may get a little hard and feel a little daunting but that doesn't mean it's impossible. I'm just happy it's not too late to start my journey.

Angelica Thomas, Grade 8
Ralph Waldo Emerson Middle School, CA

Going to 8th Grade

"Top dogs of Reagan County Middle School," is what I said at my house that morning. "I'm going to be an 8th grader. Sports and classes are going to more fun than 7th grade. I'm ready for what life throws at me!"

On my way to school I was thinking about how my classes would be and how the school looked with the new buildings. When I was dropped off at my school, it was like nothing I expected. The new classes in the new building had these whiteboards called smart boards. When I went to my first class, I knew I was going to like school more often. The classes are fun and we get to work in partners. The teachers make learning interesting, and football had new positions for defense.

In Mr. McKinzie's he tells us a story. He has so much enthusiasm. When he tells us the story, it's like taking a time machine to the olden days. In Coach Baucom's science class, it's different how he teaches this year. In his class last year we used workbooks for homework. This year we use spirals as our study guide and homework. He gives us instructions on what to do, like putting in pictures as study guides.

I thought this year, eighth grade, would be the same as seventh grade. It turns out I was wrong. Eighth grade is WAY better than seventh grade. Everybody has a day to learn.

Cody Ortiz, Grade 8
Reagan County Middle School, TX

Bandit

My dog Bandit is very athletic for a dog. He plays tetherball and soccer. When he plays tetherball we hit the ball and then he jumps and even does a twist. When Bandit plays soccer he kicks the ball with his feet when he runs. He controls the directions of the ball by his nose.

He is a husky, which means he is fast and loves it when you play with him in the winter. That is when he is most excited to play with anyone. When we play with him we have to sprint as fast as we can to catch up with him. We have to play with him for a long time until he is tired and can't play anymore. He is one of those dogs that like to play in all the seasons, not just during the warm seasons. My dog will play in any heat or coldness.

But during summer and spring, when it is really hot, we have to put out a little pool in the back yard so he can lie down in the cool pool and it is in the shade so it would not be so hot and stay cool longer. Even though we have to fill it up every day.

My dog is so much fun, but he is not the best dog to take on a walk because he will drag you throughout the neighborhood. That is why my dog is different from all of the other dogs.

Matthew Boyd, Grade 8
St Elizabeth Ann Seton School, TX

Friendship

"You only meet your once in a lifetime friend, once in a lifetime" (*Little Rascals*). Friendship is a special relationship between a group of people. Companionship is something that is viewed differently by one other. Most people treasure their relationship with their friends but others are unappreciative and take it for granted. We all need to realize how important friendships are and hold on to them.

To me, friendship is really important. Without my best pal, I would be devastated. We have gone through many obstacles in our lives, but we have managed to remain friends.

In my opinion, a true friend walks in when others walk out. Friendship is meant to be trustful, honest, and cherished. A true friend is one who is supportive and understanding; a buddy does not talk behind one's back and keeps secrets. You shouldn't take advantage of your friendships. Your friends are the ones who will help you throughout your life, and if you are one of those people who are ungrateful of their friendships, you will end up losing your friends. Without companionship, there basically is no meaning to life.

In conclusion, friendship is the key to happiness in life. "Remember, the greatest gift is not found in a store nor under a tree, but in the hearts of true friends" (Cindy Lew).

Clarissa Cortez, Grade 9
Kaufer High School, TX

That Takes the Cake

July 3, 2009. It was my thirteenth birthday, I was at camp. After everyone sang "Happy Birthday" to me, the cook cut a huge créme white cake. Birthday girl gets first choice. I was eating my cake, talking to my friends. I was happy, until Alyssa Collins pushed me aside and ran her finger over the velvety frosting of my cake while laughing with her friends and saying, "Oh, thanks!" as if she couldn't see me. To her I didn't exist. As if she didn't care, she grabbed my cake plate out of my hand and took a big piece and smeared it in her friend's mouth. I only had one bite of my birthday cake.

When I think back to that night, I remember my self-confidence and esteem shattering like a crushed eggshell. My first reaction to what she did was anger. I felt so hot and mad that she could be so rude, especially on my birthday! Then came the sadness, rushing through me like a waterfall starting form the tip of my head crashing down to the tips of my toes. The worst part was, it seemed like she didn't even have a clue about how she made me feel. In that instant my emotions did not matter to her at all. I felt nonexistent, and that feeling is empty.

Please be conscious of the effect of how one simple action can separate one person from the crowd and make her feel unseen.

Fiona Bennett, Grade 8
Headwaters Academy, MT

The Scarlet Ibis

In the short story, "The Scarlet Ibis" by James Hurst, the narrator is an excellent brother. He spent quality time with Doodle. Also, fantastic brothers teach each other useful skills. He also provided positive support for Doodle. The narrator is a good brother.

First, brothers spend quality time with their siblings. The narrator took Doodle to his favorite spot. He is willing to push Doodle in a go-cart. Some people may believe that the narrator was a bad brother because he had originally planned to smother Doodle, however he is a good brother because he had determined that quality of life was more important than quantity of life, so he helped his brother instead. A brother must be loving to spend time with his siblings.

Second, a brother is a good brother if he teaches his siblings useful skills. The narrator taught Doodle to walk. The narrator set goals for Doodle. A brother must care if he sets goals for his siblings. The narrator is a good brother because he teaches Doodle.

Thirdly, good brothers provide positive support. The narrator never gave up on Doodle. He helped Doodle reach goals. He kept pushing Doodle. That shows that the narrator wanted to help Doodle.

In conclusion, the narrator in the short story, "The Scarlet Ibis" by James Hurst, is a great brother. He spent quality time with Doodle. He taught Doodle useful skills. The narrator provided positive support. The narrator is a great brother.

McKenzie Brewer, Grade 9
South Jordan Middle School, UT

Loose-Leaf

Sitting in English, doodling, was my newfound hobby. I loved to write, but listening to her lectures on how "our age" had turned dependent on video games was not what I had in mind. Writing, to me, was always something special that anyone with a case of sarcasm and a wild imagination could do, that's why I always believed it was my talent. All my friends were athletic super stars, but I was just OK in every sport I tried from golf to swimming. So when I found writing, I found love. Of course there were, and always will be, millions of better writers than me out there, but to know that I could come out of my shell onto a sheet of loose-leaf, made me want to do it all the time. In my 12 years of life, like everyone, I have been through some difficulties. Death, broken hearts, and other things have happened, and writing is where I can talk about it without having to drive anyone nuts with my poor-me sob story. Oh wait, did she just call on me? Her croaky voice is calling my name. Wow! What was the question? Oh no, I was daydreaming, again. Once again I am on her list. Well to the principal's office I go. Next time during English, I think I will stay in reality. Even if my imagination's more interesting.

Rylee Stewart-Kucera, Grade 7
Lewistown Jr High School, MT

The Best Camp Ever

It all started one day at 3:00 in the morning. We got all our stuff and loaded the bus to go to Discover Camp. I was tired but very excited.

On the way there, we were asleep until about 8:00 a.m. When we woke up, we ate our breakfast. The rest of the way over there, we either slept or stayed up and talked. I could not concentrate or sleep because I was thinking about what was ahead. So I just took pictures of the sleeping people and the mountains with my camera. When we finally arrived, everyone was excited and no one was sleepy!

The ladies had to check us in. Then, we went to our dorms. They were pretty nice, but I've seen better. All that mattered was that the beds were comfy.

The best part was the church. It was the biggest church I have ever seen in my life. As we walked in, you could feel the presence of the Holy Spirit. The worship service was awesome!

The whole experience was very awesome, but we had to go home. I was sad to leave because it was lots of fun and meaningful. I will keep this experience with me forever.

Kimberly Wiebe, Grade 7
Seminole Jr High School, TX

Peyton Manning

Peyton Manning was born March 24, 1976 in New Orleans, Louisiana, and right now he is playing for the Indianapolis Colts as #18 as the quarterback.

he started playing football for the Colts as the first overall pick in 1998 after a standout with a college football career with the Tennessee volunteers.

In his first season he passed 3,739 yards with 26 touchdowns and five different NFL rookie records. Also in 2008 he won 12 out of 16 games.

In one of the seasons he and his little brother Eli Manning went to the playoffs and played Manning VS Manning (Colts VS New York Giants).

When he was in college he went to the University of Tennessee and played college football before the pros drafted him.

And since then he has played for the Indianapolis Colts.

I like Peyton because my Maw Maw and I have always liked the Colts and his brother and because he is a good football player.

Lilly White, Grade 7
Deweyville Middle School, TX

A Kid

I know a kid who was born October 9, 1995. He is a really nice person, once you get to know him. He is a kind person, through some people say that he is a little weird. He is a funny person and is fun to have around. He makes the atmosphere light in a heavy situation and makes nay depressed person laugh.

He isn't all play and no work, like a clown or something. He can be very serious about the work that he does. He will focus and do it well the first time. He is a great team player and a great leader. You can really learn a few things from him. He will do his best to share real information.

I remember when that kids first moved next to me. He was pretty shy at first, but after a while he started to lighten up. He tires to be nice to everyone that he meets, such as a random person on the street. He helps me with everything, from homework to giving me ideas for a project. He is very supportive of what I do. He is a great role model and makes me want to be the best person I can be.

Byron Radosevich, Grade 8
St Thomas Aquinas School, NM

My Favorite Superstar

Troy Aikman is 42 years old. He used to play for the Dallas Cowboys from 1989 to 2000.

When he was twelve years old he had to move from Texas to Oklahoma. When he had played for Texas junior high he was pretty much a superstar. When he moved he had thought that his career was over, but to his surprise it had just begun. For a surprise he still played the rest of his junior high and high school years.

Without notice he got accepted into UCLA on a football scholarship. Not knowing what position he would play he got to play quarterback, he played that position great just like a professional. That year he went to the Cotton Bowl.

He got drafted into the NFL as a Dallas Cowboy. From 1989 to 2000, he brought the Cowboys to a three time championship. He is my favorite player because he is in the pro football hall of fame.

Dustin Eubanks, Grade 7
Deweyville Middle School, TX

Moving On

I have known my best friends for many years. My very best friends that I have known for eleven years and my other for about seven. I have known many people through out my lifetime. As I grow older I gain friends and lose friends. It happens to everyone in life. It's sad to see happen but it's something that can't be changed.

Next year I will be a freshman in high school, and like many other students, I too will be moving on. It seems that once you enter high school, your taste in friends begins to change, as well as your style. When that happens, you gain friends and meet many new people. So what happens to all your other old friends? Soon you will have not much contact with your old friends.

People grow apart and make new friends; it's life. As high school will go on I will soon be looking back at my past. I will remember all my good friends I have had in my life. I will realize the things I have lost when I entered high school. I might see my old friends there at the end. They may be there with me but then again they may not.

People go through things like this all the time and realize it's something that happens sometime during your lifetime. Hold on to your friends now but be ready to maybe lose them in the future.

Corina Little Turtle, Grade 8
Isbell Middle School, CA

The Worst Thanksgiving Ever

Last year I had the worst Thanksgiving ever! I almost lost my Grandpa on Thanksgiving.

One day after school I was surprised to see my brother, Bradley was picking me up instead of my mom. He said, "Hurry up! Grandpa is in the hospital." A shock went through my body "Oh no!" I thought. Then we went to the hospital, and my mom asked if I wanted to see my Grandpa. I said "Sure." I walked into the ER and when I saw my Grandpa I almost broke down in tears! Then the doctor came in and said that he had three heart attacks this morning. After that, the family decided to take him to Lubbock, so he could have surgery.

The next day we left for Lubbock. When we got to the hospital we checked my Grandpa in, then it was time for his surgery. The doctors decided he needed a quadruple bypass surgery.

After the surgery, they decided to put my Grandpa in the ICU. Then after a couple days it was time to take Grandpa home. I was so excited to see I could barely sit still. As a matter of fact, my cousins and I couldn't keep our eyes off the elevator. It was great to see him sitting up and not lying down when the elevator doors opened.

To this day my Grandpa and I are best friends. We always look back and say "Wow I'm so glad we survived that Thanksgiving week."

Savannah Neudorf, Grade 7
Seminole Jr High School, TX

My Family Being in War

When someone dearest to you is in a bad situation, it can affect your entire family. Many people have experienced what I am talking about. It could leave family members in a troubling situation. It could make your family grow apart.

Every man in my family that I know of has been in war. My great grandfather was in World War I. My other great grandfather was in World War II. My grandfather was in Vietnam. My pa-pa was also in the military, and my dad was in the Gulf War. There are some things my family won't talk about. My grandfather wont' even talk about what he saw overseas. My dad and my pa-pa are the only ones who will talk. My dad has told me many stories. For instance, my dad told me about 2 weeks ago about the Japanese kamikazes. The kamikazes were pilots who would do nothing but fly their planes into ships, basically a suicide.

All of this has changed my life in many ways. For instance, when I grow up I want to join the military so I can keep what is sort of a tradition going. Knowing what my parents have told me makes me eager to join.

Maybe someday I can be in the military. I would love to serve my country. Maybe someday I can serve under a famous general like my dad who served under Norma Schwarzkopf, the leader of "Desert Shield."

Kobe Roberson, Grade 8
Reagan County Middle School, TX

My Animals

I'm a very lucky girl who experiences a lot of love from my pets. I have two dogs, two rabbits, one mini toad, and one fish. Each one of my pets has a special personality.

Let me start off with the smallest one, Ted the toad. He is so small that when my dad found him, he almost mistook him for a cricket. Now the little guy preys on the tiny crickets we feed him like a lion!

Let me tell you about my indoor fish Sensei. He is a beautiful blue color with some red and has a long tail and long flowing fins. He gracefully swims in his tank like a water ballerina.

Cozy and Job are both dwarf rabbits. Cozy is not as friendly as Job, but he is special in his own way. Job is bigger than Cozy and is as black as can be. Job has a special talent; he is an escape artist, but always comes back home.

Finally, there are my two dogs, Chiquita and Feliz. They are like my little sisters and are my best friends. Chiquita is a mutt and Feliz is a Shetland Sheep Dog. They always play around with me and keep me company.

All of my pets are very special to me and play a big part in my life. I love them so much. I don't know what I would do without them.

Kristen Sanchez, Grade 7
St Thomas Aquinas School, NM

Two Vowels and a Consonant That Changed My Life Forever…Literally! AFI

I never knew that three basic, commonly used letters could have such an impact on my life. To many these three letters mean absolutely nothing but for me, these three letters have become a part of me forever.

People especially my peers stop and ask me, "What's AFI?" or "What does it stand for?" which I find funny since I feel like it's for me to know and for you to never find out, but of course I end up telling them. I feel as though after I tell them a piece of me has slipped away and is gone forever. I feel as though AFI belongs to me because if you ask anyone if they know who they are, the answer is 99.99% of the time a no.

To me AFI is not only a band but gods. I look up to Davey Havok, Jade Puget, Adam Carson, and Hunter. Their music isn't only awesome, it's lyrically powerful. I find it funny that AFI is considered an "emo" band. Instead of making me sad, AFI makes me happy and puts me in an incredible mood.

I consider myself more than a fan, I'm dedicated to this beautiful band. If this band didn't exist, I'd feel incomplete. AFI is those very rare bands that I never get bored of listening to.

I hope to continue loving this band, buy all the CDs and DVDs they've released, see them in concert, meet and greet Davey Havok, Jade Puget, Adam Carson, and Hunter and receive autographs. I also plan to get AFI's band logo as a tattoo one day. So far it's been five years (since the third grade) I've been obsessed with this band and listening to them. They'll always remain my favorite band. I love AFI, forever and for always.

Jovannah Ramirez, Grade 8
Rio Bravo Middle School, TX

Swimming in Success

When I first started on the swim team, I was mortified. Now, I am one of the coach's favorite swimmers. I have a trophy, a lot of ribbons and a medal. I've accomplished it all because I believed in myself.

The first day of swim practice, I thought swimming was going to be easy and lots of fun. I was wrong. When I first started swim practice, the water was freezing. Did I mention that we started in early April? We started off with kickboards. The drills got harder and harder as we progressed. Then we began to use pullbuoys and finally started to swim the strokes. After all of that, I could take no more. I asked if I could go to the restroom, and ran to my mom. I burst out into tears and said repeatedly, "I can't do it! I can't do it! It's too hard!" My mom said, "You just need to practice, these kids have been doing this for years."

I've been swimming for two years now and I know I will continue to get better and better. I just have to keep practicing and most importantly, believing in myself.

Haylee Passmore, Grade 7
Goodson Middle School, TX

N.Y. to N.M.

This summer I moved from Long Island, New York to New Mexico. Moving from an island to the desert is a huge difference. It is like moving to a different planet.

It all started last December when my father interviewed for a job. We had a family meeting to discuss the job and the move. We were all shocked to hear the job was in New Mexico. It was so far away and I didn't know anything about New Mexico. I thought it would be a boring place to live, especially since there was no ocean or beach. We came to visit and we saw all the outdoor activities such as, hiking, biking, exploring caves, etc. I also get to see parts of the United States that I never have been to before. People are so nice in New Mexico. I love the weather, but I do miss the rain.

It is hard leaving my friends and family behind in New York. I miss my friends a lot, but we get to talk and play on Xbox 360 and on the computer. I have made new friends here and I play flag football. Sometimes it is hard to live here but I do it because I know it is the right thing to do. People ask me, "Why did you move to the desert?" I tell them, "Why not."

Justin Feeney, Grade 8
St Thomas Aquinas School, NM

Friends Are What Make Life Fun

Having friends in my life is important to me for many reasons. Friendships are made from our early years as children through our adult years. Some of the ways that relationships we have as friends are important are because of the following: listening, having fun, compromising and sharing feelings.

Listening to your friends can help you grow closer in friendship. When you listen to your friends and what they say, it not only allows you to comprehend what your friend is saying it allows you to give them feedback. When your friend is explaining something, once they notice that you are actually paying attention they will appreciate you. When you are with your friends, you need to have a little fun every once and awhile. It wouldn't hurt to laugh and joke around with your friends. Having fun with your friends can open up your relationship. Compromising with friends is important because everyone has their likes and dislikes, but you work things out with them so you don't get into a fight with them. Everyone needs to learn how to compromise, because it is not fair when one friend gets their way all the time.

The importance of friends to me is that they are there to help me through any difficult times in my life. Friends are there to support and encourage me in all that I do. They are there to have fun with. That's why my friends are important.

Kayla Alker, Grade 7
Goodson Middle School, TX

A Growing Friendship

Jaclyn and I were destined to be friends. Because before we were even thought of our parents were friends. Jaclyn is six months older than me. She was at the hospital asleep, the day I was born. She is my best friend.

"Ring Ring," I heard the phone. I left my coloring picture on the couch and ran to answer the phone. It was Jaclyn inviting me to her seventh birthday party. "It is a slumber party!" She told me excitedly. I was thrilled. It was going to be my first slumber party.

When I got to the party everyone was already there. They were eating pizza and cake. I walked into the kitchen, grabbed a slice of cheese pizza, hurried over to the table, and sat down beside Jaclyn. She got some neat gifts such as a Ballerina Barbie, and tons of adorable jewelry. It was getting late so we laid down and watching "A Cinderella Story." I fell asleep halfway through the movie thinking about the best slumber party I have ever been to.

Six years later Jaclyn and I still love to spend the night together. We love doing crazy things and spending time together. Jaclyn, my best friend, is one of the most important things to me.

Sarah Shirley, Grade 7
Seminole Jr High School, TX

The Los Angeles Dodgers

A team that has a long history in baseball is the Los Angeles Dodgers. Last year they were the National League West Division champions as well as this year. They are supported by fans of different races. The Dodgers used to be the Brooklyn Dodgers, the Atlantics, the Grays, the Superbas, and the Robins. The club used to originate in New York. They moved to Los Angeles in 1958. At first they used to play in the L.A. Colliseum. Then they moved into Dodger Stadium after it was built. They have won 7 pennants and 6 World Series championship titles. Hopefully, this year will be good for them. The Dodgers have many great ballplayers such as: Manny Ramirez, Jim Thome, Andre Ethier, and Rafael Furcal. My two favorite players are Andre Ethier and Rafael Furcal. With these strong players, the Dodgers are on their way to the World Series. Their team batting average for this year is 29.7. They also have some great, young pitchers such as: Clayton Kershaw, Chad Billingsly, and Randy Wolf. Their pitching average is 27.8. This season, they scored 780 runs. The top home run maker this year for the Dodgers was Andre Ethier with 30 home runs. Since Joe Torre's arrival, the Dodgers have been winning more games. The Dodgers' general manager is Ned Collette. He always brings great players to the team. It's amazing how one team can bring many people together.

Rudy Soto, Grade 8
Isbell Middle School, CA

Trust

I think that trust is important to have in life. People may not see it but trust is almost everything. You use and have trust in everyday life. In the dictionary the definition of trust is, "to commit or place in one's care."

Trust is the key to all relationships, friendships, family, boyfriend or girlfriend and even a professional relationship. With my friends they can trust me not to tell their secrets, most important to keep them. With my family they can trust that I will make the right choices for myself whether it be hanging out with friends or in school to get something done. On a professional level, I'm only fourteen so to me my teachers are my professional relationship and they trust me to get my homework done on time. My coaches trust me to make the right play or score that winning point. In a boyfriend/girlfriend relationship you trust them to be faithful to you and speak the truth.

William Shakespeare once said, "Love all, but trust a few." The sad thing is, is that it's true. I wish you could trust everyone but you can't, that's why trust is so important to me.

Luna Tarango, Grade 8
Zia Middle School, NM

Mr. Zaroff, the Cheater

Mr. Zaroff has a "game" that he invented and plays every night. This "game" is cold-blooded, heartless murder. He not only slaughters trapped human beings, he cheats. Mr. Zaroff gives unfair weapons, he has a better advantage with time. He knows the island, he has Ivan and he has dogs. Mr. Zaroff is nothing more than a savage cheater.

First, the setting for the game is on a jungle island; his island! This island has dangerous animals, quicksand, and foliage you could get lost in. Zaroff has maps! How is any person going to compete with that? Not to mention that these sailors are good on the sea, not land. Zaroff is a seasoned, professional hunter. Now is that fair?

Some may say that it is fair because the hunted have a weapon. The person being hunted has a knife and Zaroff has a pistol. Zaroff has three days to hunt you. He gives you an hour head start, but one hour to the seventy-two hours he has to hunt you, one to seventy-two not very equal. Remember he knows the land, so simple for him to find you.

Third, Zaroff has his brute, Ivan and his aggressive attack dogs. Ivan is a gargantuan master that belongs to a race of savages. Ivan has little or no concept of human lives and is the only other option to the game. The dogs are trained to hunt what their master commands them to. They will kill if necessary. Who would want to end their day being chewed up by dogs?

Zaroff knows the land and he has a gun, his opponent does not. Zaroff has maps and time on his side. Lastly, he has Ivan and the dogs to assist in eliminating the grieved sailors. Zaroff is a cheater.

Olivia Motzkus, Grade 9
South Jordan Middle School, UT

Doing Your Part

I'm doing my part, are you doing yours? Every day in Africa, people are living in poverty and even dying from it. In America, we do not see the struggles of their daily life.

Poverty is a big problem. Every day thousands of people die from it. People often go without food for days on end simply because they cannot afford it. Water is also a necessity that is hard for them to attain. While we take it for granted, they often have to walk miles just to get a drink.

In Africa, people are living in terrible housing and living conditions. In America, we live in beautiful houses that far exceed Africa's. Africans often live in makeshift houses made out of any material they can find. Often, they live in houses that have leaks and holes in the roof or walls. These poor living conditions can affect their health.

Health is a major issue. They are often helpless and innocent victims of HIV/AIDS. Many factors affect this including malnutrition and poor health care. Health care is a luxury that is often unaffordable.

My family and I sponsor two children in Africa. We also make additional sacrifices so that we can send support for their community improvement projects. Some people might think we should just help our neighbors here in America. My friends in Africa are my neighbors. If everyone would do their part to help, the people of Africa would have a chance of hope.

Alex Cowan, Grade 9
North Garland High School, TX

My Loving Family

I have relatives who live all over the United States of America. From the west coast to the east coast, north to south, I have relatives on either my mother or father's side of the family. Based on the fact that I move so much, I don't usually get to see my relatives that often. But when I do, it is a great blessing to my family and me. Now that I live in New Mexico, I am a bit closer to my relatives that are on my mother's side of the family.

Just a few days ago, my grandparents (mother's parents) came out to visit us here in New Mexico. My grandparents live in Livonia, Michigan. I am glad that they came out to visit us. Their flight took around three and a half to four hours. They just got here so the fun is just beginning. This weekend I hope to do some fun things with them, including: driving up to Santa Fe and maybe go out to lunch a few times.

My grandparents are very fun to be around and I am glad to be able to spend time with them in New Mexico, where we are both new to Albuquerque. I feel that I am very fortunate to have so many loving and caring relatives that will travel great distances to see their beloved family.

Dante Brutyn, Grade 8
St Thomas Aquinas School, NM

Holly McPeak

Holly McPeak, a famous beach volleyball player, has collected seventy-two beach titles and nineteen FIVB titles throughout 1996-2008. Her birthday is July 16, 1969, in Hollywood California, Los Angeles. She's forty and she still plays today. She has won eighty Olympic beach medals throughout 1982-2008. She has won eighty out of one hundred games in her whole life.

She claims volleyball's her favorite sport and that she will not want to retire any time soon. She wants to play volleyball until she has to retire, she has been playing since she was sixteen and she wants to keep playing. As a matter of fact, she has recently played on Friday, August 28, 2009-Sunday, August 30, 2009. Holly has been to the school at the University of Phoenix. She's even played in the summer Olympics on October 17, 2007 for the United States.

If I was one of her friends I think I might stay her friend for as long as I could 'cause I like her and she seems like a nice person.

Makayla Beck, Grade 7
Deweyville Middle School, TX

Music

Although there are many important things in this world, one of the most important to me is music. Across the country, music activities are being eliminated from schools.

Music can tell you things about the world. Some songs talk about how great the world is, and others talk about things wrong with it. I agree with both types but I'm wondering what is wrong with it. Hearing that schools across the country are eliminating band makes me wonder where the funding for those classes is going. I'm in band and one day my director told me that our band receives little funding from the school. I wondered where the funding was going. Both the volleyball and football teams received new uniforms at the beginning of the year. I have no problem with that but a few weeks into the school year they were asked to turn in the their uniforms for new ones. Whether or not it was school funded I don't know. That might be where band funding is going.

Do you think Green Day or the All-American Rejects started playing songs without practice? They were probably introduced to music in school; if the funding for their school bands was cut we might not have their music. Try to imagine a world without music. What would be played during a movie? What would be played at dances?

Music is something everyone can relate to. When I hear certain songs they remind me of the moment when I first heard that song. When me and my family are on long vacations there are songs I like to listen to more than others. Participating in music at school has helped open my mind to the world of music.

Music is great but we have to protect the right to have it.

Philip Miller, Grade 8
Zia Middle School, NM

High Merit Essays – Grades 7, 8 and 9

The Best Summer Trip (For Now…)

The best trip I ever had was our 2009 summer vacation trip. We went to Canada for the first time. We went many places and visited a couple of people.

It all started on a bright summer day. When we got to New York we got a rental car and went to Niagara Falls. The site is very beautiful and wet if you are walking close to the edge of the walkway.

We then went to Duc's house. He is my dad's friend and he stayed along for most of the trip.

Now we first got a tour of Toronto, which is where Duc lives. Then we went to Montreal. It is full of beautiful buildings and scenery. We went to three other cities but I can't recall them. When we got to the mainly French speaking part we had two interpreters; my mom and another person. When we finally got back to Toronto we had only two more days.

We met Duc and he was a great man. He made us all laugh and was a great guide. We met one of my many cousin's grandmas and grandpas. Their house is huge. We met other people and my cousin's cousins. The people in Canada are very friendly.

The day we left Canada was the worst but we still were happy. My brother got a toy car in Canada. I got a new book. I think my parents had a great time and so did we.

Garreth Tran, Grade 7
St Elizabeth Ann Seton School, TX

Motocross Racing

Motocross racing is one of the best and most competitive sports. Motocross racers that are good at racing can get a good sponsor and a good team to help them with expenses. Motocross is very exciting because of all the different tracks in the United States. You never know what might happen while you're racing.

For serious racers a sponsorship can be really helpful because they provide you with trailers and free gear for racing. They pay you for things like using stickers and wearing shirts and dirt bike parts for your bike. Those are some good things about getting a good sponsor.

The thrill of racing dirt bikes is what I like the most. I love going fast on the straight aways. I love the big jumps and going to the new tracks and seeing the new gear. All these things give me an adrenaline rush.

Another exciting thing is that you never know what is going to happen when the gate drops and you go. There could be a new rider that is there, and he or she could crash or stop on a jump, or something like that could happen. I have been at a race, and a rider got stuck on the start gate. It was something that can happen to anyone good or new.

For me Motocross racing is the best because it is exciting in my spare time. If you ever get a chance to race dirt bikes I think you should do it.

Austin Horan, Grade 8
Holliday Middle School, TX

Cheer '09-'10

"Go Indians!" We all yelled while finishing our cheer. Sixth grade I tried out for cheerleading. I was really excited to be trying out with all the other girls, but unfortunately only seven girls make the squad. I made the team! So I knew then this was going to be a great seventh grade year.

It all started with summer cheer camp. I had a blast at cheer camp! Cheerleading is really important to me, so I needed to focus really hard to get all the moves down before school. Every day was fun! We practiced cheers from eight to twelve.

During the second week of school, we had our first pep rally! We couldn't wait for it, but at the same time, we were all nervous.

"Two bits, four bits, six bits, a dollar all for the Indians stand up and holler!" We had practiced for Thursday pep rally and football game. In our cheer I was put up as a flyer and they Barbie dolled Makaya. Barbie doll is when we rotate the flyer in the air; that is one of my favorite stunts.

Finally, it was Thursday! The pep rally went great for my first one. Cheerleading is really important to me and it is so fun. I am going to stay with it until the end of high school and maybe college too.

April Davis, Grade 7
Seminole Jr High School, TX

A Baseball Diamond in the Rough

It was the third game of my baseball season. I jogged out to left field and looked at the other teams' dugout. Standing at the fence was Roger Clemens. I couldn't believe it! I could meet him after the game and get his autograph. I was so thrilled that I totally forgot about the game. When I finally stopped daydreaming and focused on my job, the batter hit an easy fly out my way. My mind started to rush. What would normally be a simple play had turned into a chance to impress Roger Clemens. Suddenly I couldn't think. I just ran towards the ball and held out my glove. The ball hit it, bounced out, and rolled five feet away from me. I was stunned! I had just missed the simplest play ever, and in front of one of the greatest baseball players of all time. I couldn't see my face, but I'm certain it was as red as a rose. I was so embarrassed. How could I meet Roger after that? When the game was over, I decided it didn't matter. I grabbed a ball, borrowed a pen from my grandmother, and went over to Roger. Still feeling a little embarrassed, I asked him for his autograph. I told him, "You're the best pitcher ever!" as he was signing the ball. Then Roger said, "Thanks. You have to practice a lot to be good, but you will still make mistakes sometimes." I smiled, and my embarrassment disappeared.

Mason Samhan, Grade 7
Goodson Middle School, TX

Sweet Covered Truth

"Honesty is always the best policy" is a tried saying, but embraces an enormous amount of certainty. Though deceit often permits one to escape dilemma, the truth will always emerge. In most situations, one will discover that deceit does not present the same long-term benefits as honesty does.

Sometimes, deceit can come in the form of white lies. An example of a white lie is when someone asks if they look good in an outfit and you agree, although they are not. A white lie can ultimately shatter one's heart if they discover you deceived them. Is it worth deceit or embarrassment to inform someone that they look good when they are not, particularly when they discover it?

With regard to serious matters, however, deceit can lead to more dreadful consequences. Cheating on a test, for example, may result in failing a class and in getting into an immense predicament. If one cheats, that person is only cheating him/herself. Cheating is just like lying because one is lying by saying that he/she did the test his/herself.

Regardless of advantages to telling the truth, deceit can still be tempting. For instance, how can one explain the death of a relative or friend to an innocent child? Should children learn about death at such a young age? One is entitled to lie in an effort to shelter a child from the harshness of reality. Deceit is often used as a defensive action.

Therefore, one can view deceit as a sweet treat. It is like a cupcake that satisfied hunger and provides a good feeling. However, the cupcake can cause poor health in the future. Similarly, deceit appears to be appropriate but only holds problems in the future, particularly if you indulge.

Daylen Sisneroz, Grade 8
St Anne Elementary School, CA

Oma

My Oma (grandma) is very cool because she does a lot of things that you would never think a seventy year old person would do, she goes on fifty-mile hikes, plays pool, and dances like a 20 year old. She always has a good attitude for her grand children.

My Oma is a great hiker. One time she hiked from the top of the Sandia Mountains to the bottom. She has taken me on many hikes to the Pecos and to the Sandias!

My Oma plays pool, for an extra thing to do! One time she said, "Kevin, why don't you come over to my house and join me and my friends to a pool tournament." So I said, "This will be easy, they're all old." And the first game, I got "killed" by them. As always, though, she helped me by teaching me the rules and ways to do different things.

My Oma is a good dancer. She taught me how to dance the tango and the waltz. She has also shown me how the steps are different from others.

Tell me something is your grandma this cool?

Kevin Savela, Grade 7
St Thomas Aquinas School, NM

Friends

Friends are very important to me. Friends are people who like you for who you are and help you out in life. There are certain characteristics that I find in my friends and I have different groups of friends to do different things with.

Characteristics of a good friend would be being kind, generous, supportive, and caring. For example, if I forgot my money for lunch and I asked my friend and my friend had money, they would let me borrow some and I would pay them back. Or another scenario that shows what a true friend is would be that if I didn't understand my homework they would help me through it and explain it.

Friends are important to me because without friends I would have no fun and I would be very lonely, and being lonely is not a fun thing. I have many different groups of friends, and I enjoy doing different things with each of them. For example, I have friends on my baseball team and during trips we have lots of fun going out to eat and hanging out in hotels. I also have friends that I have grown up with through elementary school. We like to go to the local high school football games on Fridays and hang out at brunch. I think everyone needs a friend, because without friends you basically have no fun or support or anything.

Jonathan Ivankovic, Grade 7
Placerita Jr High School, CA

My Family

Family is one of the most important things to me. My family is always there for me, we do fun things together and they always do things for me. I might be mad at them sometimes, but I will always treasure them.

One reason I treasure my family is because my family members are always there for me. They always know what to say to make me laugh and make me feel better. Whether it's my dad putting a smile on my face or my mom putting my mind at ease, they always cheer me up.

Another reason why I treasure my family is that many fun memories I have are from times I have spent with them. An abundance of my loving memories with my family are from when we have been camping. Camping has been a tradition in my family ever since I was born. Another fun thing my family does is that we go to the beach. We go there for spring break and we stay at my aunt's beach house.

The final reason why I treasure my family is because they always do things for me. My parents drive me to school, my friends' houses and to guitar lessons. Also, they are the ones who pay the bills, buy the food and supply me with all of my other necessities.

It's easy to overlook how important family is, but never forget what they do for you.

Spencer Martin, Grade 8
Thora B Gardiner Middle School, OR

This Is Me

I am me. Who else could I be? I've tried to be someone else, but it never works out, and I always come back to just being me. There are many different parts of me; some that I make known, and others that I do not. Music, values, and words are a very big part of who I am. This is a sneak peak into the inner workings of me.

I can't remember a time when I wasn't around music. I thank my mother for introducing me to this world I never would have known without her expertise. I play the piano, sing, and play the guitar. I love to perform and have done so since I was capable of it. But sometimes, music isn't enough.

My family has always taught me to do what's right. Now that I'm older, I've decided what things are important to me. Family, religion, friends, and honesty have always been my biggest values.

Writing can be a wonderful way to let go of your emotions or just a way of expressing yourself. For me, writing has been a way out, a best friend, and a chore. It's taken me back through the hard times, and the good times. Words can be used to lift someone up, or to bring them down. Where would I be without my words?

In the end, all we have is who we are. I am who I decide to be. No one can change me, and I can't change them. I am I, and you are you. There is nothing in this world that can change that, and no other way that I would want it to be.

Mikayla Hassett, Grade 9
Fairfield Jr High School, UT

Sox

ROAR! The truck started its engine and pulled into the road. I ran as fast I could, my cat trailed behind me. As I turned to look at Sox, he was gone. He always trailed behind me. Where could he have gone? It was then that I realized he was gone; he didn't make it across the street.

It all started when my cat Sox was walking me home from school and we saw a big truck on the side of the street. We were crossing when the truck roared its engine. I was scared so I ran. I screamed when I noticed Sox was gone, and I was sad because he was my best friend.

Some memories of Sox make me smile. One morning I woke up and Sox was at the foot of my bed asleep, and when he woke up, he rolled off my bed. I laughed. The first day of school I noticed I was being followed, but I never knew by whom. He ran into my ankle and I knew who it was in an instant; it was my cat Sox. I was happy that my cat was brave enough to follow me to school.

When my dad noticed that Sox was following me to school and staying there all day, he was happy and had no problem with it. Until that fateful day. I still love that cat.

Jordan Foster, Grade 8
Piner Middle School, TX

Eva

The one thing that is really important to me is my best friend Eva. We do everything together.

Eva and I love going to the movies. My mom usually takes us to the one in Hobbs. Our sleep overs are always totally fun except when we play board games or card games late at night and my mom catches us.

One night on the Fourth of July Eva and I got to stay up really late. We were watching scary movies almost all night. When we decided we should go to bed we heard the front door open and footsteps toward my room. They didn't sound like human footsteps so we got really scared. "Grrrrr" is all was heard before we heard a loud scratching sound on my door. Eva and I dared each other to open the door but neither of us would do it. Eva fell asleep, but there was still a whining sound outside my door. Finally, I opened the door. All that was there was my dog scared of the fireworks that were going on next door.

Eva and I are like sisters except for the fact we have never gotten into a fight. We've had many laughs, and I look forward to much more. We will be friends forever.

Jessica Reimer, Grade 7
Seminole Jr High School, TX

Be Careful What You Wish For

Have you ever wished for something, and then it came true? I have and I definitely regret it. It didn't only hurt me, but even worse, it changed my mother's life FOREVER! All because of that dumb, thoughtless wish.

I remember things were going terribly wrong. Especially the things for the guy I liked. That's when I got mad and said, "I wish I would die." I said it without thinking and he wasn't worth it.

My mom, little brother, and I were returning home from McDonald's. There was a lot of traffic. Our truck was moving less than five miles per hour. We were on Country Club near Montoya when a minivan came flying by at forty five miles per hour and pushed us off the road. It was as scary as one of those horrifying scary movies. I was crying. I thought to myself, "God please don't let this be the end for me. I never meant what I wished for."

I thought we were going to crash into the vehicle that was coming the other way toward us. Fortunately my mom got really good control of the truck and stopped it right tin the middle of the road. I thought we were all right, but whoa was I wrong.

My mom's back was very hurt. She has a hernia and it's very complicated for her. Her health has changed completely. She doesn't want surgery because it's a very dangerous surgery. My back has a cyst, but it's not as bad as my mom's back. The accident really made me think about how precious life is. I also learned that life is too short, so take the time and appreciate.

Rebeca Baeza, Grade 7
Santa Teresa Middle School, NM

Changing the World Job: Neurosurgeon

Changing the world is all about your profession. Originally, I wasn't sure what I wanted to be when I grew up. Now, however, due to personal experience, I've narrowed it down. Recently, I met a man who has been, and will now always be, a huge inspiration to me: Dr. Richard Roberts. Dr. Roberts is one of three highly trained surgeons at Cook Children's Hospital in Fort Worth. He and his colleagues specialize in neurosurgery, surgical procedures for cranial and spinal nerve disorders. Each neurosurgeon stays on call on certain days during the week to tend to emergency patients. Dr. Roberts was on call the night of my accident, and performed my nine hour surgery.

My neck was severely broken; one of the bones almost severed my spinal cord. Ligaments were torn, disks were dislodged, and I was not supposed to survive. I should be paralyzed right now. The way I live and how I look at the world has changed completely. My faith has been strengthened, and I realized how much I'd miss being here with my family and friends. I appreciate more fully all the simple things I used to take for granted. It's a good way to look at life; thankfully. I want to give someone else another chance at life; the chance to look at a world you might have lost, and then got a second chance. I may not have the power to change the whole world, but I hope I can change someone else's.

Shannon Reilly, Grade 8
St Elizabeth Ann Seton School, TX

Motto or Mockery?

In God we trust — or do we? In the United States, suppression of public displays of faith and historical revisionism — the removal of any hint of a belief in God from history — squelch religion and leave atheism — a lack of belief in any god — as the only permitted value system for our country.

Since 1992, prayer has not been allowed at public school graduations because, according to Supreme Court Justice Anthony Kennedy, "asking public school kids to stand respectfully while others pray, psychologically coerces religious practice." And a Texas tradition of prayer before high school football games was outlawed because, according to the Supreme Court, "some fans might feel like outsiders."

Historical documents and speeches such as the Mayflower Compact and Patrick Henry's famous "give me liberty or give me death" speech are often abridged in textbooks to conceal the fact that the Founding Fathers were religious. This excerpt from Patrick Henry's speech includes in capitals the part that is usually omitted. "Is life so dear or peace so sweet as to be purchased at the price of chains and slavery? FORBID IT, ALMIGHTY GOD! I know not what course others may take, but as for me, give me liberty or give me death."

Our country's motto claims that we trust in God, but when we prohibit prayer and rewrite history, that's just a meaningless phrase. A motto is a saying to live by, and I believe that we Americans need to live by our motto: "In God we trust."

Aisha Rigert, Grade 9
Joshua Blossom Preparatory Academy, CA

Run Away Life

It was as cold as a day in Alaska in the winter. That was an unforgettable Christmas. That morning I felt very excited and cheerful about presents, but when evening came, I thought that Christmas was going to be my last.

I was sick and my forehead was becoming a sun. I fainted. Next thing I knew I was in Providence Hospital and my parents were sitting right beside me. I asked them "What happened?" They responded with a relieved look. "You fainted," they said. We called 911 and that was how I ended up at the hospital. I had been in a coma for half an hour. I was still so dumbfounded. After I woke up my mom went home to rest and my dad stayed with me there all night.

The next morning I was released from the hospital. A lot of people came to my house asking the same questions, "Do you feel okay?" They also had "get well soon" balloons and cards. I told them I felt much better. While I was in a coma, I thought I was dead, but I could feel my heart, boom-boom. My heart was a turtle.

That day I learned not to be mean to people and to live life well, because any day could be your last day.

Armando Mendoza, Grade 7
Santa Teresa Middle School, NM

An Unexpected Joy

Swish, swish, swish, swish. My running shorts speak as I run. They say, "Yeah! I have been chosen to run cross country with David!" Cross country is important to me because there really is no point in running. This means I can make it whatever I want, whenever I want. If I am sad, I can run it off. If I am angry, I can — well, you know — run it off.

For me, running is a challenge. There are goals that I set, constantly beat, and then set new ones. The beginning of the new season is probably the hardest time to set a goal because then I am just starting, and usually I am slower than I was the previous year. Also, couch-potato summers are no help to a goal.

Running keeps getting easier and easier. By the end of a season, the exhaustion at the beginning becomes an enjoyment. From starting my first year when I simply dreaded it, my want to keep running through the rest of the year urges me to set that as a goal. My emotions have switched from dreading the beginning of the season and looking forward to the end to looking forward to the beginning of the season and dreading the end.

David McLain, Grade 8
Faith Christian Jr/Sr High School, CA

Volleyball

Have you ever played a sport that you never imagined yourself playing? When I was in sixth grade, my volleyball team needed one more player to complete the team. Almost all the girls joined, but the rest of the girls refused. I didn't want to see the team not play a sport just because they didn't have enough players. So I decided to join. At the time, I didn't know *anything* about volleyball, nor had I ever played, or even thought about playing. Plus, I didn't really talk to most of the girls on the team.

On the first day of practice, I was nervous! As soon as I got dressed and got down to the practice arena, I saw all the girls on the team and the coach. He saw me and was shocked and said, "Oh my goodness! We have a new member on the team!" I grinned and he began to explain the rules of the game.

When I saw the other girls do the drills, it seemed hard, and my forearm was hurting because I'd never played the game. I practiced more than anyone on the team because I was a beginner, and I needed extra help. I practiced and practiced until I got the drills right. After a while, I started getting used to it, and I loved it! Eventually, I started talking to the other girls, and loved the sport.

When we played our first game, it was amazing! I loved the excitement and the rush of the game! I still play the game today with an undefeated record, which is so awesome! I'm so glad that I joined volleyball in sixth grade. This experience taught me two valuable lessons: Don't say you don't like something unless you try it, and practice makes perfect.

Alice Saidawi, Grade 8
Corpus Christi School, CA

Pro Dog Fighting

Pro dog fighting is cruel and inhumane. Animals are not meant to be treated poorly. All animals should get a chance to live a life of respect. God never intended for any of the animals to be treated harshly and cruelly. God has given them special gifts and we should never use it against them.

God has given animals claws, teeth, speed, and language to survive; not to fight their own kind for money. Why should people watch or pay to see dogs kill each other for pleasure? What if you were in their place? Fighting for your life and no one caring what happens to you? If you lose the fight, they can abandon you or just dump you out on the streets. Sometimes they just might kill you right there. And then go buy another dog.

The dogs that do survive have a worse end to deal with. Living the past life, most of the dogs are unstable and have killing tendencies. Any animal with that problem is a natural killing machine. If an animal like that was let out on the streets, there's no telling what damage that animal can do to anyone or anything.

Jacob Warren, Grade 8
St Elizabeth Ann Seton School, TX

Four Leafed Friend

"A best friend is like a four leaf clover, hard to find, lucky to have." (Source unknown). The term best friend can't be thrown around freely. Not anyone can be called it, they have to earn it. She knows me better than I know myself; she can read me like a book. She is my best friend.

On a warm spring day in late April 2001, I was by the sand box with my best friend Courtney. This stranger with blonde curly hair and big brown eyes came up to us. She looked at me, then turned around, and threw a spider at Courtney. From then on, I hated the girl until fifth grade when we became best friends. She reminds me almost every day that if she didn't throw the spider at Courtney, we may not have been friends.

We have so many inside jokes that to others seem stupid, but to us they make us laugh till we're blue in the face. We argue about the silliest things, but in the end we don't remember what we were even arguing about. She's always been there for me. She's been through the heart breaking moments and she'll be there through plenty more.

She is my four leaf clover, hard to find, lucky to have. I still don't know why she threw the spider, but I'm glad she did. She's my best friend now and forever. Her name is Casey Nicole Kinasz.

Kelsey Maillet, Grade 8
Thora B Gardiner Middle School, OR

What Are You?

Isn't it weird when people don't know what your race is? This is a big issue in my family. Most people just ask me, "What are you?" This happens to me so many times. I'm actually quite used to this. The answer is quite easy, although a bit hard to explain. I will start from the beginning.

My grandparents were born in China and Japan. They immigrated to Peru, and had my parents; my parents got married, moved to the USA, and had me. Simple, right? Wrong! Here's my problem: I am a girl born in the USA, whose whole family speaks Spanish (even though they're all Asian), whose friends are mostly Filipinos and Latinos, who listens to modern songs in English while listening to Peruvian folk music in Spanish. I am someone who eats a mixture of Chinese, Japanese, Peruvian, and American food. Confusing, right? I know. Most of my school friends think I'm Filipino. Some people think I'm Peruvian, and sometimes people think I'm Korean!

This may be hard to understand, but it's even worse when you are trying to explain this to someone. So whenever someone asks me what I am, instead of explaining my family history over and over again, I simply reply, "I am Chinese and Japanese, but I can speak Spanish." Simple as that.

Sophia Ynami, Grade 7
Corpus Christi School, CA

English Bulldogs

English bulldogs are very interesting dogs. Their teeth kind of pop out and they are bowlegged, but come on, they're pretty cute.

The English bulldog is the dog breed of extreme par excellence: considered by some, the most ugly and by others, the most beautiful dog. They are also one of the most funniest and photogenic.

Bulldogs are very special from other dog breeds. Among the qualities that make them stand out is their legendary patience with children and their quiet and calm behavior. They are also intolerant to heat and excessive exercising.

Even their true character is very sweet; their appearance is very different from other dogs. The bulldogs' scary and mean appearance hides the fact that they are gentle and kind. It often scares people away.

They aren't rambunctious dogs. They hardly ever bark. They only bark if there is a good, definite reason to. They have a real quiet temper. Most people think that they would be real loud and annoying. Well think differently.

As the puppy grows and matures, it should be given a minimum amount of training. It surely is not a dog that will jump at your every whim, and complete obedience is not necessary, but with a little bit of patience, it can be accomplished in no time. Bulldogs should be treated kindly but firmly.

English bulldogs make great pets. They don't bark until necessary, they are very kind and gentle, and over all, they are very cute.

Landre Griffin, Grade 8
Breckenridge Jr High School, TX

My Family

My family is very fun to hang around with. We do something different every day. Some days we will just stay home, and do something there. If we are not home, we will go out of town and go out to eat.

I have two brothers, a mom, and a dad in my family. My youngest, Carmine, is so much fun to play with. My younger brother, Seth, is fun to play with sometimes. Seth can get on my nerves every once in a while, but we do get along sometimes. My dad has his good days and his bad days. When my dad has his bad days, everyone in the house gets a little mad.

My mom and dad are always there for me. If I have anything bothering me, I can go to them. Sometimes they even know something is bothering me, when I don't tell them. I think the reason I don't tell them is because I don't feel like talking about it.

Now my family is very interesting. We could be all mad in the morning, then be all happy in the afternoon. It could also be the other way around. My family is not the most perfect family in the world, but they are unique in my eyes.

Kevin Flores, Grade 7
Seminole Jr High School, TX

Baseball Rocks!

"Home run," the umpire yelled as I hit the ball over the fence. I was circling the bases as my team was crowding home plate. I touched the plate and my teammates were hitting me on the helmet and congratulating me. "Baseball Rocks!" I thought. Then something tragic happened. I was walking to the dugout when I slipped on a bag weight. All I remember is falling to the ground in pain.

When I woke up, I was in the hospital. "What am I doing heerree!" I yelled at the top of my lungs. "When you fell you passed out and broke your leg." The doctor corrected. "I broke my leg. This can't be true. It is all a dream." "I'm sorry Nathan it is real," my dad said. "How long do I have to be in a cast?" I asked. The doctor responded, "Eight weeks just to help the bone set." The next day was the worst watching practice, people helping me with my books and worst of all kids asking me what happened.

Eight weeks later, I walked into the doctor's office. He took an x-ray of my leg and said, "Holy cow you should have taken the cast off two weeks ago." Even though I had the worst thing happen to me in baseball it is still really important to me.

Nathan Shortes, Grade 7
Seminole Jr High School, TX

My Trip to Hawaii

The best part of Hawaii was our cruise to the Napali coast. We went with an Australian family we met on the plane. It worked out well because they were the only other kids on the boat.

Once we boarded the boat we were on our journey. We went to a little snack bar below the deck that we had to walk backwards to get to. After awhile we saw a herd of dolphins. Then more and more started coming. It was fun watching them do a bunch of tricks. They would jump out of the water and do 360's.

After they left we saw some sea turtles poking their heads out of the water. They were really cool. Finally we were at the Napali coast. It was beautiful. It was just like the postcards you see. There were a bunch of underwater caves too. It was awesome.

Once we turned back, we had lunch and we went snorkeling. The captain explained the rules and my dad and I went down the slide to the ocean. My little sister threw bread in the water which attracted all the fish. We heard someone yell, "Sea turtle!" and we swam and saw it was huge. I was right above the sea turtle.

The cruise was a blast. It was so fun going to see the Napali coast. The only way to see the Napali coast is on a boat or in a helicopter. I'm glad we got to see it.

Andrew Burdick, Grade 8
Monte Vista Christian School, CA

Softball

Softball is a worldwide sport that was invented by George Hancock in Chicago, Illinois. This means it originated in America. Softball is a very physical sport and you get a lot of exercise. Softball would be considered a very emotional sport because many people get different emotions if they win or lose their game. Softball is a sport that is played with 8-9 players. It is a popular sport, especially in the United States.

I really enjoy this sport of softball; this sport is a way I like to have fun. It is also one of my hobbies. Not only do I have fun playing this sport, I also get enough exercise that is needed in a day. In softball, you use a lot of physical and mental work. Something I like about this sport is that it is a team sport. You need to play as a team in order for you to win. Another thing that I like about softball is that during a game you get to cheer on your teammates and encourage them.

I like softball because I'm very good at it and because I meet new people. Softball can be hard when you first start playing but as time progresses, you manage to get better, but only if you try hard and put your heart into it. I would say the best part about this sport is that you meet new people. These people are sometimes your friends for life.

Felicia Magana, Grade 8
Isbell Middle School, CA

Thailand

Happiness filled throughout me and I felt like a beam of sunshine, waking up behind the clouds. This emotion filled day was spent my first day with my family in Thailand. Immediately we were greeted with hugs and words unknown. Nobody spoke English, but that link and inner connection of just being family made us understand one another. Extraordinary memoirs were shared throughout my whole visit, I'm truly lucky to have an astonishing family tree.

They took us everywhere to the zoo, the mall, the floating market, the shops, and temples. My favorite reminiscence was at a temple; we took a picture at the same place my great-aunt took a picture at. It happened to be the framed picture we worshiped at her funeral.

My Cousin Nun trained me to ride a bike, it was a grueling task, but we managed. (My dad died before he had the chance of doing so). One day we even played soccer with her neighborhood friends. It was a great sentimental feeling of thrill to play the game I have a passion for with my new friends and family.

Encountering my Thai family has made an impact on how I look at things now. That fourth grade summer was filled with many remarkable memories that I will cherish forever. Even though we were parting, happiness was inside my heart, and I was appreciative to have met them at last.

Serena George, Grade 8
Thora B Gardiner Middle School, OR

The Day My Grandma Died

It was October a few days after my birthday. My great grandma had been in the nursing home. I knew her time was soon I just didn't know this soon.

I was playing in the front yard with my cousin when she did something funny. I wasn't aware that my laugh would turn into a cry as my aunt told me that my great grandma had just died. I was so shocked I didn't know how to react. It felt like a piece of me was taken and would never come back. Finally reality caught up with me; and I just cried. I couldn't hold it in. I knew not to be sad because she had gone to a better place, but my heart was grieving.

As I got to my dad's house, he told me the funeral would be in three days. It felt like three days were like three minutes. Finally my mom came and got me out of school to take me to the funeral. When I got there, I met my dad then they started playing the music. While she was put in the ground, it didn't feel right. My grandma never thought negative. She always saw the good things in life. Now that was all over.

After the funeral, I went to her house. As I walked inside, I thought how this house filled with laughter, joy, and Grandma's cookin'. Now it's filled with sadness and sorrow. Still I will not forget my grandma.

Kason Rosalez, Grade 7
Seminole Jr High School, TX

Everyday Angels

In your lifetime, you will meet someone who you wish you could be more like. Someone who never seems to do anything wrong and always knows what to say. During my short time on this Earth, only one person comes to mind. Her name is Angela, but I know her by a simpler name. I know her as Mom.

My mother means the world to me. She always stays with me, through thick and thin. She helps me with whatever problems I may have, both in school and out. When I am in doubt, she is there to support me. When I fall she is there to catch me. She has given me everything I need: a home, a family, but most importantly, love. My mom gives me her unconditional love each and every day. Even with two other brothers, I never feel like I am left alone or ignored. Whenever I see her I always feel at home. When she talks to me, I have no doubt in my mind that I am blessed to have such a wonderful mother.

People like my mom are everywhere. We see them at home, school, work, or the local grocery store. They are the people you always feel a close bond to. These people are the ones who you look at and just smile because you know them. Some consider them as good people, others role models, but I have a different name for them. I call them our "Everyday Angels."

Jacob Chandler, Grade 8
St Elizabeth Ann Seton School, TX

The Three Things I Like About America

America is the land of freedom. You have the freedom of having food, we also have the freedom of choice, and the freedom of education.

One of the things I like about America is that we have food. I'm thankful for that because in some other countries they don't have food. Another reason is that some people die from starving.

Another thing that I like about America is that we have the freedom of choice. What I mean is that we can marry whoever we want. You can also choose the way you want to live.

The third thing I'm thankful for is that we can have an education. We can go to college. We can also study what we are interested in without paying tuition. In other places you have to pay to study. We can also pick what career we want. These are the three things I'm thankful for.

I love living in America because of the freedoms I have. I have the freedom of choosing who I want to marry. I also have the freedom of having food, and the freedom of education.

Ivan Quinones, Grade 7
Santa Teresa Middle School, NM

Beginnings of Middle School

The first day of middle school was awkward and weird. I had a lot of impressions on people I saw in the hallways but really it caught my attention on how everyone was so quiet. To be honest, the people that I thought were different from me are now my friends in seventh grade. The bell rang and the pressure was on. Everything was nice and easy.

My schedule was very simple. First I went to math and science, then off to physical education (PE). After that I had lunch, then Avid which so far was my favorite class. Finally, I had language arts and history. School started on Wednesday, and the only thing we did in class was to learn the teacher's class rules and procedures. Then we started real Math and everything else.

Middle school has one of everything: bullies, cliques, punks, skater boys, normal kids, and of course girly girls. That's how life is. Kids just want to make fun of you so your friends sometimes betray you. Some examples are weird shoes, pants, shirts, socks and even underwear. This is true and I've seen it. That can't let you fall into the place where you start trying to be like them and think like them, because that can affect your grades. All this can happen in one week. Let's just look at the bright side and always think positive, because it's just middle school.

Marcos Cervantes, Grade 7
Isbell Middle School, CA

North Carolina

Have you ever seen the largest personal residence in the United States? Have you ever seen an enormous lighthouse that was painstakingly moved a mile inland? If you want to see these amazing sites you need to travel to majestic North Carolina. North Carolina is a great place to live because the educational system is helping children to succeed, there are wonderful historic sites to see, and amazing athletic events.

North Carolina is helping children to excel through its educational system. The schools have strict policies on advancement to the next grade. There are writing assessments in the fourth, seventh, and tenth grades the students have to pass. If a student does not pass, he is not advanced to the next grade. Also, there are math and language arts assessments that have to be taken every year. The students must pass these tests to move to the next grade.

Historical sites are found everywhere in North Carolina. There are many lighthouses scattered on the North Carolina coast. Also, the first airplane flight took place at Kitty Hawk, North Carolina. One can go and see the Lost Colony of Roanoke, where the settlers from England disappeared. The Biltmore, the largest personal residence in the United States, can be found in Asheville, North Carolina. This house even has its own bowling alley in the basement. North Carolina is home to the NASCAR Hall of Fame, the Carolina Panthers, and the Bobcats. Remarkable North Carolina is the place to be!

Scott Gardner, Grade 9
South Jordan Middle School, UT

Consequences

My mom always tells me that I shouldn't do anything without first thinking about the consequences. My dad always tells me that pride comes before a fall — the more the pride, the bigger the fall. When I was four years old, I made good progress learning to ride my 'tike' bike and was finally able to ride it without training wheels. Unfortunately, one day, I forgot my parent's advice. It was a sultry summer day; my parents helped me park my bike and went indoors while I was supposed to remove my helmet. However, in a moment of overconfidence, I decided to take my brother's slightly bigger bike for a spin.

Before I knew it, I was zooming down the driveway and the concrete ground was rushing underneath me. I screamed loudly as if I was the master of screaming to get my parents' attention. They sprinted down the stairs and the driveway. But the damage was already done. I fell down and not only scarred my knees but was also quite shook up.

Ever since that day, I have had two very important lessons etched into my skin and memory. First, I should think of possible consequences to any actions that I may want to take before doing anything. Second, I learned that pride comes before a fall. These lessons keep me levelheaded as well as keep my self-confidence intact. My scars definitely help me remember the lessons I learned that sunny afternoon to this day.

Aishwarya Aravind, Grade 8
John M Horner Jr High School, CA

The Piano

Pianos are very interesting instruments. They have origins in the harpsichord and the clavichord. The denotative definition of the piano is a musical instrument in which felt-covered hammers, operated from a keyboard, strike the metal strings. The piano is thought to have been invented by Bartolomeo Christofori in Italy in 1709. Christofori called his new instrument 'Gravicembalo col piano e forte' meaning a harpsichord with soft and loud.

The average piano has eighty-eight keys. There are fifty-two white colored keys and thirty-six black colored keys. The white keys are the natural keys and the black keys are the sharp or flat keys. The keys are connected to small felt covered 'hammers'. When a key is pushed, these hammers hit a string. How loud you are depends on how hard you push the key. Each key has at least one string. The amount of tension on each string is about eighteen tons when tuned to a concert pitch.

Pianos kept in a home should be tuned every four to six months. Normally, a piano takes somewhere from sixty to ninety minutes. When cleaning piano keys, use a slightly damp cloth to start with, and a dry cloth on the buff keys. If you use a cloth that is too damp, you could damage your piano.

There are several different types of wood used in the piano. Each one is chosen for its particular suitability for the application in question.

Jamie Dye, Grade 8
Breckenridge Jr High School, TX

Love

When you think about love, what does it mean? Is love, a general passion shared between two people? Does it withstand time and last throughout history? Is it something imagined up by authors and we try to apply it to our lives? We see so much heartbreak in the world around us, how can this so called love survive through all the hardships we face? Or was it never there to start out with? Are we as humans more engulfed in the romance of love? The answer is within the thoughts of each person. If anything, love is one of the only redeeming qualities we as human beings have. No matter what we try to do, it's for the love of something if not someone. Love seems to be the most concentrated essence of human nature, so pure, that we relish the very thought of it. It is our most defining moment and advancement in human nature. Love is something that can never be removed from the planet on which we stand. If all else fails, someone, somewhere will be affected by love, no matter what form it may come in or even if it was by a conscious effort, it will always be there. If anything has withstood the test of time better than love, I am yet to be proven wrong. Because without my love of writing, I wouldn't be telling you this now.

Alyson Ludlow, Grade 9
South Jordan Middle School, UT

Jesus Christ

Have you ever felt lost and lonely, like nobody cares about you? Well, there is someone out there named Jesus who died on the cross to save us all. Jesus cares about everyone.

When I was seven I started going to a church with my family. I didn't even pay attention. It was hard to listen because the preacher had a weird accent. My parents didn't believe some of the preaching the church did, so we started going to a different church called First Baptist.

The First Baptist Church was a lot better than the first church we went to. They played more music, I could understand the preacher, and my parents and I believe everything they do. The best part is that they have events. The church takes the kids to different places to do fun activities. One of them was called a youth rally that was held here in town at the community building. A band called Ornans Floor played for us. After the band had played a couple of songs, a guy started preaching to us about God. When he finished preaching, I had learned a lot of things. That's when I accepted Christ.

I am glad I accepted Christ into my life. He comforts me when I am sad or if anything is wrong with me. I don't know where I would be without Jesus Christ.

Angel Aguilera, Grade 8
Reagan County Middle School, TX

Willie

Two years ago my mom brought me to a friend's house. I had no idea why, being so I didn't know them that well. My friend's mom told me to hop on this skinny thoroughbred named Willie. A couple of weeks later my mom let me lease him. After I got him I wanted to sell him right away. I kept falling off of him and it was starting to get annoying. I finally learned how to just ride it out.

About a year after I got Willie, he hurt himself and I couldn't ride him for three months. Luckily, some friends of mine let me borrow their horse for competitions. After I brought Willie back to his normal exercise routine, I started to compete in shows for the Dallas Hunter Jumper Scholarship Circuit. We have had a lot of wins so far and are currently in first for Puddle Jumpers and second for Schooling Jumpers.

Willie is definitely the best horse for me and I love him. There is a magical bond between horse and rider in the show ring and at home. He is probably the best companion I could have and I hope to do so much more with him.

He has taught me so much as a rider and as a student. He has taught me responsibility and not to be boastful. Looking back on when I first got him makes me laugh because now I would never sell him.

Remington Willkie, Grade 8
St Elizabeth Ann Seton School, TX

Too Long

I believe the school day should be reduced to five hours per day by reducing wasted time and unnecessary classes. A cut in school hours can be done very easily and may even improve our education. A reduction in school hours would also improve family life.

I do not believe a seven hour school day helps kids to become smarter. In fact, I believe it makes kids dread the long agonizing hours they are made to sit still and focus. How long can a kid actually focus? I know from personal experience that by lunch time I am done focusing and I just want to go home.

The school day should begin at eight o'clock and end at one o'clock. The subjects taught should be math, science, English/literature, social studies, and religion. Some of the time wasters that could be cut out are "specials," P.E., lunch, and recess. Not only are they unnecessary but costly for the schools.

Since everyone has to attend school, why not at least make it worthwhile for all? The seven hour school day is just too long. Although kids need to go to school, they also need to play, exercise and get the proper amount of sleep. I believe a five hour school day is the right amount of time to allow kids to focus on learning and still have time to be a kid. I know I would be happier, healthier and smarter with a five hour school day.

Michael Ouellette, Grade 8
St Elizabeth Ann Seton School, TX

My Grandma

Think about someone that you really love. Now think and ask yourself, what would I do if something bad was to happen to them? I never did until my grandma had a stroke.

One day, in August, my family was at my aunt's house. We had invited everyone to go, but my grandma was the only one that didn't go. We told her it was ok if she didn't want to go. After a while my grandpa told my mom to get my grandma out of their house for a bit, so my mom went tot pick her up. So my mom took off in her car and went to go get my grandma. At my aunt's house, my grandma was walking around for a while, but the whole time we were there we never noticed that the right side of her face was dropping or that she was limping until my mom asked my grandma what was wrong. My grandma responded that she didn't feel well and felt pressure on her face. My aunt and mom quickly rushed her to the E.R. At the hospital they told us that they were going to have to transport her to Shannon in San Angelo. Quickly.

Once she had her treatment and right before we left the doctor told us that she had a minor stroke and could not at any time be alone. Now I know that what hurts one hurts all not just a couple. So now everywhere we go we can't take too long or my grandma will get sick.

Jazlyn Galindo, Grade 8
Reagan County Middle School, TX

Splattered Birthday Party

It was a sunny happy day on my birthday on October 28, four years ago. My best friend got hit in the face by a golf club. I was playing Jurassic Park or something. Several questions raced around my mind like jockeys on stallions. How did he get hit? Who hit him? Is he okay? It all started with a KACHUNCK!!!

From a golf club and a scream an octave higher than it should've been; I saw something that is burned into my memory forever. Dominic was sprawled out on the ground writhing in pain and clutching his nose, blood was trickling down like a spilled glass of really thick Hawaiian Punch.

Who was to blame for this horrific accident? It was none other than his little brother Freddy. I knew that his nose was broken. When he returned to school he filled me in on the details. I almost didn't want to know but I was right; he had broken his nose. There is also a story form the victim of this accident so if you want to hear it from Dominic's point of view read his essay. Mini Golf is a dangerous game of life and pain.

Author's Note: Dominic and I are still friends and he has made a full recovery (considering he had a couple years to recover).

Harrison Benway, Grade 7
Santa Teresa Middle School, NM

Being Yourself

A million different things are important to me such as family and friends, but more than anything, I think it is very important to always be myself. I believe the best quality a person can find in a person is if they can be genuine around all kinds of people. Acting like another person will get you nowhere except for exactly where the other person is. How boring would it be to have the same life as somebody else? That is why you have to be your own person and not try to act like the kids you think are better. What is wrong with being different?

Being comfortable with yourself is a very valuable trait that one can have. Being yourself determines who you make friends with, because you spend time with who you can be yourself around. It also determines what kind of job you will feel comfortable with in the future. I think being yourself is so important because if you do not, then it is hard to know yourself and become your own unique person. When I can be myself, I know I'm relaxed and I know that I don't have to act like somebody I'm not.

As we all probably know, it's not always easy to be genuine all the time, but I try to not act like other people and find the unique things about myself.

Nicolette Young, Grade 8
Zia Middle School, NM

Hanging with My Friends

There are a lot of things I like to do with my friends. First, I like to go see scary movies at the movie theaters. When we see scary movies they always get way more scared than me and I feel really brave. After the movie is done we go to Round Table and eat pizza like pigs. We always have a great time when we go to the movies.

Another thing I like to do in my free time with my friends is go shopping. I like to shop till I drop with them because they have good sense of style. When I go shopping with them they always choose the right clothes for me to wear. Sometimes when I can't decide what clothes to choose they give me their honest opinion and that helps a lot.

Finally, the last thing I like to do with my friends is have slumber parties. When we have slumber parties we always have a great time. We have pillow fights. We hit each other so hard but we handle it. Then we do each others make up. It's really funny because some of my friends don't like wearing make up but we convince them to wear it. Then when we're done having fun we put on a scary movie or we tell scary stories. We get really scared so that we scream and our moms have to come and shut us up. It's really fun hanging out with my friends in my free time.

Guadalupe Fernandez, Grade 7
Isbell Middle School, CA

My Best Friend

It was the middle of the year and I was the new kid. I had just been enrolled in public school. I was use to wearing uniforms and all of a sudden I was wearing my every day clothes; I felt out of place. The first few days where especially difficult, since the school had just started their ITBS testing! I sat alone most recesses, and then one day a girl in my class, named Mikayla, started hanging out with me. At first I didn't understand why. We started hanging out every day. We sat under the same slide singing different songs, such as, "Pocket Full of Sunshine." Before we knew it, we became really good friends.

As the months flew by, we were like sisters. We had sleepovers almost every weekend. We shared clothes and spent holidays together. All of a sudden it was the last day of school and we were being separated. I was going to St. Thomas Aquinas School and she was going to James Monroe Middle School. We thought it was the end!

Summer came and we spent time together, like it was the last time we would see each other, but really it wasn't! School started again, but we still had sleepovers and always talked. Then, one day we decided to make a deal; we swore that we would never forget one another, and ever since we have been best friends.

Summer Davis, Grade 7
St Thomas Aquinas School, NM

Life Treats Me Well

Life treats me well because I was lucky enough to be born in the USA. I am very glad to have a twin brother that is nice to me and makes me feel good. I am fortunate to have a home, an awesome family and a lovable dog that is always by my side. The one thing I love the most is my family. My parents love me so much that they give me health care and things I need for school.

Life treats me well because I don't starve or beg for money on the streets. Life treats me well because with all the bad viruses going on in the world I have vaccinations to help me stay well.

Life treats me well because God keeps my home and family safe. Life treats me well because I live in Las Cruces, NM where we don't have tornadoes, hurricanes, earthquakes, tsunamis and other large natural disasters.

Life treats me well because I have friends, teachers, and family who help me do my very best. I am grateful to have an education and learned how to play a musical instrument.

Life treats me well and someday I plan to pay it forward and help other people so that life would treat them well too.

Garrett Bensley, Grade 8
Zia Middle School, NM

The Expressions of America

Although we say we value freedom of expression, most of us aren't very tolerant of those who express unpopular ideas or act in nonconforming ways. People can be incredibly judgmental towards those who think differently. Politics, religion, and clothing are the most basic forms of expression, yet people are treated harshly because of them.

Religion has been and will be an issue forever. A Middle Eastern complexion and belief in Allah, rather than God, are thought to be signs of terrorists. Any religion that is a minority is treated cruelly, whether by water cooler gossip or dirty looks on the walk outside to get the paper.

Politics, possibly the most controversial topic in society, has had its effect on acceptance, too. For years, advocates for women's or African American rights struggled to be treated the same, despite their beliefs. Sometimes people hold on so tightly to their opinions that wars are fought and lives are lost.

Clothing can allow people to express their ideas and customs. When an Indian woman walks around in a sari, pedestrians gaze at her, seeing only a strange dress. It is part of many cultures to wear traditional attire, but we find it odd to wear anything that isn't from a magazine.

Sometimes we forget what people have gone through to give us rights. The ability to express ourselves is part of the appeal of America. So, rather than looking down upon those who differ in opinion, we should consider them part of America.

Marisa Brown, Grade 8
Holliday Middle School, TX

My Family and I

My family and I may not get along, but I still love them, and they will always be there for me to love and support me. One of my favorite things about my grandparents is that they encourage me in sports, and cannot forget about the homework. I am very happy to have parents to support me, and put a roof over my head. My bedroom is one of my favorite places to just get away from everybody, and when I am in my room, I love to listen to music, and also go on the computer.

A favorite vacation that I went on with my grandparents is when we went to Disneyland for the first time on my 10th birthday. It was one of the best experiences I have had. Another one is when we go camping at the beach. When we go to the beach, I love to go boogie boarding. That is one of my favorite things to do. I feel so free, and I don't have to worry about life! I really appreciate my family because they are there for me, and buy the things I need, and without them I don't know what I would do.

Jenna Ray, Grade 8
Thora B Gardiner Middle School, OR

The Wound That Can't Be Fixed

My dad always tells us to be careful, but he should be careful himself. It started like a normal day, dad woke up, dressed, ate and left to work. He was making a wall using 2x4 wood. He had to cut them because they were too big. He used a skill saw to cut the wood. It had a huge knot and when the blade touched it, the sharp blade cut between his pointing finger and his big finger. He wrapped one towel on the cut and another on his hand to stop the bleeding.

He went to the car to get Tylenol to ease the pain. He said it didn't hurt. It took him time to get to the hospital, but he couldn't get treatment. He needed a specialist. They took him to Los Angeles. The paramedics asked him, "Can you feel it when I touch your finger?" or, "Can you move it?" They then cleaned the wound and he had surgery at 7:00. The doctors put him under anesthesia. They had to use a microscope to stitch his veins. He woke up with a cast. The doctor gave him morphine for the pain, but he didn't come home for two days.

After a month with a cast, they took it off. The doctors put two huge, metal pins in his finger to reconnect the bone. He went back six times to see if it was healing. He stayed home for two months which was a problem. He's the one who paid the bills. I was sad because he didn't talk much after what happened. He had to do some therapy to get his muscles back to normal. My dad's a strong, handsome, great father and that's why I love him. I wouldn't have it any other way.

Luis Ramirez, Grade 8
Charles Maclay Middle School, CA

Infant Murderers

What value does life have? Some people like to imagine that our world is peaceful and nothing horrible ever happens. In reality, our world isn't peaceful or safe. I know this from just watching the news. How can a place be considered "safe" when these women are having and killing their babies. Is this a description of a safe place?

I feel that if people are going to kill their infants they shouldn't be allowed to reproduce. I honestly feel that nothing can be worse then killing your child. How these people live with themselves and can cause their babies pain is way beyond my comprehension. I know that I'd never be able to live with myself if I inflicted pain on my child.

What's going on with these people to make them think it's okay to hurt their children? I know that no one's perfect, but when it comes to a baby (your own child) you just don't put them in danger. Parents you're supposed to keep children safe and love them no matter what.

Let me ask this question again, "Is our life and world safe?" When I think about it my answer is no it isn't safe. When people kill their own family and are able to live with themselves no one's safe. These people need help either emotional or physical help. And think about this question as well, "What value does life have?"

Benita Martinez, Grade 9
Kaufer High School, TX

The Destruction Derby

I learned about the destruction derby in September of 2009. The destruction derby is a motor sport usually presented at county fairs. In demolition derbies, racers do not race against each other. They try to destroy the other cars. It consists of five or more drivers competing and the last driver whose vehicle is still able to drive moves on to the finals. The last one in the finals that is still drivable is the winner.

Demolition derbies can be very dangerous. Drivers are required to sign a waiver to release the event holder in case of injuries. Most demolition derbies are held on dirt tracks or in a field that is usually soaked with water. This causes the area to become muddy, which helps to make the vehicles slower.

The vehicles are stripped of interior fixtures trim, plastic, lights, and glass. Additional modifications include trimming sheet metal from around the wheel wells, removing parts of bumpers, welding the doors shut, and relocating the battery and gas tank are part of the preparation to enter your car. To make the cars last longer, some drivers bend and notch frames, notch trunk lids, and rear coil springs are replaced with leaf springs. Roll bars, fire extinguishers, and other safety equipment is installed in the vehicle. I like the destruction derby. It is an exciting and dangerous sport.

Gibran Steen-Mcneely, Grade 8
eScholar Academy, CA

Experiences in Nature

You can hear all things around you. The birds are chirping outside. The wind chimes in the distance, clanging an almost familiar tune. Leaves rustling in the trees. Nature…it's everywhere you look.

God's creation is a wonder to us all. Nothing can add up to its beauty. It fills all of you. Your mind is cleared of almost everything. This experience is like no other that you will ever feel.

In our fast-paced lifestyle we can sometimes forget its natural beauty. If we just stop for even a minute we can take so much in. No one can ever take in too much nature. We can learn so much also. Can one imagine what it was like before all of our modern world? What would it be like without buildings, trains, cars, roads? Just nature.

If we just learn to love it we're fine. Trees can be better than TV. Just laying in the cool green grass with the cool breeze lightly blowing so you can enjoy it. We can love so much. Nature is a thing you can touch, feel, experience, unlike other things such as video games or television. God gave us this beautiful world to enjoy so get out and enjoy it!

Monica Fleming, Grade 8
St Elizabeth Ann Seton School, TX

Freedom

We live in one of the world's greatest countries where we are free to express ourselves and to express our ideas, the best thing of living in America is our freedom they've given us.

One freedom I appreciate is how you may dress, the second freedom is you get to choose your own job, and my last freedom I appreciate is to choose your own optional marriage.

One freedom is choosing how you can dress, you can dress however you want, not like other countries that some people just use a sash or a robe to go outside or to eat at restaurants.

Second freedom is you get to choose your own job, you aren't given an assigned job that you don't like, like working on a farm instead of working on the job you always wanted.

Third freedom is to choose your own husband or wife, when you get married or when someone becomes your soul mate, you can learn how they are with people and how they really act.

If someone chooses your husband or wife and they're ugly, you wouldn't like to be with them because you don't know them or they may be alcoholics.

All of these great opportunities of freedom I enjoy for this wonderful country.

I love the freedom because I live in America, I'm an American citizen, and to be in one of the greatest countries known to all mankind!

Erik Nuñez, Grade 7
Santa Teresa Middle School, NM

My Golden Treasure

Ever since my first scream my family has loved me. My little brother is always making me laugh.

My parents have been there for me even when I yell at them about how annoying they are and how much they invade my space. But hey they are my family. My dad has taught me how to cook, fish, and ride my bike. I remember when I was learning to ride my bike, I was trying to balance. I started to pedal and got up to speed, but I didn't know how to brake. I was going too fast and toward a metal chain link fence. Then all of a sudden I was flying above my bike as it ran into the fence. My dad had picked me up and saved me from running into the fence. My mom talks with me about "girl issues" like when I am having problems with my friends or a guy. She gives me advice on how to get through it.

"Show Time" is my brother Philip's nickname. He is always goofing around and being the center of attention. He gets on my nerves, but he is my baby brother. Philip is always being himself and being hilarious. He is my best friend, we hang out, sit on the couch and watch TV.

Family can be annoying, but they are always there for me. We have fun together and they are always making me laugh. I love my family.

Alex Pompel, Grade 8
Thora B Gardiner Middle School, OR

Life

Life is, according to the Webster's Dictionary, "the time from your birth until your death." Many people dream about life and what is to come. I might dream a little, but I mostly think of what parts of life I value. I would divide my life into three valuable components: family, education, and sports. All of these are important in my day-to-day living.

There are many reasons why family is important to me. One would be that they provide me with love, care, and protection. They provide almost everything in my life. I would not be able to live without the support of my family, which I love very much. Now on to education… Education is one of the key components of life. Education can help me get a good job later in life. It can help me be successful overall. Finally, for me sports are critically important to my life. I play sports just to have fun and get exercise. Although I participate in what might be considered the less common sports of tennis, ping-pong, and paintball, I also play soccer. These sports are important because I know I will have fun whenever I play them. To me it is important to have fun.

In conclusion, family, education, and sports are all important to me. They are important because I would fall apart and not be able to live without them. These few things create and enrich my life and make it what it is.

Sonia Garcia, Grade 8
Zia Middle School, NM

Through a Child's Eyes

Everything seems different through a child's eyes. They see things as simple, yet complex. A butterfly to us may seem simply an animal flying by, but ask a child and they will tell differently. They might see a fairy with beautiful wings, or they see inspiration. The world is so much more than it seems to a child. They observe every detail and every aspect as if inspecting every stitch in a quilt. A child's imagination is something you cannot obtain, but it is something we lose as we get older. We begin to criticize and think that everything must have an explanation. Our imaginations are replaced with logic. If we were to see everything from a child's point of view it would be an entirely different world. Things would seem more thrilling and magical. The saying, "stop and smell the roses" could apply to this. Sometimes you just need to stop and look at life through your childlike eyes. Everyone has them, sometimes they are just deep down within us. Sometimes we just need to grow down instead of growing up. If everyone did this every now and then, the world and its beauty would be much more appreciated. So I ask you, next time you see a butterfly flutter by you, next time you see Mother Nature's work, or next time you stop to smell the roses, look at all around the world through your child eyes.

Madeline Muskrat, Grade 8
St Elizabeth Ann Seton School, TX

Military Kid

Being a military kid has its ups and downs. There are many emotions people feel living in a military family, such as confidence, trust and pride. Children who are born into a military family have to grow up dealing with a lifestyle that they didn't even ask for. However, they will always find that good things come out of it.

When growing up as a military kid, you don't realize the actuality of it. You think it's a normal life because you've never experienced how the average kid lives. Of course, you move to different states and even countries, but you learn to adjust and create new relationships. When you're young, you don't mind the moving, because it's easy to make friends. As you grow, it's harder and harder to leave friends behind. With this being the main hardship, there are twice as many benefits.

You get to see the world in an all-expense paid trip, learning history and many unique features. You develop strong and close bonds with your family and siblings, who soon become your best friends. Being a military kid strengthens character and personality. You become much stronger as an individual and learn to trust and help people. Many people say that they're lucky they have an average life, but they don't know what they're missing! I for one consider myself blessed and lucky to be born as a military kid, and I will cherish the blessing forever.

Parker Magness, Grade 8
St Thomas Aquinas School, NM

Freckles

Six years ago, my little sister would enjoy calling my grandpa to tell him the next time we would go to his house. We would always expect a call from him. So we weren't surprised when Grandpa gave us a call on a Saturday night, the night before Mother's Day. He called to say that his dog, "momma," had just had a litter of eight puppies. I cannot say how excited we were when we heard the news.

On Mother's Day, we had gone to my grandma and grandpa's house to see the brand new pups. We had picked our favorites and named them. I remember, my older sister Adrienne's favorite was a brown male dog and my little sister Victoria's favorite was the runt of the litter, which she named Tiny. My favorite was a small, white female dog with brown spots that I thought looked like freckles, which led to her name Freckles.

We couldn't wait for the weeks to pass on by so we could finally pick one to bring home. Finally, the day came and we had chosen a dog. It was Freckles. I as so happy! I knew that we had made the right choice. My older sister was upset thought. The whole ride home, Adrienne was crying. So was Freckles.

Now Freckles is six and we love her very much. She is for sure the best dog that we could ever have.

Marissa Baldasti, Grade 7
St Elizabeth Ann Seton School, TX

Unexpected Fun

There we were getting ready for my 12th birthday party in March. It was freezing weather and my mom, being a mother, was taking so many pictures of Ryan, Spencer, my brother A.J., my dad, and me. I thought we would freeze before we would make it to the car. Finally, after twenty minutes, we hopped into the car and headed to Gat Splat Paintball Indoor Paintball Field in Lewisville.

We got there about forty minutes later. We rented our guns and our needed gear. The first few games were pretty fun. Then one of them was unexpectedly won. I was busy covering some new guys. Then I couldn't find my brother. Ryan said he couldn't find him and it was the second round; so, I thought he got hit and left the field. We tried calling him; but, he didn't answer. Then out of nowhere, he popped out of a long bunker called "snake". It was perfectly set out as if we had planned it. He was on the right side, and we were on the left. The other team didn't know how to shoot in covered positions. So when they came out, we saw them and picked off everyone of them. We played about six hours total. Yes, it was a long time, but when you have fun, it goes by fast. At the end of the day we were all exhausted, but we all had a blast!

Adrian Sison, Grade 7
St Elizabeth Ann Seton School, TX

Four Brothers

Do you have any brothers? I have four brothers and there are many good and bad things about that.

My brothers' names are Ryan, Russell, Rainier, and Reggie. As you can see, all of our names start with an R. It is a good thing to have brothers, because they will protect me and always support me.

My brothers are unique and smart. My oldest brother, Ryan, is a doctor of pharmacy and is currently working for Kaiser Hospital. My second oldest brother, Russell, is graduating from nursing school this year and actively participates in body building. My third oldest brother, Rainier, is graduating from high school, is on the varsity wrestling team, and going off to college next summer. My fourth oldest brother, Reggie, is a high school freshman and is on the junior football team. I am the only girl in the family of five, and the youngest child.

Although I have four amazing brothers, it is difficult at times. Being the only girl, I get picked on constantly by all of my brothers. My brothers will practice their wrestling moves on me, use me as a punching bag, and they hog the bathroom.

I like having four older brothers, even though they constantly pick on and make fun of me. After all, I know that in the end, my brothers will always be there for me. I am very proud of my four big brothers!

Rachelle Tanega, Grade 7
Corpus Christi School, CA

A Bloody Birthday

Blood was running down my leg and tears down my face. Still in shock from what had happened, neither my mom or I were speaking. Both of us were laying in different ambulances with blood on our faces, legs, and on my mom's back.

It was about six at night when we left to get my grandma because it was her birthday. Little did we know we would never get there. As we were driving my mom screamed, then everything went black. I don't remember anything until I woke up on the side of the street with blood on my clothes, like someone splattered red paint on me. When I looked at my legs, one of them was stuck between the curb and the luggage rack on the top of the car. Then it hit me, my mom was nowhere to be seen, but thankfully, the next minute I heard her calling me. I yelled back. She was trying to get the car off my leg when six people arrived and helped her. They called the ambulance and told us they had seen the entire crash. The driver who hit us was stopped and jailed for DWI. I learned that I should never drive while drunk, or ever drink at all.

Stephen Sommerville, Grade 7
Santa Teresa Middle School, NM

Kawashima Hospital

On a cold December afternoon in Japan, my family went to Kawashima Hospital to meet my dad's friends and to see the place where he once worked. This hospital was opened by Gorou Kawashima, the father of my dad's friend. When Gorou Kawashima died, his sons, Yasuo Kawashima and Sadao Kawashima, inherited and continued running the hospital. Sadao, my dad's friend, currently works in the hospital as a doctor. The color of the hospital is blue and white, and the hospital itself is very large. The hospital is three stories high, around thirty meters wide, and around ten meters in length. This is the hospital my dad worked at while studying for his doctorate. My dad had a hard life in Japan because my dad was poor, but Sadao Kawashima became my dad's benefactor and helped him out. Now my dad has very fond memories of the hospital and is very thankful of Sadao Kawashima.

We walked through the glass door of the hospital and looked around inside. The hospital was lighted well enough to see down the hallway, but the patient waiting area was dimly lit. We looked around the hospital and waited for Yasuo and Sadao. After waiting for a quarter of an hour, we met him inside the hospital. We rode in his car and went to a restaurant for dinner. This is the first time I met Yasuo and Sadao Kawashima.

Dingbo Shi, Grade 9
Clear Lake High School 9th Grade Center, TX

The Swine Flu

Swine flu...is it just the flu, or is it something we should be scared of? Many people are overreacting to the swine flu. So far, it's not any different from the regular flu.

Is this another type of flu or is it a very serious problem? People are getting freaked out because there have been some cases where people have died from swine flu. No more people have died from the swine flu than from the flu.

Everybody hates shots. But everyone is going to get them. Do we even know if they work? Are they harmful to us? Well there have been some doctors who have said that there are a lot of harmful things in the vaccination shot and not enough research has been done on it.

Yes, everybody is aware that numerous people are getting the swine flu. It's not worth closing down the schools for it. It's understandable that the school board wants to keep the students healthy, but is it really necessary to close the schools? By closing the schools you are just making the students lose days out of their school year and they're going to have to make it up on their holidays and their school days. We all know that nobody wants to do that.

In conclusion, the swine flu isn't something we should be scared of. Just take precautions, wash your hands, and don't share drinks or food with anybody.

Abbi Ritchie, Grade 8
Holliday Middle School, TX

My First Deer Hunt

Last year I came home from school and found out that I was going on my first deer hunt. I was so excited! I couldn't believe that I was going.

When we got to camp we had about three hours of daylight left. So my dad said that we should go to the stand. Right after we got in the stand, a huge deer stepped in the clearing. I grabbed my gun and got ready to shoot. "You ready?" I said. "Yep," said my dad. Boom! The sound of the gun filled the stand. "You missed," my dad said. "Let's go in."

The next morning I got up at 5:30 a.m. and got in my stand. When it became daylight, we noticed that there was a bunch of deer right in front of us. As I looked, I noticed that there was a nice buck about a hundred yards away. I got my gun ready. Suddenly it was as if time was repeating itself. "You ready?" I said. "Yep," my dad said. Boom! The gun went off. "You got him!" said my dad. That buck had nine points! Boy, was I happy.

After we field dressed him, which is the nasty part, we took him to camp. Then, we loaded up to head home. That was the happiest time of my life.

Derek Cox, Grade 7
Seminole Jr High School, TX

Never Forget the Good Times

I didn't realize that my best friend was gone forever. You might think that he was an ordinary friend, but to me he was my role mode. He always taught me something and always made me laugh. I will never forget him and I will always hear him say, "Never forget the good times."

We had always known that he was diagnosed with lung cancer, but I didn't realize that it had gotten worse until I saw him. He was really sick and was sent to the hospital. We waited an eternity when they finally said he was going to be fine, but of course they were just bluffing. When we visited him again he had all these tubes that were giving him medicine, then a few days later we received a sad phone call.

It was my aunt she said he had gotten worse and was sent to a special hospital in El Paso. The next morning he was gone, gone forever. But before he left he had given my grandma a paper. The words on the paper said, "Never forget the good times," at the funeral everyone cried, it seemed that every tear felt like a never ending river, because I had lost my best friend in the whole universe.

So ever since then I made a promise to myself I would never, ever, ever forget him, and I would always appreciate and love my friends and family, but lastly the most important promise that I made to him was that I would "Never forget the good times."

Alejandra Martinez, Grade 7
Santa Teresa Middle School, NM

Baseball: America's Pastime

Crack! The ball rockets off the bat and starts to climb higher and higher into the stands. "Peanuts, cracker jacks," a vendor's voice rises high above the hum of the crowd. "You're worthless! Just go back to AA," says a heckler from a crowd. These are all different kinds of sounds from a ballpark that make the experience worthwhile. Baseball has been considered one of America's national pastimes for a while. From senior citizens playing to a young toddler playing tee-ball, baseball can stick with people for their entire lifetime. That is why I love to play it and why it will probably stick with me for a long time to come.

To succeed in baseball you must practice hard, want to win and play like a champion. It doesn't matter if you are good or not, because if you work extra hard, there is always room to improve. Baseball can be fun and serious at the same time as long as you always want to win. To win, you have to be determined and always work hard. All of these traits make up a quality baseball player.

Baseball is important to me because it will always be there for me. Also, it is a sport I love and something I am good at. As long as that all stays the same, baseball will always remain one of the top things I love.

Justin Braun, Grade 8
Palm Desert Charter Middle School, CA

Three of a Kind

I've been told I'm one-of-a-kind, but that's only true to a certain extent — because I have best friends that are just like me. Whether it's their love of singing, art, or doing goofy, childish things in public, my friends are perfect matches for me.

Last year, I met Shannon. With her big hazel eyes and long blonde hair, she is beautiful — and tons of fun. She shares my love of country music, and can usually be found with a song on her lips and a poem on her paper. She's a great artist, and loves to sketch whatever comes to mind. She also knows how to make me laugh, no matter what.

I've known Abby since I was seven years old, and we became best friends instantly. Abby has deep brown eyes and black hair — an Ecuadorian beauty. She's a huge help when it comes to Spanish homework, and she knows how to lighten any tense moment with a single smile. She's an amazing friend — and believe me, inside jokes come easily for the two of us!

The three of us together are an unstoppable trio. Whether we're trying on prom dresses at the mall or just hanging out, we can make every day an unforgettable one. The funniest thing is how people tend to refer to us as Lindsey-Abby-Shannon, without a breath in between. They say it as if we were a single person. You know what? We practically are.

Lindsey Faust, Grade 8
St Elizabeth Ann Seton School, TX

The Sports Life

Baseball and basketball are two of my favorite sports. I have played each of these sports for several years, both on recreational and select teams. Through these experiences, I have learned quite a bit about both of these sports. In this paper, I will discuss the similarities and differences between basketball and baseball.

Baseball and basketball are similar because they are team sports, not individual. Both sports use a ball to score points. Each sport has officials who judge the games. To become a strong player, you must put a lot of time and effort into perfecting your skills. Basketball and baseball offer opportunities for college scholarships, and for the very best players, a chance to play professionally in the MLB or NBA.

Even though basketball and baseball have similarities, they are very different. In baseball there is no time limit; there are nine innings vs four quarters in basketball. A basketball team has five players on the court and baseball needs nine players. The score of a basketball game is much higher than a baseball game. Basketball is a much faster-paced game with many more opportunities to get points. Players need more endurance in basketball to run up and down the court. Also, height matters in basketball. Taller players have a better chance of getting rebounds, giving their team additional chances to score.

Although I have played both sports, I like baseball better. I enjoy hitting the ball and running the bases.

Chris Kotch, Grade 8
St Elizabeth Ann Seton School, TX

My Brother Luis

My brother's name is Luis Andres Vizcaino. He was born on February 6th, 1986. He is my big brother. At a very young age he struggled with his academic marks while he was in middle school. He also had problems with staying out of trouble. Luis was in and out of S.A.C. throughout middle school for vandalizing school property, fighting, and talking back to teachers. All this lead him to getting sent to KEYS and a juvenile detention center.

My brother finished middle school at the juvenile detention center. Becoming a freshman at Americas High School, he began to take charge of everything. He straightened out his academic marks in school, and also started to act very responsible and independent. He grew up to be an excellent young man. Luis finished high school in the year of 2006. Many people changed their perspective of him and realized that he was just a misunderstood child back then, now a young man, they see he has so much potential to show the world.

Luis chose to join the United States Marine Corps, once he graduated from high school. He officially became a United States Marine in 2008. He is now stationed in Okinawa, Japan. He certainly is a long way from home, but he still is close in our hearts. We really do miss him very much, and we hope he will come home real soon.

Brenda Vizcaino, Grade 8
Rio Bravo Middle School, TX

My Dad

My dad, Ray, is a role model for me. He is a role model because he enlightens people's days. He is nice to everyone he meets and is a great father. He is always at my side. He assists me with homework when I have questions and he encourages me to be a role model. He teaches me the importance of being successful in academics, practicing my Catholic religion, by going to church, as well as enjoying sports; he is truly the best!

My dad lightens people's days by helping them and being funny to get them to smile. He is always happy. There are times when I come home sad because I did not do so well. He will make me smile by helping me understand what to do if the situation arises again.

My dad always is there to comfort people as they go through hard times. He helps people who may be lonely or hungry. He always comforts me when I am not feeling well. In the end, he has me laughing and smiling. My dad is an awesome father. He has helped me in so many ways. My future plans are to attend the University of Southern California and study in the medical field. My dreams are to be either a dentist, oral surgeon or an orthodontist.

Marcos Ray Serna, Grade 8
St Thomas Aquinas School, NM

My Wonderful Family

What is the most important thing in your life? Well, the most important thing in my life is…MY FAMILY! When no one else is there for me, I can depend on my family.

God is part of my family. I have faith in Him and I always look up to Him. In heaven, with God, I have three very special members of my family. I feel their presence when I'm in a tight spot, two of them are my grandpas and one is my uncle Joey. Their deaths have brought us all closer and that's most likely why I depend on my family so much. Two other amazing people I look up to are my parents. They always give me support, even if I fail. My little brother brightens my day and makes me smile. He is such a blessing. If I need someone to talk to, I turn to my little sister. When having a hard time with friends and school, I can talk to her. Aunts, uncles and cousins give me moral support and I usually have a really good time with them. I'm very close to all of them.

My grandmas are there for additional support or that last minute ride home from school or activities. All of these people are with me through thick and thin. I am so proud to call them FAMILY. They are truly what matters to me and what my life is all about.

Maria Stout, Grade 8
Zia Middle School, NM

Traditional Academic Courses vs Extra-Curricular Classes

Schools should put as much emphasis on subjects such as music, physical education or visual arts, as they do not traditional academic courses such as English or math. Extra-curricular classes are tremendously important to the student body.

Education is important, but extra-curricular classes are just as important to the students. Some students can easily understand math, English or science. Other students can understand band or visual arts better than traditional academic courses.

Students tend to try harder and do their best in their favorite class, whether it is in a traditional or extra-curricular class. The reason is students tend to spend more time doing what they enjoy.

Extra-curricular activities tend to get a higher percent of college scholarships than traditional academic courses. One reason for this is the harder a student works in their favorite class, their knowledge from that class will continue to grow with time. College scouts want to find students who are willing to work hard. They also want students who do more than just the traditional academic courses. This shows the scouts that the students are willing to do more than the average student.

Schools should put more emphasis on subjects such as music or physical education as they do on traditional courses. The importance of these subjects to the students is tremendously important to the student body.

Audrey Lillie, Grade 8
Holliday Middle School, TX

Family Christmas

When Christmas comes, we always go see family. We go to our Granny Joy's house. It's out in the country in Denver City. I'm always asking my mom "When are we going to Granny Joy's?" I love going to her house!

When we go there for Christmas all my family goes. I have so many cousins when we're all together. She cooks a home cooked meal every year for Christmas like corn, turkey, and mashed potatoes. She cooks a lot of other things too. When I'm there I always eat cookies and drink chocolate milk. My mom always says stop, but Granny Joy lets me.

The first thing we do when we get there is play. Then, we get cleaned up and eat. After we eat we play while the parents play board games. Then, we open our presents. We open them youngest to oldest so I'm third to last. I hate it because they take forever.

After everyone opens their presents we play. One time I got a baby doll when I opened up my present! It was so fun that Christmas because I love baby dolls! I have a blast when we go there for Christmas. My family means so much to me.

Randee Thomas, Grade 7
Seminole Jr High School, TX

Field Trips

Schools shouldn't omit field trips because of the educational possibilities. It indeed helps students by letting them interact with learning.

In many ways, field trips are advantageous to students. Students who go on educational field trips have been shown to learn the subject easier and faster. It also helps them understand the subject and how it came about. Field trips are highly educational in ways that classrooms sometimes aren't. For example, students can interact with the process of learning and experimenting.

Students like field trips because they are exciting. They teach kids of all ages that learning can be exciting. The Omni Museum in Dallas and Fort Worth has many informative exhibits that are fun. Students who go to field trips quite often with their school like doing more school related things, such as UIL. The schools in the U.S. have practically omitted the advantages that come with field trips by going on fewer and fewer field trips every year.

Field trips to places like museums in Washington, D.C. are convivial and highly enlightening. Videos and dinosaur facts have proven to be better than classroom boredom.

Schools shouldn't omit field trips because of the educational advantages they bring to some children. Don't let the U.S. take those away from your child.

Tyson Trotter, Grade 8
Holliday Middle School, TX

My Music

Do you like music? I love my music. I don't care for my brother's or my mom's. How does it make you feel? It helps me concentrate and relax. I get my homework done in a timely manner. I think I get better grades. I turn it on when my brother is getting on my nerves so I stay calm. It helps me get to sleep faster at night.

I have two things that I care for. One is my music and the other is books. I adore my music more than my book because I can shut out the world. I got an iPod for Christmas last year. It was the best gift ever. Music is my safe haven. I retreat to my zone when I put my earplugs in. I can take my iPod everywhere I go. I thought my world was going to come to an end when I washed my iPod in the washer. It was in my pants pocket.

There are all kinds of different music. My dad always has the radio on hard rock. My mom has shown me the love she has for country music. I prefer the rock. Without music the world would be boring and lifeless. I think I would be an angry person if I could not have it. You can find me listening to music at the end of the school day to the end of my day. I hope others share the passion for music as I do.

Wyatt Hinze, Grade 8
Thora B Gardiner Middle School, OR

My Dog

My dog, Betsy, is the best friend I've ever had in my entire life. She is faithful, loving, and always there for me. She is a golden retriever/lab mix. We purchased her when she was two months old. Now she is four, turning five in February.

Because my parents are divorced, I usually get lonely but ever since I got a dog, I'm not. She is a vastly playful dog, and my dad comes home late, so I never feel lonely. Somehow she knows when I'm sad. She lies down next to me and puts her paw on me as if she were comforting me or trying to cheer me up. She is also clever. I taught her how to sit, lie down, crawl, shake, and give me a high five. She taught herself how to open my bedroom door even when it is completely closed. She also taught herself how to steal treats from the box, which I think is funny. She is very protective. When someone she doesn't know or recognize comes to our house she starts barking, and she is very cautious of their movements because she doesn't want them to hurt us.

She has impacted my life by making me a more responsible person. Since she belongs to me, I have to take care of her. Also, she is a trustworthy dog and having her has given me a friendship that cannot be replaced.

There is no true friend like man's best friend.

Sarah Nieto, Grade 8
Reagan County Middle School, TX

My Cousin's Wedding

"Are we there yet?" I asked my dad. My family and I were on our way to Canada. My cousin Elfriede's wedding was in two days. "No just a few more minutes," my dad said. I hadn't seen my cousin in two years!

When we arrived at her house, I jumped out of the car and ran to the door. After everyone said hi and gave each other a hug I went to play with Elfriede's sister, Eveline.

On the day of the wedding everyone got into the car and we drove to the church. My little sisters were the flower girls. Eveline and I helped serve the food.

When the bride walked down the aisle the ceremony began. Eveline and I began serving the food. We had Mexican food for supper. After eating, some friends and relatives shared stories about Elfriede's childhood. Then they played a game.

In this game they placed two chairs on the center of the room, facing opposite directions. The bride would sit in one chair and the groom in the other. Then the groom had one of the bride's shoes and the bride had one of the groom's shoes. Then somebody would ask questions like "Who eats more?" and they would lift the shoe of the person who they think it is.

After the wedding everyone went home. I had a lot of fun.

Brenda Froese, Grade 7
Seminole Jr High School, TX

A Cat Named Kirino…

I never thought it would happen that way. Just to touch and feel the last heartbeats he would ever have in his life. He was in pain and crying like never before. They don't really have nine lives.

The day before this tragedy I had been mean to the cat. He had eaten the bologna from my sister's and my sandwiches. We screamed at him so badly than my sister and I went for other lunches while the cat purred in her arms, she told him "not right now, I am eating!" He came to me and I said "Back off. You are going to give me allergies again!" That night I slept on the couch waiting for daddy to come home. Early that Saturday morning a tragedy happened. I got awakened by tears. I went outside. My mom and sister were there, our cat in a box with broken bones. His jaw broken open, his tongue coming out, his bones of his spine were popping out. He had been crushed by a car. He was covered with blood!

I reached out and touched his fur gently. I was over my allergies for the first time in five years and yesterday I had been mad at him. I was crying like never before. I reached out for his ear and whispered "I love you kitty, I am sorry!" I heard "meow" like if he understood.

We took him to the vet. He needed to go. I knew it would be forever. I knew it was the last time I would see him. He was going to heaven now and forever. So remember, always love your pets. You never know when they will leave. R.I.P. my kitty Kirino. Love you!

Esmeralda Verduzco, Grade 7
Santa Teresa Middle School, NM

Siblings

Do you have a brother? A sister? Do you get along with them? Let me tell you about my brother Chris. Chris and I don't get along very good. He is 18 years old, 6 years older than me. I love my brother so much but we just don't like to communicate. It feels weird to talk to Chris because we are not used to making a conversation. I would rather just leave it like that. It's hard for him too because he is a dad. So he needs to spend more time with his daughter than his sister. Hopefully things will work out and just be good to each other.

We have many differences but not a lot of what people except. My brother likes to be violent and I would rather be playing video games with him like we used to. I would also like to be hanging out with him, going to different places. I feel sorry for the people who don't have any siblings at all. For example my cousin has no siblings what so ever, so she invites me and my sisters almost every weekend to her house.

If you have any siblings then just talk to them enjoy that you have them. Some siblings can be mean some can be nice. Their can be all sorts of different siblings. That's why siblings are so important. I love all my siblings.

Sarah Sigala, Grade 8
Isbell Middle School, CA

Friends

Friends come and go. As we grow older through elementary school we meet new friends. Friends are people whom you can rely on. I'm sure you have experience friendship too.

When I first met my best friend Courtney, I was in sixth grade. We did almost everything together. About every Friday we would go to Dairy Queen after school and stay there for an hour. After Dairy Queen we would walk around town. We stayed out until one of us had to go. Then on Saturday we stayed out all day. Sometimes we would go to the South Park and play basketball and then we would go to my house and prank call people from my phone. We stayed up until six in the next morning, and we would not wake up until the afternoon.

Once I heard Courtney was moving, I cried. I was losing my best friend. She told me she was leaving at the end of July. I told her we have to spend as much time together as we can. The month went by fast. We bought gifts for each other before she left. That was the last day I saw my best friend.

After my best friend moved away I knew there were more friends out there. We have been talking every night since she moved. I miss her, but I know she is always there for me when I need her.

Anna Perez, Grade 8
Reagan County Middle School, TX

Power Behind the Throne

Given some time and school, I can change the world by working behind the scenes. Just think of one of the places you visit most during your day. GOOGLE!!! As of July 2009, Google was the world's most visited website. If I work at Google, I am changing the lives of kids and adults alike. If a student is writing a report for a major grade, he needs information. Where does he or she get it? Google! A good grade can mean excelling in school and make him or her one of tomorrow's key leaders. The same goes for adults, just at a present standpoint.

If I worked at Google, I would make applications for the main website. For instance: Bing, G-mail, and YouTube. I would be making life easier and more enjoyable for the majority of humankind. Another type of job at Google Inc. is being a person who makes the complicated algorithms that find the data inputted. These people are the people that need to really enjoy numbers and math.

Given the question, "What job would you take to change the world?" a lot of people would say being the president or the pope. Just by working at a website's company, I am changing the world and no one knows it. So next time you log on to Google, make sure to think of the person who helped you make your report, type your résumé, or just give you some pointless information.

Taylor Willenbring, Grade 8
St Elizabeth Ann Seton School, TX

Christmas with My Family

One Christmas I went to my Nana and Tata's house. My whole family was there and we did more things than we thought we would. On the 3rd night I was there my family and I made Tamales! It was messy. At first all the stuff to make them looked really gross. We had made tons, around 200! (I think mine were the best!) When they were all done we finally went to bed. When I got up I saw about a quarter of my family in the living room (which would be considered big to other families), it was a surprise. When I got dressed my cousins and I went to the backyard and hung out. When it was dinner time everybody swarmed to the food, I was the last one. But I at least got some tamales, they were really good. After that we talked, laughed, and smiled at what everybody had to say. After the party I went to bed hoping I would get some sleep but we went to midnight Mass so I was extremely sleepy. Then I went to bed, I was awoken by the sizzle of bacon and my baby cousin Rayna. Then I remember it was Christmas. We had a delicious breakfast. After that we opened presents in the living room. Once we were all done with the presents everybody was filled with smiles and cheer on their faces. Then I realized this was the best Christmas.

Cara Gobea, Grade 7
St Elizabeth Ann Seton School, TX

Him!

Have you ever liked anyone since elementary school? I have, there's this guy I've liked him for the longest time!

I remember the first time he talked to me. It was a Monday because that's the weekend before I had gotten a haircut. It was really crazy, punk-rock but, still so cool! He went up to me saying "Hey cool hair!" "Thanks!" I said and walked off.

In the seventh grade we started talking a lot, and got really close. One time my friend asked if I liked him, I blushed meaning of course yes! And it had turned out that he had liked me too!

The day he asked me out I remember as if were yesterday. My friend asked me what I would do if he asked me out I told him that I would say yes! Later on that day the guy I liked came up to me before baseball and softball practice. We small talked for a while then he asked me the question I had been dying to hear since 5th grade. "Will you go out with me?" I didn't hesitate at all, I said "Yes!" He kissed me on the cheek and walked off.

We stayed together most of the summer and got back together the beginning of 8th grade. Unfortunately, we had drama and broke up. We're still not together but I still love him with all my heart and I wish that he does too!

Desiree Rios, Grade 8
Rio Bravo Middle School, TX

Laugh at Yourself

There I was, standing at the top of the tallest sand dune with the predatory eyes of a tiger. I took off with my board down the ghostly white sand dunes without a care. My cousin, in the distance, watched me with his dark, intimidating eyes. I maneuvered the dozens of yards of sand, until the menacing, yet unsuspecting white rock popped out. Can you guess what happened?

The family settled in for the trip to White Sands and we were ready to go boogie boarding. We took turns riding through the sand. Most of my family played for awhile, but soon returned. Only my cousin and I remained.

An evil and somewhat modest rock tripped me and the board down the tallest sand dune. The rock seemed to jump with joy as I lost control, crashed and landed on my head three times.

When you think of an accident, you think of blood, broken bones and such. When I had my accident, I wasn't hurt in that way. I felt stricken for a moment, then felt embarrassed, especially when a "true" rumor was spreading around the settlement area, telling that I had a complete wipeout.

My pride got in my way, so I felt like I really couldn't approach the rest of my family and friends. I literally felt like I was at death's door. I slowly walked to the campsite and during that time, I thought to myself, "People are laughing at your mistake. If I was there, I would laugh about the other persons' mistake as well. Don't care what people say about you. In fact, laugh as well. Laugh at yourself."

This is what I did and I enjoyed my day. Many other people made worse mistakes. We shared our laughs.

Sean Palmer, Grade 7
Santa Teresa Middle School, NM

Becoming a Vet

"Study Study Study," is what I tell myself all the time. I need to study because I want to become a vet when I grow up. Being a vet is my ultimate goal.

Personally, I think that I am blessed to have such a background of vets. My dad was a vet. My mom was a vet. Hopefully someday I'll be a vet too. My parents really inspire me and support me. I have got to the point now that anytime an animal gets hurt, I take care of it. I have learned the basic things, and even some things that a real vet doesn't know. I study vet skills so that I can get a head start on college (which I will go to for 6 years) so that I will know things that others don't know.

When I go to zoos or animal refuge parks or camps I feel that I should be a vet. It also helps me because it shows me what I might have to take care of. Like I said being a vet is my ultimate dream. I still try to study every day, and any animal I meet that is in need of help I try to help it.

Miranda Freeman, Grade 7
Seminole Jr High School, TX

The Ultimate Best Friend

I've always known there's a difference between good friends and best friends. From the beginning of seventh grade until now as en eighth grader, I've realized that our best friends are the ones we must have while our good friends come and go. As I come to this realization I can think of only one, Nico. He has many wonderful qualities as a guy and a best friend.

Nico's one of those guys that you always want to be around. He is the kind of person that will fill in one of those awkward silences with a random comment or joke. The life of the party is Nico, or better yet, he is the party. This great guy has always been a fun, easy to love person, which is why we've been friends for so long.

I have known Nico since we were adorable little kids in preschool. We ended up going to different schools when we were in kindergarten through second grade. My third grade year I went to his school and I was so excited to see my long lost friend. In about sixth grade was when it started getting hard for me to hang out with him because everyone assumed we liked each other. But Nico's and my bond was too tight for anyone to break it with their accusations. That's what made our friendship even stronger. We're still best friends to this very day. I know that Nico is the ultimate best friend!

Kaitlin Smith, Grade 8
Thora B Gardiner Middle School, OR

Halloween Costumes

We all want to choose the perfect one. But sometimes our parents get in the way, so we can't usually get the costume we want.

For example, they say it's too expensive, it's ugly, or they just don't want to buy the costume. That is what they did to me. All I wanted to be was a vampire in 3rd grade, but all they got me a cheap flower princess costume instead! I was really mad at them, but I was also grateful that they at least got me a costume (even though it wasn't the one I wanted).

4th grade was different because they bought me the costume I wanted. It was an evil fairy costume. The dress was Tinker Bell-like with skulls on it. I liked it so much that I wore it in 5th grade too! In 6th grade, I didn't dress up for Halloween because I didn't want to. All I wanted to do was give out candy to trick-or-treaters.

Now this year I want my parents to buy me the costume I want. I want to be a vampire. Ever since I was in 3rd grade, I've always wanted to be a vampire. I think the costume is scary and awesome.

In conclusion, you can't always get what you want. But be grateful, because most kids don't have the chance to buy a costume.

Denise Hernandez, Grade 7
Isbell Middle School, CA

Simple Love

Love is not complex but simple. It is in the heart of every person of every race. It lives in us even when you don't think it can. It can heal old wounds or new ones. It can overwhelm and fill you up. It brings back life to people. It makes you feel content and joyous. It can boil over and be shown to others or be kept a secret in the deepest part of you. It is all right, no one can escape its steel clutches. Do not try to escape, but accept the fact and move on. Love lives on in everyone, even the ugly. Love can be a single flame or a large bonfire. You may think of love as hearts and arrows. Others may think of a mother and her child. But I think of love as an outlet to feelings. Someone you love that loves you back will not laugh or mock you, but instead raise you up and cherish you. They love you through thick and thin. They love you when you're happy or sad. The love for someone else must be shown. Don't let it eat you up. Remind them or tell them you love them. They will accept your feelings if they care. Love is the key to the door of life. Unlock it and live fully. Hate is not the answer. Remember love is simple if you can handle it.

Lyndsay Christensen, Grade 8
St Elizabeth Ann Seton School, TX

It's Not Like That

Cheerleading is an underestimated sport. It's belittled by simple-minded people all over the world. It infuriates me that people don't even think of cheer as a sport, that it's not hard, that anyone can do it! People think that cheerleading is all about ditzy girls saying auspicious rhymes and wearing exiguous skirts. They think cheerleaders are stuck up and pompous and that they have enough influence to command and bully the student body of their school. People think cheerleaders only date football and basketball players or else arrogant fools, and that they get bad grades and have loaded parents that give them unlimited access to that cute, little plastic card that grants them their wishes, but it's not like that, not by a long shot.

Did you know cheerleaders have to do gymnastics, so they must be flexible, and they perform complicated stunts that require lots of strength and focus? Was it common knowledge to you that the first cheerleader was a guy and the world of cheer has extensively reformed into the *sport* it is today? Did it even cross your thoughts that cheerleaders don't only cheer at football games, but compete with other teams like every other sport? Most importantly was the fact dismissed that cheerleaders' personalities differ just like everyone else's? The discrimination and stereotypes of cheer prevent people from seeing the discipline and hard work that are the foundation of cheerleaders today. If you open your eyes maybe you'll get a glimpse of the exceptional *sport* of cheer.

Kendall King, Grade 7
Placerita Jr High School, CA

Christmas

Have you ever had a feeling about loving something so much, you count down the days until the event happens? Or you go shopping months and months earlier for decorations and presents. Well that's how I feel about Christmas.

The first thing that I really like about Christmas is the smell, the smell of pine trees after it rains. I also like the smell of the food, but the desserts are the best. One last smell I like is the smell of candles that make you feel like you're in the country on a Christmas day. Another reason why I think Christmas is important is because of the decorations. I think ornaments look really nice when they're snowflake shaped and they sparkle. The lights on the outside hanging on the house get me into the mood. One last thing I like about Christmas is the presents. I like the way they look when they're neat and orderly under the tree by each person. My favorite part about opening presents is when everyone is so surprised with what they got. Unless you looked early.

Finally, the most important reason why I like Christmas is because my whole family gets together. So after all the things I listed think about what you really like. If you don't like Christmas what is truly important to you?

Jamie Jeffers, Grade 8
Zia Middle School, NM

Skateboarding

Skateboarding is a very exciting sport. It is very fun if you know how to do many tricks. You can skate on many different obstacles. If you are not coordinated then it is really hard to skate. It is also very fun to watch professionals skate because they do many amazing tricks and stunts.

Doing tricks on a skateboard is fun and it gets you excited if you land really hard tricks. If you know a big variety of tricks it is more fun to skate because you do different activities with friends. You can do different types of tricks on different types of terrain. When skating on flat ground most people do more flip tricks or grind while skating in half pipes or bowls there are more grinds and grabs. There are many different types of obstacles you can skate on. There are two main types of skating obstacles, and they are called street and vert. Street consists of flat ground skating like stairs, boxes, and rails. While vert consists of bowls, quarter-pipes, and half-pipes.

If you try to skate and you are not coordinated, it will be harder to skate as somebody who is coordinated will be better. If you are coordinated it is easier to skate because skating consists of foot work. To do certain tricks you need to move your feet a certain way. Professional skateboarders are fun to watch because they are really good and can sometimes do really good tricks.

Cody Acevedo, Grade 8
Isbell Middle School, CA

My Experience Being on a Swim Team

My favorite sport is swimming. I got started swimming through my mom. She signed me up for swimming lessons because she wanted me to learn how to swim. When I started swimming, I was put in the highest level. After four weeks, I tried out for the swim team. I skipped two teams and got put on blue. I worked very hard to get on a higher swim team. After a month, I was ready for my first swim meet. The swim meet I went to was in Grapevine, Texas. It was scary going for the first time. There were many people there and it was very crowded. At the swim meet, we did warm ups; we had to put twenty people in each lane. I did two events: 50 freestyle and 50 backstroke. I did a good job for my first meet.

After another month, I skipped the levels white, red, and bronze. I got to the Age group 1 team. At first, it was tiring, but I built up my strength and my speed. Then I got used to swimming on the team. I have been swimming on the team for more than a year now. I hope to go to higher teams soon and be on the high school swim team. I enjoy swimming very much and I hope to keep swimming for a long time.

Victoria Rosario, Grade 7
St Elizabeth Ann Seton School, TX

Don't Put Me in a Music Box!

Preppy or goth? Punk or rocker? Fitting into a social group or clique is important for many students in middle school. Some may disagree, but I think that everybody judges other people and puts them into a clique based on their music choices. When one thinks of Taylor Swift or Miley Cyrus, one thinks "prep," but mention Slipknot or Korn and goth comes to mind. Is it true that music choices define people? No! One would be surprised to find out what other people listen to.

In my experience, a student who is a prep, or is the popular cheerleader type, does not listen only to the above-mentioned artists. Many of my preppy friends enjoy some of the same music that I do, and I am not preppy. One of my prep friends has many styles of music on her playlist. Another listened to one of my Kerli CDs and enjoyed it.

The same can be said about goths, rockers, and punks. As a punk myself, I love listening to Kerli, Korn, and Evanescence. But I also like the Black-Eyed Peas, and Carrie Underwood. Another friend, who likes heavy rock, also enjoys listening to country and even hip-hop! How can you categorize people based on music? People cannot be defined by a genre of music. On my iPod I have alternative, country, dance, metal, pop, hip-hop, rock, and soundtracks, yet I am only in one clique. In conclusion, don't judge people based on the music they listen to.

Elisabeth Greene, Grade 8
Zia Middle School, NM

The Common Good

The people who must affect me most are my parents. They help me through the rough times and guide me through the good. They impact my life more than any other people in my life. My mom and dad both work to send my two sisters and I to a nice school. My family members are all Christians so we all go to Mass on Sundays.

My dad is a hardworking man, he takes initiative in everything he does. He spends quite some time at his work, usually from morning to late dinner. Dad was born and raised in Wisconsin then he moved to Texas and married my mom. We spend a lot of time together on the weekends, especially on sports.

My mom also works a job. Her life is a little more compact than my dad's. She has to work her job, run errands, pick up my sisters and I from school, and help clean the house. Mom keeps working so my family can have a smooth and easy life. My mom and dad both have to sacrifice their life so that we can have a good childhood.

David Reynolds, Grade 8
St Elizabeth Ann Seton School, TX

School Electives

Schools today should stress the importance of students taking subjects such as music, arts, and physical education as they do on the traditional subjects like English and math. We should treat sports and music the same way we do our core subjects like reading and science. Kids would be healthier, more knowledgeable, and would enjoy school more.

If schools were to encourage music and sports they would get their exercise every day, which would help kids fight diabetes. It would also help kids that are heavy to lose weight. Another thing is it would help kids relieve stress and be able to carry on with their everyday lives.

Another reason schools should urge students to focus on subjects like sports and music more is that it will make them a well-rounded student. When they get into high school, students will be focusing on college more, and doing one of those subjects would look good on a college application. Also, you can possibly receive a college scholarship for doing a sport or being in band.

My final reason that schools should focus more on their students' electives is that kids have a great deal of fun doing things like sports and band. They would much rather do that than math or science. For example, there are a bunch of athletic kids who love sports and would play it 24/7, and there are quite a few kids who have a passion for arts.

In conclusion, if schools were to focus more on students' electives than their core subjects kids would be healthier. They would also be a better-rounded student and have an opportunity to get a college scholarship, and they would have a lot more fun and enjoy school more.

Tyler Judd, Grade 8
Holliday Middle School, TX

Books

I slowly draw in my breath as I scan the many shelves in the library. The numerous colored bound spines stretch before me as I begin my search for a new and exciting tale to indulge in. I give a resolute wave to the curly haired librarian and dash towards one of my favorite sections, fantasy. I glide down the stretching aisle, waiting for my eyes to catch an intriguing picture or word that will launch my plunge into a new adventure. I see it, roughly stuffed between what looks like a towering Moby Dick and a feeble paperback, is a slightly frayed hard back with curly letters weaving down its spine and horned yellow fairies dancing in and out of the picture. I find myself gently sliding the book from its hidden place, and making my way to my favorite plush chair. As I turn to page one to start yet another journey, I flashback to the many others that I have had in this very place, and I realize, this is where I belong.

Over the years as I have made my way through book after book, I find my knowledge growing and growing, even if in some of the smallest ways. Some books have been intense enough to alter one of my opinions completely, while others have added to my strength. Books have made me who I am today and I plan for them to make me who I am tomorrow.

Savanna Turpen, Grade 8
Zia Middle School, NM

Is It Love?

What is love? Love is described as a number of emotions related to an intense feeling of tender affection for somebody. At the young age of thirteen, the diversity of uses and meanings, combined with the complexity of the feelings involved can be very confusing. As for myself, I wonder if I have been struck by the love bug.

I think I have fallen in love. We go to the same school and we have been talking to each other for quite some time. We can be ourselves when we are around each other. I like everything about her, her beauty, smile, personality, sense of humor, and I really enjoy being around her.

She gives me a feeling that I have never felt before, you know that ticklish feeling in your stomach that people call butterflies. I believe that she knows how I feel about her and I have a feeling she pretty much feels the same way about me.

I know that people say that we are too young to understand what love is. Call it puppy love or what you wish, but I think that this is the real thing. I think I have found the right girl for me.

So I really don't know, maybe we are too young and are silly to think we are in love. But for now, I need to enjoy the feeling that I get when I'm around her and admit that I have indeed been struck by the love bug.

Steven Velazquez, Grade 8
Rio Bravo Middle School, TX

Priceless Memories

It was hard to think of things that money can't buy. Everything I could think of was something that could be bought with money. Then it came to me that nothing can buy my memories, happiness, or peace. I have wonderful memories of my childhood. The trips with my family and friends make me think about how happy I was. Money can't buy peace. Even with all the money that has been spent in the actual war in the Middle East, there is still no peace.

My family and I like to go to San Diego every time we have vacations. We go to Sea World or the Miramar Air Show. My mom visits her friend, too. My memories of these vacations are priceless. I love watching the animals, and the shows are very funny at Sea World. At the Miramar Air Show I have seen my favorite airplanes. I have touched them and even been inside some of them. My brother and my dad like airplanes too, so we share the memories together. My mom likes the shows too, also likes meeting with her friend. These are memories which money can't buy.

Peace is among the most desired gift that money can't buy. We hear about all the money that our country spends sending troops to the Middle East to defend our peace, but the daily news relates that more and more are killed. Money can't buy peace, love, or tolerance, but forgiveness does.

George Stoute, Grade 8
Our Lady of the Rosary School, CA

Global Warming

Global warming is an important current issue.

Most of us know that Al Gore won a Nobel Peace Prize for the prevention of global warming. My opinion is, Al Gore is a hypocrite. He preaches about conserving our earth and climate change, but he himself owns private jets that pollute our environment. I really don't think he deserves a Nobel Peace Prize.

Climate change has happened in the past. The earth has had several major ice ages and a lot of small ice ages. Earth also has had warming periods, as well as ice ages. North Africa used to be rainforest, and now most of North Africa is desert. Climate change is a natural thing and we shouldn't waste billions of dollars to try to prevent an event that just naturally happens. Thousands of years ago they didn't have gas powered vehicles or factories giving off smog, and climate change occurred. So that tells you right there that global warming is just a huge myth that costs a whole lot of money.

Al Gore also says to go and buy solar power systems. Solar power energy systems cost thousands of dollars to mount on the roof of your house. Where I live, I don't get much sunlight, so for me that is a total waste.

Global warming is a natural thing because it has happened before. Hopefully, Americans will come to know that there is nothing to worry about.

Samuel Gomez, Grade 8
Corpus Christi School, CA

My Purity Ring

My birthday is July twenty-fifth. I turned thirteen this year. I asked my parents for a purity ring. A purity ring is a ring that symbolizes my love for the Lord and myself. It's a promise I made to Christ that I will respect myself, keep my abstinence, and do, listen, and see pure things. I believe a purity ring is very important because you should treat yourself as a treasure.

My parents personalized my ring. It has a ruby in the center, two larger diamonds on each side, and smaller diamonds surrounding the entire ring. The ruby represents my birthstone and Proverbs 31:10 "A wife of noble character who can find? She is worth far more than rubies." The two larger diamonds represent my parents, and the smaller diamonds are the constant light and protection that God gives me, and all the graces He has given me that I am grateful for.

Purity rings aren't only for women. Men also have these rings, they are called chastity rings. Chastity rings serve the same purpose as purity rings. I admire the Jonas Brothers. I like their music. I also like that they set a good example by each wearing a chastity ring.

Last summer my family and I were invited to a beautiful wedding at the Arboretum in Dallas, Texas. The couple both had *rings*, and they exchanged them after saying their vows. I was astonished. From that day, I've always wanted a husband who would do the same.

Daniela Frangione, Grade 8
St Elizabeth Ann Seton School, TX

Spay and Neuter

Most of the animals at the pound are there for one reason, their owners did not spay or neuter. In six years one dog and her puppies can have as many as 67,000 puppies! One cat and her kittens can have as many as 420,000 kittens! That is a lot of animals, most of which will end up in the pound.

There are many reasons people don't spay and neuter. A common reason is that they think that their animal is very special, but in truth all animals are very special. Animals have less chance of infection, cancer and many other problems if spayed before their first heat. Animals are also less likely to bite, spray, run away and get in to fights. Animals that are spayed or neutered are also more likely to live longer.

There are a lot of cases of accidental breeding; spaying and neutering can easily prevent this. Each year 6-12 million dogs and cats are put to sleep. Most shelters can only find homes for 10% of the animals. That is a lot of unwanted critters, and every time a pet has babies the number of unwanted pets go up.

One of the most important things you can ever do for your pet is get them spayed or neutered. So please for the sake of all the animals, and the world, Spay and Neuter!!!

Michailia Massong, Grade 9
Home School, AK

Music and Me

On a Christmas morning, 2003, I ran downstairs very early, to open Christmas presents. After I begged my parents to get out of bed and come downstairs, I saw a huge present sitting right in front of the Christmas tree. After ripping up the wrapping paper, I saw my first introduction to music. An electric keyboard and it changed my life.

I would later get lessons, and learn how to properly play the piano. Then I started listening to more rock bands like The Beatles and The Who. After three years of learning the piano, I decided I wanted to learn something new, so I picked up a guitar.

Music has affected my life greatly, mostly in academics. Music takes time, practice, and hard work, which is very much the same as school. In fact, my grades would not be as good as they are if I had never gotten into music. Music has given me better opportunities in life, and makes me try harder in everything I do.

I've been playing the guitar for a few years and play in the school's jazz band. But it all started that Christmas morning. If I wasn't playing music, I would probably be doing another hobby, but I know it wouldn't bring me as much joy as music and knowing how to play an instrument.

Sean O'Connell, Grade 8
North Layton Jr High School, UT

My Giving Tree

A giving tree is someone who gives with no expectations in return. An amazing example of this was my mother. My mother possessed three of these important qualities. She gave everything she had to others, she was strong and brave, and she was a great mom. She was one of the strongest and bravest people I knew. In October of 1997 she was diagnosed with stage 4 esophageal cancer. She endured some of the worst months of her life. It was hard for her and our family and friends to see her suffer. She stayed strong though, not for herself, but for us.

My mother also made it a point to give to others. She spent many years giving back at our church and helping with Meals-on-Wheels. Although she had cancer she still made it a point to raise me. When she became too weak and ill to keep up with me, my dad would just put me on her lap and we would talk. My dad offered to take her to MD Anderson in Houston when she got worse. She refused to go there, wanting to stay home. She kept living her normal life at home and continued to raise me. After 9 painful months my mom died. She died on October 13, 1998 when I was only two and a half years old. She lived an awesome life and lived it mostly for others not herself. I love my mom and hope to be just like her.

Caitlin Rodgers, Grade 8
St Elizabeth Ann Seton School, TX

Guitarist for Life

It was a day like any other. I was in school with my friends Ana, and Beatriz her sidekick. That day we were talking about reveries we've had. I said, "Won't it be cool to be roommates in college?"

Beatriz said, "Yup, except for the going to college part."

Then I noticed that Ana was in her own little world. I asked, "What's wrong?"

"Nothing, I'm just thinking about rock bands."

"OH!" After that Beatriz said, "Hey we should start a band." As soon as Ana heard that she had such an impulse for that to happen.

She said, "That could actually happen. I could play guitar, Beatriz the drums and you could play the bass." Beatriz and I accepted.

When Ana wanted something she perseveres. I admire Ana since the first day I met her in second grade. She is a person you can look up to.

After school we went to Mr. Smith's music class. His classroom was full of all kinds of instruments. I told him, "Mr. Smith can you teach us how to play an instrument? I want to learn how to play the bass, Ana the guitar, and Beatriz the drums."

"Sure. Next week we start a new semester so you can be in my class."

"Okay," I said.

A week passed and we had music. We started learning how to play. Weeks passed and Mr. Smith heard Ana play and said, "You're a natural!"

Yesenia Perez, Grade 8
Charles Maclay Middle School, CA

Mine Forever

It was another Wednesday night and I was upstairs in my room working on my math homework. I was on my last math problem having trouble concentrating when I heard the familiar jingle. I spun around in my chair and saw Tiger's old and comforting furry face poking in my doorway. He always knows when I need him.

As Tiger proudly jingles over to me, I cannot help but to remember the time I first laid eyes on his angel face. It was one warm September day in Broad Brook, Connecticut, when my mom took my brother and me to the local animal shelter. Although I was only five years old. I knew he was meant to be with me from the moment I set eyes on him.

As time went by, Tiger and I grew closer and closer. A few years after this adoption, my family and I moved to Texas. It was a big adjustment not only for me, but also for Tiger because he was a country cat. It has been over a year since our move and Tiger and I have become inseparable. He is my study buddy and partner in crime! The best part about Tiger is that he is mine forever!

Katie Ouellette, Grade 7
St Elizabeth Ann Seton School, TX

What's Worth Waiting For?

The most important thing worth our waiting for is love. Love is important to every person that falls into it. It is not always genuine at a young age, but as we grow older we ascertain it as vital. Love is everywhere and in everything, young and old, new and trite. People learn and have learned many things from love, and individuals at a young age do not yet realize what love has to offer. Love is when we melt in the presence of our soul mate, when we get the feeling that nothing else matters except for that one person. Love, said by many people, is almost like a shock, an aspect of the human condition that is worth anticipating.

Love has benefits and liabilities, though it becomes a salient aspect of life. Most don't fall in love until a later age, but everyone who experienced love at least once realized that it is special. Love leads its people into happiness and satisfaction, but also altercations, melancholy times, and dissent. Love is all you need, a famous old quote by the Beatles, tells that with love, our lives should be perfect. The quote by the Beatles may sound spurious, but love equalizes differences between people and draws them together. What we don't always perceive is that love is everywhere in everybody, though not always noticeable or easily understood. Love is, in the beginning, inconspicuous and esoteric, but one of the things that is worth our waiting.

Sara Glueck, Grade 8
St Rita Elementary School, CA

A Game to Remember

The tennis match looked bleak. With a score of six-two, the other team was dominating. My doubles partner was tired, she wanted to rest. Sweat was running down my face from the scorching heat of the sun. It was my serve, and we wanted to win. I tossed the ball up into the air. Bending my knees and loading the racket behind my head I was ready to hit the ball. BAM, my body exploded forward as I slammed the ball toward my opponent. The ball went flying past his reach. Ace! We were back in the game.

At the beginning of the match Molly and I walked onto the court with extreme confidence. We met the other players, warmed up, and started playing. The first two games, Molly and I were unbeatable. But then, we started to think and got cocky. The other team was playing great and was unstoppable. They won six games in a row. I was so angry and frustrated that I thought we could never win.

Molly and I started to stop thinking and started playing. We would hit the ball past the players on almost every point. We won five straight games. It was forty-thirty, my serve; and ace! We had done it, we came back from an almost unbeatable game. Now that is a game to remember.

Tyler White, Grade 9
South Jordan Middle School, UT

Jesus Christ

Have you ever felt like you're not cared about? Well, it's not true. The man who died on the cross for us does care about you, and His name is Jesus.

I began to attend church in the sixth grade. I never understood what they were talking about. All I did was mess around. One day at an event we call "The Lock-in," what Josh my youth leader said caught my attention. We started talking about giving my life to Christ. He helped me with my decision to get baptized.

After being baptized, sharing Jesus felt natural. I started to invite my friends and family to come learn with me. My actions also changed, and they needed to change.

Waking up early in the morning for church is so hard, and on Wednesdays I'm so busy. Although after a while, I got used to it. I never miss church.

My favorite thing about church events such as youth camps, lock-ins, and just Bible study is that I know Jesus is watching me. When I sing a song at an event, I feel the power of Jesus flowing through me, and when I pray I feel Jesus using me as a microphone.

All these things have changed the way I feel and act. I was lonely and never cared, but now I'm always happy and act right. Jesus Christ cares about us all.

Thomas Croghan, Grade 8
Reagan County Middle School, TX

Heartbroken

Have you ever been heartbroken because a loved one has passed away? It is very painful and leaves a scar in your heart, but as the time passes it goes away.

I still remember of that time. I was 9 to 10 years old. Whenever there was a funeral I didn't know why people were crying and dressed in black. All this was strange to me I didn't understand anything of this. I would see the priest praying, flowers around the coffin. Instead of me crying I was playing with my cousin.

Until one day we got news that my grandpa had died. My mom was very sad, and when she told me I didn't feel any emotion toward the news. The next day we went to his funeral to see him inside his coffin. I saw all my family members crying and putting flowers in his coffin. After the funeral was almost over, my uncles picked up the coffin to put it inside the car.

We followed the car to the graveyard. My uncles put the coffin down so that everyone could see him one last time. One last time I went next to the coffin for one last time. This time was different I felt pain and my heart burning inside of me. I was crying and finally felt the way each grownup has felt.

Alexander Galarza, Grade 8
Rio Bravo Middle School, TX

Music

From Ludwig Van Beethoven to Brokencyde, music has evolved throughout the centuries and affected the lives of many. I am also one of that crowd. In an unforgettable memory, music molded my personality creating the person I am today.

As my little brother was screaming along with the *SpongeBob SquarePants* theme song, I dragged myself to my bedroom and dropped my patterned, filled to the zipper, backpack.

Seth burst in crying, "Sissy! Are you okay?!"

I groaned and explained it was merely my backpack.

Once he had gone, I collapsed on the bed still thinking of those echoing words she said.

"I HATE YOU! AND I NEVER WANT TO SEE YOUR FACE AGAIN!"

After finishing my homework, I flicked through the TV channels hoping to find *something* worth watching. Passing yet *another Drake and Josh* rerun, then, a sound caught my interest. It sounded like the light strumming of a guitar.

As I listened, it seemed that the vocalist was harmonizing the trials for my day. Like best friends ventilating, her voice sang words of comfort. She sang of a day going into crisis. Also, though times may be bad; tomorrow can always change. I couldn't help but join in.

"I can hear you say!" I chanted, "It's a brand new day!"

Abruptly, I stopped and grinned. I didn't feel sad anymore. I knew now that if I was ever down, music would help me through. Music can calm a rampaging rhino. It can calm a complicated teenager, too.

Vanessa Soto, Grade 8
Reagan County Middle School, TX

Love

Love is an amazing thing at one point in life everybody goes through it. I've heard many stories about it, but since I'm too young I haven't found my prince charming yet. Fortunately I've grown up with my uncles and aunts and my parents and they've been married for a long time now. And when I see them I see how much they love each other.

I like reading romance stories and movies, sometimes I cry but I still love to watch them. My grandparents have been married for 50 years now. And they still love each other. Love is something everybody goes through and it can be something really beautiful. Love can mean many things, like your family, friends, pets. Sometimes people get divorced, but that doesn't mean that there's probably someone out there that can be the love of their lives. For love there's no ages. Someone 80 years old can actually still be in love with someone. I honestly think that loving someone is wonderful, and when I finally experience it, it is going to be something great!

Susana Zavala, Grade 8
Rio Bravo Middle School, TX

Missing You

Do you miss someone that left you or died? I do, a lot!

This past summer I had a big tragedy in my family. My great-grandma passed away in a car crash. When I first heard she died from a phone from the hospital I was shocked and disappointed. When my great-grandma died I felt like nothing else in the world mattered. I love her so much and miss her a lot, I can't believe she is not with us anymore. I wish I would have spent more time with her, but she lived so far away. If I would have had another chance I would have spent every second of my life with her. She was the reason I would wake up every Sunday wanting to go to church with her. She was always smiling, always up and running, she may have been an older woman but she was really healthy.

My great-grandma means the world to me. When I heard she died all I wanted to do is find a way to bring her back to life. I want her back with us I miss her. Now I can't do anything about it she is gone forever but will always stay in my heart, and she is in a better place now, Heaven. I miss my great-grandma.

I miss you!!!

Paulette Estrada, Grade 8
Rio Bravo Middle School, TX

Why I Love Music

Music is very entertaining. I hear music every single day. There are different types of music that I love. Music can be played with all kinds of instruments. The major thing I love about music is to sing! There is a lot of music to choose from. Some people prefer certain kinds of music. I love all of them! I can dance to the beat of any kind of music. Some music is played with instruments, like the piano or guitar. It helps to keep the beat for most songs.

Music is all over the place. There is good and bad music. I mostly dislike country music, but a few country songs are really good. I hear music in stores, houses, malls, and parties.

Listening to music is what I do every day! Sometimes music helps me speed up with something I am doing, or sometimes slow down. The music I love to hear helps me focus more on what I am doing. When I listen to the type of music that I do not love, I feel like I lose energy.

Music is fun when I sing a long. Singing is so amazing! I love to sing along to my favorite songs. Without any music in my life, I would be sad because music helps me throughout my day!

Music is very fun and entertaining! Without music, dancing would be dull and boring. Music is wonderful. I hear it almost everywhere! I love music because it always brightens up my day!

Janessa Madarang, Grade 8
Corpus Christi School, CA

My Parents

Being a parent is the hardest thing on Earth. I know this because I usually see my parents struggling. My parents have two sons and two daughters. I am one of their two daughters.

As we were driving down the streets of Mexico we came to a stop. Suddenly we heard kids crying. We turned to the left, to the right…two twelve year olds were sitting in a small box near the sidewalk. Nothing to keep them warm, just a shirt and shorts. Beside them was an old raggy towel torn up as if a dog had just attacked them, scars head to toe. We parked the car beside the sidewalk. Moments later the kids had told us how they ended up in the streets. They said their mom died of cancer, and their father left them at age four. That night my aunt had an extra bedroom for the two kids to sleep in.

We had to leave the next day, so we left them money for the kids. They are now fifteen and go to school. They later found out where their dad had been all these years. I am very happy for my parents because they helped these teenagers.

Lots of kids don't have homes to live in. This made me think about how lucky I am to have a roof over my head, clothes, and parents alive, healthy, and caring.

Luz Cervantes, Grade 8
Reagan County Middle School, TX

Two Minutes from Death

Has there ever been a time when you were about two minutes from dying? Has there ever been a time when your dad saved your life? Well in my life, this has happened.

It was a different morning than usual. My sister and I were going to our grandparent's house for the day. We had one minute to get dressed before we had to walk out the door.

As soon as we get to our grandparent's house, my sister wanted to watch TV. Instead, I decided I wanted to go upstairs. My grandpa told me to be careful because the stairs are really steep. As I started heading up the stairs, my foot slipped and I started rolling down. Then, everything went black.

Before I knew it, I was in a helicopter and I saw my dad and some stranger next to me. I heard my dad tell me that I had a slight concussion and I was going to be ok.

As we went through the doors of the hospital, I saw my mom. Another stranger came up and asked me if I felt any pain in my head. Of course, I said yes. The doctor told my dad that it could have been a lot worse but to be grateful that it wasn't.

As soon as I woke up, I saw my mom lying right beside me. She explained to me what happened that day. If it wasn't for my dad, I wouldn't be alive.

Clarissa Arguijo, Grade 9
Kaufer High School, TX

Family

My family is awesome, fun, and great to be around all the time. My mom is a beautiful, loving, sweet, crazy, fun mom. I'm glad that she is my mom and that she is in my life. If she never existed, I would fail in life because she cheers me up when I'm down. She's always here for me and gives me great advice. She's an angel.

My loving step dad is great! He's like a real dad to me because my mom got a divorce with my real dad. I hardly even see him or talk to him. Now my step dad is like my real dad to me. I'm glad Scott is in my life. He has changed my life since he met my mom and I. He is always here for me and helps me when I need help, and cheers me up when I'm down.

Also my funny, cute, adorable sister named Emma. She is ten months old and now is starting to walk. She can crawl to places fast now and is talking a lot more. She's like a doll.

I like to hang out with my family all the time. On Thanksgiving, we eat and pig out with the rest of the family. In December my family and I get together with some family that we haven't seen for a long time and open presents and have a BIG dinner. On Christmas we open presents, then we get together with my aunt, uncle, my cousins and my grandparents too.

We sometimes fight but we get through it and we still love each other. So I mostly treasure my family and the great times we've had.

Melia Vega, Grade 8
Thora B Gardiner Middle School, OR

A House Boat Trip

Last summer my family and I went on a house boat vacation for a week at Shasta Lake. There was my mom, my brother Kyle, my two cousins James and Jackie, my aunt Judy, and her boyfriend Mike. We all packed a lot and had spent a lot of money, but I think it was worth it. Although loading and unloading was not fun, we still had a great trip.

The first day wasn't much fun because we had to find a spot for everything we had to bring. But after that, we were able to swim a little and relax. The next day we all got to ride the jet skis and go tubing. That night I had some of the best steak I've ever eaten. It might have tasted better because I was on a house boat for the first time, but it was pretty darn good.

After the first couple of days we finally got into the hang of things and we had everything planned out for the rest of the trip. We saw lots of wild life, like deer and bears. The deer came right next to the house boat, which was really cool. Thankfully, it wasn't the bear. When it was the last day, I couldn't believe that the trip was just about over. It was disappointing, but I still think it was the best vacation I have ever had.

Chris Lasater, Grade 8
Long Valley Charter School, CA

She Is the One

"Mommy, Mommy! Can we go look at kitties?" I said when I was five years old. For my fifth birthday I wanted an orange and white striped tabby with green eyes named Ashley. So, one day my mom and I went to a pet store; we were "just looking" as my mom made very clear. Inside the store we went. The sign in the store said "kittens for sale." There were tons of orange and white striped tabbies with green eyes!! I was so overwhelmed with all of the excitement. I was looking at all of the precious kittens, but one in particular came right up to the glass of the cage and stared right at me! She was the one, and she also just happened to be a female as well! She even came to me to look at me and meow. "Mommy Mommy! It's Ashley." She was the absolute one. My mom went to go get the lady who worked there, I stayed behind and never took my eyes off of her. The lady went back behind the glass to get Ashley; she almost took the wrong one but we stopped that from happening. Mom and I went into the visiting room and I looked at her she looked at me, we both nodded our heads yes. The day we took my little Ashy cat home. I was a very happy little five year old girl.

Sarah Cervantes, Grade 7
St Elizabeth Ann Seton School, TX

Friends

Do you have friends? Have you ever wondered how things would be if you had no friends? Well I have really good friends. I've never thought on how things could be different without them. Nobody does.

Everyone has their own definition of the word friendship. To me friendship means someone who will be there for you. Someone who will always have the right advice, tell you the truth even if it hurts, and help you be the best you can be. This would be my definition of friendship because of my friendship with my friends.

If I had no friends I wouldn't be the same person. It would probably be hard to trust someone because you always trust your friends with your secrets. You would definitely be a quiet person if you had nobody to talk to. At school the only good thing would be you'd get good grades. There would be a small chance of a person with no friends wanting to interact with others in sports or any other activity.

The one thing you should try to do is to not leave someone out. Just imagine how that person feels how you would feel if you were all alone. All you need to remember is to have a friend you need to be a friend. When you actually think about it and put yourself in that position everything can change. You might have thought friends aren't anything but they can make a big change in a person's life.

Denise Garcia, Grade 8
Stacey Middle School, CA

Wondrous Eagles

Eagles get to soar through the sky. While soaring through the sky, they get to see some of the most amazing things on the planet. Eagles are also considered a part of America's history. They are the base symbol for the greatest country on the Earth, America. Symbolizing unity and peace, they bring people together from all over the world. Eagles are able to soar all over this wonderful world; over the forest green grass and crystal clear oceans. Their glorious life is not so easy though. Eagles also have to provide for, and take care of their family and home. They have to fly over open plains and vast forests for their meal that day. When eagles finally see something that their family can eat, they will swoop downward and catch it viciously. Eagles will fly over many trees and mountains to finally find a good area to build a nest for their family. Once they finally build a nest, they'll feed their young and rest easy. At the climax of the day eagles will fly back to the nest and get ready for their next day. The best part about being an eagle is probably having the freedom to fly anywhere that they want to. I think that they are the greatest animals on Earth!

Robert Martinez, Grade 8
St Elizabeth Ann Seton School, TX

Appreciation

Appreciation is a powerful thing. According to the American Heritage Dictionary, appreciation has five definitions.
1. The act of estimating the qualities of people or things.
2. Gratefulness; gratitude
3. A delicate perception
4. An expression of criticism
5. A rise in value or price

My favorite definition of appreciation is number two. It is the one I can most relate to. Like for instance, I appreciate my family. I am grateful for them and I have gratitude that they are MY family, no matter how much they can sometimes get on my nerves. I love them and can't think how I could ever live without them.

We can apply appreciation in our lives every day! We can appreciate even the simplest things that we take for granted — like television, or computers, or mp3 players, or even our cell phones.

The time I learned my lesson about appreciation was the time I experienced going without fun for a whole month. I was grounded for my disobedience. This act made me lose my shoes, my jewelry, my TV time, and my computer time for 30 days. Because, I had to go without these things for so long, I appreciated them so much more after I got them back.

So, appreciate even the littlest things in life while you can. Someday, you just might have to live without them.

Mia Valdez, Grade 7
Valdez Christian Academy, TX

Breathe

Have you ever stood at the ocean's shore? Have you ever felt the cool, salty breeze or watched the fiery sun submerge itself into the waters? If you have, you've felt the serenity, the calm, the wonder. But have you ever thought about who created it all?

The most meaningful thing in my life is God. He's my Father, my one true friend, and He's the reason I'm on this wondrous Earth — my ticket to existence. He hears me when I cry out. He picks me up when I've been knocked down, and His blessings are nearly inconceivable. I know I'm never alone with Him. I can read the Bible and feel He is right next to me. He's an unfailing amazement, and I cannot even begin to grasp how He created such a large, mysterious universe.

But that's how I like to think of Him. Large. Intriguing. Unimaginable. Even though I can't see Him, I know He's there. He's like the glittering stars — far away but shining with light — and without Him, my life would be a black hole. I would keep getting sucked in, never able to break free from the encroachment that's holding me back or see the hope in different things.

I have Him, though, and even with that knowing, I still have to remind myself to breathe. To smile, to let go, and just know that He is there to catch me when I fall.

Konner McLaughlin, Grade 8
Piner Middle School, TX

My Awesome Friends

Hanging out, having fun, playing games and being goofy are what true friends do. Sticking up for each other is what a true friend does. My friends and I know so much about each other. We know what we've been though in our lives. We know what all of our favorite things to do are such as, going to the movies, going to the mall, and just hanging out at each other's houses and having fun. When anyone of us is sad or upset about something that has gone on in our day or at home we always find a way to cheer one another up. Waking up every day knowing that they are always there for me is an awesome feeling. Having them by my side and them going through everything with me is such a sacrifice they are willing to make. My friends Savannah, Kelsey, Caroline, and Katie are always there for me. We as friends are very close to one another. Savannah is the type of person that you can come to when you are sad and tell you anything. Kelsey is the funniest person you can ever meet, and when you're sad, she'll cheer you up. Katie is so awesome; she's the coolest friend you can ever have. Finally, Caroline is the type of person you can hang out with and have ultimate fun. Being with all of them is a blessing. I couldn't ask for better friends.

Romeo Ayala, Grade 8
Faith Christian Jr/Sr High School, CA

Appreciated Soldiers

Why should we appreciate soldiers? Soldiers risk their lives everyday. They willingly sacrifice their lives for us each day. They leave families behind when they go off to defend our country. In the most recent war between Afghanistan and the U.S., we already have lost many soldiers. Soldiers do not have to volunteer to protect us, they choose to.

Everyday soldiers go out into different places, unfamiliar places. They do not know if the will live that day, but they still do what they have to do to defend our country. In some places, there may even be a battle or a surprise attack with deadly weapons, and they may not live through the battle. If you had to leave your family to protect someone that you do not know, would you leave? Soldiers leave behind children, husbands/wives, parents, and brothers and sisters, just to protect you. They don't have to, but they do it any ways. In the war against Afghanistan, which continues to proceed, the United States military has lost 4,337 soldiers. This means someone has lost a family member, and is now grieving.

We all need to appreciate the sacrifices, such as losing family members, which soldiers make everyday to protect our country. The recent war is not over, and we still need to show gratitude in the people who fight in it. Soldiers don't have to fight for us; it is a decision that they make and we need to recognize and appreciate it, more than anything.

Catherine Aranda, Grade 9
Weber Institute of Applied Sciences & Technology, CA

LeBron James

It would be an understatement to say that LeBron James had a difficult childhood. He was born December 30, 1984 in Akron, Ohio. LeBron's mother Gloria was sixteen years old at the time and his father Anthony McClelland was an ex-con who deserted LeBron and his mom. Gloria single-handedly raised LeBron James. Things became complicated because of Gloria's boyfriends. One of them, Eddie Jackson, who played a pivotal part in the career of LeBron, was also an ex-con. But his presence ensured that young LeBron James would not feel the absence of a father. LeBron was a natural athlete. He participated in football and basketball. In his school years the most important man came into his life. Frankie Walker was his basketball coach in school. Besides coaching LeBron, he invited him to stay with his family so LeBron could live a normal life without the specter of drugs and violence hovering over him. By 8th grade LeBron was six feet tall, could play all five positions, and had a sixth sense for the game. When he was a sophomore in high school he led his team to two consecutive championships. He was already making covers of sports magazines. NBA rules are the only thing that stopped him from entering the 2002 draft. LeBron has become one of the best overall basketball players the world has seen. He is the best passer in the league. He is a basketball legend, with a long ways to go in his career.

Clay Boaz, Grade 8
Breckenridge Jr High School, TX

The Death Bed

Death is something everyone deals with. It don't matter how old or how young. The sad things is, is when you hear about it.

It happened that summer of 2008; we were at a hockey game in Oklahoma. It had just started to be one of the best days of my life. The game had just started, and everyone was excited until we got the phone call. It was my aunt she was telling us that Grandpa was in the hospital sick. We left right then, we went to the hospital. My grandpa looked terrible he could hardly speaks. Then the test results come back. He was not going to make it! The doctor said he would probably be gone within an hour. He had happened to live longer than they thought because; he had made it through the night. The next morning at 6:30 am he was gone.

I still remember his death till this day. We don't go to Oklahoma because of those terrible memories it brings back. We don't even speak of his name anymore. When I saw him lying in that bed it broke my heart. I try to forget about it. It's like a tattoo that could only be surgically removed.

Life is precious you should hang onto it as long as you can. Even though it has its ups and downs.

Cheyenne Scott, Grade 8
Reagan County Middle School, TX

The Hunt

I remember my first hunting trip as if it were yesterday.

Our family hunts in the hill country of Central Texas. The property is rocky but has a dense forest which makes it easier to hide and wait for the deer.

We start our day at five a.m. I managed to drag myself from my bed and get dressed. We wear camouflage so we can blend into the forest and not be noticed by the wandering deer.

When we were sitting quietly in the stands, every minute felt like an hour. Then, we spotted a large buck across the meadow. KA-BOOM! My dad's rifle went off! The bullet soared toward the deer. Once the bullet hit the deer, down it went. We trudged through the forest to locate the fallen deer.

My dad took out his knife and started the cleaning process. When I saw him starting to cut the deer, I said "Oh, that is gross! Can't we just leave the animal here?" My dad said, "Son, it is not right to kill a living creature just for the joy of it. There should be a purpose. The deer provides meat for us to eat."

This hunting experience changed my life. I will remember what my dad told me that day — "It does not matter if we shoot anything or not, the important thing it is that I get to spend some time out here together with you."

Michael Dow, Grade 7
Goodson Middle School, TX

The Finish Line

If people could be the definition for words, Libby Riddles would be the definition for will-power. In 1985, she drove a sled dog team 1,012 miles across Alaska, becoming the first woman to ever win the Iditarod Race. With only her dogs as company through the distance between the checkpoints of the race, she had to listen to her own wit and the instinct of her dogs for survival and a winning title. This was a huge risk! If she got lost in the wilderness of Alaska, she could be lost forever.

Can you imagine facing the dangers of Alaska, all alone, even in the darkness of night, trying to find the trail, and facing the bitter cold for 1,012 miles? She made risky decisions, for her own good, and the good of her dogs. She ran out into a blizzard, while all other competitors stayed inside, and that action put her miles in front of everyone, taking her to the finish line.

Libby Riddles did the impossible. She is my hero and role model. Her story helps me overcome obstacles that may seem impossible. She risked everything for one accomplishment, which reminds me I have to give my all to succeed. She helps me reach for my dreams, even the most extraordinary ones, and her extreme determination helps me achieve them. After all, her dreams came true.

Kelli Reagan, Grade 8
St Thomas Aquinas School, NM

People

People, we have roamed this planet for thousands of years, we come in different shapes, sizes, colors, hair follicles, noses, eyes, mouths (lips), etc. (you get the idea). But we're not just some organism roaming the earth, we are something greater than life itself, without us life would (I think) not be as great, (but of course we would not know because, well, we wouldn't be here). Anyway, what I'm trying to say is that the human "element" if you will, is greater than any…well…actually there is no word that doesn't fit a human, for we are all weird, different, smart, foolish, impaired, and beautiful, in our own unique way. For what drives us humans is (I think) a mystery, for it is up to us to fulfill our own mystery (a.k.a. destiny). In the end humans are all incredible, foolish organisms, roaming the planet for who knows what reason. Doing our part individually and as one nation together, no matter how big that ocean might be separating each nation, or how small each person is, we are all people doing our part, favoring each other in one way or another, because when one thing or another threatens our human existence, no matter all the wars, all the violence that shadows our unique past, in the end we will band together and exceed our existence rather than perish. For the human element is, and shall be forever one national spirit that thrives in all of us today. So I ask you fellow reader, are you ready to fulfill your mystery?

Ian Murphy, Grade 8
Rio Bravo Middle School, TX

Mystery Love Story

Some say love is a mystery, it's a feeling, it's a thought. I was in love. I never knew love was something real. Like many people say "love is blind," well I was blind.

To me this love was real, I adored him he was my life! My best friend/boyfriend was like the sweetest guy to me and I didn't notice or see it till we broke up. I would wake up every day hoping to see his face even his smile oh my, how his smile made my day. The one thing that kept me on my tippy toes was knowing that he would be there to make my day.

When I was with him it seemed as all problems went away and my only focus was on him. Someday soon enough you let go of them, an you lose everything that was ever important to you. In my eyes I saw him as an angel from heaven as everyone else saw him as just him, a boy that was nothing and that I was dumb for liking him. Till one day I thought to myself what time I was wasting these past six months. Looking back on it he was the most amazing guy I'd ever met.

I lost him. My biggest regret was losing him, I actually loved him though now he loves someone else and I might too. But no matter what crosses my mind any day, anytime I'll always love my mystery love story.

Briana Ramirez, Grade 8
Rio Bravo Middle School, TX

Christmas Eve

It is the night before Christmas…Christmas Eve is one of the most exciting nights of the whole entire year. On Christmas Eve, my family and I have a big celebration at my aunt's house. Which, we will be leaving for in about an hour. At my aunt's house we have a big dinner, with my parents, grandparents, aunts, uncles, and cousins. After we have all eaten and have had the most chocolaty desserts, we all gather in her living room. In her living room we have tons of presents, all different shapes and sizes. With all of these gifts we play White Elephant, a fun, exciting game.

"Julia get in the car, we are leaving for Aunt Joanna's now!" my mother exclaims. I was excited we were finally leaving.

We are there; we all get out of the car and ring the door bell. My cousin opened the door for us to enter. Right in front of our eyes, when we first walked in, is a 20 foot tall Christmas tree! The tree had various types of ornaments on it. The ornaments had many different colors and shapes. After staying at the party for about two hours, we started to head home. When we finally got home, we got ready for bed. We closed our eyes and waited for Santa to come the next morning.

Julia DeBlassie, Grade 8
St Thomas Aquinas School, NM

Becoming an 8th Grader

Have you ever thought you would never pass 7th grade? I did; one time I was failing and my grades weren't even in the 50s. The teachers told me that I would not pass the third six weeks.

During basketball season I failed my report card. When Coach Prentice captured my grade, he told me, "If you fail one more time, I'm going to kick you off the basketball team." After he told me that I promised myself that I would try harder. I tried hard the next week, and I was improving a whole bunch. By the end of the six weeks, I was passing all my classes.

By then it was close to the TAKS test, and I was anticipating it. But I still needed a whole lot of work for my math. So I had somebody tutor me in math. Ever since the tutor helped me, I did better. Then I was getting B+, A-, and A+ on my report cards.

It was time, TAKS was starting. The first TAKS was math. I answered my questions with positive answers. On each question it took me three to five minutes. The day later I had another TAKS. Two to three months later I found out that I failed both TAKS but still tried to pass to the 8th grade, and I did.

Try harder to meet your goal. Make a better effort in all classes. Success can come to anyone at any time.

Jason Rodriguez, Grade 8
Reagan County Middle School, TX

Two Tablespoons of Sugar, and 1 1/2 Cups of Hard Work

The fresh smell of sweetness consumes me, warmth radiates from its center, and as it touches my lips, my brain is engulfed by one, delicious thought: Blondies. Blondies are made of the same ingredients as brownies, but they have a butterscotch flavor; and for me, they are "to die for." They are almost as fun as they are to eat as they are to bake. Ever since I visited the Hyatt hotel's very own kitchen on a preschool field trip and received a chef hat with my name on it, it has been my passion to cook.

I love to make a variety of things, from pumpkin pie to spaetzle, for not only is it fun relaxing, and blissful, it is an important life skill. I often bake with my mom, for she is a self-taught, culinary genius with 101 tips and tricks of the trade. Whenever we cook, we make a delectable treat to share with friends and family. We often make our special, homemade bundt cake whenever a new neighbor moves in on our street. It's always a great success.

I believe cooking is a great way to express who you are, and I always put a piece of myself into whatever goes in the oven. Without a cook in the house, food would be bland and meals uneventful. Cooking can bring people together, and could make the world a better place. In the words of chef Julia Child, "Bon Appetit!" and let's get cooking!

Ricky Novaes, Grade 7
Placerita Jr High School, CA

Sending Smiles

We each can take part on making the world we live in a better place. To do this, one can make random acts of kindness for those around you. Sometimes it could be just smiling at the person walking past, sometimes it's more. It could be unique and fun.

I think it's exciting and it's very unpredictable, since you could practically do anything to make someone happy. It changes the world by creating smiles and it brings joy to others. It doesn't seem like much, but the little things you do all add up. You can change the world little by little; one person at a time. There's so much hate in this world, even a smile could make someone's day.

Some people make acts of kindness and don't even know it. It's a chain reaction. If you make someone happy, they will be in a good mood, and make someone else's day. The simplest things you do can help someone out. Even if it's just babysitting for your friend; it counts. It isn't only rewarding to the person you're helping, but it's also rewarding to you. You feel good knowing that you did something to help someone out.

Some people don't think they can do anything to change the world. They think they won't make a difference because they are so small in such a big world. But that's not true. Everyone can make a difference. You can change the world one person at a time.

Adrienne Baldasti, Grade 8
St Elizabeth Ann Seton School, TX

The Mall

The clothes and shoes are just half the greatness of the mall. There are many ways to have an enjoyable mall experience. You can shop, get something to eat at the food court, or see a movie.

At the mall there are many things you can do to have fun. One thing to do is shop. Shopping can be boring if you don't have a friend, so you have to make sure to invite a couple of friends. You can always buy dresses, shirts, jewelry.

Another fun thing to do at the mall is to see a movie. When you pick a movie make sure that you know what genre you are in the mood for. When you watch the movie make sure you buy a lot of candy and popcorn.

When you go to the mall make sure you have a good lunch at the food court. When you go to the food court you have lots of choices. Some choices are Chinese, hamburgers, pizza, pasta, smoothies, and ice cream. Whatever you choose you are definitely going to have something delicious.

The mall is a place full of fun, food, and friends. When you go to the mall you are definitely going to have a great time, and maybe buy some great items!

Catherine Grinzewitsch, Grade 8
St Michael's Episcopal Day School, CA

I Love My Glasses

Glasses have been around since the year 1275. Over the years kids make fun of people with glasses. Some people get offended when kids make fun of them so they end up not wanting to wear them no more. For example Mr. Lopez calls me four eyes and he takes it as a joke but I don't. There are lots of different kinds of glasses. Some people need glasses to see better and there are also reading glasses. I use glasses because I need them to see farther.

There are different contacts depending on your eyesight. Lots of people prefer to wear contacts than glasses. Some contacts are hard to put in. There are different colors for contacts. I have never tried on contacts because I think they're hard to put on. You can do more sports with contacts than you can with glasses. For example in soccer when you run with your glasses they can fall and break. Some contacts you can sleep with, some you can't. Some advertisements say you can get 6 pairs of contacts and with glasses you can't.

Glasses have different designs. Some glasses are thicker than others. There are also small glasses and little glasses. There are round ones, square ones and oval ones. They have different kinds of frames. The frames come in different colors. Even though I don't like contacts I still love my glasses.

Jahayra Avila, Grade 8
Isbell Middle School, CA

My Best Friends

Friends are splashes of colors designed to enlighten someone's world adding enthusiasm and humor to every aspect of your life. A friend changes your life forever, and they're always there for me. Right by my side through the tough times that seem to drag on forever. All the stress or drama that I have to cope with on a daily roller coaster ride, is easily melted away like the sun warming up thick sheets of ice. It's so nice to have people who understand who I am. My favorite memories include my friends. All the laughs we've shared couldn't possibly compare to anything else I've experienced before. Many of the places I've gone to my friends have been right by my side. From football games to haunted houses with all the other vivid memories in between, they will forever be there. Of all the friends who've run in and out of my life, two have and will always have had a special place in my life. I found my life changing in 4th grade. I met this girl who I knew would forever and always be my best friend, and just recently I grew another amazing friendship with an even more amazing person. Thank you Erin and Rachael for sticking by me, refusing to let go, and for forever being my best friends. My life has changed so much because of the lasting impression these two colorful people have created. Now, my world will never be dull, dark, or gray.

Gabie Barrera, Grade 8
Thora B Gardiner Middle School, OR

Pedro Fregoso

Pedro Fregoso was my grandpa. He was born in Mexico and lived there his whole life. He grew up in a poor family. All they had to eat was beans.

Every time his parents had enough money they would give him a peso. He would go to the store and buy himself two oranges and one egg, he would eat it raw. He wouldn't go buy himself marbles. He would go, buy food that smelled like oranges.

His family was so poor Pedro didn't go to school. They couldn't afford good shoes. So they bought him sandals, sometimes he was barefoot.

When he grew up he was a policeman. He quit the job and meet Elpidia, which is my grandma. They started dating and weird things happened. Like one time they were walking together and a black coffin popped out of nowhere.

When they got married, even stranger stuff happened. One time Elpidia was washing, when she was finished, she entered her room and a skull rolled from one corner to the other side of the creepy room. When she was putting the clothes away, something pushed the squeaky closet door and hit her. She went to go tell Pedro, "A ghost just hit me with the door!"

Pedro went outside to see what it was. He went around the house to look, when he was looking he saw a shadow. It was about eleven feet tall and then it disappeared. Pedro died on November 6th of 2004.

Eliseo Fregoso, Grade 8
Charles Maclay Middle School, CA

Is It Love or Just a Crush?

Everyone has to have a love in their life. Either they love someone or someone loves them. In my opinion, romance is one of the reasons why Earth is so peaceful. When you have someone to love, it just brings happiness to your life because they're the reason why you want to wake in the morning. When you find that true person you love, you know it's right because you get this feeling in your stomach every time you see his or her face. When you really love that person, you just always want to smile every time you're with them. When you're young you really don't know what love is you just think you know. I don't know what love really feels like or what it really is but I do believe in true love. One day I want to wake up in the morning and see my partner next to me. One day I want to know what it feels like to have that one person that really cares for me and not just pretend. I want to look at someone the way my mom looks at my dad. When someone is in love, they only see that other person and no one else. If you don't feel that with your partner that you're with right now, then it's not really love it's just a crush.

Nicole Gabaldon, Grade 8
Rio Bravo Middle School, TX

Happiness

Happiness is that overwhelming joy, the inexplicable smile on your face, and uncontrollable laughter. For me, happiness is the aroma of home-baked pies, bargain hunting with my aunts, the never-ending adoration from my puppy, sparkly Christmas trees, the laughter of my nephew, and the proof that I am right. What brings joy is different for everyone. Some girls may delight in making their hair just perfect while others find that the adrenaline rush from running up and down the soccer field is the greatest natural high that exists and other people just love reading. But no matter what the form, happiness is always better shared. My gut hurts more when I'm laughing with my sisters, music has a stronger beat in a crowd of dancing people, and Gramma's fresh baked cookies are tastier when sharing them with cousins. Really, happiness can be anything. It might be the whack job you call your best friend or a bowl of Rice Crispies. "Happiness is anyone and anything at all that's loved by you." (Happiness from *You're a Good Man, Charlie Brown*).

Christy Glad, Grade 9
Fairfield Jr High School, UT

What's Important

Have you ever wondered what the world would be like without creativity? It would be a blank and lifeless place that constantly drove beings to suicide. We often take creativity for granted, but it alone is what gives the world ideas, life, and separation from animals.

The ideas that humanity imagines are what power decisions and light the world. Some ideas are what created things that we use every day, such as clothing, video game consoles, cars, and pencils. Someone, somewhere 'thought' these things up, experimented, and thus created something that humanity counted on.

If we were to think of the world without creativity, we would imagine a lifeless planet. Creativity is what spawned art, hunting, religion, language, inventions, and other important things. To be deprived of it would result in a dead, monochromatic world bloated with beings who looked, thought, and acted the exact same as others. Stifling creativity causes a dull and boring world that lies full of empty shells called 'humans.'

It separates us from animals in several ways. The biggest example of this is that we want things to change. Animals go through the same routine: survival. It's something that we're already covered in.

Therefore, creativity plays a huge part in the play of my life. I want to stand apart with my ideas, bright attitude, and ability to be distinguished from animals. Creativity is massively important and is what drives me to stand out.

Kyleigh Pearson, Grade 8
Zia Middle School, NM

The Importance of Family

Even though the word "family" means people who live under the same roof, I believe that it means people who love each other deeply with all their heart. Although some children only have a mother, father, or a grandparent, the child should always know someone loves them. Four people who have impacted my life are my mom, dad, sister and my granny. From the loved ones mentioned above, my life lessons were taught by different family members in different ways.

First of all, my role models and life teachers are my mom, dad, sister and my granny. My mom, Debbie is my best friend, she has taught me life lessons that I will carry to the grave. The second person is my dad, Dennis, who has encouraged me to be a hard worker and has taught me you can be a small fish in the sea and grow up to be a friendly shark. One word that describes my sister is fun; Brittney can spark up my day and make me laugh, even if I am going through a crisis. The last person is my granny, Wanda who may not be alive anymore, but she taught me so many lessons while she was alive that have influenced who I am today.

In conclusion, I feel my life is unique. My mom, dad, sister and my granny are all wonderful and have touched my life, provided guidance and always surround me with love no matter what comes my way.

Aitiana Zamora, Grade 8
Zia Middle School, NM

Being an American

Being an American is very important to me. To me, the value that is most essential to being an American is courage. Courage is important because without it we would not have any bravery, and would probably be afraid of everything that comes our way. It is truly very important.

A lot of our founding fathers had to have courage in order to run the country. If, in the past, one of our presidents had to make a speech on television in front of millions of people, the president would have to exercise courage to be successful in addressing the nation. Courage could get you to where you want to be in life just like the presidents. To most of our presidents, courage was mostly important because running the country is mostly based on that.

The Declaration of Independence basically states people wanting their freedom and that they do not want to be treated as if they were owned. For all the very important people that signed it, they needed to have courage to speak for themselves. Honor, love, and dedication are all very important values. For me, however, courage is most essential. It can be expressed in many different ways by different people. A lot of us think it could be honesty or something else, but for me it will always be courage.

Cecilia Corona, Grade 7
Anthony Charter School, NM

African Elephants

African elephants are one of the most endangered animals in the world. They have been killed for many years. They are endangered because their beautiful tusks, made of ivory, are a prized possession to many people. Their tusks and large ears sell for a lot of money. African elephants are very beautiful and it would be sad to see them go, forever. We do not want the African elephant to become extinct for many reasons.

The African elephant is the largest land animal in the world. When an endangered animal goes extinct, it means that all of the people born after the animal becomes extinct will have never gotten the chance to see it and its beauty. All we would be able to do is see the image of it on the computer. It is even more special if you could see it in person. If the African elephant becomes extinct that means that all of the people who took advantage of the African elephant and killed it for its tusks are the people to blame for the extinction of the African elephant.

People should start making piano keys of plastic instead of ivory to help save the African elephant. One third of all trees in Africa forests depend on elephants to help pass seeds through the elephant's digestive system to plant more trees. If the African elephant becomes extinct it would ruin the circle of life.

Abbey Bland, Grade 8
St Michael's Episcopal Day School, CA

The Power of Love

Love is the most powerful thing in the universe and heavens. It is the most sought out topic everywhere you look: in old novels, new novels, young people, old people, in the past, present, and, undoubtedly, future.

In the Greek myth of Demeter and Persephone, Demeter was outraged that Zeus had let Hades, the Underworld King, steal their daughter, Persephone, away into his dark kingdom without her knowing. She told him, "I will show you the power of my love and it will defeat that of force!" Finally, Zeus gave in to Demeter's demands and made a compromise between Hades and Demeter because Demeter's love was so powerful, even he didn't know how to stop her. Thus showing that as mighty as Zeus may be, love was stronger.

A world without love is pointless, as shown in *The Giver* by Lois Lowry. The 'community' was very controlled; there was no weather, no color, no death, and most appalling of all, no love. Sure, they had a word for what we would describe as 'preferably like,' but there wasn't any real emotion behind it. They think of love as we think of eating fruits — some people like them, but others just eat them because they have to. A mere shaking of hands compared to a hug or kiss, but they weren't even allowed to touch anyone not in their family!

Love is the basis of life, for without love, there would be no life with such great emotions as we have.

Vanessa Lam, Grade 9
Downey High School, CA

Enjoying Your Job

Job satisfaction is more important in a career than a high salary and fringe benefits. Some studies show that when you like your job you don't use as many sick days.

Job satisfaction is an important part in working. One reason is because if you don't like the job, then you're not necessarily going to be good at your job but it wouldn't be your favorite thing to do. So if you like your job and you are good at it, and then you will get paid.

Job satisfaction is essential because if you can't do the job, then you are either not going to be paid well, or you get fired. If you get fired then that might lead to depression. Depression might lead to suicide and then you would not have to worry about getting a new job.

When you are in an occupation that you like then you will probably be in a happy mood; therefore, if you're in a happy mood, you will be less likely to have family troubles. When you're in a happy mood, it makes your life much easier.

Although many people would say that the money is the most important part in a job, they also say money can't buy you happiness. This is why I believe job satisfaction is important.

Emilee Erwin, Grade 8
Holliday Middle School, TX

Becoming an 8th Grader

The beginning of anything new can make you feel butterflies in your stomach. Moving up to a new grade level can be difficult. I've learned that everybody has to grow up someday. Being an 8th grader can make you feel important.

It all started one Monday morning at 5:30 am. Mom hollered at us to wake up. I was the first one to wake up. I still couldn't believe we were going back to school. We all got dressed and ready to go. My brothers and I said bye to Mom and left. Dad took us to the bus stop. We had to ride the bus because, we live out of town. The bus arrived and we all left. After a tiring 30 minutes, we arrived at school. I saw all my friends sitting at the table eating breakfast. They all said hi. I did not eat breakfast because, I was so nervous. I was waiting anxiously for the bell to ring to go to first class.

"Rong rong," the bell rang.

We all went to our first class. I was so relieved because I didn't have to wait anymore. My friends and I talked the whole class period. Next we all went to second, third, fourth, sixth, seventh and eighth period classes.

Becoming an 8th grader really impacted my life it is showing me new things. Eighth grade is not as hard as people say it is.

Teila Jimenez, Grade 8
Reagan County Middle School, TX

Baseball Is Not Simple

Baseball is a sport which requires strategic thinking. It isn't just hitting, throwing, and catching. There is a lot more to it. When playing defense, the catcher does the most thinking. He must analyze each player on the team he is about to play, to find their weaknesses. During the game, the catcher must decide what pitch and location the pitcher should throw to the batter. The infielders must also know what to do, such as when they can square up on a ball or when they need to charge the ball and throw it on the run. Infielders must know who needs to hold the base runner on base, and make any other quick decisions. The outfielders must know where to throw the ball based on where the runners are. On a fly ball the outfielders need to decide who has a better position to catch the ball, and they need to know where the wall is so they don't run into it.

Offensively, the batter needs to know what pitches to expect in different counts. The base runner must know what the count is so he knows when there is a good time to steal. He must be prepared to dive back if the pitcher tries to pick him off.

If you thought that baseball was a very simple sport you should reconsider that thought. In fact, baseball is known as the thinking man's sport.

Jack Mahoney, Grade 7
Placerita Jr High School, CA

Environment

Have you ever thought about the world you're living in, and how it's giving us a home? What have we done in return? Not much. Sure we recycle sometimes, but not everyone does. Some people just care about the money, and leave the world in pollution. They don't care if the polar bears are going extinct; they'd rather get money than let amazing animals like polar bears live on. We should all take part in saving our world. Earth is the one providing us shelter, food, anything we need to survive. Since we aren't taking care of our world, more natural disasters are occurring. If we don't stop destroying Earth now, it will be flooded by melting glaciers or maybe something worse, like an ice age.

Helping Earth is simple; we just *all* need to do little things, and the world will change little by little. All of us recycling will reduce trash by much. If we don't use cars as much, Earth's atmosphere would be unpolluted and clean. Instead, we could walk, ride a bike, carpool, etc. There are other ways you could help stop pollution. You could get solar powered panels if you really want to help the planet (and it saves money). Saving the planet is simple, you just have to do simple things. Start helping now.

Joseph Lee, Grade 7
Placerita Jr High School, CA

Something Worth Being Passionate About

Every story begins somewhere; mine just happens to begin in a simple middle school classroom, where I am learning things that I once thought were so far in our race's past that they weren't worth learning about. When my social studies teacher introduced the topic of genocide in Africa I thought we were getting ready to study something that happened many years ago, and then he opened up Google Earth and showed us destroyed villages all throughout the Darfur region of Sudan. Now, I didn't know Sudan was even a country, much less that a horrible war was going on over there! After weeks of studying I learned so much about the people of Darfur and all that they have faced in the last years. I felt as if they were part of my own family; which made it that much harder learning about all the atrocious things that they had to suffer: war, violence, pain, death, starvation, and so much more! Imagine having your six month old baby being burned in your home and you not being able to do ANYTHING about it! After hearing all about these horrible things I felt as though I needed to take action and this is where you come in, spread the word! Tell your friends, start to fundraise for Anti-Genocide organizations, and spread this story. Anything is possible if we all unite to better our communities and our world!

Sky Mihaylo, Grade 9
West Albany High School, OR

Being the Only Daughter

Being the only daughter is like being a lucky girl. A lucky girl gets everything she wants and anything she wants. I love to get new jackets, new shoes, new clothes and many more things.

It all started on December 4, 1995, at 4:00 am. The nurse told my mom to push one more time, and there I was Mommy's little sunshine. The name is Emily Joseline Gallegos Balderas. I have a mommy, a daddy, and two very annoying brothers. Their names are Alfonso Gallegos and Cristian Gallegos. Even though they are very annoying, I still love them. I love my mommy so very much, she's the one who gives me everything I want. I love my daddy even though I'm not really a daddy's girl.

The good thing about being the only daughter is that I get to get everything I want. Getting everything and anything I want is so cool. I get my own cell phone, a flat screen TV, my own big room and anything a little girl dreams of having in her life. The bad thing about being the only daughter is that my big brother is always picking on me, even though sometimes he makes me laugh, I love my brother. Me and my little brother are always fighting. He always makes me mad, and I hate being mad. I like to be happy and have a big cheesy smile on my face. Sometimes I wish I had a sister, but at the same time I don't, I love to be the only daughter.

Emily Joseline Gallegos Balderas, Grade 8
Reagan County Middle School, TX

Normal…with a Twist!

My name is Elizabeth. I love to sing, read, help, and participate in school functions. I am in the eighth grade at Saint Elizabeth Ann Seton. I also have Type 1 Diabetes.

As you can see, I am just like any other 13-year-old girl. There are just some other things I have to do to make sure I am healthy. I have to monitor my blood sugar by pricking my finger to make it bleed. I also have to take an insulin shot based on the numbers of carbohydrates I consume. I also must take extra care of my eyes, feet, kidneys, nerves, heart, blood vessels, and gums.

Something that is very important for people with diabetes is self-awareness in symptoms of high or low blood sugar. The symptoms of high blood sugar are extreme thirst, frequent urination, dry skin, being hungry often, blurry vision, very tired, slow-healing wounds, and rapid weight loss. Symptoms of low blood sugar are shakiness, fast heartbeat, sweating, dizziness, anxiousness, hunger, blurry vision, weakness or fatigue, headache, and being irritable.

One thing that really bothers me is the fact that when people think of diabetes they think that the person with diabetes can't consume any sugar or carbohydrates. This statement is not true at all. It is also not true that eating too much sugar causes diabetes.

I believe that I have definitely grown up since my diagnoses 1 year and 4 months ago. Living with diabetes can be tough but it is definitely manageable.

Elizabeth Seyer, Grade 8
St Elizabeth Ann Seton School, TX

The Diversity of the Word Parent

What does the word parent mean to you? The definition of this word is, one who begets, gives birth to, or nurtures and raises a child; a father or a mother. Yet, one interprets this word differently depending on what life has had to offer us. Many people agree with the denotation of the word parent. "To me parents are those who raised me," states Lupita and Martin. Parents are people who guide you throughout life. It's someone who loves their child no matter what and takes care of them. Watching and nurturing one's own child is what a parent is. "Because my parents are there since I was an infant I must say that I consider them my teachers on life" confesses M.C. Armando. "Parents are the people that I know are there for me no matter what I do. They are there for me through any situation, be it physically, mentally or spiritually," says Martin Cuellar. Despite the fact that the word parent is usually positive to all, part of the population feels extremely different. Some parents are overbearing, demanding, and contradicting. Many parents say that grades truly do not matter; yet, once report cards come along it's a different story. "Parents are usually never satisfied with anything we do," said Lupita Espinosa. In conclusion, different people have gone through different experiences making their view of the one word parent diversely unique. Some experiences are positive while others are negative making their knowledge and feelings towards the word resemble their experiences. *But we still love them.*

Martin E. Cuellar, Grade 8
Rio Bravo Middle School, TX

Global Warming

Global warming is what is important to me. Pollution is part of global warming and a major part of it. Pollution is caused by hair spray, old cars with the gas we use, and chemicals. The way to stop global warming in the world is use less of these items. To gain more oxygen may help us breathe better so we should plant more trees.

Pollution is about killing our ozone layer. The ozone layer keeps us safe from the sun's harmful rays. The ozone layer is dying and the sun's rays are melting the ice caps that would soon flood the world. If the ice caps melt the animals living on them would extinct.

The way to slow it down or prevent it is to use green energy. The way to stop global warming is in everyone's hands because everybody needs to help. We need to build more windmills because that's green energy. Everyone needs to recycle to help out the environment. So as you can see it doesn't take one person to cause global warming, it takes everyone. Then it's not going to take one person to stop global warming, it's going to take everyone's help for this goal.

Gabriel Medina, Grade 8
Zia Middle School, NM

Bethany Hamilton

Born on February 8, 1990 on the island of Hawaii, Bethany Hamilton started surfing at a young age. By age seven she entered her first longboard and shortboard division and won. She also won the "15 and under" and "12 and under." Her parents are very proud of her.

After a while she got used to going to competitions and just went surfing all the time. One specific day, she went surfing with her friend Alana. It was just like any other morning when out of nowhere a 15-foot tiger shark came and bit Bethany's left arm off two inches just before the shoulder, and she also lost 60% of her blood. It was very fatal. Bethany was immediately rushed to the hospital and placed into surgery. It took a while before she would be released from the surgery. The doctor said that the surgery went very well and Bethany would be fine.

Bethany took a while to recover from the surgery and she still surfs. In 2004 she won an award for best comeback athlete of the year. She is my favorite because she came back after a really bad accident and surfs like it never happened.

Emily Ashworth, Grade 7
Deweyville Middle School, TX

My Artistic World

Drawing is something I enjoy doing for many reasons. When I draw, I feel as though I can escape to a different place, like nothing can hold me back.

Art is like another world to me. Once I'm involved with art, I feel like I've gone somewhere else. I like to use my talent with art to escape from the real world and get lost in another. That's the fun thing about art; with it you can create a whole different world, and claim it as your own.

The best times to escape from the real world to fantasy land are when bad things are going on and when I'm upset or when I'm really happy about something. When I feel either of these, I draw till I've calmed down.

My artistic needs are sometimes hard for me to control. I draw on anything with any colored ink that I have. Sometimes I draw when I shouldn't. Drawing is irresistible sometimes, so I draw until my need to draw is gone.

My favorite thing about art is that I can draw anything I want and use it as my own code for something so that nobody understands why I drew a particular thing. With art I can be as secretive as I want to be, and even have my own secrets drawn out without anyone knowing.

There are many reasons to love art, and that's another thing I love about it: its many reasons to be loved.

Monica Lazo, Grade 8
Corpus Christi School, CA

My Way of Life

Click click go the bottoms of my banana yellow shoes. Walking through the jungle grass, the sprinkle of dew sprays lightly on my kneecaps. My purple frostbitten fingers are the only things I can see. Frozen right through the core of my bones, yet I continue to move forward with exhilaration and determination kindling the fire within my heart. Startling my eyes is a soccer ball that I move down field anticipating many screams and cheers.

Not just a game, it's a way of life, a passion, a dream. I look forward to the early mornings, the desert sun, and new challenges, mainly because I know that nothing feels better than to run on a field. I put my heart and soul into every moment, pushing and shoving, and to say I gave it my all. Sometimes I do well, and other times not so well. I am not a player but an artist.

Play with passion. I have a dream to make it big. There may be ups and downs on this bumpy roller coaster ride but I know I will do anything to make my dream become a reality. No matter what your dream is, you can't get far if you don't take the next step to success. So take that step, speak with your last breath, work even though there is nothing left, and open your eyes to a life of success.

Eleni Kutay, Grade 7
Placerita Jr High School, CA

Life's Values

As life goes on, I wonder more and more what is most important me. Most things have some meaning, but few are truly important. In my eyes, some of the only values that have true importance are education, family, and enjoying life.

Education is important to me, as it is the foundation of a successful life, and should be treated with seriousness. Education will let me, or anyone else for that matter; pave the way to a successful and enjoyable career. This will allow me to make a living and support a family when I become an adult.

Next, family is important to me because it is an outlet of love and care. My family encourages me to do my best, and provides me a kind and safe environment. They always encourage to do the best I can and will guide me on the way to a successful career. They have always been kind in the things they ask me to do and I hope they are there for me for a very long time.

Finally, in my thoughts of important values, is just sitting back and enjoying life every once in a while. Relaxing after a day of hard work takes my mind off day-to-day stress allowing me to keep doing my best. Also, spending money here and there for enjoyment is no sin either. As my parents say "life is short, so enjoy it while you still can!"

So in conclusion, much of life's values are meaningful, but only some like education, family, and enjoying life are truly important to me. Values like this will help you achieve your dreams and help you deal with life's challenges.

Isaac Kassim, Grade 8
Zia Middle School, NM

My Other Half

There are a million things I could write about, but I will write about my favorite, my twin. I love my twin, even though she says I don't show it. She is there when I need her and when I don't. When I want something really bad she gives it to me even if it means sacrificing something she wants. This may sound lovey-dovey, but my twin is my precious gift from heaven God has granted to me, and I have to cherish her. She sticks up for me and gets me out of trouble, even if it means she gets the blame. The saddest part about this is that I never tell her how much she means to me, when clearly she shows me how much she loves me every day.

My twin is loving, kind, responsible, and loyal. I am very glad to be able to tell you about her. My twin says I light up her life, and that I'm very special to her. Most people say we are alike, but we aren't, because she's noble, self-sacrificing and sweet, and I am selfish. She hates when we fight, and she gets sad if we don't make up.

I love her and I always will, because even though she doesn't know it, she lights up my life.

Leticia Diaz, Grade 8
Our Lady of the Rosary School, CA

My Passion

Music is something beautiful and very strong. Why you ask? Because music can represent many things. It can represent your state of mind, your feelings, or maybe how you feel about someone. I say music represents everything in life as we all know it. I even have a little saying, "Music is beautiful, music is life, just don't abuse it, cause it's a terrible sight." Which means that you can express yourself through music, but I just don't misuse it because it can affect the way people look at you.

Songs, sounds, the things you hear can be made into any kind of rhythm. Everyone says (almost everyone) that I have a talent when it comes to music. I can be able to compose good songs on a computer program called Garage Band. And I am a quick learner when I try to play any instrument, but so far I know how to play only one instrument, guitar.

I know at least a few songs on my guitar, but I learn very quickly. But besides me playing the guitar, every word that I said in this story is true. Songs, music, and putting songs together is mostly what I do best. I am also thinking of having a career as a musician or anything that can involve music as the main subject of the job. If anyone has a love for music like I do then they should play the instrument that they like. Music is my passion.

Oswaldo Covarrubias, Grade 8
Rio Bravo Middle School, TX

My Tae Kwon Do Life

If you are in the seventh grade and start Tae Kwon Do, it's going to be a little hard. Since everyone is ahead of you, you might want to speed up the belt process by working harder, because I am only a yellow tip (belt) even though I'm thirteen.

However, I've learned quite a bit. If you don't already know Tae Kwon Do, the belts are a system of their own, with my belt being the second lowest, so you have to earn your respect. I can still remember my first belt test as if it was two months ago.

First in a belt test you usually have to show off your kicks by doing different drills and routines. Then, we show our motion blocks, which are all 5 blocks in one move.

Then, forms. Forms are routines of kicks, punches and blocks. Usually twenty or more steps long.

Then we do…board breaking. When I broke my first board, it was about one inch thick cedar, and I figured out I had more power than I thought!

Board breaking is probably one of the very few fun parts of a belt test.

For those who are thinking of learning Tae Kwon Do, stick with it, and work hard.

Aaron Hernandez, Grade 7
St Elizabeth Ann Seton School, TX

Sports

Ahh…Sports, my favorite thing to do in the summer…of course in school, too. Do you like to play sports too…?

One day I made it to All-Stars in baseball, and we had a tournament in Big Lake, Texas. It was a long hot day. Then at night we were playing for the ship (championship). We had to play Ozona in the rain. It was cold and the grass was slippery.

At the time I was playing right field. The guy that was up to bat was a good home run hitter. My heart was pumping as well as my teammates' hearts. The first pitch came and…"SMACK" he hit the ball straight to left field. I ran up to it, and then the unthinkable happened. I had slipped and fell on my back. Then as I lay there, everybody starts to cheer and I wondered why. I sat up, looked in my glove, and smiled. I had caught the ball, that moment I felt like a super hero. At first I thought I missed it. In the end I acted like I was really happy, but I was super excited. I didn't get the golden glove like I had hoped, but I got a second medal for playing well. That was the last All-Star game I played in. After that I went home with a big smile on my face, and I left the field with the game ball.

Geovanna Carrasco, Grade 8
Reagan County Middle School, TX

Alaska: The Best Place in the World to Vacation!

Alaska is the best place to vacation because of its natural beauty and wildlife. In Alaska, you can see many varieties of wild animals in their habitats. You can see all sorts of mountains, glaciers, and forests beyond your front porch. In Alaska, the weather is also great.

You can go hiking out in the woods and see a lot of animals in their natural habitats. You can see squirrels, moose, black bears, deer, birds, and many other animals. You can get really close to the animals without getting hurt as long as you don't scare them, make them mad, or get close to their babies.

If you go up towards Tok (in northern Alaska), on the way you can see beautiful glaciers, mountains, forests, and even some minor volcanoes. On both sides of the road is a gorgeous forest full of wildlife! There are rivers formed from melting glaciers. The water is a pretty turquoise color!

The weather in Alaska is gorgeous. The temperature in the winter can get down to -30F, but if you are properly dressed it can be fun playing in four feet of snow. In the summer, it can get up to about 80F. This feels really good and is also warm enough to go swimming in a pool with a couple of your friends.

Remember, if you have a choice to vacation anywhere in the world, choose the best and only the best, Alaska. Alaska is the final frontier where everything is great.

Demetri Haskell, Grade 8
Holliday Middle School, TX

Me and My Sister

Hi, my name is Gilbert Joe II, and I am going to tell you my favorite thing to do. I like to play with my baby sister. Her name is Esperanza. She is my youngest sister. She is fun to be with. I also have another brother and sister, but I am not naming them in the story. Esperanza was born on February 26, 2008, three days before my birthday. I was the first to carry her around the house.

The first thing we do is walk up the hill at our ranch to look around places. Next thing we like to do is talk to each other and I teach her new things when I am with her. Third thing I love to do is play with her anywhere we go. Last thing I do with my sister is to kick back with her and watch TV. This is what we like to do when I watch her.

So these are my favorite things to do with my sister Esperanza. I am the oldest in my family and it is sometimes hard being a role model, but, I love my sister so much that I won't let anything happen to her. She is 1 and a half years old and she is my best friend. This is my story about us.

Gilbert Joe II, Grade 7
Pine Hill Schools, NM

New Mexico the Beautiful

New Mexico is beautiful in every way you look at it. Its Watermelon Mountains glisten in the sunlight and the mightily flowing river runs through the center of the humble town of Corrales. The town so eloquent and peaceful, it remains the highlight of Albuquerque. You can spend your afternoon at the riverside watching the cottonwoods sway back and forth to the rhythms of the howling wind. New Mexico, both gorgeous and ever peaceful, is my home town and will always be.

Capture and visualize in your mind an orange flickered sunset with splashes of pink, and red. An incredible brightly glowing moon, resolute and patiently waiting for you to take it home and make it yours. A crystal clear creek in the mountains filled with rainbow trout. Several trees and elegant flowers rest and grow just beside the stream where a picnic can be held.

Hundreds and thousands of acres across the nation are often unnoticed, but New Mexico is usually one of those amazing states that is seen for its elegance and beauty, and will always be.

Savonn Currence, Grade 8
St Thomas Aquinas School, NM

Lost Leg

I will never forget this day or forgive my brother for what he did. He changed my life. This memory haunts me. It will never erase!

The day was hot, and it was summer time. I went to feed my hamster, Sally. I went to her cage and saw she wasn't there. I knew right away my sister had her. I ran to her room as fast as I could. I saw she had something in her hand and, so I snatched it from her.

My sister was angry, and I am telling you, she was angry. When I looked at my hand it wasn't Sally. It was her Barbie doll. She hit me hard on my head, and yelled "Why did you do that for? You'd better get out before I hit you again and it won't be pretty, trust me!"

I knew then my brother probably had Sally. I looked everywhere and then I heard him, "Wee! Let's do that again! Why won't it go, stupid car why won't you drive." I ran outside and took the car away from him.

I looked at him then down at the car and right in the middle was Sally. She looked at me with pain so I took her out and ran inside. I found my parents and told them what my little brother had done. My parents were angry, and worried about Sally.

They took Sally, to help her stop her bleeding. Then I took her back to her cage. I put her back and I was watching her. I saw she was limping. When I looked closer I gasped. She had lost her leg! My heart was broken, I knew from that day on I would never forgive my brother for what he had done to Sally!

Chris Holsapple, Grade 7
Santa Teresa Middle School, NM

America

I love America because they have safe jobs that don't need to be closed down because of extortion. There is a lot of food you can eat so you don't have to starve to death. I also appreciate the doctors because they can help you if you are sick or injured.

One of the things I like about America is that you have a little job and you don't have to worry about people coming to hurt you. In other places this is why a lot of people close their business down and don't have any money. Here the jobs are safe and pay you well to feed your family and yourself.

The second thing is that you have any money you can get help from the government. In other countries like Africa, the people starve to death. The babies and children are skinny and have diseases because they can't afford medical help, or medicine.

The third thing I really appreciate are the doctors and hospitals. Some people in the U.S. don't like shots but the kids in Africa that really need them. But they don't have all this stuff that cures us and medicine that prevents us from getting sick. So I think we should really be thankful for the help we get.

All of these reasons are why I love America. It is safe, we have freedom, and we don't have to worry of getting hurt, or starve to death because thanks to all of the help we have here, the word "danger" doesn't exist. This is America.

Jennifer Campos, Grade 7
Santa Teresa Middle School, NM

The Joys of Family Holidays

On my dad's side of my family there are eight brothers and sisters, so obviously I have many cousins. My grandparents own a family farm in Missouri and we visit them about twice a year. Every year we go to meet all of our family for Thanksgiving and the 4th of July. Thanksgiving is always fun because it's a holiday that is all about eating! There is the original farmhouse, the bunk house, and the new farmhouse. It's always fun to visit for the major holidays when all the family is there because the girl cousins all get to stay in the original farmhouse, and my Aunt Pat always brings junk-food and sodas for us! Even though I enjoy Thanksgiving, the 4th of July is even more fun! Since we have a farm with many acres in the country, we can set off our own fireworks! We also have this big cork table with a lot of holes in it, and we put bottle rockets in all the holes then we set it off as the Grand Finale! Last 4th of July it went off for about ten minutes! One time though, my little cousin John-John got hit by a bottle rocket, but he was fine in the end. All of these are great traditions and memories that I hope I never forget. They are definitely my favorite times of year.

Amelia Arth, Grade 7
St Elizabeth Ann Seton School, TX

That Was Scary!

One of the scariest moments in my life is when 9/11 happened. My mom was in New York City when this happened. I remember being in school and I was in kindergarten. I did not know what was happening, but all I know was something was wrong. I did not know that it was a terrorist attack on the World Trade Center. It was early in the morning when my dad came to pick me and my brother up from school. He told us that there has been a terrorist attack on the World Trade Center. We were driving home when we called our mom to see if she was okay. She ended up being just fine and came home in a couple of days after the attack.

I had figured out that us, the people, are not as safe as we think. We can still be attacked just like every other nation in the world. We have to fight for our freedom and we can't just sit around. Many men and women are dying for our country. We cannot let them die in vain.

Chris Sarrat, Grade 8
St Elizabeth Ann Seton School, TX

Choices

Life is full of decisions that are good or bad. Two paths are drawn when you get at an age where your choices start to take a huge toll in your life. One leads to success and enlightenment, and the other to death and destruction to the mind and soul.

The road to destruction is the road best not taken. Walking down this path will lead to depression, fear, and even death. Violence is also a part of the road to destruction. Violence leads to crime, crime leads to punishment and eventually death. Eventually you'll meet your demons and they will be the death of you.

The road to enlightenment is the path that should be taken but is skipped more than it should. Taking this path will grant you many things with perseverance. If you try hard enough anything is possible. Going down this path you will even meet true love.

In conclusion life is teeming with choices that shape up your life. Some of these choices have consequences, because life is not an easy thing to go through.

Jacob Phetteplace, Grade 8
Zia Middle School, NM

Best Friends

I've heard, "Friends comfort you when you cry, but best friends already have the shovel to bury the person who made you cry." No one literally has a shovel to bury someone, but she does talk to the person and sees if she will talk to you and work things out. Everyone wants a friend, but everyone needs a best friend to depend on. A best friend is one who will stick with you even when you are in trouble. She praises you when you are right and encourages you to do right when you are wrong. A best friend always tells you the truth.

Imagine the world with no friends. A best friend is one of the simple ways of making it through life safely and happy. What would we do without friends? This world would be a very troubled and unhappy place. When you have a best friend she will always listen to you and help you.

It makes a difference on who your best friend is though. You have got to chose wisely because if you are hanging out with the wrong type, you will get hurt or you might turn around and hurt someone else because of what you are learning as you hang out with those people.

A best friend is like the color of your world. Without colors, everything is boring and sad looking. That is why God made friends.

Emily Capaul, Grade 8
Faith Christian Jr/Sr High School, CA

Full House

Normally, a house would hold your immediate family: a mom, a dad, a little sister, and an older brother, sometimes even a dog. But my house is different. I live with fifteen other people, all family. It can be hectic here, but that's why I love it. It's my home!

I live with my mom, my dad, my brother, three aunties, an uncle, seven cousins, and my grandma. Growing up in a huge home like mine is never boring. There is always someone to talk to or play with. And I love how it feels to come home from school to the familiarity of all the noises and people. Everything just makes me feel safe.

But there are a few downsides. Like most people, I like to sleep in on weekends, but sometimes they wake up too early, and I hear talking, and footsteps running through the hallway. Other times, I just want to be alone. But someone always has to ask me something or wants to play, so I lock myself in my bedroom. But what bothers me the most is that we can be WAY too loud!

But with everything that's wrong, sometime good comes along with it. Sure, it annoys me a bit, but I've learned to cope with it. Having so many people around is great because some of the people I care about the most are always near.

I live in a house full of people I love, and it's the best feeling ever!

Samantha Geronimo, Grade 7
Corpus Christi School, CA

Heroes

Growing up, every kid has an idol. One that they listen to and try to follow in their footsteps. These people, these idols, are our heroes. They may sometimes disappoint us, but they will always remain in our hearts. My hero is none other than the amazing, kindhearted man known as Ralph Lauren.

Ralph Lauren is one of the most famous fashion designers in the world! And the most amazing part is that he started from almost nothing. He grew up in a family that was just barely sufficient, his dad was rarely home so he and his brothers were raised by his mother and lacked many things that most kids were able to have. Lauren didn't even finish college! Even though so many things were depriving him of becoming successful, he was still able to defeat the odds and fulfill his lifelong dream of becoming a famous designer.

Ralph Lauren is, for a fact, one of the most inspirational people alive. Even if you have never heard of him, he might have affected you. Have you ever needed to wear something semiformal or just nice for a restaurant, and you didn't want to wear a button down shirt? Chances are, you ended up wearing a polo, which was created by none other than Ralph Lauren. Another great thing about him is that he donates thousands of dollars every year to different charities! I dream of one day becoming as amazing as Ralph Lauren.

Alexandra Luna, Grade 8
St Elizabeth Ann Seton School, TX

The Real Me

When you go to school or with your friends, are you being yourself or are you being who your friends think you are? I want to answer yes; however, there isn't anything different from me to the next girl.

I might have all the clothes in the world, all the shoes, and all the friends but what is the point if they don't reflect the real me. My friends see me as shy and reserved, however this is not the real me not even close. I lead them to believe this because I'm always at my desk quiet and ready to work. At lunch, I don't go crazy and I hardly talk. The more I realize who I really am the more I want to be the real me. I don't just want to be another face in a crowd I want to stand out or at least be true to myself.

I want to be me, a wild, energetic, fun loving, and talkative girl. Little by little, I started to let myself out. "Sorry Angeline and Celeste!!!" but instead of reacting the way I thought they would (meanly) they acted just as they always had. They are really good friends. Now I can truly be myself and not worry about anything. I really hope I don't forget this; it is an important thing to me. For all of you who know me PLEASE don't let me forget.

Lynette Rodriguez, Grade 8
Zia Middle School, NM

5,728 Miles Isn't So Far Away

"Fao, I don't know what I'm going to do. He was so mad at me, he didn't even say goodbye!" I wailed, tears slipping down my face, as I remembered how my father had yelled at me. Then he hung up the phone without even saying goodbye.

"Nandra," Fao said using the nickname he'd made up for me. "Nandra, don't worry about him. He's just annoyed because his own personal life is going wrong, so he's taking it out on you. Just think, outside of your country in a small town called Marsala in Sicily, Italy, there is a boy who loves you more than you could ever dream possible. Hun, that boy is me," he finished. Even though we were on the phone, I could tell he was smiling.

That is why Fao is my best friend. He is always ready to support me and save the day. I've only known him for six months, but as far as I'm concerned, I grew up with him.

Some might ask, "But if he lives in Italy, how do you keep in touch with him?" We may be 5,728 miles apart, but that doesn't make any difference to us. Day or night, if I need him, he's there. If he needs me, I'm there.

We may be in different countries, but that doesn't change how much love we have for each other. You know what they say, 'Distance makes the heart grow fonder.' Fao and I are living and breathing proof.

Alexandra Burns, Grade 8
Piner Middle School, TX

The Fuzziest Easter Present

One warm day, three days before Easter, my mom came home from work. She waited outside in the car while my brother ran outside to her. She told him to go get me from inside. He came inside quickly and told me to come out. I walked outside lazily, thinking I would have to carry in some groceries, or something. My mom told me to come around the passenger's seat. I walked over and opened the door. She looked up from her phone and told me to look at the seat. "You got me a scarf!?" I exclaimed. Mom looked at me like I was crazy, "Poke it," she said. All I did was stare at the fuzzy bundle on the passenger's seat. I slowly moved my hand and poked the little fuzz ball. It squirmed slightly, so I poked it again. After a few seconds of moving and squirming a small head popped up. This made me jump a bit. I looked at my mom and she smiled. "A puppy!" I said. "Can we keep it?" my brother asked. "Well of course, silly," Mom said.

As we walked inside, my mom holding the puppy, my grandma saw us and walked over. "How cute!" Grandma said. My grandpa came over from his chair. "Oh, no, another dog." We named the dog Abby, she is totally crazy. Abby is the fuzziest Easter present.

Courtney McDonald, Grade 7
St Elizabeth Ann Seton School, TX

The Fantastic Woman Rosa Parks

I think Rosa Parks is a fantastic role model for us to follow because she stood up for what she believed in and didn't back down. Rosa was an African American civil rights activist and the United States Congress calls her the, "Mother of the Modern-Day Civil Rights Movement." During Rosa's time, certain seats were reserved for white people, and black people had to either move or leave the bus if they weren't enough seats for white people. On December 1, 1955, in Montgomery, Alabama, the bus driver James Blake ordered that Rosa parks give up her seat for a white passenger. When Rosa refused, James called the police. When many people questioned why Rosa didn't give up her seat, she replied, "I would have to know for once and for all what rights I had as a human being and a citizen." Rosa was arrested and fined for not following the rules and codes. She and her husband lost their jobs and faced punishment and fines. Rosa later received many awards, like the Presidential Freedom Medal, The Martin Luther King Jr. Award, and the International Freedom Festival Award. She also published books, had streets named after her, and had a Super Bowl played in her honor. I think Rosa Parks had courage above what any of us could ever imagine. We need to be more like Rosa in our everyday battle against things that go against what we believe in, for example the battle for the sanctity of life.

Alexis Sanchez, Grade 8
St Thomas Aquinas School, NM

Why I Like Hamburgers

Hamburgers are juicy and tasty. They're good grilled or pan-broiled. You could make hamburgers in less than 30 minutes. Just grab ground beef, season it, make the ground beef into thick patties, and cook! Let the smell of the smoke drift you away into the heavens.

My favorite kind of hamburger is a double cheeseburger plain. I don't like lettuce, onions, tomatoes, or pickles. They're just gross. I like my burger with just the meat, melted cheese, and a crunchy bun. I usually help my mom make them. She always says I should try it with all the fixings. I think she wants me to eat much healthier.

There are many types of burgers. My favorite spot for a burger is Joe's Cable Car in San Francisco. They have an extensive menu of burgers, all gourmet delights. My favorite is the Fresh Ground Beefsteak, which is the most popular.

When you order at Joe's, you can choose among a four-ounce, six-ounce, or eight-ounce burger. They will cook it just the way you like it: rare, medium rare, medium, medium well, or well done. You can also choose your cheese from their abundant varieties. I like American cheese because it has no sharp taste or odor. Cheese, mustard, or ketchup should never cover the flavor of the meat, in my opinion.

Forget apples — if I could have my way, I'd eat a burger every day! I don't think it would keep the doctor away, but I would be a very happy boy.

Christian Rose, Grade 8
Corpus Christi School, CA

An Emotional Day

My dad was wonderful and mysterious. Also there might be something you don't understand, so I will try my best to make it be neat.

My dad was sick in the beginning of 2004. With a sickness called pneumonia. He had to be in the hospital for quite a while. After that, the doctors said he was supposed to go through surgery. We found out that he was cut from his belly button on down his leg to his foot.

When we arrived at home he looked strange. So one day he was having this strange and quick heart attack. The ambulance drove him to the hospital and the nurses couldn't find what was wrong with him, so they drove him to Lubbock. When we arrived at Lubbock we were at the Covenant Hospital. They took him to a room called the ICU. The doctors said that he was too sick to go home, also his heart was doing bad. The doctors told my mom and my brother to come in the room, because he was throwing up blood. The doctors tried to do something to stop it, and they couldn't. So at 4:00 a.m., the doctors asked my mom if they could take him off of Life support, she said, "he wouldn't want a life on a machine." So that is the story of a sad and emotional day.

Susie Neufeld, Grade 7
Seminole Jr High School, TX

Death

Death has a tendency to change people for better or worse. It can bring out the good memories after someone dies, sometimes we remember the worst. When someone dies, we remember how they die. How they die can affect and change the way we continue to remember them. When Officer Joe Harris died, over the summer, it was a very sad time for a lot of people, especially at my school. Once a week he used to come and teach the 7th and 8th grades. He shared much more than safety with us he shared his life with us. When he died he died he gave his life to save his partner. He died a hero. When we hear his name now and in the future, we should remember him for his patriotic and heroic acts and what he stood for. He was a man who would give his life for his country and stand up for his fellow man. When he goes in the history textbook of our great state of New Mexico just as others have. He will be remembered for his love of God, country and family. I don't know if everyone will feel the same as me but I know when I read the book, or the magazine article, I will remember him as a hero.

Ambrose Kupfer, Grade 8
St Thomas Aquinas School, NM

Benefits from Household Chores

Children learn responsibility and the value of work by being required to do household chores, such as making beds, washing dishes, and taking care of pets. It helps them be more responsible, gets them used to working, and parents get more respect.

Doing chores can help children learn a lot of responsibility. It helps get them ready for when they move into their own house. I sure don't want to live in a house where the dishes aren't clean and the beds aren't made. Also, Mom isn't always going to come and clean your house for you, so it's a good idea to learn how to be responsible while young.

It can also get children used to the idea of working. You're going to need a job for money, so it's a good idea to start getting used to being told what to do. You will also become more organized because you're used to everything being neat.

Parents also benefit from children doing chores. They can earn more respect from their children. They will also listen more. And, if the children do what they are supposed to do, the parents can trust them more to do many things.

In conclusion, children learn responsibility and the value of work by doing household chores. With every chore they do, the children are becoming more responsible. They are learning about the value of work, and the parents are earning a great amount of respect. These are all important things to have in life.

Tara Henderson, Grade 8
Holliday Middle School, TX

Being a Big Sister

Sometimes when you least expect something to happen, a couple of minutes or days later that thing happens. Most of the time you may not know how to react. In this case it's supposed to be good.

"Merry Christmas!" my mom and dad exclaimed as they both handed my sister Stephanie and I cards. I was hoping there was money in it, but once I opened it, there was a whole other surprise. "I'm going to be a big sister! Agh!" I yelled joyously. "I can't believe it. Finally, I've been waiting ten years for this!"

As the months went by, my mom's stomach grew bigger and bigger. I got to feel things that were so unreal. I was so amazed by how fast babies grow in just nine months. We found out he was a boy, so we named him Adriano Jose after a bull rider, but we call him A.J. for short.

One night when I was asleep, I was awakened by my dad who yelled "Wake up. Your mom is having the baby!" We were packed and off to the hospital. It was a long wait for him to get here, but at 1:13 p.m. he was born. "Wow!" There he was six pounds eleven ounces. "This is the beginning of a new life."

Happiness comes in many different ways no matter what it is. This has changed my life completely. I feel much happier with him in my life. He is a character.

Leanna Torres, Grade 8
Reagan County Middle School, TX

My Gift

In our generation many people have a common bond of having food allergies. When people have these food allergies they feel that it makes them less of a person, but it really makes them stronger, and more unique than everyone else. It makes people stronger because they have to deal with things that other people would never even think of having to deal with. This includes being excluded from things, being made fun of, and not being accepted by other people. Dealing with these things helps you to be a better person, and helps you grow into someone beautiful.

I have had my share of these experiences. I am allergic to all dairy and egg products. I have been made fun of by people, but I have also met people who will stand up for me, and will not let anything bad happen to me. I also have been excluded from things such as dances and parties. When kids bring in cupcakes for their birthday, I am usually the only one there not eating. When these things happen it makes you want to cry, or crawl up in a shell and go home. But then you realize that you have to be strong and help yourself. A lot of people say, "Why me God? Why did you pick me out of all people to have food allergies?" And I say why not me?

Erin Hoffman, Grade 8
St Elizabeth Ann Seton School, TX

My Favorite Grandma

My favorite grandma has left us. She was the sunshine in my day. My brother couldn't figure out what happened. My grandma lived in Hawaii. I didn't see her often, once or twice a year. We didn't go often because of school. I didn't want to take time off because I didn't want bad grades, so summer was all.

She was the only family left on my dad's side. My dad was adopted. In 2003 my papa died. My dad left 3 days before to Hawaii for his funeral. It turns out that he died of heart failure from diabetes. My grandma was lonely so 6 months later she got a Maltese named RJ.

She died three and a half years ago. In late May 2006 she found out that she had colon cancer. She went on dialysis, after a while she didn't want to anymore because she had to go to the emergency room four times. She stopped in July. I went to the hospital where she was. My brother visited. We brought him home. I wanted to stay at the hospital. At 12:30 p.m. on July 24th she died. That was the only time I've ever seen my dad cry.

She was my favorite nana, but God wanted her and she left us for a while. Now we're a broken chain, but piece by piece we will join until we're together again. If my tears could build a stairwell I would walk to Heaven and bring her back again.

Sami Crozier, Grade 8
Thora B Gardiner Middle School, OR

A Journey to a Dog

My family relocated from Ohio to Texas three years ago. My dad had promised that after we moved we could finally get a dog. We bought two puppies from a rescue shelter. I named them Rocco and Bella. They were brother and sister and had been found barely alive under a decaying porch. They were part poodle and Chihuahua, and very cute. We noticed that they both had some spots on their body without fur. We figured it was a lack of care; however everyone in our family soon began getting spots and itching. My mom called the shelter and the lady there said it was probably ringworm from living outside. She told us to bring them back and she would get them well and then give them back to us. She had them for a week. We called every day to see how they were doing. One day she didn't return our call. We received an e-mail telling us that Rocco and Bella had passed away. We were so sad. I kept their pictures hanging on my wall for months. A year later, on Super Bowl Sunday, we drove out to a Waffle House in a country town to meet a breeder and bought a toy poodle. When we took her home, my dad thought she looked like a wet rat; but I was so happy because I knew she would be mine forever. Bella Boo number two still sleeps with me every night and is my special pet.

Maryssa Buffano, Grade 7
St Elizabeth Ann Seton School, TX

Trip to California

After I was born, we moved to California. On the trip to California, we had to pass through several other states. We passed through New Mexico and there were a bunch of different gangs with guns along the walls and several different types of weapons on their front porches to use in a gang fight. My brother started crying because one of the gang members threw a rock into our back window. I was crying because I was just a little baby and I did not know what was happening to my family.

After finishing our trip through New Mexico, we had to travel through Arizona. Arizona was nicknamed the "Journey of Heat" by my dad. We were traveling through the Arizona desert when we ran out of gas. Lucky for us, there was a town not too far away. I was crying because I was hungry and we did not have any water for my baby formula.

We went into the town and my dad went into the store while we sat outside. When he came out with water, my brother was not there. My dad asked my mom where he went and she said, "He asked to run to the end of the street and back." My dad got us into the car while my mom made some formula for me. My brother was out of breath and I was really tired.

Jesse Vazquez, Grade 8
Long Valley Charter School, CA

Assassin

I believe Lee Harvey Oswald assassinated President Kennedy and police officer J.D. Tippit. I believe that he shot Kennedy because, firstly, the shots came from the spot where he worked. Also, police found a high-powered rifle and three empty cartridge cases near where he worked. Oswald was in possession of the rifle, and had his fingerprints on it. Oswald had also purchased it under a false name. Oswald also shot police office J.D. Tippit, with more than ten horrified witnesses watching, showing that he was prone to bursts of extreme violence.

I believe the assassination was not a conspiracy, for if you looked at Lee Harvey Oswald's childhood, you will observe that he resented working with others, so as such, he was an outcast. Also, he despised authority or leadership of any kind, showing he probably would not be part of a mob. Oswald also disliked democracy, and favored Marxism, or communism. Some people suggest that Oswald worked for Russia, for he lived some of his life there, but I disagree, for like I said before, he resented leadership. Oswald also did not interact a lot with the Russians. I believe President John Fitzgerald Kennedy's assassin was Lee Harvey Oswald, and he acted alone.

Conner Prachyl, Grade 8
St Elizabeth Ann Seton School, TX

Baseball Techniques

Baseball is a very complex sport that is difficult to master. But several players have used their abilities to go professional. This includes batting, base running, and fielding.

First of all, batting is very complicated. You have to have a stance about a little farther apart than your shoulders. Have the bat up on your shoulder, pointing toward the sky. The most important part about batting, I think is to watch the pitcher release the ball from his hand and follow it all the way to where it hits the bat.

Base running is a mind game. You have to be smart and know what signs that the pitcher gives you to steal the base. If the pitcher doesn't give you a second look when he should and you have a good lead, you should steal the base right as he starts his motion of throwing the ball.

Finally, the most important part of playing baseball is fielding. You have to know what is going on at all times. You have to know where to throw the ball if it is hit to you. To field a ground ball, you have to get in front of it and bend your knees so when the ball hits your glove, you can trap it with your other hand and make a throw to the base.

By following these three things, one can become a professional baseball player.

Geoffrey Luoma, Grade 8
St Michael's Episcopal Day School, CA

The Tornado

My name is James and I was born in Little Rock, Arkansas. In May of 2000, I was just hanging out at the house when the TV said something that made my parents *flip out!* A tornado was coming our way. It was about 10 miles long, as a crow flies. Come on! I was four, I didn't know what the heck was going on. Then my mom started to pack a quick diaper bag for my baby brother. Within seconds the blue sky became a deep gray. Then the power went out and we were unable to see the warnings on TV. The rain was coming down hard and side ways. Mom tried to get us to the storm cellar; however, the tornado came too fast to get there. As we stepped on our porch the lawn furniture blew off the deck never to be seen again. My dad pulled us from the doorway and we huddled on the living room floor covering our heads. Mom began to cry, she thought we were going to die. Forty-five seconds later, we heard a *smash* and a *Crack!* Stunned by the sound, my eyes were closed. I slowly opened them only to find a nightmare. Some how I knew it was over when the sound was gone. Outside stop signs were bent to the ground. The cotton gin was destroyed… all gone, our tree destroyed completely. I am no longer four now, but I still remember that devastating day.

James Bruce, Grade 7
Long Valley Charter School, CA

My Grandma

My grandma is really special to me I remember when I was little she used to take care of me. When she stayed with us we would sleep together. We used to call each other comadres. Also we would play tea party, just me and her.

One week she stayed with us but she was getting old I could see it, and I was getting bigger. I took her to the restroom because she couldn't walk that much. I helped my mom take care of her like showering my grandma and making food for her. It was fun. We laughed a lot.

One week later when she left, my aunt called and said my grandma was in the hospital. My father was upset because that was his mother so we all went to the hospital. I was upset too I wanted to cry.

When we got here the doctors said she has a blood clot in her brain. Then my mom, dad, and me went inside to see her. I remember that she looked pale and really sick. I tried talking to her because the doctors said she could hear, although she was asleep.

The last words I said to her was "I love you with all my heart, grandma." I remember she moved her hand. Each day I miss her more and more. Now we visit her in her grave to remember my grandma. "I miss you Grandma."

Melissa Valle, Grade 8
Rio Bravo Middle School, TX

Who I Look Up To

Throughout my life there are a lot of people who walk in and out of it, but the people that really love me and care about me are the ones that stay in my heart and I appreciate the most.

In my family, there was a person that I really admire a lot. She was funny, kind, happy, hard worker, and she cared about others. Her name is Valeria and she is my sister.

Valeria was diagnosed with cancer when she was 15. When the doctor told us, my family and I, what she had, it was a total shock. All of us couldn't believe it, but Valeria always had a positive attitude.

Valeria spent almost two years in the hospital, and we could take her out and go home whenever the doctor said we could, but almost every time we took her home she would get very sick and we would have to take her back to the hospital.

In the hospitals people suffer a lot. It is very hard to be inside a hospital with a disease, taking a lot of medicines. Valeria suffered all that, but she was always smiling and saying that she was fine and she would be better after she take a nap and eat better. She would always say that because didn't want anyone to be worried or sad.

Valeria passed away when she was 17. She was really strong to support that for two years, that's why I look up to her a lot.

Susana Muniz, Grade 8
Rio Bravo Middle School, TX

Visiting Home

Today is the day I visit my old house back in Chapin, S.C. When we moved, I was very attached to my old house. It was more than just a house. It was my childhood, my memories, my home.

"Yay!" I yelled as we came to a stop in the driveway. I looked up to see a tan house. I was a little upset to see all the new things like the new color of the house, the mistreatment of the flowers and bushes, and the hideous pool that was once beautiful. I walked straight over to the green, murky pool. I remember all the memories that we left, as a tear rolled down my cheek. The new owner was a slob.

I then walked over to Ginger's grave. Ginger was our two year old, expensive puppy who was killed by a car. I missed her. I looked everywhere but could not find the grave. I then realized it had been blown over. As the tears coursed down my cheek, my dad walked over and said, "I'm so sorry, Elizabeth."

As we drove off, I sat in the back seat crying. I will miss everything that was once ours in that house. That day my life was crushed.

Elizabeth Gillespie, Grade 7
Seminole Jr High School, TX

Megan Edwards

Megan Edwards has had an interesting life. When she was 8 years old, her life revolved around skating. Megan also has a twin sister, her name is Mandy.

Megan started skating because her dad decided she and Mandy needed something to keep active. After they started skating, they went to the World Championships in Denver. That was when Megan and Mandy decided that was what they wanted to do.

Megan's first skating competition was when she was 8 or 9. She competed for 13 years. In the 13 years that she competed, she had 9 different private coaches. When Megan and Mandy were 12, they lived with their coach and family so they could continue to train after their parents moved.

Megan and Mandy once competed against each other. Megan beat Mandy and they did not talk for a week. When Megan was at the pre-juvenile level, she was the regional champion. Even though she stopped competing, Megan completed her testing and reached gold level in Moves in the Field and Free Skate. Megan is now a 2nd level certified rated coach in Moves in the Field and free Skate.

Megan choreographs all of the skating teams programs and teaches spins. Mandy is the jump coach and helps perfect programs. The skaters have learned over the years that Megan is most happy when she has her coffee and Mandy is most happy when we work hard.

Paige Mascarenas, Grade 7
St Thomas Aquinas School, NM

World of Memories

Everyone has their own treasures. For me personally it holds everything I need to get through the years with. It's where I'll find safety from arriving storms and I'll find joy. Every special moment is captured. It's overflowed with pictures of cheerful times; my photo album.

The world of memories lays just ahead when I open it. That's where I fall into memory land. The land that holds memories of me as a child throughout my lifetime. Every page holds something. Events that'll be there whenever I open it. As I look through my photo album, there are pictures of events that can never be replaced. The pages pull me in and I rediscover events. Even when I forget those events, there will always be my photo album. As I look through the album, I see relatives that passed away. It brought tears of sorrow to my eyes. Even if it's overflowing with cheerful times, there's always some pictures that can bring tears. That's my treasure, the place where I get pulled in and rediscover life.

When I see my photo album I'll get flashes of my life. That's where I'll find happiness and sometimes even sadness. I can open it and I'll be away from danger, I'll be safe from anything. My treasure is always the place I can remember the good times and even the bad times in life. The photo album is that place.

Tracy Khang, Grade 8
Thora B Gardiner Middle School, OR

President Kennedy Case

There are many things that most people know about the John F. Kennedy assassination, but there are also details that have been left out and stored away for the public not to see. The lone aspect that I would like to learn more about from this Texas historical moment would be what the FBI investigators additionally found out about Lee Harvey Oswald. I would first want to know what other things they found at his residence, for example contacts of other people, suspicious items, and plans for the assassination. I think this would help me to understand what kind of person he was and actually what was going on in his head.

I would additionally want to know what they discovered with the mysterious address they found on the package for Lee Harvey Oswald's gun. All we know is that it is a Chicago address. I want to know more about if they followed up on it and if they made any crucial discoveries. This would be very interesting because it could possibly lead to figuring out if Oswald acted alone. Or, indeed he was working with something much larger than himself. With this information I think it could get people closer to knowing what really happened that day, and if there was really al second assassin behind the fence of the Grassy Knoll.

Stephen Jolissaint, Grade 8
St Elizabeth Ann Seton School, TX

My Unique Abilities

My essay is about how, for me, I have well you can say unique abilities. When I was little I was able to see these weird objects. They would be ghostly looking figures or probably figures of my imagination. When I was about 8 years of age I would hear things when nobody else would hear and they would call me weird or say that I was crazy. To me, my close friends, and my parents, it was a gift. My parents would call me to help them with chores and I wouldn't hear a thing, but when they didn't call me I would ask them if they had called me and they would say no. I have too good of an imagination. If I was sitting in a car and had nothing to do, my mind would take over and I wouldn't have known. I would imagine things that no other person would think of or would ever have thought of. I would tell my cousin all the cool ideas that I had in my head for drawings that I would make, but my imagination is so good I couldn't even get close to drawing them. My whole life for me is filled with these abilities and have sometimes helped me get through some tough times in my life.

Jason Kenyon, Grade 9
Weber Institute of Applied Sciences & Technology, CA

My Great-Grandfather

My great-grandfather was born on April 19, 1925 in McAllen, Texas. He had four sisters and three brothers. Great-grandpa was the second to the youngest of the boys. He told me that when he was growing up times were very hard. Their house was very small for eight children. His mom would make shirts and pants for the boys, and dresses, skirts, and blouses for the girls. My great-grandfather had a job after school delivering newspapers. He only went to school till the age of sixteen and then when he turned seventeen he left to the navy. He was a WWII veteran of the United States Navy and served on the LST1081. When he was in the Philippines he brought home a machete. I remember when he would show the machete to us and I would get scared because it was a very sharp blade and was very shiny. He was a lot of fun to be around. My grandpa and I would always have competitions to see who could eat the most jalapenos. I would call him Grandpa Starchy because he loved baked potatoes. People said I look like him when he was young. He had colored eyes but one of his eyes was blue and the other green. That's why I think I have colored eyes. After he came from the service he got a job at the Monitor newspaper in McAllen for two years. Then he moved to El Paso and started working at the El Paso Times and Herald Post. He retired after thirty-seven years. He was married to my great-grandma for fifty-nine years. He passed away on April 2, 2007. I miss him and we will always miss him. I LOVE YOU GRANDPA STARCHY.

Brandon Valenzuela, Grade 8
Rio Bravo Middle School, TX

Friends Forever

It's always great to have someone there for you. Someone you can always depend on, and a friend, is the perfect person for that. I have a lot of great friends, and they all mean so much to me.

Kindergarten is the first day of school, when you see all your future friends for the first time. Sara Stone was in Mrs. Nichol's class with me, and boy did we argue! We would be the best of friends, then the next second we were archenemies. We even got in a fist fight once and had to go to the Counselor's office! At recess, Sara and I would play on the monkey bars, and occasionally attend "cheerleading classes" which one of our friends named McKaylee forced us to do. It wasn't fun, but I survived Kindergarten.

In third grade I was so upset because none of my friends were in my class. That was until I met Julie. I don't know exactly when we started hanging out together, but we just instantly clicked. We started inviting each other over a lot, and I even went to Mr. Gatti's with her for her birthday. In fifth grade a girl named Baylee was in my class. We were great friends too, and just like Julie I never thought we would be.

So this is why my friends are important to me. We have been through a lot together. It's great to have friends.

Jaclyn Beaty, Grade 7
Seminole Jr High School, TX

Destination: Shelton

My family, which consists of Mom, my sister Sheila, Sydney the boxer, and I, usually go to Shelton, Washington every summer in our comfortable, dependable 1996 Dodge Caravan to visit relatives. We wake up around 6:00 a.m., already packed, so all we have to do is load up in the car and go. We leave around 7:00 a.m. and take 395 North to Susanville and then maneuver our way through the monotonous mountain passes to I5 in Redding.

Mom usually drives, so the rest of us are snuggled up in our own cozy cocoons while the curvy roads carry the rest of us through la-la land. By the time we reach Redding, we're all awake and ready for a "rest stop," which means we have had enough rest and need food and a stretch.

From there we spend copious hours in the car listening to bad music or whatever we can find on the radio in that area. We play silly road games like "I Spy" or "Twenty Questions" until we can't stand it any longer. We stop every few hours to stretch and "take care of business," and by about 6:00 p.m. we start looking for a motel. This is my favorite part of the first leg of this journey because Mom knows what we like, and she makes sure we always get it… a motel with an indoor pool!

Tyler Oliver, Grade 8
Long Valley Charter School, CA

Sally: Feline Comedian

Who is able to wake up someone by merely opening a door? Who likes to look out any window? Most people can do these things, but can a cat? I know one cat who can. Do you?

I have a cat named Sally. She is nine years old and is still as playful as a kitten. Sally will lounge in any chair that you are about to sit in. She enjoys being outside, then pretends to desire to be inside. She will wait for a while, then stretch and slowly come inside after you have become extremely impatient.

When my dad whistles "The Snake Charmer," Sally will come to him and give him a fascinating stare. It is hilarious when she stares at our answering machine when a recording of my dad whistling is played. She will occasionally nibble or paw at my dad, or the answering machine, when "The Snake Charmer" is whistled.

Sally will crawl in the four inch space between my father's extremely tall desk and the wall. (That's where all the computer cables are! Ah!) Then my mom will say in a firm voice, "Sally, get out of there." Sally will politely obey. Do you know who the cat is that will wake up someone by opening a door and enjoys gazing out the window? If you guessed my cat, Sally, your answer is correct.

Jessica Andersen, Grade 8
St Elizabeth Ann Seton School, TX

Rosita

Just like many others, I have a family pet. But it's not a dog or cat. Instead I have a parrot. My parrot's name is Rosita, and my family has had her since my mom was eight years old. Every day when I get home from school after sports practices, I usually go to the kitchen to grab a snack, and say hello to Rosita.

Except Rosita isn't the type of parrot you would think she is. She has always been quite aggressive and angry at times, and even when my mom was a kid, she wasn't even able to pet her or else she would end up being bitten by Rosita's sharp beak! But that's not all; she's also really loud and yells constantly, whether I'm on the phone or doing my homework. She just won't stop, even if I beg her to!

Everyone usually has something in their house that helps them truly realize that they are finally "home." It can be family members, or a special possession. But for me, whether Rosita is screaming her head off or is quietly sleeping, I feel a sweet tenderness that helps me realize I am home when I see her!

My family has moved several times when I was a baby, and every single time we moved and found a new place, when I saw Rosita there in a comfy corner on one side of the kitchen, then I would know, "I'm home."

Sarah Abughrib, Grade 7
Corpus Christi School, CA

The Day Pikachu Ruled the World

At the age of 6, I remember my dad bringing a Pikachu costume from Tijuana. I wanted him to bring me something else, but I was still excited. When he gave it to me he told me I had to wear it for Halloween. I was so happy that I was going to be Pikachu for Halloween.

When it was Halloween I went with my uncle to go ask for candy. It's very very fun to go with my uncle because he has three kids. He is also a very funny guy. I really like trick-or-treating, especially when I was a little kid. It was so fun trick-or-treating with my Pikachu costume. I'm really looking forward to going trick-or-treating this Halloween. Last Halloween I didn't go trick-or-treating. My mom told me to give away the candy when people came. That was still fun, because I was eating candy from the bowl.

The day that I wore my Pikachu costume was one of the best Halloweens and one of the best days of my life. I really loved that day and I wished it would never finish. I wish I could have another day like the one I had on that Halloween. That was the day Pikachu ruled the world.

Humberto Zacarias, Grade 7
Isbell Middle School, CA

Pensive Confusion

People have created an organized and stable system where "knowledge" is used to advance society. But to me, at times, "knowledge" does not clarify anything; only, it makes me more confused.

To live in a world where there is a set system of laws seems to be simple and uniform, but complicated. Words make me wonder why they mean what they mean and how people are able to communicate through a line of symbols. Taking apart a word, examining each stroke drawn to craft a word makes me wonder how it was coined, with what inspiration. Then all the meanings of words that I had memorized throughout my life dissolve into an opaque soup where all I can see is darkness. Used for clarification, words ironically confuse me more.

Occasionally, I wonder who I could be if I had a different father or vice versa. Would I be who I believe I am? Would I live up to the same dream? A whole parade of questions run through my mind and makes myself foreign as though there was an "other me" peering at me. Engulfed by confusion, I think sourly of how this world would even bother to function without my existence. These possibilities all just jumble my own self and it takes me minutes, even hours, to remember who I am and gratefully return to life.

I admire civilization's systems. However, confusion can always take place instead of certainty when thinking beyond what is known or stated.

Sara Pak, Grade 9
Diamond Bar High School, CA

The Academic Internet

It is essential to use the internet as a tool for school and research, but it is even more important to use it safely. The internet can sometimes have horrific content such as inappropriate images and ghastly terms. There are ways to prevent these appalling events from happening, such as preparing the children for some things that may appear. But to get away from even having to do that you can put up security walls for your computer and internet. The internet is a great tool for research, but you must be careful of what lurks beyond.

A good way to prevent children from finding shocking content on the internet is to first prepare them by telling them that there is some inappropriate content and that they must be careful. A way to get around having to tell them is by setting up a school security system blocker on each computer, or a fire wall. This helps prevent the popups and prevents children from going onto websites that may not have appropriate terminology. Either way it's important to protect the kids.

The internet is a resourceful device but you have to know how to prepare yourself. Using these tips and ideas can help to make the internet a more wisely used tool in schools if used securely. You don't want to catch the kids off guard, and you can help protect them.

Maddison Johnson, Grade 8
St. Michael's Episcopal Day School, CA

No Ordinary Day

A certain impulse suddenly came through my body as I entered the hot room filled with people and their body heat. An intuition surged through me as if I knew I was going to be nervous. I looked towards the backstage where my teacher stood cheering me on with a huge smile.

I complied with the first verse of the Six Flag theme song, with my instrument in hand with pride in my eyes. The perpetual chant as my bow hit the strings of my violin. When I looked out into the audience I saw my mother rocking to the rhythm of the irresistible sweet sound.

The ecstasy in her eyes as she hummed the song quietly with her feet tapping on the ground. The pervading audience's joyful smiles. I see my impudent competitors seated with hands swing against their chest. Lip poked out with a blunt frown.

As I arrived at the ending of the song I immediately clutched my violin, stroking the bow once more to make the ending sound interesting. A powerful applaud emerged through the crowd. The announcer then said, "Give it up for Ms. Specialjoy Alexander."

As the show was over I ran to the front of the auditorium where I met my mom with open arms and a huge grin. No ordinary day that I feel this way.

Ms. Specialjoy Alexander, Grade 8
Charles Maclay Middle School, CA

My Family

The average American family usually consists of four people: the two parents and two kids. If this statement is true, my family would be far from average.

My family is made of eight people total. There are my parents and my five siblings. I have four brothers and one sister. You know, some people say rude things or throw dirty looks, but if those people only knew what they were missing, they wouldn't be so quick to judge.

People think having a big family is a bad thing or a hassle. I guess it could be a hassle sometimes, but most of the time it can be an adventure. I am the oldest child in this unique family. This means I have something to do all the time and I'm the one who is always there to help out. The best thing of all, though, is I have the chance to watch my siblings grow. I think this is awesome, because I get to be an element in their lives and I guess to help form them into who they become. I get to be a major part of someone's life!

I'm proud of the family I have and I will always be. So next time someone says something rude or gives my family a dirty look, I'll be laughing, and I'll also make sure I pray for those people because they don't know what they're missing.

Josiah Fredette, Grade 8
St Thomas Aquinas School, NM

Discovering Volleyball

This past summer, I discovered volleyball! There was a sports camp nearby that offered volleyball so I decided to try it! It was so much fun being on a volleyball team that very quickly I developed a passion for volleyball!

To play volleyball, I had to learn how to serve, set and spike. There are two types of serves: underhand and overhand. I tried both but decided to use underhand. When I served, I bounced the ball for good luck then threw it up in the air, hit it hard and over the net it went! After three times over successfully, I pumped my hands with joy!!! Setting was the easiest — I hit the ball high over my head so my teammates could spike it down hard — usually unreturnable!!!

My favorite part of volleyball was being on a team! On the team, I played in every position on the court. I really enjoyed all the positions! I also enjoyed working with my teammates, cheering them on and loved winning the games!! When we were losing, we called a time-out. In these few minutes, we psyched ourselves out and most of the time we made a comeback and won!

This summer was my first time on a volleyball team. I had a wonderful time and developed a deep passion for the sport. I hope to be on a volleyball team for many years to come!

Doreen Pacini, Grade 7
The San Francisco School, CA

My Puppy Casper

Puppies are so cute, most of my friends and I agree. From last centuries dogs are known as men's best friend. Since I could remember my family has always had a dog for a pet. The one I loved the most was Casper.

The first time this puppy arrived at our home was the happiest day. He was so white, so small and delicate, I had started to love him. As a family we decided to call him Casper. He was playful day and night, but sometimes he got out of hand.

My step-dad will always play with the dogs, sometimes biting them. We surely didn't like biting Casper, he was our beloved dog. My mother will tell him, "Hey that's a dog, not a hot dog. Leave him alone!" I would laugh and take Casper away from him.

Suddenly something terrible happened, he got really sick. He didn't eat his favorite food or drink water, so we gave him medicine hoping he would get better. One day I woke up, to find out Casper was dead. I cried and cried. He was my adorable dog.

All I could wish for was for it to be all a dream, that he would wake up and play with me like always. Later that day we had a small funeral, I think it was the hardest thing ever. Now I remember him as my childhood best puppy, I will never forget him. R.I.P.

Michael Carrasco, Grade 8
Rio Bravo Middle School, TX

The Hospital

I was born in a hospital thirteen years ago. I don't remember much about being there then, but I have seen some pictures. Last week I had to go to the hospital again and I wasn't too happy about it. I think it is the smell that hits you as soon as you enter the automatic doors that gives you a bad feeling, or maybe it is the disgusting food they serve, or is it the sick feeling in your stomach of not knowing what is coming next.

First, I thought I was going to have my own room, not the case. I did not have to wear that hospital gown that doesn't really tie up, I could get into bed in my pajamas. My head was aching, which is why I was there in the first place. I tried to sleep, which wasn't easy. Every hour a nurse would come in take my temperature, check my medicine, and ask me how my head felt on a scale of one to ten.

The day my doctor told me I could go home, I was excited! As they took my IV out I was relieved to know that I was going to be okay. My mom and I gathered up my things and headed for the elevator. I glanced back at the little curtained off section of the room that had become my world for three days and three nights and thought, I still don't like hospitals.

Caroline Elmets, Grade 8
St Michael's Episcopal Day School, CA

A Little Sense of Humor

"Common sense and a sense of humor are the same things, moving at different speeds. A sense of humor is just common sense, dancing." William James spoke these excellent words. Humor is a desperate ingredient for even the least bit of sanity to exist in one's life. Humor is a miracle that God gave so that we could always find some little way to relax when everything else is going too chaotic for us to handle.

When you laugh with a friend so hard or for such a long time that your stomach hurts or you just make up a quick and witty comment on the spot, these make someone else smile. Humor helps me get though the day. Humor is knowing when to make a joke or laugh at one. It's like a much-needed breath of fresh air.

Keeping humor in life is so easy. Having a friend around to make you laugh, or even a quirky little pet to keep you smiling, humor is so easily found and you never really have to look for it. As William A. Ward said, "A well-developed sense of humor is the pole that adds balance to your steps as you walk the tightrope of life." Never go anywhere without a little sense of humor.

Kaitlyn Houston, Grade 8
Faith Christian Jr/Sr High School, CA

Mom Losing Her Baby

Oh, where do I begin? Everyone has those days. You know, like the kind that you just beg to end. I've had many of those "terrible days," you're not the only one, but there was a day when I really wished that I was dreaming.

May 2, 2008 — Isaiah, my baby brother, was pronounced *dead*. He passed away due to a circulatory problem; his bloodstream didn't supply his heart with sufficient blood. So with every breath he took, his life was gradually slipping away from him, and no one knew, until it was too late. I was traumatized, I just didn't want to accept the truth. The doctors came into the waiting room and asked if anybody wanted final words before they took Isaiah away. When it was my turn I picked him up, held him firm, and I never wanted to let go…I just wanted to awaken from this nightmare.

Death is everywhere, but no one ever thinks their families are going to be next. This ill-fated day impacted me when I realized God's reasons are way beyond our understanding. I couldn't have done anything to stop this day from occurring or make the situation preventable. I cried many times before I realized that Isaiah is in a better place now, in God's hands. And someday I'll be reunited with him and with anticipation I'll get to hold him once more.

No matter what family always stays with you, even in your heart.

Gloria Mendoza, Grade 8
Reagan County Middle School, TX

The Big Monster

If we make our funniest or special moments memorable, then we could share them with our friends. This is one of my best memorable moments.

It all happened in one rainy, dark night of November. My family and I were moving to our new home, the grey apartments off Dromfield St. We didn't have our beds set, so we had to sleep on the floor that cold night.

When we were in a deep sleep, suddenly my mom woke up in a strange way. Then she pulled up the fluffy blankets. That's when my sister and I woke up wondering what was happening. "Did you feel the tiny cold feets?" my mom asked.

"No," we responded, "But could we just go to sleep again, it's one in the morning and tomorrow we have to do a lot of work."

It remained silent for awhile then we heard a squeaky noise, that freaked us out. We didn't know what it was, so we ran to the door like if our lives depended on it. We paused and thought for a second. We realized that our actions were lame. We decided to go inside the room, and turn on the lights. What we saw made us laugh perpetually. It was my little, light brown, hamster in the middle of the room.

Anayeli Montano, Grade 8
Charles Maclay Middle School, CA

Officer Joe Harris

When someone dies, it can leave a person wondering, why them? Others might think, it was their time to pass, but when a best friend dies, you just cry and hope to wake from the nightmare soon. You might ask why it was them and not you. My best friend died a while ago, he was the nicest man anyone had ever met. He was known as the spunky cop with a big heart, and a stomach to match.

Officer Joe Harris was that man. I remember the first day that I met him; I was afraid of what might happen. Would he call on me for something? What about my dad, would he ask about him in front of everyone? None of these questions arose, he just taught us, and talked about his "wonderful family." And I came to know that at his funeral, the saddest day of my life. The day I couldn't stop crying. The day my life took a turn for the worst.

His smile was contagious, no matter who you were, or how sad you were. During the days of our "law related education," I was the happiest I had been in a long time. But during the funeral, I realized, what if he survived the gun shot, he would've had to quit the job he loved, and still be in pain. Now, he's in Heaven, making everyone smile and laugh. So, now when it rains, I ask myself, what joke is he telling now?

Helena Genco, Grade 8
St Thomas Aquinas School, NM

Hunting

Hunting is a great sport. It is very hard to get up early in the morning and drive out into the field before dawn, but it is also very fun. When I went with my grandfather to go on his hunt when I was six, I was fascinated with it and received my license the next year. I have been hunting every year since. Some of the things I have hunted and killed are: antelope, oryx, and elk.

Antelope have inhabited the southern plains of New Mexico since before Columbus discovered the Americas in 1492. Oryx are not native to North America, and it was not until a professor had them brought over from Africa about fifty years ago, and let them loose on White Sands Missile Range. The climate here is perfect for them, so they lived. They still have very tough hide, a result of their species being in Africa and being attacked by lions.

This requires me to use a large rifle, with a lot of takedown power. Elk are native to New Mexico, but due to unregulated hunting, their species went extinct about a century ago. Theodore Roosevelt had some individual animals brought over from Colorado, and let them loose on the land. They have since populated the land, and people are not allowed to hunt them with a permit. Hunting is a great sport for anyone who has patience, and enjoys being outdoors.

Liam Moots, Grade 8
St Thomas Aquinas School, NM

Christmas in Buffalo

One of my favorite holidays is Christmas because I love putting up the Christmas tree and being with my family! Last December we went to Buffalo, New York to celebrate Christmas with my dad's side of the family. When we got there it was snowing everywhere! It was really nice to see my family again! A few days before Christmas we went to a ski lodge and had our own skiing lessons. We had a really fun time! My little brother, Daniel, was giving the guy a hard time and we kept falling at first. My sister and I caught on pretty quickly but my two brothers weren't doing that well.

On Christmas Eve we went to my Aunt Liz's house for dinner and my cousin Nick was telling us that he would stop smoking for the New Year. He went to the garage and Daniel and I caught him smoking! Daniel called him a smoker and a liar! That was pretty funny!

Finally, it was Sunday, the day we had to go back home. We went to the airport and got on the plane, but when the pilot found that the windshield was cracked we all had to go back into the airport. We were stuck in there for about an hour and had to stay an extra day in Buffalo but we still had a good Christmas! It was my first time skiing and being out of town for Christmas!

Cathryn D'Amore, Grade 7
St Elizabeth Ann Seton School, TX

My Uncle

It was me, Jakey (my uncle), and Nick (my cousin) always playing around. We would do everything together. Jakey would do amazing pro wrestling moves to us on our trampoline. In Canada, we raced down a really super big hill beside our house. We were flying down on our sleds going so fast we almost flew into the air. Me and Nick fell off sometimes but that was because Jakey hit us off.

Jakey loved playing video games a lot just like Nick and me so we played often. Video games weren't the only thing we did though. Jakey was only 13 so he still lived with his parents, and my grandparents have a big house. In my grandparents' house, we played hide and go seek which was really hard because they always hid upstairs. Hide and go seek upstairs was so hard because there was no electricity in some of the rooms and you can turn on the main lights from upstairs or downstairs.

The last time I saw Nick was two years ago at another one of my uncle's funeral. Three years ago Nick's parents became Jehovah's Witnesses and he was not allowed to visit non Jehovah's Witnesses. I get lonely sometimes because it's only me and Jakey. My uncle Jakey will always be a very important person to me.

Tony Klassen, Grade 7
Seminole Jr High School, TX

It's All About Basketball

"Number Nine takes a three to tie the game and banks it in! This is unbelievable! This game is going to overtime!" yelled the game announcer over the PA system. The crowd went wild. This was during the season tournament at AK middle school in 2008. Everyone congratulated me for my three pointer.

The reason basketball is so important to me is because since I was three years old, the only craze I wanted to do was basketball and to watch were athletes playing basketball since I couldn't yet. The game of basketball has been everything to me.

It's been my refuge, the place I've gone if I needed to find comfort and peace. It's been a source of intense pain but also a source of joy and satisfaction. It's been a relationship that has evolved over time and has given me the utmost respect and love for the game.

The game of basketball has given me the optimism and desire to achieve my goals with perseverance and a positive attitude. It has provided me a platform that allows me to share my love and passion of basketball with many other kids that I call my friends. I hope I can make it to the NBA. I have faith in my dreams. For I believe as Michael Jordan, a great leader once said "Limits, like fears are often just an illusion."

Deep Bhatti, Grade 9
Faith Christian Jr/Sr High School, CA

Forlorn Faces

Pets are an important part of our lives, they are always there for us, and they never leave our side. That has to make a person wonder why someone would abuse their pet. Some of the people in this world find it amusing to see another creature in pain, but it's not amusing. It's wrong and it's sick! These people kill over one-thousand five-hundred helpless creatures every year.

Dog fighting, setting cats on fire, and beating a pet are the most common forms of abuse someone will use, aside from neglecting or abandonment. The only possible reason someone could do this is if they were mentally ill, and even then it's still wrong, and they have no right. It is mind blowing at how someone could look at an animal's forlorn face as they beat it or set it on fire and find amusement from it. Or for those who neglect their pet, they are no better, even if they could not afford to take care of them. If it came to that point they should do the right thing and give the animal up instead of forcing it to suffer and die a slow, painful death and all their owners do is watch.

It's unacceptable to let these living creatures suffer for our own sick, demented pleasure, or simply because we knew we couldn't take care of them. Dogs are considered man's best friend. It makes one wonder, why would a man kill his best friend?

Parker Acevedo, Grade 8
Nobel Middle School, CA

The Lord's Little Blessing

What is important to me is my family. I'm sure there are a lot of people who choose to write about their family; however, I believe my family is truly special. It all started in the spring of 1996, when my mom had her fourth kid, a girl, my little sister. When she was born the doctors quickly realized something went wrong with her development, but they could not find diagnoses for her disease. The doctors told my mother that my sister, whom my mom decided to name Laura, would not live for any longer than six months. My mom did not accept what they said and gave Laura as much love and attention as she could, and before long Laura had outlived her six-month deadline. However, she was not physically growing, but she did keep aging. Soon six years had passed, but she grew no bigger than a newborn baby. We were all concerned. We knew nothing we could do could change Laura's predicament, so we decided to make the best of it. However much we loved her, we knew her time on earth would be limited, and on a cold day in February the Lord decided to take His little angel home. Even through the hardships of dealing with a special sister, my family stuck through it all, and that is the reason why my family is important to me.

Jackson Wyers, Grade 9
Pine Tree High School, TX

Disneyland

When I went on vacation with my aunts, cousin, mom, and sister to Disneyland this fall for the first time, we had a blast. First we went on a ride called Spaced Mountain, which was one of my favorites. Next, we went on Buzz Lightyear. That was pretty fun and I got a high score. After that we went on Indiana Jones, which was my favorite ride. It felt like you were driving off terrain in a vehicle while inside of a dark cave attempting to find your way out. It was very exciting because of the sharp turns, unexpected drops, and objects coming towards you such as a loose boulders, you even get attacked by what appeared to look like natives. We ate lunch at a pizza and pasta buffet. Next, we went on the Haunted Mansion but because we went there near the month of October, it had a Nightmare Before Christmas theme. Prior to that we went on a ride in California Adventure called Soarin' Over California. We went on the Peter Pan Adventure. Last but not least we went on the Matterhorn. I liked it very much because of the surprises. It was much like a cave that you would weave in and out of. While inside, Yetis would pop out at you. Though we weren't able to see many Disney characters, we had lots of memorable events. I hope I am able to go again.

Alyssa Lauffer, Grade 7
St Elizabeth Ann Seton School, TX

My Grandpa

Anytime you have someone you love very much, and they just pass away it's never easy to forget them. You will always have the memories you had together in your heart. At least you know someone special is always watching over you.

It was September 18, 2009. It couldn't have been a better day. I had passed my spelling test and my AR test. It was the best day until school let out, and as I was waiting for my mom I had a bad feeling in the pit of my stomach. When I saw my mom I knew my gut was right. She was driving faster than normal, which made me worry. When she picked me up she said something terrible happened, and then we were off to Dallas, Texas. Earlier that day my grandpa had been airlifted there.

When we got to Dallas, I witnessed needles being inserted in to my grandpa. It was scary; I had not seen anyone in so much pain. All my family dropped to the ground; his pulse went dead. I was so upset. He was the one person I truly loved. A couple days later we had the funeral, and I was so upset I couldn't go. There lay Gene Edward Freeman may he R.I.P.

He was a great man and someone you could trust. I would do anything in the world to get him back. You never really know what you've got until you lose it.

Eddie Ortiz, Grade 8
Reagan County Middle School, TX

Guilty Pleasure

I think reality TV is more entertaining than scripted television because to people, it is funny to watch people embarrass themselves. People are always curious about other people's lives and what they go through, and this gives us the pleasure to watch from our homes. My mom and I have totally separate lives. I go to school, and then volleyball, and then I do my homework. My mom goes to work, runs errands, and makes dinner. But every Thursday night we are both on the couch watching the "Real Housewives of Atlanta."

The show "Real Housewives of Atlanta" is about a group of five socialites in Atlanta and their day-to-day life. They get into cat fights, and are very loud and energetic. I think that it is a "guilty pleasure" because it is almost like you are snooping into another person's life and it is funny. It is amusing to watch people's crazy antics, which they go through every day.

I think that reality TV appeals to multiple age groups because it is not like cartoons, or dramas. It can be everything put into one show. That is why I think that reality television, and more specifically the "Real Housewives of Atlanta" is both mine and my mom's "guilty pleasure."

Jaitika Singh, Grade 8
St Michael's Episcopal Day School, CA

My Favorite Animal

The Bengal tiger is my favorite animal, but they are almost extinct because people are hunting them down.

These rare tigers are only found on the other side of the world, in the desert regions of India and in Burma, and Nepal. In 1990 the Bengal tiger population of India was estimated to be at 40,000-50,000 by 1972 this number dropped alarmingly to 1,850. But a good conservation program has increased the population to about 4,000 Bengal tigers.

Something I like about the Bengal tiger is its behavior. They are solitary and nocturnal, they do not like to share their space with other tigers. All tigers mark their territory by using their very strong urine and they screech with serve as a warning to other tigers nearby.

The Bengal tiger is strong enough to drag huge animals a long way. A single tiger can pull a water buffalo that weighs more than a ton! That's how much it would take 13 men to move such an enormous weight. If a tiger is really hungry it could even attack a bear but that could be a mistake because a bear is twice as big as a tiger. This tiger can eat about 100 pounds of meat just in one sitting! This is about one-fifth of its total weight, but of course a tiger has to eat a lot because it often goes several days without eating anything.

As you can see the Bengal tiger is amazing and I hope that because of humans they don't go extinct.

Neftali Arevalo, Grade 7
Isbell Middle School, CA

Hawaii Vacation

My love for surfing started when I was little. One day my uncle took me out to the beach in Waikiki. He brought with him two surf boards and some wax for each of them. He told me that he was going to teach me how to surf and I was cool with that.

On my first attempt he basically pushed me into the wave and I had no idea what I was in for. As I caught the wave, I lost my balance but I did not fall. At that time I did not know how to stop so I just rode the wave in, all the way to the shore. After three more attempts I did not lose my balance at all. I never found a way to stop, so I invented my own way. When I feel like stopping, I will cannon ball into the water, and it stops the board cold.

To top if off we went to Germaine's Luau. They had all the food we could eat including poi, manapuas, salads, and many more. They buried the pork in a toasty pit and we even saw them lift the pork straight out of the ground. There were fire dancers that did some pretty insane moves. It had been one amazing day and I would love to do it again.

Kai Paresa, Grade 8
Monte Vista Christian School, CA

Express Yourself

Recall an Obama speech. The powerful words can excite you. But when, you are shy and bashful like me, you don't want to give speeches. What is something that you do, that makes your voice heard? Whether you are shy or talkative, everybody has a way of communicating to the world.

Here are some of the most common ways we talk to the world. One of them is smiling. From Iceland to Argentina smiling means the same thing. Anybody can smile. Just by smiling, you may brighten someone's day.

Another way is through art. Most art has a message or emotion the artist wants to express. I remember getting depressed after seeing this painting of a paralyzed woman who could not walk. Artists can express their ideas through art.

In addition, people talk to the world by writing. People send their messages through folklore, stories, or essays. In *To Kill a Mockingbird* the message was it's important to have empathy for people. Most books that have received awards have an important message.

Although I have only named a few, there are several ways to communicate to the world. As for me I do not know how I can best communicate to the world. I think most people also don't know how to communicate to the world. So the next time you feel that you cannot speak your mind, there is someway you are being heard because everybody has a way to communicate to the world.

Amanda Holloway, Grade 7
Washington Middle School, WA

Is Your Little Brother Necessary?

Crash! Weeks of hard work, revision, and imagination shatter as they hit the floor. Your little brother was responsible. You think you can live without him, think again. Sure, he's annoying, but he can also be a great friend.

Yes, little brothers are annoying, it's true. Little brothers break things a lot. My little brother is constantly breaking my LEGO creations. Have you ever heard this line, "Can I play too? Please?" It happens a lot. Sometimes having a friend over isn't a good thing. Every time I have a friend over I hear this phrase over and over.

When little brothers aren't being annoying the can actually be fun. Video games sometimes aren't fun without someone to whop. When he isn't breaking anything he is actually a great building partner. Together we can build almost anything.

Little brothers are fun to be around, most of the time. What? Fun to be around? Sure. You can bug them when they have a friend over. And when you are bored they are there, most of the time. My little brother leaves for a week each summer and when he is gone I am so bored. "What about your other friends?" Yeah, but it's just not the same. Yes, little brothers are annoying. Sure, they break stuff, but I couldn't live without mine!

Caleb Sale, Grade 8
Thora B Gardiner Middle School, OR

The Roller Coaster of Life

Not many people can get over all their fears in one day, but then not everyone is like me. I used to be very afraid. In the morning I thought that I might forget everything, and when I came home from school, it crossed my mind that anyone in my family could die right now for any reason. To make a long story short, I was afraid of anything and everything.

I tried to overcome my fears, but they did not go away. I couldn't go on like this forever, and I didn't. One day, we decided to go to Cliff's, a local amusement park, with my cousins. I didn't want to go on any rides that went more than ten feet high. Eventually, my sister and cousins dragged me onto rides that were out of my comfort zone, and I started to really have fun. Towards the end of the day, I realized if I didn't focus on my fears, I had much more fun.

Finally, my sister dragged me on to the biggest roller coaster in the park. I was terrified! As the ride started, I wasn't scared at all, it was the most fun I had ever had. When I got off the ride, I realized that life is like a roller coaster; sometimes it's fun, then it could make your head spin, and the track isn't always smooth, but the end usually turns out great. Since that day, I have been able to enjoy the roller coaster of life.

Nicole Klein, Grade 8
St Thomas Aquinas School, NM

Cats

Animals are great, but my favorite animals are cats. I think cats are great, but many people think dogs are better. The cat can be an awesome pet too. There are many reasons why cats can make great pets.

Cats are easy to take care of and they pretty much take care of themselves. You don't have to worry about them when you're on vacation. All you have to do is get someone to feed it every day. Cats don't exercise so you don't need to take them outside to walk, they sleep all day.

Cats can come in many shapes and sizes. You can choose a furry cat or one with less fur. Maybe you can get a small kitten or an adult cat. You can get a gray kitten or an orange, white, brown, and red cat. Cats also have many names like calico, tabby, etc. There are also cats that can't be pets. There are the tigers, lions, snow leopards, leopards, cheetahs, mountain lions, etc. These cats are wild animals and are bigger than regular house cats. Many people are dog lovers, but cats can be just as lovable as dogs.

Overall, I think cats can be wonderful pets. If you have a cat, you also have a best friend.

Johanna Contreras, Grade 7
Isbell Middle School, CA

Imagination

Imagination. What would the world be without it? Imagination is needed for the world to officiate. Would we be able to ride a train? Drive a car? Fly an airplane? No, without imagination we would be on the same level as animals.

Imagination helps provide meaning to experience and understanding knowledge. It is a fundamental facility through which people make sense of the world. We encounter everything with our imagination. The things that we see, touch, and hear coalesce into a "picture" into our minds. Most famous inventions or products were created from inspiration from someone's imagination. Without imagination, there wouldn't be a cure to a disease, a new discovered planet, or even something as simple as jokes or laughter. Even the great Albert Einstein once said, "Imagination is more important than knowledge. Knowledge is limited. Imagination encircles the world."

As you can see, imagination, is very substantial in all of our lives. It's a powerful, potent force that defines and governs everything we do. It creates and allows us to embrace our most important aspect of existence; humanity.

Christina Granillo, Grade 8
Zia Middle School, NM

World History

World history is one of the most important subjects you can learn in school. English and math are very important, but so is history. You learn how nations rise and fall; who or what cause this downfall, their culture, and their literacy.

World history can and will repeat itself and a prime example of this is revolution. Multiple countries came into existence because of a revolution, and it's all for the same reason: the government taking control of their rights and taxes to get more money. The United States is one example of this, and India, South Africa, and others came into existence the same way, rebellion.

Countries learn from others' mistakes. They learn who would make a good leader, technology, warfare, and economy. These are just a few examples of things countries could learn by studying world history.

Another thing you can learn is about the culture of other countries. You would need to know this so if you do go there, you would know all their customs and beliefs. For instance, calling someone a goat in an Arab country is the worst insult you can ever call an Arab. You might want to know cultural differences before you go to a foreign country so you don't accidentally insult someone. These are just a few reasons why world history is important. Learning about culture differences and from the mistakes of the past are examples of why history is just as important as English or math.

Tippie Ray, Grade 8
Holliday Middle School, TX

In Their Shoes

Have you ever questioned what it would be like to live in someone else's life? Would it be more fun or easy going? At points in our life we all want to be someone or something else.

When my mother was young she lived in a household where she was beaten. She always reminds me, "You're lucky with the life that you've got." Yet even after this has been said I complain; about chores, and babysitting. I'm still trying to learn to shut my mouth. Because she is right, I do have it easier compared to most. We all have trials to get through. One trial is no more important than the next. Remember you aren't the only one with something hard to face.

Take for instance the addict; knowing the drug is killing them, yet not quitting because of how hard it might be. Maybe the old man realizing his life has floated past him without meaning and no way to go back and change it. Or possibly the bird, with freedom hovering on its wings while in flight. Then it is shot down to feed the starving family of six.

Your life escapes you between open fingers unexpectedly. Don't waste your life on what's not good enough. Make it good enough for you. Find the sole light in the darkness. When your world is crashing around you, don't crumble under the weight, stand and take the pain. Who knows — perhaps you will win.

Ashten Warren, Grade 8
Canyon View Jr High School, UT

My Family!

A day in my family is chaotic. There is something always going on and something new happening such as sports and fun trips. My mom always makes sure I have what I want or need for anything.

I play soccer and volleyball. I have practice every day and my mom is always there to take me or even my brother. My mom also makes sure I'm not late to any of my games. I'm always up to try new things and sometimes we do it as a family.

Trips are a big thing. Every year we go to Las Vegas, Nevada. My favorite memory of going to Las Vegas is having all the family on Thanksgiving sitting around the table together. Another place we have gone was California. There are so many great memories from there. One of my favorites is when it was all rainy outside. We stayed in and played games instead of going out.

My family is always there for me but my mom is there the most. If I need something for school she will take me to the store and get it. If I want to do another sport, she will always find a way to fit it in her busy schedule.

Even though my family is chaotic they are always there for me. If I need something or someone I know I can go to them and we also have a great time together for the most part.

Samantha Bain, Grade 8
Thora B Gardiner Middle School, OR

Family

People are happy when they see their families. Family sometimes upset you, and other times you have fun times. Family teaches you lessons the hard or easy way.

I woke up Saturday morning. I screamed, "Yea." I woke up everybody in the house. I felt as excited as if I had a thousand cups of coffee. Today was the day of my family reunion. We all got our orange Hernandez family reunion shirts on and got ready for a day in the park of fun and games. We arrived at the Brown Plaza Park in Del Rio, Texas. Most of my family was already there. We played volleyball. It was orange team against the yellow team. I had my game face on and was ready to play. My uncle Jesse kept falling down like a hammer hitting a nail. I burst out laughing, "Ha." My family, the orange team, own. The next sport was basketball. It was gray team vs. orange team. My dad uncle jumped in the center of the court. I got the ball and I flew down the court like a bird. So I acted like I was going to shoot a layup jump, stopped, and shot. We won a trophy for best overall winners.

I think that was a fun time, and I look forward to the family reunion next year in March. I hope to have as much fun next year with all the sports. I really got to know everyone in my family.

Jalisa Hernandez, Grade 8
Reagan County Middle School, TX

My Older Sister

If any of you have an older sister, you know what I deal with every single day. She picks on you, she is often too occupied with other things to help you with whatever you need, and of course, she is loving (at times).

Like all sisters, my sister and I have our bad days and our good days. Sometimes on our bad days we fight with each other and scream at each other. Also when she is moody, she messes around with me and I respond in kind to that. Other times she just gets on my last nerve. But on our good days, we really show that we care about each other, and we get along perfectly. On my birthdays she is really nice to me, and she doesn't fight with me.

Deep deep *deep* down, I really love my sister, even though sometimes I don't really show it. If I had the choice to exchange my sister for any other girl to be my sister, I wouldn't do it. I love my sister deep down, in spite of her flaws.

Marcela Alvarez, Grade 8
Corpus Christi School, CA

The Heart Attack

"Can I get Tony with his things please," the intercom spoke out. I got my materials and took off to the office. I saw my mom standing there, and I asked her what happened. She answered, "Your grandpa just had a heart attack."

It started like any other day. I woke up, got washed up, then I got dropped off at school. Everything was good and then around 2:30 P.M., I got called to the office and my mom told me.

"What!" I yelled.

"Your grandpa had a heart attack, and we need to leave now so we can get to Houston as soon as possible." my mom explained.

We got home, and we packed about a weeks worth of clothes because we knew we were probably going to be there awhile.

We took off, and 8 hours later we were there at the Methodist Hospital. We arrived at about one or two in the morning. As soon as we entered we went straight to ICU. My grandpa looked ill and weak. We talked to the doctors, and they said he needed to rest and that he needed an operation. They said there was a chance he couldn't make it. My grandpa was so worried. We calmed him down and a week later he was in the surgery room. The doctors said, the operation was a big success. Now he spends his days in Diboll with my family every day.

You never realize how much you care about someone until you lose them or get close to losing them. Love your friends and family and appreciate them.

Juan A. Encinas Jr., Grade 8
Reagan County Middle School, TX

A Hunter Forever

Nicholas was sitting close to the warm campfire waiting for daylight to break. When he sipped his nice cup of hot chocolate, he asked his father when they would start hunting for elk. His father told him when the time is right, then they would go. Nicholas nodded and continued to sip his hot chocolate. Finally the sun began to come over the horizon and Nicholas was filled with joy! He grabbed his coat and rifle and headed into the beautiful forest of New Mexico with his dad, ready to start the hunt.

They set up a tree stand right up by a watering hole. Then they were set, ready for whatever passed by them. Suddenly, a giant bull elk walked up to the watering hole. When Nicholas spotted him, he gasped. He told his father that was the one. He loaded his rifle and raised it, ready to take a shot. Right when the bull elk looked up and grunted, BOOM! Nicholas fired. The bullet struck the elk and it fell to the ground. Nicholas and his dad came down from the tree stand and went to see their trophy. When they reached the elk, Nicholas was so excited, he shouted, "I'll be a hunter forever!"

Nicholas Chavez, Grade 8
St Thomas Aquinas School, NM

Life Is Not a Movie

Film and television studios in the U.S. nearly always want to dish up a sunny view of life because American audiences would rather not be reminded of problems in society. In real life, the final scene is not always what we want to see.

Films depict the villain getting punished and the hero victorious, which often happens. Sometimes, the bad guy is not so easily captured. Movies and television shows make it appear very easy to solve the crime, but it is actually more complicated. Occasionally, the good guys don't win.

Films and television depict war as a glorious adventure with the war hero returning home to live a happy, normal life. Some of the unfortunate consequences of war may be omitted. Audiences don't want to see the hero killed, left emotionally or physically disabled, or unemployed.

Movies and television portray families as having problems, but they usually work together, and everyone ends up happy. Unfortunately, this doesn't always happen in real life, even though it should. Family members are sometimes hesitant to compromise. They may not be brave enough to face problems and work out solutions.

The film and television industries usually try to paint a sunny, unrealistic view of life. In real life, solutions to problems are not always easy to uncover. The end result may be favorable, or it may be unfavorable. Without God guiding our steps, it could be a dismal picture.

Colton Dedmon, Grade 8
Holliday Middle School, TX

Little Monsters That Took All of Me

They are small, like little monsters that are living with me, who came unexpectedly. All they seemed to want was my tender care, like a loving mother is supposed to care for her children as if there won't be sunrise tomorrow.

First they started by taking away my sleep with their desperate cries in need of my attention, as if they get some type of joy or good feelings with just being with me and looking at me. Like a child around its mother.

They seemed to want all of my time! They are indescribable!

They crawled into bed with me like bed bugs, you don't know when they arrived but you know you woke up with them in your bed. They took away my beauty sleep, and they want whatever I have, they copy everything I do. They have even begun acting like me. They have become two little monster mes!! They absolutely took away my time, they have taken all my attention. They do so much they make me lose focus! These little monsters are driving me insane!

They took my heart. All my love…they took all of me!!!! These little monsters are creepy, like when they creep upon me unexpectedly. These little monsters seem to always follow me like when trouble finds me…these little monsters want to be like me…like the girls at school that hate to love me.

But though they came uninvited, they are welcome and are loved…my daughters.

Maria Hernandez, Grade 9
REACH High School, TX

My Grandpa

My grandpa changed my life forever. I was his only granddaughter and he treated me like a princess. He was a manager of a motel called, The Sunset. Every time I went to visit him, I would see him behind the counter or cooking food on the grill by the pool. Two years ago he was diagnosed with lung cancer. He was in the hospital for a long time. After a few months, we though the was recovering. He wasn't; he passed away in his sleep. It broke my heart to hear he was gone. He will always have a place in my heart. There are trees in my uncle's backyard that my grandpa plated. Those three trees symbolize his grandkids: my brother, my cousin, and me. Because God loves someone, He will stop the pain and let them be with Him forever.

After he passed away, I knew God would make my grandpa's life better; he would have no more worries. I knew that he would watch me from Heaven with most of his family. My grandpa inspired me to reach for what I want and to not let anything stand in my way. He changed my life, but since the day he died, I have thought about the kinds of things we could have done. When God takes me, I will be able to do those things.

Alexis Farah, Grade 8
St Thomas Aquinas School, NM

How Basketball Changed Forever

Michael Jordan changed the game of basketball forever. This man never made a mistake, he was unstoppable when he was coming down the court. He was and still is the greatest basketball player who has ever played. He was a god when it came to basketball.

Michael Jordan was an outstanding player, both on defense and on offense. Whenever he and his team had the ball and was taking it down the court he would always get the ball and score. He would always jump right over the players and dunk the ball! He also had an outstanding jump shot. He got the ball no matter what. He was unstoppable.!

Another great thing Michael Jordan was good at was defense, no one could get behind or around him. If he was on the court the other team would not score at all. Before the other player would know it Michael Jordan came flying over them and blocking the ball from going into the hoop.

Michael Jordan is, and will always be, the greatest basketball player, no basketball player will ever come close to being as good as Michael Jordan. There will never be a basketball player like him.

Joseph Padilla, Grade 8
St Thomas Aquinas School, NM

Toucans

The toucan, a colorful, intelligent, and playful bird, is one of the many extraordinary animals living in the rain forest today. It is also one of the world's most popular birds. It got its name from "tupano" by the Tupi Indians of Brazil. The toucan is one of the noisiest birds in the jungle. They are related to woodpeckers. There are almost 40 types of toucans, ranging in height from 7 inches to more than two feet, and weigh about 20 ounces. It has a short, thick neck with a large, lightweight, and multicolored beak.

The toucan's bill is used to squash its fruit and berries that it eats. Being an omnivore, the toucan's diet mainly consists of fruit, nuts, small animals' eggs, insects, small birds, and lizards. Toucans build their nests inside trees, and usually live in small flocks or pairs. They are mostly found in South and Central America, in the canopy section of the rain forest. Toucans are extremely important to have in the rain forest because they help grow food by scattering seeds from the fruits that they eat.

Once every year, toucans lay about 2-4 eggs inside their nests. As the young toucan grows, its beak slowly grows and develops more color. They do not become full-grown until several months later. Toucans are very common household pets. They live for about 15-25 years. Even after the toucan dies out, it will live on, and always be remembered as one of the world's most popular and cherished birds.

Sophie Hasuo, Grade 7
Placerita Jr High School, CA

Bully

I'm in 8th grade now. I know what's right but before I was bullied nobody helped me when I was down. I saw that everybody was scared of them too but didn't want to get beat up so I was mad and I chose to do the same thing bully.

It was a new year and I was ready. I beat up kids I got in trouble I didn't care, all I cared about is respect and I got it. I was happy nobody talked back they did what I said and then I found out the truth and I was shocked.

It was not respect they were not my friends they were scared of me and I stopped. I said sorry to the kids who I hurt and I started to stand up for those who got bullied it worked they stopped but I started to tell the kids to stand up for each other. It's like you take a stick alone you can break it easy but put more in and it never breaks. So stand up for those who need help I now know that I needed help but nobody helped me so it's wrong. Bullying doesn't get you respect it gets people to stop liking you so don't do the same thing I did and stop bullying from happening.

David Medina, Grade 8
Canyon View Jr High School, UT

Empires Rise and Fall with Technology

Have you ever wondered why we have items today that other people in the past haven't had? This is where technology comes in. When people progress through time, technology advances as well. Over time, empires would rise and fall by weapons, transportation, and communication.

In the 9th century, Chinese scientists found gunpowder. The Chinese harnessed gunpowder, made it into fireworks and explosives, and then shortly thereafter they made guns and cannons with gunpowder. In the 1300s, news spread through Europe about this development. Wars erupted with guns and cannons and the castles became obsolete. Regimes with castles soon fell, and the whole world changed.

In the 15th century, Leonardo Da Vinci drew the first idea for an airplane and in 1907, the Wright brothers flew the first plane. These were biplane fighters, which were then further developed in World War I. In World War II, bombers were developed with two wings, and the Nazis developed the first jet fighter. This advancement helped deliver supplies and troops faster as well as destroyed cities.

In the 1800s, people could only communicate by mail. This changed when the telegraph was developed and helped people communicate from far away. In the 1900s, people developed phones and Internet, which enabled people to communicate from across the globe. It also became strategic for the military to use in radar and missiles.

In conclusion, as man progressed and advances were made in the areas of weapon, transportation, and communication, empires grew and divided.

Austin Beaart, Grade 7
Placerita Jr High School, CA

Helping Out

Helping your parents is the best thing you can do. Parents need help in all ways. Physical and emotional are just two of the ways you can help.

I started helping my mom when I was eight years old. It was fun because in the little farm that I lived in there was usually nothing to do. There weren't any kids my age there I could pay with. There wasn't mainly anything to do. The only people there were my godmother's children.

Often my mom had something for me to do around the house. Cleaning my room and taking out the trash were two things I always had to do. Whenever there wasn't any work, I would go outside and play basketball on a basketball court that my brother and I helped my dad build. It was boring though because I didn't have anyone to play with. I usually was the only one who helped because my brother was at football practice, and my sister was at her friend's in Rankin.

I helped my mom when she was sad or mad. When she was sad I asked her what was wrong and we would sit down and talk about it. I sometimes had the answers, and it would help her a little.

Eventually I moved to Big Lake, and now I don't help her that much. You know I think it's time I should start helping again. Every time I would help her, it would feel rewarding.

David Garcia, Grade 8
Reagan County Middle School, TX

We Are All Perfect in God's Eyes

Do you ever think that you are different? That you don't quite fit in? Have you ever felt that you were too tall, too short, too fat, or too thin? If you are too dark, or too white, I know where you are coming from, because I always feel the same way. I've spent my life feeling that I am different because my mom is Caucasian and my dad is Hispanic. I've always felt that I am judged by people.

I have since learned that it doesn't matter what you look like; it matters what is inside of a person. You don't have to hangout with the popular kids. Don't let it bother you if people tell you that you are ugly, because deep down inside, you are a beautiful person. Follow your dreams, even if it is becoming a scientist, a model, or anything that you want to be. I am always told that you can count all your true friends on one hand. A true friend will never put you down.

Friends should only like you for who you are, not what you can give them. So the next time you feel down and people are picking you apart, look deep inside yourself and remember that you know more good things about yourself than anyone does, except God. You are perfect the way God made you, and that's great. Remember that you have good friends you can count on.

Cortney Garman, Grade 7
Long Valley Charter School, CA

An All-Nighter

Have you ever tried pulling an all-nighter? I have. If you didn't know what an all-nighter is, it means staying up the whole night. I spent an all-nighter with my friends, Kheelan and Khrizia. Kheelan is like a little brother to me, while Khrizia is like a big sister.

One day, when my parents decided to have a little gathering at home, my mom invited Khrizia's family over. I was really excited because I hadn't seen them in a long time.

The moment I saw them, I ran to give them a hug. After I hugged Kheelan, he rushed upstairs because whenever he used to come over, we would always play Pac-Man on the Playstation 2. After an hour of playing Pac-Man we decided to play foosball. We were all hungry, so we grabbed some food. When our moms saw us eating, they kept laughing at us because we filled our whole plates.

After we all finished eating, Khrizia suggested to watch some funny videos on YouTube. We watched a lot of hilarious videos, and it almost made me cry laughing.

All three of us started to feel really tired. When I looked at the clock, I noticed it was 3 a.m.! We hadn't noticed because we all had such fun. When they had to leave, we all felt really sad. We promised each other we would have another all-nighter very soon.

Erika Olazo, Grade 8
Corpus Christi School, CA

Organ Donors

Many people never wonder about what happens to them after they have passed away. I feel everyone should stop and take time to think about becoming an organ donor and giving the gift of life back to others.

About five years ago my dad received an organ from a donor so I now understand the importance of donation. Even though my family and I can praise the Lord every day for letting my dad have another chance at life, I am devastated to know about the young man who was in killed in a car accident who also had young children just as my dad did. I know the young man did not have to choose to be an organ donor, but he did. My condolences are with his family and especially his children. I couldn't imagine the thought of losing my dad. We are very thankful for the donor and may God bless his family throughout their lives.

Ever since the surgery many of my family members and friends have committed themselves to becoming organ donors. Although there are also hundreds of thousands of people around the world who have also committed, there is still not enough awareness about the importance of organ donations. Everyone should give it a thought and hopefully decide to give the gift of like back to someone just like my own dad was given.

Shelby Szteiter, Grade 9
Kaufer High School, TX

Unity: President Obama's Speech

"Our patchwork heritage is a strength, not a weakness." This is what President Obama, forty-fourth President of the United States, announced to the world. He told them firmly that Americans stand united; that unity is our strength and the bringer of peace and a golden age.

Our strength, our unity lies on working together, like the tightly interwoven mechanism of a clock. It is through our unity that we persevere through the hardships of civil war and segregation "emerg[ing] from that dark chapter stronger and more united," We lock arms and push forward, learning and depending on each other. The hardships we face forms bonds that shall never be broken because of our unity. Dumbledore in J.K. Rowling's *Harry Potter and the Goblet of Fire* (the fourth book) declares: "I say to you all, once again, we are only as strong as we are united, as weak as we are divided, We can fight, only by showing an equally strong bond of friendship and trust. Differences of habit and language are nothing at all if our aims identical and our hearts open." Heart stirring, mind blowing, his words echo President Obama's: that together, no matter what, we will be strong.

Therefore, unity is one of the only things that can achieve peace. It is by far the feeling most needed to be attained. Instead of just tolerating each other we should learn each other for who we are. That is how unity is the way we can survive, in happiness.

Paula Quach, Grade 8
Jefferson Middle School, CA

The Best Concert Ever

Last year I in September I went to a Linkin Park concert with my aunt and cousin. Linkin Park's opening act was Green Day, and a lot of the people got excited when they came out. They played a few songs like '21 Guns' and 'American Idiot.' While they were playing someone in the general admission, where the crowd was going crazy, had to be taken out because they attacked a person. Green Day got a lot of attention after that happened. The second band, U2, was extremely boring to me. I didn't pay much attention while they were playing. They are pretty big in America and the UK but not many people liked them. U2 played about fifteen songs before they left.

A few more bands played but I can't remember most of their names. They were all really good though. After a few hours Linkin Park came out. They played a few songs the best ones were 'What I've Done' and 'Tried so Hard'. They played for about two hours before the concert finally ended.

Before they left they thanked us for coming to the concert and listening to them play. The security guards all came and escorted us to the exit and then to our cars. In my opinion it was a very good concert.

Dylan Byrum, Grade 8
Isbell Middle School, CA

The Youngster

Life is actually fun for me being the youngest in the family. I have a twenty-six year old sister who lives in Indiana, another sister who is twenty-three, and a brother who is twenty-one. The rest of us live in Texas. I am a girl who is twelve and in seventh grade. When I was born on November 21 my brother was nine, my sister was eleven, and my other sister was fourteen! I was born and the doctor told my mom that I was a girl. My mom told my dad and my family, but when my brother found that out he started bawling because he was hoping to get a little brother. Any ways, I was born and he forgot about that. He was still happy to have a new member to the family. I like to be the youngest, even though sometimes it is not that fun because they treat me like a slave. I don't do what they say; I learn to live with it and move on. On weekends I stay home with my parents while the others are out doing their own thing. It's not boring because my parents try to make it fun. I love being the youngster of the family because I am more spoiled than the others! Not that matters, it only matters that you have a family that loves you and always will.

Melissa Kaminski, Grade 7
St Elizabeth Ann Seton School, TX

Begging, Working, Receiving a Black Lab

In life you have to work, hard, for the things you want and need. It takes many people years to learn this lesson, but I have figured it out. Of course, the answer was, for the millionth time, NO! My endless pleading was like fighting against someone with a newly sharpened sword with a butter knife. My father's iron will always win in the end. To get a puppy, I tried everything; putting a stuffed dog on his keyboard, mailing him a letter, even putting pictures of dogs on his immaculately made bed! Nothing worked; I was an ant trying to move a fifty ton brick wall. Refusing to give up, I stubbornly declared that I would personally raise all funds.

After what seemed like millennia, the iron was cracking, and finally cracked in half. My dad agreed, not knowing what he had gotten himself in to. Overjoyed, I thanked him profusely.

Doing many arduous jobs, I slowly earned two hundred dollars' worth of change and dollar bills. Finding A.K.C. lab puppies for two hundred was difficult, but possible. My dad was shocked, but could he turn me down? We went to the breeders' house and picked a female black lab I named Jazzy, due to constant wiggling.

By getting Jazzy, I have learned that you have to work hard for things. This isn't easy. Jazzy is very important and special to me. This petite dog has a larger than life personality, she's loyal, and overall, the perfect best friend!

Danielle Shaver, Grade 8
Thora B Gardiner Middle School, OR

All 'Bout Courtney Thompson

Courtney Thompson is a pro volleyball player. She went to Kentlake High School. Thompson was born November 4, 1984, in Bellivard. She went to the University of Washington. Courtney played for the Huskies and went to the NCAA Tournament.

Courtney Thompson also plays basketball and softball. Thompson is very athletic, and has two brothers that are also athletic: Craig, a WW graduate, and Trevor, the captain of the Senior baseball team at the United States Naval Academy.

Her sophomore year, she led the Huskies volleyball team to the semifinals of the NCAA Tournament, and her freshmen year she set the record of her school-best 1,643 seasons total. Courtney started playing volleyball in 2005, and she has gotten very far for only four years of playing volleyball. Thompson is still playing volleyball today and is still doing great. Courtney Thompson is still my favorite volleyball player because she has gotten a lot of awards and she is a very interesting person to read about, and she has a lot of interesting facts about her past life.

Lenzi Hutson, Grade 7
Deweyville Middle School, TX

Sylvia Carrete

Sylvia Vargas Carrete was born on October 7, 1944. She was born to a Mexican mother and Italian father in Mexico. My grandmother as a child growing up in Mexico was poor. Her childhood was full of heartbreak and disappointment as her dad left when she was 6 years old. My grandmother moved to El Paso, Texas, and as a teenager she went back and forth from Juarez, Mexico to El Paso. When she was 16 years old, my grandpa met my grandma. They were married six years later and her life began. She settled in El Paso and later my grandpa's work took them to Chicago, Illinois. After moving back to Texas, she had her first son; a year later she had her first daughter. Two years later my grandparents moved to California where she had her last child and raised them together. She lived there for 22 years and then moved to Albuquerque to join my grandpa and a new business. After many years of not having much money and her going without Christmas presents for herself, or food so that her children didn't have to go without anything, the business in Albuquerque began to make life comfortable. Grandma always talked about God and how He would never leave us without what we needed. Food, happiness, and each other. My grandma made everything special and she found the good in everything. Six years ago she was diagnosed with cancer and died last year from her cancer. I miss her very much but I know she is with God and I will always remember my grandmother and that with God all things are possible.

Zachary Quezada, Grade 7
St Thomas Aquinas School, NM

Someone Special

I'm sure there is at least one person who is special to somebody in their life. But have you ever thought what it would be like if you lost that person? Well I didn't, but I learned a very important lesson. It is something that I will remember for the rest of my life.

That special person was my grandma. Her name was Victoria, but everyone called her Vicky. She raised me for the first five years of my life. I learned much from her that has helped me live my life better. But as I got older I began to spend less time with her and I wouldn't appreciate her as much. Little did I know that I would be facing a nightmare that would change my life forever.

It started out as a minor cold that turned into a word that now sends a cold shiver down my spine every time I hear it — Cancer. When she told me, it seemed like my heart stopped beating and I began to cry. Vicky told me that everything would be okay. This made me feel better, but I had no idea what was really coming. On January 21, 2007, Vicky passed away from lung cancer.

It was a long, cold, lonely winter for me, but I guess you can say it was worth it. I learned that you should always appreciate the people that are close to you because you never know when you're going to lose them.

Adrian Arvizo, Grade 8
Rio Bravo Middle School, TX

Surviving HMS

There are many confusing rules to learn at our school; it is important that you know them to "survive." Some of these things are learning the correct side of the hall to stay on, how to act appropriately, and how much time you will have in between each class.

First, we have many students in our middle school because we count sixth graders as junior high students. In between each period, students swarm the halls in a hurry to get to class. It is easier for everyone to stay on the right side of the hall to avoid chaos and lunch detention slips.

Next, it is important to remember that you have four minutes to get to and from each class. Use your time wisely and don't even try to make it to the bathroom because it won't happen.

Please don't forget about our school's reputation of discipline. If you try to act courteously and responsibly, the teachers will adore you. You will have a hard time if you are disrespectful and juvenile. Always have good sportsmanship towards visiting teams and reply with Yes, sir, No, sir to all of your teachers.

I'm sorry for asking so much of you, but it becomes less difficult with practice. Try to be determined and make exceptional grades and do everything the best you can.

Amber Loyd, Grade 8
Holliday Middle School, TX

The Day I Killed a Sawhorse

Last weekend my dad and I went down to grandpa's to work on our projects. My grandpa is the owner of a huge piece of land. I can drive tractors, quads, and the shaker. We use them to harvest the walnuts. We went down to work on the shaker. We got it running and waited a while to let it warm up. My dad hopped into the driver seat then I asked, "Can I drive?" My dad told me the shaker had no brakes and no power steering, but I still wanted to drive.

As I hopped into the driver's seat and turned it on, I noticed grandma was drying raisins and apricots on her drying racks. My dad also told me to watch the back of the shaker because the wheels turn from the back. I looked down and saw the drying rack. Then I heard an unbearable sound. Crunch! "Oh no!" I yelled.

My grandma was right behind me. "What happened?" she said. Needless to say, my dad took over driving the shaker, while I replaced the sawhorse that had turned to dust when I drove over it.

So the moral of my day is never drive without brakes or power steering. Thankfully, no raisins, apricots, or people were harmed that day, only a saw horse.

Jonah Bennett, Grade 9
eScholar Academy, CA

First Impressions

First impressions can either be good or bad. They can also be true or false. I have made a few different impressions on people. I also know that people have made impressions on me. I know I have been wrong a few times.

One impression I have made was on one of my friends. When I first saw her in class, I thought she was weird. But then we started talking and now we are really good friends. Another impression I have made was on one of my sisters friends. I met him and for some reason I just didn't like him. He and my sister were really good friends so I tried to be nice and like him but for some reason I still didn't. Then there was an incident where someone came between their friendship and they didn't talk for a while. I had always told my sister I didn't like him. Now they are friends again and I'm glad they are but I still kinda dislike him.

After I made those impressions I realized that I was wrong to judge the people without really knowing them. Also I shouldn't make impressions on people on how they act or look or by what I've heard about them. I think it's wrong for people to make impressions. From now on I'm not going to make impressions on people. I don't think anybody should make impressions on people whether they know them or not.

Laura Solis, Grade 7
Isbell Middle School, CA

Free Will

My take on free will is that everyone should retain independence. The citizens of the United States of America have the option to constitute good or bad decisions. What most people don't understand is that all decisions have consequences. The definition of consequence is: As a result. I find that numerous people think consequence only to mean bad; but consequence could mean good or bad results.

Classmates of mine always question my decision to live an honest life. I choose to make good decisions that have my, my family, and others' best interests in mind. In school one day, a boy asked to copy my paper. I said no, it was cheating. He insisted that it was helping. I stuck with my answer, "No." He eventually found someone else to copy off of. He called her "the nice person" and me "the mean person."

If I had let him copy my work, who would benefit? Not me, certainly. But most definitely, not him; now he probably will keep cheating and won't reach his full potential. He might pass the class, but dishonestly; he wouldn't have earned it. My decision to say no will leave me a consequence of a clear conscience.

Free will is the core to our democracy. Without it, we wouldn't have our government. I say we use our free will to help the world; to reach our full capacity and transform the world for good.

Kayla Klingbiel, Grade 8
Union Middle School, UT

My Family

My family is really important to me. We all go out to eat and go to each other's games, concerts, and graduations. My family is made up of me, my sister, my dad, my mom, and my two dogs.

My sister's name is Stacy. She is a sophomore at Hart High School. Stacy also plays volleyball and is in show choir. My sister can be annoying a lot but we get along sometimes.

My mom played college softball and basketball as CSUN and she is now the recreation services manager for the city of Burbank. My mom takes me and my sister to all our tournaments and games.

My dad was a firefighter for the city of Glendale and now teaches civilian emergency services. He also takes my sister and me to practices, games, and tournaments. He calls himself the chauffeur.

My family always has dinner together every night and talks about how our day went. We go to plays, musicals, and sports games. My family has a lot of barbecues with friends and family. We sit around our fire pit and make s'mores. I realized that without my family I wouldn't have all the things I have today like playing club soccer, club volleyball, and I wouldn't have all the fun I have when we just sit around and talk with my aunt, uncle, and cousins. My family is the most important thing to me in the whole world.

Erin Indermill, Grade 7
Placerita Jr High School, CA

My Life

My life is like honey. Sometimes I go to Juarez to visit my uncles and grandparents. At the time I go to Juarez I start to get scared, because all the things that are happening over there. People getting killed, people stealing cars, and a lot more things. I would like that everyone be happy. To stop killing, and burning, and cutting human bodies. All the people that are doing all that things need to stop and think about all the kids that are over there seeing, hearing, when they kill people. That is why young teenagers start to get along with bad people, or start to do their own gangs.

In the United States it is like other world, here in the United States is different. The government and the police know what to do in an emergency or how to investigate the criminals. I think that my life is better here because you can go outside or to the movies with your friends, but in Juarez you are not comfortable you can't go outside, or with your friend to the movies. They are killing in movies, concerts, or in the Internet rooms.

I would like to be twenty-two and make my uncles and grandparents come here to the U.S. and live happy forever. To stay out of the criminals. Some young kids are turning criminals, but not me because my parents teach what is right for me and what is wrong for me. I am going everywhere with what they had taught me. I would be an engineer, counselor, or a police officer because I like to help people.

Christian Delgado, Grade 8
Rio Bravo Middle School, TX

My Best Friend

My best friend is someone I love with all my heart. He always asks me if I need help with my Spanish homework. I'm always important for him it doesn't matter if he's sad, mad, tired or even sick. He always brings happiness to my life. We always talk about our problems. He is not with me at this time.

My best friend is my dad. He lives in Mexico because of some personal problems. Sometimes we don't talk in days. I don't get to see him with frequency because he always goes out of town. When he goes out he calls and says, "see you next week" I tell him "ok but take care."

When he gets back he calls me and asks me if I want to go out to the movies or the amusement park. We also like to see the *WWE* which is a wrestling show. We have a blast together.

When it's time to go back to my house I cry a lot and I give him a big bear hug. It's very hard leaving away from my dad. I dream that we live together in the same house. And I hope that dream comes true in the future. My dad is my best friend and I would never change him for someone or anything.

Oscar Vielma, Grade 8
Rio Bravo Middle School, TX

Unexpected Victory

3, 2, 1, beep! The buzzer sounded and I was tossed into a swarm of pushing girls. From the sideline I noticed my dad cheering me on, with his video camera in hand. He was taping my first cross country meet at Bear Creek, actually the first time I've ever done anything competitive. After a few minutes I could hear heavy breathing, and then suddenly the crowd fell back. I was just half way through the race when I noticed that only a couple girls had kept their original pace. To my surprise I wasn't tired yet, so I kicked it up and I passed the leaders. I knew I had to stay strong and imagined crossing the finish line. Coming around the final corner, I could see the colorful flags marking the finish line, and the cheers were becoming louder. Striding past the finish I felt a sensation I'd never experienced. It was a mixture of joy, pride, and relief. I always imagined that getting first place at something would be so cool, but I never dreamed it would happen to me. Especially since I had not trained for this race. And when people asked me how I beat 150 competitors, I didn't know how to reply because all I did was just run as hard as I could. Even when I feel exhausted and want to stop, I've learned it pays off to keep going…with three scoops of Baskin Robbins chocolate ice cream and a blue ribbon!

Madison Gilcrease, Grade 7
Goodson Middle School, TX

My Jolly Time of Year

There are so many holidays in the year. I love all of them, but Christmas is my favorite holiday of them all. I like that it is in winter because it is chilly outside. I love the winter.

Christmas is the time of year when everyone is jolly and joyful. It is when everyone is dressed up in their coats, gloves, and scarves during this chilly weather. All the adults are a little stressed out trying to get all their Christmas shopping done because they know that Christmas is near. All the kids are so excited for Santa Claus to come visit their house with their presents that they have wanted for a very long time.

I love Christmas Eve. I just love getting all warm and cozy in my pajamas and watching my little siblings with their huge smiles across their faces that are filled with joy and excitement. Everyone gets in their bed early, anxious for Santa to come with our presents. Usually one of us wakes up really early in the morning and goes into each other's room. We wake each other up one by one. We all walk down the cold stairway together and look under the Christmas tree and see all those presents waiting for us. We all open our presents, then eat the special meal that our mom makes, and then go to Christmas Mass. That is why I love Christmas so much!

Jamie Huntzinger, Grade 7
St Elizabeth Ann Seton School, TX

Washington D.C.

My trip to D.C. was a great experience. It was the first time I had the opportunity to fly and I flew alone. It was really cool. While I was there, I had the opportunity to do and see many things. The downfall of the trip was having to walk everywhere. Another bad thing about the trip was the time change.

Some of the monuments were taller than I thought. One example is the Washington Monument; I thought it was only like one hundred feet tall, but it's actually close to six hundred. Another monument that was taller than I thought was the Vietnam memorial. I didn't think it was taller than six feet; it seemed close to twelve. Some of the war memorials were surprisingly long. One of the war memorials was pretty cool. Instead of having names on the wall, the Korean War memorial had faces from pictures taken during the war.

The trip to D.C. was a cool experience. I got to see some really cool things and meet some cool people. One of the most exciting things I saw was when my group went to the gate of the White House. I saw the president's dog run across the front lawn. By the end of the trip I was so tired I could barely even stand without falling asleep. When I got home all I wanted to do was go to sleep, but I had to stay up and tell my mom about the trip.

Cody Jacobs, Grade 8
Long Valley Charter School, CA

Becoming a Sister

Brothers are very annoying, they are always bothering you, and they don't listen to you. I have 2 little brothers of my own and they just don't know when to leave me alone.

I remember when my two little brothers were born. One of my brothers was born on, March 23, 2000, and the other one was born on April 1, 2004. When I was little I used to get in the playpen and play with them. My mom would always have to get after me, because I was in there with them. We would play with the little toy cars, stuffed animals, and play house.

As soon, as we started getting older and grew apart from each other. We are always at each other's throats. We get on each other's nerves, we don't get along at all and they never want to listen to me. They always think they are their own bosses. I would tell them to do something, and then they do the opposite of what I told them to do. It really makes me mad that they would do that to someone who is trying to help them stay out of trouble, and they keep doing it. I hate that my mom always takes their side when I do something to them, because the only time I do anything to them is when they do it to me first. Becoming a sister really changes your life.

Alexus Barajas, Grade 8
Reagan County Middle School, TX

Christmas Vacation

Last Christmas my family and I went to Disney World in Florida. We drove from Texas to Florida; it took about 13 hours to drive. When we got to Disney World the first park we went to was Disney Studios. It was so much fun! Disney Studios was all about the process of movie making and you can watch movies there. The 2nd day we were at Disney World it was Christmas, so we went to the Magic Kingdom. When we were about to go into the Magic Kingdom, the worker at the booth in the parking lot said we can't go in because the parking spaces are all filled, so we had to go to Epcot instead. While we were about to buy the tickets to Epcot, a worker told us that the Magic Kingdom was now open. So we drove back to the Magic Kingdom and it was open. While we were there it was so crowded because of the parades during Christmas. So when we got there, we saw a parade with all the Disney characters on floats. Since it was Christmas, the whole park was open until 2 A.M. At midnight we saw amazing fireworks, and when they started shooting all the fireworks it looked like it was daytime. That day was amazing and I hope to go to Disney World again.

Dianne Espiritu, Grade 7
St Elizabeth Ann Seton School, TX

Planet Earth

Something that is very important to me, most people take for granted. It is something that all living things, could not live without, and yet most people give little thought to it. Every single thing uses it on someway or somehow. The Earth is highly important to me.

There are hundreds of reasons why Earth is important to me. I think the Earth is an extraordinary creation, which should be cared for with the same compassion as we do for our own families. A difficult thing for people to understand is that the Earth is like a fragile flower. Too much sun or water could kill the flower. It is the same exact concept with the Earth. "Polluted by his own it happens all the time. Son turns on his father, just so that he can have his glory." once said by my father. If too much distraction is done the Earth will no longer be able to support life, and die. Another reason why, I care so much for the Earth, is because it is my home. My home is the most beautiful miracle that has ever been.

Whenever I look up at the sky I'm at peace. The Earth should be important to everyone, it protects you, your family, and me. Next time someone thinks of the Earth, they should think, wow I'm lucky. Be grateful for what you have. The Earth is important, it's no just that your grandson won't see a polar bear it's that his great-grandson won't see the light of day.

Jennifer Krueger, Grade 8
Zia Middle School, NM

High Merit Essays – Grades 7, 8 and 9

Up to the Moon

I watch the slow rise and fall of the child's chest as he breathes deeply. I see a peaceful slumber smile cross his face. I hear the lullaby tape playing in the CD player and whisper the words to the song, "I love you up to the moon. I love you big as the sky. I love to watch you sleep, and hold you when you cry."

All my life I have loved to baby-sit, hold a new born baby in my arms, or run around with a toddler just for fun. Even at age four, whenever I was at church and one of the babies needed to be fed, I begged the mother to let me feed him. I don't understand why, but watching these children grow and start to achieve their goals brings me sheer happiness.

I wonder what it will be like to have a child of my own. Will I love watching him grow up or want him to stay young forever? Will I be ready to carry the responsibility for another life? I cannot even imagine the love I will feel for him. I know that it will be a long while before I have my own baby, but I cannot help but wonder how I will feel singing to my own child, "I love you up to the moon. I love you big as the sky."

Lydia Buerer, Grade 9
Faith Christian Jr/Sr High School, CA

My Sister Going to the Air Force

Have you ever had a loved one join the Air Force or the Army? I have when my sister left. I still remember the day my sister joined the Air Force.

She left the Monday before Thanksgiving 2007. My dad drove her to San Angelo to meet her recruiter. We didn't see her again until January 3, 2008, when she graduated basic training. The first glimpse we got of her was when she was marching onto the parade grounds with her flight. It was very cold, and we were huddled up drinking hot chocolate. My sister somehow seemed different, and we were proud of her.

After spending a couple of days with her, we came home, and she flew to her tech school in California. Meagan finished tech school in August 2008. She then came home for 10 days. It was really nice to have all of us together again.

Meagan is currently stationed in Colorado. She works with NASA on satellites. She is not allowed to tell us exactly what she does as it is classified information. She has been stationed at Schriever AFB for over a year now. I am jealous of her because she gets to see snow in Colorado.

Since my sister has joined the Air Force, I have experienced many feelings. I was sad to see her leave, however, I am extremely happy when we get to see her. I am very proud of her. Just because somebody leaves doesn't mean they will not come back.

Zackary Pool, Grade 8
Reagan County Middle School, TX

America's Veterans — Our Country's Heroes

Veterans Day is an American holiday that honors military veterans. This special day honors men and women in uniform who have protected our country and kept us safe from terror. On this day, we not only honor military veterans, but we also honor their families for the sacrifices they have made for our country.

On September 11, 2001 while getting ready for school, I heard my mom scream while watching the news. The news was reporting that the terrorist attacks had taken place in New York. I was too young to understand everything that was happening and my mother did not want to scare me. Watching her reaction and then coming to school and seeing all of the sad faces, I knew something was wrong. My parents told me that everything would be okay because we are a strong country, and they said we would be protected.

Shortly after the 9/11 terrorist attacks, the United States launched a war against terrorism in Afghanistan. Many soldiers have been killed in the war because they were brave enough to defend our country and keep us all safe.

I now realize that our military does many things on a daily basis to protect our country from harm, and living through the experience of 9/11 has given me a great appreciation for our soldiers and veterans. I now truly understand the meaning of Veterans Day and why we honor them.

Brocke Stepteau, Grade 8
St Elizabeth Ann Seton School, TX

Friends

Having friends is important to me. Having friends is something good to have. Without friends you would be lonely, you would be bored at school or anywhere without friends. When you have friends you have somebody to talk to and hang out with. Maybe you can tell your friends anything because you know you can trust them. Your friends are people who you can tell anything to without being afraid that they are going to tell somebody else. Telling your friends your secrets, you can tell your friends your deepest secrets. When you have friends you don't feel left out. Your friends are there for you through anything. Friends do not talk about you behind your back, they will never say anything mean to you or about you. Friends do get in arguments but it doesn't mean that they will never talk to you again. Real friends will always talk to you even when you guys get in arguments. Friends that just walk away and don't even try to talk about the problem aren't real friends. Some people really trust their friends, people that can't trust their friends aren't real friends. Friends don't say anything to get you mad they don't lie to you they speak the truth. That's why having friends is important to me. Without friends I think people would be bored and lonely. Friends are important.

Chastidy Barreras, Grade 8
Zia Middle School, NM

Change

This essay is on change, and how it's a good thing and how the fear of change can be overcome. Change is inevitable, so as we go on we must adapt.

Change is when our life turns for the worst or for the better. We learn to go along or to move around the change. Sometimes we choose differently, and change the things that would happen to fit our needs, when we do this we do it for a better cause, but most times it affects others.

Often we think of the outcome of our situation, or rather how it will end. We can only predict this and situations that we might face. The best thing to do is to follow what we think is best. In times whether we choose an act or don't choose an act, the decision will shape the future.

The world around us is filled with change and opportunities that will decide ours, and the youth's future. We can help each other every day to make the right choices that will help us through a rough time.

As we go on with our lives we have to face change, and if for the better or good, we can endure it to the end. And I would like to end this with one of my favorite quotes. "You can't direct the wind, but you can adjust your sails."

Evan Hansen, Grade 8
Canyon View Jr High School, UT

Trip to the Bahamas

It was seven days before the first day of school was to start. I wasn't ready for my summer to end. I knew that once school started the fun was over. I was looking for one more thing to top the summer off. So my parents said "hey guys lets go to the Bahamas and stay at Atlantis." I was so excited; I couldn't wait to start packing my bags! So we decided to leave the next day.

We got to the airport and found out the flights were full, but luckily we were the last four people to get the seats on the plane. We finally got to the Bahamas and the second I got there I knew I was gonna go and hit the water park! They had so many water rides. There was the Leap of Faith, which was huge and you went sliding through a tank of sharks. Then there was the Abyss. It was pitch black and we went down it. Then there was the Challenger where you would be able to race down the water slide with anyone.

We went every day to the waterpark and every day to dinner; there was tons to choose from! The Miss Universe models were staying in the same wing as us, and we were able to see them. But soon it was time to end our fun in the Bahamas. So we had to go back to Texas and return to school!

Lauren Ondarza, Grade 7
St Elizabeth Ann Seton School, TX

Breathtaking Books

Although there are a great number of items in my life that I value, one of the most important to me is books. No matter what the circumstances may be, I can always lose myself and find total peace in a well-written book. My mind journeys over to this new, captivating land, and I find myself relating to, even sympathizing with, a wide assortment of characters.

Novels can hold me in many different ways. They may be suspenseful and spooky — the kind of book that can be read under the covers with a flashlight late into the night. They could also be full of interesting characters which I might find myself laughing or crying with. I even find myself thinking of what I might say to them if that particular person were right alongside me.

Over the course of a dull day, I find my eyes and mind darting to that unfinished, lovingly worn book lying on the table; inviting me to accompany it on a well traveled, and exciting journey. I may have read that particular book dozens of times, and know what will happen next, yet will be surprised and even more pleased with the outcome than before. But, I must pull myself away, and resort to the everyday mundane tasks stretched out before me. Even as I am prevented from reading, my subconscious is trying to figure out what will happen the next time I travel to this literary dimension that is so important to me.

Kimi Stevenson, Grade 7
Placerita Jr High School, CA

No Phones Allowed

Kids having cell phones at school is not only unnecessary, but also very distracting. Students would not focus on their schoolwork, and they could even use their phones to cheat on a test.

One reason cell phones should not be allowed is that students would use their phones to cheat. They could easily pull out their phone and text someone to give them the answer. They could even look up the answer online if their phone has the Internet.

Another reason is that their phones are unnecessary. Why would you text or call someone when they are already right there in the classroom? Even if the person you want to text is not in the classroom, you could still talk to them in between classes or at lunch. There's no reason to have a text during class.

The final reason is that cell phones distract the students. They would be too concerned with texting their friends instead of doing their assignments. Students would not listen to their teachers because they would be texting someone.

As you can see, there are many reasons why students should not be allowed to have cell phones at school. From cheating on a test to not paying attention in class, students are bound to not do very well in school if they were allowed to have and use cell phones.

Mariah Hoffman, Grade 8
Holliday Middle School, TX

My Cousin

Ring! Ring! Ring! I answered the phone. It was my aunt. I never thought what she told me could ever happen. She told me my cousin had died.

I remember when we were little. He would always make me laugh. He was full of life. Every day was a new adventure for him, he had lost his mother and baby brother a while back. He loved to ride horses. Everyone loved him, he was easy going, he hardly ever was mean to anyone.

Well when they first told me, I was shocked. I couldn't believe it! They told me when the funeral was. I asked, "How did he die?" They said, "He was riding his horse and when the horse stood up he fell, then the horse fell on top of him."

The day of the service, I went. It was weird not seeing him run to me, giving me hugs. When I finally got the guts to go see him, I stayed up there with him for 2 hours. I decided to talk to him. I told him how much I loved him. Then they came and took him away.

The next morning, I woke up and took a shower. I was getting ready to go to the cemetery, and say my final good-byes. When we got there, everything was set. We said our final good-byes. Then we left.

Up to this point, I still cry, but it's gotten better. I will never forget how important my cousin was to me.

Sierra Talamantes, Grade 7
Seminole Jr High School, TX

History of Post-It Notes

Post-It notes were invented by Spencer Silver in 1790. Silver had first invented a type of glue. This glue would stick, but not very well. He tried to sell it, but nobody wanted it. I mean, it had no purpose. People thought that it had no reason to be invented. (You might as well sell a pen with no ink.) So, he put his idea away. Silver's friend was having a problem with his books. (This was the next step.) His friend would always complain about his book markers falling out of his books when he opened them. What he needed was some glue that he could use to glue his pages together, but he didn't want to ruin his books. He told Silver about his problem, and Silver knew just the thing! Silver told his friend about the glue he had invented, and that it would most likely work. So, they used his glue and glued two pages together. It worked! Then, he put some glue on one of his book markers, and that worked too! Silver had made just the thing! He sent them to offices and they loved them so much that they kept ordering more! In that time, they were just a plain yellow color, now they come in all different shapes, sizes, colors, and designs! Silver's product worked its way up into one of the top-selling products ever! Still today, they are very popular and used in just about every office!

Alexandria Sims, Grade 7
Breckenridge Jr High School, TX

Soccer

My life has been blessed with many things and many people. My family is one of them. One of the blessings I am most grateful for is my ability to play soccer. It has had a great influence on my life. I have been playing almost all of my life, along with all of my other siblings play. I'm grateful for this because I have so much happiness when I play and I always look forward to playing whenever I can. I'm pretty good at it.

I have played on four different teams throughout my career. The first team I was on was a really good team but everyone on the team was older than me. The second and third team I was on weren't very good. We hardly won any games. I learned, playing on those teams, that winning isn't everything. Sure, winning is always more fun and everyone would prefer to win than lose, but if you always win, you don't learn as much as you do when you lose. Losing made me a better player

I learned to be competitive and to be my best. My current team is very good. We win a lot! I enjoy soccer very much. It has had a positive influence on my life. It is the thing I really enjoy doing.

David Gros, Grade 8
St Thomas Aquinas School, NM

At the Louvre

Many people are quietly gazing at the paintings on the wall in amazement. The Louvre, located in France, is one of the world's biggest art museums. It is full of art from all over the world. Many water fountains and a medieval building adorned with sculpture surround the main entrance to the museum, a glass pyramid. Inside the Louvre, there are two famous pieces of art, the *Mona Lisa* and the *Venus de Milo*.

The *Mona Lisa* is an oil painting and portrait by Leonardo da Vinci, who lived in medieval times. She wears a black gown and has a mysterious smile. With her arms folded in front of her, and the background different on each side, she looks out at the crowd knowingly. The whole face, especially the eyes, is painted with detail.

The *Venus de Milo* is somewhat different, however. This figure, carved out of white marble, is the work of an anonymous artist who, people believe, lived in ancient Greek. While her arms are cut off, the figure is still very detailed; you can see every fold on the fabric and the strands of hair on her head. She looks at the crowd with a solemn and unsmiling face. There is also a robe draped across her. However, these two pieces of art are equally amazing and breathtaking. These masterpieces show the quality of two exceptionally skilled artists. People who come here to see the art in the Louvre will be wowed even more.

Ted Shi, Grade 7
Westbrook Intermediate School, TX

Goalie

Here we are at another soccer game. I am playing midfield, my favorite position, and I call for the ball. My teammate passes me the ball, I shoot, I SCORE! The crowd goes crazy, the score is now 10-9 for us. The whistle blows and it's half time. Everyone rushes in for water and their next position. I am sitting on the bench waiting to be called as midfield when I hear, "Maddy, goalie." I had just heard my least favorite word ever.

The whistle blows and now it's time to be goalie. As I put my gloves and penny on, I say to myself, "I can't do this."

30 minutes later I blocked 3 goals and let 4 in, but luckily my teammates scored 3 goals. The score is now 13-13 and there are 10 minutes left. I am still holding up pretty well, but to make sure we win I have to block the rest of the goals from the other team. One minute left and the score is the same. The other team is coming at me. They keep getting closer, they shoot...The crowd is standing with their mouths wide open, I jump in the air at a diagonal angle, I'm spread out ready to block. It's coming closer and closer, the ball gets to my hands...and CRACK...my finger...broke. I broke my finger and I didn't even block the goal. The whistle blew and the referee yells, "GAME, score 14-13." We lost.

Madison Halboth, Grade 7
St Elizabeth Ann Seton School, TX

Who Am I?

Who am I? That's the question most teenagers ask themselves. For me, I know who I am, who I'm supposed to be. But why am I different? What makes me special, what makes me stand out?

When I was in fourth grade, I was determined that I wanted to be a veterinarian. And that I would also be the first woman to find a cure for cancer. Then, as I got older, thoughts started scrambling through my head. An interest for politics, and chemistry popped inside my brain and all of those days promising everyone I was going to be vet were over. I decided I wanted to do something greater than a cure for cancer; I wanted to find a cure for one of the most deadly viruses in the entire globe, AIDS.

I'm in the seventh grade now, three years have passed. My mind is zipping through all the choices I have to make until the end of high school. I'm planning on using this essay for my college interview. I want to get into an Ivy League, which means I have to be perfect. I have to be different. I have to stand out. Which brings me back to the beginning. Who am I? I'm a girl with a future.

Cinthia Moncores, Grade 7
Goodson Middle School, TX

Inspirational

One of the most inspirational people in my life would have to be my great-grandmother, Angeline Hajek. She was a strong, brave woman always willing to benefit the other people in her small town of Seymour, Texas. She would go to her Catholic church every Sunday, and would almost always give a donation to her small parish, even if she needed the money herself.

Every day, she would make three home-cooked meals for her family, always adding a little love. We would say grace and dig in to her wonderful meal. She would also make delicious pies, cakes, cookies, and preserves for after our dinner. She would can the peaches and pears by hand. She would even make her own homemade pickles!

Whenever I needed help, she would always give me advice. She listened to my problems and loved to help. She loved to laugh and was very strong in her faith. She lived life to its fullest, never doubting God. She gave her all, even in her fight with cancer. She passed away in January of 2007. She was a very inspirational woman in everything that she said, did, and was as a person. I am so blessed to have had her in my family and I will never forget the special memories we shared. I know that she is watching from Heaven and guiding me through my life, which I hope will be as inspirational as hers.

Jordan Bailey, Grade 8
St Elizabeth Ann Seton School, TX

National League West Champs

On Oct. 3rd, 2009, we headed for Dodger Stadium in Los Angeles. It was the second to last game of the season for the team. They had needed only one game, to clinch the division; that was a week ago.

Now on this 2nd to last game of the season, they are only one game ahead of the Colorado Rockies, who they were playing that night. You have to understand that the games they lost all week were against last place teams or close to last. They had just finished a five game losing streak with those teams.

When we arrived it was sold out; we already had our tickets. We had great seats in the infield reserve section on the third base side. It was a sea of Dodger blue, myself included. What a show of support by the Dodger fans.

Clayton Kershaw, the 21 year old pitcher did a great job for the Dodgers. He struck out 11 batters and shut out the Rockies through six innings. One of the surprises of the night was Manny Ramirez. He had struck out four times the day before, but this night he got a base hit.

Manny, Kemp, Belliard, Pierre, Blake, and others helped the Dodgers beat the Rockies five to nothing. The Dodgers became the National League West champs, with the best record in the National League. This gave the Dodgers home field advantage on October 7 against the Cardinals in the first round of the playoffs.

Cody Haas-Tellez, Grade 8
Palm Desert Charter Middle School, CA

Being an American

The civic value that I feel is most important to being an American is behaving justly. Many people want to be American people and ship illegally across the United States border. That is why we have border patrol police officers. The people who signed the Declaration of Independence made freedom and justice possible. We fought wars to keep justice.

We fought wars to keep freedom for the people who couldn't grasp it. Freedom is the most important thing in the United States. To keep it fair, we still have laws but they're fair laws. Some of our laws are freedom of speech, no illegal substances, no murder, and no stealing.

Hope to find cures is coming faster and faster in the United States. We need hope to be American. We are American not American't! We will find a cure for cancer one day. We will find a cure for AIDS one day. We will find cures for everything one day! The day we get the cure for everything is the new beginning.

America is the best place to live! We have laws, freedoms, and justice. That is the reason I live here, because I was born here. You have to be legal to live in America. This is why I'm thankful to be American. I don't need a green card or food stamps, I have a family that has a job and lives happily, because we are thankful for where we live. We don't abuse the fact that we are American and others are not, but we do think that it is fair that others have a place to live.

Bryce Lobb, Grade 7
Anthony Charter School, NM

Introduced to Skateboarding

One day I rode my first skateboard and as soon as I got one it I knew I would be doing this for a long time. At first I started riding Walmart Monguse boards, those were the cheap useless boards beginners ride when they're starting to learn. Then in like a month or two I got my first pro deck, it was a Blind. Later on when I started getting better doing the basic tricks like kick flip, pop shuvit, big spin, nolies, 180s I started entering comps in beginners division. Winning most of them I began to learn more intermediate tricks like 360 pop shuvit, dubble flip, nilie heel, swich heel, nolie varial heel, and fs flip n bs flip. Those are most of my intermediate. Right now I am still an intermediate skater but I'm trying to learn more advanced tricks. This very moment I am doing everything to learn harder tricks. Also, did I tell you the grinds and grabs I already know, well here they are, in grind, 5-0, 50-50, nose grind, krook, salad, and blunt. And grabs, air walk, method, melon, indy, cannon, benihana, and roast beef. Well there you have what I know right now but wait a year or two and you will see how good I will be.

Luis Aragon, Grade 8
Rio Bravo Middle School, TX

Me Moving!!

My name is Domitille de Thé. I am from France and will be returning there next year. Before coming to the United States I lived in Spain for three years and then in France for five years. This is how the story about me moving to the United States goes. When I was nine years old, one day my father came to me and said, "We are moving to the united States." We moved from our apartment in June with great emotions. We had been living there for so long. We spent our summer in France bidding farewells to family and friends. Finally on August 3rd 2006 we took the plane to leave our country. When we arrived I was very excited. Something that I think is very funny is that when someone talked to us we'd say: "no understand." After about three weeks in the hotel we could finally move to our own house. We visited the house and I was amazed by our pool and yard. It was the first time we ever got to live in a house. I thought about the past and the future. I missed the past but looked forward to the future. My first year was like a nightmare. I didn't understand anything and I had a lot of homework each day. Now here I am at Saint Elizabeth Ann Seton with nice friends and I am able to speak English (thankfully) better than four years ago. I love the United States!

Domitille de The, Grade 7
St Elizabeth Ann Seton School, TX

Z Is for Zebra

My favorite wild animal is a zebra. They are really cool animal. They are a type of wild horse that lives in the grasslands, savannas, woodlands, scrublands, and mountains in Africa. There is three extant species of the zebra. The one that is mainly known is the Grey's Zebra.

The zebra has been my favorite animal since I was little. Every zebra is different because no zebra has the same exact same print. The print is really weird because every one thinks that it is white with black stripes, but it is really black with white stripes. If you were to shave a zebra it would be completely black. The Grey's Zebra is endangered due to poachers and loss of habitat.

A male zebra is called a stallion, and a female is called a mare. Something weird about them is that they sleep standing up. Zebras can run really fast. They can run up to 40 miles per hour. The smallest species is the mountain zebra. Something strange about new born zebras is that they can run one hour after they are born.

My favorite animal is the Zebra. They are really cool because if you were to shave a zebra it would be completely black. Their lifespan in captivity is about 40 years. In their natural habitat it's about 15 to 20 years.

In conclusion, zebras are my favorite wild animal. Be sure to save them so the future children can enjoy them.

Rebecca Scott, Grade 7
Isbell Middle School, CA

What's the Deal with Moms?

They are always telling you what to do! Kids say that they hate their moms or they think bad things about them. Some tell their friends stories of what their mom won't let them do, like not let them have any privileges, ground them or tell them they have to go to bed early because of school.

Don't you hate it when moms always get psyched for your first day of school and they always want to take your picture of how cute they think you are? Then you end up getting all embarrassed and they smother you in kisses and you can't wait for it to all be over. Moms will never change. When you turn sixteen, they will always call you their baby and I doubt they're going to ever stop.

The point of having a mom is to let your anger out on someone. Who else are you going to talk about your problems with? Who will tell you that you forgot this and say they love you and all the gushy stuff? You may hate it but deep down you really love them. When the time comes and you get older, you're going to feel guilty about all the things you said or ever did and you're going to go right up to your mom and tell her that you love her. Mom, I love you!

Laurel Winnegge, Grade 7
Long Valley Charter School, CA

Church Is Not a Sleeping Matter

Some people sleep, some don't care or just don't understand it, but don't judge church because of maybe something you've heard. You can really learn something new every day. I love church so much it's like a super strong string that can't be cut. Some churches just read out of the Bible. At my church, Prince of Life Lutheran Church, we play games that interact with what we learned or learn from each other. What makes those things fun is friends and learning something new.

What also makes church important to me is learning. Learning does sound boring but at church it's not math and science. It's the way of life. Church makes me feel relieved from homework or politics. To me it's a breath of fresh air. In addition to learning about the Bible you can learn about you or maybe a gift God gave you.

After all the education comes the exciting things! Learning could be entertainment but going to concerts, doing holiday activities and spending it with friends is much better. One of my favorites is the Halloween Spectacular. We go to a haunted corn maze and spend the night at church. Even though it's scary we all stick together with God. During the summer we go on mission trips. Mission trips are a lot of fun and it's good to help people. So next time you go to church don't fall asleep because you can learn something new every day and that's what is important to me.

Nikki Brees, Grade 8
Thora B Gardiner Middle School, OR

School Hours

United States public schools should not extend their hours. We already go from 8:00-3:10. That is plenty of time to learn.

Some adults might think two more hours of school won't hurt. If they were thirteen again, they wouldn't want to extend school hours. When they were in school, they hated it. A lot of kids do; it's normal. If we went to school for longer we would have no social life. The only time we could talk is during break and lunch.

Longer school hours mean less time to sleep and do homework. If we have no time to do homework we will be turning in late work, and trust me — teachers hate it when you don't have your work in on time. It would also cut into our time to sleep. When we don't get enough sleep it turns us into monsters. Monsters are vicious, and nobody likes them.

Teachers don't want to extend school hours, either. They also want to go home and see their family, and friends. They have a life too you know. It may also cause the teachers to want to quit. Then you might have to close the schools. Then the kids would have to transfer, and schools would become over populated with kids.

We would turn in lots of late work, and we would have no time to do homework or sleep. No teachers or parents want that to happen.

Makenzie Baker, Grade 8
Holliday Middle School, TX

Having Great Parents

Everyone loves their parents whether they know it or not. For some people it takes a real eye opener for them to realize that they really do love their parents. This wasn't the case for me. I knew from the very beginning that I loved my parents no matter how mad I got at them.

It started the night before my first football game. I was so nervous I couldn't even pick up a fork to eat my dinner. After I finally managed to eat something, I took a hot shower and headed off for bed. I laid there for what seemed like hours, I tossed and turned, but I just couldn't get to sleep. After about three hours, I nodded off into a deep sleep. Before I knew it, it was time to get up and get ready for school. I was so tired I even tried to put my shoes on the wrong feet. All that day my mom was telling me to just relax and I would do great. My dad even stopped by the locker room to wish me good luck!

Both of my parents are always encouraging me to do my best. After every game they always tell me how good I did and what I can do to get better. I consider myself to be the luckiest kid on earth because my parents are always there for me no matter what.

Justin Pullig, Grade 8
Reagan County Middle School, TX

Pandas: The Awesomest Animals Ever!

Pandas are great animals. They are very rare and cute. Since I was little I always wanted to go to China and adopt one. Many people thing that pandas are lazy, worthless animals but they are the most interesting animals EVER! People think pandas don't do anything but pandas are very had working. They feed their baby cubs. They are very loving animals. Since pandas are very rare it is very urgent to help save them. They need our help because if we don't help them they are going to become extinct!

A panda looks like this: big, black and white, fuzzy fur, chubby. Pandas eat bamboo. Bamboo is a long stick with leaves. Pandas are giant. They are as big an American Black Bear. Pandas are the second most threatened species in the world. There are two types of pandas. There are the "Giant Panda" and the "Red Pandas." The Red Pandas kind of look like foxes. They have long tail and are reddish brown. Red pandas are cute. But I like giant pandas better. Pandas live in the forest of China. Pandas first appeared about 2-3 million years ago. Pandas only breed once a year. Pandas can't go without food for more that 5-6 hours. Some people call pandas "Big Bear Cats."

Pandas eat bamboo, sugar cane, rice gruel, a special high-fiber biscuit, carrots, apples, and sweet potatoes. They are very smart animals that need our help. We need to do the best we can to make them live longer.

Daisy Duran, Grade 8
Isbell Middle School, CA

Tony Romo

On April 21st, 1980 in San Diego one of the greatest Dallas Cowboys quarterbacks was born and his name was Tony Romo. Tony Romo was a great Dallas Cowboys quarterback. In 2003 Tony was finally signed by the Dallas Cowboys as a free agent who was now soon to be an American football quarterback of the NFL.

In 2008 Tony led the Dallas Cowboys to a 28-10 win over the Cleveland Browns. During the 3rd quarter when Linebacker Willie McGinest hit Tony in the chin with his helmet he had to have 13 stitches for his injury. Tony broke his little finger during the 2008 season. He was out for the following three games.

Despite the fact of Tony's injuries he would not let this stop him. On December 19th, 2002 he was the first player in eastern Illinois and Ohio valley conference history to win the Walter Payton award. Tony was a strong athlete. He would not let injuries or the press take him down. To me Tony Romo is the greatest quarterback of the NFL because he plays the game that he loves and does not back down to anything. That is why I think Tony Romo is the greatest Dallas Cowboys quarterback and he still plays to this day.

Nocona Holland, Grade 7
Deweyville Middle School, TX

The Replacement

I had a dog since I was 2 years old. Her name was Annie. She was always there for me. It was like she understood me, and was the best. But on New Year's Day of 2008 she had died. I was in complete shock and was lonely. I knew I would never get another dog that would replace her. It was just very unlikely.

I had gotten many other dogs after her including a yellow lab, and a German Sheppard puppy. I thought that one of those dogs would be the replacement, but they were both returned because my parents couldn't handle it. About a year and a half later, around May of 2009, my dad had a patient come in, and she asked him if he wanted a yellow lab. So we visited this dog at a shelter, and my brother fell in love with it. They asked me if I wanted her, so I said yes because my brother wanted it. I did not like her at first, but later she had ended up liking me the most. I had then realized that this would be the replacement. Her name is Sunny. She is very much like my other dog who died, and she understands me like Annie had. She is still my dog today, but I still miss Annie and I will always remember her.

Bilito Starck, Grade 7
St Elizabeth Ann Seton School, TX

Decision Making Process

Decision making is an important process that can affect you in good ways or small ways. Decisions are something we do every day. Whether decision of what to wear, or something big like what house to buy. There is something you need to consider when you are about to make your decision.

One thing you should consider and think about is your attitude. Will you react bad if something doesn't go your way, or will you accept it? Another is if you have adaptability if your decision goes bad can you quickly use a back up plan and adjust your plan? If your decision goes with your attitude and you always have a backup plan. You are safe and prepared to continue with your choice. Unfortunately there is something that can make your decision harder. That thing is obstacles. Obstacles block you from making your decision or making it come true. Obstacles can be big or small and can be difficult to overcome. The way to overcome your obstacle is state your obstacle, think of how to solve it. Then do it. If it doesn't work try another way to unblock your path. Also if you need help making a decision use the seven step decision plan to help you, or ask someone for their opinion.

Attitude, adaptability, and obstacles are important in decision making. When you make your decision make sure to consider these things and your decisions will work out fine.

Lorenzo Beltran, Grade 8
Rio Bravo Middle School, TX

My National Tournament

My basketball games are important to me because my team and I had to go to Corsicana for the national tournament. A lot of our fans were going to support us. The only way to go to the national tournament is to come in first or second in regionals. Last year we got third place in nationals and this year we were hoping to do better.

After a long drive from Brownfield, TX, we made it to our hotel. The next morning we anxiously got ready to play. We won our first game against Fairfield. Our second game was against Kerrville since they also won their game so they might be a little harder or a lot harder than Fairfield was. The only way to be eliminated from this tournament is to lose two games. Anyway, we ended up losing against Kerrville and had to play Fairfield again. We won against Fairfield, again, and now they were out of the tournament. Next we played Denver City. They were the only team we lost to in regionals. They were really hard. We lost to them by three points, we came in eighth place.

I was proud, my coach was proud, and my team was proud that we tried our hardest. We are proud that we got to go there from a long way away and we tried our hardest but didn't reach our goal.

Braeden Spence, Grade 7
Seminole Jr High School, TX

Family

You know that feeling you get when you're losing someone? It feels as if no one else feels what you feel. I have felt this way before, but there are always people who will be there for you.

I'll never forget that Thursday afternoon when I was at the hospital because my grandma was very sick. My mom seemed very sad. I didn't see why because my grandma was going to get better, or that's what I thought.

Later my mom was talking to me. She was telling me about how my grandma wasn't going to get better. That's when it hit me, "Mom, is she going to die?" I asked.

"Yes," she answered with teary eyes.

I was very sad the rest of the day. My mom kept telling me that it was going to be okay and that she was going to be in a better place where she didn't have to suffer. Still I couldn't help being sad. The thought of losing her was just too much to bear. When I saw her in the room she looked like she was in so much pain, and she could barely even talk. It was scary as the days went by knowing what was going to happen. On Sunday morning when she passed away it was one of the saddest days ever.

From this experience I learned how important family is, and how hard it is losing someone. I learned that family is always an important part of life.

Abigail A. Robles, Grade 8
Reagan County Middle School, TX

Why I Love My Brother

People often ask me why I love my brother. Here are the many answers to that question. I will say that I love him because he is funny, lovable, and very creative.

I think he is funny because he would always tickle me and he would always make me laugh when I am sad, or even when I'm doing my homework. He is very lovable because he would always hug me, or kiss me on the cheek. He also says "I love you," out of nowhere. He is very creative, because he can draw anything. He loves art. He loves to draw. He can draw SpongeBob, flowers, cars, houses, and butterflies. Ask him to draw something and he will draw it.

He is so friendly to others that people want to grab him and just give him a big hug. Everyone thinks that my little brother is super cute, especially me. He loves everything. He loves watching TV, drawing, and playing with his toys. He especially loves drawing and watching SpongeBob SquarePants.

My brother is the best brother anyone can have. Even though we squabble, we still will always love each other. We love doing things together. We love drawing, pretending we are going around the world, and most especially, we love being together. I could never live without my brother. He is very special to me. He makes me happy. He loves me, and I will always love my little brother, all our lives long.

Jemm Magaling, Grade 7
Corpus Christi School, CA

$20 in the Ocean

When I was in second grade we went to Hawaii for my grandma and grandpa's 50th Anniversary. When we got off the plane we were so excited and my mom, dad, my brothers, and I ran to the rental car place. Once we got the keys to the rental car we were so excited! But once we got on the road we were very confused. The streets all had really odd names that looked the same. Eventually we got to the hotel and the worker at the front desk gave me a balloon. My brothers and I scurried to get changed into our swimsuits. Finally when my mom, dad, and brothers were ready we all jumped into the ocean. The part of the ocean we were in had really cloudy water. I was wearing my lucky pair of goggles and my mom said "You won't be able to see anything in that dirty water." I didn't care so I went back underwater. It only took about two seconds for me to pop up and scream happily "I found a twenty dollar bill!" My entire family was shocked and told me I could keep it because there is no way of knowing who owned the twenty dollar bill. I remember the twenty dollar bill was in perfect shape the only thing wrong with it was it needed to dry. That one twenty dollar bill made me one of the happiest second graders alive.

Theresa Jablonski, Grade 7
St Elizabeth Ann Seton School, TX

My Friend

I used to have a friend that made me laugh so hard that I would cry, he was nice, funny, and smart, he was the only guy that I have ever trusted. Elementary was great, we used to play tag and basketball, I would always win. Then came middle school and things changed, we would still hang out but it was different, this time we would say hi in the hallways but that was about it, but the day came when we didn't know each other, he changed, he became friends with the "emo kids" and I was friends with the normal kids, we wouldn't say much, actually we wouldn't say anything. Seventh grade came along, the best year time of my life, I made new friends and there's where I met my boyfriend, but my friend was still missing, I missed laughing with him, all I can do is remember the good times we had. Then last but not least, eighth grade, it's not that bad, sometimes I'm like "dude today sucks." I still don't talk with my old friend; I have only one class with him, sometimes we make eye contact and all I can do is look away, and go on with my life. It was like if it was yesterday that we were talking about the future, and what we would do, but those memories are slowly fading away. I didn't only lose a friend; I lost a part of me.

Jacqueline Ramos, Grade 8
Rio Bravo Middle School, TX

Wet 'n Wild

It was the day that I have been waiting for all summer. We were going to Wet 'n Wild. I loved swimming and I was good at it. I was like a seal and I had a talent for holding my breath forever under water. Wet 'n Wild was perfect for me. However, when we got there, let's just say sometimes special talents can turn against you.

We paid and got our bracelets. We went to the tables by the wave pool. This was our usual spot. Then we all went our separate ways while our parents stayed at the tables by the wave pool. My cousins and I went on the Amazon. It was fun! They wanted to go again but I said I didn't want to. I went back to the wave pool. I arrived just in time to catch the waves. I jumped right in. As I jumped the waves, I decided to see how long I could hold my breath. I took a deep breath and went right under the next wave. I could hear a whistle go "eee." I didn't think it was for me and kept up with my challenge. A few seconds later, a girl started to poke me. I looked up and I saw everyone staring at me.

They thought I was drowning! It was the lifeguard that had pulled me up. I was so embarrassed! I felt like a man standing in his underwear and everyone was staring at him. After that I didn't go into the water at all! I did learn something that day. Never show off your talents in public, especially mine!

Dimitri Viramontes, Grade 7
Santa Teresa Middle School, NM

Individuality

Individuality is a part of us that seems to be lacking in so many of our lives. We don't try to stand out, we try to fit in, we try to be like everyone else. There's just one problem, we're not the same, not every one looks alike so why try to be identical? The problem with the lives of so many people in the world is that they don't want to be themselves, they want to be someone else. People do things to act more like someone else or look more like someone else.

Some think if someone does drugs they should try it too. If someone is underage and they're drinking that it wouldn't hurt if they took a sip either. Few think that just because people are wearing these jeans they have to wear them to, they see a celebrity wearing a pair of shoes, they then have to have them too. People cut there hair, change there clothes, and act a different way just to fit in with a crowd. Why change who you are, are you ashamed of yourself? Why change who you were born to be?

Individuality means to be different or separate from one another. Individuality is something that's your own, it's something that distinguishes you from others. Why would you try so hard to act like someone else when it's easier to just be yourself? Why act like a snob when you're a totally different person? Make a difference, be the person you were meant to be.

Lindsey Murillo, Grade 8
Louis Pasteur Fundamental Middle School, CA

My Girl

My girl is what is important to me. Though I won't say her name, not because I am embarrassed, but because I didn't get her permission. So you won't know who she is. She is my star in the dark and my sun on a cold winter morn. She is the wind in my hair and the mist in my face. She is my comfort in times of trials, the love of my life. Without her I am nothing but a sad, lonely, screwed up kid with a lot of problems in life. Even though I only see her at school, she is with me always when I need her to be.

She lives in the country and I live in the city. Though there is a gap between us in space and time, I would travel a thousand miles to see her smile. When she is sad, I am depressed. When she is happy, I am joyful as a lion to a feast. This sensation has grown on me so much that the once bitter heart inside of me has turned to mud, and I have begun to speak freely about what I think of her, and she has done the same to me.

Hopefully sometime in my high school years, I want to give her something special, something she will remember for the rest of her life. Maybe it could even be a purity ring of some sort. What I do know is I will never forget her and all she has done for me and my spiritual fire inside.

Aidan Greathouse, Grade 9
Faith Christian Jr/Sr High School, CA

Be Water Wise

Have you ever wondered, how planet Earth would be without water? The world is losing one of its biggest natural resources. Water is very helpful to every living species on Earth. There are many animals in danger of extinction because they need water to survive as well as human beings and plants. Our total required amount of water is 2.5 liters a day.

Water is all around us in the air and in the ground. It's in milk, vegetables, fruits, meats, leaves, trunks, roots and branches of a tree, it's even in stones. Many people don't notice what big impact water is in our lives. We drink it, wash things with it, we need it to cook, play in, and to water plants. Water is also needed to transport people or cargo on ships or boats. More plants and animals live in water than on land.

There are many great lakes that are losing at least 2.5 billion gallons of water a day. Water can be easily polluted and it is very difficult to get it cleaned, but there are many ways we can try to stop it like conserving water by turning off the tap when running water is not necessary, by being careful of what you throw in your sink or toilet, use environmentally friendly household products, taking great care not to over use pesticides and fertilizers, and by not littering in rivers. These are only many ways to prevent water loss.

Nayra Perez, Grade 8
Isbell Middle School, CA

How to Prepare for High School Football

All great players start at one point, and this is the start of my football career. When I sign up for football in high school there are things that should go through my mind. First, I should get in the mood of becoming tough and ready for football. Second, I should worry about getting the wide receiver spot. I think this will be a tough thing to accomplish.

There are several ways I need to become prepared for tackle football. The first thing is I need to eat healthy foods. I also need to condition so I'm in shape when football season comes. I also need to become mentally strong and take yelling from my coaches. Being tough is an important element of football.

There will be lots of people trying for the wide receiver position. In order to get this position I need to practice drills that will make me catch better and run faster. Getting on the coaches good side is always a win-win. If I bring the players together, the coach could see a leader in me. If I get the spot I want in football, it will make the game more enjoyable.

As you can see I have my work cut out for me. If I work out it will make football easier for me. If I give it my all every day I'll get my wide receiver spot. My football career starts here and you may see me in the NFL one day!

Grant Peszynski, Grade 8
St Michael's Episcopal Day School, CA

Scarlet Ibis

Have you heard the quote: "You can do anything you put your mind to?" This describes the narrator in this story who is a good brother. Good brothers teach each other important skills. They take each other on adventures, and they protect each other.

First, the narrator taught his brother Doodle important skills by encouraging him to walk. Doodle knew from his brother that he could do anything if he kept trying. Doodle learned to walk, run, box, row a boat, and swim. Doodle learned to do the things that normal kids do. Some people think that the narrator is a horrible brother for pushing Doodle too hard; however, the narrator is a loving brother for teaching Doodle important life skills.

Second, good brothers take each other on adventures. The narrator loved Doodle enough to pull him around in a wooden go-cart when he went places. He took Doodle to Old Woman's Swamp, which is where Doodle learned to walk and do other activities.

Finally, good brothers protect each other. The narrator loved Doodle. He watched out for him. He made sure his brother was safe. He would make sure Doodle was making progress. He always seemed to know where Doodle was. Good brothers watch out for each other.

Good brothers love each other simply because they're brothers. Good brothers teach each other life skills. They take each other on adventures, and they protect each other. This is why the narrator in *The Scarlet Ibis* is a good, loving brother.

Gentry Lange, Grade 9
South Jordan Middle School, UT

My Wonderful Life

My family is always there for me no matter what. They care for me and support me. I love to hang out with them all the time. They make me laugh. I have a blast spending time with them.

When I am down my brother makes me laugh. When I am bored out of my mind and have nothing to do my sister comes up with something extraordinary and exciting to do, and whenever I need something that's what my mom and dad are for. Together we are a family. We may have our bad times but we still love each other. I love my family; I know I can count on them.

I love my friends, I couldn't ask for better people to have in my life. They support me all the time. If I do something wrong they would help me get through the problem, and not judge me. I enjoy hanging out with such wonderful people. We go to parties together, shopping, even travel together. I absolutely enjoy having fun with them. My friends and family are a part of my life I don't know what I would do without.

Carolina Rumyantsev, Grade 8
Thora B Gardiner Middle School, OR

A Friendship

From coloring books and colors scattered across the floor to magazines and lip gloss. Through all the years, a best friend remains a constant. Silly as ever, me and my buddy were inseparable. Life changes, the world changes each day. The one thing that you can count on is a friend.

I remember my first day of preschool. I was so excited to meet new kids. Being an only child, I got lonely at times, and I was ready for a change. As I hung my bag on the shelf, I noticed the girl standing next to me. We said hello to each other, and eagerly asked if we could be friends. Looking back at that now, I can't help but laugh. Even though I was so young I knew that friendship would help me get through life. As the years went on that same girl, Alyssa, and I became the best of friends. We went from being grossed out by boys, to actually admitting that we had a crush on them the whole time. It was so bubbly to talk about such girlie things. She was like my sister, and I looked up to her and felt like she was family. There was a strong pull that can't really be put into the right words. I now realize that is true friendship. Though we're in different schools now, we will always have that friendship. Life would be a scary place without a companion to confide in.

Odette Perez, Grade 9
Kaufer High School, TX

Where's My Dog

One day I was on my way to school and my dog was following me. I said "Go home, Pal!" He just barked. Then I said "Now!" So he darted off down the street. Then all of a sudden, a big blue and white van came up and people got out and took him! When I got to school, I called my parents. They said, "We can get you another dog." "Why?" I asked. "Let's just look for him." They said that it would be too much trouble to go through for a dog.

When I got home, I walked up to my room and wrote in my diary, "I hate my parents!" I decided to run away and find my dog that night. When everyone went to sleep, I went outside. As I started to walk away, I heard my parents come to our front door. It slowly creaked open. I hid behind the bushes. They didn't see me, so I jumped out and started to walk again. About an hour later, I heard some barking, and I looked in a backyard. There was Pal! I was so excited, but I still had to find a way to get him out.

After I hopped the fence, I untied him and threw him over. We went happily home. When I got home, I told my mom and dad what had happened. They were mad and happy.

Aliyah Hawkins, Grade 7
Seminole Jr High School, TX

School Is Cool

Every day I go to school. At school I hang out with my friends, participate in activities, and listen to my teacher so that I can learn. education is an important part of my life.

School is important to me because I have friends there. James is my best friend. He is funny and awesome to talk to and hang out with. Ron is a cool friend too. He jokes with James and I. Michael was my best friend, but he moved to a new school in Reno. Mike and I used to do our math, reading, and spelling together. I miss the old days. I look forward to seeing my friends at school every day.

Every week at school I have an art class with many different activities. I like listening to my art teacher about all the ways to use colors, shading, and styles of art. This helps me with my own drawings of dinosaurs and characters that I create. School gives me an opportunity to better my drawing skills.

Learning is influential because I would like to go to college and study animation. College will be an important part of my life because I want to be a comic book writer and artist. after I am finished with my comic book story I want to publish it at a cartoon company so I can sell my comic book story to Cartoon Network. Every day I am at school, my teacher teaches me skills that prepares me for future education.

Kevin Basurto, Grade 8
Long Valley Charter School, CA

You Call This Cheerleading?

Last year in the 7th grade I had decided to become a cheerleader for school. So, over the summer I had taken some tumbling classes for our back-to-school pep rally. My tumbling classes were good and I gained my round off back handspring. About two weeks before school started our cheer team had a two day clinic to learn our pep rally routine. After two days we had learned a good dance routine that I thought was sure to impress our school.

Finally, the pep rally day had come and we were all very nervous. The moment had come for us to begin our pep rally. I had practiced my round off back handsprings at recess and they were strong. Although in the pep rally my landing was awful. I got over that quickly and had to go straight into the routine. Our routine had no timing and we were all hitting motions at different times. Even though we had a lot of failures we celebrated anyway because we had finished our very first pep rally.

Many weeks later at one of our cheer practices we received a DVD of our pep rally and I was really anxious to see it. On the DVD you can hear a student from a younger grade yelling out, "You call this cheerleading?" which I thought was hilarious. Even though it was an insult, I could not stop laughing! I hope the next pep rally goes better than our first.

Rachel Townsend, Grade 8
St Elizabeth Ann Seton School, TX

Save the Animals

Animals are awesome! But we, the people are killing or destroying their homes they live in. So I say to do something about this, like when we are at the beach don't leave your trash. Green sea turtles are dying because of people that don't think that they are killing such beautiful animals. Soon all the Green sea turtles will die and there will be no more.

California sea lions are dying by people that go fishing and just leave their fishing nets in the ocean. What they don't realize is that they are killing the animals. The sea lions are thinking that the fishing nets are jellyfish. Then, they get caught and can't escape and die. Everyone can do something to prevent these animals from dying.

Pandas are cute but they are disappearing because people are destroying their homes and then they die. It's not fair that they are dying because people don't think that will affect the pandas. Pandas have a low reproductive rate so they don't reproduce fast. China don't you care that your pandas are dying because of you.

Not only are these animals dying but polar bear are dying. Polar bears are drowning because polar caps are melting. We are not only destroying the planet but everything that lives on Earth. Everyone should clean after themselves. Mama polar bears are not returning to the baby polar bears because when they go look for food they're drowning because there are no polar caps to float on.

Paola Torres, Grade 7
Isbell Middle School, CA

The Sun and the Moon

Surya. Everyone has told me that was a pretty name. But that's all they said. Pretty. I've never really heard anyone say anything else except for pretty. Okay, maybe some people have said that's a *nice* name, but that's about it.

You know what, now that I think about it, a few weeks ago there was a boy in my P.E. class who asked what my name was, and I said, "Surya," and he said, "That's an *exotic* name." I remember it made me feel really happy that he didn't say the one word that I despise the most.

Pretty. Ugh, how I hated that word. I remember for the longest time when I was little I used to hate my name so much. Why? Because Surya is a boy's name. Surya means Sun God, not *Sun Goddess*. And my name isn't like Taylor, where it can be a girl's or a boy's name. My name is more like a Bob; it can only be a boy's name. My sister always used to tease me so it didn't really make me feel better. My mom would say, "At least none of the American kids will know it's a boy's name," and I would say, "Yeah, but the Indian kids will." And when I say Indian I don't mean Native American.

Sometimes I wish I had my sister's name, Divyana. We call her Divya for short. Divya means divine, like the moon. I wish my name meant the moon.

Surya Baraiya, Grade 9
Hemet High School, CA

Strict = Good?!

One day in 2001, I was going to school in first grade. I was going to St. Johns in Fort Worth, Texas. I had met my teacher, Mrs. Lanzarati, two days before and she seemed pretty nice *at first.* When I got to class, I kissed my mom goodbye, and sat in a desk. It turns out that the nice teacher I was expecting on the first day of grade school was the strictest teacher in the entire school. Every morning I would get so nervous I would get sick. I made my mom walk me in and would not let go of her arm when it was time to go. I thought every day, "Here comes another nightmare."

Now, I am 13 years old and remember everything that she taught. She was so strict that she sent a kid back to kindergarten. However, she was so strict that it made me learn a lot. Even though she was, for a fact, the strictest teacher, she made the learning connect in my mind. As I grew to know and appreciate her, and her way of teaching, I felt a warm part of my heart open to her. By the time I actually wanted to go to her class in the morning, the year was over and I was going to second grade. That year made it possible for me to get to second grade a lot easier. Second grade was like a review for me because of Mrs. Lanzarati.

Andrew Ryan, Grade 8
St Elizabeth Ann Seton School, TX

Academic Requirements

Students should be required to meet a certain academic requirement, such as passing all courses maintaining a 'C' average, in order to participate in extracurricular activities.

If you don't maintain a 'C' average in high school you may become a drop out. You may just not care anymore and drop out. Once you drop out, you won't be able to get a very good job.

If you don't maintain a 'C' average you could get caught up in the wrong crowd and start doing drugs, smoking, and drinking. Once you have started doing those things, you won't be able to stop. Once you're a part of those kids, no one will ever look at you the same way.

Teachers will have more respect for you if you maintain a 'C' average or higher. You will also have more privileges, such as more extracurricular activities or student council, if you meet the right requirements. Your coaches, if you play sports, will have more respect for you if you do well in school.

In conclusion, if the kids maintain a 'C' average, then they should be able to participate in extracurricular activities. If they drop below a 'C' average then they should be kicked out of whatever extracurricular activity they're participating in.

Brayden Boyd, Grade 8
Holliday Middle School, TX

My Inspiration

Have you ever known someone who changed your life just by being themselves, or who inspired you to be the person you are today? My inspiration was my cousin Matthew. He was born on March 25, 1986, to his wonderful parents, and a younger sister, Tiffany. He always loved music and earned an Associate of Science degree in recording arts, and actually produced some music for a very popular band, Metallica.

When he was twenty-one years old, he joined the U.S. Air Force. Later, he was diagnosed with lung cancer and had to be treated with chemotherapy several times. He battled with it for two years; it would go away and then come back. Doctors said he had only a certain amount of time to live. I believe that when God wants you, he will take you with Him. Some days were either better or worse than others for Matthew. Most days were so painful; the worst he'd ever experienced. No matter what he always tried to smile for his family and friends.

On June 7, 2009, God took him to Heaven. He will never be forgotten because he impacted many people. I've never met anyone so brave, especially for someone still so young. He accomplished much in such a short life. He learned all God wanted him to. For most of us, it takes longer. He was amazing, brilliant, unselfish, and a loving person, who will never be forgotten.

Daniella Armijo, Grade 8
St Thomas Aquinas School, NM

Little Surprises

Have you ever got more than one surprise in one day? I have. It could be pretty exciting and appalling. This is a story of how I actually got three surprises in one day.

It all started out on a warm and cloudy Saturday morning. I got ready for a volleyball game at the Y. We got to the gymnasium early so I practiced with my teammates. The game started early and finished within half an hour. It was as short as a catnap. During the game a timeout was called. During that timeout, my dad called me over and told me I was going to get a surprise after the game. I was excited and couldn't wait.

I was glad the game finished early. I ran outside and I was a free soul. As we drove off to my surprise I tried to figure out what it was. The car ride seemed like hours. It felt like we were driving to Maine.

Finally, we turned into some neighborhood streets and stopped in front of a house. We got off and went in where a portly woman was happy to see us. She went into a room. "Meow." My eyes got big as the lady brought out two beautiful kittens. They were my surprises.

We left and along the road was a small black kitten. My dad pulled over and we picked him up and took him home with us. We were actually going to keep him! In one day I got three kittens. I was happier than a bird with a french fry.

Michelle Duran, Grade 7
Santa Teresa Middle School, NM

Forever and Always

Forever and always.

This is a great explanation of a family. There are plenty of different names for a family, like…a support system, household friend, caregiver and many more.

Your family will be there for you forever and always. You do everything with your family. My family and I are going to Disneyland. It has amazed me how much time and work my parents have put into the trip. It has shown me that they love me and care for me. It makes me respect them and show my love for them even more than I do now. No matter what, your family will be there for you when your eyes are wet, or if you are shaking with fear. Your family cries together, mourns together, and enjoys the special moments together. There is a very famous quote that I love. "Life is not measured by the number of breaths we take, but by the moments that take your breath away." I love this quote because it means to savor the special moments. You make plenty of moments with your family. Savor them, and be grateful for them.

I love my family. They are my support system, household friends, and my caregivers. They will be there for me. Forever and always.

Riley Calder, Grade 8
Canyon View Jr High School, UT

We Are All Different

Do you ever wonder if people will hate or pick on you about what you like to do or what you want to be when you are older? Well, I have. Sometimes, when I tell people I want to be a kindergarten teacher or I like to go fishing, they give me a funny look or tell me I'm weird.

I don't worry about what people think about my goals, plans, and hobbies. You shouldn't either. Don't change your mind or lie to people when they ask you what you want to do when you grow up. Also, don't lie about your hobbies or what you like to do, even if they look at you funny.

We are all different. We all like different things. We are individuals. Do not care what people think. It doesn't matter what they think. You can be whatever you want to be if you believe in yourself and ignore what people say or think. We are meant to be different, to think differently, and to like different things.

If someone laughs at you when you tell them what you like to do, then they are not your friend. All of us have different ideas. If your friend comes up to you and tells you their plans and what they want to be, don't laugh or copy them. If you believe in yourself and put in a little effort, you can do whatever you want, and be whoever you want to be.

Tiffany Tong, Grade 7
Long Valley Charter School, CA

Family and Friends

Your family and friends are always there to help you through the tough times in your life, but there are some ways that your family and friends are different. There are also ways they are the same.

My family and friends do so many things for me; they make me happy, they support me, and most of all, they love me. There are times when I can only tell certain things to my family, rather than my friends, because it would be more personal. They can understand and relate to me so well, that they can always help me with all my problems. There are also times when I could only tell certain things to my friends, because I would be afraid of what my family would say. They would give me advice on what and how to deal with a situation.

I would always choose my family over my friends because sometimes you don't exactly know who your real friends are. People sometimes would be your friend only so they can get what they want. My family knows me better than anyone else, and I have a strong bond with each one of them.

There are some things only your family could do for you, and there are also things only your friends can do. Either way, my family and friends are the most important people to me, and I would hate to lose any one of them.

Roni Nievera, Grade 7
Corpus Christi School, CA

Why Do You Need to Go to School?

There are many reasons a person should go to school. For one, you need to go to school because it's the law. You would also want to go to school so you can learn to read and write. You should do well in all subjects so that when you're in high school you can apply for scholarships to go to good colleges. Another reason you need to go to school is that when you graduate from college you can apply for a high paying job that interests you.

School also teaches you many values in life. respect is one of them. You need to learn respect when you're young because you need to be respectful to your parents, guardians, and even teachers, or you might get in big trouble. You also need to be respectful of others if you want them to be respectful of you. When you have a job you have to be respectful to your co-workers and your boss or you could get fired.

School teaches you many things that you need in life such as respect. Friendship, honesty, integrity, teamwork, communication and social skills can also be learned in school. It also helps you learn more in English, literature, mathematics, history, and science. If you want to succeed in life, you need to get a good education.

Blake Gollhofer, Grade 7
St Elizabeth Ann Seton School, TX

The Killer Tree

It was around Christmastime, and I was going to have the best Christmas ever. Have you ever had two emotions ripping you apart? That is how I felt on this anything but ordinary day.

It all started in the morning. The spirit of Christmas was in the air. It was a perfect day to invite my friend to come play with me.

I quickly went to the phone and dialed the number that I had dialed so many times before. I could hear the ring in the earpiece and became more and more anxious with every ring. After what seemed like forever, someone answered on the other line. "Hello?" said the familiar voice of my friend. When I gave him the opportunity to come play with me, he readily agreed. After receiving permission from his parents, my friend Tim, got on his iron horse and rode as fast as a horse to my house.

Upon his arrival, Tim asked me what we should do first. There were so many things to do, but I thought that we should play my Playstation. We played this until it started getting late, and then we decided to pretend to be tornadoes.

We were raging tornadoes spinning and spinning around the room. I started getting dizzy. It just so happened that we were in the formal room with the Christmas tree. Everything was blurry, but the last thing I saw was green.

Luckily, I dodged the killer tree before it fell on me. I felt so bad. I also felt like laughing because how often do seven-year-olds go around knocking Christmas trees on top of themselves? In the end, I learned to be careful where and what kind of things I do because everything is breakable. Even people!

Jacob Wilson, Grade 7
Santa Teresa Middle School, NM

Things That Make Me Happy

My family makes my happy because they're always there for me when I need them. They always keep me happy.

The one thing that is important to me is my mom. Moms are always at home waiting for you. She's always there to tell me stories and good night.

Learning makes me happy because learning teaches many things. Learning makes me happy because it will affect my future. Teachers make me happy because they are there to teach students about history, reading, and so much more.

Friends make me happy because friends are there for you so you won't be alone. I once said to my friend that I was there for him and I would never leave him alone.

Ice cream and candy make me happy cause they are so good. Everybody likes them. I feel joy when sweet things are in my mouth that taste good. These are things that make me happy.

Aden Delgado, Grade 8
Rio Bravo Middle School, TX

Fruits

The sweet juice of an apple squirted in my mouth as I took the first bite of it, with each bite of the apple my taste buds flooded with the joy of the natural sugar. It had been awhile since I had eaten any kind of fruit and both my body and mind craved some kind of fruit deeply. When I finished the apple (including the center, stem, and seeds) I realized that I still craved some kind of fruit. I dug into the refrigerator and looked through the pile of fruits. I found a bag of frozen berries all mixed together, and I immediately devoured half of the whole bag. My hands were stained with the colors of the berries and both my lips and face were also covered with the dark red the berries left.

After I washed my stained face and hands, my thoughts drifted to fruits once more. Not that I had wanted to eat fruits again, but I had wondered why they were so good. Fruits are so wonderful in every way I couldn't think of how the world would manage without them. They are so delicious and different in their own ways that I would consider them to be a treasure, something that's so precious that I would get a sudden feeling of sadness every time I finished one. They are a gift from trees and bushes that grow among their leaves, waiting to be picked from the stem or branch that holds them.

Stephen Lares, Grade 8
Rio Bravo Middle School, TX

Don't Fail the Earth

The earth has been here for thousands of years. Some people don't even realize that they are polluting it and some animals are very close to extinction. Later in life some people won't even be able to see some of the animals we are able to see today. For example the polar bears and the bald eagles are very close to extinction there are not many left in the world because of pollution. There are actually people that care a lot about the environment and try to stop all the littering and polluting in the world but they can't do it alone so they need everyone's help. If the people would have stopped pollution in the beginning then we would have probably been able to see some dinosaurs today. People should really try harder in taking care of the earth because we are in big danger of having a flood or other disasters.

There are also some factories like the machine factories, and beer factories, those are the ones really polluting the earth. So if you would still like to be able to see all the wonderful animals we see today we should really help out the earth. There are some people that think it is so hard to do all these things but it isn't because if you're recycling all the glass, plastic bottles, and cans in your house then you are helping the earth.

Veronica Perez, Grade 8
Isbell Middle School, CA

Hope

Hope is something you believe in; it's a positive outcome related to any circumstances or events in your life. Hope is also feeling the joy wanting something that can be given to or that a certain event will always turn out for the best. That's why I like Pandora because even though she opened the box and let out all the horrible energies that make our world the way it is today; she kept one thing safe in the box…HOPE!!!!

I like to think that hope is real because every once in a while I hope everything will come out good for me and my family. Even though me and my family have had so many frustrations, hope will always be there waiting to rise through to our present and future. A good example of hope should be my mom because she hopes to be able to meet the day when she can say I have done everything for my kids. Even though being a single parent doing everything she does just hoping to get to see me and my brother one day at our real home; I believe if my mom really didn't have hope she wouldn't care to see us better ourselves and grow as a family.

Hope to me and my family is not giving up when something goes wrong, but to learn from it and try to exceed our hope to one day say "That's my…family!" without being afraid.

HOPE!

Victoria Estrada, Grade 8
Rio Bravo Middle School, TX

High-tech Suit Ban

FINA, the international swimming federation, has decided to ban nearly 150 new high-tech suits. These suits include the Speedo LZR Racer, Arena X-Glide, Jaked, and TYR A7. All of the suits listed above, and many more were worn at the 2008 Beijing Olympics and the 2009 World Championships. Between those two meets, over 100 world records were not only beaten, they were shattered.

For males, FINA has also decided to ban suits that extend above the navel and below the knee. For females, the suit cannot cover the neck, reach past the shoulder, or continue below the knee. I think this is a good idea because it refocuses the competition back on the swimmer, not the suit.

I personally raced in the Speedo LZR Racer and felt a different level of buoyancy in my upper legs. With that suit I dropped nearly 8 seconds in my 200-meter backstroke. I do not like to think that the suit makes you race faster. Knowing that, it made me feel like I didn't deserve the time I achieved.

FINA realized the same basic thought. So many of these swimmers are dropping time, achieving never before thought of feats. Because of this, and many studies, FINA has chosen to ban these suits starting January 1, 2010. One question that is yet to be answered is what FINA will do with all the new world records set in these high-tech suits.

Cole Cogswell, Grade 7
Placerita Jr High School, CA

The People That Complete My Life

It all started out with a simple Uno game, followed by cheating and switching cards, finally so much laughter that I could not hold it in. This happened on our trip back from Shasta Lake. I was in the car with my "trip" friends Tyler, John, and Joe. I could never imagine how I would survive without the friends I make.

Whether I have friends I will know all my life, or friends I meet on a trip, only to see them for a week, I feel God has blessed me to make friends wherever I go. Before my friends and I had our out of control card game, we were coming from a wakeboarding trip with our youth group. Throughout this trip I spent so many hours with each of them, enjoying the worship, standing on the wakeboard, and eating the water after falling off of the tube. At the beginning of the whole trip, I did not even think I would have this much fun.

Eventually, we came to the end of the trip, but not the end of our friendships. We all got along with each other and enjoyed every minute. Even though I may not see some of them again, I will surely remember, and keep them in my prayers.

Austin Best, Grade 8
Faith Christian Jr/Sr High School, CA

Take It All In

There are many times in a person's life when they forget to stop and take in all of their blessings. One of the greatest blessings we have is our role models. to many, a role model is someone famous or someone who receives media attention. Not for me. My role model is a humble religion teacher at my private school named, Kenneth Cantwell.

You may wonder, why such a common person? A man of his stature is most definitely uncommon actually. This man has shown me the true measure of a man; every day he continues to shine. He is a very bold man that sticks to a firm set of rules. He respects life and has experienced the sadness of death and still is a very upbeat man and amazing person. When I grow up, I want to be remembered in the same way many people think of him now.

I try as much as possible to be like him, even at my age. Cantwell inspires me to stick to a firm purpose in life and to keep the faith, even if someone else doesn't think it's cool or in style or whatever. The future is coming up really quickly and I believe we could all use more "Cantwells" or role models in our lives. I wish to be a role model one day and inspire many childrens' lives. Even the smallest act of kindness will go farther than we could even imagine.

Peter Walden, Grade 8
St Thomas Aquinas School, NM

Sticks and Stones

Citrus, mint, chocolate, lime. Not those garish candies that sit on grocery counters, peeled back by greedy hands and eagerly eaten. They're worse — they sit in the glass-partitioned section that rises just above eye level; they come in strangely straight rectangular boxes, and are stamped with names like "Marlboro" and "Havana." Yes, cigarettes — but don't be tempted, because beneath all of the high pricing, the kiddy flavors, and the pristine packaging, there lays row after row of killers. "Cancer-sticks," they are called by many, and for good reason: the leading cause of lung cancer is proven to be smoking. In fact, Dr. David E. Larson writes that each year smoking kills more Americans than the number that died of Americans in WWII and Vietnam combined. It is scientifically proven that each cigarette a person smokes shortens their life by ten minutes. If there is so much overwhelming evidence against smoking, then why do so many reach for the boxes behind the glass partition almost daily? Why is it even legal? Many claim that it alleviates their stress, helps them lose weight, and the saddest reason of all: because "everyone else does it;" when in fact the reason why so many smoke is because cigarettes contain nicotine, a highly addictive drug. And once hooked, it is very difficult to extract oneself from the excruciatingly tight grip of smoking — which is why prevention is indeed the best medicine in this case. So say no and save yourself the trouble, along with time.

Stephanie Guo, Grade 8
Carmel Valley Middle School, CA

Small School, Big Opportunities

Despite what some people may believe, attending a small school can make a person "well-rounded," as opposed to attending a larger school. Even though there is a larger variety of classes and extracurricular activities, there are more opportunities at a small school.

Going to a school with fewer people can help you make friends with everyone. Also, you know all the teachers, and all the teachers know you.

Having fewer people means smaller classes. With smaller classes, it seems like there is almost "one-on-one time" with the teacher. Also, you can't get away with much. You can't skip class, and there is no way around turning your homework in. If a teacher tells you to do something and you don't do it, they are going to find out. Kids our age need that.

When there are more people in your athletic classes, you have less chances of getting to be on a team. At smaller schools, they almost always need players, so everyone will get to play. Student council, yearbook staff, and band are other examples of extra curricular activities. Since there are less people, everyone can do something.

Bigger doesn't always mean more opportunities for people. As you can see, there are a lot of advantages to going to a small school.

Samantha Schade, Grade 8
Holliday Middle School, TX

Fired Up, Ready to Go

I will never forget where I was on January 20th, 2009. It was freezing cold that day, but nothing could have stopped us, especially not the weather. We bundled up in hats, scarves, gloves and overcoats and headed to the Metro Station that would take us to into the heart of Washington DC and to Barack Obama's Inauguration.

My heart was pounding with anticipation as my mom and I stepped off the train. "This is it." I thought to myself. "Today will change history forever." The next few hours were spent in a blur of waiting in crowds to get through the security screening and trying to keep warm. We were packed into that safety checkpoint like teenagers in a mosh pit but the experience we had there was most unlike that of a concert. There was no pushing or shoving and I didn't hear a single rude word. People where introducing themselves to complete strangers!

This was not a normal crowd. This was a crowd moved by the idea of peace, hope and change. That day I realized just how amazing this election was. It had joined together all kinds of people from all over the world. Barack Obama accomplished a great thing that day. He showed America that it's not about color or gender; it's about who you are inside. And we should never forget that.

Freya Jamison, Grade 9
Capital High School, WA

Canine Einsteins

Border Collies are the most intelligent dogs in the world. They have been known for their intelligence when learning difficult tricks, herding sheep, and dealing with different situations.

It's not always easy living with a Canine Einstein. Border Collies have a willingness to learn new things like turning on a TV or opening a garden gate. These could be bad things to teach your dog.

Some Border Collies have also learned human words. One woman taught her dog Snap the different names of his body. Now he can point them out on command. Another woman, Cathy, was taking her dog, Jefferey to the vet one day when a nurse gave him a rawhide bone. Jefferey didn't like to chew on things, but he took it out of courtesy. The nurse left, and Jefferey put the bone in Cathy's lap. A piece of the rawhide fell, so he picked it up. Cathy was curious, so she knocked it off again. Jefferey glared at her and picked it back up to put in Cathy's lap. He wouldn't let go until he was sure she wouldn't bother it again.

They have done all these things over these years, and yet it still shocks people. So over all, Border Collies really are the most intelligent dogs in the world.

Taylor Wike, Grade 8
Holliday Middle School, TX

You

Being your own best friend is all about feeling comfortable in your own skin, it's okay to say no, it's okay to have your own ideas, or disagree; it's a way to find out who you are. It's about liking yourself, and it's not always easy to like yourself all the time. You are not going to like yourself every day, as your body and mind ages, you also age in wisdom and comfort, as you grow older you will journey through the process of self discovery. Some people come into your life and then leave for a reason. You will always have yourself in your life, and you need to be confident and comfortable with who you are. Follow something you are passionate about, explore and discover something new. Reach out and try new things. Don't be afraid to let yourself be free and experience life and all the things it has to offer because you only live once; get the most out of your life. Tell people the truth and listen to what other people have to say; although it might be boring to you, it is interesting to them. Do something you love, not something you will regret. Stick to your gut and be who you are, not what others want to see. Watch your surroundings and grow from your mistakes. Do not think too much about the abhorrent things in life, your fear is just getting to you. Stay true to who you are.

Avery Stray, Grade 8
St Rita Elementary School, CA

Soul Soothers

What is important to me? Out of millions of things I managed to pick just one. It isn't a specific, because for everyone it is different. In your life you will go through a raging roller coaster of emotions. You can be anything from infuriated to depressed to ecstatic. There is such a wide array of emotions, but a large portion of the time you are at the extreme of an emotion.

That is when you need your soul soothers. When you're cheerful to celebrate, extremely irate to calm down, and extremely sad to cheer up.

For some it is music, friends, praying, poetry, painting, or a variety of other hobbies it all depends on who you are. One of my favorites is music. When your day has been amazing and you are going to explode with joy you can turn music on and it rejoices with you. If you are sad and you want something to offer you sympathy or to uplift you turn on the music, and you can listen to it like a poem with instruments. If you are flaming angry and you need to calm down, but sitting with someone telling you "Calm down, calm down, breathe deeply" is only feeding the fire you can crank up the music and simmer yourself down. Music is one of my favorite soul soothers because one it is not fickle, judging, and is always around you even if it is just the sounds of nature. So take a second, listen.

Cassandra Ekdawy, Grade 9
Faith Christian Jr/Sr High School, CA

A Clairvoyant World

The Vehement stares of those around you and the anxious sound of turning stiff pages. You wonder in awe what could capture them and lure them to be their prisoners. You begin to ask a nearby friend when they put up their index finger and whisper "shh." Now I will tell you what the cause is of all this peace and intense air even though it is a secret of mine, well kept, it must come out to the world.

Reading. Reading? Reading! Blank pages soon covered with these strange black symbols known as letters that is their interest. Is it a fantasy or a mystery that draws them in? There is only one way to know. To me a book is like food to my soul or a soft caress to my heart. There is a spectacular place that is unlike any other. The library for me is simply 'Heaven on Earth'.

Read always and enjoy those authors who we are so fortunate to have. I recommend one thing: Do not read while driving or riding your bike. Let's just say you cannot multitask when you are reading. Escaping to a distant place is something I do often. No one is saying escape reality, of course, but take a vacation. Enjoy the charismatic world and tell me how it is.

Kacee Guerrero, Grade 9
Mueller Park Jr High School, UT

Camp, the Impact on a Teenager's Life

I started going to camp when I was nine years old. I've made dozens of friends that I never see in the winter, but once June rolls around, we all reconvene back at camp. Some of the greatest life lessons I've learned, came from camp. Our counselors taught us about life, friendship, how to avoid bears and how to pull off a prank without getting caught.

I miss camp during the winter, and often think about it. I keep a journal that I've made into a scrapbook, with fragments of stuff from camp and pictures of all my friends. I like to reminisce and laugh at what I've said. I bring my experiences to school whenever I play a prank or tell a story. I learned how to resolve "girl drama" without hard feelings. I learned to flirt without showing that I have major "camp goggles" for someone and how to play sports with the guys without looking ridiculous. My friends and I all support and lean on one another at camp. We keep each other grounded.

We play games like capture the flag and tackle an incredibly crazy challenge course that forces us to work as a team. Camp helped me realize who I am as an individual with a heart and soul. In conclusion, camp has dramatically changed my life and keeps me out of trouble in the summer. Camp has made me the confident, head strong, crazy, curious, daring, and unique teenage girl that I am today.

Jessica Busby, Grade 8
St Michael's Episcopal Day School, CA

When Winter Arrives

Winter is here when the last leaf has fallen from the old oak. Thin sheets of ice cover the small, deserted pond. Humans leap, jump, dance. The blades slice through the ice and sketches are formed. You know winter has arrived when children's laughter fills the air, and their pink noses shine. Winter is inside me, it will never leave.

There are leaves in me… gently rocking back and forth, falling, as if swaying to their mother softly singing them a goodnight lullaby. Resting on many different dew laden fields, composed, calm, motionless, tranquil, peaceful. Staying a bright, marvelous color, that always seems to match their mood.

There is a hearth in me… welcoming and warm. Giving. Occasionally crackling in rage but eventually dying down to a soft simmer no matter what the motive. The hearth is always willing to burn hatred and accept forgiveness.

There are snowflakes in me… graceful ballerinas who prance down from the sky twirling on their toes, each one unique. Tickling your nose as they take their final bow. When lying on the earth, they soon turn to angels, where they stay until they melt away. The snowflakes create a blanket over all that surrounds us, protecting us for the surprises that wait.

Winter never leaves me. Even when the snow says good bye and the flowers say hello. Even when the bird's singing comes to life again and the sun filled the sky. Winter never leaves me; it will always stay, for without winter, you are without me.

Madeline de Figueiredo, Grade 7
Lindero Canyon Middle School, CA

Dancing Queen!

"Dancing is like dreaming with your feet!" says Constanze. I have to agree with this quote and that dance is something that interests me strongly.

Dance is a good way to express yourself. When you're upset and you dance, it seems as though the negative washes away and you become upbeat. It gets you "in the groove" and up and alive.

Another reason why dance interests me is because it makes you move. Rather than sitting on the computer, you could be getting fit and learning new dances.

My final reason why dance interests me is because as silly as it sounds, it prepares you for school dances. Instead of making a fool of yourself at prom, you can learn how to dance and I guarantee that it will improve your dancing skills and you will fit in.

In conclusion, I think dance is a good sport to be interested in because of all of the benefits, and there are many types of dances to dance to.

Holly Paterson, Grade 7
Goodson Middle School, TX

Dezz!!!

Well I want to write about some girl…her name is Deseray Arispee. I love that girl. She is so funny, cool, adorable, crazy and fun to be around with. We got really close this year. She comes to Rio Bravo like me and she's an 8th grader like me. Every time I am sad or something she makes me happy! And I started being dumb with her. I love it when we are together cause we always do stupid stuff. I would do anything for her. We promise each other that we would be best friends forever. I hope she does not break her promise because I know I am not going to break it. Yeah we fight sometimes but we don't stay mad at each other that long. The longest we have been mad at each other was like two hours. I don't think it was that long. I have never had a best friend or friend like Dessi. I really care about her. And I would always be there for her no matter what. Thanks to her I'm not a bad girl any more. Cause last year I was really bad. I changed a lot because of her. So I just wanted to write this because I want people to know that there are true friends out there you just have to look for them.

Abbie Resendiz, Grade 8
Rio Bravo Middle School, TX

Being an American

For me, I would choose honor as the most essential value to being an American. I feel that honor is the most essential value because, if you don't honor America, why are you here?

People honor America all the time; they even do it in their average, everyday, ordinary lives. They do this by respecting things like: the flag, elders, the president, and the troops who risk their lives for America.

According to *Webster's International Dictionary*, honor means: showing great respect or self-respect. I exercise honor by saying the Pledge of Allegiance instead of just standing there during the morning announcements. Also, I exercise honor by trying to not let the flag touch the ground, by respecting the flag, and by honoring my parents. I also honor America by honoring the troops who protect America by respecting them. When there are drives at my school I always try to help out.

George Washington honored this country by willingly fighting Great Britain, with many soldiers, so that America could be its own independent country. Then, during the Revolutionary War, he honored this country again by signing the Declaration of Independence, which said "we mutually pledge to each other our lives, our fortunes, and our sacred honor."

In the Bible there is a verse that reads, "Honor your father and your mother so that you may live long in the land…" I honor my parents just as well. That is why I chose honor to be the most essential value to being an American.

Christian Miller, Grade 7
Anthony Charter School, NM

The History of Golf

Golf, the greatest game ever played. A lot of people know nothing about the history of golf. Where it was first played, what it's played with, etc.

The exact origins of golf are unknown, the most widely accepted theory is that it was invented in Scotland during the high Middle Ages. The first female to play golf was Queen Mary. She was the queen of Scotland. The oldest golf course is St. Andrews, it's also in Scotland. It's known to be one of the most natural golf courses in the world.

The equipment and scoring of golf is very simple. In golf the lowest score wins. You're either over par or under par. Par is usually seventy two strokes. In England during the eighteen hundreds and throughout the nineteen hundreds, golf clubs were made out of wood. The golf ball as we know it was invented in 1903. The first two piece golf ball was invented by Spalding in 1971.

Golf is going to be a sport again in the Olympics, during 2016 at Rio de Janeiro. The most famous and exclusive golf course in the world is Augusta National. It's also home to the most famous caddie master, Freddie Bennett. The Masters golf tournament is played here each year.

Golf is important to me, because it's a sport I can play for the rest of my life. You also don't have to be big or small to play golf either.

Alec Winfrey, Grade 7
Seminole Jr High School, TX

Believe in What You Achieve

Never give up on chasing your dreams. Keep your mind open and be creative in showing what you can do that will take you to bigger and brighter things in life. To achieve these goals, you can keep trying, like if you have a job don't quit when it gets hard, and just keep trying to work things out. I remember at times when I don't want to do my homework, but I have to do it because it depends who you'll be in life like someone who is going to do their job right. Also to achieve it's not easy to get where you want to be in life.

If you fail a couple of times don't make it seem like you can never try it again. For example, if you don't make the cut for the basketball team that doesn't mean if you practice and get better you still won't make it the next time. If you keep your head held high you can achieve in almost anything. If you want to be a doctor, go to school and study hard. If you do these steps you will get your doctors degree and most likely become a doctor.

You can become successful in life if you keep going even when times get tough. Follow your dreams, but work hard to reach for them. Remember nobody, said it was easy, but then again no one said just give up.

Miranda Gonzales, Grade 8
Isbell Middle School, CA

There Is a God!

"Science is neutral." states professor of physics, Lawrence Krauss, during a debate with Michael Behe. Michael Behe, microbiologist at Lehigh University, has written the book, *Darwin's Black Box*, a book that disproves Darwin's theory of evolution using evidence from microscopic cell design. Behe argues that everything's designed for a purpose. A snowflake can be used as an example. When a snowflake falls from the sky, the odds that the snowflake has been created by chance is negligible. Behe quotes Richard Dockins, a Darwinian, saying, "Biology is the study of complicated things that give the appearance that they have been designed for a purpose." He also shows that a cell has many parts that couldn't have been formed without a higher power.

For example, if you took a lot of fabric, put it in a bag with a needle, shook it, clapped on it, and moved it in any way, the fabric would never become a complete blanket. In another source Behe states that cells are based on microscopic machines that help move the cells around. This shows that there must be a higher power, designing us to work the way we do. Without design we wouldn't be how we are today. If there wasn't something, i.e. a higher power, putting us in place, we wouldn't have some of the natural things we have, or be able to live how we do today. All in all, a higher power has, and is, working in us, whether we know it or not.

Raoul Bascon, Grade 8
Sts Peter and Paul School, TX

The Importance of Friends

Having friends makes whatever you are doing more enjoyable. Friends are very important because they help you through hard times, teach you how to communicate with people and when you should or should not risk something. Friends make life worth living because without friends all you would have are enemies.

Friends can always make you feel better whether it's making you laugh or texting you a compliment. Friends are the people you can trust the most because they know everything about you. They know when you are feeling down and when you need a 'just because' gift or a hug. Seeing your friend smile at you makes you feel better because you know someone cares.

Having friendships help prepare you for other relationships as well. Friendship helps you develop compromise skills, forgiveness and patience. Learning these skills takes time, and no one will be perfect at it at first. Friends are there to forgive you when you mess up and to teach you the right way to admit your faults. Arguments and apologizing makes your friendship stronger and the stronger your friendships are, the longer they last. Overall, Friends are one of the most important aspects of your life because they teach you, understand you and love you.

Sasha Foley, Grade 8
St Michael's Episcopal Day School, CA

Becoming a Big Brother

Becoming a big brother can change anyone's life. I love being a brother, you have to be more responsible, but that's okay. He is a mess and cries at night, but it doesn't really bother me. He wants everything and we tell him no, and then he starts to scream.

Scott, who was born November 29, 2005, is my little brother. He is now three and it is hard. Everything has to be his way. I ask if I can go to Dairy Queen, and he begs me to take him with me. He wants to do everything. He loves John Deere tractors. He can name all the tractors. I wanted our room to be Indianapolis Colts and instead it is John Deere.

I love playing with him, I have to admit. He plays weird games, but it is hilarious. Most of the time I have to baby-sit him whenever my mom goes to church meetings. He always wants to fight, and he can hit really hard.

My little brother means a lot to me and always will. Scott and I are very close, and I love him a lot. When we adopted him, I could tell it was going to make a really big impact on my life, and it has. I wish sometimes I didn't have to go to school because I know Scott misses me, and I definitely know I miss him.

Skyler Jones, Grade 8
Reagan County Middle School, TX

My Sisters Being Born

I remember that day April 26th. I remember like it was yesterday. That day that my family and I brought them home.

Since they came home from the hospital, it has been extra loud all throughout the house, and if one starts to cry, so would the other one. Having to change their diapers was not very fun either, but I'm glad that those days are over.

Rebeca and Raquel are my little sisters. They are twins and are as adorable as a box of newborn puppies. It was only my brother and I but then the twins came along and that really impacted my life. Since they were born, I have learned how to take care of babies, and I became more mature. I was no longer the only girl anymore, which definitely changed the way I thought about them. I became even more excited because I would be able to do their hair, which was a big thing for me because my brother didn't let me do his hair. But I did feel sorry for my brother because he was praying that my mom would have a boy and a girl, but he said that it was okay and that he was happy that he had two new sisters.

I'm really excited and I can't wait to see them grow up. I just don't want them to grow up too fast. And my mom is always telling me the more people the better.

Judy De Leon, Grade 8
Reagan County Middle School, TX

Soccer

Soccer is my favorite sport I have been playing it for a long time. I'm going to talk about times that I have played soccer and why I like it.

I have liked soccer since I was in 1st grade. Every year in my school we would do a championship at the last day of school. My team would always win because all my team likes soccer like me.

I like soccer because the first time I played it I was in first grade and I was good. Most of my friends liked soccer so I started playing with them. I also like it because I made more friends playing it. Soccer helped me get friends and I'm good at it.

I have been on soccer teams, and I like it. If I grow up and I still like soccer I would want to be a good soccer player on a team. I have also been on school soccer teams and I'm going to join this year too.

In the end I hope to keep playing soccer all my life. I would really like to be in a professional team when I grow up. My goal would be that. I don't think anyone likes soccer like I like it.

Cesar Trujillo, Grade 8
Rio Bravo Middle School, TX

Morning

Each and every morning brings a day to remember. I have something fun or thrilling to do, besides going to school. Every morning, I get up at about 7:00, sometimes even later. Most of the time I am awakened by the sound of my little brother crying which is around 6:00 or maybe by the screaming and yelling of my mother or grandma telling me, "You're gonna be late for school! If you're not out there by the time I'm ready to leave, I'm leaving."

After this rude awakening, I get up ever so slowly from bliss of my bed and jump into the cold waters of my shower. The reason it's cold is because my brother, Natowa, is an early bird, gets up before me and uses all of the hot water. But all in all, the cold shower helps me wake up. After about five minutes in the Arctic of my bathroom, I get out and brush my pearly white teeth with the best toothpaste in the world, Crest.

It's now about 7:08 and I go into my room. Once in my room I start to get dressed. Sometimes if I get dressed fast I lay back in bed and fall asleep again. Other times I try to get in the kitchen and eat breakfast. Most of the time breakfast isn't cereal; it's cold leftovers. After, I run out the door and am on my way to school. And that's what every morning is like for me.

Kietzecume Garcia, Grade 8
St Thomas Aquinas School, NM

Music: Then and Now

It's no doubt that the music industry has totally changed since it first began. Supposedly, an artist's purpose is focused more on money than their love of music. If you turn on the radio today, you can easily point out the songs that have been overproduced; you rarely hear a real voice. Whereas decades ago, you could tell that the artist had a legitimate talent. To hear the difference, you only have to switch stations — new to old.

Apparently, in this day and age, the only object musicians think about is money; any person with a voice can make millions. The reason is studios enhance the voice digitally so it's "catchy." But the truth will eventually be revealed when they sing live. They will either sing horribly, or lip-synch. Singers from the past sang amazingly live or recorded. The reason for this is the technology was not as advanced; plus, the artist had genuine, real, talent. These songs are now present day hits as well, and make plenty of money.

The companies that decide to alter a singer's voice are cheating out music lovers. Sure, they make catchy hits, but the truth is that voice doesn't exist. The raw voice is completely different from the one on the track. Years ago, the artist's voice always sounded beautiful. Now, the listeners are disappointed because they know their songs are illegitimate. But, the truth is that the record companies may force the artist to go digital — against their will — for the money.

Maxi Wilson, Grade 8
St Michael's Episcopal Day School, CA

Inspired

The most inspirational people in my life are my grandparents. They are the most loving, giving, and generous people I know and they have given up so much to help my brother and me. Zachary and I lived in Cancún, Mexico for almost nine years and things were pretty rough for us. My parents were busy trying their hardest to make the best of our situation while my brother and I were missing a lot of school. They decided that it was time for a little help and that's when my grandparents stepped in.

The goodbyes were tough but we knew they weren't forever. After waving to my parents until my hands hurt, my brother and I climbed on the plane with our grandmother. That's when the adventure began. My grandparents were on the brink of retirement with countless ideas on how to spend their days and savings. But many of those dreams were put on hold because two young children were coming to Texas. It was hard on all of us to get accustomed to the new life, but through all the tears, sadness, laughs and happy moments, my grandparents were there for me in all ways imaginable. It is they I have to thank for my foundation in my morals, beliefs, and my love of learning and trying new things. This is why my grandparents are such an inspiration, and the reason I hope to one day be able to make sacrifices like they were.

Brianna Stachowiak, Grade 8
St Elizabeth Ann Seton School, TX

Genius in the Water

Me and my friend Miranda where hyped up beyond belief. We were on the way to Tourmaline Beach, our favorite spot in the whole world. When we finally arrived I wrestled into my Wet Suit and bolted down to the beach. The sand flipped up behind me as I stumbled down to the waters edge, boogie board in tow. Miranda loved surfing, so we went our separate ways. I like surfing, don't get me wrong, but I'm terrible at it. I swam out with ease and waited for a worthy wave to come my way. The waves where pretty low, so I waited a while, but then a big one started racing towards me! I kicked frantically, but the wave overtook me and I flipped under the water, then something sharp and hard slammed into my forehead and I hit the bottom of the ocean. I couldn't find the surface, I was practically screaming 'Why is there sand here!?' I felt someone grab me by my elbow and rip me up to the surface. "OMG, are you ok!?" the surfer exclaimed. He had hit me with his board. Another wave came and my boogie board, which was attached to my wrist, got ripped by it, which caused me to fly through the water. I ended up beached on the sand, gasping for air. I'm sure everyone that had seen my little show was thinking "What a genius!" and I certainly felt like, a genius in the water.

Audrie Ford, Grade 8
Heritage Christian School, CA

Me Coming to United States

When I was going to the U.S.A. it was a very difficult day for me because I wasn't going to have as much fun as I did in Mexico, also because I wasn't going to know anybody or anything.

When I barely came to the U.S.A. I was scared because I didn't know the place where we were because I was still small. I didn't like being here but I still had to stay. When I got a little older my mom put me in school. In my first day of school I was nervous because I didn't know English, but I was kind of happy because I was going to learn English and many other awesome things. The first day of class was great, but then as the days passed the teacher started to be mean to me because I didn't know English. There was another teacher that was nice to me and she encouraged me to go to school. I started to learn English as I went from kindergarten through sixth grade.

Now I'm in seventh grade and I learned that the U.S.A. isn't so bad after all, but I still miss Mexico, I miss all the good candy, and all the yummy food. I'm going to become a citizen now because my dad barely became one. Coming to the U.S.A. isn't so bad after all because you could have a good future.

Alondra Medina, Grade 7
Isbell Middle School, CA

Brady James

My favorite football player is Brady James. He is 28 years old and was born in Monroe, Louisiana on January 17, 1981. As he got older he went to LA University to play college football for LSU's football league. During that time he became the second player in LSU's history to register more than 400 tackles and became the first player to suppress 150 tackles in a season.

James was awarded first all-American linebacker since Michael Brooks in 1985. He became #56 of the Dallas Cowboys as their linebacker. Brady was the 6th middle/inside linebacker taken behind Angelo Crowell of Virginia.

When he had time to become famous he was on a sports talk radio station in Dallas along with Tony Romo, member of Omega Phi fraternity inc. In 2006 he was a co-host of "Inside the Huddle." James was named defensive MVP of the 2000 Peach Bowl.

Shauna Seaton, Grade 7
Deweyville Middle School, TX

Playing Basketball

So here we were playing basketball in our backyard. I have the ball and I'm at the back of the court. I shoot the ball but miss, but my mom doesn't get mad at me because we both aren't very good at basketball. My mom rebounds the ball and shoots; she scores! Robert gets the ball and he's not in the right position because our court only has one hoop, so he passes it to my dad; he shoots, but misses. We rebound and go all the way to the end of the court. I have the ball, I pass it to my mom to score, but she misses. I breathlessly sigh.

It's the second quarter and I have the ball once again. I try to get closer to the net, but Robert steals it from me. He shoots but misses the basket at a two-pointer shot. Robert starts off with the ball. He passes it to my dad, but my mom gets it and we score. So now my dad starts off with the ball again. He throws it to my brother who gets it and scores.

It's the last game, so we try to win it. We're tied five to five and it goes up to ten; we only have five more points to go. My mom shoots the ball and unties the game. I get the ball and shoot from the three-pointer. We win the game!!! I guess boys aren't better than girls! Hmph!

Emily Garcia, Grade 7
St Thomas Aquinas School, NM

Jeremy

I didn't think I'd remember much, but thinking about the time he and I spent together, I do.

Jeremy, ah where to start?

He's my smile on my face, the one that has my heart beating fast and I get this so called "Corriwabblez," in my tummy. He was once my perfect boyfriend who made me want to get up in the morning and rush to school just to get one of his warm hugs. His recent girlfriend treats him like crap and I know I didn't treat him any better. I'm sorry I didn't see how lucky I was to be with him! I guess I get hurt because he never looked at me as the way he looks at her. He's just so amazing to me and he added a little color to my world. He's always saying, "Fishes have cameras," and is always singing songs I never heard before.

And I love them!

And when I look into his green eyes it's like it's just me and him. He's my world and meeting him could be the best thing that ever happened to me. A great boyfriend and now an awesome friend!

I love you Jeremy!!!

Brianna Hawkins, Grade 8
Rio Bravo Middle School, TX

Ban Alcoholic Beverages, Legal or Not

Colleges and universities should ban alcoholic beverages on campus, even for students who are of legal drinking age. This would prevent many problems from happening at a place where people should be getting an education, not partying. Colleges should have a greater concern about this problem than what most do.

If this problem doesn't stop, eventually the campus of the college will begin to get trashy. The trash scattered out on the ground from a party isn't going to make a campus look good. I mean, who wants to go to a trashy college with a big time party reputation?

Many kids under the legal drinking age go to the parties, and I know most young college kids at a party with upperclassmen are not going to resist drinking. These young kids try to act cool, and they get out of control. This leads to serious injury, alcohol poison, or even death. I'm sure you don't want to be the next parent getting a phone call saying your kid is in the hospital. The only thing parties lead up to is trouble.

Kids staying up to party instead of sleeping, doing homework, or studying are not going to be able to get a good education. These kids are not going to be able to go to class the next morning after getting drunk the night before.

Colleges need to get control of the drinking before it controls them. That is why they need to keep all alcoholic beverages off campus.

Brennan Whitaker, Grade 8
Holliday Middle School, TX

It Was My Time

It was the Friday before my 6th grade year would end. I went to the doctors after school because I was peeing the bed, wiped out all the time, had rapid weight loss, and was drinking tons of fluid. I hadn't peed my bed in years. So, that Friday my father took me to the doctors.

I took a pee test and blood sugar test. I had large keytones and had a blood sugar reading of 500. With keytones you want small to none. Also, with a blood sugar of 500 it is as high as the machine will read until you go into diabetic shock. I could have been in the ICU in a couple of days.

I remember my doctor coming in, shaking his head, practically in tears. He said "Mackenzie the tests are not good. I'm so sorry. I'm so, so, so sorry that this is happening to you. You have type 1 diabetes." My heart dropped. "I will give you some time alone with your dad," Dr. Luck said. As soon as he left I burst into tears.

Dad took me to OHSU an hour later. I was in the hospital for 5 days. All my family from Washington came to visit me, even my Uncle Jon. He helped me out a lot, because he is a respiratory therapist.

My life has changed a lot. I have learned way more stuff than I wanted to. My dream of going into the Army was crushed. I will have to live with my diabetes for the rest of my life. Sometimes I feel high, sometimes I feel low, but at the doctor's office, and in the hospital, I knew it was my time.

Mac Morrow, Grade 7
Hazelbrook Middle School, OR

My Uncle Roger

God bless our troops! Have you ever had someone you love fight in a war? It's scary thinking about what could happen to them. My uncle's life is at risk. His name is Lieutenant Colonel Roger Farris; he is my mother's brother. He has a wonderful family who loves him and wants him to be safe. I feel all he wants to do is fight, because that's why he joined the army in the first place. He loves his country and is eager to serve, but he knows we worry about him.

Just recently, my uncle Roger was transferred to the Pentagon from Fort Hood, Texas. He moved with my aunt and two cousins to Haymarket, Virginia, near the Pentagon in Washington, D.C. He now has a big house with lots of land and a little bit of peace in his life. He likes working at the Pentagon because he used to work in Iraq away from his family for two years. He had to be away form the people he loved for that long. It was hard on his children and for him. He just recently volunteered to go back to Iraq because he knows he can make a difference there. We are all praying that God will keep him safe!

Paige Fallon, Grade 8
St Elizabeth Ann Seton School, TX

Costume

A costume makes you different. It makes you a different person. Adults and kids like dressing up. You get to be whatever you want for a whole night. Costumes have been on earth for lots of years people don't just only dress up for Halloween but for many other things.

People also dress up in plays so they could act as some one else. Actors also dress up but not with a costume, but something to change their characteristics. People in theater also use costumes to be what they're acting like. Some people could change their whole personality with a costume.

Over the years costumes have changed. Before kids would dress up like vampires and ghosts. Kids now dress up like super heroes and not scary stuff. Before costumes were simple. You could use a bed sheet as a costume. Now kids spend a lot of money. Kids still enjoy trick-or-treating. They dress up and get candy and enjoy the spirit of Halloween.

Some people criticize Halloween. They say it involves the devil. They say it shouldn't be considered a holiday. Many people don't celebrate it. Some people's houses get egged. That makes people dislike Halloween even more.

Overall I like Halloween. It's a fun time for all ages. Like kids like going trick or treating. Adults enjoy going to Halloween parties. If your costume is scary or fun Halloween is a fun time. I like going trick or treating and being with friends and family.

Alan Millan, Grade 8
Isbell Middle School, CA

Love

Have you ever tried to explain the definition of love to anyone? Could you think of anything to tell them? Love is something that you can't explain.

Love is like the wind; you can't see it, but you can feel it. It is like a rush that overcomes you when you see the face of your crush. It is the warmth you feel when you blush, or the tickling sensation when he talks to you.

Love comes in various different forms. There is the love you feel when you see your grandparents. That's love. It's love that you feel when you give your dog a belly rub, or even the love you feel when you see your little sister. That feeling that if they ever leave you, there will be a hole in your heart.

Love is measured in size and strengths. Love has different strengths because, you may feel a greater pull when one person leaves, but when the other person does, you feel nothing. It is the same for sizes. You may love someone a whole bunch, but then love the other person very little.

As you can see, there are many different ways to love a person. There is no real definition of love. Love is just a feeling, and everyone's definition of it is different. So if anyone asks you what love is, you can just say: 'It is different for you and me, and it is up to you to find out.'

Becky Coltrain, Grade 8
Holliday Middle School, TX

Technology

Ever thought what would the world be without a computer, Xbox, or iPod? Life would be really different without technology. It would be very hard to go one day without turning on the TV to watch SpongeBob, or turning on your computer to log into your Myspace. I'd be saying, "I'm not a caveman!"

Technology is everywhere. Technology is a big part of my life. The computer and instant messaging sites are good ways to communicate with friends. Texting is also a good way to communicate. I say it's one of the best ways to stay in touch with friends. Without that or a phone, the only way to communicate would be a written letter. Who has the time for that? There's no way I would want to do that.

I love video games like an imaginary brother. Life would be really boring if I didn't have my Wii and couldn't play Wii Sports Resort. That would be a bummer if I could not play any video games, especially since I'm a video game addict.

We should all be thankful that we have technology. No iPod, computer, or Play Station would exist without it. Without technology we would all be living in caves, writing on walls, and maybe working for Geico in their commercials.

Luis Wright, Grade 8
Corpus Christi School, CA

The Life of Shawn Johnson

The young American icon Shawn Johnson was born January 19, 1992. Born and raised in Des Moines, Iowa, Shawn started chasing her dream of becoming an American Olympian when she was about three years old.

Her mother said that Shawn was a very spastic child and needed something to use all that energy in. For this reason her mother signed her up for a ballet class. Shawn hated it so her mother pulled her out and enrolled her at a local gymnastics school "Chow's Gymnastics." BINGO! Shawn loved it and began enrolling in more and more classes. As Shawn got older she got better and better. When she started to compete her parents went to nearly every competition. She said they were her biggest fans and supported her all the way to the 2008 Olympics.

Weighing in at only ninety pounds, the sixteen-year-old was so dedicated to doing well at the Olympics that she trained through some bad conditions. When disaster struck and a huge flood swept through her state, Shawn still didn't give up she kept training. Even when water was pouring in her gym, Shawn did still not throw in the towel. When she went to the Olympics she won many awards, though her best one was gold in all around. I like Shawn Johnson because she never gives up, and I idolize her for all her hard work.

Taylor Kroutter, Grade 7
Deweyville Middle School, TX

Soccer

Soccer is a fun sport and has been played since the 19th century. The Federation International de Football Association (FIFA) was founded in 1904. In other countries soccer is known as football such as in England, France, Spain, and Italy. Soccer is a fun sport that can be enjoyed by all ages for any level of skill, it also is good for you because you need to keep yourself in good condition to be able to play. It's also good for you because it encourages you to work hard and inspires competitiveness.

Soccer has been enjoyed by all ages and is fun to play as well. There are leagues for varying levels of skill. So whether you've just started, or you've had a few years experience, or you've played for a long time, there are leagues for all levels of skill. They have recreational league which is for players who have just started playing the next step up is select then the highest level for teens and kids is competitive. Then there's high school and college soccer, after those it's semi-pro and pro. Soccer is fun because it can be played anywhere all you need is a somewhat flat surface and a soccer ball.

Soccer is good because it encourages healthy eating habits and constant exercise. It encourages competitiveness and hard work so you have to want to be good and improve to do well at soccer. So overall soccer is a fun sport that keeps you active.

Preston Harding, Grade 8
St Michael's Episcopal Day School, CA

Church

There is always a day you are proud of what you've done. Sometimes these days are few and far between. These are the days I will always remember.

One Sunday evening at the end of a sermon in my church, I decided to approach my priest. I told him I put my faith in Jesus and was ready to confess publicly. While walking to the podium, I was nervous about confessing in front of so many people, but in doing this I felt good inside.

I only had to do one more thing, and it was to get baptized. I walked into a white room where it was to take place. My priest put on a bright white robe and motioned me to step into the Holy Water. He gave me the oath I had to agree to and then dunked me in the water.

After doing this I was the most excited person in the room. The smile on my face wouldn't come off even if I were to get hit by a bus. I felt much joy and still do when talking about this day.

I started to get more into church and God. I went to mostly all the youth meetings and now go to church even when my parents don't. I felt like confessing really affected my life. One man told me hadn't confessed yet. This is when I knew that there is always a choice to follow your faith.

Juan Marquez, Grade 8
Reagan County Middle School, TX

Bikes

I love to ride bikes. I just landed a 360 back spin. That is hecka cool. I went to my friend's house last weekend and was riding bikes and he had a ramp. One of his friends named Daggles dared me to jump from about five feet and I did and I landed it. Then I went to my other friend's house and we were riding bikes and I landed a 360 back spin on video, I am going to put this on my MySpace. When I was at the Gridley Skate Park I was going to jump up on the Ural and do a 360 with my handle bars. But I crashed really hard. I tried it again and I landed it and my dad was there to see it.

My dream is to become pro and go to dirt racing. There are bigger jumps and grind rails and stuff like that. I want to get sponsors from Rockstar and Monster energy drinks. There is a competition in Sac I want to go to and enter in. I know that I will probably lose but it will be fun just learning new tricks.

Brandon Dunlap, Grade 9
Faith Christian Jr/Sr High School, CA

Art

Once there was a boy who loved art. In fact, he was even good at drawing, coloring, painting and sculpting. He was also in my art class, the teacher would show his work to everyone. Everyone would say, "Cool," "Wow," or "Stick with it." I even thought it was amazing. He always would be careful what he was doing, also he would always follow directions. Whenever the teacher said, "Pour a little paint into your pallets," then he would. Most importantly, he would keep his station clean, such as keeping crayons on his side of the table or paint onto the paper. Plus he was so serious about his work that he would only let himself or the teacher hold it. He was also a very nice kid, he would never gossip, he would mind his business, he would never get into fights, nor start an argument. He was a peaceful, loving, caring kid. In my opinion he seemed like a nonviolent person.

Brandi Stewart, Grade 8
Charles Maclay Middle School, CA

Index

Abraham, Matthias 98	Bangal, Michael 40	Brown, Clint 77
Abughrib, Sarah 200	Baniqued, Alyssandra 50	Brown, Marisa 161
Acevedo, Cody 172	Baraiya, Surya 228	Bruce, James 197
Acevedo, Parker 204	Barajas, Alexus 216	Brutyn, Dante 150
Adam, Logan 142	Barcelon, Jasmine May 119	Buerer, Lydia 217
Adams, Katelyn 140	Barclay, Rebecca 125	Buffano, Maryssa 196
Aduddell, Alyssa 118	Barley, Kelsey 96	Bullard, Kayla 76
Aguilera, Angel 159	Barrera, Gabie 184	Burciaga, Alexa 116
Alexander, Audrey 112	Barreras, Chastidy 217	Burdick, Andrew 156
Alexander, Ms. Specialjoy 201	Basalone, Jack 33	Burns, Alexandra 193
Alker, Kayla 148	Bascon, Raoul 236	Burns, Heath 119
Allen, Adam 61	Basquez, Courtney 10	Burns, Kristin 55
Allen, Julia 57	Basurto, Kevin 227	Busby, Jessica 234
Allison, Alexa 140	Bazan, Amber 10	Bush, Brandon 36
Alsop, Carson 13	Beaart, Austin 210	Bush, Heather 25
Alvarado, Alejandra 22	Beaty, Jaclyn 199	Bush, Kaitlin 10
Alvarez, Marcela 208	Beck, Makayla 150	Byrum, Dylan 212
Ambler, Philip 37	Bedwell, Keisha 59	Cairns, Victoria 87
Andersen, Jessica 200	Belote, Ryan 22	Calder, Riley 229
Anderson, Andrea 25	Beltran, Lorenzo 223	Camarillo, Cesar 121
Antley, Emily 66	Beltran, Stephen 137	Campos, Jennifer 191
Apachito III, Juan Pedro 108	Bennett, Fiona 145	Cannon, Destiny 70
Aragon, Luis 221	Bennett, Isaac 125	Cannon, Marnie 68
Araiza, Darlene 58	Bennett, Jonah 214	Cantu, Andrew 23
Aranda, Catherine 181	Bensley, Garrett 161	Capaul, Emily 192
Arauz, Asalia 134	Benway, Harrison 160	Carrasco, Geovanna 190
Aravind, Aishwarya 158	Bergen, Eric 91	Carrasco, Michael 202
Archer, Dylan 28	Bergmann, Chandra 70	Carrillo, Noah 107
Arevalo, Neftali 205	Berry, Bethany 30	Carter, Pamela 11
Arguijo, Clarissa 178	Berry, Carlie 106	Castaneda, Marguerite 81
Armijo, Daniella 229	Bertrand, Sean 59	Castilleja, Alexandra 11
Arras, Brenda 56	Best, Austin 232	Castro, Carolyn 53
Arth, Amelia 192	Bhatti, Deep 204	Cates, Nina 43
Arvizo, Adrian 213	Bitner, Talyne 26	Cathey, Kelsi 64
Ashworth, Emily 188	Bland, Abbey 186	Cavazos, Jonathan 41
Ashworth, Kaitlyn 133	Boaz, Clay 181	Cepeda, Armando 46
Astwood, Colton 24	Bocko, John 20	Cervantes, Luz 178
Avila, Jahayra 184	Bogdon, Ariana 52	Cervantes, Marcos 158
Avilucea, Erin 135	Boisa, Brieanna 38	Cervantes, Sarah 179
Ayala, Romeo 180	Bongbonga, Dharyl 93	Chacon, Victoria 138
Babb, Trent 72	Bookstaff, Jordan 90	Chaides-Reyes, Mikaela 134
Badillo, Humberto 29	Bosquez, Ashley 108	Chain, Sebastian 16
Baeza, Rebeca 153	Boyd, Brayden 228	Chamness, Anna 89
Bailey, Dylan 35	Boyd, Matthew 144	Chan, Leonard 77
Bailey, Jordan 220	Braaten, Cassaundra 37	Chandler, Jacob 157
Bailey, Stormi 88	Brabec, Tyler 73	Chapa, Kelly 71
Bain, Samantha 208	Braun, Justin 166	Charleston, Kryshawna 52
Baker, Makenzie 222	Brees, Nikki 222	Chase, Brieghanna 50
Baldasti, Adrienne 183	Brewer, McKenzie 145	Chavez, Nicholas 209
Baldasti, Marissa 164	Briesmaster, Morgan 88	Chen, Jessica 85
Banerjee, Ela 74	Brinson, Robert 126	Chida, Chelsea 82

Childers, Frances 138	Diaz, Leticia 189	Fredette, Josiah 201
Christensen, Cole 124	Diaz, Octavio 143	Freeland, Bailey 104
Christensen, Lyndsay 172	Dickey, Carissa 71	Freeman, Miranda 171
Clay, Patrick Dodge 137	Dimas, Jennifer 105	Fregoso, Eliseo 184
Clifford, Alison 105	Dollins, Taylor 85	Froese, Brenda 169
Coco, Lauren 59	Domingo, Joseph 51	Fuertes, Raquel 67
Cogburn, Madison 118	Dorn, Kevin 28	Furano, Olivia 140
Cogswell, Cole 231	Doucet, Tanner 129	Gabaldon, Nicole 184
Cole, Jessie 55	Dow, Michael 181	Galarza, Alexander 177
Cole, Lindsay 23	Downing, Cassie 105	Gale, Lauren 74
Cole, Michael 78	Duckworth, David 16	Galindo, Jazlyn 160
Coleman, Victoria 21	Dunlap, Brandon 241	Gallegos, Dashia 136
Coltrain, Becky 240	Duran, Daisy 223	Gallegos Balderas, Emily Joseline . .187
Contreras, Johanna 207	Duran, Michelle 229	Garcia, Celine 132
Contreras, Robert 98	Dye, Jamie 159	Garcia, David 211
Cooksey, Stephani 117	Eastland, Mallory 53	Garcia, Denise 179
Cope, Michael 16	Eaton, Chad 25	Garcia, Emily 238
Copeland, Jessica 19	Ekdawy, Cassandra 233	Garcia, Kietzecume 237
Cornejo, Jerry Ann 127	Elhalwagi, Shereef 84	Garcia, Shayla 129
Corona, Cecilia 185	Elmets, Caroline 202	Garcia, Sonia 163
Corral, Ruben 127	Encinas Jr., Juan A. 208	Garcia, Yesenia 134
Corralejo, Jonathan 33	Enns, Susie 112	Gardner, Scott 158
Cortez, Clarissa 145	Erwin, Emilee 186	Gardner, Trenton 124
Cortez, Vanessa 48	Escamilla, Jose 72	Garman, Cortney 211
Covarrubias, Oswaldo 190	Espinoza, Franklin 38	Garnica, Kandice 141
Covary, Sharon 113	Espiritu, Dianne 216	Garza, Hailey 136
Cowan, Alex 150	Espitia, Caitlyn 23	Garza, Trinda 56
Cox, Derek 166	Essman, Justin 56	Gayon, Alex 117
Croghan, Thomas 177	Estrada, Paulette 178	Genco, Helena 203
Crozier, Sami 196	Estrada, Victoria 231	George, Serena 157
Cuellar, Martin E. 188	Eubanks, Dustin 146	Geronimo, Samantha 193
Cunningham, Emilee 128	Evans, Donovan 104	Gibbon, Gracie 62
Currence, Savonn 191	Evans, Megan 116	Gibson, Katelynn 128
Cutler, Lauren 55	Fallon, Paige 239	Gilcrease, Madison 215
Cyrus, Kellie 24	Farah, Alexis 209	Gillespie, Elizabeth 198
D'Amico, Daniel 136	Farhat, Carmen 71	Gilmartin, Kevin 67
D'Amore, Cathryn 203	Faulkner, Emily 58	Gilmore, Sam 49
D'Andrea, Erika 14	Faust, Lindsey 166	Glad, Christy 185
Davidson, Maddie 50	Fedchun, Nadia 69	Glaser, Jamie 112
Davis, April 52	Feeney, Justin 148	Glaspie, Collyn 22
Davis, April 151	Ferguson, Austin 49	Glueck, Sara 176
Davis, Jenna 127	Fernandez, Brianna 13	Gobea, Cara 170
Davis, Summer 161	Fernandez, Guadalupe 161	Godinez, Lauren 80
de Figueiredo, Madeline 234	Ferris, David 32	Gollhofer, Blake 230
De La Cruz, Billy 111	Figueroa, Mary Jo 45	Gomez, Briana 34
De La Vega, Martha 82	Fileccia, BreeAna 12	Gomez, Jennifer 67
De Leon, Judy 236	Finn, Jeff .98	Gomez, Samuel 174
de The, Domitille 221	Flann, Maxwell 141	Gomez, Yesenia 134
Dean, Cody 42	Fleming, Monica 163	Gonzales, Miranda 235
DeBlassie, Julia 182	Flores, Kevin 156	Gonzales, Richard 62
Dedmon, Colton 209	Flores, Maddie 120	Gonzalez, Anthony 135
Deen, Colt 74	Flores, Matthew 107	Gonzalez, Chris 124
Delaney, Nathaniel 31	Fogel, Casey 45	Gonzalez, Jennifer 143
Delgado, Aden 230	Foley, Sasha 236	Goodman, Riley 49
Delgado, Christian 215	Ford, Audrie 238	Gothard, Emily 89
Devora, Jessica 114	Foster, Jordan 153	Goulet, Grace 113
Diaz, Josh 64	Frangione, Daniela 175	Grace, Eric 24

Index

Granillo, Christina 207
Gray, Kobie 45
Gray, Matthew 76
Greathouse, Aidan 225
Green, Alisa 26
Greene, Elisabeth 173
Griffin, Landre 156
Grimaud, Dylan 36
Grinzewitsch, Catherine 183
Gros, David 219
Guerrero, Kacee 234
Gullen, Gracie 129
Guo, Stephanie 232
Gutierrez, Nancy 71
Guzman, Skyblue 130
Haas-Tellez, Cody 220
Haggard, Savannah 32
Halboth, Madison 220
Hales, Gavin 37
Hall, Sarah 96
Hammer, Taylor 110
Hansen, Ashley 57
Hansen, Evan 218
Harding, Preston 241
Harris, Jennafer 110
Harris, Lauren 91
Harris, Stephen 64
Hart, Kierra 43
Haskell, Demetri 190
Hassett, Mikayla 153
Hasuo, Sophie 210
Hawkins, Aliyah 227
Hawkins, Brianna 239
Haws, Ty .18
Hayden, Ryan 115
Hayes, William 12
Haynes, Brenton 95
Hayworth, Caitlyn 72
Heard, Amanda 77
Helm, Paul 84
Henderson, Tara 195
Henley, Gabrielle 132
Henney, Nicholas 34
Henry, Kelsey 111
Herbert, Seth 109
Hernandez, Aaron 190
Hernandez, Abelardo 97
Hernandez, Denise 171
Hernandez, Jalisa 208
Hernandez, Maria 209
Herrera, Amber 139
Herring, Sarah 123
Hervey, Olivia 116
Hiatt, Rachel 80
Hickey, Bryan 88
Hilton, Ryan 43
Hinze, Wyatt 168

Hise, Jessica 51
Hise, Mary 86
Ho, Jonathan 77
Hoffman, Erin 195
Hoffman, Mariah 218
Hoffman, Paul 18
Hogan, Jake 109
Holland, Nocona 223
Holloway, Amanda 206
Holm, Camille 85
Holsapple, Chris 191
Horan, Austin 151
Houston, Kaitlyn 202
Hsu, Kevin 40
Huber, Veronica 117
Huff, Jonathan 63
Huntzinger, Jamie 215
Husman, Tanner 126
Hutson, Lenzi 213
Ibarra, Vanessa 131
Indermill, Erin 214
Ivankovic, Jonathan 152
Jablonski, Theresa 224
Jackson, Carley 121
Jackson, Rikki 83
Jacobs, Cody 216
James, Aaron 96
James, Gloria 127
James, Samuel 130
James, Tayler 100
Jamison, Freya 233
Jeffers, Jamie 172
Jeffers, Kinsey 20
Jennings, Joey 94
Jensen, Shae 30
Jilani, Bilal 41
Jimenez, Teila 186
Joe II, Gilbert 191
Johansen, Catrine 64
Johnson, Callie 42
Johnson, Connor 133
Johnson, Maddison 201
Johnson, Paige 142
Jolissaint, Stephen 198
Jones, Ashley 86
Jones, Kristen 30
Jones, Skyler 236
Jones, Tatum 124
Jones, Tennyson 50
Jorgensen, Jenessa 27
Juarez, Abraham 137
Juarez, Christian 142
Judd, Tyler 173
Jurado, Andrew 122
Kade, Bradley 40
Kaminski, Melissa 212
Kasperitis, Kaitlyn 86

Kasperitis, Kimberlyn 75
Kassim, Isaac 189
Keating, Kevin Michael 65
Keiper, Chris 97
Kenagy, Andrea C. 73
Kenyon, Jason 199
Keough, Nicholas 106
Khang, Tracy 198
King, Kendall 172
Kirby, Kent 17
Kirmse, Kara 92
Klassen, Tony 204
Klein, Nicole 206
Klingbiel, Kayla 214
Koedyker, Seth 128
Kolmannskog, Thea 91
Kopper, Brandon 91
Kotch, Chris 167
Krebel, Hannah 134
Kroutter, Taylor 240
Krueger, Jennifer 216
Kupfer, Ambrose 195
Kutay, Eleni 189
Lackey, Paige 63
LaFleur, Zackry 125
Lam, Vanessa 186
Lang, Christopher 126
Lange, Gentry 226
Larcade, Kalee 79
Lares, Stephen 231
Lasater, Chris 179
Lauffer, Alyssa 205
Lazo, Monica 189
Lear, Lauren 94
Lee, Angela 97
Lee, Joseph 187
Lentzner, Ashley 108
Lentzner, Kevin 117
Lester, Sarah 32
Lie, Ethan 21
Lillie, Audrey 168
Limhengco, Winston 127
Limon, Rey 93
LiRocchi, Caydon 62
Little Turtle, Corina 147
Liu, Brittany 27
Livesey, Jessica 65
Lizama, Sabrina 86
Lobb, Bryce 221
Logan, Kyle 29
Logan, Madison 133
Loo, Beverley 128
Looney, Stephanie 38
Lopez, Adrian 139
Lopez, Amri 104
Lopez, Stephanie 60
Lowry, Tanner 143

Loyd, Amber 213	Medina, David 210	Neria, Laura 142
Lucero, Tera 132	Medina, Gabriel 188	Nettles, Shalyn 14
Ludlow, Alyson 159	Medina, Octavio 15	Neudorf, Savannah 147
Ludwick, Chance 135	Mendez, Daisy 15	Neufeld, Susie 194
Lujan, Frankie 129	Mendoza, Armando 154	Ngo, Myvy 57
Luna, Alexandra 193	Mendoza, Gloria 202	Nguyen-Okwu, Leslie 68
Luna, Miguel 120	Meyer, Torrey 129	Nielsen, Hannah 65
Luoma, Geoffrey 197	Meza, David M. 74	Nieto, Sarah 169
Madarang, Janessa 178	Micheletti, Kimberly 99	Nievera, Roni 230
Madrigal, Marcy 44	Mihaylo, Sky 187	Nijim, Chad 56
Magaling, Jemm 224	Millan, Alan 240	Nisbet, Rebecka 121
Magana, Felicia 157	Miller, Alex 35	Noel, Macaulay 111
Magness, Parker 164	Miller, Cheyenne 90	Norton, Jim 89
Mahoney, Jack 187	Miller, Christian 235	Novaes, Ricky 183
Mahood, Dylan 76	Miller, Meaghan 17	Nua, Samantha 137
Maillet, Kelsey 155	Miller, Philip 150	Nuñez, Erik 163
Maldonado, Jimmy 46	Miranda, Joanna 143	O'Baker, Kevin Brandon 58
Malone, Maddison 51	Mitchell, Aaron 15	O'Connell, Sean 175
Manganiello, Joseph 106	Miyashiro, Analisa 27	Ochoa, Joshuah 116
Manry, Benjamin 31	Mohler, Jessica 21	Ochoa, Natali 122
Maples, Chuk 47	Mohr, Krystine 84	Okazaki, Raina 81
Marcelli, Ann 119	Moncores, Cinthia 220	Olazo, Erika 211
Maricle, Tyler 40	Mondejar, Cindy 12	Olivas, Bianca 108
Marquez, Juan 241	Montano, Anayeli 203	Oliver, Tyler 199
Martin, Amber 123	Montano, Angelica 69	Omiya, Samantha 107
Martin, Kelsey 110	Montano, Oscar 60	Ondarza, Lauren 218
Martin, Spencer 152	Montez, Caleb 98	Ong, Kimberly 28
Martinez, Alejandra 166	Montoya, Mariah 76	Oradiegwu, Jennifer 26
Martinez, Benita 162	Moore, Brandon 83	Orozco, Elsa 105
Martinez, Martha 72	Moots, Liam 203	Ortega, Andrea 115
Martinez, Miriam 61	Morales, Ericka 135	Ortiz, Cody 144
Martinez, Robert 180	Morales, Sly 95	Ortiz, Eddie 205
Martinez, Ross 78	Morazán, Michelle 21	Ortiz, Micheal 107
Mascarenas, Paige 198	Morris, Alisha Brooke 11	Ortiz, Priscilla 47
Massong, Michailia 175	Morris, Ruth 20	Ouellette, Katie 176
Mathis, Maryssa 60	Morrow, Austin 66	Ouellette, Michael 160
Matsumura, Jenna 33	Morrow, Lindsey 26	Owens, Brian 92
Mattice, Caitlyn 130	Morrow, Mac 239	Pacini, Doreen 201
McBride, Cheryl 100	Morse, Summer 39	Padilla, Joseph 210
McBride, Shannon 24	Morstad, Mckenzie 111	Padilla, Nathalia 114
McCaskill, Ebony 23	Mortensen, Matthew 80	Paganin, Sofia 113
McCollough, Lauren 131	Mosley, Dustin 83	Pak, Sara 200
McCracken, Jason 49	Motzkus, Olivia 149	Palagi, Andie 109
McDaniel, Brandon 61	Mouton, Giraud 114	Palmer, Sean 171
McDonald, Courtney 194	Mow, Lauryn 81	Paresa, Kai 206
McFadden, Cierra 97	Muery, Heidi 121	Parga, Crystal 138
McFarland, Sapphire 79	Muniz, Susana 197	Parks Jr., Steven 67
McGuire, Molly 39	Munoz, Anthony 126	Paskett, Kyle 92
McKamy, Jessica 54	Muñoz, Leslie 105	Passmore, Haylee 148
McKinley, Megan 43	Murillo, Lindsey 225	Paterson, Holly 234
McLain, David 154	Murphy, Ian 182	Patoc, Aileen-Ann 92
McLain, Katherine 19	Murphy, Shannon 39	Patterson, Brian 24
McLane, Holley 94	Murray, Kara 53	Pavik, Jason 66
McLaughlin, Konner 180	Murray, Taylor 63	Pearce, Lily 141
Meadows, Rachel 89	Muskrat, Madeline 164	Pearson, Kyleigh 185
Meas, Shawn 48	Navarrette, David 112	Peavler, Jacqlynn 90
Medina, Alondra 238	Nerenberg, Natasha 139	Peel, Meridith 110

Index

Pense, Daniel 69
Perez, Anna 170
Perez, Nayra 226
Perez, Odette 227
Perez, Veronica 231
Perez, Yesenia 176
Peszynski, Grant 226
Peterson, Justin 106
Petruska, Adam 138
Peyatt, Alyssa 13
Phan, Katrina 14
Phelps, Cole 126
Phetteplace, Jacob 192
Philipp, Faith 84
Pisano, Theresa 83
Polly, Kaitlyn 96
Pompel, Alex 163
Pool, Zackary 217
Porter, Michael 62
Prachyl, Conner 196
Prokop, Sofia 87
Puente, Onassis 108
Pullig, Justin 222
Quach, Paula 212
Quezada, Brisa 116
Quezada, Zachary 213
Quinones, Ivan 158
Radosevich, Byron 146
Ramirez, Briana 182
Ramirez, Joshua 75
Ramirez, Jovannah 148
Ramirez, Luis 162
Ramos, Jacqueline 225
Ramos, Jaimie 140
Ramsey, Zach 70
Ray, Jenna 162
Ray, Tippie 207
Reagan, Courtney 81
Reagan, Kelli 182
Reddy, Pooja 44
Reed, Marley 140
Reigh, Brian 141
Reilly, Shannon 154
Reimer, Jessica 153
Rendeiro, Melissa 15
Resendiz, Abbie 235
Reyes, Ryan 42
Reyna, Gabriel 131
Reynolds, Britt 14
Reynolds, David 173
Rigert, Aisha 154
Rios, Desiree 170
Ritchey, Payton 19
Ritchie, Abbi 165
Ritchie, Shon 107
Rivera, Cindy 144
Roberson, Kobe 147

Robinson, Hailey 13
Robles, Abigail A. 224
Rodgers, Caitlin 175
Rodriguez, Alondra 118
Rodriguez, Jason 183
Rodriguez, Jose 25
Rodriguez, Lynette 193
Rodriguez, Maddison 35
Rodriguez, Sagrario 75
Rodriguez, Tammy 90
Rodriguez, Yutaka 87
Romani, Jullisa 113
Rosalez, Kason 157
Rosario, Victoria 173
Rose, Christian 194
Rossow, Sophia 22
Rubio, Jari 118
Ruiz, Lucas 19
Rumyantsev, Carolina 226
Rush, Taylor 44
Ryan, Andrew 228
Saelee, Cindy 29
Saenz, Jessica 51
Saidawi, Alice 155
Sale, Caleb 206
Sales, John Paul 120
Samaniego, Franchesca 11
Samaniego, Jasmin 109
Samay, Alexander 104
Samford, Miranda 20
Samhan, Mason 151
Sanchez, Alexis 194
Sanchez, Kristen 147
Santillan, Evelyn 12
Sarrat, Chris 192
Saucedo, Cynthia 125
Savage, Nikki 95
Savastru, Andrei 30
Savela, Kevin 152
Sbrocca, Marie 46
Schade, Samantha 232
Schorn, Kelley 122
Schulik, Joshua 99
Schwartz, Jenifer 44
Schwartz, Kim 54
Scioli, Keith 36
Scott, Cheyenne 181
Scott, Rebecca 221
Seaton, Shauna 238
Segal, Sara 82
Serna, Marcos Ray 167
Seyer, Elizabeth 188
Shams, Saad 79
Shaver, Danielle 212
Shaw, Christian 115
Shi, Dingbo 165
Shi, Ted 219

Shihabi, Danny 131
Shirley, Sarah 149
Shoemake, Talon 132
Sholtis, Alexandria 69
Shortes, Nathan 156
Sigala, Sarah 169
Sigl, Jake 59
Silva, Ashley M. 136
Sims, Alexandria 219
Sims, Jennifer 66
Singh, Jaitika 205
Sisneroz, Daylen 152
Sison, Adrian 164
Smith, Brianna 123
Smith, Kaitlin 171
Smith, Michal 37
Smith, Samantha 45
Solis, Laura 214
Sommerville, Stephen 165
Sorensen, Ashley 42
Sorensen, Lynda 11
Sosa, Marcela 122
Soto, Latasha 73
Soto, Rudy 149
Soto, Vanessa 177
Southall, Hannah 41
Speers, Lauren 34
Spence, Braeden 224
Spencer, Jennifer 128
Stachowiak, Brianna 237
Stafford, Kolby 78
Stanger, Nicole 80
Stapleton, Kindra 95
Starck, Abby 131
Starck, Bilito 223
Steen-Mcneely, Gibran 162
Stefoglo, Alina 27
Stepteau, Brocke 217
Stevens, Alissa 115
Stevens, Branda 31
Stevens, Wyatt 112
Stevenson, Kimi 218
Stewart, Brandi 241
Stewart, Jordan 99
Stewart-Kucera, Rylee 145
Stone, Michael 18
Stotler, Rachel M. 133
Stout, Maria 167
Stoute, George 174
Stray, Avery 233
Strong, Marla 68
Sutton, Lauren 41
Symister, Savannah 121
Szteiter, Shelby 211
Talamantes, Sierra 219
Tanega, Rachelle 165
Tanner, Branson 34

Tansiongco, Jordan	63	Wade, Tracy	61
Tarango, Luna	149	Wait, Toni	47
Thomas, Angelica	144	Walden, Peter	232
Thomas, Divya	109	Walker, Shanise	65
Thomas, Philip	87	Warman, Zachary	28
Thomas, Randee	168	Warner, Ryann	78
Thorpe, Mark	75	Warren, Ashten	207
Todd, Michael	16	Warren, Jacob	155
Tong, Tiffany	229	Waters, Emily	130
Toon, Riley	88	Weisbeck, Shanna	17
Torgerson, Julie	114	West, Briatni	82
Torres, Karina	119	Wheeler, Mollie	17
Torres, Leanna	195	Whitaker, Brennan	239
Torres, Paola	228	White, Chelsea	54
Torres, Willie	117	White, Lilly	146
Torrez, Lauren	114	White, Tyler	176
Townsend, Rachel	227	Whitman, Emilie	32
Tran, Garreth	151	Wickliffe, Eva	46
Trembley, Ember	48	Wiebe, Kimberly	146
Trinh, Jake	99	Wike, Taylor	233
Trosclair, Alexis	111	Wilde, Meridith	94
Trotter, Tyson	168	Willenbring, Taylor	170
Trujillo, Cesar	237	Williams, Reed	57
Truong, Dustin	38	Willis, Chauncey	51
Turpen, Savanna	174	Willkie, Remington	159
Ulibarri, Rosa	138	Wilson, Eliza	48
Uribe, Maritza	58	Wilson, Jacob	230
Valadez, Arturo	120	Wilson, Maxi	237
Valdez, Mia	180	Wilson, Shayne	133
Valencia, Trigal	139	Wimberley, Leslie	93
Valentine, Ariel	120	Windham, Clint	93
Valentine, Emily	144	Winfrey, Alec	235
Valenzuela, Brandon	199	Winnegge, Laurel	222
Valle, Melissa	197	Winters, Victoria	79
Van Gelder, Jessica	15	Wolter, George	104
Van Ryn, Nathan	60	Worley, Katie	39
Vance, Ashley	36	Wright, Callum	54
Vance, Jarod	47	Wright, Luis	240
VanRij, Jordyn	123	Wyers, Jackson	204
Vargas, Brando	55	Yamane, Kelli	53
Vasko Jr., Thomas	10	Yang, Jia-luen	119
Vasquez, Veronica	35	Ynami, Sophia	155
Vassar, Jessica	68	Yoshihara, Jordan	18
Vazquez, Jalen	85	Young, Clayton	73
Vazquez, Jesse	196	Young, Nicolette	160
Vega, Melia	179	Zacarias, Humberto	200
Velazquez, Steven	174	Zamora, Aitiana	185
Veloro, Kyle	130	Zaragoza, Ezequiel	106
Verduzco, Esmeralda	169	Zaugg, A.J.	135
Verma, Neil	52	Zavala, Susana	177
Vielma, Oscar	215	Zepeda, Matthew	33
Villagrana, Nicolas	125	Zhang, Samantha	70
Villalon, Kathryn	29	Zizzi, Olivia	31
Villanueva, Anica	137		
Viramontes, Dimitri	225		
Vizcaino, Brenda	167		
Vorwaller, Scheridan	124		

Author Autograph Page

Author Autograph Page

Author Autograph Page

Author Autograph Page

Author Autograph Page

Author Autograph Page

Author Autograph Page

Author Autograph Page

Author Autograph Page

Author Autograph Page